Problem Solving with Java™

Elliot B. Koffman

Ursula Wolz

Addison
Wesley

Boston San Francisco New York
London Toronto Sydney Tokyo Singapore Madrid
Mexico City Munich Paris Cape Town Hong Kong Montreal

Executive Editor	Susan Hartman Sullivan
Executive Marketing Manager	Michael Hirsch
Production Supervisor	Marilyn Lloyd
Project Management	Argosy Publishing
Composition and Art	Argosy Publishing
Copyeditor	Nancy Young
Proofreader	Janet Renard
Indexer	Elliot B. Koffman
Text Design	Sandra Rigney
Cover Design	Gina Hagen Kolenda
Cover Photo	Photo Disk ©2002
Design Manager	Gina Hagen Kolenda
Prepress and Manufacturing	Caroline Fell

Access the latest information about Addison-Wesley titles from our World Wide Web site: http://www.aw.com/cs

Many of the designations used by manufacturers and sellers to distinguish their products are claimed as trademarks. Where those designations appear in this book, and Addison-Wesley was aware of a trademark claim, the designations have been printed in initial caps or all caps.

The programs and applications presented in this book have been included for their instructional value. They have been tested with care, but are not guaranteed for any particular purpose. The publisher does not offer any warranties or representations, not does it accept any liabilities with respect to the programs or applications.

Library of Congress Cataloging-in-Publication Data

Koffman, Elliot B.
      Problem Solving with Java / Elliot B. Koffman and Ursula Wolz. – 2nd ed.
          p. cm.
        ISBN 0-201-72214-3
1. Java (Computer program language) I. Wolz, Ursula. II. Title.

QA76.73.J38 K64 2002
005.13'3--dc21   2001045827

ISBN 0-201-72214-3
12345678910-DOC-04030201

DEDICATION

To Elliot's family:
Caryn, Debbie, Robin and Jeff, Richard, Jacquie, and Dustin

and to Ursula's family:
Jim, Chris, Henry, Kathy and their little girl

Preface

This textbook is intended for a first course in problem solving and program design with Java (CS1). It assumes no prior knowledge of computers or programming, and for most of its material, high school algebra is sufficient mathematics background. A limited knowledge of discrete mathematics is desirable for a few sections.

Problem Solving and Program Design

The primary emphasis in this text is on **problem solving** with Java. We accomplish this by selecting features of the language that lend themselves to good program design. We also emphasize abstraction and follow a standard five-step approach to program design (problem specification, analysis, design, implementation, and testing). We have modified this time-tested approach for software development to the object-oriented paradigm. We follow it faithfully in the solution of more than 20 case studies throughout the book. Ten of the case studies are new to this edition.

Classes and Objects Early

Students use predefined classes like `String` and `Math` to write small applications in Chapter 2. They begin to write their own worker classes to model real-world objects in Chapter 3. Examples are a `FoodItem` class, a `CoinChanger` class, a `Circle` class, and a `Washer` class. Methods are introduced in Chapter 2 and thoroughly covered in Chapter 3.

Object-Oriented Programming (OOP)

We continue to use worker classes in applications and discuss OOP concepts in an informal manner. We provide a detailed discussion of OOP in Chapter 6. We introduce class hierarchies, inheritance, interfaces, and abstract classes by studying several case studies that use these features.

Standard Input/Output Stressed

We use standard Java for input and output. Starting in Chapter 1, we use class **JOptionPane** (part of **Swing**) for windows-based input and output and we use the console window for more extensive output. In Chapter 3, we provide an optional package with static methods for input (based on **JOptionPane**) that simplifies data entry with dialog windows. The input methods check for number format errors and can check for range violations. Most programs in the book use standard Java I/O methods, but students can use the optional package if they wish.

This is a departure from the first edition, which utilized a nonstandard graphical user interface (GUI) package. Our experience is that many of the benefits of this package can be derived through class **JOptionPane**. Many Java programming instructors preferred to teach standard methods rather than rely on a nonstandard package. We hope that we have met the needs of most users by relying on standard input/output and by also providing an optional nonstandard package that is simpler to use.

Applets and Applications

We focus on applications in Chapters 2 and 3, where we attempt to teach the basics of simple programs that calculate results. We use applications rather than applets because we don't want students to have to deal with the details of providing a GUI. We introduce applets, HyperText Markup Language (HTML), and graphics programming using the AWT Graphics class to draw simple graphical patterns in Chapter 3. When we cover GUIs in Chapter 7, we use **Swing** components (see below).

Control Structures and Indexed Data Structures

In this edition, we cover selection and loop control structures together in Chapter 4. However, the control structures are not intermixed. We complete the selection control structures before we begin loop control structures, so instructors can separate these structures if they wish to.

We study arrays in Chapter 5, along with other Java indexed data collections, the **Vector** class and **ArrayList** class. We also discuss wrapper classes for the primitive types in this chapter.

GUIs

We revisit applets and HTML in Chapter 7 when we describe how to build GUIs using **Swing** components. We also show how to use class **JFrame** to write applications that have GUIs. We show several examples of GUIs in both applications and applets.

Exceptions and Streams

Chapter 8 is a new chapter on exceptions and streams. Knowing how to catch and throw exceptions is critical to stream processing, so we begin the chapter with a discussion of exceptions. The chapter covers streams of characters, binary streams, and streams of objects.

Coverage of Advanced Topics

Chapters 9 and 10 concern themselves with more traditional aspects of programming often found in CS2: recursion and processing linked data structures. We develop classes for linked lists, stacks, queues, and binary search trees. We define the node structure in inner classes. We also show how to use the `LinkedList` collection class and the `ListIterator` class. Many CS1 courses would not include this advanced material.

Flexibility of Coverage

There is sufficient material in the textbook for one and a half semesters or for two quarters. We consider Chapters 1 through 7 the core of the book, and they should be covered by all students. The first four chapters (through control structures) must be covered in sequence:

1. Introduction to Computers, Problem Solving, and Programming

2. Using Primitive Data Types and Using Classes

3. Object-Oriented Design and Writing Worker Classes

4. Control Structures: Decisions and Loops

The next three chapters deal with arrays, OOP, and GUI design, and they can be covered in a variety of ways:

5. Arrays and Vectors

6. Class Hierarchies, Inheritance, and Interfaces

7. Graphical User Interfaces (GUIs)

Faculty who want to cover GUIs earlier can cover Chapter 7 first, omitting the few examples that involve arrays. Similarly, faculty who want to cover OOP details earlier can introduce the fundamentals of using arrays (Sections 5.1–5.3) and then cover Chapter 6 in detail. Then continue with the rest of Chapter 5 or Chapter 7.

Chapter 9, Recursion, could also be introduced earlier. Sections 9.1–9.3 could be covered after Chapter 4 and the rest of the chapter could be covered after Chapter 5.

Pedagogical Features

We employ several pedagogical features to enhance the usefulness of the book as a teaching tool. Discussion of some of these features follows.

End-of-Section Exercises: Most sections end with a number of self-check exercises, including exercises that require analysis of program fragments as well as short programming exercises. Answers to odd-numbered self-check exercises appear at the back of the book; answers to other exercises are provided in the Instructor's Manual.

End-of-Chapter Exercises: Each chapter ends with a set of quick-check exercises with answers. There are also chapter review exercises with solutions provided in the Instructor's Manual.

End-of-Chapter Projects: There are several projects at the end of each chapter that are suitable for programming assignments. Answers to selected projects appear in the Instructor's Manual.

Examples and Case Studies: The text contains a large number and variety of programming examples. Whenever possible, examples contain complete class or method definitions rather than incomplete fragments. Each chapter contains one or more case studies that are solved following the software development method.

Syntax Displays: The syntax displays describe the syntax and semantics of each new Java feature complete with examples.

Program Style Displays: The program style displays discuss issues of good programming style.

Error Discussions and Chapter Review: Each chapter ends with a section that discusses common programming errors. Chapter reviews include a table of new Java constructs.

Appendixes and Supplements

Appendixes: The text concludes with several appendixes covering the Java language, HTML, unicode, Borland JBuilder, resources for finding out more about Java, and a summary of Java class libraries.

Packages and Classes: Further information about this textbook can be found at www.aw.com/cssupport. You will be able to download package psJava and source code for all the classes provided in the textbook.

Instructor's Manual: Access to an online instructor's manual is available through your Addison-Wesley sales representative. The Instructor's Manual contains answers to selected exercises and projects and is available to qualified instructor's only.

Acknowledgments

There were many individuals without whose support this book could not have been written. These include the principal reviewers of this edition and the first edition:

Julia E. Benson, DeKalb College

Richard J. Botting, California State University, San Bernadino

Tom Cortina, SUNY at Stony Brook

Robert H. Dependahl, Jr., Santa Barbara City College

Bill Grosky, Wayne State University

Stanley H. Lipson, Kean University of New Jersey

David Mathias, Ohio State University

Bina Ramamurthy, SUNY at Buffalo

Stuart Reges, University of Arizona

James Svoboda, Clarkson University

John S. Zelek, University of Guelph

Several students at The College of New Jersey (TCNJ) and Temple University helped with the development of the textbook. They include Brice Behringer, Greg Bronevetsky, George Drayer, William Fenstermaker, Mark Nikolsky, Brian Robinson, and Michael Sipper from TCNJ and N.D. Brabham, Yadh El Afrit, Thaung Ngwe, Blossom Pinheiro, Brian Rubin, John Salmon, and Saritha Somasundaram from Temple.

We are also grateful to our colleagues who provided valuable insight and advice. In particular, we want to acknowledge Joseph Turner of Clemson University and Penny Anderson and Shawn Sivy from The College of New Jersey.

There are several individuals at Addison-Wesley who worked very hard to see this textbook completed. They include our sponsoring editor Susan Hartman and her very able assistant Elinor Actipis. Among their many contributions, Susan and Elinor worked with us and the principal reviewers to help refine our manuscript.

Finally, we would like to acknowledge the help and support of our families. The members of Ursula's household, her husband Jim, son Christopher, and father Henry, were all very understanding about her preoccupation with this book over the past year as were Elliot's wife Caryn and his children Deborah, Richard, and Robin and grandson Dustin. We are grateful to them all for their love and support.

EBK
UW

Contents

Chapter 10 Linked Data Structures   623

Introduction to Computers, Problem Solving, and Programming

Since the 1940s, the computer has dramatically changed the way we live and how we do business. Computers provide instructional material in school, print transcripts, prepare bills and paychecks, reserve airline and concert tickets, allow us to bank and shop conveniently, and help us write term papers and books. The Internet and, more recently, the World Wide Web give us access to information on computers all over the world.

Although we often are led to believe otherwise, computers cannot reason as we do. Basically, computers are devices for performing computations at incredible speeds (more than 1 million operations per second) and with great accuracy. To accomplish anything useful, however, a computer must be provided with a program, that is, a list of instructions. Programs are usually written in special computer programming languages such as Java, which is the subject of this book. The Java programming language is a key component of programming on the World Wide Web.

1

In this chapter, we introduce you to the computer and its components. We also present an overview of programming languages. Finally, we describe a method for developing software (programs), and we use it to write a first Java program.

1.1   Overview of Computers

In our everyday life, we come in contact with computers frequently, and you may have used computers for word processing or for exploring the **World Wide Web**. You may even have studied programming in high school. But computers weren't always seen as accessible to everyone. Not long ago, most people considered computers to be mysterious devices whose secrets were known only by a few computer wizards.

Mainframe and Minicomputers

The first electronic computer was designed in the late 1930s by Dr. John Atanasoff at Iowa State University. Atanasoff designed his computer to assist graduate students in nuclear physics with their mathematical computations.

The first large-scale, general-purpose electronic digital computer, called the ENIAC, was completed in 1946 at the University of Pennsylvania. The United States Army funded its design. The ENIAC weighed 30 tons and occupied a 30- by 50-foot space. ENIAC was used to compute ballistics tables, to predict the weather, and to make atomic energy calculations.

These early computers used vacuum tubes as their basic electronic component. Technological advances in the design and manufacture of electronic components led to new generations of computers that were considerably smaller, faster, and less expensive than previous ones.

Up to 1970, most computers were very expensive and were used primarily by the government, universities, and large companies. The main applications of computers were performing scientific calculations and business data processing operations. Most of these computers were large **mainframe** computers, but smaller computers called **minicomputers** were used in research laboratories and for special applications such as controlling a power plant or controlling a complicated manufacturing process.

Sharing Computer Resources

In this period, there were many more computer users than computers. A technique called **time sharing** was developed to allow many users to simultaneously access a mainframe or minicomputer. The problem with time sharing is that you have to wait your turn to use the computer resources. Because the computer is so fast, computer users often don't even realize they are taking turns. However, during peak periods waiting times can become excessive. Furthermore, if the computer stops working (an event called a crash), all users are affected because they must wait for the computer to be restarted.

Microcomputers

In the 1970s, the Altair and Apple computer companies manufactured the first **microcomputers**. In a microcomputer, the computer processor (a **microprocessor**) is fabricated on a single electronic component called a **computer chip**, which is about the size of a postage stamp. Their affordability and small size enable computer chips to be installed in watches, pocket calculators, cameras, home appliances, automobiles, and, of course, computers.

As microprocessors became more powerful and less expensive, computer usage changed. Instead of many users simultaneously sharing a single mainframe computer, office workers have their own **personal computers** on a desktop, **portable computers** that can be carried in a briefcase, or both. Today, there are **palm computers** that fit in your hand and allow you to connect to the Internet and to other, more powerful computers.

Although microcomputers do not have the huge resources of minicomputers and mainframes, they provide their users with dedicated resources. Waiting your turn is no longer an issue. Also, if one machine crashes, others are not affected. The major disadvantage of early personal computers or workstation computers was that they were isolated from the vast resources of the larger machines. In the next section, we see how computer networks solve this problem.

EXERCISES FOR SECTION 1.1

SELF-CHECK

1. List the different kinds of computers from smallest to largest.

2. Why do you think that, in a time-shared environment, each computer user is unaware that others are also using the computer?

1.2 Computer Components

A computer system consists of two major components. The first is **hardware**, the actual equipment used to perform the computations. The second essential major component is **software**, the programs. **Programs** enable us to communicate with a computer by providing it with the list of instructions it needs to operate.

Despite significant variations in cost, size, and capabilities, modern computers resemble each other in many basic ways. Essentially, most consist of the following hardware components:

◆ Main memory

◆ Secondary memory, which includes storage media such as hard disks, floppy disks, and CD-ROMs

◆ Central processor unit

◆ Input devices, such as a keyboard and a mouse

◆ Output devices, such as monitors and printers

◆ Network connection, such as a modem or network interface card

Figure 1.1 shows how these components interact in a computer when a program is executed; the arrows connecting the components show the direction of information flow.

Figure 1.1   Computer components

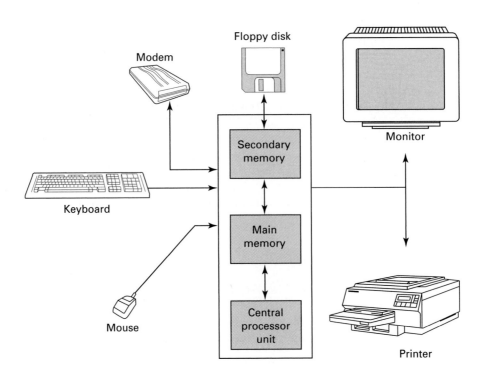

The program must be transferred from secondary memory (usually a disk) to main memory before it can be run. Data must be supplied from some source. The person using a program (the program user) may supply data through an input device.

Data may also come from a data file located in secondary memory, or it may come from a remote machine via the network connection. The data are stored in the computer's main memory, where they can be accessed and manipulated by the central processor unit. The results of this manipulation are stored in main memory. Finally, the information (results) in main memory may be displayed through an output device, stored in secondary storage, or sent to another computer via the network.

In the remainder of this section, we describe these components in more detail.

Memory

Memory is an essential component in any computer. Before discussing the types of memory—main and secondary—let's first look at what it consists of and how the computer works with it.

Anatomy of memory

Imagine the memory of a computer as an ordered sequence of storage locations called **memory cells** (see Fig. 1.2). To store and access information, the computer must have some way of identifying the individual memory cells. Therefore, each memory cell has a unique **address** that indicates its relative position in memory. Figure 1.2 shows a computer memory consisting of 1000 memory cells with addresses 0 through 999. Most computers have millions of individual memory cells, each with its own address.

The data stored in a memory cell are called the **contents** of the cell. Every memory cell always has some contents, although the contents may not be meaningful to us. In Fig. 1.2, the contents of memory cell 3 is the number **−26** and the contents of memory cell 4 is the letter **H**.

A memory cell can also contain a program instruction. Cells 6 through 8 in Fig. 1.2 store instructions to add two numbers (from cells 1 and 3) and to save the result in memory cell 1. The ability to store programs as well as data in memory is called the **stored-program concept**: a program's instructions must be stored in main memory before they can be executed. We can change the computer's operation by storing a different program in memory.

Bytes and Bits

A memory cell is actually a grouping of smaller units called bytes. A **byte** is the smallest addressable unit of memory. A byte is also the amount of storage required to hold a single character (for example, the letter **H** in cell 4 of Fig. 1.2) using the most common computer code for representing characters (**ASCII**; American Standard Code for Information Interchange). The number of bytes a memory cell may contain varies from computer to computer.

Figure 1.2   1000 memory cells in main memory

Address	Contents
0	–27.2
1	354
2	0.005
3	–26
4	H
5	400
6	RTV 001
7	ADD 003
8	STO 001
. . .	. . .
998	X
999	75.62

A byte is composed of even smaller units of storage called bits (see Fig. 1.3). The term **bit** derives from the words *binary digit* and is the smallest element a computer can deal with. Binary refers to a number system based on two numbers, 0 and 1; therefore, a bit is either a 0 or a 1. Generally there are 8 bits to a byte.

Storing and retrieving information in memory

Each value in memory is represented by a particular pattern of 0s and 1s, that is, bits. The pattern can be used to represent a number, a character such as the letter **H**, or an instruction such as **ADD 003**. A computer can either store or retrieve a value. To **store** a value, the computer sets each bit of a selected memory cell to either 0 or 1; storing a value destroys the previous contents of the cell. To **retrieve** a value from a memory cell, the computer copies the pattern of 0s and 1s stored in that cell to another storage area for processing; the copy operation does not destroy the contents of the cell whose value is retrieved. The process described is the same regardless of the kind of information—character, number, or program instruction—to be stored or retrieved.

Main memory

Main memory stores programs, data, and results and is made of electronic circuitry in the form of computer chips. In most computers, there are two types of main memory: **random access memory (RAM)**, which offers temporary storage of programs and data, and **read-only memory (ROM)**, which stores programs or data permanently.

Figure 1.3   Relationship between a byte and a bit

RAM temporarily stores programs while they are being executed (carried out) by the computer. It also temporarily stores data such as numbers, names, and even pictures (called graphics or images) while a program is manipulating them. RAM is usually **volatile memory**, which means that when you switch off the computer, you will lose everything in RAM. To prevent this loss, you should store the contents of RAM in secondary memory, which provides for semipermanent storage of data, before you turn off your computer.

ROM, on the other hand, stores information permanently. The computer can retrieve (or read) information in ROM but cannot store (or write) information in these memory cells, hence its name, read-only memory. Because read-only memory is not volatile, the data stored in ROM do not disappear when you switch off the computer. Most modern computers contain an internal ROM that stores the *boot instructions* needed to start up the computer when you first switch it on.

Usually a computer contains much more RAM than internal ROM; also, the amount of RAM can often be increased (up to a specified maximum), whereas the amount of internal ROM is usually fixed. When we refer to main memory in this text, we mean RAM because that is the part of main memory that is normally accessible to the Java programmer.

RAM is relatively fast memory; however, it is limited in size and is not permanent memory. Next, we introduce secondary memory, which, although slower than RAM, is both larger and more permanent.

Secondary memory and secondary storage devices

Secondary memory, through secondary storage devices, provides semipermanent data-storage capability. Secondary storage often consists of a magnetic medium such as tape or disk. Audiocassette tapes are an example of a magnetic medium on which music is stored. Computer tapes and disks store digital information instead (sequences of 0s and 1s). Magnetic media can easily be erased and recorded over.

The most common secondary storage device is a **disk drive**; it stores and retrieves data and programs on a disk, transferring the data between secondary memory and main memory. A disk is considered semipermanent storage because its contents can be changed.

Information stored on a disk is organized into separate collections called **files**. One file may contain a Java program. Another file may contain the data to be processed by that program (a **data file**). A third file could contain the results generated by a program (an **output file**).

The two most common kinds of magnetic disks for personal computers are **hard disks** (also called fixed disks) and **floppy disks**. Most personal computers contain one hard disk that cannot be removed from its disk drive; therefore, the storage area on a hard disk can be shared by all users of the computer. A hard disk can store much more data than can a single floppy disk, and the CPU can access that data much more quickly. Normally, the programs that are needed to operate the computer system are stored on its hard disk.

A floppy disk is a small Mylar sheet coated with magnetizable material and housed in a hard plastic container. Floppy disks are used primarily to store programs and data for individual users and to move small amounts of information between personal computers that are not easily networked. A computer user may have several floppy disks that can be inserted into a computer's floppy disk drive. Another portable, magnetic storage device is a Zip disk. These disks and their supporting drives store much more data than floppy disks and access it more quickly.

Another common storage device is the CD-ROM. A CD-ROM drive accesses information stored on plastic disks that are identical to compact disks (CDs) used in a CD audio player. Lasers are used to store binary information on a CD (a process called **burning a CD**) and optical technology is used to read that information. A CD-ROM provides a convenient way to store data that does not change. For example, commercial software products, images, sound (such as music), and large quantities of text such as encyclopedias are often provided on CD-ROMs. These disks are less expensive and more reliable than magnetic media. Many computers have CD-RW drives, which means they can write information onto a CD as well as read it. Some computers have drives that combine CD-RW capability with digital video (DVD).

Central Processor Unit

The **central processor unit (CPU)** has two roles: coordinating all computer operations and performing arithmetic and logical operations on data. The CPU follows the instructions contained in a computer program to determine which operations should be carried out and in what order. It then transmits coordinating control signals to the other computer components. For example, if the instruction requires getting data from a user, the CPU sends the necessary control signals to the input device.

To execute a program stored in main memory, the CPU retrieves each instruction in sequence (called **fetching an instruction**), interprets the instruction to determine what should be done, and then retrieves any data needed to carry out that instruction. Next, the CPU performs the actual manipulation, or processing, of the data it retrieved. The CPU stores the results temporarily in main memory, but it can also store them in secondary memory for later use.

The CPU can perform such arithmetic operations as addition, subtraction, multiplication, and division. The CPU also can compare the contents of two memory cells. For example, it might determine whether two values are equal and, if not, which memory cell has the larger value. The CPU can make decisions based on the results of that comparison.

Input/Output Devices

We use **input/output (I/O) devices** to communicate with the computer. Specifically, these devices allow us to enter data for a computation and to observe the results of that computation. The most common input device is a **keyboard** (see Fig. 1.4). The most common output device is a **monitor** (display screen).

A computer keyboard resembles a typewriter keyboard. When you press a letter or digit key, that character is sent to main memory and it is also displayed on the monitor at the position of the **cursor**, a moving place marker. A keyboard has extra keys for performing special functions. For example, on the computer keyboard shown in Fig. 1.4, the 12 keys in the top row labeled F1 through F12 are **function keys**. The activity performed when you press a function key depends on the program currently being executed; that is, pressing F4 in one program will usually not produce the same results as pressing F4 in another program. Other special keys enable you to delete characters, move the cursor, and enter a line of data you typed at the keyboard.

Another common input device is a mouse. A **mouse** is a pointing device. Other kinds of pointing devices are touch-sensitive screens (such as used in many automated teller machines) and the joy-sticks used with video games. A mouse is a hand-held device containing a rubber ball. When you move the mouse around on your desktop, the rubber ball rotates. As the ball moves, so does the **mouse cursor** (normally a small rectangle or an arrow) displayed on the monitor's screen. You can use the mouse to select an operation by moving the mouse cursor to a word or picture (called an **icon**) that represents the computer operation you wish to perform. You then press or click a mouse button to activate the operation selected.

A monitor provides a temporary display of the information that appears on its screen. If you want hard copy (a printed version) of some information, you must send that information to an output device called a **printer**.

Figure 1.4   Keyboard for IBM-type computers

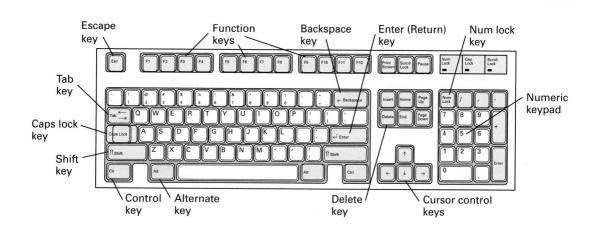

Computer Networks

Network technology was invented to connect computers together in order to share resources. Unlike a mainframe, which is a single computer shared by many users, a **computer network** consists of many computers that share resources. Within an organization, a **local-area network (LAN)** allows many personal computers to access sharable resources from a larger computer called a **server**. A network that links many individual computers and local-area networks over a large geographic area is called a **wide-area network (WAN)**. The most well-known WAN is the **Internet**, a network of university, corporate, government, and public-access networks. The World Wide Web is supported on the Internet.

Today, most computers are connected to a network and to the Internet. Computers can be networked with hardware connections and cables that transmit digital signals (sequences of 0s and 1s) directly, or through telephone lines and **modem**s (short for **modulator/demodulator**). The modem at the sending computer converts **digital signals** into **analog signals** (see Fig. 1.5) that can be sent over telephone lines. The modem at the destination computer converts the analog signals back to digital form that can be understood by the destination computer.

By sharing resources through networking, computer users get the best of both stand-alone personal computers and large mainframes. For example, many academic computer laboratories arrange their computer hardware in a LAN so that students can work on individual machines for word processing or programming tasks and can also retrieve course materials from a central source. If a computer within the network crashes, the users are not all affected, as is the case with time sharing.

The World Wide Web

The World Wide Web (the Web) was introduced in 1989 and is one of the most popular applications of the Internet. The Web was developed at the European Laboratory for Particle Physics (CERN), which was interested in creating an effective and uniform way of accessing all the information on the Internet. You can use the Web to send, view, retrieve, and search for information.

A Web page is a single document or file stored on a computer that is connected to the Internet. Usually Web pages are in a special format called **Hypertext Markup**

Figure 1.5   Digital and analog signals

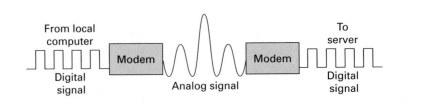

Language (HTML), which we will introduce in Chapter 4. You can easily interconnect documents on the Web by inserting links in one document that connect it to another. Anyone can create Web pages and there are no controls or checks for accuracy, so you should take this into account when accessing information on the Web.

To access the Web, you need a program called a **Web browser**. You use the browser to display the text and graphics in a Web document and to activate the links to other documents. Clicking on a link to a document causes that document to be transferred from the computer where it is stored to your own.

Programming for the Web

The Web has dramatically transformed the way people do business and get entertainment. Also, it has forced programmers to think about programs in new ways. Because networks consist of many different kinds and sizes of computers, all information and programs on the Web must be usable without modification by a variety of computers. A user of a Macintosh computer should be able to explore the Web in the same way that a Sun or IBM-compatible computer user does. Consequently, there is a need to write programs that can run on any of these machines so that the look and feel don't change substantially across computers (creating what is called **platform independence**).

The Web has also intensified the use of **multimedia**, the full integration of text, graphics, sound, video, and animation. For example, people use the Web to listen to music before they buy it or to view video clips of a news broadcast. Coordinating the programming of all of this material requires careful analysis of very complex problems involving huge amounts of data. For example a 10-minute video clip requires more storage capacity than that of the entire hard disk of a 1980s personal computer.

One of the reasons for the popularity of Java is that Java is the first programming language to exploit the networked programming environment. Java programs are platform independent. Also, you can embed special Java programs called **applets** in Web documents or Web pages. An applet enables a Web document to calculate and display information graphically or to interact with a user through a graphical user interface (GUI). We will have more to say about platform independence and applets in Section 1.5.

EXERCISES FOR SECTION 1.2

SELF-CHECK

1. If a computer were instructed to sum the contents of memory cells 2 and 999 and store the result in cell 0, what would be the contents of cells 0, 2, and 999 in Fig. 1.2?

2. One bit can have either of two values, 0 or 1. A combination of 2 bits can have one of four values: 00, 01, 10, 11. List all of the values you can form with a combination of 3 bits. Do the same for 4 bits.

3. List the following in order of smallest to largest: byte, bit, RAM, hard disk, floppy disk.

4. Explain the purpose of main memory, secondary memory, CPU, and the disk drive and disk.

5. What do you think each of the instructions in memory cells 6 though 8 in Fig.1.2 mean?

6. Explain the difference between the Internet and the World Wide Web.

7. For each device, indicate whether it usually provides temporary, semipermanent, or permanent storage: ROM, RAM, floppy disk, Zip disk, CD-ROM, hard disk.

8. Which storage component from the list in question 7 does a word processor use to store a letter while it is being typed? Which does it use to store the letter after you are finished? Which is used to store a software package you purchase? Which would you use to store some very large files you no longer need?

9. List some of the roles that a computer can play in a network.

10. Explain in your own words why platform independence is desirable.

11. What features of Java make it desirable for programming on the World Wide Web?

1.3 Computer Software

In the previous section we surveyed the components of a computer system, components referred to collectively as hardware. We also studied the fundamental operations that allow a computer to accomplish tasks: repeated fetching and execution of instructions. In this section we focus on these all-important lists of instructions called computer programs or computer software. We will consider first the software that makes the hardware available to the user.

Operating System

The collection of computer programs that control the interaction between the user and the computer hardware is called the operating system (OS). The operating system of a computer is often compared to the conductor of an orchestra because it is the software that is responsible for directing all computer operations and managing all computer resources. Usually part of the operating system is stored permanently in a ROM chip so that it is available as soon as the computer is turned on. A computer can look at the values in ROM but cannot write new values to the chip. The ROM-based portion of the OS contains the instructions necessary for loading into memory the rest of the operating system code, which typically resides on a disk. Loading the operating system into memory (RAM) is called **booting the computer**.

Some of the operating system's many responsibilities include the following:

1. Communicating with the computer user: receiving commands and carrying them out or rejecting them with an error message

2. Managing allocation of memory, processor time, and other resources for various tasks

3. Collecting input from the keyboard, mouse, and other input devices and providing this data to the currently running program

4. Conveying program output to the screen, printer, or other output device.

5. Accessing data from secondary storage

6. Writing data to secondary storage

In addition to these responsibilities, the operating system of a computer with multiple users must verify each individual's right to use the computer and must ensure that each user can access only data for which he or she has proper authorization.

Table 1.1 lists some widely used operating systems. An OS that uses a **command-line interface** displays a brief message called a **prompt** that indicates its readiness to receive input, and the user then types a command at the keyboard. Figure 1.6 shows entry of a UNIX command (`ls temp/misc`) requesting a list of the names of all the files (`Gridvar.c`, `Gridvar.exe`, `Gridok.dat`) in subdirectory `misc` of directory `temp`. In this case, the prompt is `mycomputer:~>`. (In this figure, input typed by the user is shown in color to distinguish it from computer-generated text.)

Table 1.1 Some widely used operating systems characterized by interface type

Command-Line Interface	Graphical User Interface
UNIX (or Linux)	Macintosh OS
MS-DOS	Windows 95/98/2000
VMS	Windows NT
	OS/2 Warp
	UNIX + X Window System

Figure 1.6   Entering a UNIX command to display a directory

```
mycomputer:~> ls temp/misc
Gridvar.c        Gridvar.exe      Gridok.dat

mycomputer:~>
```

In contrast, operating systems with a GUI interface provide the user with a system of icons and menus. To issue commands, the user moves the mouse cursor to point to the appropriate icon or menu selection and clicks a button once or twice. Figure 1.7 shows the result of "double clicking" on the "My Computer" icon at the top left of a Microsoft Windows desktop. The window with the white background and label "My Computer" appears on the screen. It has a menu line with the words "File," "Edit," "View," and "Help." This is a **pull-down menu**—clicking on the menu item View causes the list of choices shown in Fig. 1.7 to appear on the screen. The window also has icons with labels such as "3½ Floppy (A:)," "(C:)," "(D:)," "Control Panel," and "Printers." The first three icons represent secondary storage devices (floppy disk A:, hard disk C:, and so on). Double clicking on any of these devices brings up another window showing the directory for that device.

GUIs have made it much easier for people to interact with computers; however, compared to older text-based interaction, it is more difficult to program GUIs directly. The object-oriented approach to programming (discussed shortly) helps manage the complexity of programming with GUIs. Java is an object-oriented programming language that contains a standard set of classes such as windows. The programmer does not have to build GUI objects from scratch but can use predefined classes to do complicated things like displaying a window with buttons in it.

Application Software

Application programs are developed to assist a computer user in accomplishing specific tasks. For example, a word-processing application such as Microsoft Word or WordPerfect helps to create a document, a spreadsheet application such as Lotus 1-2-3 or Excel helps to automate tedious numerical calculations and to generate charts that depict data, and a database management application such as Access or dBASE assists in data storage and quick keyword-based access to large collections of records.

Computer users typically purchase application software on disks or CD-ROMs and **install the software** by copying the programs from the disks or CD-ROMs to the hard disk. When buying software, you must always check that the program you are purchasing is compatible with both the operating system and the computer hardware you plan to use. Programmers use programming languages, the subject of the next section, to write most commercial software.

Programming Languages

Developing new software requires writing lists of instructions for a computer to execute. However, software developers rarely write in the language directly understood by a computer because this **machine language** is a collection of binary numbers. Another drawback of machine language is that it is not standardized: There is a different

Figure 1.7   Effect of selecting "My Computer" icon

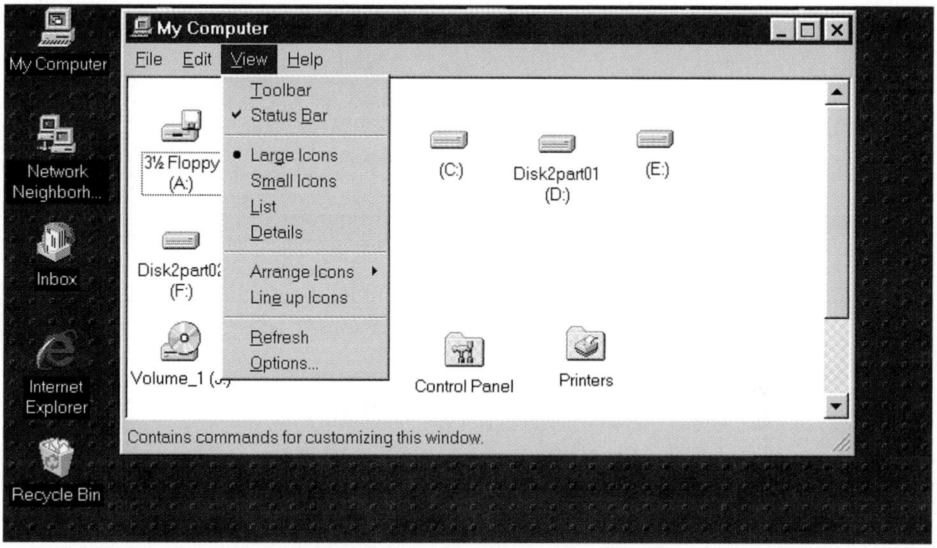

machine language for every type of CPU. This same drawback also applies to the somewhat more readable **assembly language**, a language in which computer operations are represented by mnemonic codes rather than binary numbers, and variables can be given names rather than binary memory addresses.

Table 1.2 shows a small machine language program fragment that adds two numbers and an equivalent fragment in assembly language. Notice that each assembly language instruction corresponds to exactly one machine instruction: The assembly language memory cells labeled **A** and **B** are space for data; they are not instructions. The symbol **?** indicates that we do not know the contents of the memory cells with addresses 00000100 and 00000101.

To write programs that are independent of the CPU on which they will be executed, software designers use **high-level languages**, which combine algebraic symbols and English words. For example, the machine/assembly language program fragment shown in Table 1.2 would be a single statement in a high-level language:

```
a = a + b;
```

This statement means "add the data in memory cells **a** and **b**, and store the result in memory cell **a** (replacing its previous value)."

Table 1.2 A program in machine and assembly language

Memory Addresses	Machine Language Instructions	Assembly Language Instructions
00000000	00010101	RTV A
00000001	01010110	ADD B
00000010	00110101	STO A
00000011	01110111	HLT
00000100	?	A ?
00000101	?	B ?

There are many high-level languages available. Table 1.3 lists some of the most widely used ones, along with the application areas that first popularized them.

Object-Oriented Programming

Table 1.3 lists two object-oriented languages: C++ and Java. Object-oriented languages are popular because they can make it easier to reuse and adapt previously written software.

An **object** is an entity characterized by a **state** and a **behavior**. The state can be encoded into a computer program as data; the behavior can be encoded as **methods** that perform essential tasks.

As an example of an object, consider a specific automobile, for example, a yellow 1999 Volkswagen Beetle. You may visualize a vehicle with four wheels, a steering wheel, a rounded body shape, a yellow color, and room for four passengers. These are the attributes, or data, of this automobile. Other attributes are the fact that it has an engine, its fuel efficiency (value is 38.5), the time in seconds to accelerate to 60 miles/hour (value is 9.5), and stopping distance from 60 miles/hour (value is 135.5

Table 1.3 Common high-level languages

High-Level Language	Original Purpose
BASIC	Simple language intended for student use in school work
C	For writing system software
C++	Extension of C that supports object-oriented programming
COBOL	For performing business data processing
FORTRAN	For engineering and scientific applications
Java	A highly portable object-oriented language used for programming on the Web
Lisp	For artificial intelligence applications that require manipulating abstract symbols
Pascal	For teaching students how to program in a careful, disciplined way

feet). You can also imagine the automobile's behavior or the actions associated with operating it, such as starting the engine, driving forward, driving in reverse, and stopping the automobile. These activities are analogous to methods.

A class is a prototype or model (abstraction) of a general automobile. The class describes the properties (attributes) of a general automobile but does not have any data associated with it. Table 1.4 shows some attributes of the class automobile and two objects of that class.

Classes can have other classes as components. For example, a car has an engine and wheels. Both of these components can be defined as separate classes.

These basic principles help programmers organize their solutions to problems. In particular, rather than starting each program from scratch, programmers use object-oriented programming because it encourages reuse of components (classes) that are already written. They can use existing classes as components of new classes and activate methods that were programmed for the existing classes.

EXERCISES FOR SECTION 1.3

SELF-CHECK

1. What do you think the five high-level language statements below mean?

    ```
    x = a + b + c;            x = y / z;
    d = c - b + a;            z = z + 1;
    kelvin = celsius + 273.15;
    ```

2. List two reasons why it would be preferable to write a program in Java rather than in machine language.

3. What are the two basic parts of a class?

Table 1.4 The relationship between a class and objects of the class

Class automobile	Object yourCar	Object parentsCar
Color	Red	White
Make	Toyota	Buick
Model	Celica	LeSabre
Year	1995	2001
Engine	Four-cylinder engine	Six-cylinder engine
Fuel efficiency	38.5	25.5
Time in seconds to 60 mph	5.5	7.5
Number of passengers	2	5
Has driver's seat (true or false)	True	True
Has rear seat (true or false)	False	True

4. How can existing classes be used by a programmer?

5. Explain the difference between class and object. Which represents an abstract object? Which represents an actual object?

I.4 Processing a High-Level Language Program

Because a computer can only understand machine language instruction, each instruction in a high-level language program must be translated into machine language before it can be executed. The original high-level language program is called the **source program**; the machine-language translation is called the **object program** (no relationship to an object of a class). The system program that performs this translation is called a **compiler** (see Fig. 1.8).

In languages like C and C++, the translation is done one time and the resulting object program can be run as often as needed. The user of a program is unaware of the compile process. The object program is delivered to the user as the final product. The software developer decides which machines to support and guarantees that the object program works correctly on those machines.

Cross-Platform Transparency and the Java Virtual Machine

Networks, and especially the World Wide Web, have encouraged the concept of **cross-platform transparency**. This means that an application program must run correctly regardless of what machine (platform) you use. This creates a special burden for the

Figure I.8   A unique C compiler for each computer

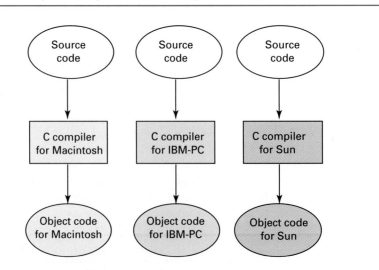

software developer, who must verify the correctness of object code for every machine on the network.

The Java language uses a model that relieves the developer of this burden and solves some other network-related problems as well. The Java compiler does not compile source code into machine language for any particular computer. Instead, the Java compiler creates object code (called **byte code**) for a simulated computer called the **Java Virtual Machine**. This "machine" is actually an **interpreter** program that translates each byte code instruction into the machine language for a particular computer and then executes it. Figure 1.9 shows the relationship between source code, the compiler, byte code (object code for the Java Virtual Machine), and the interpreter. The software developer can compile Java source code once (into byte code for the Java Virtual Machine) and know that it will run on a variety of computers. Files that contain Java source files have names that end with the extension `.java`. Files that contain byte code have names that end with the extension `.class`.

You may be wondering what the difference is between a compiler and an interpreter because both translate instructions in one computer language to another. The primary difference is that a compiler translates the entire program and creates an object program before it begins to execute individual instructions, whereas an interpreter interleaves translation and execution. An interpreter translates the first instruction, executes its machine language equivalent, translates the second instruction, executes it, and so on.

The Java compiler and interpreter are part of the Java Development Kit (JDK), which can be downloaded from the Sun Microsystems Web site (www.sun.com) and installed on any computer. There is also a Java Software Development Kit (SDK),

Figure 1.9   The Java Virtual Machine model

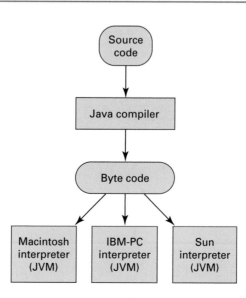

which contains other useful software tools. Similar tools are often included in an Integrated Development Environment (IDE) such as the one on the CD included with this book. An IDE combines an editor, Java compiler, and other Java support tools that will help you build and test Java programs.

Applets and Applications

A side benefit of the virtual machine approach is that it supports **applets**, Java programs that run as part of a World Wide Web page. An applet is stored at a remote site on the Web but is executed on the user's local computer (see Fig. 1.10). Because the Web supports platform transparency, an applet can run on any machine that is able to access its Web page. Without the virtual machine concept, the Web site would need a different object code file for the applet for each kind of platform. When a user requested a program, the Web site would have to identify the type of computer the user has and send the appropriate object code.

With platform transparency the Web site can send the same object code program for an applet to all users regardless of the user's computer. The local machine and its byte code interpreter handle the details of executing the application. This kind of compartmentalizing and distribution of responsibility is a fundamental principle of network, GUI, and object-oriented programming.

A **Java application** differs from an applet in that it does not need to be part of a Web page to be executed. A Java application is not part of a Web page and runs like any other program that runs on a particular computer. In this text we will initially focus on applications rather than applets because they are less complicated and permit us to concentrate on the important concepts of programming and problem solving.

Figure 1.10   **Accessing an applet from a remote computer and running it**

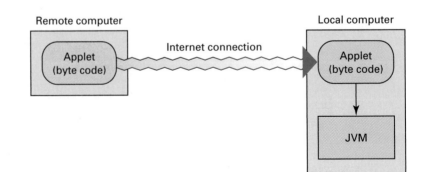

EXERCISES FOR SECTION 1.4

SELF-CHECK

1. Explain the difference between compiling a C program and compiling a Java program.

2. What is the difference between a Java language statement, a byte code instruction, and a machine language instruction? Which do you create, which does the Java compiler create, and which does the Java Virtual Machine (interpreter) create?

3. What are the advantages of a virtual machine?

4. Explain the difference between an applet and an application.

1.5 The Software Development Method

Programming is a problem-solving activity. If you are a good problem solver, you have the potential to become a good programmer. Therefore, one goal of this book is to help you improve your problem-solving ability. Problem-solving methods are covered in many subject areas. Business students learn to solve problems with a *systems approach,* whereas engineering and science students use the *engineering and scientific method.* Programmers use the *software development method.*

In object-oriented design the focus is on selecting and implementing classes. Wherever possible, we want to reuse existing classes as is or use them as components of new classes or modify them to create new classes. This approach lets programmers (software designers) use classes as off-the-shelf components to design and build new software systems just as hardware designers use off-the-shelf electronic circuits and components to design and build new computers. Incorporating these ideas into the software development method gives us a methodology for object-oriented design:

1. Specify the problem requirements

2. Analyze the problem and identify the classes that will be needed

3. Design the classes to solve the problem by

   a. Locating relevant classes in existing libraries

   b. Modifying existing classes where necessary

   c. Designing new classes where necessary

4. Implement the new and modified classes

5. Test and verify the completed program

6. Maintain and update the program

We describe these steps in more detail next.

Problem

Specifying the problem requirements forces you to state the problem clearly and unambiguously and to gain a clear understanding of what is required for its solution. Your objective is to eliminate unimportant aspects and zero in on the root problem. This is not as easy as it sounds. You may find you need more information from the person who posed the problem.

Analysis

Analyzing the problem involves

- Identifying the problem **inputs** (i.e., the data with which you have to work)
- Identifying the problem **outputs** (i.e., the desired results)
- Identifying any additional requirements or constraints on the solution
- Identifying the processes that transform the inputs into outputs

You should also identify the classes that will participate in solving the problem. Sometimes the description of a class will be obvious; other times it will feel somewhat contrived, especially for very small problems that involve simple arithmetic calculations. Typically, for larger problems, when you really understand the problem, the classes you have identified make a lot of sense.

You should also develop a list of problem variables and their relationships. These relationships may be expressed as formulas. In some situations, you may have to make certain assumptions or simplifications to derive these relationships. The process of extracting the essential problem data and their relationships from the problem statement is called **abstraction**.

Design the Classes

Designing the classes to solve the problem requires you to identify existing classes that you can use as is, to identify classes you wish to modify, and to identify classes that you will write from scratch. This is often the most difficult part of the problem-solving process. Many programmers are tempted to write all of their classes from scratch. This is because it is more fun to solve small problems on your own than to try to find existing solutions elsewhere.

For each class you have identified, you want to identify the data it stores and the methods it has for operating on its data. You also want to keep track of its interaction with objects of other classes.

Many of our problems will involve at least two classes: we will use a *worker class* that represents the object we are modeling. Then we will identify a *user interface class* or *application class* that interacts with the user (you or someone else) to get the problem inputs and to display the problem outputs and results. In this way, we separate the tasks associated with the worker class from those that are performed by the user interface class. This **separation of concerns** is an important aspect of object-oriented design.

Most computer problems consist of at least the following subproblems:

1. Get the data (input), typically asking a user.

2. Perform computations that are required.

3. Display the results (output) in a meaningful way.

Generally, the worker class will contain method(s) for performing subproblem 2, and the application class will contain methods for performing subproblems 1 and 3.

Implementation

Implementing the solution involves writing the new classes in Java. For classes you are modifying, you must write code that describes your modifications.

Writing a class consists of identifying the data to be stored in the class and writing the methods (operations) of the class. Prior to writing a method, we recommend that you write the list of steps or **algorithm** performed by that method.

Testing

Testing and verifying the program requires testing the completed program to demonstrate that it works as desired. Don't rely on just one test case—run the program several times using different sets of data, making sure that it works correctly for every situation required in the problem statement or provided for in your solution.

Maintenance

Maintaining and updating the program involves modifying a program to remove previously undetected errors and to keep it up-to-date with changes in its environment. For example, changes in government regulations or company policies may require modifications to existing systems. Maintenance may also involve adapting the code to integrate it with new kinds of computers and operating systems. Twenty years ago no one thought that programs would remain in use more than 5 years. As we approached the year 2000, many older programs were still in use and showed little signs of becoming obsolete. Consequently, a massive and expensive effort was required to make these programs "Y2K compatible."

The problem resulted because many of these older programs were written when computer storage space was at a premium, at a time when program designers stored only the last two digits of a year instead of all four digits. These programs represent the year 1999 using the digit pair 99 and the year 2000 using the digit pair 00, which is smaller, not larger, than any other two-digit pair. This discrepancy can lead to errors in calculations that are based on the current date or on the elapsed time in years. This points out that it is generally not wise to introduce inaccuracies in a program just to save some memory space or computer time and that programs should be written with the future in mind.

Applying the Software Development Method

Now let's walk through a sample case study to illustrate the software development method. Don't worry about understanding the details just yet. We will explain them in the next chapter. Our immediate goal is to demonstrate the software development method and to show how it helps us organize and develop solutions to programming problems.

CASE STUDY SHOWING YOUR NAME IN STARS

PROBLEM   A goal of many actors is to "see their name in lights" on Broadway. As novice programmers, your goal is more modest—to see your name in stars. You need to write a program that reads your name and displays it surrounded by stars.

ANALYSIS   The data for this program consists of your name. The output is your name in stars. To make it a bit more impressive, we will show three lines with your name in stars. The data requirements are listed below.

Data Requirements

> *Problem Input*
> Your name
>
> *Problem Output*
> Three lines showing your name in stars

DESIGN   We need to create two new classes to solve this problem, but we will be able to use a Java class that has methods for interacting with the user through dialog windows. We need a class that provides storage for your name and knows how to surround it in stars. This will be our worker class, `NameInStars`. We also need an application class that interacts with the user. The role of the application class is to get your name, store it in an object of type `NameInStars` (also called an **instance** of `NameInStars`), ask that object to surround your name in stars, and then display the result. The main method in class `ShowNameInStars` performs these tasks. We describe the two classes next.

Class NameInStars	Class ShowNameInStars
Data Fields	**Data Fields**
Your name	An object of type NameInStars
Methods	**Methods**
Surround your name in stars	The main method
Classes Used	**Classes Used**
—	NameInStars, JOptionPane

The class definitions show that class **ShowNameInStars** (the application class) uses class **NameInStars** and class **JOptionPane** which is part of Java. The worker class **NameInStars** has a method for surrounding a name in stars. The application class **ShowNameInStars** has a main method, which is where a Java program begins execution. As we will see in Section 2.5, class **JOptionPane** has methods for interacting with the user through dialog and message windows.

IMPLEMENTATION   Fig. 1.11 shows class **NameInStars**. It has a data field (**name**) to store your name and a method **surroundNameInStars()** to surround it in stars. Fig. 1.12 shows class **ShowNameInStars**, which contains a main method. When you run the application, the main method uses the **JOptionPane** method **showInputDialog()** to read your name. Next, it creates an object **you** of type **NameInStars**, and finally it uses the **JOptionPane** method **showMessageDialog()** to display your name surrounded in stars. We will explain these statements in Chapter 2.

Figure 1.11   Class NameInStars

```
public class NameInStars {
   // data fields
   private String name;

   // methods
   public NameInStars(String n) {
      name = nam;
   }

   public String surroundNameInStars() {
      return "*****" + name + "*****\n" +
             "*****" + name + "*****\n" +
             "*****" + name + "*****";
   }
}
```

Figure 1.12   Class ShowNameInStars

```
import javax.swing.*;

public class ShowNameInStars {

    public static void main(String[] args) {
        // Get the user's name
        String userName = JOptionPane.showInputDialog("Enter your name");

        // Create a NameInStars object that stores the user's name.
        NameInStars you = new NameInStars(userName);

        // Display your name in stars three times
        JOptionPane.showMessageDialog(null, you.surroundNameInStars());
    }
}
```

TESTING   Fig. 1.13 shows a sample run of the application class
ShowNameInStars. As shown in Fig. 1.13, a dialog window appears asking the user
to "Enter your name." When the user types in a name and presses Enter or clicks on
the OK button, a message window appears that displays the user's name surrounded
in stars three times.

Object-oriented programming allows us to compartmentalize a problem solution
into separate classes and to concentrate on one class at a time. A powerful thing about
object-oriented programming is that a lot of messy detail can be hidden within
classes and methods. In Fig. 1.12 we use methods **showInputDialog()** and
showMessageDialog() of the predefined class **JOptionPane**. We don't need to
know how these methods work to use them in our program.

Figure 1.13   Sample run of application class ShowNameInStars

EXERCISES FOR SECTION 1.5

SELF-CHECK

1. List the steps of the software development method.

2. What is an algorithm?

3. In which phase are algorithms developed? In which phase do you identify the problem inputs and outputs?

4. Why is software maintenance important?

5. Describe what information you specify about a class in the design phase.

PROGRAMMING

1. Change class **NameInStars** in Fig. 1.11 so that the application in Fig. 1.12 will display **Hello** *your name* twice where your name is stored in an object of this class.

1.6 Professional Ethics for Computer Programmers

We end this introductory chapter with a discussion of professional ethics for computer programmers. We hope that this first course will spark an interest in a career in computing or, at least, give you the desire to be more involved in computing as you continue your college education. Like other professionals, computer programmers and software system designers (called software engineers) should follow certain standards of professional conduct.

Privacy and Misuse of Data

As part of their jobs, programmers may access large data banks (or databases) that contain sensitive personnel information, information that is classified "secret" or "top secret," or financial transaction data. Programmers should always behave in a socially responsible manner and not retrieve information that they are not entitled to see. They should not use information to which they are given access for their own personal gain or do anything that would be considered illegal, unethical, or harmful to others. Just as doctors and lawyers must keep patient information confidential, programmers must respect an individual's right to privacy.

A programmer who changes information in a database containing financial records for his or her own personal gain is guilty of **computer theft** or **computer fraud**. An example would be changing the amount of money in a bank account. This is a felony that can lead to fines and imprisonment.

Hacking Is Irresponsible and Illegal

You may have heard stories about "computer hackers" who have broken into secure data banks by using their own computer to call the computer that controls access to the data bank. Some individuals have sold classified information retrieved in this way to intelligence agencies of other countries. Other hackers have tried to break into computers to retrieve information for their own amusement or as a prank or just to demonstrate that they can do it. Regardless of the intent, this activity is illegal, and the government will prosecute anyone who does this. Your university now probably addresses this kind of activity in your student handbook. The punishment is probably similar to that for other criminal activity, because that is exactly what it is.

Another illegal activity sometimes practiced by hackers is attaching harmful code, called a **virus**, to another program so that the virus code copies itself throughout a computer's disk memory. A virus will cause sporadic activities to disrupt the operation of the host computer. For example, unusual messages may appear on the screen at certain times. Viruses can also cause the host computer to erase portions of its own disk memory, thereby destroying valuable information and programs. Viruses are spread from one computer to another when data are copied from the infected disk and processed by a different computer. Certainly, these kinds of activities should not be considered harmless pranks; they are illegal and should not be done under any circumstances.

Plagiarism and Software Piracy

Another example of unprofessional behavior is using someone else's programs without permission. Although it is certainly permissible to use modules in libraries that have been developed for reuse by your own company's programmers, you cannot use another programmer's personal programs or programs from another company without getting permission beforehand. Doing this may lead to a lawsuit, and you or your company may have to pay damages.

Another fraudulent practice is submitting another student's code as your own. This, of course, is plagiarism and is no different from copying paragraphs of information from a book or journal article and calling it your own. Most universities have severe penalties for plagiarism, which may include failing the course and/or dismissal from the university. You should be aware that even if you modify the code slightly or substitute your own comments or different variable names, you are still guilty of plagiarism if you are using another person's ideas and code. To avoid any question of plagiarism, find out beforehand your instructor's rules with respect to working with others on a project. If group efforts are not allowed, make sure that you work independently and submit only your own code.

Many commercial software packages are protected by copyright laws and cannot be copied or duplicated for use on another computer. Therefore, it is illegal to make additional copies of protected software for use elsewhere, a practice called **software piracy**, and if you do this, your company or university can be fined heavily for allowing this activity to occur. Not only is software piracy against the law, but using software copied from another computer increases the possibility that your computer will receive a virus. For all these reasons, you should read the copyright restrictions that pertain to a particular software package and adhere to them.

Misuse of a Computer Resource

Computer system access privileges or user account codes are also private property. Such privileges are usually granted for a specific purpose. For example, you may be given a computer account for work to be done in a particular course or, perhaps, for work to be done during the time you are a student at your university. The privilege is to be protected; it should not be loaned to anyone else and should not be used for any purpose for which it was not intended. When you leave the institution, this privilege is normally terminated and any accounts associated with the privilege will be closed.

Computers, computer programs, data, and access (account) codes are like any other property. If they belong to someone else and you are not explicitly given use privileges, do not use them. If you are granted a usage privilege for a specific purpose, do not abuse the privilege or it will be taken away.

Legal issues aside, it is important that we apply the same principles of right and wrong to computerized property and access rights as to all other property and privileges. If you are not sure about the propriety of something you are thinking about doing, ask first. As students and professionals in computing, we need to be aware of the example we set for others. As a group of individuals who are most dependent on computers and computer software, programmers and programming students must respect the rights of others. If we set a bad example, others are sure to follow.

CHAPTER REVIEW

1. The basic components of a computer are main and secondary memory, the CPU, and input and output devices.

2. Main memory is organized into individual storage locations—memory cells.

   - Each memory cell has a unique address.

   - A memory cell is a collection of bytes; a byte is a collection of 8 bits.

   - A memory cell is never empty, but its initial contents may be meaningless to your program.

   - The current contents of a memory cell are lost whenever new information is stored in that cell.

■ Programs *must* be copied into the memory of the computer before they can be executed.

■ Data cannot be manipulated by the computer until they are first stored in memory.

3. Information in secondary memory is organized into files: program files and data files. Secondary memory stores information in semipermanent form and is less expensive than main memory.

4. Mainframes and minicomputers accommodate multiple users simultaneously through a technique called time sharing. Personal computers can work alone or can access the resources of larger computers if they are connected to a network.

5. A network is a collection of computers that are linked together. Networked computers share resources such as files and printers.

6. The Internet is an interconnected collection of computer networks. The Internet supports the World Wide Web, a collection of linked documents on computers throughout the world that can be accessed using a Web browser.

7. A computer cannot think for itself; you must use a programming language to instruct it in a precise and unambiguous manner to perform a task.

8. Two categories of programming languages are machine language (meaningful to the computer) and high-level language (meaningful to the programmer). A third category, assembly language, is similar to machine language except that it uses special mnemonic codes for operations and names for memory cells instead of numeric addresses.

9. You use several system programs to prepare a high-level language program for execution. The computer *operating system* enables you to access these programs. An *editor* enters a high-level language program into memory. A *compiler* translates a high-level language program (the source program) into the object program.

10. The Java compiler translates a Java source program into byte code. The Java Virtual Machine (interpreter) translates each byte code instruction into machine language instructions for a particular computer or platform. The machine language instructions for the current byte code instruction execute before the next byte code instruction is translated.

11. Applets are Java programs that can be inserted into a Web page. When a Web page with an applet is downloaded to a computer, that computer's browser causes the applet to be executed.

12. Programming a computer can be fun if you are patient, organized, and careful. Following the software development method for solving problems using a

computer can be of considerable help in your programming work. Five major steps in the problem-solving process must be emphasized:

- Problem specification

- Problem analysis

- Program design

- Program implementation

- Program testing

13. Follow ethical standards of conduct in everything you do pertaining to computers. This means don't copy software that is copyright protected, don't hack into someone else's computer, and don't submit someone else's work as your own or lend your work to another student.

✔ **QUICK-CHECK EXERCISES**

1. The _____ translates a(n) _____ into byte code.

2. The _____ or _____ translates byte code into _____.

3. A(n) _____ interleaves translation with execution, whereas a(n) _____ _____ the entire program first and then executes the _____.

4. A high-level language program is saved on disk as a(n) _____ file.

5. The _____ program is used to create and save the source file.

6. Computer programs are _____ components of a computer system, whereas a disk drive is a(n) _____ component.

7. Determine whether each characteristic below applies to main memory or secondary memory:

   a. Faster to access

   b. Volatile

   c. May be extended almost without limit

   d. Less expensive per byte of storage

   e. Used to store files

   f. Central processor accesses it to obtain the next machine-language instruction for execution

   g. Provides semipermanent data storage

8. A(n) _____ network, or _____, would be found in a single computer laboratory, whereas the Internet is an example of a(n) _____ network.

9. A(n) _____ converts _____ signals to _____ signals for transmission over _____ .

10. In object-oriented programming, a(n) _____ is the model or prototype for an actual _____ .

11. List the six phases of the software development method outlined in this chapter.

ANSWERS TO QUICK-CHECK EXERCISES

1. compiler, Java program

2. interpreter, Java Virtual Machine, machine language instructions

3. interpreter, compiler, compiles, object program

4. source program

5. editor

6. software, hardware

7. main (a, b, f), secondary (c, d, e, g)

8. local-area network, LAN, wide-area network

9. modem, digital, analog, telephone lines

10. class, object

11. problem specification, analysis, design, implementation, testing, maintenance

REVIEW QUESTIONS

1. List at least three kinds of information stored in a computer.

2. List two functions of the CPU.

3. List two input devices, two output devices, and two secondary storage devices.

4. What are the different categories of programming languages and why are they needed?

6. What is the difference between applets and applications?

7. Why is Java used for programming over the Internet?

8. Explain the relationship between memory cells, bytes, and bits.

9. Explain the difference between Java applets and application programs.

10. What processes are needed to transform a Java program into machine language instructions?

11. What are the differences between RAM and ROM? Which contains the instructions that execute when you first boot your computer? Which can be extended? Which contains information that does not disappear when you turn off your computer?

12. What is the major reason for the popularity of object-oriented programming? Name two object-oriented programming languages.

2

Using Primitive Data Types and Using Classes

In this book, we will write programs that process two kinds of information: numeric information and sequences of characters or text. We will also write programs to manipulate objects that store collections of these basic kinds of information. This chapter begins to explore how these kinds of information are represented and manipulated using the Java primitive types and the `String` class.

In this chapter, we focus on using classes that are part of Java, rather than writing our own classes. We describe two useful Java classes: `JOptionPane` and `Math`. Class `Math` enables us to perform mathematical computations.

Class `JOptionPane` is part of a package called `swing` that was added to Java in version 1.2. `JOptionPane` contains methods that make it relatively easy to interact with a program user to get program data (input) and to display program results (output). We also show how to use methods `print` and `println` (not part of `JOptionPane`) to display output in the console window.

We also solve a case study in this chapter. The solution involves three classes: `JOptionPane`, `String`, and an application class.

2.1   Primitive Data Types

The Java compiler needs to know what kind of information is stored in each memory cell of a program. It also needs to know what operations can be performed without error on that information. Data types help the compiler with this task.

Data Types, Variables, and Declarations

A **data type** represents a particular kind of information and specifies the operations that can be performed on that information. In Java, some data types are built into the language and others are defined by Java programmers.

We use **variables** for two purposes in Java: to reference objects and to store values in memory. The term *variable* indicates that the object referenced or the value stored can change. A **declaration statement** is a program instruction that tells the compiler the name of a variable and its data type. A variable whose data type is a class type can reference an object (instance) of that class type. We illustrate this later for the `String` class, which is part of Java.

Java has eight built-in data types, called primitive types. A variable whose data type is a primitive type stores a primitive type value instead of referencing an object. We will use just four primitive data types in this book: `int`, `double`, `char`, and `boolean` because these types are sufficient to represent all the data we will process. Table 2.1 describes the kind of value that can be stored in each of the primitive data types.

◆◆ EXAMPLE 2.1 ───

Each of the statements below declares a variable that stores a primitive type value. Notice that a semicolon is used to terminate each Java declaration statement.

```
int kids = 2;
double bankBalance = 500.45;
char firstLetter = 'a';
boolean married = true;
```

Although not required in a data declaration, we have specified the initial value to be stored in each variable. Each initial value appears as a constant or **literal** after the = sign. The data type of each literal must match the data type of the variable in which it is stored (see Table 2.1).

Table 2.1 Primitive data types and values

Data Type	Kind of Value Stored
`int`	Integers—simple numbers that do not contain fractional parts such as 516,222 (written in Java without a comma between 6 and 2), and –52. *Other primitive types used to store integers are `byte`, `short`, and `long`.*
`double`	Real numbers—numbers that can include fractional parts such as 2.5, 3.66666666, –.000034, and 3,555,640.0 (written in Java without commas). *Another primitive type used to store real numbers is `float`.*
`char`	Characters—all of the symbols that can be produced by pressing keys on a keyboard. *Characters are used to produce human readable text such as English sentences.*
`boolean`	Boolean values—the values `false` and `true`. *This data type is named after the English mathematician George Boole, who developed a two-valued algebra.*

Syntax Displays

The syntax of a language defines the rules for expression in the language. For each new Java construct introduced in this book, we provide a **syntax display** that describes and explains its syntax and shows examples of its use. In the first syntax display, we discuss the italicized elements, *typeName*, *variableName*, and *value* in the interpretation section. The brackets in **[= *value*]** show that this part is optional.

Variable declaration

    Form: `typeName variableName [ = value];`
    Example: `int pennies;`
               `int kids = 3;`

    Interpretation: The data type of *variableName* is specified as *typeName* where *typeName* is either predefined in Java or is the name of a class that has been defined by Java programmers. If *typeName* is a primitive type and *value* is specified, it must be a literal (constant) of data type *typeName*. If *typeName* is a class type and *value* is specified, it must be a object of data type *typeName*.

Primitive Type `int`

In mathematics, integers are positive or negative whole numbers. A number without a sign is assumed to be positive.

Because of the finite size of a memory cell, not all integers can be represented using type `int`. In Java, you write integers (and all other numbers) without commas. Some valid integers are

```
-10500     435     15     -25
```

We can perform the common arithmetic operations (add, subtract, multiply, and divide) on type `int` data. For example, the expression 15 + 25 has the value 40. We discuss these operations in detail later in this section.

Primitive Type `double`

A real number has an integer part and a fractional part separated by a decimal point. Some valid real numbers are

```
-10.5     .435     15.     -25.1234
```

We can use scientific notation to represent very large and very small values. In normal scientific notation, the real number 1.23×10^5 is equivalent to 123000.0, where the exponent 5 means "move the decimal point 5 places to the right." In Java scientific notation, we write this number as `1.23e5` or `1.23e+5`. If the exponent has a minus sign, the decimal point is moved to the left (e.g., `0.34e-4` is equivalent to `0.000034`). Table 2.2 shows examples of both valid and invalid `double` values. We can perform the common arithmetic operations (add, subtract, multiply, and divide) on type `double` numbers.

Table 2.2 Valid and invalid `double` values

Valid	Invalid
`3.14159`	`-15e-0.3` (`0.3` invalid exponent)
`0.005`	`12.5e.3` (`.3` invalid exponent)
`.12345`	`.123E3` (needs lowercase **e**)
`12345.0`	`e32` (doesn't start with a digit)
`16.`	`a34e03` (doesn't start with a digit)
`15.0e-04` (value is `0.0015`)	
`2.345e2` (value is `234.5`)	
`1.15e-3` (value is `0.00115`)	
`12e+5` (value is `1200000.0`)	

Primitive Type `boolean`

Unlike the other data types, the `boolean` data type has just two possible values: `true` and `false`. We can use this data type to represent conditional values so that a program can make decisions. Type `boolean` operators allow you to manipulate `boolean` values. We discuss them in Section 4.2.

Primitive Type `char`

Data type `char` represents an individual character value—a letter, a digit, or a special symbol. Each character is unique; for example, the character for the digit zero (`'0'`) is distinct from the character for the letter "oh" (`'O'`), even though they might look identical. We use apostrophes to denote character literals.

Java uses a coding scheme for characters called Unicode (see Appendix B), which has 65,536 unique characters. This allows symbols from languages around the world to be represented in a Java program. Unicode uses 2 bytes to represent each character, whereas the more common ASCII (American Standard Code for Information Interchange) code uses only 1 byte.

Java uses a special set of symbols, called **escape characters**, to represent special characters. Each escape character is written as a literal consisting of a backslash \ followed by another character. Table 2.3 shows some common escape characters. The first two escape characters represent characters that control the appearance of text that is displayed: \n (new-line) and \t (tab). The last three escape characters are used to represent characters that are delimiters or special characters in Java: \", \', and \\.

Table 2.3 Java escape characters

Escape Character	Meaning
\n	New-line
\t	Tab
\"	Double quote
\'	Single quote
\\	Backslash

Data Types Enable Error Detection

Data types allow the compiler to detect erroneous operations in a program. For example, if a statement attempts to add two `boolean` values, the Java compiler displays an error message telling you that this is an incorrect operation. Similarly, if you try to store the wrong kind of value (for example, a `double` value in a data field that is type `int`), you get an error message. Detecting these errors keeps the computer from performing operations that don't make sense.

You might wonder whether you can convert from one primitive data type to another. The answer is "Yes, sometimes." For example, it is obvious that an integer can be converted into a real number with a fractional part of zero. But if you convert a real number into an integer, do you truncate (remove) the fractional part or do you round it to the nearest integer? We discuss the rules for conversion between primitive types in the next section.

EXERCISES FOR SECTION 2.1

SELF-CHECK

1. List four kinds of primitive data.

2. **a.** Write the following numbers in normal decimal notation:

   ```
   103e-4 1.2345e+6 123.45e+3
   ```

   b. Write the following numbers in scientific notation:

   ```
   1300 123.45 0.00426
   ```

3. Indicate which of the following values are legal in Java and which are not. Identify the data type of each valid value.

   ```
   15    'XYZ'    '*'    $ 25.123    15.    -999    .123
   'x'   "X"    '9'    '-5'    true    'True'
   ```

4. What would be the best data type for storing the area of a circle in square inches? How about the number of cars passing through an intersection in an hour? The first letter of your last name?

5. Distinguish between character (**char**) and integer (**int**) types.

6. Why is type **boolean** needed?

7. Indicate whether each assignment below is valid, and indicate the result of each valid assignment. Assume **r** is type **double**, **i** is type **int**, **b** is type **boolean**, and **c** is type **char**.

a. r = 3.5 + 5.0;	f. r = c;
b. i = 2 * 5;	g. c = 's';
c. c = 'my name';	h. r = i;
d. c = "y";	i. i = r;
e. b = boolean;	j. r = 10 + i;

2.2 Processing Numeric Data

To solve many programming problems, you will need to write arithmetic expressions that manipulate integer or real data. Table 2.4 shows all the arithmetic operators. Each operator manipulates two operands that may be variables or other arithmetic expressions. The operators may be used with both real and integer types. The +, −, and * operators behave as expected. When the operands are integers, an integer result is produced. When the operands are real numbers, a real result is produced. We discuss the division operator / and remainder operator % next.

Table 2.4 Arithmetic operators

Arithmetic Operator	Meaning	Example
+	Addition	5 + 2 is 7.
		5.0 + 2.0 is 7.0.
−	Subtraction	5 − 2 is 3.
		5.0 − 2.0 is 3.0.
*	Multiplication	5 * 2 is 10.
		5.0 * 2.0 is 10.0.
/	Division	5.0 / 2.0 is 2.5.
		5 / 2 is 2.
%	Remainder	5 % 2 is 1.

The Division and Remainder Operators

The division operator behaves differently depending on whether its operands are integers or real numbers. If one or both operands are real numbers, the division operator gives a real number as its result. If both operands are integers, the division operator performs **integer division** and it gives an integer as its result. Consider the following variables:

```
int x = 5;
double r = 5.0;
```

The expression r / 2 or r / 2.0 gives the result 2.5. The expression x / 2 gives the result 2, which is the integer part of 2.5. The fractional part (0.5) is lost. However, the expression x / 2.0 gives the result 2.5 because the divisor is real and real division is performed.

The % operator is the remainder operator. It returns the remainder of the division. For example, x % 2 returns 1, which is what is "left over" after the integer division. The remainder operator can also be used with real operands, but we don't recommend doing this.

Assignment Statements

Normally an **assignment statement** such as

```
x = y + z;
```

is used to store the value of an arithmetic expression (**x** + **y**) in a primitive type variable (**x**). The symbol = is the **assignment operator**. If variable **x** is a primitive type, you should read this statement as **x** *gets the value of* **y** + **z**, or **x** *is assigned the value of* **y** + **z**.

Assignment statement

    Form: *variable = expression;*
    Example: x = y + z;

    Interpretation: If *variable* is declared as a primitive type, the value of the *expression* is stored in *variable*. If *variable* is a declared as a class type, a reference to the object formed by *expression* is stored in *variable*. The data types of *expression* and *variable* must be the same.

◆◆ EXAMPLE 2.2 ────────────────────────────────

In Java you can write assignment statements of the form

```
sum = sum + item;
```

where the variable **sum** appears on both sides of the assignment operator. This is obviously not an algebraic equation, but it illustrates a common programming practice. This statement instructs the computer to add the current value of **sum** to the value of **item**; the result is then stored in **sum**. The previous value of **sum** is overwritten, as illustrated in Fig. 2.1. The value of **item**, however, is unchanged.

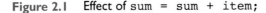

Figure 2.1   **Effect of sum = sum + item;**

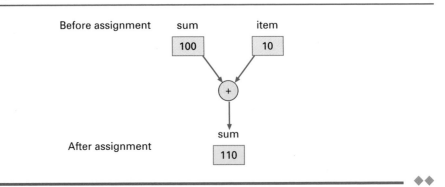

◆◆ EXAMPLE 2.3 ────────────────────────────────

You can also write assignment statements that assign the value of one variable to another variable. If **x** and **newX** are type **double** variables, the statement

```
newX = x;
```

copies the value of variable **x** into variable **newX**. The statement

```
newX = -x;
```

instructs the computer to get the value of **x**, negate that value, and store the result in **newX**. For example, if **x** is 3.5, **newX** is −3.5. Neither of the assignment statements above changes the value of **x**.

Because Java represents the values of each data type differently, the value being assigned must be **assignment compatible** with the variable receiving it. For now, this means that the variable and value must be the same type, unless the value is type **int** and the variable receiving it is type **double**.

── ◆◆

Data Type of an Arithmetic Operation

How does Java determine the data type of the result of an arithmetic operation? The following rule applies:

The type of the result of an arithmetic operation is **double** if an operand is type **double**. If both operands are type **int**, the result is type **int**.

This means that if **i** is type **int** and **x** is type **double**, any expression involving **i** and **x** as operands gives a type **double** result. For example, the expression **i * x** gives a type **double** result. To calculate this result, Java multiplies the type **double** equivalent of **i** (a real number with a fractional part of zero) by the type **double** value stored in **x**. An expression with all type **int** operands is a type **int** expression. However, an expression with one or more type **double** operands is a type **double** expression.

Mixed-Type Assignment Statement

When an assignment statement is executed, the expression is first evaluated and then the result is assigned to the variable preceding the assignment operator =. Either a type **double** or a type **int** expression may be assigned to a type **double** variable.

◆◆ EXAMPLE 2.4 ────────────────────────────────

The following statements are valid:

```
int m = 3;
int n = 2;
double y = m + n;      //assigns 5 to y
                       //stored as a real number
double x = y + m / n;  //assigns 6.0 to x
```

In the last statement, the expression **m / n** involves two integers and gives an integer result (**1**). This value is converted to its type **double** equivalent before being added to **y** (type **double**). Notice that the type conversion is done after the two integer values are divided and not before. If it were done before, real division would give a result of **1.5** and the value **6.5** would be stored in **x**, not **6.0**. We will see shortly why division is done before addition.

◆◆

Java does not allow a type **double** expression to be assigned to a type **int** variable because the fractional part of the expression cannot be represented and will be lost. This means that the following mixed-type assignment statements are invalid if **count** is type **int** and **average** is type **double**.

count = 3.5;	*invalid—assignment of* **double** *value to* **int** *variable*
count = count + 1.0;	*invalid—1.0 is* **double**, *so result is* **double**
count = average / count;	*invalid—result of division is* **double**

Each statement above causes this error message:

```
Error: Incompatible type for =. Explicit cast needed to convert
double to int.
```

Casting Operations for Type Conversion

You can use **type casting**, or **casting**, to create a value of one data type from another. For example, if **x** (type `double`) is `7.8`, the expression

```
(int) x
```

evaluates to `7`, the type `int` value formed by truncating or removing the fractional part of **x**. If **m** is type `int`, the assignment statement

```
m = (int) x;
```

is valid and assigns the integer value `7` to **m**.

Similarly, you can use type casting to create a type `double` value from a type `int` value. If **m** (type `int`) has the value `6`, the result of the expression

```
(double) m
```

is the real number equivalent to `6`, or `6.0`, which has a fractional part of zero.

Expressions with Multiple Operators

In our examples so far, most expressions had a single operator; however, expressions with multiple operators are common. To understand and write expressions with multiple operators, we must know the Java rules for evaluating expressions. For example, we stated in Example 2.4 that the operator `/` was evaluated before `+` in the expression **y + m / n**. This is because Java uses the same rules as algebra to determine the order of operator evaluation.

Rules for Evaluating Expressions

    a. *Parentheses rule:* All expressions in parentheses are evaluated separately. Nested parenthesized expressions are evaluated from the inside out, with the innermost expression evaluated first.

    b. *Operator precedence rule:* Operators in the same expression are evaluated in the order determined by their precedence (from highest to lowest):

Operator	Precedence

`–` (unary minus)
`*, /, %`
`+, –`
`=`
	Highest precedence
	
	Lowest precedence

c. *Left associative rule:* Operators in the same expression and at the same prece-dence level (such as + and –) are evaluated in left-to-right order.

These rules will help you understand how Java evaluates expressions. Use paren-theses as needed to specify the order of evaluation. Often it is a good idea in compli-cated expressions to use extra parentheses to document clearly the order of operator evaluation. For example, the expression

```
x * y * z + a / b - c * d
```

can be written in a more readable form using parentheses:

```
(x * y * z ) + (a / b) - (c * d)
```

◆◆ EXAMPLE 2.5 ───

The formula for the average velocity, v, of a particle traveling on a line between points p_1 and p_2 in time t_1 to t_2 is

$$v = \frac{p_2 - p_1}{t_2 - t_1}$$

This formula can be written and evaluated in Java as shown in Fig. 2.2. You read this evaluation tree from top to bottom. Arrows connect each operand with its oper-ator. The order of operator evaluation is shown by the number to the left of each operator; the letter (a, b, or c) to the right indicates which evaluation rule applies.

Figure 2.2   Evaluation tree for v = (p2 − p1) / (t2 − t1);

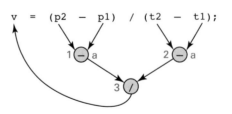

◆◆ EXAMPLE 2.6 ───

Consider the expression

```
z - (a + b / 2 ) + w * y
```

containing `int` variables only. The parenthesized expression `(a + b / 2)` is evaluated first (rule a) beginning with `b / 2` (rule b). Once the value of `b / 2` is determined, it can be added to `a` to obtain the value of `(a + b / 2)`. Next the multiplication operation is performed (rule b), and the value for `w * y` is determined. Then the value of `(a + b / 2)` is subtracted from `z` (rule c). Finally the result is added to `w * y`. The evaluation tree for this expression is shown in Fig. 2.3.

Figure 2.3   Evaluation tree for z - (a + b / 2) + w * y

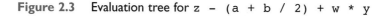

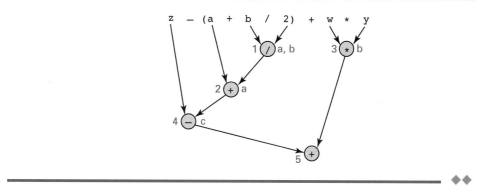

◆◆ EXAMPLE 2.7 ────────────────────────────────────

If `x` (value is `7.8`) and `y` (value is `3.6`) are both type `double`, the expression

```
(int) (x + y)
```

forms the sum `x + y` (result is `11.4`) and then uses casting to create the type `int` result `11`. If `m` is type `int`, the assignment statement

```
m = (int) (x + y);
```

is valid and assigns `11` to `m`.
    The parentheses around `(x + y)` are required in the above statement. If you remove them, the type cast operation (highest precedence) occurs before the addition, so the expression

```
(int) x + y
```

adds the result of the casting operation `(int) x` (value is `7`) to `y` (value is `3.6`). Therefore, the above expression gives the type `double` result `10.6`.

◆◆

Writing Mathematical Formulas in Java

You may encounter two problems in writing a mathematical formula in Java. First, multiplication often can be implied in a formula by writing the two items to be multiplied next to each other, for example, $a = bc$. In Java, however, you must always use the * operator to indicate multiplication, as in

```
a = b * c;
```

The other difficulty arises in formulas with division. We normally write the numerator and the denominator on separate lines:

$$m = \frac{y - b}{x - a}$$

In Java, however, the numerator and denominator are placed on the same line. Consequently, we use parentheses to separate the numerator from the denominator and to clearly indicate the order of evaluation of the operators in the expression. The above formula would be written in Java as

```
m = (y - b) / (x - a);
```

Table 2.5 shows several mathematical formulas rewritten in Java.

Table 2.5 Mathematical formulas as Java expressions

Mathematical Formula	Java Expression
1. $b^2 - 4ac$	b * b - 4 * a * c
2. $a + b - c$	a + b - c
3. $\dfrac{a + b}{c + d}$	(a + b) / (c + d)
4. $\dfrac{1}{1 + x^2}$	1 / (1 + x * x)
5. $a \times [-(b + c)]$	a * (-(b + c))

The points illustrated in these examples can be summarized as follows:

◆ Always specify multiplication explicitly by using the operator * where needed (formulas 1, 4).

◆ Use parentheses when required to control the order of operator evaluation (formulas 3, 4, 5).

◆ Never write two arithmetic operators in succession; they must be separated by an operand or an open parenthesis (formula 5).

Unary minus

The fifth Java expression in Table 2.5 uses a unary minus to negate the value of **(b + c)** before performing the multiplication. The unary minus has only one operand and has the highest precedence. Also, unary minus operators are right associative.

◆◆ EXAMPLE 2.8 ───

Figure 2.4 shows a Java program that declares two numbers (**num1, num2**) and computes and displays their sum, difference, product, and quotient. The first line of the program identifies it as the Java class **TwoNumbers**. The second line starts the definition of the main method where program execution begins.

The statements in the main method execute in sequence. Each statement beginning with **double** declares and assigns a value to a type **double** variable. The statements beginning with **System.out.println** cause information to be displayed in the **console window** (see Fig. 2.5). Each line in the console window begins with the sequence of characters enclosed in quotes. This sequence of characters is followed by the value of an arithmetic expression (for example, the characters **Sum is** are followed by the value of **(num1 + num2)**. We explain how this happens in the next section and in Section 2.4.

Figure 2.4   **Class TwoNumbers**

───

```
public class TwoNumbers {

  public static void main(String[] args) {
    double num1 = 8;
    double num2 = 6;

    System.out.println("First number is " + num1);
    System.out.println("Second number is " + num2);
    System.out.println("Sum is " + (num1 + num2));
    System.out.println("Difference is " + (num1 - num2));
    System.out.println("Product is " + (num1 * num2));
    System.out.println("Quotient is " + (num1 / num2));
  }
}
```

───

Figure 2.5   Sample run of class `TwoNumbers`

```
TwoNumbers

First number is 8.0
Second number is 6.0
Sum is 14.0
Difference is 2.0
Product is 48.0
Quotient is 1.3333333333333333
```

EXERCISES FOR SECTION 2.2

SELF-CHECK

1. **a.** Evaluate the following expressions with `7` and `22` (both type `int`) as operands.

   ```
   22 / 7    7 / 22    22 % 7    7 % 22
   ```

   Repeat the exercise for these pairs of integers:

   b. `15, 16`

   c. `3, 23`

   d. `-4, 16`

2. Draw evaluation trees for the following expressions. What is the value of the last one?

   ```
   1.8 * celsius + 32.0
   (salary - 5000.00) * 0.20 + 1425.00
   10 % 4 + 1 / 2
   ```

3. Given the declarations

   ```
   double pi = 3.14159;
   int maxI = 1000;
   double x;
   double y;
   int a;
   int b;
   int i;
   ```

indicate which statements are valid and find the value of each valid statement. Also indicate which statements are invalid and explain why. Assume that **a** is 3, **b** is 4, and **y** is -1.

a. `i = a % b;`

j. `i = (maxI - 990) / a;`

b. `i = (990 - maxI) / a;`

k. `x = a / y;`

c. `i = a % y;`

l. `i = pi * a;`

d. `x = pi * y;`

m. `x = pi / y;`

e. `i = a / b;`

n. `x = - y * a / b;`

f. `x = a / b;`

o. `i = (maxI - 990) % a;`

g. `x = a % (a / b);`

p. `i = a % 0;`

h. `i = b / 0;`

q. `i = a % (maxI - 990);`

i. `i = a % (990 - maxI);`

4. Write an assignment statement to implement the following equation in Java.

$$q = \frac{kA(T_1 - T_2)}{b - ac}$$

5. Let **a**, **b**, **c**, and **x** be the names of four type **double** variables and let **i**, **j**, and **k** be the names of three type **int** variables. Each of the following statements contains a violation of the rules for forming arithmetic expressions. Rewrite each statement so it is consistent with the rules.

a. `x = 4.0 a * c;`

d. `k = 3(i + j);`

b. `a = ac;`

e. `x = 5a / bc;`

c. `i = 2 * -j;`

f. `i = 5j3;`

6. Assuming **x** is type **double**, **n** is type **int**, and **ch** is type **char**, write the assignment statements described below. Use type casting where necessary:

a. Assign `x * 1.5` to n.

b. Assign `n + 1` to ch.

c. Assign ch to x.

d. Assign the sum of n and ch to x.

PROGRAMMING

1. Modify the Java class in Fig. 2.4 to compute and display `num2 - num1` and `num2 / num1`.

2. Write a class called `ThreeNumbers` that finds the sum and product of three numbers.

2.3   Introduction to Methods

Figure 2.4 uses two methods: `main()` and `println()`. You can think of the methods of a class as determining the operations that can be carried out by the class. For example, method `main()` specifies what happens when you run class `TwoNumbers`; method `println()` causes information to be displayed in the console window. To help you identify method names in this text, we will follow each method name with parentheses.

Calling or Invoking Methods Using Dot Notation

To execute the statements in a method, we must **invoke** or **call** the method. We usually call or invoke methods for one of the following reasons:

◆ To change the **state** of an object; that is, the information that is stored in an object

◆ To calculate a result

◆ To retrieve a particular data item that is stored in an object

◆ To get data from the user

◆ To display the result of an operation

When a method is called to calculate a result or to retrieve a data item stored in an object, we say that the method **returns a result** or value. For all the other reasons listed above, the method is **executed for its effect**.

Method `main()` is automatically called by the operating system when we attempt to run a class, so we don't need to call it. However, we must call method `println()` when we want to execute its statements. Each call to method `println()` changes the state of the console window by adding information to it. The console window is the Java object referenced by `System.out`.

A call to an object's method has the form

```
objectName.methodName()
```

This form is called **dot notation** and it tells the Java compiler to call method *methodName()* of object *objectName*. Programmers often say that method *methodName()* is applied to object *objectName*.

We also write method calls that have the form

`objectName.methodName(argumentList)`

In this case, we must evaluate the `argumentList` of `methodName()` and pass this information to the method. An `argumentList` can contain a single argument or multiple arguments separated by commas. In Fig. 2.4, each call to method `println()` has the form

`System.out.println(argumentList)`

where `argumentList` is a single argument. This tells Java to call method `println()` of object `System.out` using the argument shown in parentheses. The argument is evaluated and the result is appended as a new line to object `System.out` (the console window). In Section 2.4, we show how this evaluation is performed.

Method Arguments Are Like Function Arguments

A method argument provides information or data that a method needs and is like a function argument in algebra. In algebra, the notation $f(x)$ means that f is a function with argument x, and the result of evaluating function f depends on the value of its argument x.

◆◆EXAMPLE 2.9 ─────────────────────────────────────

If $f(x)$ is $x^2 + x + 1$, $f(0)$ is the value of $f(x)$ when x is 0:

- ◆ $f(0)$ is 1 $(0 + 0 + 1)$
- ◆ $f(1)$ is 3 $(1 + 1 + 1)$
- ◆ $f(2)$ is 7 $(4 + 2 + 1)$

── ◆◆

◆◆EXAMPLE 2.10 ───────────────────────────────────

Functions can have multiple arguments:

$$f(x, y) = 3x + y$$

In this case, the function reference $f(2, 3)$ is the value of function f when its first argument (x) is 2 and its second argument (y) is 3. Verify that the value of $f(2, 3)$ is 9.

── ◆◆

Instance Methods versus Class Methods

There are actually two kinds of methods in Java: instance and class. Method **print-ln()** is an **instance method** because it belongs to an object instance and is applied to an object (**System.out**). **Class methods** belong to the class rather than to individual class instances (objects) and therefore are not applied to an object. We also use dot notation to call class methods, but we prefix the method name with the class name instead of an object name:

ClassName.methodName(argumentList)

Method **main()** is a class method, but we do not call it. We will see examples of other class methods in Sections 2.5 and 2.8.

Method call

Form: *objectName.methodName(argumentList)*
            ClassName.methodName(argumentList)

Example: `System.out.println("I like studying Java")`
            `Math.sqrt(15.0)`

Interpretation: Apply method *methodName* of object *objectName*, passing in the value of each argument in *argumentList*. The first form is used to call instance methods and the second form is used to call class methods.

Note: If a function has no arguments, you must provide an empty pair of parentheses after the function name when you call it.

EXERCISES FOR SECTION 2.3

SELF-CHECK

1. For the function shown in Example 2.9, what is the value of *f*(5)? *f*(7)?

2. For the function shown in Example 2.10, what is the value of *f*(5, 3)? *f*(7, 1)?

3. What is a class method? What is an instance method? How do you call a class method? How do you call an instance method?

PROGRAMMING

1. Write the following method calls:
    a. Call method **doubleIt()** of object **x**. Assume **doubleIt()** has no arguments.
    b. Call method **makeBigger()** of object **y**. Assume **makeBigger()** has the integer 7 as its single argument.

c. Assume method **f()** is a class method of class **Algebra** that returns a real numbers as its result. Write a statement that calls method **f()**, passing it the integer arguments 5 and 3. Assign the result of the method call to variable **z** (type **double**).

2.4 The String Class

Java provides the **String** class as a data type that can be used to store and manipulate sequences of characters. We generally use the **String** class to process text data instead of the more limited **char** data type, which stores only single characters. **String** variables can reference objects that contain sequences of characters.

Declaring String Variables

The declaration statements

```
String name;
String flower;
```

declare two variables, **name** and **flower**, that can reference **String** objects. However, no **String** objects currently exist, so **name** and **flower** have no value.

Using Constructors to Create String Objects

The statements

```
name = new String("Dustin");
flower = new String("Rose");
```

create two **String** objects using the **new** operator. The process of creating an object using the **new** operator is called **instantiation**. An object is said to be an **instance of a class**. The first **String** object contains the letters **Dustin**, and it is referenced by variable **name**; the second **String** object contains the letters **Rose**, and it is referenced by variable **flower**.

The **new** operator allocates storage for a new object of type **String**. It calls a **constructor**, which is a special method that has the same name as the class. The constructor method stores the initial data in the object. The part of the constructor call in parentheses is the **constructor argument**, and it provides information that the constructor needs to set up the object. In the first call above, the argument is the **string literal "Dustin"** and it specifies the sequence of characters to be stored in the new object.

Class instantiation

Form: *variableName* = new *className*(*arguments*);
Example: flower = new String("rose");

Interpretation: An object of class *className* is created and will be referenced by *variableName*. The data type of *variableName* must be type *className*. The constructor *className* is called and stores the data specified by the *arguments* in the new object. Use empty parentheses **()** to indicate that there are no **arguments**.

Combining Variable Declaration and Object Creation

We often use a single statement to declare the data type of a variable and to create the object it references. The two statements

```
String name = new String("Dustin");
String flower = new String("Rose");
```

have the same effect as the four statements shown earlier.

If you already declared **name** as type **String**, it would be invalid to use the statement

```
String name = new String("Robin");    // invalid—name declared twice
```

to cause **name** to reference a different **String** object because Java would consider this a second declaration of variable name (only one declaration is allowed). However, the statement

```
name = new String("Robin");
```

is valid and causes **name** to reference a new **String** object containing the characters **Robin** instead of the first **String** object containing the characters **Dustin**. Figure 2.6 shows the status of variables **name** and **flower**.

Reference Variables

When we allocate storage for a variable that is a primitive type, the corresponding memory cell stores a primitive value of the designated type. However, the memory cell associated with a variable that references an object stores a **reference** to other memory cells that store the object's data and methods. By *reference* we mean the address of the first memory cell that stores the object's information. We use an arrow in Fig. 2.6 to indicate that a variable stores a reference to an object.

Because **flower** in Fig. 2.6 is a variable that references an object, we sometimes call **flower** a **reference variable**. Sometimes we will refer to the second object shown in Fig. 2.6 as object **flower**. Technically speaking, it is really the object referenced by **flower**.

Figure 2.6 Two variables of type String

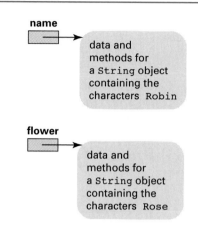

Special Properties of Strings

Strings are different from other classes that you will create. For one thing, the characters stored in a String object cannot be changed. For most classes you write, you will be able to change the data stored in an object.

You can create a new String object just by writing the sequence of characters it contains as a literal (value) in a Java statement. For example, you can replace the statements

```
String flower = new String("Rose");
String name = new String("Robin");
```

with the simpler statements

```
String flower = "Rose";
String name = "Robin";
```

We will use String literals to designate new String objects rather than explicitly calling the String constructor. However, you must use constructors to create objects of other class types.

String Operator + and String Assignment

Another difference between String objects and other objects is that you can use the operator + to manipulate String objects. You can manipulate other objects only through methods.

When used with String objects, the operator + means **concatenate**, or **join**, and is called the **concatenation operator**. The expression

```
name + " " + flower
```

creates a new **String** object that contains all the characters contained in its three **String operands**. For the declarations shown in the preceding section, the new **String** object contains the characters **Robin Rose**. The **String** expression

```
flower + " " + name
```

creates a new **String** object that contains the characters **Rose Robin**. The statement

```
String fullName = flower + " " + name;
```

declares **String** variable **fullName** and causes it to reference the **String** object with characters **Rose Robin**.

Comparison of **String** and **Character** Data Types

Be careful not to confuse **String** objects with character values. For example, the literal **"X"** denotes a **String** object that contains the single character **X**, whereas the literal **'X'** is the character **X**. Because a **String** object can contain one or many characters, we will generally process text data using strings, not characters.

◆◆EXAMPLE 2.11 ───

The statements

```
char digit = '3';
String numberStr = digit; // error—incompatible types
```

is not valid in Java. You cannot assign a type char value to a type **String** variable. However, you can use the statement

```
String numberStr = "" + digit;
```

to accomplish this. The concatenation operator joins the **empty string** **""** to the character in **digit**, creating a **String** object that contains the same character as digit. This object is referenced by **numberStr**. We discuss concatenating strings with other primitive types in the next section.

─── ◆◆

Concatenating Strings with Primitive Types

We can concatenate strings and primitive type operands. In Fig. 2.4, in the statement

```
System.out.println("First number is " + num1);
```

the method argument is a string expression. This expression creates a new **String** object that contains the characters **First number is** followed by the digit characters that represent the value of **num1**. If **num1** is **8**, the new **String** object contains the characters **First number is 8**. Method **println()** displays its **String** argument as a new line in the console window (object **System.out**). In this example, the concatenation operator has one operand that is type **String** and one that is type **double**.

◆◆EXAMPLE 2.12 ─────────────────────────────────

Assume **x** (type **int**) is **5** and **y** (type **int**) is 7. The expression

```
x + y + " is the sum of x and y"
```

creates a **String** object that contains the characters **12 is the sum of x and y**. The left operator **+** forms the sum **(12)** of its two integer operands. The right operator **+** concatenates the characters representing the sum with the characters in the **String** literal **" is the sum of x and y"**.

◆◆

◆◆EXAMPLE 2.13 ─────────────────────────────────

Assume **x** (type **int**) is **5** and **y** (type **int**) is 7. In the expression

```
"The sum of x and y is " + x + y
```

the left operator **+** (concatenate) is evaluated first and it forms a **String** object that contains the characters **The sum of x and y is 5**. Because of this, the right operator **+** also means concatenate, not add, so we get a **String** object that contains the characters **The sum of x and y is 57**.

We can use parentheses to ensure that the right operator **+** means add. In the expression

```
"The sum of x and y is " + (x + y)
```

the right **+** operator is evaluated first, giving a value of **12**. Therefore, the expression result is a **String** object that contains the characters **The sum of x and y is 12**. If you look back at Fig. 2.4, you will see that each arithmetic expression in an argument for method **println()** is enclosed in parentheses.

◆◆

String Methods

Java provides methods in the **String** class (see Appendix C) to perform some common **String** operations. Table 2.6 describes some of them: **length()**, **charAt()**, **subString()**, and **indexOf()**. The table shows that methods can have the same name but different argument lists. For example, methods **subString()** and **indexOf()** can be called with either one or two arguments. This feature is called **method overloading**.

Table 2.6 String methods

Method Call	Description
"This String".length()	Finds the length of string **"This String"**. Result is **11**.
"This String".charAt(6)	Gets the character in string **"This String"** at position 6, where the first character is at position 0. Result is **'t'**.
"This String".subString(5)	Gets the part of string **"This String"** starting at position 5 through the end of the string. Result is **"String"**.
"This String".subString(5, 7)	Gets the part of the string **"This String"** starting at position 5 up to, but excluding, position 7. Result is **"St"**.
"This String".indexOf("is")	Determines the position of the first occurrence of **"is"** in **"This String"**. Result is **2**.
"This String".indexOf("it")	Determines the position of the first occurrence of **"it"** in **"This String"**. Result is **–1** because **"it"** is not found.
"This String".indexOf("i", 5)	Determines the position of the first occurrence of **"i"** in **"This String"** starting the search at position 5. Result is **8**.

◆◆EXAMPLE 2.14

If the variable **saying** references a **String** object containing the characters **Java is fun!**, the method call

```
saying.length()
```

applies method **length()** to the object referenced by **saying**. The result of this operation is the integer **12**, the number of characters contained in the object referenced by **saying**.

◆◆

◆◆EXAMPLE 2.15 ─────────────────────────────────

The method call

```
saying.charAt(0)
```

applies the method **charAt()** to the object referenced by **saying**. The argument **0** tells the method which character (the first) will be the result of applying this method. This expression returns the first character (the letter **J**) stored in **saying** (the characters **Java is fun!**).

◆◆

◆◆EXAMPLE 2.16 ─────────────────────────────────

The expression

```
saying.charAt(saying.length() - 1);
```

returns the last character (the symbol **!**) of string **saying**. This is an example of **composition of method calls**. The inner method call **saying.length()** finds the number of characters in the string **saying**; this number, **less 1**, is the argument for method **charAt()**.

◆◆

Method subString()

Method **subString()** gets a portion of a string (called a **substring**). If this method has a single argument, that argument will be the starting point of the *substring*, which extends to the end of the string. If the method call has two arguments, the first is the starting point for the substring to be retrieved and the second is the ending point, as explained in the next examples.

◆◆EXAMPLE 2.17 —————————————————————————————

The method call

```
saying.subString(5)
```

returns a **String** object containing the characters starting at position 5 of **say-ing**. The result is a **String** object containing the characters **is fun!**.

—————————————————————————————————— ◆◆

◆◆EXAMPLE 2.18 —————————————————————————————

The method call

```
saying.subString(0, 4)
```

returns the substring of **String** object **saying** starting at position **0** up to, but not including, the character at position **4**. The result is a **String** object containing the four characters **Java**. Notice that the state of **String** object **saying** is not changed by this method call or by any of the others shown in this section (that is, it still contains the characters **Java is fun!**).

—————————————————————————————————— ◆◆

Method *indexOf()*

Method **indexOf()** searches a string to find the first occurrence of a *target string* (the method argument). If the target string is found, **indexOf()** returns its starting posi-tion (a value greater than or equal to zero) in the string being searched. If the target string is not found, **indexOf()** returns a value of **-1**.

If method **indexOf()** has only one argument, the search always starts at position 0. However, you can use a second argument to specify a starting position that is dif-ferent than 0.

◆◆EXAMPLE 2.19 —————————————————————————————

The expression

```
saying.indexOf("Java")
```

returns a value of 0. The expression

```
saying.indexOf("java")
```

returns a value of **-1** (case matters). The expression

```
saying.indexOf("Java", 1)
```

also returns a value of **-1** because the search starts at position **1** (the first letter **a** in **Java is fun!**).

◆◆

◆◆EXAMPLE 2.20 ─────────────────────────────────────

Children enjoy speaking "pig Latin." This is a play on English in which each word in a sentence is modified as follows: If the first sound is a consonant sound, put it at the end of the word and add "ay" to it. For example, "cat" becomes "atcay." We can do this by constructing a string from the second letter to the end of the input word, the first letter of the input word, and the literal "ay." We can describe this process by the "formula"

second letter to the end of the word + first letter of the word + "ay"

where + means concatenate. We can use methods **subString()** and **charAt()** to get the indicated parts of the string. If we want to express the contents of variable **word** in pig Latin, we can rewrite the above formula as the expression

```
word.subString(1) + word.charAt(0) + "ay"
```

Remember, the second letter is at position 1, not 2.

◆◆

Storing the Result of a Method Call

We use assignment statements to store the result of a method call. For example, the method call below

```
int posBlank = text.indexOf(" ");
```

returns the position of the first blank in the string referenced by **text**. If **text** references a **String** object containing the characters **Mickey Mantle**, the method result (**6**) is stored in **posBlank** (type **int**). The statement

```
String firstName = text.subString(0, posBlank);
```

applies method **subString()** to the **String** object referenced by **text**. It returns a reference to a **String** object containing the characters in positions 0 through 5 of this string: **Mickey**. Variable **firstName** (type **String**) references this object.

◆◆EXAMPLE 2.21 ──────────────────────────────────

You would like to change a name that is written in the form *lastName, firstName* to one that is in the form *firstName lastName*. You can do this by finding the position of the comma and then forming a new string that joins the characters that follow the comma (*firstName*) with the characters that precede the comma (*lastName*). The statements below accomplish this.

```
String author = "Wolz, Ursula";
int posComma = author.indexOf(", ");
String name = author.subString(posComma + 2) + " " +
              author.subString(0, posComma);
```

The result of the call to method **indexOf()** is the position in **String author** of the comma and is then stored in **posComma** (value is **4**). The last statement joins the characters starting at position 6 (**Ursula**) with the characters that precede the comma (**Wolz**). A space is placed between these two substrings. **String name** references the object that contains the characters **Ursula Wolz**. These statements would do the same thing to any name stored in this format in **String author**.

── ◆◆

Displaying the Result of a Method Call

You can reference a **String** method inside the argument expression passed to method **println()**. In this case, Java must execute the **String** method and get its result before executing method **println()**. For example, the statement

```
System.out.println("The first blank is at position " +
                   text.indexOf(" "));
```

displays in the console window the characters **The first blank is at posi-tion** followed by the result of method call **text.indexOf(" ")**.

EXERCISES FOR SECTION 2.4

SELF-CHECK

1. Evaluate the string expressions and method calls below.

    a. `"value of x is " + 5 * 7`

    b. `"value of x is " + 5 + 7`

    c. `"value of x is " + (5 + 7)`

    d. `"This String".charAt(0);`

2. For each expression below, assume the declaration

   a. `String test = "This String";`

   b. `test.charAt(0);`

   c. `test.charAt(test.length());`

   d. `test.subString(0);`

   e. `test.subString(4, test.length() - 1);`

3. Write statements to do the following:

   a. Assign to **word2** the first through fifth characters of string **word1**.

   b. Assign to **word2** the string consisting of the letter **A**, the substring of **word1** consisting of the third through fifth characters inclusive, and the letter **z**.

   c. Assign to **word2** the substring of **word1** starting with the fifth character and ending with the last character.

   d. Assign to **word2** the last half of string **word1**.

2.5 Input/Output with Class `JOptionPane` and Method `println()`

A primary goal of object-oriented programming is to write error-free code. One way to accomplish this goal is to reuse, whenever possible, code that has been previously written, tested, and debugged. This practice is called software reuse.

To facilitate software reuse, the Java language developers provided collections of classes called **packages** that perform useful functions that are not included in the language. Also, programmers often write their own collections of classes and packages that they can reuse in future programs.

`import` Statement

If you want to use a package that has been previously defined by either the Java system or by other programmers, you need to tell the Java system how it can access the package and its classes. You do this by placing an **import statement** at the beginning of a file that needs to access a package. If you place the line

```
import javax.swing.*;
```

at the beginning of a source file, you will import the **swing** package, which became part of Java in version 1.2. The **swing** package and its many classes facilitate building GUIs.

The **import** statement above gives access to *all the classes* defined in package **swing**. If you want to access only class **JOptionPane**, you can use the statement

```
import javax.swing.JOptionPane;
```

import statement

Form: `import package;`
Example: `import javax.swing.*;`
           `import javax.swing.JOptionPane;`

Interpretation: The **import** statement makes the class or classes in the specified package accessible to the classes that are defined in the current source file. The symbol * is a wildcard, and we use it to indicate that all the classes in a directory or folder can be accessed, not just a particular one.

Reading Data Using `JOptionPane.showInputDialog()`

Java provides class **JOptionPane** (part of package **swing**) for easy input and output of information. By **input** we mean interacting with a program user to get program data, and by **output** we mean displaying a value on the screen. The **JOptionPane** class makes it easy to create dialog windows for input and message windows for output.

Method **showInputDialog()** is a class method that displays dialog windows and returns data typed into them by the program user. The method call

```
JOptionPane.showInputDialog("Enter your name")
```

pops up a dialog window (see Fig. 2.7) that is similar to ones you may have seen in commercial software. The method returns a reference to a **String** object that contains the characters typed in the data area (currently blank). The statement

```
String name = JOptionPane.showInputDialog("Enter your name");
```

causes the variable **name** to reference this **String** object.

You can use statements similar to the one above to read primitive type data values entered by the program user. However, the data entered and stored in the **String** object must be converted to the desired primitive type. Fortunately, Java provides the necessary conversion methods.

Figure 2.7   A dialog window

◆◆EXAMPLE 2.22 ————————————————————————————

Use the statement pair

```
String str1 = JOptionPane.showInputDialog("Enter your age");
int age = Integer.parseInt(str1);
```

to store an integer in **age**. The character(s) typed in by the user are stored in a **String** object referenced by **str1**. The method call **Integer. parseInt(str1)** converts this string to a type **int** value, which is stored in **age**. If the conversion cannot be done because the string contains letters or other non-numeric characters, an error message will appear in the console window and your program will stop execution. Method **parseInt()** is a class method defined in class **Integer** (see Section 5.8).

◆◆

◆◆EXAMPLE 2.23 ————————————————————————————

Use the statement pair

```
String str2 = JOptionPane.showInputDialog("Enter your salary");
double salary = Double.parseDouble(str2);
```

to store a real number in **salary**. The character(s) typed in by the user are stored in a **String** object referenced by **str2**. The method call **Double. parseDouble(str2)** converts this string to a type **double** value. If this cannot be done, an error message will appear in the console window and your program will stop execution. Method **parseDouble()** is a class method defined in class **Double** (see Section 5.8).

◆◆

◆◆EXAMPLE 2.24 ────────────────────────────────

Use the statement pair

```
String str3 = JOptionPane.showInputDialog("Enter a letter");
char initial = str3.charAt(0);
```

to store a single data character in the variable **initial** (type **char**). The method call **str1.charAt(0)** returns the first character in the string typed in by the user. This character is stored in variable **initial**.

── ◆◆

Displaying Results in the Console Window

Earlier we showed how to use method **println()** to display information in the console window (**System.out**) using statements such as

```
System.out.println("First number is " + num1);
System.out.println("Second number is " + num2);
System.out.println("Sum is " + (num1 + num2));
```

Method **println()** takes a single argument of any primitive or class type. In the statements above, each argument is a **String** expression. The argument is displayed on a separate line of the console window.

You can also use method **print()** to display information in the console window. The difference between **print()** and **println()** is that **print()** does not insert a new-line character after the information in its argument is displayed. This means that the information shown in the console window after the execution of the *next call* to **print()** or **println()** will appear on the same line as the information displayed by the *current call* to **print()**.

◆◆EXAMPLE 2.25 ────────────────────────────────

The method calls

```
System.out.print("First number is " + num1);
System.out.println(", second number is " + num2);
```

display the value of **num1** and **num2** on the same line in the Java console window. If **num1** is 8 and **num2** is 10, the console window will show the line

```
First number is 8, second number is 10
```

── ◆◆

Displaying Results Using `JOptionPane.showMessageDialog()`

As an alternative to using the console window for program output, you can use method **showMessageDialog()** in class **JOptionPane** to display message windows. If **num1** is 8, the statement

```
JOptionPane.showMessageDialog(null, "num1 is " + num1);
```

displays the message dialog window in Fig. 2.8. The first argument has the value **null**, which means that it does not reference any object. Because the first argument is **null**, the message window is displayed in the center of the screen. The second argument is the string to display in the window, **"num1 is " + num1**. The second argument must be a string expression or an object.

Figure 2.8   A message window

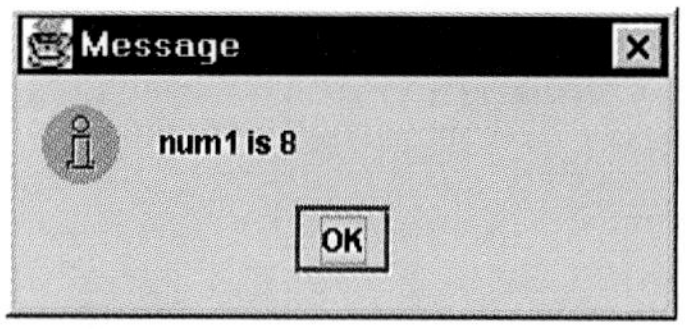

◆◆EXAMPLE 2.26

If **num1** is 8 and **num2** is 6, the statement

```
String message = "num1 is " + num1 +
                 "\nnum2 is " + num2;
```

creates a **String** object containing the characters **num1 is 8\nnum2 is 6**. Recall that the escape character **\n** represents the new-line character. The statement

```
JOptionPane.showMessageDialog(null, message);
```

creates the window in Fig. 2.9—a message window showing the string referenced by **message**. Notice that the string is displayed on two lines.

Figure 2.9   A message window with two lines

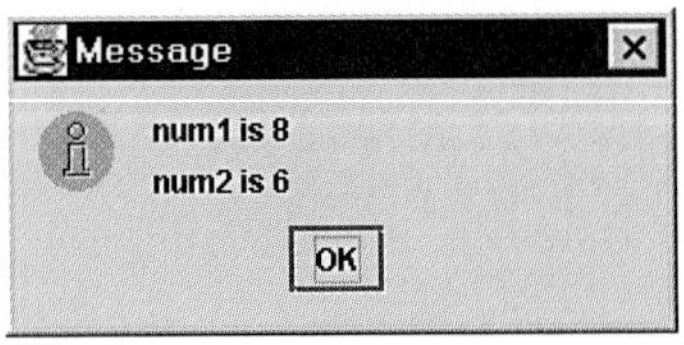

◆◆EXAMPLE 2.27

Class **TwoNumbersDialog** (Fig. 2.10) imports class **JOptionPane** of the swing package. Method **main()** calls method **showInputDialog()** to read two numeric strings (**num1Str** and **num2Str**). These strings are converted to type **double** numbers (**num1** and **num2**). Next, we store in string **message** the two numbers and their sum, difference, product, and quotient. Finally, we call method **showMessageDialog()** to display **message** in a message window. Compare this class with class **TwoNumbers** shown earlier (Fig. 2.4).

Figure 2.11 shows a sample run of class **TwoNumbersDialog**. It shows the two dialog windows used for data entry followed by the message window that displays the program results. Table 2.7 summarizes the input/output methods.

Table 2.7   Input/output methods

Method Call	Behavior
`System.out.println("x is " + x);`	Displays the characters **x is** followed by characters that represent the value of **x** in the console window. The output line is terminated.
`System.out.print("the results are: ");`	Displays the characters **the results are:** in the console window. The output line is not terminated.
`JOptionPane.ShowMessageDialog(null, "x is " + x);`	Displays the characters **x is** followed by characters that represent the value of **x** in a message window centered in the screen.
`JOptionPane.ShowInputDialog("Enter x:")`	Displays the prompt **Enter x:** in a dialog window. Returns a **String** object containing the characters entered by the user.

Figure 2.10   Class `TwoNumbersDialog`

```java
import javax.swing.JOptionPane;

public class TwoNumbersDialog {

  public static void main(String[] args) {
    String num1Str =
        JOptionPane.showInputDialog("Enter first number");
    double num1 = Double.parseDouble(num1Str);

    String num2Str =
        JOptionPane.showInputDialog("Enter 2nd number");
    double num2 = Double.parseDouble(num2Str);

    String message = "First number is " + num1 +
                     "\nSecond number is " + num2 +
                     "\nSum is " + (num1 + num2) +
                     "\nDifference is " + (num1 — num2) +
                     "\nProduct is " + (num1 * num2) +
                     "\nQuotient is " + (num1 / num2);

    JOptionPane.showMessageDialog(null, message);
  }
}
```

Figure 2.11   Sample run of `TwoNumbersDialog`

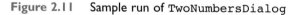

EXERCISES FOR SECTION 2.5

SELF-CHECK

1. Call method `showInputDialog()` of class `JOptionPane` to perform each of these operations. If necessary, follow each statement with one that converts the string returned to the required data type.

   a. Read a type `double` value into variable `age` using the prompt `Enter your age`.

   b. Read a type `char` value into variable `choice` using the prompt `Enter your choice`.

   c. Let `str` reference a `String` object containing the characters entered in response to the prompt `Enter your name`.

   d. Read a type `double` value into variable `Sal` using the prompt `What is your salary?`

2. Write method calls that ask the user to do the following:

   a. Enter a real number between −5.5 and 7.7.

   b. Enter a person's first initial (uppercase letter).

   c. Enter a positive integer less than 100.

   d. Enter your astrological sign.

3. Write statements to display the following lines in a single message window using method `showMessageDialog()`:

`Hi, I am _____ and`	*insert string* **name** *where shown*
`my address is _____.`	*insert string* **address** *where shown*
`My age is _____ but I feel`	*insert value of* **age** *where shown*
`much older today.`	

PROGRAMMING

1. For the method `main()` that begins

   ```
   public static void main(String[] args) {
     int x;
     double y;
     char z;
   ```

   write statements that use class `JOptionPane` methods to read and store data typed in by a program user into the variables shown.

2. For the method in programming exercise 1 above, write statements that display the values of the three data fields in a meaningful way in separate message windows. Write statements that display them in separate lines of the same message window.

3. Modify class **TwoNumbersDialog** to read three data values entered by the program user and to display the results in a message window.

2.6 Problem Solving in Action

Throughout this book, we use the first five steps of the problem-solving method as shown in Section 1.5. Each problem solution, presented as a Case Study, begins with a *problem statement*. As part of the problem *analysis*, we identify the data requirements for the problem, indicating the problem inputs and the desired outputs. We also identify the classes that will be needed. Next, we *design* these classes. Finally, we *implement* the classes using Java. We also provide a sample run of the program and discuss how to *test* the program.

CASE STUDY A PIG LATIN TRANSLATOR

PROBLEM   Write a program that reads in a word and displays it in pig Latin.

ANALYSIS   The problem input will be the word that is read and the problem output will be its pig Latin form. We know from Example 2.20 how to build the pig Latin form.

Data Requirements

> **Problem Input**
> An English word

> **Problem Output**
> Its pig Latin form

Relevant Formulas and Relationships

> pig Latin form = second letter to the end of the word + first letter of the word + "ay"

Identify the Classes

Three classes are needed. The Java **String** class is used to store a word and its pig Latin form. Class **JOptionPane** is used to provide methods for interactive input/output. A third class, **PigLatinApp**, interacts with these two classes.

Figure 2.12   Class PigLatinApp

Data Fields	
None	
Methods	**Behavior**
main()	Interacts with the program user to get the word; builds and displays its pig Latin form
Classes Used	
String, JOptionPane	

DESIGN   Class pigLatinApp is an application class. An **application class** contains a method called **main()** that is used by the Java interpreter as a starting point for program execution. Typically, method **main()** calls methods of one or more **worker classes**. In this case, the worker classes are defined by the Java developers: String and JOptionPane. Figure 2.12 describes class PigLatinApp. The main method invokes the methods of the worker classes in the correct sequence to solve the problem. The algorithm for method **main()** follows:

   *Algorithm for **main()***
   1.   Get a word to translate to pig Latin.

   2.   Store the word and its pig Latin form in a message string.

   3.   Display the message string.

IMPLEMENTATION   Figure 2.13 shows a file (**PigLatinApp.java**) with the same name as the class it defines (class **PigLatinApp**). The extension **.java** identifies the file as a Java source file. Class **PigLatinApp** contains an application class with a main method. Recall that the statements in **main()** execute in sequence. We discuss the statements in this file in the next section.

TESTING   Figure 2.14 shows the dialog and message windows that appear when you run the application class in Fig. 2.13. To test this program, try running it with a number of different words. Try running it with consonant pairs such as "th" at the beginning.

Figure 2.13   Generating pig Latin form of a word

```
/*
 *  PigLatinApp.java        Authors: Koffman and Wolz
 *  Generates the pig Latin form of a word
 */

import javax.swing.JOptionPane;

public class PigLatinApp {

  public static void main(String[] args) {
     // Get a word to translate to pig Latin
     String word = JOptionPane.showInputDialog(
                    "Enter a word starting with a consonant");

     // Store the word and its pig Latin form in a message String
     String message = word + " is " +
             word.subString(1) + word.charAt(0) + "ay" +
             " in pig Latin";

     // Display the message String
     JOptionPane.showMessageDialog(null, message);
  }
}
```

Figure 2.14   Dialog windows for `PigLatinApp`

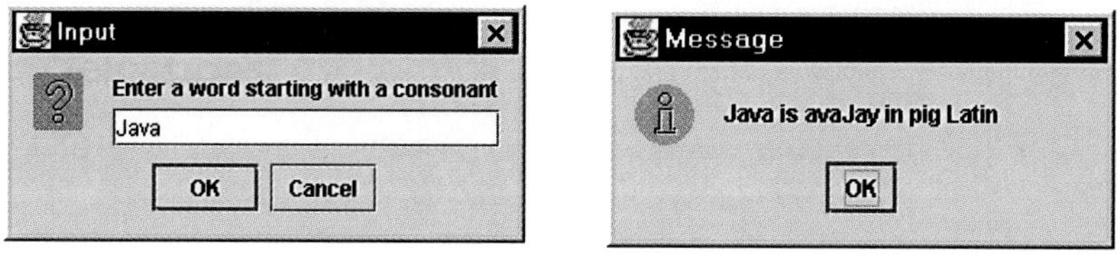

EXERCISES FOR SECTION 2.6

SELF-CHECK

1. Show how the characters contained in the stings referenced by **word** and **message** change when **Love** is read into **word**.

PROGRAMMING

1. Rewrite method **main()** in class **PigLatinApp** (Fig. 2.13) to display the word and its translation in separate message windows.

2. Rewrite method **main()** in class **PigLatinApp** (Fig. 2.13) to display the results in the console window as well as in a message window.

3. Add comments to method **main()** in class **TwoNumbersDialog** (Fig. 2.10).

2.7 Anatomy of a Program

Reading Java source code is a skill that you should acquire. You can learn a lot by studying good code.

Comments

The first thing to notice is that some text looks like English. Lines that begin with **//** are comments. Comments that begin with **//** only extend to the end of the line.

Each Java file that you write should begin with a comment that lists your name, the date the file was created, your instructor's name (if the file is for a class assignment), and a description of the assignment. You can surround a comment that extends over many lines using a single pair of **comment delimeters**, **/***, ***/**, as shown at the beginning of Fig. 2.13. Don't leave a space between the slash and asterisk.

```
/*
 * PigLatinApp.java      Authors: Koffman and Wolz
 * Generates the pig Latin form of a word
 */
```

Programmers use comments to make a program easier to understand. Comments may describe the purpose of the program, the use of identifiers, or the purpose of a program step. Comments are part of the **program documentation** because they help others read and understand the program. The compiler, however, ignores comments, and they are not translated into machine language.

A comment can appear by itself on a program line, at the end of a line following a statement, or even embedded in a statement. In the following variable declaration, the comment follows the declaration statement:

```
double sqMeters;     // length in sq. meters
```

Class Definitions

There are two viewpoints for studying a program. You can try to determine what will happen when the program executes, or you can look for the parts of the program. It is easier to see what a Java program will do after you have identified the major parts.

A Java program is a collection of class definitions. You can identify the role of each class by looking for the class in which program execution begins. In the case of a Java application, this is the class that contains a **main** method. In Figure 2.13, there is only one class definition, so this part is easy.

A class definition tells the compiler what a class is all about. Classes can be almost anything a programmer can imagine. Consequently, there must be a form in which to describe a new class to the compiler. A class definition has the following form:

1. A header declaration

2. The class body

    a. The data field declarations of the class

    b. The method definitions of the class

The name of the class being defined follows the word **class** in the header declaration:

```
public class PigLatinApp {
```

The word **public** indicates that class **PigLatinApp** has public visibility. A class with **public visibility** can be referenced by any other class that we create. If the word **public** is omitted, the class can be referenced only by other classes in the same package as the current one. The default package is the current folder or directory.

The body of the definition, surrounded by the delimiters **{** and **}**, follows the header declaration. The class body contains the data field declarations and method definitions. These can be in any order; however, we prefer to list the data field declarations first. Class **PigLatinApp** does not declare any data fields, and it defines only one method, **main()**.

Simplified class definition

    Form: **[*visibility*] class *class-name* {...}**

    Example: **public class PigLatinApp {...}**

Interpretation: The word `public` specifies that class *class-name* has public *visibility*. The square brackets indicate that the *visibility* may be omitted. If so, the class can be referenced only by other classes defined in the same package as this one. The symbols `{...}` mean that the body of the definition appears as a sequence of statements delimited by curly braces.

Definition of Method `main()`

A method definition describes a process or action in Java. Methods operate on the information stored in an object's data fields. A method definition contains a header and a body (enclosed in braces `{}`), just like a class definition:

> *method header* `{`
> *method body*
> `}`

You can learn quite a bit about a method from its header. It gives the method name, the data type of the value returned by the method (if any), and its parameters in parentheses. A method gets information through its **parameters** and it may produce an output through its **return value**.

Method `main()` always has the following header:

```
public static void main(String[] args) {
```

The keywords `public static void` have the following meaning:

♦ `public` means that the method can be accessed outside of the class (`main()` is called by the operating system).

♦ `static` means that `main()` is not applied to an object when it is invoked.

♦ `void` means that `main()` does not return a result but is executed for its effect.

The parameter list (`String[] args`) indicates that method `main()` has a collection of `String` objects as its parameter. You must declare the parameter list for `main()` as shown even though we do not refer to it in the method body.

The Body of Method `main()`

The first statement in `main()`

```
String word = JOptionPane.showInputDialog(
              "Enter a word starting with a consonant");
```

pops up the first dialog window shown in Fig. 2.14. The result of this method call is a reference to a `String` object that contains the characters typed in by the program user in the blank space for data entry. Through the assignment operation, `String` variable **word** references this object.

Notice we begin the string literal on a new line. All characters in a literal must be on the same line.

The statement

```
String message = word + " is " +
        word.subString(1) + word.charAt(0) + "ay" +
        " in pig Latin ";
```

stores the English word and its pig Latin translation in the string referenced by **message**. Next, we display the string **message** in a window.

Program Style and Programmer Conventions

Throughout the discussion so far, you saw that the Java compiler imposes rules on what you may do. The syntax of the language creates a discipline for expressing solutions. But programmers also use **conventions** to make code more readable for humans. The compiler does not concern itself with conventions. You do not need to follow these rules to make the program run; however, they are critical to maintenance. Without them, others may not be able to read your code easily.

In your initial programming experience you will find conventions coming from at least three sources:

1. Conventions from the originators of the language, such as how to name objects, data fields, and methods.

2. Conventions established in this text, such as how to lay out the spacing in your code.

3. Conventions established by your instructor, such as how to document your programs.

Of course, you can ignore conventions and simply "do your own thing." In practical terms this creates more work for you and other programmers. You may be asked to rewrite code, or others may require more time to understand your unique style. Also, ignoring conventions may lead to lower grades on programming assignments.

Placement of opening and closing braces for class and method definitions

A program that "looks good" is easier to read and understand than one that is sloppy. Most programs will be examined or studied by someone other than the original programmers. In the real world, only about 25 percent of the time spent on a particular program is devoted to its original design or coding; the remaining 75 percent is spent on maintenance (i.e., updating and modifying the program). A program that is neatly stated and whose meaning is clear makes everyone's job simpler.

Programmers adopt consistent conventions in the placement of opening and closing braces that surround the body of class and method definitions. Our preference is to place the opening brace on the same line as the class or method header and to align the closing brace with the first letter of that line. The fragment below shows just the four lines in Fig. 2.13 that contain braces.

```java
public class PigLatinApp {
   public static void main(String[] args) {
      . . .
   }
}
```

Although this is our preference, many programmers prefer to put the opening brace on its own line. Using this style, each opening brace would align with its corresponding closing brace.

```java
public class PigLatinApp
{
   public static void main(String[] args)
   {
      . . .
   }
}
```

It makes very little difference which convention you adopt, but whichever one you choose, use it consistently.

Line Breaks in Programs

Java ignores line breaks, so a Java statement can extend over more than one line. A statement that extends over more than one line cannot be split in the middle of an identifier, a reserved word, or a literal. If a long string literal does not fit on one line, rewrite it as two or more smaller string literals joined by the concatenation operator.

You can write more than one statement on a line. For example, the line

```java
int x = 5;   double y = 5.3;
```

contains two statements that declare and initialize values. A semicolon follows each statement. We recommend that you place only one statement on a line because it improves readability and makes it easier to maintain a program.

Blank Spaces and Lines in Programs

The consistent and careful use of blank spaces can improve the style of a program. A blank space is required between words in a program line. Use blank lines between sections of a program, methods, and algorithm steps in a method.

The compiler ignores extra blanks between words and symbols, but you may insert space to improve the readability and style of a program. You should always leave a blank space after a comma and before and after operators such as `*`, `-`, and `=`. However, do not insert blanks before or after the dot symbol (`.`). Be careful not to insert blank spaces where they do not belong. For example, the identifier `startSalary` cannot be written as `start Salary`.

Java Keywords Revisited

All Java statements in Fig. 2.13 contain one or more words, special symbols (for example, `=`, `+`, `-`), and punctuation symbols (such as `;`). Some words have special meaning in Java and are called **keywords** or **reserved words**. Table 2.8 describes some common keywords you have seen so far. Appendix B summarizes all the keywords in Java.

Table 2.8 Some Java keywords

Keyword	Meaning
`boolean`	The data type used for storing and processing boolean values.
`char`	The data type used for storing and processing single characters.
`class`	Indicates the start of a class definition.
`double`	The data type used for storing and processing real numbers.
`import`	Makes the classes in a particular package accessible to the classes in the current file.
`int`	The data type used for storing and processing integers.
`new`	Creates a new object instance.
`public`	Accessibility is unrestricted.
`static`	There is exactly one method or data field with this identifier for the class. A static method is not applied to an object.
`void`	Method returns no value.

Identifiers

The other words in a statement are identifiers. An **identifier** is a word that the compiler recognizes as the name of a datum (data field or variable), a method, a class, or an object. Declaration statements are used to tell the compiler the names of all identifiers and how they will be used.

You have some freedom in selecting identifiers. The syntax rules and some valid identifiers follow. Table 2.9 shows some invalid identifiers. Java is case sensitive, which means the case of a letter matters (i.e., **R** is not the same as **r**).

Syntax Rules for Identifiers

1. An identifier must begin with a letter, the underscore character (_), or the dollar sign ($). We recommend you begin all identifiers with a letter.

2. An identifier must consist only of a combination of letters, digits, underscore characters, and dollar signs.

3. A Java reserved word cannot be used as an identifier.

4. An identifier can be any length.

Valid Identifiers

```
Letter1,  _letter,  $inches,  ForEver,
ThisIsAVeryLongOneButItIsVALID
```

Java programmers generally follow well-established conventions in choosing identifier names (see Table 2.10). They use nouns to name classes (for example, **String, Automobile**). Each word in a class name, including the first, begins with an uppercase letter (**SavingsAccount**).

Programmers also use nouns to name variables and objects (for example, **miles, kids,** and **flower**). They use verb phrases (**showInputDialog**) and prepositional phrases (**toMiles, toString**) to name methods. This guideline makes sense because a data item name represents some information and a method usually performs an action. The identifiers that name data fields and methods generally start with lowercase letters, but each new word begins with an uppercase letter.

Finally, some identifiers represent values that are to be treated as constants. These values should not change as the program executes. Use names with all uppercase letters for constants and the underscore symbol between words (for example, **FEET_PER_METER**).

Table 2.9 Invalid identifiers

Invalid Identifier	Reason Invalid
1Letter	Doesn't begin with a letter
new	Reserved word
final	Reserved word
Two*Four	Character * not allowed
Joe's	Character ' not allowed

If you follow these conventions, your code will be easier to read, but these conventions are not rules imposed by the Java compiler. To differentiate between a method reference and a data field reference in Java code, you should know that parentheses must follow a method name but not a data name (for example, `toMiles()` is the name of a method and `miles` is the name of a variable).

If you mistype an identifier, the compiler may detect the mistake as a syntax error. If so, it will display an error message during program translation such as `unidentified variable`, `missing method`, or `missing object`, depending on how it interpreted the identifier. Because mistyped identifiers sometimes resemble other identifiers, avoid picking similar names.

PROGRAM STYLE: *Selecting Names in a Java Program*

The Java compiler differentiates between uppercase and lowercase. This means that you cannot write `CLASS` when you mean `class`.

Try to pick meaningful names for identifiers. For example, the identifier `salary` would be a good name for a variable used to store a person's salary, whereas the identifier `S` or `Bagel` would be a bad choice. It is difficult to form meaningful names with

Table 2.10 Java conventions for identifiers

Identifier Type	Convention	Examples
Class name	A noun that starts with uppercase; begin a new word with an uppercase letter.	`PigLatinApp`, `String`, `InOut`
Variable or data field	A noun that starts with lowercase; begin a new word with an uppercase letter.	`sum`, `miles`, `kilometers`, `squareFeet`
Method	A verb phrase or prepositional phrase that starts with lowercase; begin a new word with an uppercase letter.	`showInputDialog`, `print`, `toString`
Package	A noun that starts with lowercase; begin a new word with an uppercase letter.	`swing`, `psJava`
Constant	A noun that has all uppercase letters. Use underscore symbol between words	`PI`, `FEET_PER_METER`

fewer than three letters. On the other hand, typing errors become more likely when identifiers are too long. A reasonable rule of thumb is to use names having 3 to 10 characters.

EXERCISES FOR SECTION 2.7

SELF-CHECK

1. What are keywords?

2. Why shouldn't you use a keyword as an identifier?

3. Which of the following identifiers are (a) Java keywords, (b) valid identifiers, and (c) invalid identifiers?

```
new     private   Bill    program   Sue's   Rate
Start   extends   static   XYZ_123   123_XYZ
ThisIsALongOne    Y=Z    Prog#2    'MaxScores'
```

4. List the keywords in Fig. 2.13. For each identifier, determine whether it refers to a class, a method, or a data field.

5. Discuss the validity of this statement: Programmers should comment each and every line of their program so that it will be easier for someone else to understand.

2.8 Numerical Computations with Class Math

You will write many programs that perform mathematical computations. In this section, we introduce some methods of class **Math** that perform some common operations. We start with method **sqrt()**, which performs the square root computation. Method **sqrt()** is defined as a class method in the **Math** class. The expression part of the assignment statement

```
double y = Math.sqrt(x);
```

activates the code for method **sqrt()**, passing the argument **x** to the method. After method **sqrt()** executes, the method result (a type **double** value) is assigned to variable **y**. If **x** is **16.0**, the assignment statement above is evaluated as follows:

1. Method **sqrt()** computes the square root of **16.0**, or **4.0**.

2. The method result, **4.0**, is assigned to **y**.

You cannot instantiate class `Math`. This means that you cannot declare objects of type `Math`. We show how to use the class methods in the next examples.

◆◆EXAMPLE 2.28 ───

If `w` is `9.0`, the assignment statement

```
z = 5.7 + Math.sqrt(w);
```

is evaluated as follows:

1. `w` is `9.0`, so method `sqrt()` computes the square root of `9.0`, or `3.0`.
2. The values `5.7` and `3.0` are added together.
3. The sum, `8.7`, is stored in `z`.

◆◆

◆◆EXAMPLE 2.29 ───

The program in Fig. 2.15 displays the square root of two numbers (`num1` and `num2`) and the square root of their sum. We call method `sqrt()` three times. Each call returns a type `double` result, which is part of the argument string for a call to method `println()`:

```
System.out.println("The square root of " + nl +
                   " is " + Math.sqrt(nl));
```

The arguments for the first two calls to `sqrt()` are type `int` variables (`n1` and `n2`); the third call is a type `int` expression (`n1 + n2`). Fig. 2.16 shows a sample run.

◆◆

Methods in Class `Math`

Table 2.11 lists the names and descriptions of some of the methods in class `Math`. Most of them perform common mathematical computations.

Methods `abs()`, `max()`, and `min()` can take arguments of any numeric type; they return a value of the same type as the argument. Method `round()` takes a type `double` argument and rounds it to the nearest integer value. The remaining methods (except for `random()`) take type `double` argument(s) and return a type `double` value.

The argument for `log()` and `sqrt()` must be positive. Methods `min()`, `max()`, and `pow()` take two arguments.

Figure 2.15   Class SquareRoot

```java
/*
 * SquareRoot.java      Authors: Koffman and Wolz
 * Demonstrates square root method (Math.sqrt())
 */

import javax.swing.JOptionPane;

public class SquareRoot {

    public static void main (String[] args) {
        // Get two numbers.
        String n1Str =
              JOptionPane.showInputDialog("Enter first number");
        int n1 = Integer.parseInt(n1Str);

        String n2Str =
              JOptionPane.showInputDialog("Enter second number");
        int n2 = Integer.parseInt(n2Str);

        // Display square root of each number and of
        //   their sum in console window.
        System.out.println("The square root of " + n1 +
                        " is " + Math.sqrt(n1));
        System.out.println("The square root of " + n2 +
                        " is " + Math.sqrt(n2));
        System.out.println("The square root of their sum is " +
                        Math.sqrt(n1 + n2));

    }
}
```

Figure 2.16   Sample run of `SquareRoot`

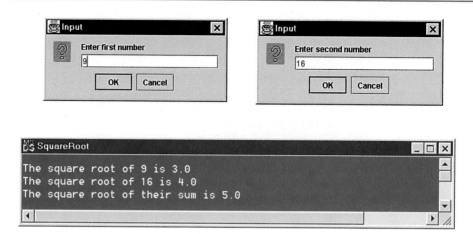

Table 2.11   Some methods in class `Math`

Method	Purpose	Argument	Result Type
abs(x)	Returns the absolute value of x.	any numeric type	same as argument
ceil(x)	Returns smallest whole number ≥ x.	double	double
exp(x)	Returns e^x where e = 2.71828...	double	double
floor(x)	Returns largest whole number.	double	double
log(x)	Returns the natural logarithm of x (base e) for x > 0.0.	double	double
max(x, y)	Returns the larger of x and y.	any numeric type	same as argument
min(x, y)	Returns the smaller of x and y.	any numeric type	same as argument
pow(x, y)	Returns x^y. An error will occur if x = 0 and y ≤ 0, or x < 0 and y is not a whole number.	any numeric type	double
random()	Returns a pseudorandom number between 0.0 and 1.0.	none	double
rint(x)	Returns the closest whole number to x.	double	double
round(x)	Returns the integer value closest to x.	double float	long int
sqrt(x)	Returns the positive square root of x for x > 0.0.	double	double

◆◆EXAMPLE 2.30 ───────────────────────────────

We can use the **Math** method **sqrt()** to compute the roots of a quadratic equation in x of the form

$$ax^2 + bx + c = 0$$

The two roots are defined as

$$\text{root}_1 = \frac{-b + \sqrt{b^2 - 4ac}}{2a}$$

$$\text{root}_2 = \frac{-b - \sqrt{b^2 - 4ac}}{2a}$$

when the discriminant ($b^2 - 4ac$) is greater than zero. If we assume that this is the case, we can use the following assignment statements to assign values to **root1** and **root2**:

```
// Compute two roots, root1 and root2, for disc > 0.0.
disc = b * b - 4 * a * c ;
root1 = (-b + Math.sqrt(disc)) / (2 * a);
root2 = (-b - Math.sqrt(disc)) / (2 * a);
```

─── ◆◆

The method **random()** generates a random number. A **random number** is a number that is selected from a specified range of numbers (the range is 0.0 to 1.0 for method **random()**). Each of the numbers in the range is equally likely to be selected. Random numbers can be used to simulate the toss of a coin (two possible values) or the throw of a die (six possible values). (Technically, method **random()** returns a **pseudorandom number** because, unlike real random numbers, the numbers it generates will eventually repeat.)

◆◆EXAMPLE 2.31 ───────────────────────────────

Fig. 2.17 shows a Java application that provides drill and practice in multiplication. The statement

```
int multiplier = (int) (10 * Math.random() + 1);
```

assigns a random integer between **1** and **10** to **multiplier**. The result returned by **Math.random()** (a real number between **0.0** and **0.99999...**) is multiplied by **10**, yielding a real number between **0.0** and **9.99999....** We add **1** to this number and use the typecasting operator (**int**) to extract the integral part of the result (an integer between **1** and **10**). If the value returned by **Math.random()** is **0.473, multiplier** is set to **5**. In the statement

```
int multiplicand = (int) (10 * Math.random() + 1);
```

we do the same thing to get a random integer value for **multiplicand**.

Assume that **multiplicand** is 6. The product **30** is stored in **product**, and the user is asked to answer the question

```
What is 5 * 6
```

Regardless of whether the user is right or wrong, we display a message window with the correct answer (see Fig. 2.18).

In a better drill and practice program, the program would compare the correct answer to the user's answer and would display an appropriate message. You will learn how to do this in Section 4.8.

Figure 2.17   Class `ArithmeticDrill`

```java
/*
 * ArithmeticDrill.java      Authors: Koffman and Wolz
 * Generates and solves a multiplication problem.
 * Uses Math.
 */

import javax.swing.JOptionPane;

public class ArithmeticDrill {

    public static void main(String[] args) {
        // Generate 2 random integers
        int multiplier = (int) (10 * Math.random() + 1);
        int multiplicand = (int) (10 * Math.random() + 1);

        // Calculate the product
        int product = multiplier * multiplicand;

        // Ask the user for the product
        String answerStr =
            JOptionPane.showInputDialog("What is " + multiplier +
                                        " * " + multiplicand);

        // Display the answer
        JOptionPane.showMessageDialog(null,
                "The correct answer is " + product);
    }
}
```

Figure 2.18   Sample run of `ArithmeticDrill`

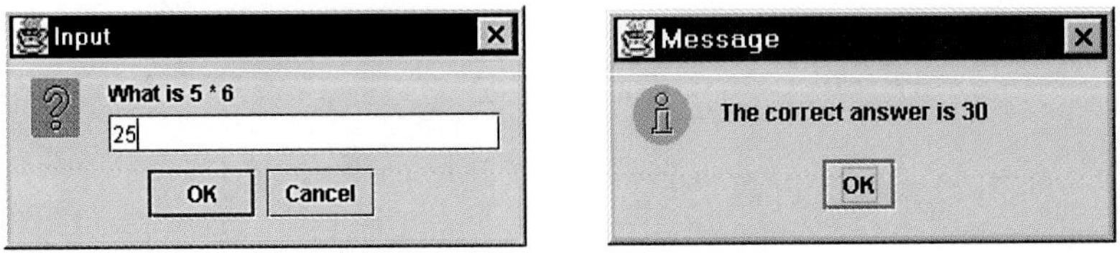

Methods That Return Whole Numbers

Table 2.11 lists three methods, `floor()`, `ceil()`, and `rint()`, that return a type **double** whole number based on their type **double** argument. You can think of methods `floor()` and `ceil()` as returning the whole numbers (type **double**) that bracket a type **double** value: `floor(x)` returns the largest whole number less than or equal to **x**, and `ceil(x)` returns the smallest whole number greater than or equal to **x**. Fig. 2.19 shows the relationship between a real value and the whole numbers that bracket it. The *x*-axis shows the whole numbers from −3 to 3 in increasing order.

Method `rint()` (round integer) returns the nearest whole number corresponding to its type **double** value. If the fractional part of the argument is **0.5** or larger, `rint()` rounds up; otherwise, it rounds down (e.g., `rint(7.4)` is **7.0** and `rint(7.5)` is **8.0**). Method `round()` performs the same operation as `rint()`; however, it returns a type **int** value instead of a type **double** value (e.g., `round(-7.4)` is −7 and `round(-7.6)` is −8).

◆◆EXAMPLE 2.32 ────────────────────────────

You may want to round the value of a real number **x** to two decimal places. The statement

```
x = Math.rint(x * 100) / 100.0;
```

accomplishes this. If **x** is **56.57832**, the method argument is **5657.832**. Method `rint()` rounds its argument value to **5658.0**. Dividing this result by **100.0** gives **56.58**.

◆◆

Figure 2.19   Methods `floor()` and `ceil()` with arguments `-2.4` and `2.8`

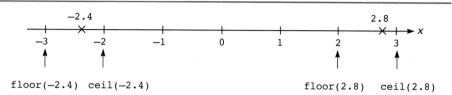

EXERCISES FOR SECTION 2.8

SELF-CHECK

1. Rewrite the following mathematical expressions using Java methods:
   a. $u + v \times w^2$

   b. $\log_e (x^y)$

   c. $(x - y)^3$

   d. $|xy - w/z|$

2. Evaluate the following method calls and indicate the type of the result:
   a. `Math.floor(-15.8)`

   b. `Math.round(-15.8)`

   c. `Math.round(6.8) * Math.sqrt(3)`

   d. `(int)-15.8 * Math.sqrt(3)`

   e. `Math.sqrt(Math.abs(Math.round(-15.8)))`

   f. `Math.round(3.5)`

   g. `Math.sqrt(3.0)`

   h. `Math.floor(22.1) * Math.sqrt(3)`

   i. `Math.floor(3.2)`

   j. `Math.ceil(3.2)`

PROGRAMMING

1. Write statements that read values into **x** and **y** and compute and display the absolute difference (e.g., if **x** is 7 and **y** is 9, the absolute difference is 2).

2. Using the `round()` method, write a Java statement to round any real value **x** to the nearest three decimal places.

3. Write a complete Java program that prompts the user for the cartesian coordinates of two points, (x_1, y_1) and (x_2, y_2), and displays the distance between them computed by using the following formula:

$$distance = \sqrt{(x_2 - x_1)^2 + (y_2 - y_1)^2}$$

2.9 Common Errors and Debugging

As you begin to program, soon you will discover that a program rarely runs correctly the first time it executes. In fact, errors are so common that they have their own special name—bugs—and the process of correcting them is called **debugging** a program. (According to computer folklore, the first hardware error was caused by a large moth found inside a computer component.) To alert you to potential problems, we will provide a section on common programming errors at the end of each chapter.

When Java detects an error, an error message is displayed indicating that you have made a mistake and describing what the likely cause of the error might be. Unfortunately, the error messages are often difficult to interpret and are sometimes misleading. As you gain experience, you will become more proficient at locating and correcting errors. Depending on the development environment you are using, you may have a lot of support in tracking down errors or virtually none. Many Integrated Development Environments (IDEs) contain a "debug" mode that lets you execute the statements of your program step by step, run the program to a particular point and then stop, or select particular variables for viewing. Even without a debugger, there is a lot you can do to view your program using simple tools.

There are four kinds of errors: syntax, system, run-time, and logic errors. Depending on the kind of error, you use different techniques to determine exactly what is wrong and to fix it.

Syntax Errors

A **syntax error** occurs when your code violates one or more grammar rules of Java. Such errors are detected and displayed by the compiler as it attempts to translate your programs. If a statement has a syntax error, it cannot be translated and your program cannot be executed. Finding and removing syntax errors, one at a time, can be time-consuming. Table 2.12 describes some syntax errors you may encounter and some possible error messages.

Table 2.12 Some common syntax errors

Syntax Error	Sample Message
Using an operator with an incorrect data type (for example, using arithmetic operator * with `char` or `String` data)	`Incompatible type for *`
Forgetting to declare a variable or data field or misspelling its name	`Undefined variable`
Declaring the same variable twice	`Duplicate definition of variable`
Use of an expression type in an assignment statement that is not assignment compatible with the variable type	`Incompatible type for =`
Missing string delimiter	`String not terminated at end of line` or `';' expected`
Forgetting to define a method, misspelling its name, or using the wrong type argument	`Method is not defined`
Using an argument of the incorrect type in a method call	`Incompatible type for method`
Omitting an object name before a call to a public method from a class in which the method is not defined	`Method not found` or `Can't make static reference to method`

Incorrect data types

The table shows that improper use of a data type often causes a syntax error. Some examples are

- Use of arithmetic operators with character or string data, except that + (concatenate) can be used with string data.

- Assigning a value of one type to a variable of another type, except that a type `int` value can be assigned to a type `double` variable.

- Returning a result from a method that is the wrong data type.

Incorrect use of quotation marks

Improper use of quotation marks with a character or string literal also causes a syntax error. Make sure you always use a pair of single quotes or apostrophes to delimit character literals and a pair of double quotes to delimit strings. Also, a string literal must fit on one line.

Errors in use of comments

Beware of dangling comments. If the compiler seems to have lost large segments of your code, you probably began a /* comment and didn't end it properly or didn't end it in the right spot.

Beware of dangling comments of another sort. Make sure that a comment following // does not end up on the next line. For example:

```
// This is a very long and involved comment that
accidentally ended up here.
```

The **accidentally** will be viewed as part of your code and confuse the compiler.

Errors in use of methods

Be careful about the data types of arguments you pass to methods. If you provide the wrong type argument, the compiler will tell you that the method does not exist. For example, if you use the incorrect method call ″happy″.charAt('a'), the compiler will tell you that method **String.charAt(char)** is not defined.

Errors in use of class Math

Math is a special kind of class that contains only class methods. You cannot instantiate an instance of this class. Attempting to do so will cause a compiler error.

System Errors

System errors are also detected during compilation. The compiler may be unable to locate the object file for the current class (**no object file error**) or it may not be able to access the classes in a package you are using because of a class path problem.

No object file error

One common error occurs when the application class and the file containing it have different names. Sometimes this is due to case sensitivity. Make sure that the name of each class exactly matches the name of the file in which it resides.

Class path (source path) errors

Class path errors are also quite common. The class path tells the compiler where to look for a file if it is not stored in the same folder as the application class. Place all the files that you create for a particular application in the same folder. Make sure the path to this folder is part of your system class path. Also, include a path to any user-defined packages that you intend to access as part of your system class path (see Appendix A). Make sure a source file begins with **import** statements that correctly specify the path to any packages (user-defined or defined by the Java system) that are referenced in that source file.

Run-Time Errors

Run–time errors are detected and displayed by the computer during the execution of a program. A **run-time error,** or **exception,** occurs when the user directs the computer to perform an invalid operation, such as dividing a number by zero or manipulating undefined or invalid data.

◆◆EXAMPLE 2.32 ─────────────────────────────────────

When method **main( )** executes, **x** is set to an initial value of 0.

```
public class RunTimeError {

  public static void main(String[] args) {
    int x = 0;
    x = 10 / x;
  }
}
```

A run-time error occurs when the assignment statement executes. The error message

```
java.lang.ArithmeticException: / by zero
```

indicates an attempt to divide by zero (value of **x**), an invalid operation.

◆◆

Data entry errors are common run-time errors. They are caused by reading data of the wrong type into a variable. An example would be reading a real number or a character into a string that is being converted to a type **int** variable (for example, reading **5.0** instead of **5**). When the string is converted (using **Integer.parseInt( )**), a **NumberFormatException** error will occur.

Another common run-time error is **arithmetic overflow.** This error occurs when a program attempts to store a value that is too large in a variable. Sometimes this error does not get detected by Java and just causes an incorrect computational result.

Logic Errors

Logic errors occur when a program follows an incorrect algorithm. Because logic errors usually do not cause run-time errors and do not display error messages, they are very difficult to detect. The only sign of a logic error may be incorrect program output. You can detect logic errors by testing the program thoroughly and comparing its output to calculated results. You can prevent logic errors by carefully desk checking the algorithm and the program before you type it in.

Debugging Using Method `println()`

Because debugging can be time-consuming, plan your program solutions carefully and desk check them to eliminate bugs early. If you are unsure of what a statement does or its syntax, look it up in reference material or in relevant appendixes of this book. Following this approach will save time and avoid trouble.

One simple technique for debugging involves inserting diagnostic output statements in a method to display intermediate results. You can do this by using method `println()` to display intermediate results in the console window (or by using method `showMessageDialog()`). If a run-time error occurs, an appropriate error message will appear in the console window.

EXERCISES FOR SECTION 2.8

SELF-CHECK

1. Describe the error in each statement below and its category (syntax, run-time, logic).

   a. `String name = amy;`

   b. `String sumXY = "x + y is " + x + y;`

   c. `int y = 0;`

   `int quot = x / y;`

   d. `String message = "Hello";`

   `String name = "Sam";`

   `String message = message + name;`

   e. `JOptionPane.println("x is " + x);`

   f. `int x = JOptionPane.showInputDialog("Enter x");`

   g. `JOptionPane.showMessageDialog("x is " + x);`

   h. `System.out.print("x is ", x);`

   i. `System.out.println("sum of x, y is + (x + y));`

   j. `x + y = sum;`

   k. `Integer.parseInt("2.5")`

2. Which kind of error is the hardest to detect? Which kind of error prevents your program from beginning execution? What kind of error gives you incorrect results? Which kind of error prevents your program from running through to normal completion?

CHAPTER REVIEW

1. You must declare each identifier and its data type. All identifiers begin with a letter, _, or $. The remaining characters may be letters, _, $, and digits. A keyword (reserved word) cannot be used as an identifier.

2. Java is case sensitive; thus, the identifier **Hello** is not the same as **hello**.

3. We follow the Java conventions for naming: verb phrases or prepositional phrases for methods and nouns for data fields and class names. Methods and variables start with lowercase, classes start with uppercase, and constants are all uppercase.

4. Java's data types enable the compiler to determine how to store a particular value in memory and what operations can be performed on that value. A type can be either a class or a primitive type. The four primitive types we will use are **double**, **int**, **boolean**, and **char**. The predefined class that we will use is **String**. The type of each data field in a class and each variable in a method must be declared.

5. String expressions are formed using **String** objects and the operator + (concatenate). If the operands of + are a string and a primitive type, the characters in the primitive type data are concatenated with the string.
    The characters in a string are numbered starting with 0 (the first character). We discussed four methods that can be applied to a **String** object. Method **length()** determines the length of the string. The last character is at position **length() - 1**. Method **charAt()** returns the character at a particular position of a string, method **subString()** returns a substring of a string, and method **indexOf()** searches its **String** object to find the location of its argument.
    String objects are immutable, which means the characters contained in a **String** object cannot be changed.

6. Every Java program is made up of one or more classes. A class definition includes a header, data field declarations, and method definitions.

7. An application class contains a `main()` method. The header for the `main()` method must be

```
public static void main(String[] args)
```

Method `main()` is where execution of an application class begins. The statements in method `main()` are executed in sequence, from first to last.

8. Programs typically get data from an external source and place data in some external destination. The external source for input and output is often the user of the program. You can use methods of the **swing JOptionPane** class for input (`showInputDialog()`) and output (`showMessageDialog()`). You can use methods `Integer.parseInt()` and `Double.parseDouble()` to convert numeric strings returned by `showInputDialog()` into type **int** and type **double** values, respectively. You can use methods `println()` and `print()` to display information in the console window.

9. The visibility of a class, method, or data field describes who may access it. Public visibility means any class may access it.

10. A method definition specifies its visibility, its return value, its name, its argument list (all in the header), and the statements that make up its body.

11. We recommend that you set up one folder for saving all your Java projects (for example, **myprojects**). Save all the files for each Java project in its own separate folder.

12. Java includes a package of predefined methods in class **Math** that can simplify mathematical computations. Use the prefix **Math.** in a call to any of the class methods defined in class **Math**. You cannot instantiate this class.

13. A program that contain no errors is extremely rare. The Java compiler helps you locate and correct syntax errors during compilation. Run-time errors or exceptions are attempts to perform invalid computer operations and are detected during program execution. Logic errors are discovered by carefully examining a program's results. They are not detected by the compiler or the run-time system.

New Java constructs

Construct	Effect
`import` Statement	
`import ourStuff.*;` `import ourStuff.Koffman;`	Placed at the top of a class definition file, it gives access to all classes within folder `ourStuff`. The second form gives access only to class `Koffman` in folder `ourStuff`.
Class Definition	
`public class Fabric` `   {. . .}`	Defines a class named `Fabric` with public visibility.
Variable Declaration	
`double sqMeters;` `String name;`	Declares `sqMeters` to be type `double` and name to be a variable that references a `String` object.
Object Creation	

`myFlower = new`
`   String("rose");`
`herFlower = "marigold";`
	Creates two new `String` objects. The one referenced by `myFlower` contains the characters `rose` and the one referenced by `herFlower` contains the characters `marigold`. Both `myFlower` and `herFlower` must be previously declared as type `String`.

Instance Method Call	
`System.out.println` `   ("Hi World")`	Calls method `println()` of object `System.out` (the console window).
Class Method Call	
`Math.sqrt(x + y)`	Calls method `sqrt()` of class `Math`.
`main` Method Definition	
`public static void main` `   (String[] args) {. . .}`	Defines the main method for an application class.

✔ **QUICK-CHECK EXERCISES**

1. How can you tell whether a class is the application class or a support (worker) class?

2. Explain the differences between the following statements:

```
import someLib.*;
import someLib.AClass;
```

3. List four categories of primitive data types of Java and their names in Java.

4. Explain why different data types are necessary.

5. What value is assigned to **x** by the following statement?

```
x = 25.0 * 3.0 / 2.5;
```

6. What value is assigned to **x** by the statement below, assuming **x** is 10.0?

```
x = x - 20.0;
```

7. Show the output lines displayed by the following lines when **x** is 5 and **y** is −20. How would the output change if the parentheses around **(x + y)** were omitted? If **Print** were changed to **println**?

```
System.out.print("The final total is: " + (x + y));
System.out.println(", x is " + x + " and y is " + y);
```

8. Write statements to prompt for and read an integer data value and store it in **num** (type **int**).

9. Indicate which type of data you use to represent the following items: number of children at school, a letter grade on an exam, your full name, the average numeric score of all students who took the last computer science exam, and whether you are single.

10. Write statements to find the position of the first comma in the string referenced by variable **sentence** and store its position in **pos1** (type **int**). Continue with questions 11 and 12.

11. Write statements to find the next comma and store its position in **pos2** (type **int**).

12. Write statements to store the characters before **pos1** in a **String** object **startStr**, the characters between **pos1** and **pos2** in a **String** object

midStr, and the characters after **pos2** in a **String** object **endStr**. Do not store the commas that are at positions **pos1** and **pos2** in any of these strings.

ANSWERS TO QUICK-CHECK EXERCISES

1. The application class is the only one that contains exactly one definition of the method **main()**.

2. The first statement imports all classes in folder **someLib**; the second statement imports only class **AClass** in folder **someLib**.

3. Integer (**int**), real (**double**), boolean (**boolean**), and character (**char**).

4. Data types tell the compiler what kind of storage space to allocate and what kinds of operations are allowed for a particular data item. In this way, the most space-efficient data type can be selected and memory allocation can be efficient. Data type conflicts that are detected by the compiler tell the programmer about possible coding errors.

5. `30.0`

6. `-10.0`

7. `The final total is: -15, x is 5 and y is -20;`

   Without parentheses around `(x + y)`:

   `The final total is: 5-20, x is 5 and y is -20;`

   Using **println()** instead of **print()**:

   ```
   The final total is: -15
   , x is 5 and y is -20;
   ```

8. `numStr = JOptionPane.showInputDialog("Enter an integer");`
   `int num = Integer.parseInt(numStr);`

9. `int, char, String, double, boolean`

10. `int pos1 = sentence.indexOf(",");`

11. `int pos2 = sentence.indexOf(",", pos1 + 1);`

12. `String startStr = sentence.subString(0, pos1);`
    `String midStr = sentence.subString(pos1 + 1, pos2);`
    `String endStr = sentence.subString(pos2 + 1);`

REVIEW QUESTIONS

1. Create an algorithm for shopping for groceries; that is, list the steps that are necessary to determine what supplies you need and the steps needed to purchase them. What kind of "data" does a problem like this one have?

2. What kind of information should be specified in the comments that appear at the beginning of a program?

3. Check the identifiers that you can use in a program:

____ `income`	____ `two fold`	____ `Hours*Rate`	____ `MyProgram`
____ `1time`	____ `C3PO`	____ `readOneLine`	____ `public`
____ `new`	____ `income#1`	____ `void`	____ `Program`
____ `tom's`	____ `item`	____ `variable`	____ `pi`

4. List four categories of primitive data types of Java.

5. Name two keywords for visibility. Explain how each has an impact on a class, method, or data field. Which keywords will we use for classes? Which for class methods? Which for class data fields?

6. Explain the difference between a class definition and a data declaration.

7. Explain how you get an integer value from a user and store it in a type `int` variable. What methods will be called?

8. Explain the difference in the way you call a class method and an instance method. If a program uses the conventions for naming identifiers described in this book, how can you determine whether an identifier is a method or a data field?

9. Explain how you can use methods `print()` and `println()` while debugging a program. What kind of errors can they help you detect? What is the major difference between these methods? Are they instance methods or class methods?

PROGRAMMING PROJECTS

For each project listed here, use the software development method to identify the data requirements, formulas, and classes needed to solve the problem. Then write each application class.

1. The formula for converting from Fahrenheit to Celsius is

   Fahrenheit = $1.8 \times$ Celsius + 32

   Write a program that will convert from Celsius to Fahrenheit. Write a second program that will convert from Fahrenheit to Celsius.

2. Write a program that converts a number of seconds into the equivalent hours, minutes, and seconds.

3. Write a program that reads two data items and computes their sum, difference, product, and quotient.

4. Given the length and width of a rectangular yard, and the length and width of a rectangular house situated in the yard, compute the time required (in minutes) to cut the grass at the rate of 2.3 square meters a second.

5. Write a program that calculates the cost of an automobile trip given the distance traveled, the average cost of a gallon of gas, and the EPA mileage rating for your car in miles per gallon.

6. Write a program that reads in the numerators and denominators of two fractions. The program should print the product of the two fractions as a fraction and as a percent.

7. Write a program that reads the number of years ago that a dinosaur lived and then computes the equivalent number of months, days, and seconds ago. Use 365.25 days per year. Test your program with a triceratops that lived 145 million years ago and a brontosaurus that lived 182 million years ago. *Hint:* Use type **double** for all variables.

8. Arnie likes to jog in the morning. As he jogs, he counts the number of strides he makes during the first minute and then again during the last minute of his jogging. Arnie then averages these two and calls this average the number of strides he makes in a minute when he jogs. Write a program that accepts this average and the total time Arnie spends jogging in hours and minutes and then displays the distance Arnie has jogged in miles. Assume Arnie's stride is 2.5 feet. There are 5280 feet in a mile.

9. Write a program that reads in a string containing exactly four words (separated by * symbols) into a single **String** object. Next, extract each word from the original string and store each word in a String object. Then concatenate the words in reverse order to form another string. Display both the original and final strings. *Hint:* To extract the words, you should use the **indexOf()** method to find each symbol * and then use the **subString()** method to get the characters between the * symbols.

3

Object-Oriented Design and Writing Worker Classes

So far you have seen examples of Java programs that were written as application classes. For each application, we wrote a class with a `main` method that created and manipulated one or more worker objects of predefined types such as `String`.

In this chapter, we focus more on object-oriented design. We will learn how to write classes and define methods that perform different kinds of operations. We call these classes **worker classes** or **support classes** because they support the **application class** or **client class**. We can reuse these classes in other applications just like the predefined classes `String`, `JOptionPane`, and `Math`. As we mentioned earlier, class reuse is a very important aspect of object-oriented programming.

The chapter ends with optional material that your instructor may prefer to skip for now. The first optional section shows how to format program output using class **DecimalFormat** or **NumberFormat**. We also describe our own class **KeyIn** for simplifying program input.

The second optional section discusses how to draw graphics patterns and designs using the Java Abstract Window Toolkit (AWT). We introduce Java applets, which are classes that can be instantiated by a Web browser or applet viewer, and we show how to incorporate a Java applet in a HyperText Markup Language (HTML) file.

3.1   A First Worker Class: Class FoodItem

Many food markets or supermarkets these days have automated checkout systems. The checkout clerk moves the item over an optical scanner that reads its barcode. The system prints a description of the item and its price on your sales slip and adds the item price to your total purchase amount.

Let's consider how we might write a class **FoodItem** to represent an item in a supermarket. We need to store a description of the item (a string) and the item size and price (both real numbers). We show how to do this next.

Review of Class Definitions

We stated in Section 2.7 that a class definition has the following form:

1. A header declaration

2. The class body

    a. The data field declarations of the class

    b. The method definitions of the class

The **data fields** of a class (also called **instance variables**) store the information associated with an object of that class. The data fields may be referenced throughout the class. The values stored in an object's data fields represent the **state** of that object. We declare class **FoodItem** and its three data fields next:

```
public class FoodItem {

    // data fields
    private String description;
    private double size;
    private double price;
```

A data field declaration resembles a variable declaration except that it begins with the **visibility modifier** `private`. A **private data field** can be accessed directly in the class in which it is defined, but not outside the class. Other classes can manipulate data field `price`, for example, only through the methods of class `FoodItem`, which we provide. Because the class designer writes the methods that determine how private data fields can be manipulated, the class designer can ensure that they will be manipulated in a safe and predictable way.

Data field declaration

> Form: *[visibility]* *typeName* *datafieldName* = *[value]*;
> Example: `private int pennies;`
> `private String month;`

    Interpretation: The data type of *datafieldName* is specified as *typeName* where *typeName* is either predefined in Java or is the name of a class that has been defined by Java programmers. If *value* is present, it must be a literal of data type *typeName*. The *visibility* may be specified as **private** (accessible only within the class), **public** (accessible anywhere), or **protected** (accessible only within the class and by subclasses of the class). If omitted, the data field has **default visibility**, which means it can be accessed by any class in the same folder as the current class. For now, we will use private visibility for data fields.

Giving a Data Field an Initial Value

You can give a data field an initial value when you declare it. For example, if every item costs $1 in your store, you might want to declare data field price as

```
private double price = 1.0;
```

We will explain other ways to give a data field an initial value shortly.

Method Definitions

Recall from Section 2.7 that method definitions have the form

> *method header* {
> *method body*
> }

where the method header gives the method name, the data type of the value returned by the method (if any), and its parameters in parentheses. So far you have seen the header for method `main()`:

```
public static void main(String[] args)
```

The next syntax display gives a more formal description of a method header.

Method header

Form: *visibility* [static] *resultType*
methodName([*parameterList*])

Example: `public static void main(String[] args)`
`private double getPrice()`
`private void setPrice(double aPrice)`
`private String toString()`

Interpretation: Method *methodName* returns a value of type *resultType*. The method parameters appear in the optional *parameterList*. This list contains individual data declarations (data type, identifier pairs) separated by commas. Empty parentheses `()` indicate that a method has no parameters. The method definition specifies *visibility* with modifier keywords (for example, `public`, `private`) that precede the *resultType*. If present, the keyword `static` indicates that the method is a class method.

The visibility specifies whether the method may be called from outside the class (**public visibility**) or just within the class (**private visibility**). Most of the methods we write will have public visibility.

The word `static` indicates that a method is a class method, not an instance method. Most of the methods we write will be instance methods, so the word `static` will not usually appear.

The result type can be a primitive type such as **double** or it can be a class type. If a method does not return a result (for example, method **main()**), the result type must be declared as **void**.

The parameter list consists of parameter declarations separated by commas. A parameter declaration specifies the parameter's data type and name. The parameter list is optional; however, the parentheses that enclose it are required. An empty pair of parentheses signifies that the method has no parameters.

Methods for Class `FoodItem`

Next, we turn to writing the method definitions for class **FoodItem**. For most classes, we need to provide methods that perform tasks similar to the first four items in the list below:

1. A method to create a new **FoodItem** object with a specified description, size, and price (*constructor*)

2. Methods to change the description, size, or price of a **FoodItem** object (*mutators*)

3. Methods that return the description, size, or price of a **FoodItem** object (*accessors*)

4. A method that returns the object state as a string

5. A method that calculates the unit price of an item (price divided by size)

The method that performs task 1 is called a **constructor,** and it must have the same name as the class. The methods that perform task 2 are called **mutators.** Programmers often give them names that begin with **set**. Mutator methods are **void** methods; they change an object's state but do not return a value. The methods that perform task 3 are called **accessors.** Programmers often give them names that begin with the word **get**. The method that performs task 4 usually has the name **toString()**. In addition to these general methods, we need to provide methods that perform the special operations associated with a class. For example, we might want to provide a method that calculates the unit price of each item (task 5 above).

You can usually write the method header from a description of what the method does. Table 3.1 shows the form of the method header for each method described above. It also shows the data type and name of each parameter. Notice that a constructor method does not have a result type.

Fig. 3.1 shows class **FoodItem** with method definitions. The order in which we list the methods in a class is immaterial and does not determine their order of execution. In fact, many of the methods in a class do not execute in a particular application program that uses the class. To execute or invoke a method, we must provide a proper method call in method **main()** or in some other method that is part of a sequence of method calls initiated by the **main()** method. Each method in Fig. 3.1 is an **instance method** and can therefore be invoked only by applying it to a class instance.

Table 3.1 Method headers for class `FoodItem`

Method	Description
`public FoodItem(String desc,` `        double aSize, double aP)`	Constructor—creates a new object whose three data fields have the values specified by its three arguments
`public void setDesc(String desc)`	Mutator—sets the value of data field `description` to the value specified by its argument; returns no value
`public void setSize(double aSize)`	Mutator—sets the value of data field `size` to the value specified by its argument; returns no value
`public void setPrice(double aPrice)`	Mutator—sets the value of data field `price` to the value specified by its argument; returns no value
`public String getDesc()`	Accessor—returns a reference to the string referenced by data field `description`; has no parameters
`public double getSize()`	Accessor—returns the value of data field `size`; has no parameters
`public double getPrice()`	Accessor—returns the value of data field `price`; has no parameters
`public String toString()`	Returns a string representing the state of this object; has no parameters
`public double calcUnitPrice()`	Returns the unit price of this item; has no parameters

Figure 3.1   Class `FoodItem`

```java
/*
 * FoodItem.java    Authors: Koffman and Wolz
 * Represents a food item at a market
 */
public class FoodItem {

  // data fields
  private String description;
  private double size;
  private double price;

  // methods
  // postcondition: creates a new object with data field
  //   values as specified by the arguments
  public FoodItem(String desc, double aSize, double aP) {
     description = desc;
     size = aSize;
     price = aP;
  }

  // postcondition: sets description to the argument value
  public void setDesc(String desc) {
     description = desc;
  }

  // postcondition: sets size to the argument value
  public void setSize(double aSize) {
     size = aSize;
  }

  // postcondition: sets price to the argument value
  public void setPrice(double aPrice) {
     price = aPrice;
  }

  // postcondition: returns the item description
  public String getDesc() {
     return description;
  }

  // postcondition: returns the item size
  public double getSize() {
```

Figure 3.1   **Class `FoodItem`**, *continued*

```
      return size;
  }

  // postcondition: returns the item price
  public double getPrice() {
     return price;
  }

  // postcondition: returns a string representing the item state
  public String toString() {
     return description + ", size : " + size +
            ", price $" + price;
  }

  // postcondition: calculates and returns the unit price
  public double calcUnitPrice() {
     return price / size;
  }
}
```

Constructor Method

We repeat the **constructor** method next.

```
public FoodItem(String desc, double aSize, double aP) {
   description = desc;
   size = aSize;
   price = aP;
}
```

Recall that a constructor executes when a new object is created and initializes its data fields. A call to this constructor always follows the word **new** and has the form

```
new FoodItem("apples, Macintosh", 2.5, 1.25)
```

The effect is to create a new **FoodItem** object whose description field stores a reference to a **String** object containing the characters **apples, Macintosh**. The **size** is **2.5** (inches) and the **price** is $**1.25** (per pound).

void Methods

The mutator methods are all **void** methods. When method **setDesc()** is called, the assignment statement

```
description = desc;
```

stores the value passed to parameter **desc** in data field **description**. Programmers say that *void methods are executed for their effect* because they do not return a value; however, they may change the state of the object to which they are applied or cause some information to be displayed.

Some other **void** methods we have seen are **main()**, **println()**, and **showMessageWindow()**. Method **main()** does not return a value. Its body determines the effect of executing an application. Methods **println()** and **showMessageWindow()** cause some information to be displayed to the program user.

The return Statement

Each method in Fig. 3.1 that is not a **void** method or a constructor returns a single result. These methods contain a statement starting with **return**. For example, in method **getPrice()** (result type **double**), we use the **return statement**

```
return price;
```

to specify that the method returns as its result the value of data field **price**. Accessor methods **getDesc()** and **getSize()** use similar **return** statements.

In method **calcUnitPrice()** (result type **double**), the statement

```
return price / size;
```

specifies that the method result is the quotient of **price** divided by **size**. For example, if an item costs $1 and its size is 10 (for 10 ounces), its unit price will be 0.10 (ten cents an ounce).

By convention in Java, a **toString()** method returns a reference to a **String** object that represents an object's state. In method **toString()** (result type **String**), the expression following **return**

```
return description + ", size : " + size +
       ", price $" + price;
```

specifies what characters will be stored in the **String** object returned as the method result. This **String** object will start with the characters in **description** followed by the characters **, size :** followed by characters representing the value of data field

size followed by the characters , price $ followed by characters representing the value of data field **price**. A sample result would be a **String** object containing the characters **Saltine crackers, size: 16, price $2.45**.

return statement

Form: **return** *expression*;

Example: **return x + y;**

Interpretation: The keyword **return** tells the compiler that the **expression** that follows is returned as the method result. The data type of the **expression** must be assignment compatible with the type of the method result as specified in the method header.

You must use a **return** statement to exit from a method whose type is not **void**. A syntax error occurs if the expression is not assignment compatible with the method's result type. A syntax error also occurs if the Java compiler determines that it is possible to exit the method without executing a **return** statement.

Calling Methods

Because a **void** method does not return a value, a call to a **void** method is a Java statement all by itself. If **myCandy** is type **FoodItem,** an example would be

```
myCandy.setDescription("Snickers, large");
```

Because a non-**void** method returns a value, a call to a non-**void** method should occur in an expression:

```
"price is $" + myCandy.getPrice()
```

The result returned by the call to method **getPrice()** (type **double**) is appended to the string that starts with the characters **price is $**.

Postconditions

Each method definition in Fig. 3.1 begins with a comment called a **postcondition**. A postcondition is a condition that must be true after the method executes and is a part of the **class documentation**. The class documentation is the set of comments that describe the operation of the class methods to a programmer who might want to use the class.

What guidelines do we use to write postconditions? If the method returns a result, we describe what the result will be:

```
// postcondition: returns the item price
public double getPrice() {
```

If the method does not return a result but just changes the state of an object, we describe how the state changes:

```
// postcondition: sets price to the argument value
public void setPrice(double aPrice)
```

Locality of Method Parameter and Variable Declarations

A method's parameters can be accessed only within the method body. Therefore, we can access parameter **aPrice** only in method **setPrice()**. The same statement is true for any variables that may be declared within a method body. Those variables can be accessed only within the method body.

Argument/Parameter Correspondence in Method Calls

We stated earlier that information is passed to a method through the arguments used in a method call. The arguments consist of a list of expressions, variables, or values separated by commas. The number of arguments in the argument list should be the same as the number of parameters in the parameter list. The data type of each argument in the call should correspond to the data type of its corresponding parameter in the parameter list. Argument correspondence is determined by position in each list (that is, the first argument in the argument list corresponds to the first parameter in the parameter list, and so on). If a method has no parameters, its parameter list will be written as **()** and the empty argument list **()** should be used in each call.

Remember, we call an instance method by applying it to an object (instance) of its class. We illustrate how to use the methods of class **FoodItem** in the next examples.

◆◆ EXAMPLE 3.1 ───────────────────────────────

If **snack** is type **FoodItem**, the method call

```
snack.setPrice(2.65);
```

calls the **setPrice()** method of object **snack**, passing the argument **2.65** to parameter **aPrice**. In the method body, the statement

```
price = aPrice;
```

stores **2.65** in data field **price**.

◆◆

◆◆ EXAMPLE 3.2 ─────────────────────────────────

The statement

```
FoodItem myCandy = new FoodItem("Snickers", 6.5, 0.55);
```

creates a new **FoodItem** object referenced by variable **myCandy**. The three arguments shown are passed to the constructor for class **FoodItem** with header

```
public FoodItem(String desc, double aSize, double aP)
```

establishing the argument/parameter correspondence in Table 3.2. The constructor stores the following values in the data fields of object **myCandy**:

```
description: a reference to "Snickers"
size: 6.5
price: 0.55
```

Table 3.2 Argument/parameter correspondence for FoodItem("Snickers", 6.5, 0.55)

Argument	Parameter
"Snickers"	desc (references "Snickers")
6.5	aSize (value is 6.5)
0.55	aPrice (value is 0.55)

◆◆

You should recognize that a syntax error would occur if we placed the string argument in a different position. If the string argument were the second argument instead of the first, we would get the syntax error **method FoodItem(double, java.lang.String, double) not found in class FoodItem**. This message means that there is no definition for a method named **FoodItem** with parameters in the order **double, String, double**. (The notation **java.lang.String** means that class **String** is part of package **java.lang**.)

If we reversed the order of the second and third arguments by mistake, we would not get a syntax error. However, incorrect values would be stored in data fields **size** and **price**.

◆◆ EXAMPLE 3.3 ─────────────────────────────────

Figure 3.2 shows an application class **TestFoodItem** whose purpose is to test the methods of class **FoodItem**. Method **main()** creates two different **FoodItem** objects, **myCandy** and **mySoup**. Each object has storage for its own data fields and the methods of class **FoodItem** can be applied to each object. Figure 3.3 shows the console window after the execution of class **TestFoodItem**.

Figure 3.2   Class `TestFoodItem`

```
/*
 * TestFoodItem.java    Authors: Koffman and Wolz
 * Tests class FoodItem
 */
public class TestFoodItem {

  public static void main(String[] args) {
    FoodItem myCandy = new FoodItem("Snickers", 6.5, 0.55);
    FoodItem mySoup = new FoodItem("Progresso Minestrone", 16.5, 2.35);
    System.out.println(myCandy.toString());
    System.out.println("-- unit price is $" +
                    myCandy.calcUnitPrice());
    System.out.println(mySoup.toString());
    System.out.println("-- unit price is $" +
                    mySoup.calcUnitPrice());
  }
}
```

Figure 3.3   Execution of class `TestFoodItem`

The execution of method **main()** causes the four lines shown in the console window to be displayed. The first of these four lines is displayed by

```
System.out.println(myCandy.toString());
```

It shows the state of object **myCandy**, the result of applying object **candy**'s **toString()** method. The second line is displayed by

```
System.out.println("-- unit price is $" +
                  myCandy.calcUnitPrice());
```

It shows the string formed by appending the result returned by **myCandy**'s **calcUnitPrice()** method to the characters **-- unit price is $**. The third and fourth lines show the result of performing the same operations on object **mySoup**.

Arguments Are Passed by Value

In Java, primitive type arguments are **passed by value**. This means that the value of each argument is passed to its corresponding parameter and a separate copy of that value is stored locally in the method parameter. If the method happens to change a parameter value, the local copy is updated but the argument value is not.

◆◆ EXAMPLE 3.4 ─────────────────────────────

In Fig. 3.4, assume argument **sal** corresponds to parameter **salary** (type **double**) of method **increaseSalary()**. Figure 3.4b shows the values of **sal** and **salary** after executing the statement

```
salary = 1.10 * salary;
```

in method **increaseSalary()**. The value of **sal** (the argument) is unchanged.

Figure 3.4 Effect of increasing salary by 10% in method `increaseSalary()`

(a) Before increasing salary	
Argument	*Parameter*
sal	salary
1200	1200
(b) After salary = 1.10 * salary;	
Argument	*Parameter*
sal	salary
1200	1320

◆◆

Transfers of Control during Method Call and Return

During compilation of a class, each method is translated into a sequence of byte code instructions. Each call to a method is translated as an instruction that transfers control to the byte code instructions for that method. When the compiler reaches the end of a method definition, it inserts an instruction returning control from the method back to the calling instruction. At this point, the compiler does not know which instruction will be the calling instruction, but it can still insert the instruction that returns control.

Fig. 3.5 shows the transfers of control that occur when the **main** method in Fig. 3.2 executes the statement

```
System.out.println(myCandy.toString());
```

The execution of this statement begins by transferring control to object **myCandy**'s **toString()** method because the argument for method **println()** must be evaluated before it can be called. After the code for method **toString()** executes, control is returned to the calling instruction in the **main** method. Continuing the execution of this statement, the main method transfers control to method **println()**. After the code for method **println()** executes, control is returned to the calling instruction in the **main** method. Because execution of this statement is now complete, the next statement in the **main** method executes.

Figure 3.5   Transfers of control for `System.out.println(myCandy.toString());`

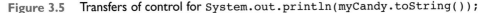

Statement in main method	Methods called

```
System.out.println(myCandy.toString());
```

Transfer to method **toString()** of object **myCandy**
Execute method body
Return control to calling statement
Transfer to method **println()** of object **System.out**
Execute method body
Return control to calling statement

Encapsulation

Mutator methods **setDesc()**, **setSize()**, and **setPrice()** change the state of a data field. Because all data fields have private visibility, another class that is a **client** (user) of class **FoodItem** cannot access a data field directly. To change a data field value, the client must invoke one of the mutator methods. To retrieve a data field value, the client must invoke one of the accessor methods.

This is the principle of **encapsulation:** A class encapsulates data fields and methods together in the same Java entity. The data fields have private visibility, but the methods have public visibility. This ensures that the data fields will always be manipulated in a safe and predictable way.

Fig. 3.6 is a diagram of the object referenced by **myCandy** that illustrates the encapsulation of its data fields and methods as a single entity. Data field **description** references an unnamed object of type **String**. The characters stored in this object can only be manipulated through its methods (**charAt()**, **indexOf()**, and so on).

Figure 3.6   Diagram of object referenced by myCandy

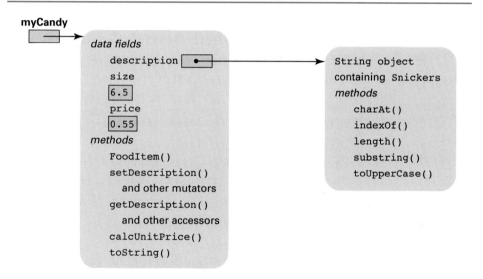

EXERCISES FOR SECTION 3.1

SELF-CHECK

1. For Example 3.3, what would be the effect of the following method calls?

   a. myCandy.toString()

   b. myCandy.getPrice()

   c. myCandy.calcUnitPrice()

   d. myCandy.setPrice(0.50)

2. Add statements to method **main( )** in Fig. 3.2 to do the following:

   a. Change the description of **myCandy** to **"Snickers, large"**. Also, change the size to 10.0 and the price to 0.95.

   b. Display the total cost of purchasing three Snickers bars and two cans of minestrone soup in the console window. Make sure you use the prices stored in objects **myCandy** and **mySoup** in your calculations.

   c. Create a new **FoodItem** object that represents an 8-ounce hamburger that costs $1.75. Calculate and display the unit cost of the hamburger.

PROGRAMMING

1. Write a new method **raisePrice( )** with a type **double** argument for class **FoodItem** that raises the price of an object by a specified percentage (the method argument).

2. Add a data field **cost** to class **FoodItem** that is the actual cost to the supermarket of a food item. Add methods **setCost( )** and **getCost( )** and also add a constructor with four arguments. Add a method **calcProfit( )** to compute the profit **(price — cost)** on a sale of an item.

3. Write a class **Date** that represents a day of the year. Your class should have a type **String** data field for month and type **int** data fields for day and year. Write a constructor for this class, and accessor and mutator methods and a **toString( )** method. Also write a **reset( )** method that changes the **Date** object to which it is applied back to the first day of the year.

3.2 A Worker Class That Manipulates **String** Objects

In our next case study, we will design both a worker class and an application class. Both classes store and manipulate type **String** objects.

CASE STUDY FINDING THE WORDS IN A SENTENCE

PROBLEMS We want to write a program that gets a sentence and displays the first three words in the sentence on separate lines. To simplify the task, we assume that the sentence has at least four words.

ANALYSIS To solve this problem, we need to be able to get the first word of a sentence and the rest of the sentence that follows the first word. Once we have done this, we can get the first word from the rest of the sentence, which will give us the second word, and a sentence that begins with the third word, and so on. Table 3.3 illustrates this process. The data requirements for this problem follow the table.

Table 3.3 Finding the words in a sentence

Sentence	First Word	Rest of Sentence
`This is a great day.`	`This`	`is a great day.`
`is a great day.`	`is`	`a great day.`
`a great day.`	`a`	`great day.`

Data Requirements

> ### *Problem Input*
> A sentence
>
> ### *Problem Output*
> The first three words of the sentence

Two classes are needed. A worker class **WordExtractor** must store a sentence (the problem input) and be able to get its first word and the rest of the sentence. An application class **WordExtractorApp** is a client of the **WordExtractor** class and also class **JOptionPane.** Both new classes use the **String** class.

DESIGN

Class `WordExtractor`

The **WordExtractor** class needs to store a sentence. It also needs a method to get the first word (**getFirst()**) and one to get the rest of the sentence (**getRest()**). Figure 3.7 shows the description of class **WordExtractor**.

Figure 3.7 Class `WordExtractor`

Data Fields	Attribute
`String sentence`	Reference to the string whose first word is to be extracted
Methods	**Behavior**
`void getFirst()`	Gets the first word in **sentence**
`void getRest()`	Gets the rest of the string referenced by **sentence**
`String toString()`	Represents object's state
Classes Used	
`String`	

The algorithms for the instance methods of class **WordExtractor** follow.

Algorithm for `getFirst()`

1. Find the position of the first blank in the sentence.

2. Return the characters up to the first blank.

Algorithm for `getRest()`

1. Find the position of the first blank in the sentence.

2. Return the characters after the first blank.

Class `WordExtractorApp`

Class `WordExtractorApp` is a client of class `WordExtractor`. It also interacts with the program user through class `JOptionPane`. Figure 3.8 shows its description.

Figure 3.8   Class `WordExtractorApp`

Method	Behavior
`main()`	Gets the sentence from the user and removes its first, second, and third words; shows the user the results
Classes Used	
`WordExtractor, JOptionPane`	

The application class contains a **main** method where program execution begins. An interesting way to solve this problem is to create three **WordExtractor** objects. The first one will store the original sentence. We can get the first word and create a second **WordExtractor** object that stores the rest of the sentence. We can get its first word and create a third **WordExtractor** object that stores the rest of the sentence, and so on. The algorithm follows.

Algorithm for `main()`

1. Read in a sentence.

2. Create a **WordExtractor** object that stores the input sentence.

3. Write the first word to the console window.

4. Create a **WordExtractor** object that stores the sentence starting with the second word.

5. Write the second word to the console window.

6. Create a **WordExtractor** object that stores the sentence starting with the third word.

7. Write the third word to the console window.

8. Write the rest of the sentence to the console window.

IMPLEMENTATION   We define each class in its own file. Class **WordExtractor** (see Fig. 3.9) has a single data field: the sentence whose first word is being retrieved. We can use the **String** class **indexOf()** and **substring()** methods to perform the algorithm steps for methods **getFirst()** and **getRest()**. The constructor method **WordExtractor()** defines the initial state of a new object. Method **toString()** returns the string referenced by **sentence**. We did not define a **getSentence()** method because method **toString()** can be used for this purpose. Method **setSentence()** updates the value of the data field.

The constructor has a **String** parameter. Data field **sentence** of the new object is set to reference the **String** object passed as the constructor argument.

Method **getFirst()** is preceded by the comment

```
// precondition: sentence has at least two words separated by a blank
```

A **precondition** is a logical condition that should be true at the time the method is called. This comment indicates that **getFirst()** should be called only when data field **sentence** contains two or more words. If you call the method when its precondition is not satisfied, the method may not execute correctly.

The method body declares a local variable **posBlank** (type **int**). This variable can only be referenced within method **getFirst()**. The statement

```
int posBlank = sentence.indexOf(" ");
```

stores the position of the first blank in **posBlank**. The statement

```
return sentence.substring(0, posBlank);
```

returns a **String** object containing the characters in the first word.

Method **getRest()** declares a different local variable named **posBlank**, which is also set to the position of the first blank. The statement

```
return sentence.substring(posBlank + 1);
```

returns an object that contains the characters after the first word in **sentence**.

Figure 3.10 shows class **WordExtractorApp**. The statements

```
String sent =
        JOptionPane.showInputDialog("Enter at least 4 words");
WordExtractor wE1 = new WordExtractor(sent);
```

create a new **WordExtractor** object **wE1** whose data field **sentence** references the string typed in by the user. The statement

Figure 3.9   Class `WordExtractor`

```java
/*
 * WordExtractor.java    Authors: Koffman and Wolz
 * Represents a class that extracts a word
 */
public class WordExtractor {

    // Data field
    String sentence;

    //Methods
    public WordExtractor(String str) {
        sentence = str;
    }

    public void setSentence(String str) {
        sentence = str;
    }

    // precondition: sentence has at least two words separated by a blank
    // postcondition: gets the first word of sentence
    public String getFirst() {
        // Find the position of the first blank in sentence.
        int posBlank = sentence.indexOf(" ");

        // Return the characters up to the first blank.
        return sentence.substring(0, posBlank);
    }

    // precondition: sentence has at least two words separated by a blank
    // postcondition: gets the part of sentence after the first blank
    public String getRest() {
        // Find the position of the first blank in sentence.
        int posBlank = sentence.indexOf(" ");

        // Return the characters after the first blank.
        return sentence.substring(posBlank + 1);
    }

    public String toString() {
        return sentence;
    }
}
```

Figure 3.10 Class `WordExtractorApp`

```java
/*
 * WordExtractorApp.java      Authors: Koffman and Wolz
 * Extracts 3 words from a sentence.
 */
import javax.swing.JOptionPane;

public class WordExtractorApp {

    public static void main(String[] args) {
        // Read in a sentence.
        String sent =
                JOptionPane.showInputDialog("Enter at least 4 words");

        // Create a WordExtractor object that stores the input sentence.
        WordExtractor wE1 = new WordExtractor(sent);

        // Write the first word to the console window.
        System.out.println("first word: " + wE1.getFirst());

        // Create a WordExtractor object that stores the sentence
        //   starting with the second word.
        WordExtractor wE2 = new WordExtractor(wE1.getRest());
        // Write the second word to the console window.
        System.out.println("second word: " + wE2.getFirst());

        // Create a WordExtractor object that stores the sentence
        //   starting with the third word.
        WordExtractor wE3 = new WordExtractor(wE2.getRest());
        // Write the third word to the console window.
        System.out.println("third word: " + wE3.getFirst());

        // Write the rest of the sentence to the console window.
        System.out.println("rest of sentence: " + wE3.getRest());
    }
}
```

```
System.out.println("first word: " + wE1.getFirst());
```

writes its argument string to the console window. Notice that we do not store the string returned by method **getFirst()** in a local variable; instead, we use the string result as an operand in the argument expression for method **println()**. This practice is very common in Java programming. The statement

```
WordExtractor wE2 = new WordExtractor(wE1.getRest());
```

creates a new **WordExtractor** object that stores the characters in the rest of the sentence, starting with the second word (the **String** object returned by **wE1.getRest()**).

TESTING   A sample run is shown in Fig. 3.11. To test this program, try running it with a number of different sentences, but make sure each sentence has at least four words.

Figure 3.11   **Sample run of class WordExtractorApp**

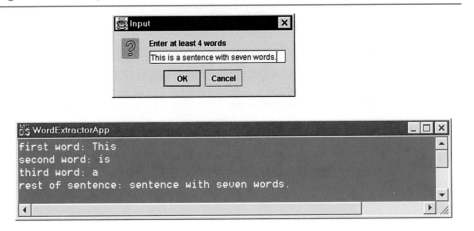

PROGRAM STYLE: *Using Multiple Objects versus Reusing One*

There is usually more than one way to solve a problem. Because class **WordExtractorApp** needed to extract three words, we decided to use multiple objects of type **WordExtractor**. When we create each object, we pass the constructor a different string to be stored. Consequently, when we apply methods **getFirst()** and **getRest()** to each object, we get a different result. We could also have solved this problem by creating a single object. We could use method `setSentence()` to update its value after extracting each word (see Programming Exercise 1 in Exercises for Section 3.2). Neither solution is "better"; they are just different approaches.

EXERCISES FOR SECTION 3.2

SELF-CHECK

1. Trace the execution of class `WordExtractorApp` for the sample run. Show each method call that occurs, its argument, and its result (or its effect if it does not return a value).

PROGRAMMING

1. Modify the application class so that it uses just one object and stores new information in this object after each word is extracted.

2. Write an application class that displays every other word in the input sentence.

3.3 A Worker Class That Processes Integers

In the next case study, we consider designing a class that represents a common machine that you might find in a bank or a supermarket: a coin changer. Coin changers accept a collection of coins and print out a receipt showing the value of that collection.

CASE STUDY DESIGNING A COIN CHANGER

PROBLEM   A common problem is to determine the value of a collection of coins. Our goal is to write a class that simulates the behavior of a coin changer. Instead of pouring a container of coins into a hopper, the user will provide the number of each kind of coin as input data.

ANALYSIS   The first step in solving this problem is to determine what a coin changer must do. It must accept a collection of coins and compute the value of the coins in dollars and cents. For example, if a collection contains 5 quarters and 3 pennies, its value is $1.28 (1 dollar and 28 cents in change). The problem inputs will be the number of each kind of coin, and the problem output will be the value of the coins in dollars and change.

Data Requirements

Problem Inputs

The number of pennies
The number of nickels
The number of dimes
The number of quarters

Problem Output

The value of the coins in dollars and change

Relevant Formulas and Relationships

A penny is worth 1 cent
A nickel is worth 5 cents
A dime is worth 10 cents
A quarter is worth 25 cents
A dollar is worth 100 cents

We need a worker class, **CoinChanger**, that knows how to calculate the value of a collection of coins. The worker class must store the quantity of each coin (the problem inputs). Besides calculating the total value in cents, it must be able to compute the equivalent amount in dollars and change. We also need an application class that interacts with the program user and with a **CoinChanger** object.

DESIGN

Class CoinChanger

We need to store the number of each kind of coin in a **CoinChanger** object. We can use mutator methods (**setPennies()**, etc.) to do this. Also, the **CoinChanger** class must be able to calculate the value of a coin collection in cents, so we need a method **findCentsValue()** to perform this calculation. Similarly, we need a method **findDollars()** to find the value in dollars and a method **findChange()** to find the leftover change (for example, 327 cents is worth 3 dollars and 27 cents in change). Lastly, we need a method **toString()** that represents the information stored in a **CoinChanger** object in a meaningful way (see Fig. 3.12).

Let's look at the algorithms for the methods of class **CoinChanger**.

Algorithm for *setPennies()*

1. Store the number of pennies.

Algorithm for *findCentsValue()*

1. Calculate the total value in cents using the formula

$$total\ cents = pennies + 5 \times nickels + 10 \times dimes + 25 \times quarters$$

Figure 3.12   Class `CoinChanger`

Data Fields	Attributes
`int pennies`	Count of pennies
`int nickels`	Count of nickels
`int dimes`	Count of dimes
`int quarters`	Count of quarters
Methods	**Behavior**
`void setPennies(int)`	Sets the count of pennies
`void setNickels(int)`	Sets the count of nickels
`void setDimes(int)`	Sets the count of dimes
`void setQuarters(int)`	Sets the count of quarters
`int findCentsValue(int)`	Calculates total value in cents
`int findDollars()`	Calculates value in dollars
`int findChange()`	Calculates leftover change
`String toString()`	Represents object's state
Classes Used	

`ChangeCoinsApp`

Algorithm for *`findDollars()`*

1. Get the integer quotient of the total value in cents divided by 100 (for example, the integer quotient of 327 divided by 100 is 3).

Algorithm for *`findChange()`*

1. Get the integer remainder of the total value in cents divided by 100 (for example, the integer remainder of 327 divided by 100 is 27).

Algorithm for *`toString()`*

1. Represent the state of the object (the number of each kind of coin).

Class `ChangeCoinsApp`

Next we design the application class **`ChangeCoinsApp`**. Figure 3.13 shows its description.

The algorithm for method **`main()`** follows.

Algorithm for *`main()`*

1. Create a **`CoinChanger`** object.

2. Store the number of each kind of coin in the **`CoinChanger`** object.

3. Display the value of the coins in dollars and change.

Figure 3.13   Class ChangeCoinsApp

Method	Behavior
`main()`	Gets the number of each kind of coin, stores this information in a `CoinChanger` object, calculates and displays the value of coins in dollars and change

Classes Used
`CoinChanger, JOptionPane`

IMPLEMENTATION   Figure 3.14 shows class `CoinChanger`. There are four type `int` data fields. Method `findCentsValue()` returns the value in cents of a `CoinChanger` object. Methods `findDollars()` and `findChange()` both call this method and process its result. Method `findDollars()` returns the integer quotient of this result divided by 100; method `findChange()` returns the integer remainder of this result divided by 100. Notice that there is no constructor for this class; we discuss why we did not have to define a constructor in the next section.

Figure 3.15 shows class `ChangeCoinsApp.` In method `main()`, we use the statements

```
String numStr = JOptionPane.showInputDialog("Number of pennies");
int num = Integer.parseInt(numStr);
cC.setPennies(num);
```

to read the count of pennies and store that value in object `cC`. We use similar statements to store the counts of the other coins. The count of each kind of coin is stored in a `String` object referenced by `numStr`, and the corresponding integer value is stored in `num`.

Figure 3.14   Class CoinChanger

```
/*
 * CoinChanger.java    Authors: Koffman and Wolz
 * Represents a coin changer
 */

public class CoinChanger {
  // Data fields
  private int pennies;
  private int nickels;
  private int dimes;
  private int quarters;
```

Figure 3.14 Class `CoinChanger`, *continued*

```
// Methods
public void setPennies(int pen) {
  pennies = pen;
}

public void setNickels(int nick) {
  nickels = nick;
}

public void setDimes(int dim) {
  dimes = dim;
}

public void setQuarters(int quart) {
  quarters = quart;
}

// postcondition: Returns the total value in cents.
public int findCentsValue() {
  return pennies + 5 * nickels + 10 * dimes + 25 * quarters;
}

// postcondition: Returns the amount in dollars.
public int findDollars() {
  return findCentsValue() / 100;
}

// postcondition: Returns the amount of leftover change.
public int findChange() {
  return findCentsValue() % 100;
}

public String toString() {
return pennies + " pennies, " + nickels + " nickels, " +
      dimes + " dimes, " + quarters + " quarters";
}
}
```

String **message** is constructed so that it shows the state of object **cC** (returned by **cC.toString()**) followed by the value in dollars (returned by **cC.findDollars()**) and cents (returned by **cC.findChange()**). We use the escape character \n in the string **"\nCoin collection value is $"** to start a new line when **message** is displayed.

Figure 3.15   Class ChangeCoinsApp

```
/*
 * ChangeCoinsApp.java    Authors: Koffman and Wolz
 * Application class that uses class CoinChanger
 */
import javax.swing.JOptionPane;

public class ChangeCoinsApp {

  public static void main(String[] args) {

    //Create a CoinChanger object.
    CoinChanger cC = new CoinChanger();

    // Store the number of each kind of coin in the CoinChanger object.
    String numStr = JOptionPane.showInputDialog("Number of pennies");
    int num = Integer.parseInt(numStr);
    cC.setPennies(num);

    numStr = JOptionPane.showInputDialog("Number of nickels");
    num = Integer.parseInt(numStr);
    cC.setNickels(num);


    numStr = JOptionPane.showInputDialog("Number of dimes");
    num = Integer.parseInt(numStr);
    cC.setDimes(num);

    numStr = JOptionPane.showInputDialog("Number of quarters");
    num = Integer.parseInt(numStr);
    cC.setQuarters(num);

    // Display the value of the coins in dollars and change.
    String message = cC.toString() +
                "\nCoin collection value is $" +
                cC.findDollars() + "." + cC.findChange();
    JOptionPane.showMessageDialog(null, message);
  }
}
```

TESTING   Figure 3.16 shows the message window displayed during a sample run of class `ChangeCoinsApp`. Make sure it runs properly when one or more coin counts are zero. Also, try running it with a combination of coins that yields an exact dollar amount with no change left over. For example, 35 nickels and 25 pennies should yield a value of 2 dollars and no cents. Then increase and decrease the amount of pennies by 1 (26 and 24 pennies) to make sure that these cases are also handled properly.

Figure 3.16   Sample run of `ChangeCoinsApp`

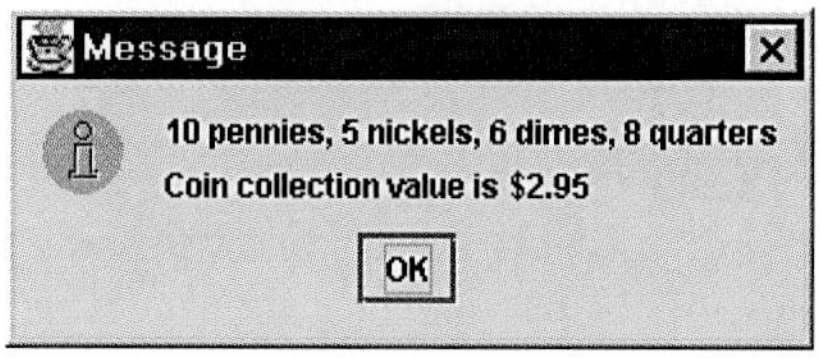

PROGRAM STYLE: *Storing Only Essential Data in an Object*

Those of you who are familiar with programming in other languages might wonder why we didn't introduce a data field in class `CoinChanger` for storage of the total value in cents. This would enable us to calculate it once (using method `findCentsValue()`) and store it instead of calculating it each time we need it (in methods `findDollars()` and `findChange()`). We don't store the total value in cents because it is not an essential attribute of a `CoinChanger` object. If we stored it, we would need to update its value each time we changed the count of one of the coins; otherwise, the information stored in the object would not be accurate or consistent. For these reasons, object-oriented programmers prefer to allocate storage only for essential data fields. We recommend you follow this convention and use methods to calculate intermediate results as you need them rather than storing them in an object.

EXERCISES FOR SECTION 3.3

SELF-CHECK

1. Trace the execution of class `ChangeCoinsApp` when the data values entered are 200, 30, 5, 8. Show the sequence of method calls and indicate the result of each method call.

PROGRAMMING

1. Add a method to class **CoinChanger** that "dispenses change" using the fewest coins. For example, if the value computed for change is 92 cents, this method should return a **String** object that contains the characters

   `quarters: 3, dimes: 1, nickels: 1, pennies: 2`

3.4   Review of Methods

Constructor Methods

A constructor method always has the same name as the class. It should have public visibility and does not have a result type because it does not return a value.

We stated that every class must have a constructor method that is called when an object is created. However, we did not define a constructor for class **CoinChanger**. The reason is that the compiler provides a default constructor (constructor with no parameters) for each class that does not define any constructors. The default constructor initializes each data field to its default value. Table 3.4 lists the default values for data fields.

Table 3.4   Default initialization for data fields

Data Field Type	Default Value
`int`	Zero
`double`	Zero
`boolean`	`false`
`char`	The first character in the Unicode character set (called the null character)
A class type	`null` (no object referenced)

Constructors with parameters initialize data fields to the corresponding argument values. Figure 3.17 shows two constructors for class **CoinChanger**. The first is the no parameter constructor. The second constructor has four parameters, one for each data field. If you write one or more constructors for a class, the compiler will not provide a default constructor, so you must define it yourself if you need it. When a new **CoinChanger** object is created, the argument list used with the constructor determines which constructor is invoked.

Figure 3.17   Two constructors for class `CoinChanger`

```
public CoinChanger() {
}

public CoinChanger(int pen, int nick, int dim, int quar) {
    pennies = pen;
    nickels = nick;
    dimes = dim;
    quarters = quar;
}
```

Accessor Methods

We have stated that the data fields of a class normally have private visibility. If the class is used to support another object such as an application, the application object cannot reference the support object's data directly. For example, a user of class **CoinChanger** (Fig. 3.14) might want to use the count of pennies in a calculation or display this value. To enable this to happen, the class designer must provide **public accessor methods,** or methods that return the values stored in an object's data fields. Figure 3.18 shows the accessor method that returns the type **int** value stored in data field **pennies**. Accessor methods are sometimes called getter methods and should begin with the word **get**.

Mutator Methods

Just as we need to access an object's private or protected data from another object, we sometimes need to store data in an object's private or protected data fields. We use **mutator** (or **modifier**) **methods** to do this. The void method **setPennies()** stores the value of its argument **pen** in data field **pennies** (Fig. 3.19). It is common practice to have several different mutator methods in a class. Mutator methods are sometimes called setter methods and should begin with the word **set**.

Figure 3.18   Accessor method `getPennies()`

```
// Accessor
// Returns the value stored in data field pennies.
public int getPennies() {
    return pennies;
}
```

Figure 3.19   Mutator method `setPennies()`

```
// Mutator
// Stores its argument value in data field pennies.
public void setPennies(int pen) {
   pennies = pen;
}
```

String Objects Are Immutable

Unlike the classes that we define ourselves, **String** objects are immutable, which means that we cannot change the characters stored in a **String** object. If we attempt to do so, Java creates a new **String** object that stores the modified string.

◆◆ EXAMPLE 3.5 ─────────────────────────────────────

In method **main()** of Fig. 3.20, variable **x** references a **String** object containing the characters **apple**. **String** method **toUpperCase()** forms a new **String** object that stores all uppercase characters. Applying this method to the **String** object referenced by **x** creates a new **String** object that stores the characters **APPLE**; however, the characters contained in the original **String** object do not change. The console window will display the two output lines

```
APPLE
apple
```

The first line above shows the uppercase characters contained in the new **String** object returned by the method **toUpperCase()**; the second line shows the lowercase characters, which are still stored in the **String** object referenced by **str**.

Figure 3.20   Class `TestStringMutation`

```
public class testStringMutation {

  public static void main(String[] args) {
    String str = "apples";
    System.out.println(str.toUpperCase());
    System.out.println(str);
  }
}
```

◆◆

Calling One Instance Method from Another

Earlier, we defined method `findDollars()` (Fig. 3.21) as an instance method of class `CoinChanger` (Fig. 3.14). The `return` statement calls method `findCentsValue()`, which is also defined in class `CoinChanger`. Method `findCentsValue()` is an instance method, but it does not appear to be applied to any object. In actuality, method `findCentsValue()` is applied to the same object as its caller, which we denote as "this object" or "the current object."

Use of Prefix `this` with a Data Field

In our constructor and mutator methods, we have been careful to use parameter names that are similar, but not identical, to data field names. For example, in method `setPennies()` shown in Fig. 3.19, we used `pen` as the parameter. You may be wondering if you can use `pennies` as the parameter name. The answer is Yes, but if you do, the identifier `pennies` will refer to parameter `pennies`, not data field pennies. The local declaration for pennies as a parameter *hides* the data field pennies. However, you can use the prefix `this.` to refer to data field pennies (that is, `this.pennies`). Fig. 3.22 shows a version of `setPennies()` with pennies as the parameter.

Class Methods versus Instance Methods

So far we have defined one class method, `main()`. We can define a method as a class method only when it does not manipulate any data fields. Class methods manipulate information passed as arguments. We use the modifier `static` to indicate that a method is a class method.

Figure 3.21   Method `findDollars()`

```
// postcondition returns the coin value in dollars
public int findDollars() {
   return findCentsValue() / 100;
}
```

Figure 3.22   Method `setPennies()` with parameter pennies

```
// Mutator
// Stores its argument value in data field pennies.
public void setPennies(int pennies) {
   this.pennies = pennies;
}
```

Because class methods are not applied to objects, we don't need to instantiate an object to call a class method. The class name is used as a prefix when a class method is called (for example, `Math.sqrt()`). Of course, we don't call method `main()`; it is called by the operating system and is the method where execution of a Java program begins.

◆◆ EXAMPLE 3.6 ───

Figure 3.23 shows class **ChangeCoinsAppTwo** (a revision of **ChangeCoinsApp**), which defines a static method **readInt()** to return an integer data value entered by the program user. The method parameter represents a prompt and is displayed in a dialog window when the statement

```
String intStr = JOptionPane.showInputDialog(prompt);
```

executes. The method returns the type `int` value corresponding to the characters entered by the program user. In method **main()**, you can use the statement

```
cC.setPennies(readInt("Number of pennies"));
```

to call method **readInt()** and to store the value it returns in data field **pennies** of object **cC**. The class name is not required as a prefix in the call to method **readInt()** because the method call occurs in class **ChangeCoinsAppTwo**. Notice that the value returned by method **readInt()** is not stored locally in method **main()** but is just passed as an argument to method **setPennies()**.

─── ◆◆

PROGRAM STYLE: *Minimizing Use of Local Variables*

At the end of Section 3.3, we indicated that we only store essential information in an object. We take the same approach in method **main()** in Fig. 3.23. Instead of using local variables to store the problem inputs, we read them and pass them on to the mutator methods (for example, **setPennies()**). This reduces our need for local storage and makes the program a bit more compact and easier to read. We did use a local variable **message** to store the string that represents the problem output. In this case, we felt that using a local variable was better than inserting this rather lengthy string expression directly in the call to method **showMessageDialog()**.

Figure 3.23   Class `ChangeCoinsAppTwo` with `static` method `readInt()`

```
/*
 * ChangeCoinsAppTwo.java    Authors: Koffman and Wolz
 * Application class with readInt() method that uses CoinChanger
 */
public class ChangeCoinsAppTwo {

  // methods

  // postcondition: Displays prompt in a dialog window and
  //   returns an int value corresponding to
  //   the characters typed in by the program user.
  private static int readInt(String prompt) {
    String intStr = JOptionPane.showInputDialog(prompt);
    return Integer.parseInt(intStr);
  }

  public static void main(String[] args) {
    //Create a CoinChanger object.
    CoinChanger cC = new CoinChanger();

    // Store the number of each kind of coin in the CoinChanger object.
    cC.setPennies(readInt("Number of pennies"));
    cC.setNickels(readInt("Number of nickels"));
    cC.setDimes(readInt("Number of dimes"));
    cC.setQuarters(readInt("Number of quarters"));

    // Display the value of the coins in dollars and change.
    String message = cC.toString() +
                    "\nCoin collection value is $" +
                    cC.findDollars() + "." + cC.findChange();
    JOptionPane.showMessageDialog(null, message);
  }
}
```

Problem Inputs, Problem Outputs, Method Inputs, Method Outputs

If you look closely at the definition for method **readInt()**, you will see that it returns as its result the data entered by the user (a problem input). So the problem input is actually an output (result) of method **readInt()**. A value returned by **readInt()** is then passed on as an argument (method input) to one of the mutator methods (for example, **setPennies()**). Similarly, when we want to display some information (a problem output), we pass that information as an argument to method `println()` or to method `showMessageDialog()`. So a problem output is actually an input argument to these methods. This may seem strange at first, but it is perfectly reasonable. A piece of information stored in memory may serve different roles when it is processed by different methods.

Another seeming inconsistency is that method inputs, unlike problem inputs, are not read by a method but are passed to a method through its argument list. Beginning programmers sometimes make the mistake of reading the inputs for a method as the first step in the method body instead of passing information through an argument when the method is called.

EXERCISES FOR SECTION 3.4

SELF-CHECK

1. What is an accessor?

2. What is the default constructor?

3. Design a class **Box** that calculates the volume and surface area of a box given its height, width, and length. The volume is defined as the product of the height, width, and length. The surface area can be calculated by summing the areas of the six sides. (*Hint:* There are actually only three unique sides.) Include the following constructors:

    ```
    Box()      // unit box (height, width, length = 1)
    Box(int side) // cube, height = width = length = side
    Box(int squareBase, int hei) // width = length
    Box(int hei, int wid, int len) // 3 different dimensions
    ```

    Include accessors and mutators for each of the data fields you define.

4. Design a class that has class methods for converting between radians and degrees. 2π radians = 360 degrees. π is defined in class **Math** and is referenced as **Math.PI**.

5. If data fields are declared public, do you think you need accessors and mutators? How does this affect the reliability of code? List the pros and cons of the two approaches: **public** data fields vs. **private** data fields with accessors and mutators.

6. Both mutators and constructors enable you to store data in an object. How are they different?

7. At first it is rather annoying that the default constructor is no longer automatically built if you define any other constructor. There is, however, a good rationale for this. Come up with an example in which you might not want a default constructor but do want other constructors.

PROGRAMMING

1. Implement a solution to Self-Check Exercise 3.

2. Implement a solution to Self-Check Exercise 4.

3. Use your solution in Programming Exercise 2 to write an application class that displays the radians that correspond to the following values in degrees: 0, 30, 60, 90, 180.

4. Use your solution in Programming Exercise 2 to write an application class that displays degrees that correspond to the following values in radians: 0, $\pi/2$, π, $3\pi/2$, 2π.

3.5 Simplifying a Solution Using Multiple Classes

In the next case study, we show how we can simplify the solution to a problem by defining two worker classes instead of just one. In this case study we will write two new worker classes. We will see that **class decomposition** is a useful problem-solving strategy.

CASE STUDY COMPUTING THE WEIGHT OF FLAT WASHERS

PROBLEM   You work for a hardware company that manufactures flat washers. To estimate shipping costs, you need a program that computes the weight of a specified quantity of flat washers. As part of this process, you need to compute the weight of a single washer.

ANALYSIS   A flat washer resembles a small donut. To compute its weight you need to know its rim area, its thickness, and the density of the material used in its construction. The thickness and density of a washer are available as input data; however, the rim area must be calculated from two measurements that are provided as input data: the washer's inner diameter and the washer's outer diameter (see Fig 3.24). The density of the material used and the number of washers to be shipped are also inputs.

Figure 3.24   Diagram of a washer

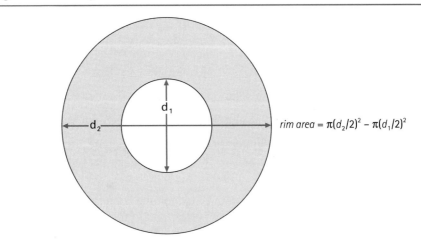

$$rim\ area = \pi(d_2/2)^2 - \pi(d_1/2)^2$$

Data Requirements

Problem Inputs

Inner radius
Outer radius
Thickness
Density
Quantity

Problem Output

Weight of batch of washers

In considering how to attack this problem, we might consider writing a `Circle` class first because a washer is really a large circle with a smaller one removed. A `Circle` class would have a data field `radius` and methods to compute its area and circumference. A `Washer` class would have an inner circle and an outer circle as its data fields. It would also have a thickness and density. It would have methods to compute the rim area of a washer and the washer's weight.

DESIGN

Class `Circle`

Fig. 3.25 describes the `Circle` class. From algebra we know the formulas for the area and circumference of a circle with radius r:

Area $= \pi r^2$
Circumference $= 2\pi r$

We can easily implement these formulas as methods.

Figure 3.25   **Class** `Circle`

Data Fields	Attributes
`double radius`	The circle radius
Methods	**Behavior**
`double computeArea()`	Computes the circle area
`double computeCircum()`	Computes the circle circumference

`Washer` Class

Fig. 3.26 describes the `Washer` class.

Figure 3.26   **Class** `Washer`

Data Fields	Attributes
`Circle inner`	The inner circle
`Circle outer`	The outer circle
`double thickness`	The washer thickness
`double density`	The material density
Methods	**Behavior**
`double computeRimArea()`	Computes the washer's rim area
`double computeWeight()`	Computes the washer's weight
Classes Used	
`Circle`	

To compute the rim area, we subtract the area of the inner circle from the area of the outer circle. The algorithms for the methods follow.

Algorithm for `computeRimArea()`

1. Calculate the area of the outer circle and the area of the inner circle and return the difference.

Algorithm for `computeWeight()`

1. Multiply the rim area by the thickness and density.

Class `WasherApp`

The application class (Fig. 3.27) interacts with the user to get the data and creates a `Washer` object. It applies method `computeWeight()` to this object to get the weight of one object and then calculates the weight of the batch of washers. It displays the results.

Figure 3.27   Class `WasherApp`

Method	Behavior
main()	Creates a `Washer` object and stores its data; gets the quantity of washers in the batch and calculates and displays the weight of the batch
Classes Used	
Washer, JOptionPane	

The algorithm for the **main** method follows.

*Algorithm for **main()***

1. Create a `Washer` object.

2. Get the washer data and store it in the `Washer` object.

3. Get the quantity of washers.

4. Calculate the batch weight.

5. Display the washer information and the batch weight.

IMPLEMENTATION   Fig. 3.28 shows the `Circle` class. Methods `computeArea()` and `computeCircum()` access the value of π (3.14159...), which is defined as a **class constant** in the `Math` class and is referenced by `Math.PI`.

Fig. 3.29 shows class `Washer`. In method `setInner()`, the statement

```
inner = new Circle(inRadius);
```

creates a new `Circle` object with radius `inRadius` referenced by data field `inner`. Method `computeRimArea()` uses the statement

```
return outer.computeArea() - inner.computeArea();
```

Figure 3.28 **Class** `Circle`

```java
/*
 * Circle.java    Authors: Koffman and Wolz
 * A class that represents a circle
 */
public class Circle {

    private double radius;

    public Circle() {}

    public Circle(double rad) {
       radius = rad;
    }

    public void setRadius(double rad) {
       radius = rad;
    }

    public double getRadius() {
       return radius;
    }

    public double computeArea() {
       return Math.PI * radius * radius;
    }

    public double computeCircum() {
       return 2.0 * Math.PI * radius;
    }

    public String toString() {
       return "circle with radius: " + radius;
    }
}
```

to compute and return the washer rim area. This statement applies method **computeArea()** to each **Circle** object and returns the difference of the outer circle area and the inner circle area.

Method `computeWeight()` calls method `computeRimArea()` using the statement

```
return computeRimArea() * thickness * density
```

The method result is the product of the rim area, rim thickness, and material density. We did not bother to show the accessor methods, but they should be included in the class.

Figure 3.29   Class `Washer`

```java
/*
 * Washer.java    Authors: Koffman and Wolz
 * A class that represents a washer
 */
public class Washer {

    // data fields
    private Circle inner;
    private Circle outer;
    private double thickness;
    private double density;

    // methods
    // postcondition: inner references a Circle object
    //   with the specified radius
    public void setInner(double inRadius) {
        inner = new Circle(inRadius);
    }

    // postcondition: outer references a Circle object
    //   with the specified radius
    public void setOuter(double outRadius) {
        outer = new Circle(outRadius);
    }

    public void setThickness(double thick) {
        thickness = thick;
    }

    public void setDensity(double dens) {
        density = dens;
    }
```

Figure 3.29   **Class** `Washer`, *continued*

```
// postcondition: Returns the difference in circle areas
public double computeRimArea() {
   return outer.computeArea() - inner.computeArea();
}


public double computeWeight() {
   return computeRimArea() * thickness * density;
}

public String toString() {
   return "inner circle, " + inner +
         "\nouter circle, " + outer +
         "\nthickness is " + thickness +
         ", density is " + density;

   }
}
```

Fig. 3.30 shows class `WasherApp`. It contains a straightforward implementation of the algorithm for method `main()`. The `main` method uses methods `readDouble()` to read the washer's inner diameter, outer diameter, thickness, and density. Each diameter is divided by 2 before being passed as an argument to method `setInner()` or `setOuter()`. It uses method `readInt()` to read the quantity of washers in a batch.

The `main` method stores the quantity and batch weight in local variables. It displays a string consisting of a description of the washers (returned by method `toString()` of class `Washer`) and the batch quantity and weight.

TESTING   Fig. 3.31 shows the output message window for a sample run of class `WasherApp`. To test it, try inner and outer dimensions that lead to easy calculations for rim area (for example, inner diameter 2 and outer diameter 4). Test the program first with a quantity of 1 and then run it with larger quantities.

Figure 3.30   Class WasherApp

```java
/*
 * WasherApp.java    Authors: Koffman and Wolz
 * A class that finds the weight of a batch of washers
 */
import javax.swing.JOptionPane;

public class WasherApp {

  // postcondition: returns a type double data value
  private static double readDouble(String prompt) {
    String numStr = JOptionPane.showInputDialog(prompt);
    return Double.parseDouble(numStr);
  }

  // postcondition: returns a type int data value
  private static int readInt(String prompt) {
    String numStr = JOptionPane.showInputDialog(prompt);
    return Integer.parseInt(numStr);
  }

  public static void main(String[] args) {
   // Create a Washer object
   Washer wash = new Washer();

    // Get the washer data and store it in the Washer object.
    wash.setInner(readDouble("Enter inner diameter in centimeters") / 2);
    wash.setOuter(readDouble("Enter outer diameter in centimeters") / 2);
    wash.setThickness(readDouble("Enter thickness in centimeters"));
    wash.setDensity(readDouble("Enter density in grams per cc"));

    // Get the quantity of washers.
    int quantity = readInt("Enter quantity");

    // Calculate the batch weight.
    double batchWeight = quantity * wash.computeWeight();

    // Display the washer information and the batch weight.
    JOptionPane.showMessageDialog(null, wash.toString() +
                             "\nThe weight of " + quantity +
                             " washers is " + batchWeight + " grams");

  }
}
```

Figure 3.31   Sample run of `WasherApp`

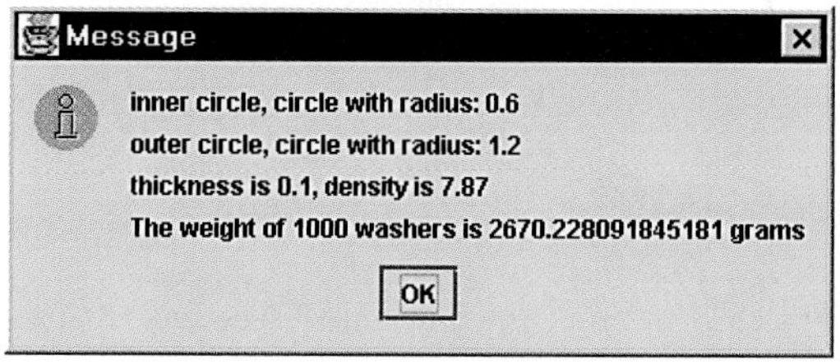

PROGRAM STYLE: *Separation of Concerns*

Each of these classes was relatively easy to design and implement. By splitting the problem solution up into three classes, we were able to keep things simple. The `Circle` class focused on those tasks that were relevant to `Circle` objects and the `Washer` class focused on those tasks that were relevant to `Washer` objects. Also, we now have two more reusable classes, `Circle` and `Washer`, which may turn out to be handy in other problem solutions.

EXERCISES FOR SECTION 3.5

SELF-CHECK

1. Explain the purpose of methods `readDouble()` and `readInt()` in class `WasherApp`. What are the advantages of using these methods? Why is the modifier `static` needed? Indicate another way that they could be called.

3.6   Formatting Output and Class `KeyIn` (Optional)

In this section we discuss Java classes that are useful during program input and output. We begin with two classes that have methods for formatting output information, thereby improving the appearance of program output. We also describe a package that has methods for simplifying program input.

Formatting Numbers with Class `DecimalFormat`

In Fig. 3.31, the value of `batchWeight` is shown to a much higher precision than is necessary. If we want to display the result to just two decimal places, we can do this using class `DecimalFormat` (imported from package `java.text`).

◆◆ EXAMPLE 3.7 ─────────────────────────────────────

Let's import class **DecimalFormat** by placing the statement

```
import java.text.DecimalFormat;
```

at the beginning of class **WasherApp** in Fig. 3.30. The statement

```
DecimalFormat form = new DecimalFormat("0.##");
```

creates a new **DecimalFormat** object **form** with the pattern represented by the string **"0.##"**. A number formatted using this pattern should have at least one digit before the decimal point and up to two digits after the decimal point. The fractional part of the number should be rounded to two digits. The method call

```
form.format(batchWeight)
```

applies object **form**'s **format()** method and returns a string representing the value of **batchWeight** formatted according to the pattern associated with object **form** (value is **2670.23**). The statement

```
System.out.println("The batch weight is " +
                    form.format(batchWeight));
```

will display

```
The batch weight is 2670.23 grams
```

If we use the pattern **"0.###"** instead, this line would be

```
The batch weight is 2670.228 grams
```

In general, using the symbol **0** before a decimal point causes a leading zero digit to be displayed. Using the symbols **00** after the decimal point causes two decimal digits to be displayed. If you use the symbols **##** instead, trailing zeros will not be displayed. Table 3.5 shows the result of associating object **form** with other patterns; Table 3.6 shows some methods of class **DecimalFormat**.

Table 3.5   Some formatting patterns for class `DecimalFormat`

Pattern for `form`	Description of Result String	Examples of `form.format(x)`
`0.00`	Place at least one digit before decimal point. Place two digits after decimal point.	`x = 0.5`, result is `"0.50"` `x = 2`, result is `"2.00"`
`0.##`	Place at least one digit before decimal point. Place up to two digits after decimal point if nonzero.	`x = 0.5`, result is `"0.5"` `x = 2`, result is `"2"`
`.00`	Place digits before decimal point if number ≥ 1.0. Place two digits after decimal point.	`x = 0.5`, result is `".50"` `x = 2`, result is `"2.00"`
`.##`	Place digits before decimal point if number ≥ 1.0. Place two digits after decimal point if nonzero.	`x = 0.5`, result is `".5"` `x = 2`, result is `"2.0"`

Table 3.6   Class `DecimalFormat` methods

Method Header	Sample Call
`DecimalFormat(String pat)`	`form = new DecimalFormat(".00");` Associates the pattern `".00"` with `DecimalFormat` object `form`.
`String format(double num)`	`form.format(x)` Returns a string based on `x` formatted to match the pattern of `DecimalFormat` object `form`.

We can use a **`DecimalFormat`** object with a pattern of `".00"` or `"#.00"` to format a currency amount (dollars and cents). A number formatted with this pattern will have always have two digits after the decimal point. We discuss another way to do this next.

         ◆◆

Class `NumberFormat`

Another way to format currency amounts is to use the **`NumberFormat`** class. If we import this class using the statement

```
import java.text.NumberFormat;
```

we can use it to format a currency amount before displaying it. Instead of instantiating class `NumberFormat`, we call method `getCurrencyInstance()` to create an object used for formatting a currency amount. For example, the statement

```
NumberFormat currency = NumberFormat.getCurrencyInstance();
```

creates an object `currency` for formatting currency amounts. The method call

```
currency.format(discountAmount)
```

calls object `currency`'s `format()` method and returns a string that represents the value of `discountAmount` in dollars. This string starts with a `$` symbol and has two digits after the decimal point. If `discountAmount` is `34.5456`, the method result is `"$34.55"`.
Similarly, the statement

```
NumberFormat percent = NumberFormat.getPercentInstance();
```

creates an object `percent` for formatting a percentage. The method call

```
percent.format(salesTax)
```

calls object `percent`'s `format()` method and returns a string that represents the value of `salesTax` as a percentage. For example, if `salesTax` is `0.06`, the method result is `"6%"`. Table 3.7 shows some methods of class `NumberFormat`.

Table 3.7 Class `NumberFormat` methods

Method Header	Sample Call
`NumberFormat getCurrencyInstance()`	`money = new NumberFormat.getCurrencyInstance();` `NumberFormat` object `money` is associated with the pattern for formatting currency values.
`NumberFormat getPercentInstance()`	`pct = new NumberFormat.getPercentInstance();` `NumberFormat` object `pct` is associated with the pattern for formatting percentage values.
`String format(double num)`	`money.format(salary)` Returns a string based on `salary` formatted to match the pattern associated with object `money`. This string starts with a `$` and has two digits after the decimal point.
`String format(double num)`	`pct.format(rate)` Returns a string based on `rate` formatted to match the pattern associated with object `pct`. This string starts with a percentage value and ends with `%`.

Class `KeyIn` Methods for Input Operations (Optional)

In Fig. 3.30, we used static methods `readInt()` and `readDouble()` to read a type `int` value and a type `double` value, respectively. As an alternative to writing these methods in each class that uses them, you can place them in your own class and import that class into an application. We have provided such a class (`KeyIn`) in folder **psJava** (Problem Solving in Java), which you can download from the Web site described in the book's preface. We encourage you to do so, because this is an excellent example of class reuse.

Class `KeyIn` has five static methods for reading input data through a dialog window: one for each of the four primitive types and one for type `String` (see Table 3.8). If you begin a new application class with the statement

```
import psJava.KeyIn;
```

you can use the statement

```
int kids = KeyIn.readInt("How many children?");
```

Table 3.8 Class `KeyIn` methods for reading data

Method Header	Sample Call
`String readString(String prompt)`	`KeyIn.readString("Enter your name")` Displays a prompt in a dialog window and returns the type `String` data entered by the user.
`int readInt(String prompt)`	`KeyIn.readInt("Enter count of pennies")` Displays a prompt in a dialog window and returns the type `int` data item entered by the user.
`int readInt(String prompt,` `int min, int max)`	`KeyIn.readInt("Number of kids?", min, max)` The type `int` data entered must lie between `min` and `max`, inclusive.
`double readDouble(String prompt)`	`KeyIn.readDouble("Size in sq. yards?")` Displays a prompt in a dialog window and returns the type `double` data item entered by the user.
`double readDouble(String prompt,` `double min, double max)`	`KeyIn.readDouble("Volts?", -12.5, 12.5)` The type `double` data entered must lie between −12.5 and 12.5, inclusive.
`char readChar(String prompt)`	`KeyIn.readChar("Enter a letter")` Displays a prompt in a dialog window and returns the type `char` data item entered by the user.
`char readChar(String prompt,` `char min, char max)`	`KeyIn.readChar("Enter a small letter", 'a', 'z')` The character entered must have a code value between `'a'` and `'z'`—a lowercase letter.
`boolean readBoolean(String prompt)`	`KeyIn.readBoolean("Is it raining?");` Displays a prompt in a dialog window and returns `true` if the user presses button `Yes` and `false` if the user presses button `No`.

to read an integer data value into variable **kids**. Method **readInt()** displays a dialog box that shows its argument as a prompt. It returns a type **int** value corresponding to the data entered.

It is easier to use class **KeyIn**'s method **readInt()** as shown above than to write your own method **readInt()** or to use the familiar statement pair

```
String kidStr = JOptionPane.showInputDialog("How many children?");
int kids = Integer.parseInt(kidStr);
```

Also, the methods in class **KeyIn** were designed to be more user friendly and are therefore less likely to cause a run-time error. If the user types in a string that is not numeric, method **KeyIn.readInt()** or **KeyIn.readDouble()** will display an error message window and then allow the user to reenter the data. However, the statement pair above will cause a **NumberFormatException** error and terminate the program. We discuss method **KeyIn.readBoolean()** in Section 4.2.

The one disadvantage of using class **KeyIn** is that it is not part of standard Java. You can only use class **KeyIn** if you have downloaded package **psJava** and the folder containing it is accessible to your Java environment.

Specifying a Range of Values

As shown in Table 3.8, you can restrict the range of values that the user can enter by providing two additional arguments to methods **readInt()**, **readDouble()**, and **readChar()**. We illustrate this next for method **readInt()**.

◆◆ EXAMPLE 3.8 ───

The method call

```
KeyIn.readInt("How many children?", 0, 10)
```

returns as its result the number typed in by the program user provided that number is between 0 and 10. If the number is negative or larger than 10, an error message window is displayed. After the user presses **OK**, the original dialog window appears again and the user is given another chance to enter a number between 0 and 10.

─── ◆◆

PROGRAM STYLE: *Defensive Programming*

Because it is relatively easy to write the standard Java statement pairs for reading numbers, you may be wondering why you should bother with class **KeyIn**. The obvious advantage is that you need to write only a single call to a class **KeyIn** method instead of using these statement pairs. The less obvious advantage is that if the program user makes a mistake and types in an invalid number, an error message will appear and the program user will get another chance to enter a correct number. Also, you can call the methods in class **KeyIn** with a second and third argument if you want to restrict the range of numbers (or character values) that a program user can enter. Taking steps like this to keep your program running properly in case of a program user error is called **defensive programming** and is practiced faithfully by professional programmers.

EXERCISES FOR SECTION 3.6

SELF-CHECK

1. Explain what each of the method calls below does.

   a. n = KeyIn.readInt("Enter your age:", 21, 100);

   b. ch = KeyIn.readChar("Enter your choice", 'a', 'e');

   c. s = KeyIn.readString("Enter your name");

   d. x = KeyIn.readDouble("What is your salary?");

2. Discuss the characters referenced by **String** res after each statement pair executes.

   a. form = new DecimalFormat(".###");

      String res = form.format(0.14159);

   b. form = new DecimalFormat("0.###");

      String res = form.format(0.14159);

   c. form = new DecimalFormat(".###");

      String res = form.format(3.14);

   d. form = new DecimalFormat(".000");

      String res = form.format(3.14);

PROGRAMMING

1. Write statements to do the following using class **KeyIn**'s methods:

    a. Enter a number between −5.5 and 7.7.

    b. Enter a person's first initial (uppercase letter).

    c. Enter a positive integer less than 100.

    d. Enter your astrological sign.

2. Write statements to do the following:

    a. Display the value of **x** with a leading digit and exactly three decimal digits.

    b. Display the value of **x** without a leading zero and up to three decimal digits (no trailing zeros).

    c. Display the value of **sales** in currency format (do this two ways).

    d. Display the value of **commission** in percent format.

3.7 Applets, AWT, and the Graphics Class (Optional)

So far all our output has been in the form of GUI windows that contain textual information. Java provides a collection of graphics methods that enable you to draw pictures or graphical patterns (computer graphics) on a drawing surface such as a computer screen. You can draw lines and various geometric shapes (for example, rectangles, circles, ovals). You can specify the position of each shape and also its color.

The Drawing Surface

In graphics programming, you control the location on a drawing surface of each line or shape that you draw. Consequently, you must know the size of your drawing surface and how to reference the individual picture elements (called **pixels**) on it.

You can visualize a drawing surface as an *x–y* grid of pixels. Assume that your surface has the dimensions 400 × 300. Fig. 3.32 shows your surface and the coordinates for the four pixels at the corners. The pixel at the top-left corner has *x–y* coordinates **(0,0)**, and the position at the top-right corner has *x–y* coordinates **(399,0)**.

Notice that Java numbers the pixels in the *y* direction in a different way than we are accustomed to. The pixel **(0,0)** is at the top-left corner of the screen, and the *y* coordinate values increase as we move down the screen. In a normal *x–y* coordinate system, the point **(0,0)** is at the bottom-left corner.

Figure 3.32   Referencing pixels in a window

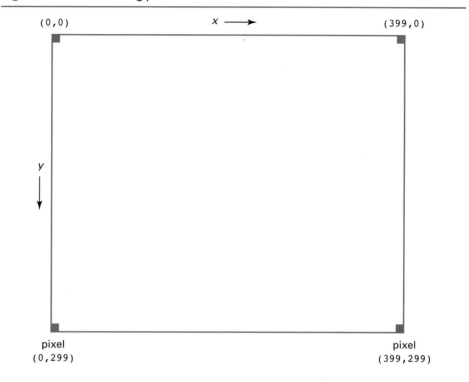

The AWT Class Library

Java provides a class library called the Abstract Window Toolkit (AWT) to facilitate graphics and GUI programming. When you wish to draw, you must import the AWT package **java.awt**. The AWT contains a hierarchy of classes for displaying windows and GUI components. The **Applet** class has an associated drawing surface that can be accessed through its **paint()** method. In this chapter we will extend the **Applet** class, inheriting its ability to draw graphics.

    We will explain applets in detail in Chapter 7. For now, recall that an application object contains a method **main()** that tells the Java interpreter where to start processing. An application class is a completely self-sufficient entity that may rely on support objects to do its job. An applet is not self-sufficient. It is intended to be a support object in a larger context such as a Web browser like Internet Explorer or Netscape. You can therefore start up an applet from a browser, or you can use the applet viewer program that is part of Java. The Java interpreter expects to process a compiled class file (a file with extension **.class**). In contrast, a browser or the applet viewer expects an **HTML file**, which is a sequence of instructions in the HyperText Markup Language (a file with extension **.html**). Appendix A includes a brief introduction to HTML.

Figure 3.33 shows a small HTML file that starts up an applet. For now, look at the text in the HTML file that is in color. These are the parts that change depending on the applet you wish to view in the browser. The file that must be loaded to start the applet follows the directive **code** =. The file name must be a compiled Java **.class** file. You must also specify a width and height (in pixels) for the applet drawing surface.

Two files play a role in the HTML page defined in Fig. 3.33. They must reside in the same folder or directory for the HTML file to work properly.

◆ *htmlFileName*.html specifies the HTML page that is displayed by the browser.

◆ *className*.class specifies the compiled applet that is to be executed.

Figure 3.33   An HTML file for the `Intersection` applet

```
<HTML>
<applet code = Intersection.class width = 300 height = 300>
</applet>
</HTML>
```

Figure 3.34 shows class `Intersection`, which draws the black and green intersecting lines shown in Fig. 3.35 and the text shown beneath them. Notice that `Intersection` must import both `java.awt.*` and `java.applet.Applet`. Class `Intersection` defines a single method, `paint()`. Method `paint()` has one argument, object g of class `Graphics` (defined in package `awt`). This object will be called upon to do the actual drawing using methods defined in class `Graphics` (`setColor()`, `drawLine()`, and so on).

The first line in the class definition

```
public class Intersection extends Applet {
```

ends with the words **extends Applet**. This means that class **Applet** is the **parent** (or **superclass**) of class `Intersection` (and class `Intersection` is a **subclass** of class `Applet`). In practical terms this means that an object of class `Intersection` is a kind of `Applet` object and can do everything an `Applet` object can do, and possibly more. Therefore, the browser can instantiate an `Intersection` object, and all the methods defined in the `Applet` class can be applied to an `Intersection` object. A `paint()` method is defined in the `Applet` class, but the definition of method `paint()` in class `Intersection` *overrides* the definition of method `paint()` in class `Applet`. This means that the `paint()` method defined in Fig. 3.34 executes whenever an `Intersection` object is sent the `paint()` message.

In Java, all classes defined by a programmer extend some already defined class. If the header does not explicitly include the reserved word **extends**, the class extends the superclass of all classes, class `Object`.

Figure 3.34   Class Intersection

```
/*
 * Intersection.java    Authors: Koffman and Wolz
 * An applet that draws intersecting lines
 */
import java.awt.*;
import java.applet.Applet;

public class Intersection extends Applet {

  public void paint(Graphics g) {

     //Draw a black line from (0,0) to (300, 200)
     g.setColor(Color.black);
     g.drawLine(0, 0, 300, 200);

     //Draw a green line from (300, 0) to (0, 200)
     g.setColor(Color.green);
     g.drawLine(300, 0, 0, 200);

     //Write some text
     g.drawString("Black and green intersecting lines", 75, 250);
  }
}
```

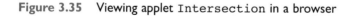

Figure 3.35   Viewing applet Intersection in a browser

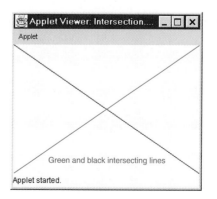

Table 3.9 Color constants (defined in class `Color`)

Color	Color Object	RGB Value
Black	Color.black	0, 0, 0
Blue	Color.blue	0, 0, 255
Cyan	Color.cyan	0, 255, 255
Gray	Color.gray	128, 128, 128
Dark gray	Color.darkGray	64, 64, 64
Light gray	Color.lightGray	192, 192, 192
Green	Color.green	0, 255, 0
Magenta	Color.magenta	255, 0, 255
Orange	Color.orange	255, 200, 0
Pink	Color.pink	255, 175, 175
Red	Color.red	255, 0, 0
White	Color.white	255, 255, 255
Yellow	Color.yellow	255, 255, 0

Each call to method `setColor()` (defined in class `Graphics.`) sets the color to be used by all drawing methods until the next call to `setColor()` occurs. Therefore, the first call to `drawLine()` (also defined in `Graphics`) draws a black line and the second call to `drawLine()` draws a green line. Table 3.9 shows the standard color values defined as constants in class `Color` (indicated by the prefix `Color.`). You can even "mix" your own colors by specifying the strength of the red, green, and blue components using integers from 0 to 255 as arguments to the constructor method for class `Color`:

```
Color myColor = new Color(75, 30, 255);
```

Method `drawLine()` has four arguments. The first two are the *x–y* coordinates of the line's starting point and the last two are the *x–y* coordinates of its ending point. It "draws a line" by changing the color of all pixels in the line defined by its arguments to the current color (as set by `setColor()`).

Method Header	Behavior
void drawLine(int x1, int y1, int x2, int y2)	Draws a line with end points (x1,y1) and (x2,y2)
void drawString(String s, int x, int y)	Displays string s starting at (x,y)
void setColor(Color col)	Sets the drawing color to col

Displaying Text in Drawings

In graphics mode, you must draw characters just as you draw other shapes. The `Graphics` class provides a method, `drawString()`, to do this. In Fig. 3.34, the method call

```
g.drawString("Black and green intersecting lines", 75, 175);
```

draws each character in a string (its first argument) starting at the point whose *x–y* coordinates are specified by the last two arguments. The word **Black** starts at the pixel whose *x* coordinate is **75** and whose *y* coordinate is **175**.

Drawing Rectangles

You can use method **drawRect()** (defined in class **Graphics**) to draw a rectangle on the screen. The statement

```
g.drawRect(x1, y1, 100, 50);
```

draws a rectangle that has point **(x1,y1)** as its top-left corner and has a width of 100 pixels and a height of 50 pixels (Fig. 3.36).

Figure 3.36 Rectangle with **(x1,y1)** as top-left corner

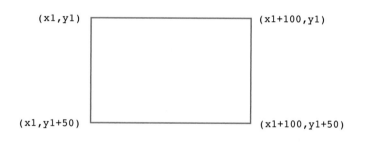

◆◆ EXAMPLE 3.9 ──

Class **House** (see Fig. 3.37) draws a house. The variables define four corner points of the house (points **(x1,y1)** through **(x4,y4)**). The two calls to **drawLine()** draw the roof as a pair of lines meeting at point **(x2,y2)**. The call to **drawRect()** draws the rest of the house.

We specified two corner points for the rectangular part of the house; however, method **drawRect()** requires the width and height of a rectangle as its third and fourth arguments. We account for this by passing the difference between the *x* coordinates as the third argument and the difference between the *y* coordinates as the fourth argument.

The statements

```
g.setColor(Color.green);
g.fillRect(x5, y5, x6 - x5, y6 - y5);
g.setColor(Color.black);
```

Figure 3.37   Class House

```
/*
 * House.java    Authors: Koffman and Wolz
 * An applet that draws a house
 */
import java.awt.*;
import java.applet.Applet;

public class House extends Applet {
   // Data fields
   // Define 4 corner points for the house
   private int x1 = 100;   // lower-left
   private int y1 = 200;   //  corner of roof
   private int x2 = 300;   // peak of roof
   private int y2 = 100;
   private int x3 = 500;   // lower-right
   private int y3 = 200;   //  corner of roof
   private int x4 = 500;   // bottom-right
   private int y4 = 400;   //  corner of house

   // Corner points for door
   private int x5 = 275;   // top-left
   private int y5 = 325;   //  corner of door
   private int x6 = 325;   // bottom-right
   private int y6 = 400;   //  corner of door

   public void paint(Graphics g) {

       g.setColor(Color.black);

       //Draw the roof.
       g.drawLine(x1, y1, x2, y2);
       g.drawLine(x2, y2, x3, y3);

       //Draw the house as a box.
       g.drawRect(x1, y1, x4 - x1, y4 - y1);

       //Draw a door.
       g.setColor(Color.green);
       g.fillRect(x5, y5, x6 - x5, y6 - y5);
       g.setColor(Color.black);
```

Figure 3.37   Class `House`, *continued*

```
       //Label the corner points.
       g.drawString("(x1,y1)", x1, y1);
       g.drawString("(x2,y2)", x2, y2);
       g.drawString("(x3,y3)", x3, y3);
       g.drawString("(x4,y4)", x4, y4);
       g.drawString("(x5,y5)", x5, y5);
       g.drawString("(x6,y6)", x6, y6);
  }
}
```

draw the door as a **filled rectangle** with top-left corner at point `(x5,y5)` and bottom-right corner at point `(x6,y6)`. The color of all pixels in this rectangle is changed to the new drawing color `Color.green.` The last statement above resets the drawing color to `Color.black.`

Fig. 3.38 shows the HTML file that loads the applet (`House.html`), and Fig. 3.39 shows the applet in a viewer. We laid out the house assuming a window size of 600 × 500. For different window dimensions, you may want to redefine the coordinates of the corner points.

Figure 3.38   HTML file for the `House` applet

```
<HTML>
<applet code = House.class width = 600 height = 500>
</applet>
</HTML>
```

Method Header	Behavior
`void drawRect(int x,` `    int y, int w, int h)`	Draws the border of a rectangle with top-left corner at `(x,y)` and bottom-right corner at `(x+w,y+h)`
`void fillRect(int x,` `    int y, int w, int h)`	Draws a filled rectangle with top-left corner at `(x,y)` and bottom-right corner at `(x+w,y+h)`

Figure 3.39 Viewing the `House` applet

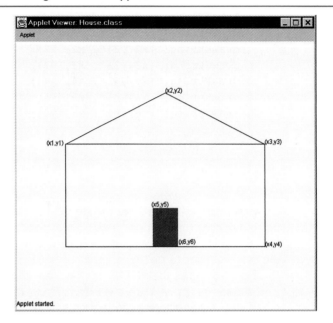

Drawing Arcs and Circles

Method **drawArc()** draws an arc. The method call

```
g.drawArc(x, y, 100, 100, 0, 90);
```

draws an arc (see Fig. 3.40) bounded by a rectangle 100 pixels in width and height whose top-left corner is point **(x,y)**. The arc begins at an angle of 0 degrees and goes for 90 degrees in a counterclockwise direction. If you imagine a clock on the screen, 0 degrees is at 3 o'clock (horizontal direction) and 90 degrees is at 12 o'clock (straight up).

Figure 3.40 Arc drawn by `g.drawArc(x, y, 100, 100, 0, 90)`

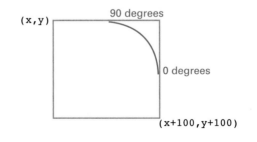

You can use this method to draw a circle as an arc of 360 degrees. However, the `Graphics` class also has a method `drawOval()` that draws a 360-degree arc within a rectangle. The two statements below draw the same circle.

```
g.drawOval(x, y, 100, 100);
g.drawArc(x, y, 100, 100, 0, 360);
```

We normally characterize a circle by its center position and radius, rather than by the position and size of its bounding rectangle, so we have to do some conversion to use method `drawOval()`. A circle with center at point `(x,y)` and radius r could be drawn inside a square whose top-left corner is at point `(x-r,y-r)`. The length of each side of the bounding square would be the same as the circle's diameter. Therefore, use the method call

```
g.drawOval(x-r, y-r, 2 * r, 2 * r);
```

to draw this circle (see Fig. 3.41).

Figure 3.41   Drawing a circle inside a square

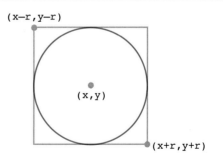

◆◆ EXAMPLE 3.10

Method `paint()` in class `HappyFace` (Fig. 3.42) draws an outer circle first (radius `headRadius`). Next it draws three smaller circles representing the eyes (radius `eyeRadius`) and nose (radius `noseRadius`). Finally, it draws the smile as an arc of 120 degrees staring at 210 degrees (8 o'clock). The arc has the same center as the outer circle, but its radius is three-fourths as large. Fig. 3.43 shows the applet. The `.html` file is left as an exercise.

Figure 3.42   Class `HappyFace`

```
/*
 * HappyFace.java    Authors: Koffman and Wolz
 * An applet that draws a happy face
 */
import java.awt.*;
import java.Applet.applet;

public class HappyFace extends Applet {
    // Data fields
    private int maxX = 500;
    private int maxY = 400;
    private int headX = maxX / 2;
    private int headY = maxY / 2;
    private int headRadius = maxY / 4;
    private int leftEyeX = headX - headRadius / 4;
    private int rightEyeX = headX + headRadius / 4;
    private int eyeY = headY - headRadius / 4;
    private int eyeRadius = headRadius / 10;
    private int noseX = headX;
    private int noseY = headY + headRadius / 4;
    private int noseRadius = eyeRadius;
    protected int smileRadius = (int) Math.round(0.75 * headRadius);

    // Methods
    public void paint(Graphics g) {
      g.setColor(Color.black);

    // Draw head.
      g.drawOval(headX - headRadius,
               headY - headRadius,
               2 * headRadius, 2 * headRadius);

    // Draw left eye.
      g.drawOval(leftEyeX - eyeRadius,
               eyeY - eyeRadius,
               2 * eyeRadius, 2 * eyeRadius);

    // Draw right eye.
      g.drawOval(rightEyeX - eyeRadius,
               eyeY - eyeRadius,
               2 * eyeRadius, 2 * eyeRadius);
```

Figure 3.42   **HappyFace,** *continued*

```
    // Draw nose.
    g.drawOval(noseX - noseRadius,
            noseY - noseRadius,
            2 * noseRadius, 2 * noseRadius);

    // Draw smile.
    g.drawArc(headX - smileRadius,
            headY - smileRadius,
            2 * smileRadius, 2 * smileRadius,
            210, 120);
    }
}
```

Figure 3.43   Viewing the HappyFace applet

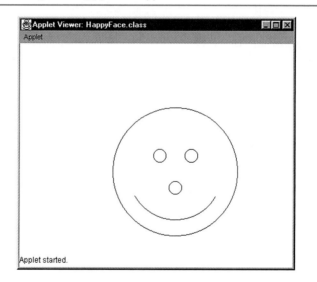

Method Header	Behavior
void drawArc(int x, int y, int w, int h, int a1, int a2)	Draws an arc inside the rectangle with top-left corner at (x,y) and bottom-right corner at (x+w,y+h). The arc goes from angle a1 to angle (a1+a2), measured in degrees.
void drawOval(int x, int y, int w, int h)	Draws an oval inside the rectangle with top-left corner at (x,y) and bottom-right corner at (x+w,y+h).
void fillOval(int x, int y, int w, int h)	Draws a filled oval inside the square with top-left corner at (x,y) and bottom-right corner at (x+w,y+h).

Drawing Pie Slices

Java provides methods to draw pie slices. A pie slice is a filled segment of a circle. The method call

```
g.fillArc(x-r, y-r, 2 * r, 2 * r, 20, 30);
```

draws the 30-degree pie slice shown in Fig. 3.44. The first two arguments specify the top-left corner of the square containing the arc, the third and fourth arguments are the length and width, the fifth argument is the starting angle (20 degrees), and the last argument is the arc length in degrees (30).

Table 3.10 provides a summary of all the methods discussed in this section. All arguments are type `int`, except for method `paint()` (argument is type `Graphics`) and method `setColor()` (argument is type `Color`).

Table 3.10   Summary of `Graphics` class methods

Method Call	Effect
`g.drawArc(x, y, w, h, a1, a2);`	Draws an arc inside the rectangle with top-left corner at (`x`,`y`) and bottom-right corner at (`x+w`,`y+h`). The arc goes from angle `a1` to angle (`a1+a2`), measured in degrees.
`g.drawOval(x, y, w, h);`	Draws an oval inside the rectangle with top-left corner at (`x`,`y`) and bottom-right corner at (`x+w`,`y+h`).
`g.drawLine(x1, y1, x2, y2);`	Draws a line with end points (`x1`,`y1`) and (`x2`,`y2`).
`g.drawRect(x, y, w, h);`	Draws a rectangle with top-left corner at (`x`,`y`) and bottom-right corner at (`x+w`,`y+h`).
`g.drawString(s, x, y);`	Displays string `s` starting at (`x`,`y`).
`g.fillOval(x, y, w, h);`	Draws a colored oval inside the rectangle with top-left corner at (`x`,`y`) and bottom-right corner at (`x+w`,`y+h`).
`g.fillArc(x, y, w, h, a1, a2);`	Draws a filled pie slice inside the rectangle with top-left corner at (`x`,`y`) and bottom-right corner at (`x+w`,`y+h`). The slice goes from angle `a1` to angle (`a1+a2`), measured in degrees.
`g.fillRect(x, y, w, h);`	Draws a filled rectangle with top-left corner at (`x`,`y`) and bottom-right corner at (`x+w`,`y+h`).
`g.setColor(Color.red);`	Sets the drawing color to `red`.

Figure 3.44   A pie slice

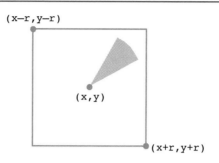

(x-r,y-r)

(x,y)

(x+r,y+r)

EXERCISES FOR SECTION 3.7

SELF-CHECK

1. In Fig. 3.42, what is the reason for basing the head radius on `maxY` and not on `maxX`?

2. Explain the relationship between a browser and an applet. Which one is the support object?

3. The method `paint()` has an argument g of type `Graphics`. Explain what this object does in the `paint()` method.

4. Show the drawing produced by the following fragment. Assume a 640 × 480 drawing surface.

```
public void paint(Graphics g) {
    g.drawOval(200, 50, 25, 25);
    g.drawLine(200, 75, 100, 100);
    g.drawLine(200, 75, 300, 100);
    g.fillArc(200, 75, 245, 295, 150, 200);
    g.drawLine(200, 150, 100, 250);
    g.drawLine(200, 150, 300, 250);
}
```

5. Write statements to add two windows to the second floor of the house in Fig. 3.39.

6. Modify the program in Fig. 3.37 so that it draws the house in the center of the screen and with the same relative size regardless of the actual drawing surface dimensions.

7. What impact does the `setColor()` method have? How long is it in effect?

PROGRAMMING

1. Write the statements to draw a tennis racket. Use a circle at the end of a thin rectangle. Color the circle yellow.

2. Write a graphics program that draws a rocket ship consisting of a triangle on top of a rectangle. Draw a pair of intersecting lines under the rectangle. Color the rectangle red.

3. Write a program that draws a pair of nested rectangles at the center of the screen. The inner rectangle should be red and the outer rectangle should be white. The outer rectangle should have a width that is one-fourth of the *x* dimension and a height that is one-fourth of the *y* dimension of the screen. The height and width of the inner rectangle should be half that of the outer rectangle.

4. Write a program that draws a male and a female stick figure side by side.

5. Write an HTML file for the **HappyFace** class. You will need to determine the height and width of the drawing surface ahead of time.

3.8 Common Programming Errors

◆ We have introduced two kinds of visibility: public and private. Make sure you declare an explicit visibility for each of your data fields, methods, and classes.

◆ Remember that if you define any constructor, the default constructor will not be built automatically for you. If you want to have the default constructor included, you must define it yourself.

◆ Be careful about the data types of arguments you pass to methods, both those in libraries and those you create yourself. If you provide an argument that is the wrong type, the compiler will tell you that the method does not exist. For example, given the method declaration

```
public void myMethod(String x) { .....}
```

the method call

```
someObject.myMethod(15);
```

causes the compiler to tell you that method **myMethod(int)** is not defined.

◆ Don't attempt to access private data fields or to call private methods outside a class. If you do, the compiler will tell you that the data field or method is not defined. You must use public methods of a class to access its private data fields.

◆ You can call a method that returns a result only from within an expression. The result returned by the method is used in the evaluation of the expression that contains the method call.

◆ If the compiler determines that a method that returns a result can be exited without executing a `return` statement, you will get a `method does not return a value` syntax error. If the method header is missing a result type, you will get an `invalid method declaration; return type required` syntax error. If the result type specified in the header does not match the type of the value returned, you may get an `incompatible types` syntax error.

◆ You can have two or more methods in a class that have the same name but different parameter lists. This is often the case for constructors. The version whose parameter list corresponds to the argument list will be executed. If this version is not provided, a `method not found` syntax error will occur.

◆ Be particularly careful when calling methods with parameters. The number of arguments in the method call and the data type of each argument must match one of the method's parameter lists. If you transpose two arguments by mistake, this error will go undetected unless it causes a data type conflict between an argument and its corresponding parameter.

◆ We introduced applets and graphics. Remember that you must import two libraries for applets to work properly:

```
import java.awt.*;
import java.applet.Applet;
```

◆ Remember that an applet may only be executed within the context of a Web browser or the applet viewer program. If you load an HTML file and the applet doesn't run, or doesn't seem to load, check the following:

  ◆ Check to make sure that the `.html` file and the `.class` file reside in the same folder. Save the `.html` file again if you modify it.

  ◆ Make sure the applet referenced in the HTML is the one you compiled.

  ◆ Check the bounds of the display area. If the bounds are too big or too small, the browser may give up and do nothing.

  ◆ Verify that the HTML syntax is correct. Even the slightest mistake will cause the browser to ignore your applet entirely.

◆ Verify that you are actually drawing within the field you expect to see. Make sure your drawing points are not negative numbers.

◆ Make sure that your background and foreground colors are not the same. If they are, you will not be able to see what you draw.

◆ Drawing may only occur within the **paint()** method or by **Graphics** methods that are called by **paint()**. If method **paint()** calls support methods to do the drawing, you must pass the **Graphics** object **g** to the support methods:

```
public void paint(Graphics g) {
  drawHead(g);
  drawBody(g);
  drawHat(g);
}
```

◆ Make sure you include an argument of type **Graphics** in each support method definition. Remember, it is the **Graphics** object that does the actual drawing. The method **paint()** receives the graphics context from the browser.

CHAPTER REVIEW

1. A Java class definition contains declarations for data fields (instance variables) and definitions for methods. Method definitions may contain their own local variable declarations as well as executable statements.

2. For the time being, data fields will have private visibility and methods will have public visibility. This means that methods can be accessed outside the class, but data fields can be accessed directly only within the class. A client of the class or an application class can access an object's data fields only through its methods. This ensures that the information stored in an object is manipulated in a safe and predictable way.

3. You create an instance of a worker class using a statement of the form

ClassName objectName = new *ClassName*(*argumentList*);

The **new** operator allocates storage for the object and the constructor initializes its data fields using values passed to the constructor through the *argumentList*. You can process this object by calling its public methods using statements of the form

objectName.methodName(*argumentList*);

4. Java creates the no-parameter constructor (the default constructor) if you don't define a constructor. A data field is initialized to its default value unless the data field declaration specifies a different value or the constructor initializes it to a parameter value. The defaults are zero for numeric data fields (`int` and `double`), `false` for boolean data fields, the smallest Unicode character for `char` data fields, and `null` for data fields that reference objects.

5. Mutator methods change the value of a data field. Accessor methods retrieve the value stored in a data field.

6. Type `void` methods do not return a result. Other methods return a result whose type is specified in the method header. A method that returns a result must execute a statement of the form

    `return expression;`

    The value of *expression* is the method result and its type must be compatible with the result type of the method as declared in the method header.

7. Preconditions and postconditions provide documentation for methods. A precondition describes the situation that must exist before a method can be successfully executed. A postcondition describes the state of the object after the method executes (for a `void` method) or the value returned by the method (for a non-`void` method).

8. A method's parameters are local declarations and can be accessed only within the method body. Any variables declared in the method are local variables and are visible only within the method.

9. You pass information to a method through argument/parameter correspondence. Each argument in the argument list is matched up with the parameter in the same position in the parameter list. The value of each argument is passed to its corresponding parameter. The type of the argument must be compatible with the type of the parameter. If the argument references an object, the parameter will reference the same object.

10. `String` objects are immutable, which means that we cannot change the characters stored inside a `String` object.

11. We can use the prefix `this.` inside a method definition to reference the current object's data fields or methods. For example, `this.aMethod()` applies method `aMethod()` to the current object.

12. We can use classes `DecimalFormat` and `NumberFormat` to format numeric information before displaying it. In class `DecimalFormat`, we specify formatting patterns using strings such as `".000"`. In class `NumberFormat`, we use

methods `getCurrencyInstance()` and `getPercentInstance()` to create objects that are used to format currency values and percentages.

13. Our package `psJava` has a `KeyIn` class for simplifying interactive input. This class defines static methods `readInt()`, `readDouble()`, `readChar()`, `readBoolean()`, and `readString()`. Each method takes a prompt string as its argument and returns the result type corresponding to the method name.

14. Each applet that you write must extend class `Applet` and contain a call to method `paint()`. The `Graphics` class provides several methods that you can call in method `paint()` to draw simple graphical patterns (see Table 3.10). Each method must be applied to the `Graphics` object that is specified in the argument list for `paint()`. The `Graphics` object does the actual drawing.

15. Use a Web browser or applet viewer to view a Java applet. You must include in the same folder as the applet `.class` file an `.html` file that can be opened in a Web browser or the applet viewer to start up the applet. If the `.html` file has a tag `<applet`, the Web browser or applet viewer creates an instance of the applet specified after `code` `=` and applies method `paint()` to the applet instance.

New Java constructs

Construct	Effect
Visibility Private	
`private double area;`	Allows access to data field **area** only through methods of its own class.
Modifier `static`	
`public static void doIt(int n) {`	Defines method **doIt()** as a class method that can be called by prefixing it with its class name.
Class Constructors	

`public MyClass(int ar) {`
    `area = ar;`
`}`
	Creates an instance of class **MyClass** and assigns to data field **area** the value of the argument passed to parameter **ar**.

`public MyClass () {}`	Defines a no-parameter constructor, which you may need to define if other constructors are defined.

New Java constructs, *continued*

Construct	Effect
Accessor Method	
| ```
public double getArea() {
    return area;
}
``` | Defines an accessor method that enables methods defined in other classes to retrieve the data in data field **area**. |
| **Mutator Method** | |
| ```
public double setArea(int ar) {
    area = ar;
}
``` | Defines a mutator method, which enables methods defined in other classes to modify the data in data field **area**. |

✔ **QUICK-CHECK EXERCISES**

1. Fill out the following table.

Visibility	*Specifies who is allowed access to data fields and methods*
public	
private	
protected	

2. Explain why explicit constructors are useful.

3. When do you need to write the no-parameter constructor and when is it defined by Java?

4. What default values are assigned to data fields?

5. What are two ways to give a data field a value that is different from the default value?

6. Explain why accessors are needed.

7. Explain why mutators are needed.

8. What does the modifier **static** mean and under what circumstances should a method be declared using the modifier **static**?

9. What is a drawing surface and which object can draw upon it?

10. What purpose is served in creating an HTML file for an applet?

ANSWERS TO QUICK-CHECK EXERCISES

1. | *Visibility* | *Specifies who is allowed access to data fields and methods* |
   |---|---|
   | public | Any method defined in any class |
   | private | Any method defined in this class |
   | protected class | Any method defined in this class or in any subclass of this |

2. Explicit constructors for a class are useful when the method creating an object instance needs to initialize its data fields.

3. You need to write the no-parameter constructor if you define any other constructors and it is possible for a client class to need a no-parameter constructor. It is the default constructor and is defined by Java only if no other constructors are defined.

4. The default values for data fields are zero for numbers, **null** for objects, the smallest Unicode characters (also called the **null** character) for characters, and **false** for boolean variables.

5. You can give a data field a value by setting it in the declaration or by passing it as a constructor argument when the object is created.

6. Accessors allow a method to retrieve the values of private data fields.

7. Mutators allow a client to update the value of a private data field.

8. The modifier **static** means that a method is a class method. A method should be declared as **static** when its actions are not tied to the data fields of an object. An example would be a method that does a calculation based only on values of its arguments.

9. A drawing surface is a device such as a display screen that can accept graphics directives and create corresponding images. In the Java AWT, the **Graphics** class is capable of drawing on such surfaces.

10. An applet is a support object for a program such as a Web browser or applet viewer. The HTML file associated with an applet contains an HTML directive that specifies which applet to load as well as the size of the applet window.

REVIEW QUESTIONS

1. What is a class method? What is an instance method? What are the advantages and disadvantages of each?

2. Explain the role of constructors, accessors, and mutators.

3. Define a class **Money** that has type **int** data fields for dollars and cents. Write a constructor with zero parameters, one parameter (the value of dollars), and two parameters. Write accessors and mutators and a **toString()** method that returns a string of the form **$dollars.cents**. Also, write a method **findCents()** that calculates the total value in cents.

4. Write an HTML file that will load an applet called **ShowName**.

5. Write an applet that writes your name three times inside a rectangle. Use a border color of red, an interior color of gray, and a different color each time you write your name.

PROGRAMMING PROJECTS

1. Write a program that computes the duration of a projectile's flight and its height above the ground when it reaches the target. Your worker class should contain data fields for the problem inputs and constant. Besides the usual constructor, accessor, and mutator methods, provide methods that implement the formulas shown below.

   ### Problem Constant

   ```
   G = 32.17     // gravitational constant
   ```

   ### Problem Inputs
   Angle (in radians) of elevation

   Distance (in feet) to target

   Projectile velocity (in feet/sec)

   ### Problem Outputs
   Time (in sec) of flight

   Height at impact

   ### Relevant Formulas
   time = distance / (velocity × cos (theta))

   height = velocity × time − × sin (theta) (g × time^2)/2

2. Four track stars have entered the mile race at the Penn Relays. Write a program that will read in the race time in minutes (**minutes**) and seconds (**seconds**) for a runner and compute and display the speed in feet per second (**feetPS**) and in meters per second (**metersPS**). (*Hints:* There are 5280 feet in 1 mile,

and 1 kilometer equals 4282 feet. Use a worker class that stores the problem inputs and has methods for calculating the total time in seconds, to calculate the speed in feet per second and to convert feet per seconds into meters per second.)

Minutes	Seconds
3	52.83
3	59.83
4	00.03
4	16.22

3. Write a program that calculates the cost of an automobile trip given the distance traveled, the average cost of a gallon of gas, and the EPA mileage rating for your car in miles per gallon.

4. In a new computer-assisted board game moves are determined by selecting a random number. However, players can influence their moves by taking a risk. The player selects a number n from 1 to 10. The computer then generates a random integer r from 1 to 10. The player's move is then $(r - n + 1) * n$. A cautious player selects 1 and always moves forward. The ambitious player selects higher numbers and may move more forward or may move backward. Write a program to determine one move in the game. Display the computer's integer selection and the move.

5. In shopping for a new house, you must consider several factors. In this problem the initial cost of the house, the estimated annual fuel costs, and the annual tax rate are available. Write a program that will determine the total cost of a house after a 5-year period and run it with the following sets of data:

Initial House Cost ($)	Annual Fuel Cost ($)	Tax Rate
67,000	2,300	0.025
62,000	2,500	0.025
75,000	1,850	0.020

To calculate the house cost, add the initial cost to the fuel cost for 5 years, and then add the taxes for 5 years. Taxes for 1 year are computed by multiplying the tax rate by the initial cost. Use a worker class called **House** with methods for performing the above calculations.

6. The Pythagorean theorem states that the sum of the squares of the sides of a right triangle is equal to the square of the hypotenuse. For example, if two sides of a right triangle have lengths 3 and 4, the hypotenuse must have a length of 5. The integers, 3, 4, and 5 together form a Pythagorean triple. There is an infi-

nite number of such triples. Given two positive integers, m and n, where mn, a Pythagorean triple can be generated by the following formulas:

Side1 $= m^2 - n^2$

Side2 $= 2mn$

Hypotenuse $= m^2 + n^2$

Write a program that reads in values for m and n and prints the values of the Pythagorean triple generated by the above formulas.

7. A class with 100 students took an exam in which grades were assigned A, B, C, D, and F. The table lists the number of students who received each grade.

Grade	Number of Students
A	20
B	30
C	35
D	10
F	5

You can create a bar graph of this data by using the **Graphics** method **fillRect()**. Each bar has a standard width. Each height depends on the number of students with that grade. Draw a bar graph of this data where each grade is represented in a different color, and each bar is labeled with the corresponding grade and total number of people.

8. Use the data in project 7 to create a line graph. Use the **Graphics** method **drawLine()** to plot the points corresponding to the number of students with each grade.

9. Use the data in problem 7 to create a pie chart. In a pie chart, the size of each "slice" should be proportional to the quantity it represents. You may find it useful to create a method that can take a percentage of a circle and return the number of degrees. For example, 25% of a circle is 90 degrees, 50% of a circle is 180 degrees.

4

Control Structures:
Decisions and Loops

In this chapter we study control structures and statements—statements that control the flow of execution in a program or method. Through the use of control statements, you enable a method to evaluate its data and to select a path of execution to follow based on the data. We study **boolean** expressions first because two important control statements rely on them.

You can incorporate decision making in algorithms using decision steps based on selection control structures. You will learn how to implement decision steps that can choose one path from among many possible paths of execution using Java's **if** and **switch** statements.

There are many situations when we would like to be able to execute the statements in a method multiple times. For example, a faculty member performs the same set of calculations on each student's data to determine a semester grade. The repetition of steps in a program is called a loop. In this chapter we describe loop forms that occur frequently in programming such as counting loops and state-controlled loops. Also, we describe two Java loop control statements, `while` and `for`, and we show how to write the common loop forms using these statements.

4.1 Control Structures

Structured programming uses **control structures** to control the flow of execution in a program or method. The Java control structures enable us to combine individual statements into a single logical unit, with one entry point and usually one exit point.

There are three kinds of control structures for controlling execution flow: sequence, selection, and repetition. Until now we have been using only sequential flow. A **compound statement** or **block**, written as a group of statements bracketed by { and }, is used to specify sequential flow. You have been using blocks all along—a method body consists of a single block. Control flows from $statement_1$ to $statement_2$, and so on:

```
{
    statement₁;
    statement₂;
    . . .
    . . .
    . . .
    statementₙ;
}
```

This chapter describes the Java control structures for selection and repetition. **Selection control structures** enable a method to select or chose one step from several alternative algorithm steps. The step that is selected depends on the input data. We introduce two kinds of statements for selection: `if` and `switch` statements.

Repetition control structures enable the programmer to specify that a block of statements should be repeated. Sometimes we specify beforehand how many times the statement block, called a **loop body**, should be repeated; sometimes we just repeat the statement block until the user presses a "Quit" button or performs some other action to signal quitting. We introduce the `while` and `for` statements for implementing loops.

4.2   boolean Expressions

A program chooses among alternative steps by testing the value of key variables. For example, because different tax rates apply to various salary levels, an income tax program must select the rate appropriate for each worker by comparing the worker's salary to the range of salary values for each income tax bracket. In Java, **boolean** expressions, or conditions, facilitate such comparisons. Each **boolean** expression has two possible values, **true** or **false**. If all workers who earn between $15,000 and $20,000 are in the same tax bracket, we need to write a **boolean** expression that is **true** for all salaries in this range and **false** outside of this range. The **boolean** expression or **condition** we are seeking is **(salary >= 15000.00 && salary < 20000.00)**. In English, we read this as "salary is greater than or equal to 15,000.00 and salary is less than 20,000.00." We learn how to write and evaluate such expressions in this section.

boolean Variables

The simplest **boolean** expression is a **boolean** variable or a **boolean** literal (**true** or **false**). The variable declarations

```
boolean leapYear = true;
boolean found;
boolean flag;
```

declare **leapYear**, **found**, and **flag** to be **boolean** variables—variables that may be assigned only the values **true** and **false**. Further, the **boolean** variable **leapYear** has the value **true**. The default initial value for a **boolean** data field is **false**.

Relational Operators in boolean Expressions

Simple **boolean** expressions that perform comparisons often have one of these forms:

```
variable   relational-operator   variable
variable   relational-operator   literal
literal    relational-operator   variable
```

Table 4.1 shows Java's **relational operators**. These symbols should be familiar, except for the **equal operator** (==) and the **not equal operator** (!=), sometimes called the **equality operators**. If **i** is type **int**, the condition **i < 3** is **true** when **i** is negative or 0, 1, or 2.

Table 4.1 Java relational operators

Operator	Meaning
<	Less than
<=	Less than or equal
>	Greater than
>=	Greater than or equal
==	Equal
!=	Not equal

◆◆EXAMPLE 4.1 ──

Assume an individual's tax rate depends on his or her salary and that single persons who earn less than $15,000 are taxed at a rate of 15%. If taxable income is stored in the type **double** variable **salary**, the **boolean** expression **salary < 15000.00** is **true** if salary is less than $15,000.

◆◆

◆◆EXAMPLE 4.2 ──

Table 4.2 lists the relational operators and some sample conditions. Each condition is evaluated assuming the variables have the following values:

x	power	maxPow	y	item	minItem	momOrDad	num	sentinel
-5	1024	1024	7	1.5	-999.0	M	999	999

Table 4.2 Some sample conditions

Condition	Meaning	boolean Value
x <= 0	x less than or equal to 0	true
power < maxPow	power less than maxPow	false
x >= y	x greater than or equal to y	false
item > minItem	item greater than minItem	true
momOrDad == 'M'	momOrDad equal to 'M'	true
num != sentinel	num not equal to sentinel	false

◆◆

Reading boolean Data

You can use method `showConfirmDialog()` of class `JOptionPane` to read data into a **boolean** variable. Figure 4.1 shows the dialog window displayed by the statement

```
int happyNum = JOptionPane.showConfirmDialog(null, "Are you happy?");
```

In this method call, the first argument, `null`, places the dialog window in the center of the screen. The second argument is a prompt. The result returned by `showConfirmDialog()` is 0 if the user presses button `Yes`, 1 for button `No`, and 2 for button `Cancel`. The **boolean** assignment statement

```
boolean happyMood = (happyNum == 0);
```

"converts" the integer result (stored in `happyNum`) to a **boolean** value. The **boolean** expression `(happyNum == 0)` is **true** if `happyNum` is 0 (`Yes`) and it is **false** otherwise (`No` or `Cancel`). Therefore, the value **true** or **false** will be stored in `happyMood` as desired.

Method `readBoolean()` (see Fig. 4.2) returns a **boolean** data value. The first statement in this method displays its argument **prompt** in a dialog window like Fig. 4.1. The **return** statement returns **true** or **false** depending on whether `Yes` is pressed (`boolNum` is 0) or `No` or `Cancel` is pressed (`boolNum` is not 0). The statement

```
boolean happyMood = readBoolean("Are you happy?");
```

displays the dialog window in Fig. 4.1. Our class `KeyIn` (in library `psJava`) contains this `readBoolean()` method.

Figure 4.1   Dialog window for `JOptionPane.showConfirmDialog(null,`
            `"Are you happy?");`

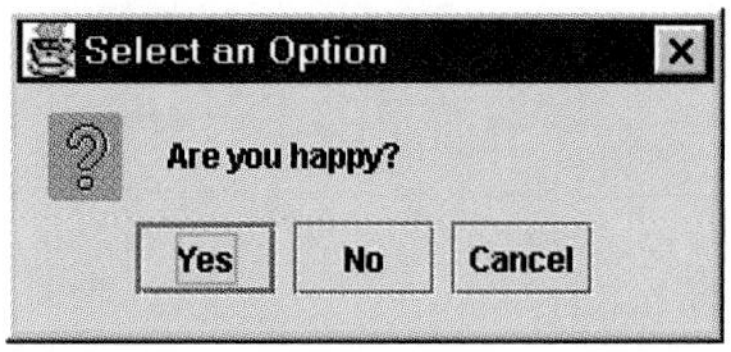

Figure 4.2   Method `readBoolean()`

```
public static boolean readboolean(String prompt) {
    int boolNum = JOptionPane.showConfirmDialog(null, prompt);
    return boolNum == 0;
}
```

boolean Operators

We can form more complicated **boolean** expressions by using the three **boolean** operators—**&&** (**and**), **||** (**or**), and **!** (**not**)—which require type **boolean** operands. Three examples of **boolean** expressions formed with these operators are

```
(salary < minimumSalary) || (dependents > 5)
(temperature > 90.0) && (humidity > 0.90)
(salary >= 15000.00) && (salary < 20000.00)
```

The first **boolean** expression determines whether an employee is eligible for special scholarship funds. It evaluates to **true** if either condition in parentheses is **true**. It will be **true** for an employee with a low salary or a large family or both. The second **boolean** expression describes an unbearable summer day, with temperature and humidity both in the nineties. The expression evaluates to **true** only when both conditions are **true**. The third **boolean** expression evaluates to **true** if an individual's salary is within the range of $15,000.00 to $19,999.99, inclusive.

Table 4.3 shows that the **&&** (and) operator yields a **true** result only when both its operands are true. Table 4.4 shows that the **||** (or) operator yields a **false** result only when both its operands are false. The last **boolean** operator **!** (not) has a single operand; Table 4.5 shows that the **!** operator yields the logical complement, or negation, of its operand (that is, if **found** is **true**, **!found** is **false**, and vice versa).

Table 4.3 The `&&` (and) operator

operand1	operand2	operand1 && operand2
true	true	true
true	false	false
false	true	false
false	false	false

Table 4.4 The || (or) operator

operand1	operand2	operand1 || operand2
true	true	true
true	false	true
false	true	true
false	false	false

Table 4.5 The ! (not) operator

operand	!operand
true	false
false	true

Type **boolean** variables can be used as operands of the **boolean** operators. You should not use relational or equality operators to compare a **boolean** variable to a **boolean** literal, as explained in the next example.

♦♦EXAMPLE 4.3 ───

If **winningRecord** and **onProbation** are **boolean** variables, we can write the **boolean** expression

```
(winningRecord && !onProbation)    // good style
```

A college team for which the expression is **true** is eligible for the postseason tournament. It has a winning record (**winningRecord** is **true**) and is not on probation (**onProbation** is **false**). Beginning programmers often write this epression as

```
((winningRecord == true) && (onProbation == false))  // bad style
```

Experienced programmers prefer the first expression because it is more concise and more readable.

                                                                                        ♦♦
───

An operator's precedence determines its order of evaluation. Table 4.6 lists all Java operators introduced so far in decreasing precedence order, from highest to lowest. Logical ! (not) is among the highest precedence operators. The relational and equality operators and logical **&&** (and) and logical || (or) are near the bottom. Notice that logical `&&` has higher precedence than logical `||` and both have lower precedence than the relational and equality operators. To prevent errors and to clarify the meaning of expressions, use parentheses freely.

Table 4.6 Operator precedence (from highest to lowest)

Operator	Description
!, + (unary), − (unary)	Logical not, unary plus, unary minus
*, /, %	Multiplication, division, remainder
+, −	Addition, subtraction
<, <=, >=,>	Relational inequality
==, !=	Equal, not equal
&&	Logical and
||	Logical or
=	Assignment

◆◆EXAMPLE 4.4 ───────────────────────────────

Java interprets the expression

```
x + a < y + b
```

as

```
(x + a) < (y + b)
```

because + has higher precedence than <. Java interprets the expression

```
min <= x && x <= max
```

as

```
(min <= x) && (x <= max)
```

because the relational operators have higher precedence than `&&`. If you remove the parentheses in the expression

```
(flag || leapYear) && switch
```

you change its meaning because `&&` has higher precedence than `||` and would be performed first.

─── ◆◆

◆◆EXAMPLE 4.5

Expressions 1 to 4 below contain a variety of operators. Each expression's value is given in the comment assuming x, y, and z are type double, flag is type boolean, and the variables have the values

x	y	z	flag
3.0	4.0	2.0	false

1. !flag   // not false is true.

2. (x + y / z) <= 3.5   // 5.0 <= 3.5 is false.

3. (!flag) || ((y + z) >= (x - z)) // true or true is
                                   // true.

4. !(flag || ((y + z) >= (x - z))) // not (false or
                                   // true) is false.

Figure 4.3 shows the evaluation tree for expression 3.

Figure 4.3   Evaluation tree for (!flag) || ((y + z) >= (x − z))

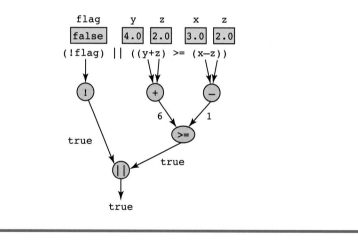

◆◆

Short-Circuit Evaluation of boolean Expressions

When evaluating **boolean** expressions involving the operators **&&** and **||**, Java employs a technique called short-circuit evaluation. This means that Java stops evaluating a **boolean** expression as soon as its value can be determined. For example, if the value of **flag** is **true**, the expression

flag || (x > 0 && y != 7.5)

must evaluate to **true** regardless of the value of the parenthesized expression following the || operator (that is, **true** || (...) must always be **true**). Consequently, there is no need to evaluate the parenthesized expression following || when **flag** is **true**. Similarly, we can show that **false** && (...) must always be **false**, so there is no need to evaluate the expression any further when an operand of the **&&** operator is determined to be **false**.

◆◆EXAMPLE 4.6 ───

If **x** is zero, the condition below

```
(x != 0.0) && (y / x > 5.0)
```

is **false**, because (x != 0.0) is **false**, so **false** && (...) must be **false**. Consequently, there is no need to evaluate (y / x > 5.0) when x is zero. However, if you reverse the order of the subexpressions

```
(y / x > 5.0) && (x != 0.0)
```

Java will evaluate (y / x > 5.0) first, leading to a division-by-zero run-time error because the divisor x is zero. This result points out that the order of subexpressions in a condition can be critical, and you can take advantage of short-circuit evaluation to guard against run-time errors.

─── ◆◆

Writing English Conditions in Java

To solve programming problems, we must write English conditions as **boolean** expressions. Often we want to test whether a variable has one of several possible values. For example, if **ch** is type **char**, we may want to know if **ch** is the letter a or A. The **boolean** expression

```
(ch == 'a') || (ch == 'A')     // true if ch is the first letter
```

is **true** if ch is the letter a or A. The parentheses are not required.
    Make sure you don't try to write this expression as

```
ch == 'a' || 'A'               // not a valid expression
```

In this case, the operand 'A' of the **boolean** operator || is type **char**, not type **boolean**. Another incorrect attempt would be caused by writing = instead of ==:

```
(ch = 'a') || (ch = 'A')     // not a valid expression
```

Each assignment has the value of the letter being assigned, so both operands of ||
would be type **char**, not type **boolean**.

◆◆EXAMPLE 4.7 ─────────────────────────────────

Many algorithm steps test whether a variable's value is within a specified range of
values. For example, if **min** represents the lower bound of a range of values and
max represents the upper bound (**min** is less than **max**), the **boolean** expression

```
(x >= min) && (x <= max)
```

tests whether **x** lies within the range **min** through **max**, inclusive. In Fig. 4.4 this range
is shaded. The expression is **true** if **x** lies within this range and **false** if **x** is outside the range. The expression

```
(x > min) && (x < max)
```

excludes the endpoints **min** and **max** from the range of **x** values for which the
expression is **true**.

Figure 4.4   Range of true values for (x >= min) && (x <= max)

◆◆EXAMPLE 4.8 ─────────────────────────────────

Sometimes you want to write a **boolean** expression that is **true** if a variable has
a value that lies outside a specified range of values. For example, you might want to
write a **boolean** expression that is **true** when **x** has a value that is not in the
shaded region of Fig. 4.4. You can write this expression by simply negating the earlier one:

```
!( (x >= min) && (x <= max) )
```

Or you can write a simpler expression by observing that the new expression will
be **true** if the value of **x** is less than **min** or if the value of **x** is greater than **max**.

```
(x < min) || (x > max)
```

This expression is logically equivalent to the earlier one.

◆◆

DeMorgan's Theorem (Optional)

You can also derive the simpler expression above using **DeMorgan's theorem**. The first part of DeMorgan's theorem states that

$!(expression_1$ **&&** $expression_2)$ equals $!expression_1 || !expression_2$

So by DeMorgan's theorem,

```
!( (x >= min) && (x <= max) )
```    equals    `!(x >= min) || !(x <= max)`

To complement each expression in parentheses on the right, reverse the relational operators (`>=` becomes `<` , `<=` becomes `>`). The expression on the right becomes

```
(x < min) || (x > max)
```

The second part of DeMorgan's theorem states that

$!(expression_1 || expression_2)$ equals $!expression_1$ **&&** $! expression_2$

So by DeMorgan's theorem,

```
!( (ch == 'a') || (ch == 'A') )
```    equals    `!( ch == 'a') && !( ch == 'A')`

To complement each expression, replace `==` with `!=`, giving

```
(ch != 'a') && (ch != 'A')
```

Comparing Characters

The order of **char** comparisons is based on the Unicode position of each character (see Appendix B). The first 128 characters of Unicode correspond to the ASCII code. These characters include the letters (uppercase and lowercase), digits, punctuation, operators, and special control characters. In these codes, the digit characters are in numeric order (`'0'` < `'1'` ...), the uppercase letters are in alphabetical order (`'A'` < `'B'` ...), and lowercase letters are in alphabetical order (`'a'` < `'b'` ...). The digits precede uppercase letters, and uppercase letters precede lowercase letters. Table 4.7 shows several examples of character comparisons.

Table 4.7 Examples of character comparisons

Expression	Value
'a' < 'b'	true
'X' <= 'A'	false
'3' > '4'	false
'3' <= '4'	true
'a' > 'A'	true
('A' <= ch) && (ch <= 'Z')	true if ch contains an uppercase letter; otherwise false

◆◆EXAMPLE 4.9 ─────────────────────────────────

In the assignment statement

```
boolean isLetter = (('A' <= ch) && (ch <= 'Z')) ||
                   (('a' <= ch) && (ch <= 'z'));
```

variable **isLetter** is assigned **true** if ch is an uppercase or a lowercase letter. The expression on the first line is **true** if ch is an uppercase letter; the expression on the second line is **true** if ch is a lowercase letter.

◆◆

Comparing Strings for Equality

You can also compare **String** objects; however, you should use methods in class **String**, not the relational operators. For example, use the **String** method **equals** (not the equality operator **==**) to compare two strings for equality. The value of the expression

```
string1.equals(string2)
```

is **true** if **string1** is equal to **string2**. Two **String** objects are equal **if** they contain the same characters and have the same length. Either string may be a variable or a literal.

◆◆EXAMPLE 4.10 ─────────────────────────────────

Given the declaration

```
String feeling = "happy is good";
```

the expression

```
"happy".equals(feeling.substring(0, 5))
```

correctly evaluates to **true**. It compares a **String** object that contains the characters in the string literal **"happy"** to one that contains the first five characters in **String** object **feeling**. Because the characters in both these **String** objects are the same, the result of the comparison is **true**.

However, the expression

```
"happy" == feeling.substring(0, 5)
```

incorrectly evaluates to **false**. The reason is that Java compares a reference to a **String** object that contains the characters **happy** to a reference to a different **String** object (the result of the call to **substring()**) that contains the same characters. Even though these **String** objects contain the same characters, they occupy different storage locations in Java. The **==** operator compares the actual memory addresses of the two **String** objects.

◆◆

Method equalsIgnoreCase()

The expression **"aces".equals("ACES")** is **false**. However, you can use method **equalsIgnoreCase()** to compare two strings for equality, ignoring case. The expression **"aces".equalsIgnoreCase("ACES")** is **true**.

Lexicographic Comparisons of Strings

Java provides a method, **compareTo()**, that you can use to compare strings lexicographically. The **lexicographic order** of two strings is the order in which they would normally appear in a dictionary. The expression

```
string1.compareTo(string2)
```

◆ Has a negative value if **string1** is lexicographically less than **string2**

◆ Has the value **0** if **string1** is lexicographically equal to **string2**

◆ Has a positive value if **string1** is lexicographically greater than **string2**

The result returned by **compareTo()** depends on the relationship between the first pair of different characters in the strings being compared. For the method call

```
"acts".compareTo("aces")
```

the result depends on the relationship between characters t and e ('t' > 'e').
Therefore, "acts" is lexicographically greater than "aces" and the above expression
has a positive value. (Its actual value is 15, which is the difference between the character codes for 't' and 'e'.)

Table 4.8 shows the result of several other string comparisons. For "1234" and
"56", the result depends on the first character in each string ('1' < '5'), not on
the strings' numeric values. The last two comparisons involve a string ("aces") that
begins with a shorter substring ("ace"). The substring "ace" is lexicographically less
than the longer string "aces".

Table 4.8 Method compareTo

Expression	Value	Reason
"XYZ".compareTo("ABC")	Positive	'X' > 'A'
"XYZ".compareTo("XYZ")	Zero	"XYZ" equals "XYZ"
"XYZ".compareTo("xyz")	Negative	'X' < 'x'
"1234".compareTo("56")	Negative	'1' < '5'
"acts".compareTo("aces")	Positive	't' > 'e'
"aces".compareTo("ace")	Positive	"aces" begins with "ace"
"ace".compareTo("aces")	Negative	"aces" begins with "ace"

EXERCISES FOR SECTION 4.2

SELF-CHECK

1. Assume x is 15 and y is 25. What are the values of the following conditions?

    a. x != y

    b. x < x

    c. x >= y - x

    d. x == (y + x - y)

2. Draw evaluation trees for the following:

    a. a == (b + a - b)

    b. (c == (a + b)) || !flag

    c. (a != 7) && (c >= 6) || flag

    d. !(b <= 12) && (a % 2 == 0)

    e. !((a > 5) || (c < (a + b)))

3. Evaluate each expression above if a is 5, b is 10, c is 15, and flag is true.

4. Evaluate the following expressions, assuming short-circuit evaluation, if **x** is **6** and **y** is **7**. Would the results be any different without short-circuit evaluation?

   a. `(x > 5) && (y % x <= 10)`

   b. `(x <= 10) || (x / (y - 7) > 3)`

5. Evaluate the following expressions assuming **ch** is `'c'`, **digit** is `'7'`, and **string1** is `"happy"`.

   a. `'a' <= ch && ch <= 'z'`

   b. `'0' <= digit && digit <= '9'`

   c. `digit < '0' || digit > '9'`

   d. `string1.equals("Happy")`

   e. `string1.equalsIgnoreCase("HAPPY")`

   f. `string1.compareTo("Happy")`

   g. `string1.compareTo("happyer")`

   h. `string1.compareTo("HAPPY") == 0`

   i. `'0' < digit && string1.compareTo("happyer") < 0`

PROGRAMMING

1. Write a **boolean** expression for each of the following relationships:

   a. **age** is from **18** to **21**, inclusive.

   b. **water** is less than **1.5** and also greater than **0.1**.

   c. **year** is divisible by **4** (*Hint:* Use %).

   d. **speed** is not greater than **55**.

   e. **ch** is an uppercase letter.

   f. **ch** is not a letter.

2. Write **boolean** assignment statements for the following:

   a. Assign a value of **true** to **between** if n is in the range **-k** and **+k**, inclusive; otherwise, assign a value of **false**.

   b. Assign a value of **true** to **upperCase** if ch is an uppercase letter; otherwise, assign a value of **false**.

   c. Assign a value of **true** to **divisor** if m is a divisor of n; otherwise, assign a value of **false**.

4.3   The `if` Statement

We use selection control structures to choose one alternative from among many. In Java, the primary selection control structure is an **if statement**. An `if` statement always contains a **boolean** expression, and it may have either one consequent or two alternatives. An `if` with two alternatives determines which of two alternative statement groups will be executed. An `if` with one consequent determines whether the consequent statement will be executed.

if Statement with One Consequent

The `if` statement

```
// Multiply product by a nonzero x only
if (x != 0.0) {
    product = product * x;
}
```

has one consequent, which is executed only when **x** is not equal to **0**. It causes **product** to be multiplied by **x** and the new value to be saved in **product**, replacing the old value. If **x** is equal to **0**, the multiplication is not performed.

if Statement with Two Alternatives

The `if` statement

```
if (gross > 100.00) {
    net = gross - tax;
}
else {
    net = gross;
}
```

selects one of the two assignment statements. It selects the first one if the **boolean** expression is **true** (i.e., **gross** is greater than **100.00**); it selects the second one if the **boolean** expression is **false** (i.e., **gross** is not greater than **100.00**). Each alternative statement is enclosed in braces **{}**.

Figure 4.5 is a flowchart of the two preceding `if` statements. In a **flowchart**, boxes and arrows give a diagram of the step-by-step execution of a control structure or program fragment. A diamond-shaped box in a flowchart represents a decision, for which there is always one path in and two paths out (labeled **true** and **false**). A rectangular box represents one or more statements.

Figure 4.5 shows that the condition is evaluated first. If the condition is **true**, program control follows the arrow labeled **true**, and the assignment statement in the

Figure 4.5   Flowcharts of `if` **statements with (a) one consequent and (b) two alternatives**

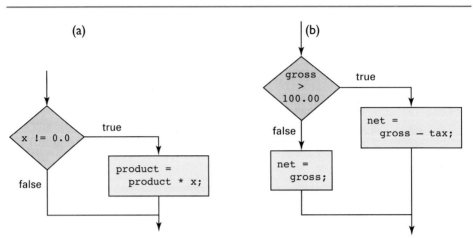

right rectangle is executed. If the condition is **false**, program control follows the arrow labeled **false**.

◆◆EXAMPLE 4.11 —————————————————————————————

Method `greeting()` (see Fig. 4.6) has an `if` statement with two alternatives. It returns either `"Hi Mom"` or `"Hi Dad"`, depending on the character stored in parameter `parentKind`.

Figure 4.6   Method `greeting()`

```
public String greeting(char parentKind) {
    if (parentKind == 'M' || parentKind == 'm') {
        return "Hi Mom";
    }
    else {
        return "Hi Dad";
    }
}
```

—— ◆◆

◆◆EXAMPLE 4.12 —————————————————————————————

In many programming problems you must order a pair of data values in memory so that the smaller value is stored in one variable (say, **x**) and the larger value in another (say, **y**). The `if` statement in Fig. 4.7 rearranges any two values stored in **x** and y so that the smaller number is in **x** and the larger number is in **y**. If the two numbers are already in the proper order, the compound statement is not executed. Variables **x**, **y**, and **temp** should all be the same data type, where the variable **temp** is used to store a copy of the original value of **x**.

Figure 4.7   if statement to order x and y

```
if (x > y) {
    // Switch x and y
    temp = x;              // Stores old x in temp.
    x = y;                 // Stores old y in x.
    y = temp;              // Stores old x in y.
}
```

Table 4.9 traces the execution of this `if` statement when **x** is **12.5** and **y** is **5.1**. The table shows that **temp** is initially undefined (indicated by **?**). Each line shows the part of the `if` statement that is being executed, followed by its effect. If any variable gets a new value, its new value is shown on that line. If no new value is shown, the variable retains its previous value. The last value stored in **x** is **5.1**, and the last value stored in **y** is **12.5**.

Table 4.9   Step-by-step trace of if statement

Statement Part	x	y	temp	Effect
	12.5	5.1	?	
if (x > y)				12.5 > 5.1 is true.
temp = x;			12.5	Stores old x in temp.
x = y;	5.1			Stores old y in x.
y = temp;		12.5		Stores old x in y.

if statement (one consequent)

Form: if (*condition*) {
                   statement$_T$;
           }

Example: if (x > 0.0) {
                   posProd = posProd * x;
           }

Interpretation: If *condition* evaluates to **true**, *statement$_T$* (the **true** task) is executed; otherwise, *statement$_T$* is skipped. *Note:* If *statement$_T$* is a single statement, the enclosing braces **{}** may be omitted.

if statement (two alternatives)

```
Form:      if (condition) {
               statementT;
           }
           else {
               statementF;
           }

Example:   if (x >= 0.0) {
               System.out.println("Positive");
           }
           else {
               System.out.println("Negative");
           }
```

Interpretation: If *condition* evaluates to **true**, then *statement$_T$* (the **true** task) is executed and *statement$_F$* is skipped; otherwise, *statement$_T$* is skipped and *statement$_F$* (the **false** task) is executed. Note: If *statement$_T$* or *statement$_F$* is a single statement, the enclosing braces **{}** around it may be omitted.

PROGRAM STYLE: *Format of the* **if** *Statement*

All **if** statement examples in this text indent *statement$_T$* and *statement$_F$*. The word **else** is typed on a separate line and aligns with **if**. The format of the **if** statement makes its meaning apparent and is used solely to improve program readability; the format makes no difference to the compiler. We place the open brace on the same line as the keywords **if** and **else**. Some programmers prefer to place it on a line by itself so that it aligns with the close brace:

```
if (x >= 0.0)
{
    System.out.println("Positive");
}
else
{
    System.out.println("Negative");
}
```

If *statement$_T$* or *statement$_F$* is a single statement, the braces **{}** around it may be omitted. For example, we could write the **if** statement above as

```
if (x >= 0.0)
    System.out.println("Positive");
else
    System.out.println("Negative");
```

The advantage to writing the braces is that they clearly indicate where the **true** and **false** tasks end. Also, we can add another statement to the **true** task or **false** task at a later time without also having to add braces. We will use both styles in the text.

Methods That Return boolean Results

Figure 4.8 shows a method `isEligibleMale()` that returns **true** if its argument (type **Person**) satisfies all the specified criteria. Assume that **MIN** and **MAX** are predefined integer constants and that the accessor methods (`getMaritalStatus()`, `getGender()`, and `getAge()`) return the expected information for a type **Person** object.

Figure 4.8   Method `isEligibleMale()`

```
// postcondition: returns true if all criteria are met.
public boolean isEligibleMale(Person p) {
    int age = p.getAge();

    return p.getStatus().equals("single") &&
           (p.getGender() == 'M') &&
           (age >= MIN) && (age <= MAX);
}
```

The **boolean** expression after **return** consists of several conditions that are operands of `&&` operators. It evaluates to **true** only if all the conditions are **true**. The expression value is returned as the method result. The method result would be **true** if the method argument represents a single male whose age is between **MIN** and **MAX**.

Programmers sometimes write the **return** statement in Fig. 4.8 using an **if** statement of the form

```
// unnecessary if statement
if (p.getStatus().equals("single") && (p.getGender() == 'M') &&
    (age >= MIN) && (age <= MAX)) {
    return true;
}
else {
    return false;
}
```

Resist this temptation. The approach shown in Fig. 4.8 is preferable.

EXERCISES FOR SECTION 4.3

SELF-CHECK

1. What do these statements display?

   a.
   ```
   if (12 < 12) {
       System.out.println("Less");
   }
   else {
       System.out.println("Not less");
   }
   ```

   b.
   ```
   var1 = 25.12;
   var2 = 15.00;
   if (var1 <= var2)
       System.out.print("<=");
   else
       System.out.print(">");
   ```

2. What value is assigned to **x** when **y** is **15.0**?

   a.
   ```
   x = 25.0;
   if (y != (x - 10.0)) {
       x = x - 10.0;
   }
   else {
       x = x / 2.0;
   }
   ```

   b.
   ```
   if ((y < 15.0) && (y >= 0.0)) {
       x = 5 * y;
   }
   else {
       x = 2 * y;
   }
   ```

3. What do these statements display when **name** is **"Chris"**?

    a. ```
    if (name.compareTo("Chris") == 0)
        System.out.println("Hi Kiddo");
    System.out.println("How was your day?");
    ```

    b. ```
    if (name.equals("Chris"))
        System.out.println("Hi Kiddo");
    else
        System.out.println("How was your day?");
    ```

4. Use indentation in the **if** statement below to improve its readability. When does the last line execute?

    ```
    // messy if statement
    if (x > y)
    {
    x = x + 10.0;
    System.out.println("x bigger");
    }
    else
    System.out.println("x smaller");
    System.out.println("y is " + y);
    ```

5. Explain the effect of removing the braces in Exercise 4.

6. What is the effect of placing braces around the last two lines in Exercise 4?

7. Explain the effect of the **if** statement below. Assume **add** is type **boolean** and the other variables are type **int**. Rewrite it using **(add)** as the condition.

    ```
    if (!add) {
        product = num1 * num2 * num3;
        System.out.println("product is " + product);
    }
    else {
        sum = num1 + num2 + num3;
        System.out.println("sum is " + sum);
    }
    ```

PROGRAMMING

1. Write Java statements to carry out the following steps:

   a. If `item` is nonzero, multiply `product` by `item` and save the result in `product`; otherwise, skip the multiplication. In either case, display the value of `product`.

   b. Store the absolute difference of `x` and `y` in `y`, where the absolute difference is `(x - y)` or `(y - x)`, whichever is positive.

   c. If `x` is `0`, add `1` to `zeroCount`. If `x` is negative, add `x` to `minusSum`. If `x` is greater than `0`, add `x` to `plusSum`.

2. Write the following methods:

   a. Write method `sameSign()` that, given two type `double` arguments, will return `true` if both arguments have the same sign and `false` otherwise.

   b. Write a second method that uses `sameSign()` and returns the actual sign (`'+'` or `'-'`). Return a blank character if the arguments have different signs.

3. Write a class that stores the names of three people (`name1`, `name2`, `name3`). Write a method for the class that rearranges the names so they are in alphabetical order (`name1 <= name2`, `name2 <= name3`).

4. Write a program that computes the area of a rectangle (`area = base × height`) or a triangle (`area = 1/2 base × height`) after asking the user what kind of figure is involved.

4.4 Decision Steps in Algorithms

Algorithm steps that select from a choice of actions are called **decision steps**. The algorithms in the following problems contain decision steps that are coded as `if` statements in Java methods.

Searching a String

Earlier we discussed comparisons of characters and strings. In the next example, we show two ways of determining if a string begins with a vowel.

◆◆EXAMPLE 4.13 ───

Fig. 2.10 showed a program that converts a data word to pig Latin using a simple rule: strip off the first character, add "ay" to it, and join it to the end of the word. You may have noticed that this rule is incorrect when a word begins with a vowel or the letter y. For example, the word "example" should not be changed to "xampleeay", but should remain untranslated. Our revised rule becomes

if the first letter is a vowel or y
   don't translate
else
   translate the word to pig Latin in the normal way

We can determine whether the first letter in a word (stored in **first**) is a vowel or y by comparing it to the letters a, e, i, o, u, y and A, E, I, O, U, Y. One approach is to evaluate the **boolean** expression

```
(first == 'a' || first == 'e' || first == 'i' || first == 'o' ||
 first == 'u' || first == 'y' || first == 'A' || first == 'E' ||
 first == 'I' || first == 'O' || first == 'U' || first == 'Y')
```

A more sophisticated approach is to use **String** method **indexOf()**, which searches a string to see if it contains a specified string or character (see Table 2.6). Method **indexOf()** returns the starting position of its argument if it is found; method **indexOf()** returns **−1** if its argument is not found. The method call

```
"aeiouyAEIOUY".indexOf(first)
```

searches the string containing all vowels and the letter y. It returns a value in the range 0 to 11 if **first** is a vowel or y; it returns -1 if **first** is not a vowel or y.

Fig. 4.9 shows a class **PigLatin** that implements this approach in **boolean** method **firstLetterIsAVowel()**. This method returns **true** if its argument string begins with a vowel or y. The class also contains a method **translateWord()**, which implements the corrected pig Latin translation algorithm.

◆◆

In the solution to the next case study, we write an **Employee** class that has two methods with decision steps.

CASE STUDY PAYROLL PROBLEM

PROBLEM Your company pays its employees time and a half for all hours worked over 40 hours a week. Employees who earn more than $100 a week pay union dues of $25 per week. Write a program to compute an employee's gross pay and net pay.

Figure 4.9   Class `PigLatin`

```java
/*
 * PigLatin.java       Authors: Koffman and Wolz
 * Class that can translate a word to pig Latin
 */
public class PigLatin {

  // Data field
  String word;      // word to be translated

  // Methods
  public PigLatin(String wor) {
    word = wor;
  }

  // postcondition: returns true if word begins with a vowel
  private boolean firstLetterIsAVowel() {
    String vowels = "aeiouyAEIOUY";
    char first = word.charAt(0);

    // Search for first letter among vowels and
    //   return true if first letter is found
    return vowels.indexOf(first) > -1;
  }


  // postcondition: translates word to pig Latin
  public String translateWord() {
    if (firstLetterIsAVowel()) {
      return word;
    }
    else {
      return word.substring(1) + word.charAt(0) + "ay";
    }
  }

  public String toString() {
    return word;
  }
}
```

ANALYSIS The relevant employee information includes an employee ID and input data for hours worked and hourly pay. The problem outputs are gross pay and net pay.

Data Requirements

> ### Problem Inputs
> employee ID
> hours worked
> hourly rate
>
> ### Problem Outputs
> gross pay
> net pay

Relevant Formulas

> gross pay = hours worked × hourly rate
> gross pay = 40 × hourly rate + 1.5 × overtime hours × hourly rate
> net pay = gross pay − union dues

We will need an **Employee** class. The **Employee** class should have data fields to store the payroll data and methods to process this data. Figure 4.10 shows a description of this class.

Figure 4.10 Class **Employee**

Data Fields	Attributes
`String empID`	Employee identification
`double hours`	Hours worked
`double rate`	Hourly rate
Methods	**Behavior**
`void setEmpID(String)`	Stores employee ID
`void setHours(double)`	Stores hours worked
`void setRate(double))`	Stores hourly rate
`String getEmpID()`	Gets this employee's ID
`double getHours()`	Gets this employee's hours worked
`double getRates()`	Gets this employee's hourly rate
`double computeNet()`	Calculates net pay
`double computeGross(double)`	Calculates gross pay given net pay (argument)
`String toString()`	Represents object's state
Classes Used	
`String`	

We also need an application class that uses class **Employee**. Fig. 4.11 shows a description of the **EmployeeApp** class.

Figure 4.11   Class EmployeeApp

Methods	Behavior
main()	Reads the employee's data and calculates and displays gross pay and net pay
double readDouble()	Returns a type double input value
Classes Used	
Employee, JOptionPane	

DESIGN   Next we design the two computational methods for the **Employee** class.

Algorithm for **computeGross()** *(class* **Employee***)*

if no overtime

    compute gross pay without overtime pay.

else

    compute gross pay with overtime pay.

Algorithm for **computeNet()** *(class* **Employee***)*

if no union dues

    net pay is gross pay.

else

    net pay is gross pay – union dues.

The decision steps above are expressed in **pseudocode**, which is a mixture of English and Java used to describe algorithm steps. The indentation and reserved words **if** and **else** show the logical structure of each decision step. Each decision step has a condition (following **if**) that can be written in English and Java; similarly, the **true** and **false** tasks can be written in English and Java.

Next, we provide the algorithm for method **main()** of the application class.

Algorithm for **main()** *(class* **EmployeeApp***)*

1.   Read and store the payroll data in an **Employee** object.

2.   Compute gross pay.

3. Compute net pay given gross pay.

4. Display the **Employee** object's state and pay amounts.

IMPLEMENTATION   Fig. 4.12 shows class **Employee**. The statement

```
private final static double MAX_NO_OVERTIME = 40;
```

declares **MAX_NO_OVERTIME** as a **class constant** with a value of 40. The modifier **final** means that the value cannot be changed and is therefore a constant. The modifier **static** means that the constant belongs to the class, not to each class instance. It would make no sense for each class instance (object) to store its own value for this constant because each value would be 40.

Method **computeGross()** uses the following **if** statement to implement the decision step shown earlier in pseudocode:

```
if (hours <= MAX_NO_OVERTIME) {
      return hours * rate;
}
else
{
   double regularPay = MAX_NO_OVERTIME * rate;
   double overtimePay = (hours - MAX_NO_OVERTIME) *
                        OVERTIME_RATE * rate;
   return regularPay + overtimePay;
}
```

If the employee works overtime, the compound statement after **else** computes **regularPay** and **overtimePay** separately and stores their values in local variables before computing and returning their sum.

The net pay computation depends on the value of gross pay. Consequently, we must compute gross pay first and pass gross pay as an argument to method **computeNet()**. The header for method **computeNet()** shows that it has a single argument:

```
public double computeNet(double gross)
```

Figure 4.13 shows class **EmployeeApp**. The constructor call creates a new **Employee** object, initializing its data fields with the input data entered by the program user. We use method **readDouble()** shown earlier (see Fig. 3.30) to read values for hours and rate.

Figure 4.12   Class Employee

```java
/*
 * Employee.java       Authors: Koffman and Wolz
 * Class that represents an employee
 */
public class Employee {

  // class constants
  private static final double MAX_NO_OVERTIME = 40; // normal work week
  private static final double OVERTIME_RATE = 1.5; // overtime rate
  private static final double MAX_NO_DUES = 100;  // max earnings before dues
  private static final double DUES = 25;        // dues amount

  // Data fields
  private String empID;
  private double hours;
  private double rate;

  // Methods
  public Employee() {}

  public Employee(String id, double ho, double ra) {
    empID = id;
    hours = ho;
    rate = ra;
  }

  public void setEmpID(String id) {
    empID = id;
  }

  public void setHours(double ho) {
    hours = ho;
  }

  public void setRate(double ra) {
    rate = ra;
  }
```

Figure 4.12   Class `Employee,` *continued*

```
// postcondition: returns gross pay
public double computeGross() {
   if (hours <= MAX_NO_OVERTIME) {
      return hours * rate;
   }
   else {
      double regularPay = MAX_NO_OVERTIME * rate;
      double overtimePay = (hours - MAX_NO_OVERTIME) *
                           OVERTIME_RATE * rate;
      return regularPay + overtimePay;
   }
}


// precondition: gross pay was calculated.
// postcondition: returns net pay.
public double computeNet(double gross) {
   if (gross <= MAX_NO_DUES)
      return gross;
   else
      return gross - DUES; // deduct dues amount
}


// Shows employee information.
public String toString() {
   return "Employee: " + empID +
          ", hours: " + hours +
          ", rate: " + rate;
}
// Insert accessor methods.
// See programming exercise 3.


}
```

TESTING   Figure 4.14 shows a sample run. To test this program, run it with several data sets that yield all possible combinations of values for the two `if` statement conditions (`true/true, true/false, false/true, false/false`). As an example, to get the condition values `true/true`, hours worked should be less than `40` and gross pay should be less than `$100`. Also test the program with a data set for which hours worked is exactly `40` and one for which gross pay is exactly `$100`.

Figure 4.13   Class `EmployeeApp`

```java
/*
 * EmployeeApp.java       Authors: Koffman and Wolz
 * Application class that uses class Employee
 */
import javax.swing.JOptionPane;

public class EmployeeApp {

  // methods
  private static double readDouble(String prompt) {
    String numStr = JOptionPane.showInputDialog(prompt);
    return Double.parseDouble(numStr);
  }

  public static void main (String[] args) {
    // Read and store the payroll data in an Employee object
    Employee programmer =
            new Employee(
                JOptionPane.showInputDialog("Enter employee id"),
                readDouble("Enter hours worked"),
                readDouble("Enter hourly rate")
            );

    // Compute gross pay.
    double gross = programmer.computeGross();

    // Compute net pay given gross pay.
    double net = programmer.computeNet(gross);

    // Display the Employee object's state and pay amounts.
    System.out.println(programmer.toString());
    System.out.println("Gross pay is $" + gross);
    System.out.println("Net pay is $" + net);
  }
}
```

Figure 4.14   Sample run of class `EmployeeApp`

```
EmployeeApp

Employee id: 0987, hours: 40.0, rate: $15.5
Gross pay is $620.0
Net pay is $595.0
```

PROGRAM STYLE: *Choosing Variable Scope*

When choosing the scope of variables (where they are accessible), we follow these principles:

1. Keep variables as local as possible.

2. Avoid making a calculation more than once.

3. Use variables sparingly.

Following principle 1, in the methods of class **Employee** we declare variables only within the block in which they are needed. For example, **regularPay** and **overtimePay** are only needed in the **else** block of the method **computeGross()**, so that is their scope. In Java, the scope of a variable is determined by the closest pair of braces that encloses that variable's declaration. If we declared them as local variables within the entire method, or worse, as class data fields, their scope would be larger than necessary. This could expose them to misuse. Program style is subjective. Other programmers might prefer to declare these variables as local variables in method **computeGross()** because this makes their declaration more apparent and there is not much likelihood of their being misused within the method.

Following principle 3, method **computeNet()** does not declare a local variable (for example, **net**) to store the method result. For example, we could have written **computeNet()** as

```
public double computeNet(double gross) {
   double net;
   if (gross <= MAX_NO_DUES) {
      net = gross;
   }
   else {
      net = gross - dues; // Deduct dues amount.
   }
   return net;
}
```

This method uses **net** to store the result and returns it at the end. Instead, in Fig. 4.13, each branch of the **if** statement returns the computed result directly, removing the need for local variable **net**. Some programmers argue that methods should only have one exit to enhance program readability and to ensure that a value of the proper type is always returned. This rule isn't necessary in Java. When a method is declared with a return value, the Java compiler guarantees that all paths through the method return a value of the proper type. Consequently, we can avoid introducing an unnecessary variable such as **net**.

Because method **computeNet()** needs the value of gross pay as data, we must use **computeGross()** to calculate gross pay first. Passing gross pay as an argument to **computeNet()** keeps us from having to calculate it a second time in **computeNet()** (principle 2). (See Self-Check Exercise 3.)

PROGRAM STYLE: *Using Constants to Enhance Readability and Maintenance*

Four constants appear in the **if** statements in Fig. 4.13. We declared them as class constants to make their purpose readily apparent to a user or reader of the class. For method **computeGross()**, we could just as easily have placed literals directly in the **if** statement, as shown next.

```
if (gross <= 100)
    return gross;
else
    return gross - 25;     // Deduct dues amount.
```

However, using constants rather than literals has two advantages. First, the original **if** statement is easier to understand because it includes the descriptive names **MAX_NO_DUES** and **DUES** rather than numbers that have no intrinsic meaning. Second, a program written with constants is much easier to maintain than one written with literals. For example, to change the dues amount to $50, you need to change only the constant declaration. However, if we had inserted the literal **25** directly in the **if** statement, we would have to change the **if** statement and any other statements that manipulate that literal.

EXERCISES FOR SECTION 4.4

SELF-CHECK

1. Change the algorithm for method **computeNet()** so that it uses a decision step with one consequent. *Hint*: Assign **gross** to **net** before the decision step and use the decision step to change **net** when necessary.

2. Predict the payroll program output when
   a. hours is **30.0**, rate is **5.00**
   b. hours is **20.0**, rate is **4.00**

    c. hours is `50.0`, rate is `2.00`

    d. hours is `50.0`, rate is `6.00`

3. In class `Employee`, method `computeNet()` has a formal argument `gross`. Would the implementation be correct if `gross` was declared as a data field of the `Employee` class? Would `computeNet()` need `gross` as an argument in that case? What would happen in Fig. 4.13 if `computeNet()` was called before `computeGross()`?

PROGRAMMING

1. Modify method `computeNet` to deduct union dues of 10% for gross salary over $100 and 5% otherwise. Also, deduct a 3% city wage tax for all employees.

2. Write an application class that uses class `PigLatin`.

3. Write the three accessor methods shown in Fig. 4.10.

4.5 Multiple-Alternative Decisions: Nested `if` and `switch`

Until now we have used `if` statements to code decisions with one consequent or two alternatives. In this section we use **nested `if` statements** (one `if` statement inside another) to code decisions with multiple alternatives.

◆◆EXAMPLE 4.14 ───

The following nested `if` statement has three alternatives. It increases one of three variables (**numPos**, **numNeg**, or **numZero**) by 1, depending on whether **x** is greater than zero, less than zero, or equal to zero, respectively. The second `if` statement (in color) is the **false** task (following **else**) of the first `if` statement.

```
// increment numPos, numNeg, or numZero depending on x
if (x > 0) {
   numPos = numPos + 1;
}
else {
    if (x < 0)
       numNeg = numNeg + 1;
    else  // x is 0
       numZero = numZero + 1;
}
```

The execution of the nested **if** statement proceeds as follows: the first condition (**x** > **0**) is tested; if it is **true**, **numPos** is incremented and the rest of the **if** statement is skipped. If the first condition is **false**, the second condition (**x** < **0**) is tested; if it is **true**, **numNeg** is incremented; otherwise, **numZero** is incremented. It is important to realize that the second condition is tested only when the first condition is **false**.

Table 4.10 traces the execution of this statement when **x** is −7. Because **x** > **0** is **false**, the second condition (**x** < **0**) is also tested.

Table 4.10 Trace of **if** statement in Example 4.14 for **x** = −7

Statement Part	Effect
if (x > 0)	−7 > 0 is false.
if (x < 0)	−7 < 0 is true;
numNeg = numNeg + 1;	add 1 to numNeg.

Comparison of Nested **if** and Sequence of **if**s

Beginning programmers often use a sequence of **if** statements rather than a single nested **if** statement. The nested **if** statement for Example 4.14 is logically equivalent to the following sequence of **if** statements:

```
// Inefficient sequence of if statements
if (x > 0)
    numPos = numPos + 1;
if (x < 0)
    numNeg = numNeg + 1;
if (x == 0)
    numZero = numZero + 1;
```

The nested **if** statement in Example 4.14 is more readable because the above sequence doesn't clearly show that one and only one of the three assignment statements is executed for a particular **x**, as the nested **if** does. With respect to efficiency, the nested **if** statement executes more quickly when **x** is positive because the first condition (**x** > **0**) is **true**, so the part of the **if** statement following the first **else** is skipped. In contrast, all three conditions are always tested in the sequence of **if** statements. When **x** is negative, two conditions are tested in the nested **if** versus three in the sequence of **if** statements. Also, if you follow this approach, you may write two conditions that are true for a particular data value and the tasks following both true conditions will execute, instead of just one.

Java Rule for Matching `else` with `if`

We use indentation and braces to convey the logical structure of a nested `if` statement to the program reader. The indentation in Example 4.14 clearly shows an `if` statement with an `if-else` statement as its `false` task. The Java compiler disregards this indentation, however, and uses its own rule for matching `else`s with corresponding `if`s: Java matches each `else` with the closest unmatched `if` that comes before it. This is analogous to the rule for matching left and right parentheses in an expression, in that an `if` is like a left parenthesis and an `else` is like a right parenthesis.

◆◆EXAMPLE 4.15 ───

In the nested `if` statement below

```
if (x > 0)
    if (y > x)
        System.out.println("y > x > 0");
    else
        System.out.println("(x > 0) and (y <= x)");
```

Java matches the `else` with the second `if`. Therefore, Java translates this statement as an `if` statement whose `true` task (following the first condition) is an `if-else` statement.

If you want the `else` to go with the first `if`, not the second, you must place braces around the inner `if` statement:

```
if (x > 0) {
    if (y > x)
        System.out.println("y > x > 0");
}
else {
    System.out.println("x <= 0");
}
```

Java translates this statement as an `if-else` statement whose `true` task is an `if` statement. Just as you use parentheses to specify the order of operator evaluation in an expression, you can use braces to clarify the structure of a nested `if` statement.

◆◆

Multiple-Alternative Decision Form of Nested `if`

Nested `if` statements can become quite complex. If there are more than three alternatives and indentation is not consistent, it may be difficult to determine the logical structure of the `if` statement. In situations like Example 4.14 in which each **false** task is an `if-else` statement, you can code the nested `if` as the **multiple-alternative decision** described in the next display.

Multiple-alternative decision

Form:
```
if (condition₁) {
    statement₁;
}
else if (condition₂) {
    statement₂;
}
else if (condition₃) {
    statement₃;
}
        .
        .
        .
else if (conditionₙ) {
    statementₙ;
}
else {
    statementₑ;
}
```

Example:

```
// Increment numPos, numNeg, or numZero depending on x.
// Display updated value.
if (x > 0) {
    numPos = numPos + 1;
    System.out.println("numPos is " + numPos);
}
else if (x < 0) {
    numNeg = numNeg + 1;
    System.out.println("numNeg is " + numNeg );
}
else {
    // x is 0
    numZero = numZero + 1;
    System.out.println("numZero is " + numZero );
}
```

Interpretation: The conditions in a multiple-alternative decision are evaluated in sequence until a `true` condition is reached. If a condition is `true`, the statement following it is executed, and the rest of the multiple-alternative decision is skipped. If a condition is `false`, the statement following it is skipped and the next condition is tested. If all conditions are `false`, *statement*_e following the last `else` is executed. *Note:* It is not necessary to have an `else` *statement*_e. In this case, nothing happens if all conditions are `false`.

◆◆EXAMPLE 4.16 ───

Suppose you want to assign letter grades based on exam scores, as shown in the following table:

Exam Score	Grade Assigned
90 and above	A
80–89	B
70–79	C
60–69	D
Below 60	F

The following multiple-alternative decision displays the letter grade assigned according to this table. For an exam score of **85**, the first `true` condition is `score >= 80`, so **B** would be displayed and program control would pass to the call to method `println()` after the multiple-alternative decision (the last line).

```
if (score >= 90)
    System.out.println("Grade is A");
else if (score >= 80)
    System.out.println("Grade is B");
else if (score >= 70)
    System.out.println("Grade is C");
else if (score >= 60)
    System.out.println("Grade is D");
else
    System.out.println("Grade is F");
System.out.println("Score is " + score);
```

◆◆

PROGRAM STYLE: *Writing a Multiple-Alternative Decision*

In the multiple-alternative decision, the reserved words `else if` and the next condition appear on the same line. All the words `else if` align with each other and with the initial `if`, and each task is indented under the condition that controls its execution.

Order of Conditions Matters

When more than one condition in a multiple-alternative decision is **true**, only the task following the first **true** condition executes. Therefore, the order of the conditions can affect the outcome.

The following multiple-alternative decision assigns grades incorrectly. All passing exam scores (60 or above) would be categorized as a grade of D because the first condition would be **true** and the rest would be skipped. The most restrictive condition (**score >= 90**) should come first, the next most restrictive condition (**score >= 80**) second, and so on.

```
// incorrect grade assignment
if (score >= 60)
    System.out.println("Grade is D");
else if (score >= 70)
    System.out.println("Grade is C");
else if (score >= 80)
    System.out.println("Grade is B");
else if (score >= 90)
    System.out.println("Grade is A");
else
    System.out.println("Grade is F");
```

◆◆EXAMPLE 4.17 ─────────────────────────────────────

You could use a multiple-alternative decision to implement a decision table that describes several ranges of values for a particular variable and the outcome for each range. For instance, let's say you are an accountant setting up a payroll system based on Table 4.11 that shows five different ranges for salaries up to $15,000.00. Each table line shows the base tax amount (column 2) and tax percentage (column 3) for a particular salary range (column 1). Given a person's salary, you can calculate the tax due by adding the base tax to the product of the percentage times the excess salary over the minimum salary for that range. For example, the second line of the table specifies that the tax due on a salary of $2,000.00 is $225.00 plus 16% of the excess salary over $1,500.00 (i.e., 16% of $500.00, or $80.00). Therefore, the total tax due is $225.00 plus $80.00, or $305.00.

The **if** statement in Fig. 4.15 implements the tax table. If the value of salary is within the table range (**0.00** to **15000.00**), exactly one of the statements assigning a value to tax will execute. Table 4.12 shows a hand trace of the **if** statement when **salary** is **2000.00**. Verify for yourself that the value assigned to **tax**, **305.00**, is correct.

Table 4.11   Decision table for Example 4.17

Salary Range	Base Tax	Percentage of Excess
0.00–1499.99	0.00	15%
1500.00–2999.99	225.00	16%
3000.00–4999.99	465.00	18%
5000.00–7999.99	825.00	20%
8000.00–15,000.00	1425.00	25%

Figure 4.15   `if` statement for Table 4.11

```
if (salary < 0.00)
   System.out.println("Error!  negative salary $" + salary);
else if (salary < 1500.00)                         // First range
   tax = 0.15 * salary;
else if (salary < 3000.00)                         // Second range
   tax = (salary - 1500.00) * 0.16 + 225.0;
else if (salary < 5000.00)                         // Third range
   tax = (salary - 3000.00) * 0.18 + 465.00;
else if (salary < 8000.00)                         // Fourth range
   tax = (salary - 5000.00) * 0.20 + 825.00;
else if (salary <= 15000.00)                       // Fifth range
   tax = (salary - 8000.00) * 0.25 + 1425.00;
else
   System.out.println("Error!  too large salary $" + salary);
```

Table 4.12   Trace of `if` statement in Fig. 4.15 for `salary` = $2000.00

Statement Part	salary	tax	Effect
	2000.00	?	
if (salary < 0.0)			2000.0 < 0.0 is false.
else if (salary < 1500.00)			2000.0 < 1500.0 is false.
else if (salary < 3000.00)			2000.0 < 3000.0 is true.
tax = (salary − 1500.00)			Evaluates to 500.00.
* 0.16			Evaluates to 80.00.
+ 225.00		305.00	Evaluates to 305.00.

PROGRAM STYLE: *Validating the Value of a Variable*

If you validate the value of a variable before using it in a computation, you can avoid processing invalid or meaningless data. Instead of computing an incorrect tax amount, the `if` statement in Fig. 4.15 displays an error message if the value of **salary** is outside the range covered by the table (**0.0** to **15000.00**). The first condition detects negative salaries; an error message is displayed if **salary** is less than zero. All conditions evaluate to **false** if **salary** is greater than **15000.00**, so the task following **else** displays an error message.

switch Statement

Java provides a convenient control structure called the **switch** statement that can be used to implement a multiple-alternative decision. Figure 4.16 shows a nested **if** statement and the corresponding **switch** statement. Both statements set the value of **price** to one of five predefined values, depending on the value of **coffeeKind**. In the **switch** statement, **coffeeKind** is the **switch selector**. Its value is compared to each **case label** (0, 1, 2, 3) and the case whose label matches the value of **coffeeKind** is *selected* for execution. This means that the statements that follow the selected case execute. If the value of **coffeeKind** does not match any of the case labels, the statements that follow **default** are executed.

The **break** statements have a very important role in the **switch** statement. Execution of a **break** statement causes an immediate exit from the **switch** statement. Without the **break** statements, execution would "fall through" to the next case (and to the one after that, and so on). This would cause all assignment statements after the selected case to execute, so **price** would always be set to **priceUnknown**. Forgetting one or more **break** statements is a common error, so make sure you include them.

Figure 4.16   Nested `if` statement and `switch` statement

Nested `if` Statement	switch Statement
| ```
if (coffeeKind == 0)
    price = priceRegular;
else if (coffeeKind == 1)
    price = priceDecaf;
else if (coffeeKind == 2)
    price = priceExpresso;
else if (coffeeKind == 3)
    price = priceLatte;
else
    price = priceUnknown;
``` | ```
switch (coffeeKind) {
    case 0: price = priceRegular;
            break;
    case 1: price = priceDecaf;
            break;
    case 2: price = priceExpresso;
            break;
    case 3: price = priceLatte;
            break;
    default: price = priceUnknown;
}
``` |

`switch` statement

Form: ```
          switch (selector) {
              case label₁:
                  statement₁;
                  break;
              case label₂:
                  statement₂;
                  break;

              ...

              case labelₙ:
                  statementₙ;
                  break;
              default:
                  statementₐ;
          } // end switch
          ```

Example:  ```
          switch (n) {
            case 1:
            case 2:
              System.out.println("1, 2, Buckle my shoe");
              break;
            case 3:
            case 4:
              System.out.println("3, 4, Shut the door");
              break;
            case 5:
            case 6:
              System.out.println("5, 6, Pick up sticks");
              break;
            default:
              System.out.println(n + " is out of range");
          } // end switch
          ```

Interpretation: The *selector* expression is evaluated and compared to each *case label*. Each *case label* is a single, constant value, and each *case label* must be different from the others. If the value of the *selector* expression matches a *case label*, execution begins with the first statement following that *case label*. To prevent executing the statements associated with another *case label*, you must place a **break** statement before the next *case label*. Control passes out of the **switch** statement when a **break** statement executes.

Note 1: If the value of the *selector* does not match any *case label*, no *statement* is executed unless a **default** case label is provided. If present, the **default** statements (*statementₐ*) are executed.

Note 2: Each *case label* must be a unique value.

Note 3: The type of each *case label* must correspond to the type of the *selector* expression.

Note 4: The *selector* type must be type `int` or `char`, and the case labels must be literals of the same type as the selector.

Note 5: If a `break` statement is missing, execution "falls through" to the statements associated with the next *case label*.

Note 4 states which data types are permitted as case labels. Notice that type `boolean`, `double` and type `String` literals are not permitted.

EXERCISES FOR SECTION 4.5

SELF-CHECK

1. Trace the execution of the nested `if` statement in Example 4.17 when `salary` is `13500.00`.

PROGRAMMING

1. Rewrite the `if` statement for Example 4.16 using only the relational operator < in all conditions. Test for a failing grade first.

2. Implement the following decision table using a nested `if` statement. Assume that the grade point average is within the range `0.0` through `4.0`.

Grade Point Average	Transcript Message
0.0–0.99	Failed semester—registration suspended
1.0–1.99	On probation for next semester
2.0–2.99	(no message)
3.0–3.49	Dean's list for semester
3.5–4.0	Highest honors for semester

3. Write a Java method to return the result (type `String`) of rolling a pair of dice. Use a random-number generator to generate the six possible values of each die and return `"You Win!"` if a 7 or 11 is rolled, `"Snake Eyes!"` if a 2 is rolled, or `"Try Again."` otherwise. *Hint:* Use `(int) (6 * random () + 1)` to determine a dice roll.

4.6 Counting Loops, `while` and `for` Statements

In this section, we will show how to use a `for` statement to repeat a block of statements (a **loop**). We begin by discussing the simplest kind of loop—counting loops.

Counting Loops

In programming, we frequently encounter situations in which we need to repeat a sequence of steps a specified number of times. For example, you may want to display a particular pattern in a graphics program four times, each time in a different position. In a payroll program, if you have three different employees, you need to repeat the pay computations three times, once for each employee. A loop that executes a specified number of times is called a **counting loop** (or **counter-controlled loop**).

We can use pseudocode to write an algorithm for a counting loop that performs the payroll computation for a group of employees.

Algorithm for payroll computation for a group of employees

1. Get the number of employees.

2. For each employee starting with the first and ending with the last
   2.1 Get the current employee's payroll data.

   2.2 Store the current employee's payroll data.

   2.3 Compute the current employee's gross pay.

   2.4 Compute the current employee's net pay, given gross pay.

   2.5 Display the current employee's gross pay and net pay.

How do we get the program to recognize when it has processed the last employee? We can introduce a variable called a **counter** to count the number of employees processed so far. The counter should have an initial value of 0. The counter value should be tested before the loop begins to execute. The next iteration of the loop (steps 2.1 through 2.5 above) should be performed only if the counter value is less than the number of employees (from step 1). Loop exit should occur if the counter value is equal to or greater than the number of employees. After each iteration of the loop, the counter value should increase by 1 to indicate that another employee has been processed. The algorithm below specifies how the counter is manipulated.

Algorithm for payroll computation with counter

1. Get the number of employees.

2. Set the counter to 0.

3. While the counter value is less than the number of employees

    3.1 Get the current employee's payroll data.

    3.2 Store the current employee's payroll data.

    3.3 Compute the current employee's gross pay.

    3.4 Compute the current employee's net pay, given gross pay.

    3.5 Display the current employee's gross pay and net pay.

    3.6 Increase the counter value by 1.

The `while` Statement

We first show how to implement a counting loop using a `while` statement, the most versatile loop control statement. A `while` statement begins with the word `while` and has the form

    `while` (*repetitionCondition*)
       statement;

where *statement* represents the **loop body**, or instructions to be repeated, and can be a statement block in braces. Loop repetition is controlled by the **loop repetition condition** in parentheses. Its value (`true` or `false`) indicates whether more repetitions are required.

The program fragment in Fig. 4.17 contains a loop that processes `numberEmp` employees. The loop body (not shown) would call methods from Fig. 4.13 that read a single employee's payroll data and compute and display that employee's gross and net pay. The last statement in the loop body adds 1 to `countEmp`, which is the count of the employees processed so far. After `numberEmp` employees are processed, the loop is exited.

Figure 4.17   Counting loop with a `while` statement

```
int numberEmp = readInt("Number of employees?");
int countEmp = 0;                     // initialize countEmp
while (countEmp < numberEmp) {     // test countEmp
    // Read pay data and compute and display current employee's
    // gross pay and net pay
    . . .
    // Add one to count of employees processed
    countEmp = countEmp + 1;       // update countEmp
}
```

loop body

The three color lines in Fig. 4.17 control the looping process. The statement

```
int countEmp = 0;                    // initialize countEmp
```

declares a type `int` variable, **countEmp** (the counter variable) with an initial value of
0. The next line

```
while (countEmp < numberEmp) {    // test countEmp
```

evaluates the loop repetition condition **countEmp < numberEmp**. If it is **true**, the
next iteration of the loop body is performed. If it is **false** (**countEmp** equals
numberEmp), the loop body is exited. The last instruction in the loop body

```
countEmp = countEmp + 1;             // update countEmp
```

adds 1 to the value of **countEmp**. After this statement executes, control returns to the
line beginning with **while**, and the loop repetition condition is tested for the next
value of **countEmp**.

If **numberEmp** is 7, the loop body is executed once for each value of **countEmp**
from 0 to 6. Eventually, countEmp becomes 7, and the loop repetition condition
becomes **false**. When this happens, the loop is exited. We could just as easily have
started the count at 1 and gone to 7. We prefer starting at 0 so that the value of the
counter variable always represents the number of employees processed so far.

The `while` statement

Form: `while (repetitionCondition) {`
              loop body
          `}`

Example: `// Write n *'s to the console.`
           `countStar = 0;`
           `while (countStar < n) {`
               `System.out.print("*");`
               `countStar = countStar + 1;`
           `}`

Interpretation: The *repetitionCondition* is tested; if it is **true**, the *loop body* is executed and the *repetitionCondition* is retested. The *loop body* is repeated as long as the
repetitionCondition is true. When the *repetitionCondition* is tested and found to be
false, the loop is exited, and the next program statement after the **while** statement
is executed. *Note:* If the *repetitionCondition* evaluates to **false** the first time it is
tested, the *loop body* is not executed.

PROGRAM STYLE: *Formatting the `while` Statement*

For clarity, indent the body of a `while` loop. If the loop body contains multiple statements, you must bracket them with braces `{ }`. Braces are not required if the loop body is a single statement, but we recommend their use. You should align the closing brace under the `w` of `while`. Sometimes programmers place the comment `// end while` after the closing brace to indicate the end of a `while` loop.

Comparison of `if` and `while` Statements

The flowchart of the `while` loop in Fig. 4.18 illustrates the execution of a `while` loop. The condition in the diamond-shaped box is evaluated first. If it is `true`, the loop body is executed, and the process is repeated. The `while` loop is exited when the condition becomes `false`.

Make sure you understand the difference between the `while` statement in Fig. 4.17 and the `if` statement

```
if (countEmp < numberEmp) {
    . . .
}
```

The compound statement after the `if` condition executes at most one time. In a `while` statement, the compound statement after the condition may execute more than one time.

Loop-Control Variable

In Fig. 4.17 the variable `countEmp` is called the **loop-control variable** because its value determines whether the loop body is repeated. The loop-control variable `countEmp` must be (1) initialized, (2) tested, and (3) updated for the loop to execute properly.

Figure 4.18   Flowchart of a `while` loop

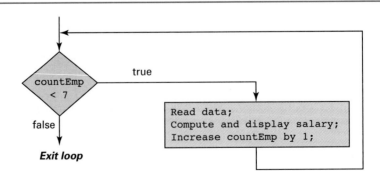

◆ Initialize—**countEmp** is set to an initial value of 0 (initialized to **0**) before the **while** statement is reached.

◆ Test—**countEmp** is tested before the start of each loop repetition (called an iteration or a pass).

◆ Update—**countEmp** is updated (its value increased by 1) during each iteration.

Similar steps must be performed for every **while** loop. Without the initialization, the initial test of **countEmp** is meaningless. The updating step ensures that the program progresses toward the final goal (**countEmp >= numberEmp**) during each repetition of the loop. If the loop-control variable is not updated, the loop will execute endlessly ("forever"). Such a loop is called an **infinite loop**.

The **for** Statement

Because counting loops are so common, most programming languages provide a special control statement for implementing them. In Java, this is the **for** statement. The **for** statement header specifies all processing of the counter variable. The **for** statement in Fig. 4.19 implements the same counting loop as the **while** statement in Fig. 4.17. The three steps listed above (initialize, test, and update the counter variable) are all enclosed in parentheses after the keyword **for**. Notice that the update step no longer appears at the end of the loop body.

We wrote the **for** statement header on three lines with comments so that you could see clearly its individual parts (*initialize*; *test*; *update*). Normally, the comments would be omitted and the **for** statement header would be written on one line:

```
for (int countEmp = 0; countEmp < numberEmp; countEmp = countEmp + 1) {
```

The initialization statement

```
int countEmp = 0;
```

Figure 4.19   Counting loop with a **for** statement

```
int numberEmp = readInt("Number of employees?");
for (int countEmp = 0;           // initialize countEmp
     countEmp < numberEmp;       // test countEmp
     countEmp = countEmp + 1     // update countEmp
     ) {
          // Read pay data and compute and display current employee's
loop      //    gross pay and net pay
body      . . .
}
```

is performed when the header is first reached. It declares `countEmp` (initial value 0) as a local variable that is visible only within the `for` statement. The testing step is performed before each iteration of the loop, including the first iteration. If the condition `countEmp < numberEmp` is `false`, the loop is exited. The update step `countEmp = countEmp + 1` is performed after each execution of the loop body.

The `for` statement

Form: `for` (*initialization statement; repetition condition; update statement*) `{`
         loop body
    `}`

Example: `// Display 10, 9, 8, . . . , 0,`
         `String temp = "";`
         `for (int i = 10; i >= 0; i = i - 1) {`
             `temp = temp + i + ", ";`
         `}`
         `System.out.println(temp);`

Interpretation: The `for` loop header summarizes the loop-control operations. The initialization statement executes when the `for` statement begins execution. Prior to each loop repetition, including the first, the repetition condition is tested. If it is `true`, the loop body executes. If it is `false`, loop exit occurs. The update statement executes after each repetition of the loop body. If you declare a variable in the initialization statement, the variable is visible only within the loop.

In the syntax display example, the loop control variable `i` gets the values 10, 9, 8, ... , 2, 1, 0, –1 and loop exit occurs when `i` is –1. The loop body appends the current value of `i` followed by a comma to the string referenced by **temp**. For example, if **temp** contains the characters 10, 9, 8 and `i` is 7, **temp** will reference a new object with the characters 10, , 9, , 8, 7, . During the last iteration of the loop body, `i` is 0, so the string that is displayed ends with the characters 0,.

◆◆EXAMPLE 4.18 ───

The fragment below uses several **String** methods listed in Table 2.6.

```
String str = "Java is fun";
//Replace each vowel in String str with a *
for (int i = 0; i < str.length(); i = i + 1) {
    if ("AEIOUaeiou".indexOf(str.charAt(i)) > -1)
        str = str.substring(0, i) + "*" + str.substring(i+1);
}
```

It replaces each vowel in a string with an asterisk. The counter variable `i` starts at 0 (the position of the first character in a string) and ends at **str.length()** — 1, the position of the last character in **String str**. Therefore, during each iteration of the loop, **str.charAt(i)** accesess the next character in string **str** (the one at position **i**). The **if** condition

```
("AEIOUaeiou".indexOf(str.charAt(i)) > -1)
```

is **true** if the character at position **i** is a vowel. If so, the assignment statement executes and **str** references a new **String** object containing the characters in **str** up to position **i**, the character *****, and the characters in **str** following position **i**. If **str** references a **String** object containing the characters **Java is fun!** and **i** is 1, **str** will reference a new **String** object containing the characters **J*va is fun!**. After loop exit, **str** will reference a **String** object containing the characters **J*v* *s f*n!**.

◆◆

PROGRAM STYLE: *Declaring Counter Variables in the* **for** *Loop Header*

In the **for** statement examples above, we declare and initialize the loop control variable in the **for** loop header. This is common practice in Java and results in the loop-control variable being visible (accessible) only in the block consisting of the loop. If you attempt to reference the loop-control variable outside of the loop, you will get an **"Undefined variable"** syntax error.

Accumulating a Sum

Loops often accumulate a sum by repeating an addition operation. In the program fragment below

```
int sum = 0;
// Read 3 integers and add them up
for (int n = 0; n < 3; n = n + 1) {
   nextNum = readInt("Enter an integer");
   sum = sum + nextNum;
}
```

the variable **sum** is an **accumulator**, a variable used for accumulating a total. In the loop body, the assignment statement

```
sum = sum + nextNum;
```

adds the next data item to the total being accumulated in sum. Consequently, the value of **sum** increases with each loop iteration. Figure 4.20 traces the effect of executing the loop with data of 10, 20, 5.

Figure 4.20   Accumulating a sum

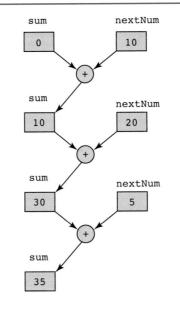

◆◆EXAMPLE 4.19

In Figs. 4.15 and 4.19, we showed an algorithm for a loop that could be used to read pay data for a group of employees and compute each employee's gross pay and net pay. Fig/ 4.21 describes class **CompanyPayroll** that has a data field **payroll** and a method **calculatePayroll()** for calculating a company's payroll that is based on these algorithms. Figure 4.22 shows the class.

In method **calculatePayroll()**, we ask the user to enter the number of employees (value of **numberEmp**) before the loop begins. The steps in the loop body are based on an earlier application that processed a single employee's payroll data (see method **main()** of Fig. 4.14). We store each employee's payroll data, in turn, in **Employee** object **programmer**. We compute the current employee's gross pay and net pay. The statement

```
payroll = payroll + gross;
```

adds each employee's gross pay to the sum being accumulated in data field **payroll**. Next, we write the current employee's results to the console window. After processing the specified number of employees, the loop is exited.

Figure 4.21   Class CompanyPayroll

Data Fields	Attributes
double payroll	The total gross payroll amount
Methods	**Behavior**
double calculatePayroll()	Calculates gross and net pay for each employee and accumulates total payroll
double readDouble()	Reads a type **double** input value
int readInt()	Reads a type **int** input value
double getPayroll()	Gets the value of payroll
Classes Used	
Employee, JOptionPane	

To run a payroll program we need an application class that contains a **main** method whose task is to invoke method **calculatePayroll()** and then display the final payroll value. Figure 4.23 shows class **RunPayoll**, and Fig. 4.24 shows a sample run of this class for two employees.

◆◆

Increment, Decrement, and Compound Operators

The earlier **for** statement examples contained update statements such as

```
countEmp = countEmp + 1;
i = i - 1;
```

Because these operations are so common, Java provides special operators that you can use to write these statements in a more compact form. The first statement below uses the **increment operator ++** to increase the value of countEmp by 1, and the second statement uses the **decrement operator --** to decrease the value of **i** by 1.

```
countEmp++;     // increment countEmp by 1.
i--;            // decrement i by 1.
```

Similarly, Java provides **compound operators** for shortening statements such as

```
payroll = payroll + gross;
```

Figure 4.22 Class `CompanyPayroll`

```
/*
 * CompanyPayroll.java       Authors: Koffman and Wolz
 * Class that can calculate a company payroll.
 * Uses class Employee and JOptionPane.
 */
import javax.swing.JOptionPane;

public class CompanyPayroll {
   // Data field
  private double payroll;    // total company payroll

  // methods
  private static double readDouble(String prompt) {
    String numStr = JOptionPane.showInputDialog(prompt);
    return Double.parseDouble(numStr);
  }

  private static int readInt(String prompt) {
    String numStr = JOptionPane.showInputDialog(prompt);
    return Integer.parseInt(numStr);
  }

  // precondition: payroll is zero
  // postcondition: payroll is sum of all gross pay amounts
  public void calculatePayroll() {
    // Process all employees
    int numberEmp = readInt("How many employees?");
    for (int countEmp = 0; countEmp < numberEmp;
        countEmp = countEmp + 1) {
      // Store the payroll data in a new Employee object.
      Employee programmer =
        new Employee(
            JOptionPane.showInputDialog("Enter employee id"),
            readDouble("Enter hours worked"),
            readDouble("Enter hourly rate")
        );

      // Compute employee gross pay.
      double gross = programmer.computeGross();

      // Compute employee net pay, given gross pay.
      double net = programmer.computeNet(gross);
```

Figure 4.22   **CompanyPayroll,** *continued*

```java
        // Add gross pay to payroll
        payroll = payroll + gross;

        // Write pay data and results to console.
        System.out.println(programmer.toString());
        System.out.println("Gross pay is $" + gross);
        System.out.println("Net pay is $" + net + "\n");
    }  // end for
  }

  public double getPayroll() {
    return payroll;
  }
}
```

Figure 4.23   **Class** **RunPayroll**

```java
/*
 * RunPayroll.java       Authors: Koffman and Wolz
 * Application class that uses CompanyPayroll
 */
public class RunPayroll {

  public static void main (String[] args) {
    // Create a CompanyPayroll object
    CompanyPayroll cP = new CompanyPayroll();

    // Calculate the payroll
    cP.calculatePayroll();

    // Display the result.
    System.out.println("Total gross payroll is " +
                    cP.getPayroll());
  }
}
```

Figure 4.24   **Sample run of class `RunPayroll`**

```
RunPayroll                                          _ □ ✕
Employee id: 1234, hours: 40.0, rate: $25.0
Gross pay is $1000.0
Net pay is $975.0

Employee id: 2345, hours: 50.0, rate: $10.0
Gross pay is $550.0
Net pay is $525.0

Total gross payroll is 1550.0
```

You can write this as

```
payroll += gross;
```

The compound operators are `+=`, `-=`, `*=`, and `/=`, written without spaces between the two operators. The first operator (`+` in `+=`) is performed on the variable being assigned (`payroll`) and the expression on the right (`gross`). The result is assigned to the variable on the left (`payroll`). If the expression on the right contains an operator, you should surround the entire expression in parentheses.

EXERCISES FOR SECTION 4.6

SELF-CHECK

1. How many times is the following loop body repeated? What is printed during each repetition of the loop body and after exit?

```
x = 3;
for (int count = 0; count < 3; count++) {
    x = x * x;
    System.out.println(x);
}
System.out.println(x);
```

2. Repeat Exercise 1 when the last statement in the loop header is

```
count = count + 2;
```

3. Repeat Exercise 1 when the last statement in the loop body is omitted.

4. What output values are displayed by the following fragment for a data value of 5?

```
int num = readInt("Enter an integer:");
int product = 1;
for (int count = 0; count < 4; count++) {
    System.out.print(product + ", ");
    product *= num;
}
System.out.println(product);
```

What values are displayed if the call to **print()** comes at the end of the loop instead of at the beginning?

5. What mathematical result does the following fragment compute and display?

```
int x = readInt("Enter x:");
int yFirst = readInt("Enter y:");
int product = 1;
for (int y = yFirst; y > 0; y--) {
    product *= x;
}
System.out.println("result = " + product);
```

6. How would you modify class RunPayroll in Fig. 4.23 to display the average gross salary and net salary in addition to the totals? Rewrite the statement in Fig. 4.22 that adds **gross** to **payroll** using a compound operator.

PROGRAMMING

1. Write a loop that displays each integer from 1 to 5 and its square on a separate line.

2. Write a loop that displays each even integer from 4 down to -6 on a separate line. Display the values in the sequence 4, 2, 0, and so on.

3. When Robin's new baby was born, she opened a savings account with $1000. On each birthday, starting with the first, the bank added an additional 4.5% of the balance and Robin added another $500 to the account. Write a loop that will determine how much money was in the account on the child's 18th birthday.

4.7 State-Controlled Loops

We can categorize most loops as either counter-controlled or state-controlled loops. In the former, repetition is controlled by a counter variable and the loop repeats a specified number of times. In a **state-controlled loop**, or **general conditional loop**, repetition stops when a state is reached that causes the loop-repetition condition to become `false`. We can express a state-controlled loop in pseudocode as:

State-controlled loop

> while stopping state has not been reached
>   Execute the steps in loop body

In our earlier counting loops to process multiple employees, the program asked the user for the number of employees to process before executing the loop. If this information is not available, we can use a state-controlled loop instead. After each employee is processed, the user can indicate whether there are more employees to process. Loop execution continues if there are more employees to process; loop execution stops when the state "there are no more employees" is reached.

In a state-contolled loop, we often use a `boolean` variable as a **loop-control variable (lcv)**. The loop-control variable controls the looping process. If the value of the loop-control variable is `true`, the loop should be repeated. If the value of the loop-control variable is `false`, the loop should be exited. The loop pattern below shows the steps that involve the loop-control variable in color.

State-controlled loop with a `boolean` loop-control variable

> Set the loop-control variable to true
> while (the loop-control variable is true) {
>   Execute the steps in the loop body
>   Update the loop-control variable
> }

In our payroll program, we can use `moreEmp` as the loop-control variable. If the value of `moreEmp` is `true`, there are more employees to process. The three steps that involve the loop-control variable `moreEmp` are

1. **Initialize**—set the value of `moreEmp` to `true`.

2. **Test**—test the value of `moreEmp` before each execution of the loop body. If `moreEmp` is `true`, the loop body executes. If `moreEmp` is `false`, loop execution stops.

3. **Update**—reset the value of `moreEmp` after each loop iteration.

The program fragment below implements these steps in Java. It begins by setting `moreEmp` to `true` because we assume there is always one employee to process. We call method `readBoolean()` (see Fig. 4.2) to update the loop-control variable.

```
boolean moreEmp = true;
while (moreEmp) {
   // Compute and display current employee's information.
   . . .
   moreEmp = readBoolean("Any more employees?");
}
```

The `while` condition tests the value of `moreEmp` before each loop iteration. The last statement in the loop body displays a dialog window asking whether there are more employees. If the user selects `Yes`, `moreEmp` is set to `true`; if the user selects `No`, `moreEmp` is set to `false`. Because the initial value of `moreEmp` is `true`, the loop body executes at least one time. The loop continues to execute until the program user selects `No`. At this point the state "there are no more employees to process" is reached.

Sentinel-Controlled Loops

Rather than ask the user if there is more data, we can designate a special data value called the **sentinel value** to stop loop repetition. If the user enters a value that is not the sentinel, the next loop iteration occurs. If the user enters the sentinel value, the loop is exited. The program should ask the user to enter the first data item just before entering the loop. The program should ask the user to enter the next data item (or the sentinel) at the end of each loop iteration. The loop pattern for a **sentinel-controlled loop** follows:

> *Sentinel-controlled loop*
>
> > Get the first data item or the sentinel
> > while the data item is not the sentinel
> > > Process the current data item
> > > Get the next data item or the sentinel

Notice that the sentinel value is not processed in the loop body. Loop exit would occur when the loop repetition test determined that the data item just read was the sentinel.

What makes a good sentinel value? The sentinel value should be a value that would not normally be entered as data by the program user. For example, in a loop that processes exam scores from 0 to 100, –1 would be a good sentinel value.

◆◆EXAMPLE 4.20 ──

Class **Exams** in Figure 4.25 contains two data fields, **sum** and **count**, that represent the sum of all exam scores and the number of students taking an exam (both initially zero). Method **findSumAndCount()** determines the sum of all exam scores and the number of students who took the exam. The loop reads each student's exam score into `score` and adds it to `sum`. The initialize and update steps both call method `readInt()` to read the next score:

```
score = readInt("Enter next score or " + SENTINEL +
                  " to stop");    // initialize lcv
```

Notice that the sentinel value is read, but it is not added to the sum being accumulated. After loop exit, the data field `sum` stores the sum of all actual student scores.

The variable `count` is not used for loop control but is used to count the number of scores that were processed. During each iteration of the loop, `count` is incremented. Method `findAverage()` calculates the average score by dividing `sum` by `count`.

```
average = (double) sum / (double) count;
```

The casting operation converts each integer value to a real number before the division; otherwise, `/` would mean integer division and the fractional part of the result would be lost. The `if` statement **guards the assignment statement** so that it only executes when `count` is greater than zero, thereby preventing a division-by-zero error.

Figure 4.25   Class Exams

```
/*
 * Exams.java        Authors: Koffman and Wolz
 * Class that can calculate average score on an exam.
 * Uses class JOptionPane.
 */
import javax.swing.JOptionPane;

public class Exams {
    // Data fields
    private int sum;        // sum of scores
    private int count;      // count of scores

    // methods
    public static int readInt(String prompt) {
      String numStr = JOptionPane.showInputDialog(prompt);
      return Integer.parseInt(numStr);
    }
```

Figure 4.25   **Class Exams,** *continued*

```
// preconditions: count and sum are zero
// postconditions: data field sum stores the sum of scores
//    data field count stores the count of scores
public void findSumAndCount() {
  int score;
  int SENTINEL = -1;    // sentinel value
  score = readInt("Enter next score or " + SENTINEL +
                  " to stop");         // initialize lcv
  while (score != SENTINEL) {          // test lcv
    sum += score;                      // add current score to sum
    count++;                           // increase count by 1
    System.out.println("score: " + score);
    score = readInt("Enter next score or " + SENTINEL +
                    " to stop");       // update lcv

  }
}

// precondition: sum and count are defined
// postcondition: Returns the average score
public  double findAve() {
  double average;        // average score

  if (count > 0)
     average = (double) sum / (double) count;
  else
     average = 0;
  return average;
}
}
```

Figure 4.26 shows an application class that tests class **Exams,** and Fig. 4.27 shows a sample run of this class.

Figure 4.26   Class TestExams

```
/*
 * TestExams.java       Authors: Koffman and Wolz
 * Application that tests class Exams.
 */
public class TestExams {

  public static void main(String[] args) {
    Exams ex = new Exams();
    ex.findSumAndCount();
    System.out.println("Average score is " + ex.findAve());
  }
}
```

Figure 4.27   Sample run of TestExams

```
TestExams
score: 65
score: 70
score: 50
score: 80
Average score is 66.25
```

Loops and Event-Driven Programming

As you will see in Chapter 7, very little "looping" is needed to manage user input when you program GUIs directly. There is an event model that manages the complex inter-action between the user and the GUI to control the repetition for you. Keep this in mind as you implement solutions based on the loop forms just discussed. In a sense we are teaching you the "old-fashioned way" of doing things. Often, as you solve one of the programming exercises, you may find that your user interface simply isn't as friendly and naturally interactive as you would like. Think about its limitations. This will help prepare you for problem solving in GUI environments.

EXERCISES FOR SECTION 4.7

SELF-CHECK

1. Trace the execution of the sentinel-controlled loop in class **Exams** (Fig. 4.25) assuming scores of 50, 70, 80, and –I.

2. Modify the loop in class **Exams** to be a state-controlled loop that uses the **boolean** variable **moreStudents** to control loop repetition. Use method **readBoolean()** to read a **boolean** data value. Show the modified algorithm and implement the loop in Java.

PROGRAMMING

1. There are 9870 people in a town whose population increases by 10% each year. Write a loop that determines how many years (**countYears**) it would take for the population to go over 30,000.

2. Write a program to maintain a checkbook. It should first ask for a balance. Then, it should ask for transactions, with deposits entered as positive values and checks entered as negative values. After each check or deposit, the new balance should be printed. Use **0** as a sentinel value.

3. Write a program segment that asks the user to enter values and prints out the number of positive values entered and the number of negative values entered. The program should stop when the user enters **0**.

4. Write a loop that displays all powers of an integer *n* that are less than a specified value, **maxPower**. On each line of a table, show the power (0, 1, 2,...) and the value of the integer *n* raised to that power.

5. Write a loop that prints a table of angle measures along with their sine and cosine values. Assume that the initial and final angle measures (in degrees) are read into **initDeg** and **finalDeg** (type **double**), respectively, and that the change in angle measure between table entries is read into **stepDeg**. *Hint:* Don't forget to change degrees to radians.

4.8 Putting It All Together

This chapter covered many of the control statements in Java. In the next case study, we develop methods that incorporate most of these control statements.

CASE STUDY   A PROGRAM FOR ARITHMETIC DRILL AND PRACTICE

PROBLEM   Your little sister would like a program that gives her some practice in solving arithmetic problems. She would like a program that can generate and solve arithmetic problems of varying difficulty and would like to be able to specify the problem type (addition, multiplication, and so on) and the difficulty level (easy, moderate, hard). Your program should generate a problem and solve it. It should also compare its solution to your sister's and let her know whether her solution is correct.

ANALYSIS   We need a class that can generate and solve simple arithmetic problems (class `MathProblem`). A math problem is represented by its operator and by its left and right operands. The class should have a constructor method to generate a simple problem and a method to solve it. The operands should be randomly generated integers. The operands should get bigger as the difficulty level increases.

We also need a class that can interact with the user to determine the type of problem she wants and to keep track of her progress. This class should compare her answers to the correct solutions and count the number of correct and incorrect answers.

DESIGN

Class `MathProblem`

The primary responsibilities of class `MathProblem` are to generate and solve math problems. We will use a constructor method to generate a problem. Figure 4.28 shows a description for class `MathProblem`.

Figure 4.28   Class `MathProblem`

Data Fields	Attributes

`char operator`
`int left`
`int right`
	The operator for the problem (+, −, *, /, %)
	The left operand
	The right operand

Methods	**Behavior**
`MathProblem(char, int)`	Generates a math problem with the specified operator and difficulty level
`boolean validOperator(char)`	Tests whether the proposed operator is valid
`int solveProblem()`	Solves a math problem
`String toString()`	Represents a math problem as a string
`String askProblem()`	Returns a string asking for the solution to a problem

The algorithms for the methods of this class follow.

Algorithm for `MathProblem()` (class `MathProblem`)

1. Store the operator.

2. Generate a random integer for the left operand that is appropriate for the difficulty level.

3. Generate a random integer for the right operand that is appropriate for the difficulty level.

Algorithm for ***solveProblem()*** *(class* **MathProblem***)*

1. switch (operator) {

       case '+': result is sum of **left** and **right**;

       case '—': result is difference of **left** and **right**;

       case '*': result is product of **left** and **right**;

       case '/': result is integer quotient of **left** divided by **right**;

       case '%': result is integer remainder of **left** divided by **right**;

    }

2. return result.

Algorithm for ***validOperator()*** *(class* **MathProblem***)*

1. Return true if the operator is '+', '-', '*', or '/'.

Class MathDrill

Class **MathDrill** must generate a series of problems (method **doMultipleProblems()**) and evaluate the student's answer to each problem (method **getAndCheckAnswer()**). Fig. 4.29 shows a description of class **MathDrill**.

Figure 4.29   Class MathDrill

Data Items	Attributes
int correct	Number of correct answers
int incorrect	Number of incorrect answers
Methods	**Behavior**
void doMultipleProblems()	Gets the data from the user, generates a new problem and its solution, gets and checks the user's answer; repeats these steps until the user is finished
void getAndCheckAnswer(MathProblem)	Solves the problem, gets the user's answer and determines whether it is correct or incorrect and increments corresponding counter
Classes Used	
MathProblem, KeyIn	

*Algorithm for **doMultipleProblems()** (class **MathDrill**)*

1. Set **moreProblems** to **true**

2. **while** **moreProblems** is **true**

   2.1 Get the operator and difficulty level.

   2.2 Create a new math problem.

   2.3 **If** the operator is valid

   Get and Check the student's answer

   2.4 See whether the user wants another problem.

*Algorithm for **getAndCheckAnswer()** (class **MathDrill**)*

1. Solve the problem.

2. Get the student's answer.

3. **if** the anwers match

   Display a congratulatory message

   Increment count of correct answers

   else

   Increment count of incorrect answers

   Display the correct answer

IMPLEMENTATION   Classes **MathProblem** and **MathDrill** are shown in Figs. 4.30 and 4.31. Figure 4.32 shows the application class **RunMathDrill**. Program execution begins with method **main()** in **RunMathDrill**. It calls method **doMultipleProblems()** in class **MathDrill** and displays the final counts of correct and incorrect answers after this method finishes.

Inside the loop of method **doMulitpleProblems()**, the statement

```
MathProblem mP = new MathProblem(op, diff);
```

calls the constructor for class **MathProblem()** to create a new math problem with operator **op** and difficulty **diff** as specified by the program user. In the constructor **MathProblem()**, the statements

```
left = (int) (Math.pow(10, diff) * Math.random() + 1);
right = (int) (Math.pow(10, diff) * Math.random() + 1);
```

define the values of data fields left and right. Method `pow()` returns 10 raised to the power `diff` (1, 2, or 3). The method result will be 10, 100, or 1000. This number is multiplied by a random integer between 0 and 1, and the integer part of the product plus 1 is assigned to left or right. For example, if method `random()` returns `0.23452`, the value assigned will be `3` (when `diff` is 1), `24` (when `diff` is 2), or `235` (when `diff` is 3).

Back in `doMultipleProblems()`, the `if` statement condition (`mP.validOp()`) tests whether the problem operator is valid (`+`, `-`, `*`, or `/`). If so, method `getAndCheckAnswer()` is called. The method header

```java
private void getAndCheckAnswer(MathProblem mP) {
```

shows that the method receives the problem to be checked as an argument. The method visibility is `private` because this method is used only within class `MathDrill`. The first statement in the method

```java
int correctAnswer = mP.solveProblem();
```

calls method `solveProblem()` (in class `MathProblem`) to calculate the correct answer and stores the result in `correctAnswer`. The `if` statement condition compares the correct answer to the student's answer, saves an appropriate feedback message, and increments either the counter `correct` or the counter `incorrect`. The feedback message is displayed and the loop continues to execute until the user indicates that she does not want any more problems.

Notice that each time the loop executes, it creates another object of type `MathProblem`. If the loop executes 10 times, storage will allocated for 10 different objects. However, variable `mP` will reference only the most recently created object. The other nine objects are not referenced by any variable, so they are no longer accessible and their storage space can be reclaimed and reallocated. We don't have to concern ourselves with this. Reclaiming storage space that is no longer needed is called **garbage collection**, and it is done automatically in Java.

PROGRAM STYLE: *Using class KeyIn*

We have tried to minimize the use of class `KeyIn` so that the programs in this book are written in standard Java. However, because class `MathDrill` calls data entry methods for three primitive types (`boolean`, `char`, and `int`), we decided to use the `KeyIn` class rather than implement the data entry methods. Method `readChar()` has not been discussed yet. It displays its argument `prompt` in a dialog window and returns the first character typed in.

```java
public char readChar(String prompt) {
   String charStr = JOptionPane.showInputDialog(prompt);
   return charStr.charAt(0);
}
```

Figure 4.30 Class `MathProblem`

```java
/*
 * MathProblem.java        Authors: Koffman and Wolz
 * Class that can generate and solve math problems.
 * Uses class JOptionPane.
 */
public class MathProblem {

    // Data fields
    private int left;         // left operand
    private int right;        // right operand
    private char operator;    // *, /, +, or -

    // methods
    // constructor
    // postcondition: stores operator and difficulty level.
    //     Sets left and right based on difficulty level.
    public MathProblem(char op, int diff) {
        operator = op;
        left = (int) (Math.pow(10, diff) * Math.random() + 1);
        right = (int) (Math.pow(10, diff) * Math.random() + 1);
    }

    // postcondition: returns the answer to the math problem
    public int solveProblem() {
      int result;
      switch (operator) {
        case '+' : result = left + right;  break;
        case '-' : result = left - right;  break;
        case '*' : result = left * right;  break;
        case '/' : result = left / right;  break;
        case '%' : result = left % right;  break;
        default: result = -1;
      }

      return result;
    }

    // postcondition: returns true if the operator is valid
    public boolean validOp() {
      return (operator == '+') || (operator == '-') ||
             (operator == '*') || (operator == '/') ||
             (operator == '%');
    }
```

Figure 4.30   Class `MathProblem,` *continued*

```
        // postcondition: returns the problem as a String
        public String toString() {
          return left + " " + operator + " " + right;
        }

        // postcondition: returns a string prompting the user
        //   to solve the problem
        public String askProblem() {
          return toString() + " = ?";
        }
      }
```

Figure 4.31   Class `MathDrill`

```
/*
 * MathDrill.java        Authors: Koffman and Wolz
 * Class that generates multiple math problems
 * and monitors the user's performance.
 * Uses class MathProblem and KeyIn.
 */
import psJava.KeyIn;
import javax.swing.JOptionPane;

public class MathDrill {
    private int correct;      // count of correct answers
    private int incorrect;    // count of incorrect answers

    // methods
    public char readChar(String prompt) {
      String charStr = JOptionPane.showInputDialog(prompt);
      return charStr.charAt(0);
    }

    // postcondition: Gives a number of arithmetic problems and evaluates
    //    the user's solution. The number of correct answers is stored in
    //    correct and the number of incorrect answers is stored in incorrect.
    public void doMultipleProblems() {
        // Generate, solve, and grade multiple math problems
        boolean moreProblems = true;
        while (moreProblems) {
          // Get new problem operator and difficulty.
          char op = readChar("Enter operator (+, -, *, /, %)");
```

Figure 4.31   **Class** `MathDrill`, *continued*

```
        int diff =
            KeyIn.readInt("Enter difficulty level - 1, 2, 3 (highest)");

        // Generate new problem based on user's specification.
        MathProblem mP = new MathProblem(op, diff);

        // If the operator is valid, get and check the student's answer.
        if (mP.validOp())
            getAndCheckAnswer(mP);
        else
            System.out.println("Bad operator - try again");

        // See if user wants another problem.
        moreProblems = KeyIn.readBoolean("Try another problem?");
    } // end while
}


// precondition: mP is a valid math problem
// postcondition: increments correct or incorrect based on user's answer.
//     Also tells user she is correct or gives the correct answer
private void getAndCheckAnswer(MathProblem mP) {
    int correctAnswer = mP.solveProblem();
    int userAnswer = KeyIn.readInt(mP.askProblem());
    String feedback;
    if (userAnswer == correctAnswer) {
        feedback = "correct, " + mP.toString() + " IS " +
                    userAnswer + " - good work";
        correct++;
    }
    else {
        feedback = "incorrect, " + mP.toString() +
                    " is " + correctAnswer;
        incorrect++;
    }
    JOptionPane.showMessageDialog(null, feedback);
    System.out.println(feedback);
}

public int getCorrect() { return correct; }

public int getIncorrect() { return incorrect; }
}
```

Figure 4.32   Class RunMathDrill

```
/*
 * RunMathDrill.java       Authors: Koffman and Wolz
 * Application that tests class MathProblem.
 */
public class RunMathDrill {

   public static void main(String[] args) {

      MathDrill mD = new MathDrill();

      mD.doMultipleProblems();

      System.out.println("You had " + mD.getCorrect() +
                         " correct answers and " +
                         mD.getIncorrect() + " incorrect answers");
   }
}
```

TESTING   To test this program, run it with several problems, choosing different degrees of difficulty. You should check that the problem operands are in the correct range and that the program generates the correct answer. Also, make sure that the counts of correct and incorrect answers are accurate. Fig. 4.33 shows the user interaction for one problem, and Fig. 4.34 shows the console window after several problems.

Figure 4.33   User interaction for a problem

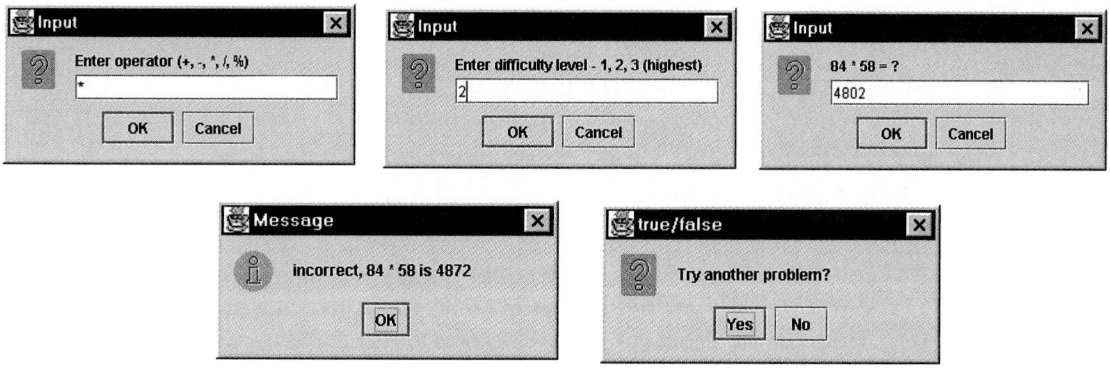

Figure 4.34   Console window for execution of `RunMathDrill`

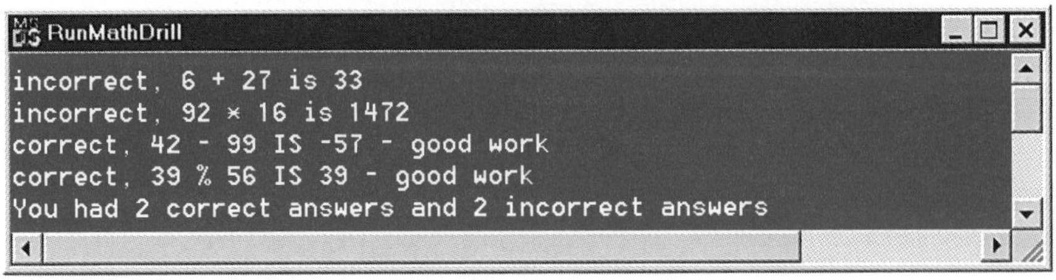

4.9   Debugging and Testing Programs with Decisions and Loops

In Section 3.8 we described the three general categories of errors: syntax, run-time, and logic errors. Sometimes the cause of a run-time error or the source of a logic error is apparent and the error can be fixed easily. Often, however, the error is not obvious and you may spend considerable time and energy locating it.

The first step in locating a hidden error is to examine the program output to determine which part of the program is generating incorrect results. Then you can focus on the statements in that section of the program to determine which are at fault. We describe two ways to do this.

Using a Debugger

Modern Integrated Development Environments (IDEs) include features to help you debug a program while it is executing. In this section, we describe these features in a general way. Specific details for Borland JBuilder are provided in Appendix A.

You can use a debugger to observe changes in variables as the program executes. Debuggers enable you to **single-step** through a program or to execute one statement at a time. Before starting execution, you indicate to the IDE that you want to debug or trace the program's execution. Instead of selecting **Run**, you select **trace into** or **step over**. The next statement to execute will be highlighted (or pointed to by a cursor arrow or both). You instruct the IDE to execute the next statement by selecting **trace into** or **step over**. As each program statement executes, the value of each visible variable is updated and you can inspect the changes. With single-step execution you can validate that loop-control variables and other important variables (e.g., accumulators) are incremented as expected during each iteration of a loop. You can also check that input variables contain the correct data after each input operation.

Some debuggers show the value of each variable that is visible in a separate window while you are debugging. You can also add the names of variables that you want to observe to a special **watch window**.

The options **trace into** and **step over** act differently when you execute a method call. The **trace into** option enables you to execute each statement in a method individually. The **step over** option executes the method as a single unit instead of tracing through its individual statements. If a method executes many times and you have verified that it works correctly, you can select **step over** instead of tracing through it.

You may not want to single-step through all the statements in your program. You can place the cursor at a specific statement and then select **Run to cursor**. When the program stops at the cursor location, you can check to see if the variables you are interested in have correct values.

You can also divide your program into segments by setting **breakpoints** at selected statements. A breakpoint is like a fence between two segments of a program. You should set a breakpoint at the end of each major algorithm step. Then instruct the debugger to execute the statements from the last breakpoint up to the next one. When the program stops at a breakpoint, you can examine the variables to determine whether the program segment has executed correctly. If it has, you will want to execute through to the next breakpoint. If it has not, you will want to single-step through that segment.

Debugging without a Debugger

If you cannot use a debugger, insert extra **diagnostic output statements** to display intermediate results at critical points in your program. For example, you should display the values of variables affected by each major algorithm step before and after the step executes. By comparing these results, you may be able to determine which segment of your program contains bugs.

◆◆EXAMPLE 4.21 ━━━━━━━━━━━━━━━━━━━━━━━━━━━━━━━━━━━

Assume the loop in Fig. 4.25 is not computing the correct sum. The diagnostic output statement in color below will display each value of **sum** and **count**. The asterisks highlight the diagnostic output in the console window and also show the diagnostic output statements in the source program.

```
score = readInt("Enter next score or " + SENTINEL +
                " to stop");        // initialize lcv
while (score != SENTINEL) {         // test lcv
   sum += score;                    // add current score to sum
   count++;                         // increase count by 1
   System.out.println("score: " + score);
   System.out.println("****** sum is " + sum +
                   ", count is " + count);
   score = readInt("Enter next score or " + SENTINEL +
                " to stop");        // update lcv
}
```

Be careful when you insert diagnostic output statements. Sometimes you must add braces if a single statement inside an `if` or a `while` statement becomes a compound statement when you add a diagnostic output statement.

After it appears that you have located the error, take out the diagnostic output statements. As a temporary measure, turn the diagnostic statements into comments by prefixing them with `//`. If similar errors occur in later testing, it is easier to remove the `//` than to retype the diagnostic statements.

◆◆

Testing

After you have corrected all errors and the program appears to execute as expected, test the program again thoroughly to make sure that it works. If the program contains a decision statement, check all paths through this statement. Make enough test runs to verify that the program works properly for representative samples of all possible data combinations. We discuss testing again in Section 6.8.

4.10 Common Programming Errors

`if` Statement Errors

You can use the **boolean** operators, `&&` (and), `||` (or), and `!` (not), only with **boolean** expressions. In the expression

```
flag && (x == y)
```

the variable `flag` must be type **boolean**. The expression would be valid without the parentheses because `==` has higher precedence than `&&`; however, the parentheses make the meaning clearer. Make sure you do not use = instead of ==; this would cause a Java syntax error.

Don't forget to use braces `{}` around a compound statement used as a **true** or a **false** task. If the braces are missing, only the first statement will be considered part of the task, and a syntax error might occur. In the incorrect fragment below, the braces around the **true** task are missing. The compiler assumes that the `if` statement ends with the assignment statement. You will get a syntax error after the line **else** because a statement cannot begin with **else**.

```
// incorrect if statement with missing { , }
if (x > 0)
    sum = sum + x;
    System.out.println("X is positive");
else
    System.out.println("X is not positive");
```

When writing a nested **if** statement, try to select the conditions so that you can use the multiple-alternative format shown in Section 4.7. If more than one condition can be **true** at the same time, place the most restrictive condition first.

Remember that the Java compiler matches each **else** with the closest unmatched **if**. If you are not careful, you may get a pairing that is different from what you expect. This may not cause a syntax error, but it will affect the outcome. When in doubt, use braces to specify your intent.

In **switch** statements, make sure the **switch** selector and case labels are of the same ordinal type (**int** or **char**, but not **double**, **boolean**, or **String**). Remember that no value may appear in more than one **switch** label. Use a **default** label to display a warning message if the selector evaluates to a value not listed in any of the case labels.

Make sure you use = and == properly. An assigment statement such as

```
int x ;
x == 5;          // should be =, not ==
```

causes the compiler error **Invalid declaration**. A condition such as (**x = 5**) in the fragment below

```
int x = 3;
if (x = 5)       // should be ==, not =
    x = 7;
```

causes a more obscure error message: **Error: Incompatible type for if. Can't convert int to boolean**. The expression x = 5 has a value of 5. The integer 5 cannot be converted to type **boolean**.

Loop Errors

Beginners sometimes confuse **if** and **while** statements because both statements contain a condition. Make sure that you use an **if** statement to implement a decision step and a **while** statement to implement a loop.

Be careful when you use tests for inequality to control the repetition of a **while** loop. For instance, the following loop is intended to process all transactions for a bank account while the balance is positive:

```
while (balance != 0) {
    double transaction = KeyIn.readInt("Next transaction:");
    update(transaction);
}
```

If the bank balance goes from a positive to a negative amount without being exactly 0, the loop will not terminate (an **infinite loop**). This loop would be safer:

```
while (balance > 0) {
   double transaction = Keyboard.readInt("Next transaction:");
   update(transaction);
}
```

If the loop body is a compound statement, make sure you enclose it in braces. Otherwise, only the first statement will be repeated, and the remaining statements will be executed when and if the loop is exited. The loop below will not terminate because the statement that updates the loop-control variable is not considered part of the loop body. The program will continue to print the initial value of **power** until you instruct the computer to terminate its execution.

```
while (power <= 10000)
   System.out.println("Next power of n is " + power);
   power = power * n;            // update power—not part of loop
```

Initialize to **0** an accumulator variable used for accumulating a sum by repeated addition. However, initialize to **1** a variable used for accumulating a product by repeated multiplication. Omitting this step may lead to incorrect results.

Be careful about the visibility of data. A variable declared in a block is only visible within that block. So if you declare a variable in a loop, you cannot reference that variable outside the loop. If you attempt to do so, you will get an **undeclared variable** error.

Off-by-One Loop Errors

A fairly common logic error in programs with loops is caused by a loop that executes one more time or one less time than it is supposed to. If a sentinel-controlled loop performs an extra repetition, it may erroneously process the sentinel value along with the regular data.

If a counting loop performs a counting operation, make sure that the initial and final values of the loop-control variable are correct. For example, the loop body below executes **n + 1** times instead of **n** times. If you want the loop body to execute exactly **n** times, change the condition to **count < n**.

```
for (int count = 0; count <= n; count++) {
   sum += count;
}
```

Checking Loop Boundaries

You should always check the loop boundaries, that is, the initial and final values of the loop-control variable. Determine the initial and final values of the loop-control variable and make sure that these values make sense. Next, substitute these values everywhere the loop-control variable appears in the loop body and verify that you get the expected results at the boundaries.

◆◆EXAMPLE 4.22 ───

In the **for** loop below

```
k = 1;
sum = 0;
for (i = -n; i < n - k; i++) {
    sum += (i * i);
}
```

check that the first value of the counter variable **i** is supposed to be **-n** and that the last value is supposed to be **n** - 2. Next check that the assignment statement

```
sum += (i * i);
```

is correct at these boundaries. When **i** is **-n**, **sum** gets the value of ^{k} squared. When **i** is **n** - 2, the value of $(n - 2)^2$ is added to the previous **sum**. As a final check, pick some small value of n (say, 3) and trace the loop execution to see that it computes **sum** correctly for this case.

─── ◆◆

EXERCISES FOR SECTION 4.10

SELF-CHECK

1. For the loop in the subsection entitled "Off-by-One Loop Errors," add debugging statements to show the value of the loop-control variable at the start of each repetition. Also, add debugging statements to show the value of **sum** at the end of each loop repetition.

2. Will the following code fragment fail? What are the loop boundaries for this code fragment?

```
for (int x = 10; x >= 0; x = Math.sqrt(x)) {
    System.out.println(x);
}
```

PROGRAMMING

1. Rewrite the loop in Self-Check Exercise 2 using a `while` statement.

CHAPTER REVIEW

1. Use control structures to control the flow of execution through a program. The compound statement is a control structure for sequential execution.

2. A `boolean` expression can appear in an `if` statement and can be written
   - Using `boolean` variables
   - Using the relational operators (`<`, `<=`, `>`, `>=`, `==`, `!=`), to compare variables and literals of the same data type
   - Using the logical operators (`&&`, `||`, `!`) with `boolean` operands

3. Use selection control structures to represent decisions in an algorithm and write them in algorithms using pseudocode. We use the `if` and `switch` statements to code decision steps in Java.

4. Tracing an algorithm verifies whether it is correct. You can discover errors in logic by carefully hand-tracing an algorithm. Hand-tracing an algorithm before coding it as a method will save you time in the long run.

5. Nested `if` statements are common in programming and are used to represent decisions with multiple alternatives. Programmers use indentation and the multiple-alternative decision form to make nested `if` statements easier to read and understand.

6. The `switch` statement implements decisions that have several alternatives. The particular alternative chosen depends on the value of a variable or simple expression (the `switch` selector). The `switch` selector can be type `int` or `char` but not type `double`, `boolean`, or `String`.

7. Use a loop to repeat steps in a program. We discussed three specific loop forms: counting loops, state-controlled loops, and sentinel-controlled loops. For a counting loop, the number of iterations required can be determined before the loop is entered. For a state-controlled loop, repetition continues until a stopping state is reached. For a sentinel-controlled loop, repetition continues until a special data value is read.

   Counter-controlled loop (counting loop) pattern
   ```
   Set counter to 0.
   while (counter < final value)
       // Do the loop processing ...
   Increment counter by 1.
   ```

State-controlled loop pattern

> Set the loop-control variable to `true`.
> `while` (*loop-control variable* is `true`)
>   `// Do the loop processing ...`
> Reset the *loop-control variable*.

Sentinel-controlled loop pattern

> Read the first value of *input variable*.
> `while` (*input variable* is not the sentinel)
>   `// Do the loop processing ...`
> Read the next value of *input variable*.

8. Use a `for` statement to implement a counting loop, and use a `while` statement to implement state-controlled and sentinel-controlled loops.

9. In designing a loop, focus on both loop control and loop processing. For loop processing, make sure that the loop body contains steps that perform the operation that must be repeated. For loop control, you must provide steps that initialize, test, and update the loop-control variable. Make sure that the initialization step leads to correct program results when the loop body is not executed (zero-iteration loop).

10. Two groups of Java operators affect variable values: the increment/decrement operators and the compound assignment operators. You can use the former to implement the update step in a counting loop; you can use the latter to accumulate a total.

New Java constructs

Construct	Effect
`if` Statement	
One Consequent	
`if (x != 0.0)` `product = product * x;`	Multiplies **product** by **x** only if **x** is nonzero.
Two Alternatives	

`if (x >= 0.0)`
  `System.out.print(x +"positive");`
`else`
  `System.out.print(x +"negative");`
	If **x** is greater than or equal to 0.0, displays `"positive"` otherwise, displays the message `"negative"`.

New Java constructs, *continued*

Construct	Effect

Multiple Alternatives

```java
if (x < 0.0) {
  System.out.print("negative");
  absX = -x;
}
else if (x == 0.0) {
  System.out.println("zero");
  absX = 0.0;
}
else {
  System.out.println("positive");
  absX = x;
}
```

Displays one of three messages depending on whether **x** is negative, positive, or zero. **absX** is set to represent the absolute value or magnitude of **x**.

`switch` Statement

```java
switch (nextCh) {
    case 'A':  case 'a':
      System.out.print("Excellent");
      break;
    case 'B':  case 'b':
      System.out.print("Good ");
      break;
    case 'C':  case 'c':
      System.out.print("Fair ");
      break;
    case 'D': case 'd':
    case 'F': case 'f':
      System.out.print("Poor ");
      break;
    default:
      System.out.print("No grade "
                        + nextCh);
} // end switch
```

Displays one of five messages based on the value of **nextCh** (type **char**).

If **nextCh** is not listed in the case labels, displays the message **No grade**.

`while` Statement

```java
sum = 0;
while (sum <= maxSum) {
  next = readInt("Next:");
  sum += next;
}
```

A collection of input data items is read, and their sum is accumulated in **sum**. This process stops when the accumulated sum exceeds **maxSum**.

New Java constructs, *continued*

Construct	Effect

for Statement

```
for (curMonth = 3;
     curMonth <= 9;
     curMonth++) {
   String prompt =
      "Sales for month ";
   monthSales =
        readDouble(prompt);
   yearSales += monthSales;
}
```

The loop body is repeated for each value of **curMonth** from 3 to 9, inclusive. For each month, the value of **monthSales** is read and added to **yearSales**.

Counting for Loop with a Negative Step

```
for (volts = 20;
     volts >= -20;
     volts -= 10) {
   current = volts / resistance;
   System.out.println(volts + ", " +
                    current);
}
```

For values of **volts** equal to 20, 10, 0, −10,−20, computes value of **current** and displays **volts** and **current**.

Sentinel-Controlled while Loop

```
int product = 1;
String prompt = "Enter number or -999";
int data = readInt(prompt);
while (data != -999) {
   product *= data;
   data = readInt(prompt);
}
```

Computes the productof a list of numbers. The product is complete when the user enters the sentinel value (**-999**).

State-Controlled while Loop

```
divisible = false;
while (!divisible) {
   String prompt = "Enter an integer: ";
   int n = readInt(prompt);
   divisible = ((n % 2 == 0 ) ||
           (n % 3 == 0));
}
```

Continues to read in numbers until a number that is divisible by **2** or by **3** is read.

New Java constructs, *continued*

Construct	Effect
Increment/Decrement	
`count++;`	Increments the value of `count`.
Compound Assignment	
`ans *= (a - b);`	Assigns to `ans` the value of `ans * (a - b)`.

✔ **QUICK-CHECK EXERCISES**

1. An `if` statement is a control statement for _____ .

2. What is a compound statement?

3. A `switch` statement is often used instead of _____ .

4. Rewrite the `if` statement condition below to prevent a possible run-time error. What error is prevented? What feature of Java keeps the error from occurring?

```
if ((j / i == 0) && (i > 0))
    System.out.println("i is a factor of j");
```

5. The relational operator `!=` means _____ .

6. Will the expression

```
!(j * i == x + y && i > 0)
```

compile without error? List the operators in this expression in precedence order, from highest to lowest. List the operators in the order in which they will be evaluated.

7. Correct the syntax errors in the following statement:

```
if (x > 25.0) {
        y = x - 25.0;
else
        y = x
}
```

8. What value is assigned to **fee** by the nested **if** statements on the left and right when **speed** is 75? Which is correct?

```
if (speed > 35)                if (speed > 75)
    fee = 20.00;                   fee = 60.00;
else if (speed > 50)           else if (speed > 50)
    fee = 40.00;                   fee = 40.00;
else if (speed > 75)           else if (speed > 35)
    fee = 60.00;                   fee = 20.00;
```

9. What output is displayed by the following statements when **grade** is **'I'**? When **grade** is **'B'**? When **grade** is **'b'**?

```
switch (grade) {
    case 'A' :  points = 4;  break;
    case 'B' :  points = 3;  break;
    case 'C' :  points = 2;  break;
    case 'D' :  points = 1;  break;
    case 'E': case 'I': case 'W' :
                points = 0;  break;
    default:  System.out.println("Bad grade");
} // end switch
if (('A' <= grade) && (grade <= 'D'))
    System.out.println("Passed, points earned = " +
                        points);
else
    System.out.println("Failed, no points earned");
```

10. Explain the difference between the statements on the left and the statements on the right. For each, what is the final value of **x** if the initial value of **x** is 0?

```
if (x >= 0)                    if (x >= 0)
    x = x + 1;                     x = x + 1;
else if (x >= 1)               if (x >= 1)
    x = x + 2;                     x = x + 2;
```

11. The sentinel value is always the last value added to a sum being accumulated in a sentinel-controlled loop. True or false?

12. What does the following fragment display?

```
int product = 1;
while (int counter = 2; counter <= 5; counter++) {
    product += counter;
}
System.out.println(product);
```

13. An erroneous loop in a program that always executes one too many times has
     a problem at the _____ . This is called an _____ error.

14. What will be displayed by the following fragment?

```
int n = 10;
for (int i = 1; i <= 10; i++) {
    System.out.println(i + ", " + n);
    n -= i;
}
System.out.println(n);
```

ANSWERS TO QUICK-CHECK EXERCISES

1. selection or decision making

2. A compound statement consists of one or more statements bracketed by { , }.

3. a nested `if` statement or a multiple-alternative decision

4. `if ((i > 0) && (j / i == 0))`

    A division-by-zero error is prevented because of short-circuit evaluation.

5. not equal

6. Yes, the operators listed in decreasing precedence are `!`, `*`, `+`, `>`, `==`, `&&`. The
    operators listed in the order of their evaluation are `*`, `+`, `==`, `>`, `&&`, `!`.

7. Remove { , } and insert a semicolon after the last statement.

8. left-`20.00` (first condition is `true`); right-`40.00` (second condition is `true`);
    `40.00` is correct.

9. When grade is `'I'`: Failed, no points earned; when grade is `'B'`: Passed,
    points earned = `3`; when grade is `'b'`: Bad grade.

10. A nested `if` statement is on the left; a sequence of `if` statements is on the right.
     `x` becomes `1` on the left; `x` becomes `3` on the right.

11. False—the sentinel should not be processed.

12. The value of `1 * 2 * 3 * 4 * 5`, or `120`.

13. loop boundary, off-by-one

14. `1, 10`

    `2, 9`

    `3, 7`

    `4, 4`

    `5, 0`

    `6, -5`

    `7, -11`

    `8, -18`

    `9, -26`

    `10, -35`

    `-45`

REVIEW QUESTIONS

1. Place the following operators in precedence order (highest first):

   `&&, ||, !, ≥, !=, +, *`

2. How does a relational operator differ from a `boolean` operator?

3. What is short-circuit `boolean` evaluation?

4. Which method will be called in the following case if `temp` is `27.34`?

   ```
   if (temp > 32.0)
      pond.notFreezing();
   else
      pond.iceForming();
   ```

5. Write a nested `if` statement to display a message that indicates the educational level of a student based on his number of years of schooling: 0—None, 1 through 5—Elementary School, 6 through 8—Middle School, 9 through 12—High School, > 12—College. Display a message to indicate bad data as well.

7. Write a multiple-alternative `if` statement to select an operation based on the value of inventory. Increment `totalPaper` by `paperOrder` if inventory is `'B'` or `'C'`; increment `totalRibbon` by 1 if inventory is `'E'`, `'F'`, or `'D'`;

increment `totalLabel` by `labelOrder` if inventory is `'A'` or `'X'`. Do nothing if inventory is `'M'`.

8. Write a program fragment that allows a user to input several pairs of values for **x** and **y** and, for each pair, computes **x** raised to the **y** power by repeated multiplication. The program should keep obtaining values from the user until a sentinel value of **0** is entered for **x**.

9. What does the value of count represent after the program fragment below executes?

```
int count = 0;
for (int i = 1; i <= n; i++) {
    int x = KeyIn.readInt("Enter an integer:");
    if (x == i)
        count++;
}
```

10. What do the values of **count1** and **count2** represent after the program fragment below executes? Explain why it is slightly more efficient to evaluate the conditions in the order shown.

```
int count1 = 0;
int count2 = 0;
for (int i = 1; i <= n; i++) {
    int x = KeyIn.readInt("Enter an integer:");
    if (x % 2 == 0)
        count1++;
    else if (x % 3 == 0)
        count2++;
}
```

PROGRAMMING PROJECTS

1. Write an applet that reads a letter C, S, or R (using `JOptionPane.showInputDialog()`) and, depending on the letter read, displays a message in a circle, square, or rectangle.

2. Write a program that reads in four words and displays them in increasing alphabetic sequence and also in decreasing alphabetic sequence.

3. While spending the summer as a surveyor's assistant, you decide to write a program that transforms compass headings in degrees (0 to 360) to compass bearings. A compass bearing consists of three items: the direction you face (north or south), an angle between 0 and 90 degrees, and the direction you

turn before walking (east or west). For example, to get the bearing for a compass heading of 110.0 degrees, you would first face due south (180 degrees) and then turn 70.0 degrees east (180.0 − 70.0 is 110.0). Therefore, the bearing is South 70.0 degrees East. Be sure to check the input for invalid compass headings.

4. Write a program that reads in a room number, its capacity, and the size of the class enrolled so far and displays the classroom number, capacity, number of seats filled, number of seats available, and a message indicating whether the class is filled. Test your program with the following classroom data:

Room	Capacity	Enrollment
426	25	25
327	18	14
420	20	15
317	100	90

5. Write a program that determines the additional state tax owed by an employee. The state charges a 4% tax on net income. Determine net income by subtracting a $500 allowance for each dependent from gross income. Your program will read gross income, number of dependents, and tax amount already deducted. It will then compute the actual tax owed and show the difference between tax owed and tax deducted, followed by the message "Send check" or "Refund", depending on whether the difference is positive or negative.

6. Write a program to control a bread machine. Allow the user to input the type of bread (white or sweet). Ask the user if the loaf size is double and if the baking is manual. Use readBoolean() to read these data into boolean data fields. The following table details the time chart for the machine for each bread type. Display an output line for each step. If the loaf size is double, increase the baking time by 50%. If baking is manual, stop after the loaf-shaping cycle and instruct the user to remove the dough for manual baking.

Bread time chart

Operation	White Bread	Sweet Bread
Primary kneading	15 min	20 min
Primary rising	60 min	60 min
Secondary kneading	18 min	33 min
Secondary rising	20 min	30 min
Loaf shaping	2 sec	2 sec
Final rising	75 min	75 min
Baking	45 min	35 min
Cooling	30 min	30 min

7. Write a program that determines the day number (1 to 366) in a year for a date that is provided as input data. As an example, January 1, 2002, is day 1. December 31, 2002, is day 365. December 31, 2004, is day 366 because 2004 is a leap year. A year is a leap year if it is divisible by 4, except that any year divisible by 100 is a leap year only if it is divisible by 400. Your program should accept the month, day, and year as integers.

8. **a.** Write a program to read in a collection of exam scores ranging in value from **1** to **100**. Your program should count and print the number of outstanding scores (**90–100**), the number of satisfactory scores (**60–89**), and the number of unsatisfactory scores (**1–59**). It should also display the category of each score. Test your program on the following data:

63	75	72	72	78	67	80	63	75
90	89	43	59	99	82	12	100	

   b. Modify your program to display the average exam score (a real number) and the smallest and largest score.

9. Modify Programming Project 8 to compute and display both the range of values in the data collection and the standard deviation of the data collection. To compute the standard deviation, accumulate the sum of the squares of the data values (**sumSquares**) in the main loop. After loop exit, use the formula

$$standard\ deviation = \sqrt{\frac{sumSquares}{n} - (average)^2}$$

   where n is the number of items.

10. Bunyan Lumber Co. needs to create a table of the engineering properties of its lumber. The dimensions of the wood are given as the base and the height in inches. Engineers need to know the following information about lumber:

   Cross-sectional area = base × height

   Moment of inertia = (base × height^3)/12

   Section modulus = (base × height^2)/6

   The height sizes are **2, 4, 6, 8,** and **10** inches. Produce a table with appropriate headings to show these values and the computed engineering properties. Do not duplicate a 2-by-6 board with a 6-by-2 board.

11. Write a program to generate a calendar for a year. The program should accept the year and the day of the week for January 1 of that year (1 = Sunday, 7 = Saturday). Remember, February has 29 days if the year is divisible by 4 and not

by 100. The calendar should be printed in the following form (for each month).

```
        January
                    1
 2  3  4  5  6  7  8
 9 10 11 12 13 14 15
16 17 18 19 20 21 22
23 24 25 26 27 28 29
30 31
```

12. A horizon effect occurs when objects get progressively smaller along a line. Write a method that draws a figure of your choosing (a house, a flower, a person, an animal). The dimensions of the figure must be variable. Start in the lower-left corner of a drawing surface and draw smaller and smaller versions of the figure on a diagonal line toward the upper-right corner of the surface. The visual effect should be of a row of your figures fading into the distance.

5

Arrays and Vectors

In our programming so far, each variable has been used to store one value or to reference one object. To solve many programming problems, it is more efficient to reference a group of data items using the same variable name rather than giving them individual names. For example, a program that processes 500 exam scores for a course would be easier to write if we gave the collection of scores the name **scores** rather than giving each score its own name (**scores1**, **scores2**, and so on). Java allows a programmer to group such related data items together into a single composite **data structure**: the **array**.

271

Arrays enable us to access all the values in a collection of data we are processing, rather than just the most recent one. For example, in the payroll program in Section 4.4, variable **programmer** could only reference one employee at a time. If we store the employee data in an array, we can access any employee's data at any time. We illustrate this in Section 5.5.

We show how to use arrays with two and more dimensions to represent information in the form of tables. We also discuss vectors, a Java data structure that simplifies some array operations.

5.1 Array Declarations

The **array** is a **data structure** in which we store a collection of data items of the same type (for example, all the exam scores for a class). By using an array, we can associate a single variable name (for example, **scores**) with the entire collection of data (see Fig. 5.1).

We can also reference individual items in the array. The naming process is like the one used to describe families and their members. "The Bush household" refers to all four members of President George Bush's immediate family, and individual names—Laura Bush, for example—designate individuals in his family.

We can perform some operations, such as passing the array as a method argument, on the whole array. We also can access individual items stored in the array (called **array elements**) and process them like other simple variables. In this section we describe how to declare arrays in Java programs and how to reference individual array elements.

Declaring Arrays

We allocate storage for arrays in Java using array declarations that specify the array element type, array name, and array size (number of elements):

Array type   Array name   Array size

↓   ↓   ↓

```
double[] salary = new double[50];
```

Figure 5.1   **Array** scores

This declaration begins with the type of the array being declared, **double[ ]**, followed by the array name, **salary**. The rest of the declaration specifies that storage for **50** type **double** values should be allocated. Java initializes these storage locations to zero.

You can also declare and initialize an array at the same time. The statement

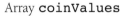

Array type   Array name   Array values

```
int[] coinValues = {1, 5, 10, 25, 50};
```

allocates storage for an array, **coinValues**, containing five integers. Each integer represents the number of pennies in one of the U.S. coins (**1** for a penny, **5** for a nickel, **10** for a dime, **25** for a quarter, and **50** for a half-dollar). Notice that you do not need to use the **new** operator or to specify the array size in this form of array declaration. Java sets the size of the array to be equal to the number of elements listed:

Array **coinValues**

coinValues

| 1 | 5 | 10 | 25 | 50 |

Array declaration

Form: **elementType[ ] arrayName = new elementType[size];**
           elementType[ ] arrayName = {initializerList};
Example: **double[] salary = new double[50];**
           int[] coinValues = {1, 5, 10, 25, 50};

Interpretation: The identifier **arrayName** represents a collection of array elements; each element can store an item of type **elementType**. The array size, or number of array elements, may be specified in the array declaration. In the second form, the array size is not explicitly specified but is implied by the size of the **initializerList** enclosed in braces. These values are stored sequentially (one after the other) in the array elements and their data type must be **elementType**.

Note 1: The **elementType** can be any primitive or class type. If the **elementType** is a class type, the array elements reference objects of the class and storage must be allocated separately for each of these objects (discussed in Section 5.5).

Separating Array Declaration and Storage Allocation

You can also declare an array and allocate storage for it in separate steps. For example, you could write the declaration for array **salary** as

```
double[] salary;
salary = new double[50];
```

where the first statement *declares* `salary` as a reference to an array of type `double` values. The second statement *instantiates* an object with storage for `50` type `double` elements; this object is referenced by `salary`. Note the importance of the empty brackets `[]` in the declaration of `salary`. If they are omitted, Java assumes `salary` is a primitive type variable, not a reference to an array.

A common technique is to prompt the program user for the array size:

```
double[] salary;
int size = readInt("How many salaries?");
salary = new double[size];
```

The value read into `size` determines the number of elements allocated to array `salary`. This approach has the advantage that the array will contain exactly as many elements as there are salary data values, no more and no less. The last two lines could be combined as

```
salary = new double[readInt("How many salaries?")];
```

Array Index

To process the data stored in an array, we must be able to access its individual elements. We access an array element by the array name (a reference variable) and the **array index** (historically called a **subscript**, from matrix algebra notation). The array index is enclosed in brackets after the array name (e.g., `coinValues[2]`).

A curious fact of Java is that we use the index `0`, not `1`, to reference the first element of an array, just as we use `0` as the index of the first character in a string. Therefore, we use the indices `0` through `4` to reference the five elements of array `coinValues` (see Fig. 5.2). Although this may seem confusing at first, you will soon get used to it.

We call a variable followed by an index in brackets (e.g., `coinValues[1]`) an **indexed variable**. An indexed variable can be used just like a regular variable. Because the elements of array `coinValues` are type `int`, we can manipulate `coinValues[1]` like any other `int` variable. Specifically, we can use `coinValues[1]` with the arithmetic operators, the relational operators, and the assignment operator. We can pass `coinValues[1]` to a method that requires a type `int` argument.

Figure 5.2   Array `coinValues` with indices

To store a value in an array element, we write an assignment statement of the form

indexedVariable = expression;

For example, the statement

```
salary[3] = 500.00;
```

assigns the value **500.00** to the element of array **salary** with index **3**.

To retrieve or access a value stored in an array element, just write the corresponding indexed variable in an expression. The statement

```
double sumFirstTwo = salary[0] + salary[1];
```

stores the sum of the first two elements of array **salary** in **sumFirstTwo**.

◆◆EXAMPLE 5.1

Let **x** be the array of real values shown in Fig. 5.3. Some statements that manipulate elements of this array are shown in Table 5.1.

Figure 5.3 **The eight elements of array x**

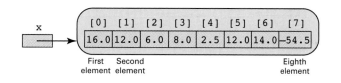

Table 5.1 Storing and retrieving values in array x

Statement	Explanation
`System.out.println(x[0]);`	Displays the value of `x[0]`, or `16.0`.
`x[3] = 25.0;`	Stores the value `25.0` in `x[3]`.
`sum = x[0] + x[1];`	Stores the sum of `x[0]` and `x[1]`, or `28.0`, in the variable `sum`.
`sum = sum + x[2];`	Adds `x[2]` to sum. The new sum is `34.0`.
`x[3] = x[3] + 1.0;`	Adds `1.0` to `x[3]`. The new `x[3]` is `26.0`.
`x[2] = x[0] + x[1];`	Stores the sum of `x[0]` and `x[1]` in `x[2]`. The new value of `x[2]` is `28.0`.

The contents of array **x** after execution of these statements are shown in Fig. 5.4. Notice that only array elements **x[2]** and **x[3]** have changed because they are the only ones that are assigned new values.

Figure 5.4   Array x after execution of statements in Table 5.1

Each index in Table 5.1 is a literal enclosed in brackets (e.g., [4]). Next, we show that an array index may be any integer expression.

◆◆

◆◆EXAMPLE 5.2 ─────────────────────────────────

The statements in Table 5.2 manipulate elements in array **x** (Fig. 5.4) where **i** is a type **int** variable with value **5**.

Table 5.2   Using index expressions with array x

Statement	Effect
`System.out.println(x[7]);`	Displays −54.5 (value of x[7])
`System.out.println(i + "\t" + x[i]);`	Displays 5, and 12 (value of 5, and x[5])
`System.out.println(x[i + 1]);`	Displays 14 (value of x[6])
`System.out.println(x[i + i]);`	Illegal attempt to display x[10]
`System.out.println(x[2 * i - 4]);`	Displays 14 (value of x[6])
`x[i] = x[i + 1];`	Assigns 14 (value of x[6]) to x[5]
`x[i - 1] = x[i];`	Assigns 14 (new value of x[5]) to x[4]
`x[i] - 1 = x[i - 1];`	Illegal assignment statement.

When **i** is 5, the indexed variable **x[i + i]** references element **x[10]**, which is not in the array. This is an **array index out-of-bounds error**.

Two different indices are used in the last three assignment statements in the table. The first assignment statement copies the value of **x[6]** to **x[5]** (indices **i + 1** and **i**); the second assignment statement copies value of **x[5]** to **x[4]** (indices **i** and **i - 1**). The last assignment statement causes a syntax error because **x[i] - 1** is an expression, not a variable.

◆◆

Array element reference

Form: *array[index]*

Example: x[3 * i - 2]

Interpretation: The *index* may be any integer expression. If the expression value is not in the allowable range of values, an array index out-of-bounds error occurs during run-time.

Arrays of Strings

We discuss arrays of objects in Section 5.5. For now, you should know that you can create and process arrays of objects just like you process arrays with primitive type elements. The statement

```
String[] friends = {"Sally", "Sam", "Jim", "Tameka"};
```

creates an array referenced by **friends**. This array has four elements (**friends[0]**, **friends[1]**, and so on), and each element references one of the **String** objects shown in the initializer list.

EXERCISES FOR SECTION 5.1

SELF-CHECK

1. Given the statements **y = x3** and **y = x[3]**, supply declarations such that these statements are valid. Assume **y** is type **double**.

2. For the following declarations, how many array elements are reserved for data and what type of data can be stored?

    a. `int[] scores = new int[10];`

    b. `char[] grades = new char[100];`

    c. `boolean[] quizAnswers = new boolean[50];`

    d. `int[] primes = {2, 3, 5, 7, 11, 13,`
       `                17, 19, 23, 29};`

    e. `String[] choices = {"Delete", "Insert", "Replace",`
       `                    "Search", "Quit"};`

    f. `double[] checks;`

       `checks = new double[readInt("How many checks?")];`

3. Provide array declarations for representing the following:

    a. The area in square feet for each of the rooms in your house

    b. The number of students in each grade of an elementary school with grade levels 1 through 6

    c. The color used to paint the 30 offices in a building with letter values assigned according to the first letter of their name (e.g., 'B' for blue)

    d. The same as part c, but store Java's standard colors instead (see Section 3.7)

    e. The names of the days of the week

    f. The names of the people in your immediate family

4. For the array in Self-Check Exercise 2, part d, indicate the effect of each statement below if it is valid. Rewrite the statements that are not valid.

    a. `int sum = (primes[1] + primes[4]) / 2;`

    b. `primes[0] = primes[9];`

    `primes[9] = primes[0];`

    c. `System.out.println("The last prime number < 30 is " +`

    `primes[10]);`

    d. `if (primes[3] == 5)`

    `System.out.println("Gotcha!");`

    `else`

    `System.out.println("Couldn't fool you.");`

    e. `primes[1 + 4] = primes[1] + primes[4];`

PROGRAMMING

1. For the array declared in Self-Check Exercise 2, part a, write statements that do the following:

    a. Store 0 in the first and last elements

    b. Display a message indicating whether the value of the third element is positive or negative

    c. Store the sum of the first three elements in the last element

5.2   Processing Arrays and Array Elements

We discuss how to process arrays and array elements in this section. Many programs require processing all the elements of an array in sequence, starting with the first element. To enter data into an array, to display its contents, or to perform other sequential processing tasks, use a **for** loop whose loop-control variable is also the array index.

The three steps for loop control are

◆ **Initialize** the loop-control variable: Because the first array element has an index of **0**, initialize the loop-control variable to **0**.

◆ **Test** the loop-control variable: Compare the loop-control variable to the size of the array. If the loop-control variable is smaller, repeat the loop body.

◆ **Update** the loop-control variable: Increase it by 1 after each element is processed to advance to the next element.

Data Field `length`

To accomplish the loop-control variable test, we take advantage of the fact that Java automatically allocates a data field **length** for each array and stores the array's size in that data field. For example, if **x** is an array, you can use **x.length** to determine its size. Notice that **length** is a data field for an array, not a method as it is for a string (i.e., if **name** references a **String** object, **name.length()** gives its size).

◆◆EXAMPLE 5.3 ─────────────────────────────────

For the array **cubes** declared as

```
int[] cubes = new int[10];
```

you can use the **for** statement

```
for (int i = 0; i < cubes.length; i++) {
    cubes[i] = i * i * i;
}
```

to store the cubes of the first 10 integers in this array. The condition

```
i < cubes.length
```

compares the loop-control variable **i** to data field **length** of array **cubes**. If the condition is true, the loop body executes and assigns i^3 to **cubes[i]**.

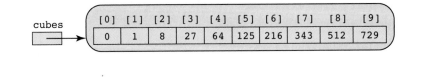

Displaying Array Elements

To display the elements in an array, you can build a string that contains all array elements, from the first to the last. The next example shows how to do this.

◆◆EXAMPLE 5.4

Fig. 5.5 shows a class **ArrayCubes** with data field **cubes**, an array of integers. The constructor with one argument

```
public ArrayCubes(int numCubes)
```

uses the statement

```
cubes = new int[numCubes];
```

to allocate storage for array **cubes**; the constructor argument is the array size. This is a common way to allocate storage for an array data field.

Method **fillCubes()** uses the **for** statement in the preceding example to store information in this array.

In method **toString()**, the **for** statement builds a string **cubeStr** that consists of the data in all array elements separated by spaces. The statement

```
String cubeStr = "";
```

initializes **cubeStr** to an empty string. In the loop body, the statement

```
cubeStr = cubeStr + cubes[i] + "   ";
```

appends the next element in array **cubes** to the string that consists of all prior elements (first "0   ", then "0   1   ", and so on). Fig. 5.6 shows an application class that uses all these methods, and Fig. 5.7 shows a sample run.

Figure 5.5   Class ArrayCubes

```java
/* ArrayCubes.java          Authors: Koffman & Wolz
 * A class that represents an array of cubes
 */
public class ArrayCubes {
  // data fields
  private int[] cubes;      // an array of integers

  // methods
  // postcondition: creates an array of size numCubes
  public ArrayCubes(int numCubes) {
     cubes = new int[numCubes];
  }

  // postcondition: Each element of cubes stores the
  //    cube of its subscript: 0, 1, 8, 27, and so on.
  public void fillCubes() {
     // Fill array cubes.
     for (int i = 0; i < cubes.length; i++) {
        cubes[i] = i * i * i;
     }
  }

  // postcondition: Creates a string containing the cubes
  //    separated by spaces
  public String toString () {
     String cubeStr = "";
     for (int i = 0; i < cubes.length; i++) {
        cubeStr = cubeStr + cubes[i] + "   ";
     }
     return cubeStr;
  }

}
```

Figure 5.6 Class `TestArrayCubes`

```
/* TestArrayCubes.java          Authors: Koffman & Wolz
 * Application for class ArrayCubes
 * Uses ArrayCubes, JOptionPane
 */
import javax.swing.*;

public class TestArrayCubes {

    public static void main (String[] args) {
        // Get array size.
        String numStr =
                JOptionPane.showInputDialog("How many cubes?");
        int numCubes = Integer.parseInt(numStr);

        // Create an ArrayCubes object with an array of this size.
        ArrayCubes aC = new ArrayCubes(numCubes);

        // Fill the array.
        aC.fillCubes();

        // Display the array contents.
        JOptionPane.showMessageDialog(null,
                        "The first " + numCubes +
                        " cubes are: \n" + aC.toString());
    }
}
```

Figure 5.7 Sample run of class `ArrayCubesTest`

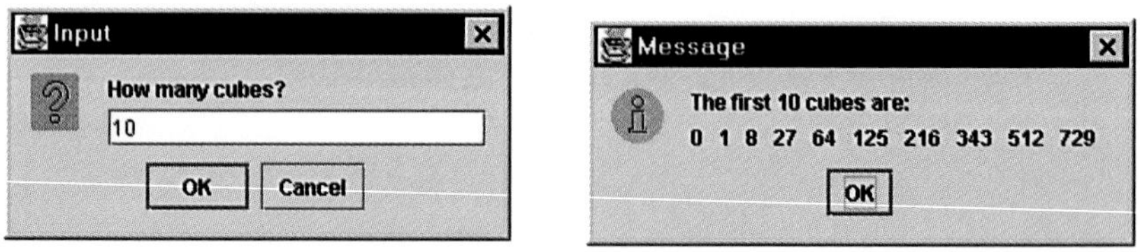

CASE STUDY CALCULATING EXAM STATISTICS

PROBLEM   Your computer science instructor needs a simple program for computing exam statistics. This program should read the scores for an exam and then compute and display various exam statistics such as the mean score, standard deviation, low score, and high score for the exam.

ANALYSIS   The problem inputs consist of the count of scores and the exam scores. The outputs are all the exam statistics.

Data Requirements

> **Problem Inputs**
>
> Count of scores
> Exam scores
>
> **Problem Output**
>
> The exam statistics

Relevant Formulas

> mean = sum of scores / count of scores
>
> $$\text{standard deviation} = \sqrt{\frac{\text{sum of squares of array elements}}{\text{count of elements}} - (\text{mean})^2}$$

DESIGN

Class `ExamStatistics`

Figure 5.8 shows a description for the `ExamStatistics` class. An `ExamStatistics` object contains storage for an array of student scores and has methods to accomplish all of the tasks listed in the problem statement. The method algorithms follow.

> *Algorithm for* **readScores()** *(class* **ExamStatistics***)*
>
> 1.   **for** each student who took the exam
>
>   Read the next score.
>
> *Algorithm for* **findMin()** *(class* **ExamStatistics***)*
>
> 1.   Set **minSoFar** to the first exam score.
> 2.   **for** each student who took the exam after the first one
>
>   **if** the current score is less than **minSoFar**
>
>   Set **minSoFar** to the current score.

Algorithm for `computeMean()` *(class* **ExamStatistics***)*

1. Set sum of scores to zero.

2. `for` each student who took the exam

    Add the current score to sum.

3. Divide sum by the number of students who took the exam.

Algorithm for `computeStandDev()` *(class* **ExamStatistics***)*

1. Set sum of squares to zero.

2. `for` each student who took the exam

    Add the current score squared to sum of squares.

3. Divide sum of squares by count of students, subtract the mean squared, and take the square root of the result.

Method `findMin()` uses the approach of "remembering" the smallest score seen so far. It begins by remembering the first score as the smallest so far. It then compares the other scores to the smallest score so far. If the current score is smaller, it remembers the current score as the smallest score so far and continues comparing this score to the others that follow. Method `findMax()` remembers the largest score so far instead of the smallest.

Method `computeStandDev()` should first compute the sum of the squares of all scores (using a loop) and, after loop exit, divide this sum by the count of students using real division. Next, it subtracts the square of the mean from this result. The standard deviation is the square root of this difference.

Figure 5.8   Class `ExamStatistics`

Data Fields	Attributes
`int[] scores`	An array of exam scores
Methods	**Behavior**
`void readScores()`	Reads the exam data
`int findMin()`	Find the smallest score
`int findMax()`	Finds the largest score
`double computeMean()`	Calculates the mean score
`double computeStandDev(double)`	Calculates the standard deviation
`String toString()`	Returns a string representing the array of scores
Classes Used	
`KeyIn`	

Class `RunExamStatistics`

Figure 5.9 shows a description for an application class `RunExamStatistics`. The application class contains a `main` method that allocates an `ExamStatistics` object and calls its methods in sequence. The value returned by each method is displayed in the console window. Because the standard deviation depends on the result of the mean calculation (returned by `computeMean()`), method `main()` should save this value and pass it to method `computeStandDev()`.

> *Algorithm for `main()` (class `RunExamStatistics`)*
>
> 1. Read the number of scores.
>
> 2. Create an `ExamStatistics` object for storing the scores.
>
> 3. Find and display the lowest score.
>
> 4. Find and display the highest score.
>
> 5. Compute and display the mean score.
>
> 6. Compute and display the standard deviation.

IMPLEMENTATION   Figure 5.10 shows class `ExamStatistics`. Method `readScores()` reads the exam data into array `scores`. The statement

```
scores[i] = KeyIn.readInt("Score for next student:");
```

prompts the user for the next score and stores the data item entered in the next array element. If you prefer not to use class `KeyIn`, you can write your own method `readInt()` (see Fig. 3.24).

Method `findMin()` returns the smallest exam score stored in the array. If the array is not empty, we store our initial guess of the smallest score—`scores[0]`. The `for` statement compares each value in the array to `minSoFar`. If the current score is smaller than `minSoFar`, we reset `minSoFar` to the current score. When we're finished checking the array of scores, we return the last value assigned to `minSoFar` as

Figure 5.9 Class `RunExamStatistics`

Methods	Behavior
`main()`	Gets the number of exam scores, creates an ExamStatistics object with an array of the proper size, calls the object's methods to find and display all statistics
Classes Used	
`ExamStatistics`, `KeyIn`	

Figure 5.10   Class `ExamStatistics`

```java
/* ExamStatistics.java          Authors: Koffman & Wolz
 * Class for storing array of scores and doing statistics
 * Uses KeyIn
 */
import psJava.KeyIn;

public class ExamStatistics {
  // Data Fields
  private int[] scores;         // scores is an array of ints

  // Methods
  // postcondition: scores references an array object with num
  //    type int elements.
  public ExamStatistics(int num) {
    // Allocate storage for the array.
    scores = new int[num];
  }


  // postcondition: reads data into array scores.
  public void readScores() {
    // Read the scores
    for (int i = 0; i < scores.length; i++)
      scores[i] = KeyIn.readInt("Score for next student:");
  }


  // postcondition: returns the smallest score.
  public int findMin() {
    // Find smallest score if array is not empty.
    if (scores.length > 0) {
      int minSoFar = scores[0];   // Remember first score

      // Remember any smaller scores.
      for (int i = 1; i < scores.length; i++) {
        if (scores[i] < minSoFar)
          minSoFar = scores[i];
      }
      return minSoFar;
    }
    else
      return 0;   // array is empty
  }
```

Figure 5.10   Class ExamStatistics, *continued*

```
// postcondition: returns the largest score.
public int findMax() {
  // Find largest score if array is not empty.
  if (scores.length > 0) {
    int maxSoFar = scores[0];   // Remember first score

    // Remember any larger scores.
    for (int i = 1; i < scores.length; i++) {
      if (scores[i] > maxSoFar)
        maxSoFar = scores[i];
    }
    return maxSoFar;
  }
  else
    return 0;   // array is empty
}


// postcondition: returns the mean of the scores
public double computeMean() {
  int sum = 0;
  for (int i = 0; i < scores.length; i++)
    sum += scores[i];

  if (scores.length > 0)
    return (double) sum / (double) scores.length;
  else
    return 0;
}


// precondition: the mean score is defined.
// postcondition: returns the standard deviation.
public double computeStandDev(double mean) {
  // Compute sum of scores-squared
  int sumSquares = 0;
  for (int i = 0; i < scores.length; i++)
    sumSquares += (scores[i] * scores[i]);
```

Figure 5.10   Class ExamStatistics, *continued*

```
    if (scores.length > 0)
        return Math.sqrt((double) sumSquares / scores.length -
                          mean * mean);
    else
        return 0;
}


// postcondition: returns a String containing exam scores.
public String toString () {

    String examStr = "";
    for (int i = 0; i < scores.length; i++) {
        examStr = examStr + scores[i] + "    ";
    }
    return examStr;

}
}
```

the smallest exam score. We can easily modify this algorithm to design method `findMax()`.

Methods `computeMean()` and `computeStandDev()` involve accumulating a sum. For `computeMean()`, we accumulate the sum of exam scores, and for `computeStandDev()` we accumulate the sum of the exam scores squared. The `if` statements at the end of these methods prevent division by zero errors when array `scores` is empty.

Figure 5.11 shows class `RunExamStatistics`.

TESTING

Figure 5.12 shows the output from a sample run. You should test the program for zero scores and for one score to make sure it handles these cases properly. Another special case would be if all exam scores were the same.

Figure 5.11   Class `RunExamStatistics`

```
/* RunExamStatistics.java          Authors: Koffman & Wolz
 * Application class for running ExamStatistics
 * Uses ExamStatistics, KeyIn
 */
import psJava.KeyIn;

public class RunExamStatistics  {

   public static void main(String[] args) {

      // Compute statistics if array is created.
      ExamStatistics ex =
            new ExamStatistics(KeyIn.readInt("How many scores?"));

      // Read the scores
      ex.readScores();

      // Show results of statistics calculations
      System.out.println("The scores are:\n" + ex.toString());
      System.out.println("\nMinimum score: " + ex.findMin());
      System.out.println("\nMaximum score: " + ex.findMax());
      double mean = ex.computeMean();
      System.out.println("\nMean score: " + mean);
      System.out.println("\nStandard deviation: " +
                          ex.computeStandDev(mean));
   }
}
```

Figure 5.12   Sample run of `RunExamStatistics`

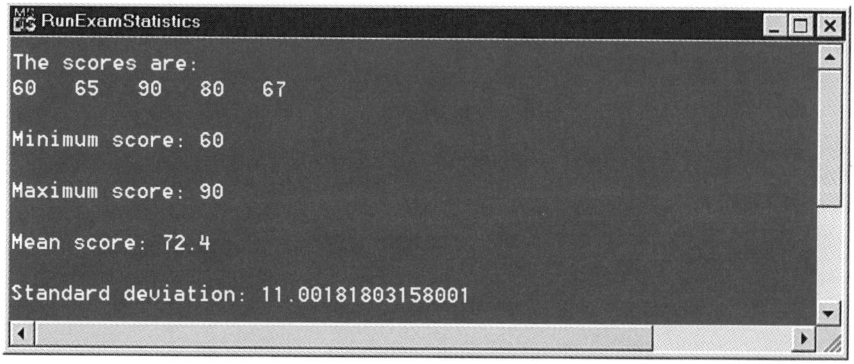

```
RunExamStatistics

The scores are:
60   65   90   80   67

Minimum score: 60

Maximum score: 90

Mean score: 72.4

Standard deviation: 11.00181803158001
```

EXERCISES FOR SECTION 5.2

SELF-CHECK

1. The following sequence of statements changes the contents of array **x** displayed in Fig 5.4. Describe what each statement does to the array and show the final contents of array **x** after all statements execute.

```
i = 3;
x[i] = x[i] + 10.0;
x[i - 1] = x[2 * i - 1];
x[i + 1] = x[2 * i] + x[2* i + 1];
for (i = 5; i <= 7; i++)
    x[i] = x[i + 1];
for (i = 3; i >= 1; i--)
    x[i + 1] = x[i];
```

2. Write program statements that do the following to array **x** shown in Fig. 5.4:

   a. Replace the third element with **7.0**.

   b. Copy the element in the fifth location into the first one.

   c. Subtract the first element from the fourth and store the result in the fifth element.

   d. Increase the sixth element by 2.

   e. Find the sum of the first five elements.

   f. Multiply each of the first six elements by 2 and place each product in an element of the array **answerArray**.

   g. Display all elements with even indices on one line.

PROGRAMMING

1. Write a loop to compute the product of all elements of an array of real numbers. Write a suitable declaration statement for this array assuming it can store up to 100 numbers.

2. Modify class **ExamStatistics** to use class **JOptionPane** methods for input.

5.3 Operations on Whole Arrays

In our examples so far, we process one array element at a time by specifying the array name and index. In this section, we show how to perform operations on a whole array. Our examples include passing an array as a method argument, assigning the values in one array to another, and copying the data in one array to another.

Declaring Arrays

Let's consider the effect of the array declarations below:

```
int[] x = {1, 2, 3, 4, 5};
int[] y = {50, 40, 30, 20, 10};
```

The declaration for array **x** creates an array object with five storage locations, named **x[0]** through **x[4]**, with the initial values shown. Java allocates one more storage location named **x**, which references these storage locations (Fig. 5.13). The same thing happens when we declare array **y** above. In this case, the cell named **y** references the array object that stores the elements of array **y** (**y[0]** through **y[4]** in Fig. 5.13).

Copying Arrays

You can copy all or some of the values in one array to another using Java's **arraycopy** method. The first statement below

```
System.arraycopy(y, 0, x, 0, y.length);
y[2] = 0;
```

uses the **arraycopy()** method to copy all elements of array **y** (the source array) to array **x** (the destination array). The second and fourth arguments indicate the first position in the source and destination arrays that are affected. The last argument specifies the number of elements to copy. Now variables **x** and **y** reference different array objects that contain the same values. The second statement changes the value of **y[2]** to **0**, but **x[2]** is still **30** (see Fig. 5.14).

You can also copy part of one array to another. The statement

```
System.arraycopy(y, 0, x, 2, 3);
```

Figure 5.13   Array objects referenced by x and y

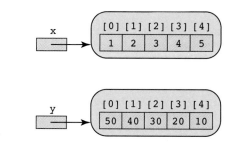

Figure 5.14 Arrays x and y after execution of `arraycopy()` and `y[2] = 0;`

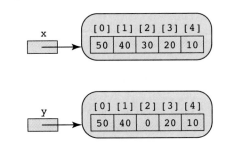

copies the first three elements of array **y** (starting with **y[0]**) to the last three elements of array **x** (starting with **x[2]**). This means that **y[0]** is copied to **x[2]**, **y[1]** to **x[3]**, and **y[2]** to **x[4]**.

Method arraycopy()

Form: `System.arraycopy(sourceArray, sourcePosition,`
        `destinationArray, destinationPosition, count);`

Example: `System.arraycopy(y, 0, x, 2, 3);`

Interpretation: Copies *count* elements from *sourceArray*, starting with the element at index *sourcePosition*, to the *destinationArray*, starting at index *destinationPosition*.

Array Assignment

You can also assign one array to another, but the effect will not be the same as for an array copy. Assume **x** and **y** reference the original array objects show in Fig. 5.13:

```
int[] x = {1, 2, 3, 4, 5};
int[] y = {50, 40, 30, 20, 10};
```

The assignment statement

```
x = y;
```

copies the address stored in **y** to **x**. Its effect is to cause both variables **x** and **y** to reference the array object originally referenced by **y**, and the array object that contained the values **1** through **5** is no longer accessible. Because **x** and **y** now reference the same array, the statement

```
x[2] = 0;
```

would change the value of **x[2]** (or **y[2]**) from **30** to **0** (see Fig. 5.15).

Figure 5.15   Effect of x = y;

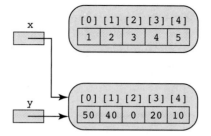

Passing Arrays to Methods

In the calls to method **arraycopy()** shown earlier, we pass arrays **x** (the destination array) and **y** (the source array) as actual arguments. When we use array **x** as an argument, what is actually passed to the method is a copy of the reference to array **x**. This enables the method to access the elements of array **x** and to change their values.

Next, we see how to declare arrays as formal parameters in methods. We begin with an example of a method that compares its two array arguments.

◆◆EXAMPLE 5.5 ——————————————————————————————

Method **equalArray()** in Fig. 5.16 determines whether its two array arguments, **a** and **b**, contain the same values and are the same length. The first **if** statement returns **false** if the actual array arguments have different lengths.

Within the loop, the **if** condition (**a[i] != b[i]**) compares corresponding pairs of array elements, starting with the first pair, **a[0]** and **b[0]**. If a pair is found to be different, an immediate return occurs with a result of **false**. If all array element pairs match, the **for** statement is exited after the last pair is tested, and method **equalArray()** returns **true**.

—— ◆◆

Argument Correspondence for Array Arguments

In the method call

```
equalArray(x, y)
```

a reference to array **x** is passed to the first method parameter, **int[] a**, and a reference to array **y** is passed to the second method parameter, **int[] b**. Therefore, during the method execution, parameter **a** references array **x** and parameter **b** references

Figure 5.16   Method `equalArray()`

```java
// Returns true if array arguments are same length and
//    contain the same values.
public static boolean equalArray(int[] a, int[] b) {
   // Check for unequal lengths.
   if (a.length != b.length)
      return false;

   // Return false if any pair doesn't match.
   for (int i = 0; i < a.length; i++) {
      if (a[i] != b[i])
         return false;
   }

   // All pairs matched.
   return true;
}
```

array **y** (see Fig. 5.17). Furthermore, `a[0]` references `x[0]` and the value of `a.length` tells us how many elements are allocated to array **x**. The `if` statement in the fragment below would display the message `Arrays x and y have same values`.

```java
System.arraycopy(y, 0, x, 0, x.length);
if (equalArray(x, y))
   System.out.println("Arrays x and y have the same values");
else
   System.out.println("Arrays x and y are not the same");
```

Figure 5.17   Argument/parameter correspondence for arrays

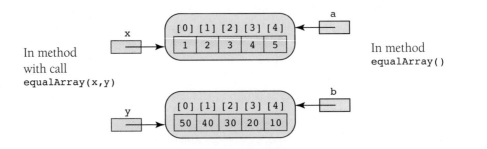

Returning an Array of Values

A Java method can return a reference to an array object. We illustrate this next.

◆◆EXAMPLE 5.6 ────────────────────────────────────

Method **getScores()** shown below is an accessor method that returns a reference to the array **scores**, an instance variable for class **ExamStatistics** (see Fig. 5.10).

```java
public int[] getScores() {
    return scores;
}
```

If **ex** is an instance of class **ExamStatistics**, the statement

```java
int[] myScores = ex.getScores();
```

stores in variable **myScores** (declared as **int[]**) the array object reference returned by method **getScores()**.

── ◆◆

◆◆EXAMPLE 5.7 ────────────────────────────────────

If **x** and **y** reference arrays of integers

```java
int[] x = {1, 2, 3, 4, 5};
int[] y = {50, 40, 30, 20, 10};
```

the statement

```java
int[] z = x + y;    // Illegal addition of arrays
```

is invalid because the operator **+** cannot have arrays as operands. You can use method **addArray()** (Fig. 5.18) to add two arrays of integer values, element by element (that is, **x[0] + y[0]** is the first element of the sum).
    Method **addArray()** has two array parameters (**int[] a** and **int[] b**) and returns a reference to an array of integers. In method **addArray()**, the statement

```java
int[] c = new int[Math.min(a.length, b.length)];
```

creates an array whose length is the same as the length of the smaller of its two array arguments. In the **for** loop, the statement

Figure 5.18   Method addArray()

```
// postcondition: returns a reference to an array that contains
//   the element-by-element sum of its array arguments
public static int[] addArray(int[] a, int[] b) {
   int[] c = new int[Math.min(a.length, b.length)];

   for (int i = 0; i < c.length; i++)
      c[i] = a[i] + b[i];

   return c;
}
```

```
c[i] = a[i] + b[i];
```

adds a pair of elements in the argument arrays with the same index. It stores this sum in the corresponding element of array **c**. The **return** statement returns a reference to the array object referenced by **c**. The assignment statement.

```
int[] z = addArray(x, y);
```

causes **z** to reference the array object containing the element-by-element sums of arrays **x** and **y** (see Fig. 5.19).

Figure 5.19   Result of z = addArray(x, y);

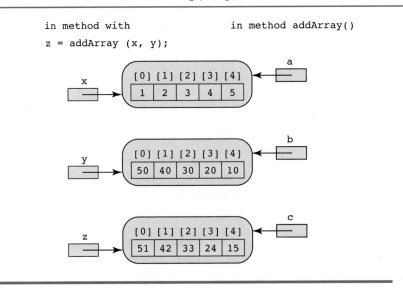

EXERCISES FOR SECTION 5.3

SELF-CHECK

1. Describe the effect of each of the statements below. Show the new values for the array modified by each statement.

```
int[] x = {1, 2, 3, 4, 5, 6, 7, 8, 9, 10};
int[] y = new int[10];
int[] z = new int[10];
System.arraycopy(x, 0, y, 5, x.length / 2);
System.arraycopy(x, 5, y, 0, x.length / 2);
z = addArrays(x, y);
```

2. When is it better to pass an entire array of data to a method rather than individual elements?

PROGRAMMING

1. Write a method that assigns a value of **true** to element **i** of its result array if element **i** of one array argument has the same value as element **i** of the other array argument; otherwise, assign a value of **false**. Assume the two argument arrays have the same length and element type **int**.

2. Write a method that reverses the values in an array. For example, if the array argument is **inArray** and the result array is **outArray**, copy **inArray[0]** to the last element of **outArray**, then copy **inArray[1]** to the next-to-last element of **outArray**, and so on.

5.4 Searching and Sorting an Array

This section discusses two common problems in processing arrays: searching an array to determine the location of a particular value and sorting an array to rearrange the array elements in numerical order. For example, we might want to use an array search to determine which student, if any, got a particular score. Or we might use an array sort to rearrange array elements so that they are in increasing order by score. This rearrangement would be helpful if we wanted to display an ordered list of scores or if we needed to locate several different scores in the array. We will write static methods to perform these operations and save them in class **IntArray** of package **psJava** (see Preface for downloading instructions).

Array Search

We can search an array for a particular value by comparing each array element, starting with the first, to the target, the value we are seeking. If a match occurs, we have found the target in the array and can return its index as the search result. If we test all array elements without finding a match, we return **-1** to indicate that the target was not found. We choose **-1** because no array element has a negative index.

In the algorithm below, the **for** loop accesses each array element and the **if** statement compares the current element to the target. If they match, the index of the current element is returned immediately. Step 3 (Return **-1**) executes after all elements in the array have been compared to target without finding a match. If two or more elements happen to match the target, the index of the first match will be returned.

Algorithm for search method

1. **for** each array element

2.   **if** the current element matches the target

>   Return the index of the current element.

3. Return **-1**.

To make sure we test each array element, the upper limit of the loop-control variable should be the index of the last value stored in the array. In a general method that examines all the elements in an array argument, we can use the array's length attribute as the upper limit. Fig. 5.20 shows such a search method. The array to be searched is the method's first argument, and the search target is the method's second argument.

Figure 5.20   Method search() of class IntArray

```
// postcondition: Returns the subscript of the first element
//    of its array argument that stores the target value.
//    Returns -1 if target is not found.
public static int search(int[] x, int target) {
    for (int i = 0; i < x.length; i++) {
        if (x[i] == target)
            return i;          //index of target
    }

    // All elements tested without success.
    return -1;
}
```

Because the search method is a class method (for class `IntArray`), we can pass it any type `int[]` array as an argument. Also, we don't need to instantiate an `IntArray` object to call the search method. In class `ExamStatistics` (Fig. 5.10), we can use the statements

```
int index = IntArray.search(scores, 100);
if (index > -1)
   System.out.println("Student " + index +
                    " is the first student with a perfect score");
else
   System.out.println("No student got a perfect score");
```

to search array **scores** and display the subscript of the first score of 100 or the message shown in the last line if no one got 100.

Sorting an Array

Many programs execute more efficiently when the data they process are sorted before processing begins. For example, a check-processing program executes more quickly when all checks are in order by checking account number. Other programs produce more understandable output if the information is sorted before it is displayed. For example, your university might want your instructor's grade report sorted by student ID number. In this section, we describe one simple sorting algorithm from among the many that have been studied by computer scientists.

The selection sort is a fairly intuitive (but not overly efficient) sorting algorithm. To perform a selection sort of an array, we locate the smallest element in the array and then switch the smallest element with the element at index 0, thereby placing the smallest element at index **0**. Then we locate the smallest element remaining in the subarray with indices **1** through **length-1** and switch it with the element at index **1**, thereby placing the second smallest element at index **1**. Then we locate the smallest element remaining in the subarray with indices **2** through **length-1** and switch it with the element at index **2**, and so on.

Algorithm for selection sort

1. For each index, fill in the array up to, but excluding, the last index.

2. Find the position (**posMin**) of the smallest element in the subarray starting at element **scores[fill]**.

3. Exchange the smallest element with the one at index **fill**.

Fig. 5.21 traces the operation of the selection sort algorithm on an array of length 4. The first array shown is the original array. Then we show each step as the next smallest element is moved to its correct position. The subarray in color represents the

Figure 5.21 Trace of selection sort

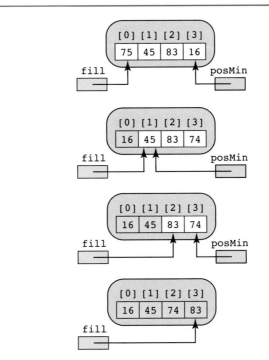

portion of each array that is sorted. Note that, at most, **length-1** exchanges will be required to sort an array.

Method **selectionSort()** in Fig. 5.22 implements the selection sort algorithm. The array to be sorted is passed as the method argument. The **for** loop *selects* the value to be placed in each array element. During each iteration, it places the next smallest value in position **fill** where **fill** starts at 0. The local variable **posMin** stores the index of the next smallest value in the array (returned by method **findPosMin()**, which is discussed next). The three statements at the end of the **for** loop exchange the next smallest value in the array (at **posMin**) with the one at **fill**.

Method **selectionSort()** is a **void** method, so it is executed for its effect. The method call

```
IntArray.selectionSort(scores);
```

rearranges the values in the array object referenced by **scores** so that they are in increasing order. After the method executes, its argument **scores** still references the same array object that it did before the call; however, the information in that object is changed.

Figure 5.22   Methods `selectionSort()` and `findPosMin()` of class `IntArray`

```
// postcondition: the values in its array argument are
//    in increasing order.
public static void selectionSort(int[] x) {

    int posMin;        //index of next smallest element
    int temp;          //temporary value for exchange

    for (int fill = 0; fill < x.length-1; fill++) {
        /* invariant:
        *    The elements in x[0] through x[fill-1] are in
        *    their proper place and fill < x.length is true.
        */
        // Find position of smallest element in the subarray
        //    starting at element x[fill].
        posMin = findPosMin(x, fill);

        //Exchange elements with subscripts fill and posMin.
        temp = x[fill];
        x[fill] = x[posMin];
        x[posMin] = temp;
    }
}


// postcondition: returns the position of the smallest
//    element in array x from x[fill] to the end
private static int findPosMin(int[] x, int fill) {
    // Assume smallest value is at position fill
    int posMinSoFar = fill;

    // Remember any smaller value found in the array.
    for (int i = fill + 1; i < x.length; i++) {
        if (x[i] < x[posMinSoFar])
            posMinSoFar = i;
    }

    // posMinSoFar is subscript of smallest element
    return posMinSoFar;
}
```

Method `findPosMin()`

In method `selectionSort()`, the statement

```
// Find index of smallest element in the subarray
//    starting at element x[fill].
posMin = findPosMin(x, fill);
```

calls method `findPosMin()` (Figure 5.22) to find the index of the smallest value in the unsorted portion of its array argument, starting at index `fill`. This method is similar to method `findMin()` in class `ExamStatistics` (Fig. 5.11). The differences are that it starts its search for the smallest value at position `fill`, not `0`. Also, it returns the *position* of the smallest value, not the smallest value.

Loop Invariants

The `for` loop in `selectionSort()` starts with the special comment below, which is the loop invariant.

```
/* invariant:
 *     The elements in x[0] through x[fill-1] are in
 *     their proper place and fill < x.length is true.
 */
```

A **loop invariant** is a statement that must always be **true** before, during, and after each iteration of the loop. Computer scientists use invariants to help prove that a loop is written correctly. The invariant summarizes the progress of the selection sort: The subarray whose elements are in their proper place is shown in the color part of array `x` in the sketch below. The remaining elements are not yet in place and are all larger than `x[fill-1]`.

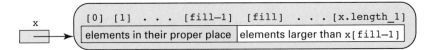

During each pass, the portion of the array in color (the sorted subarray) grows by one element, and `fill` is incremented to reflect this increase. When `fill` is equal to `x.length-1`, all the elements will be in their proper place.

Finding the Median Value in an Array

We can use method `selectionSort()` to find the median value in an array. If an array is sorted and has an odd number of elements, the median value would be the one in the middle of the array or the one with index `x.length/2`. If the array has an even number of elements, the median is the average of its two "middle" elements. Figure 5.23 shows method `findMedian()`. Notice that `findMedian()` makes a copy of its array argument and sorts the copy (array **copyX**), not the original array (see Self-Check Exercise 3 at the end of this section).

Figure 5.23   Method `findMedian()` of class `IntArray`

```
// postcondition: Returns the median value stored
//    in its array argument.
public static int findMedian(int[] x) {
  // Create a copy of array x.
  int[] copyX = new int[x.length];
  System.arraycopy(x, 0, copyX, 0, x.length);

  // Sort array copyX.
  selectionSort(copyX);

  // Return middle value or average of two "middle" values.
  if (x.length % 2 == 1)
     return copyX[x.length/2];    // odd size array
  else
     return (copyX[x.length/2 - 1] +
             copyX[x.length/2]) / 2;  // even size
}
```

EXERCISES FOR SECTION 5.4

SELF-CHECK

1. For the **search()** method in Fig. 5.20, what happens in each of the following cases?

    a. The last student score matches the target.

    b. Several scores match the target.

2. Trace the execution of the selection sort on the following two lists of integers:

    a. 10   55   34   56   76   5

    b. 5   15   25   35   45   45

    Show the arrays after each exchange occurs. How many exchanges are required to sort each list? How many comparisons?

3. Explain why we made a copy of the array argument in Fig. 5.23 before sorting it.

4. How could you modify the selection sort algorithm to get the scores in descending order (largest score first)?

5. For the arrays shown in Self-Check Exercise 2 above, what is the value of the subscript(s) of the element in array **copyX** involved in determining the result of **findMedian()**? Answer the same question if these arrays have five or seven elements.

PROGRAMMING

1. Another way of performing the selection sort is to place the largest value in index **x.length-1**, the next largest in index **x.length-2**, and so on. Write this version.

2. Modify the selection sort method so that no exchange occurs when the values at positions **fill** and **posMinSoFar** are the same.

3. Write method **searchLast()** that returns the position of the last occurrence of the target in the argument array.

5.5 Arrays of Objects

In our examples so far, we focused on arrays of numbers (type **int[ ]** and **double[ ]** arrays). You can declare arrays of any element type in Java. In this section, we see how to declare and process arrays of objects.

Arrays of Strings

Recall that Java strings are objects, not primitive types. The array declaration

```
String[] names = new String[4];
```

allocates storage for an array **names** that can reference four **String** objects. The **new** operator instantiates the array and allocates storage for the array of references. Each reference has the value **null** because we have not yet created any **String** objects. We can do this using assignment statements such as

```
names[0] = "Sally";
names[1] = "Jim";
names[2] = new String("Jane");
names[3] = names[2];
```

As a result of the last statement, elements **names[2]** and **names[3]** reference the same **String** object, the one containing the characters **Jane** (see Fig. 5.24).

We can also allocate storage for the array and create the **String** objects at the same time using an initializer list:

```
String[] names = {"Sally", "Jim", "Jane", "Jane"};
```

In this case, **names[2]** and **names[3]** reference different **String** objects that contain the characters **Jane**. As before, the size of the initializer list determines the size of the array.

Figure 5.25 shows a static method **toString()** that returns a **String** object containing the strings stored in its array argument separated by commas and enclosed in braces. For example, if string **names** above is passed as an argument to **toString()**, the **String** object returned would contain the characters **{Sally, Jim, Jane, Sue}**. The **for** statement appends each string in the argument array to **result**. A comma and space are inserted after each string except the last one.

Figure 5.24   Array of strings

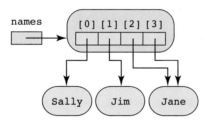

Figure 5.25   Method toString() for representing an array of strings

```
// postcondition: Returns a String representing
//    an array of Strings.
public String toString(String[] strings) {
    String result = "{";
    for (int i = 0; i < strings.length; i++) {
        result += strings[i];
        if (i < strings.length - 1)
            result += ", ";
    }

    return result + "}";
}
```

Menus

Sometimes a program user must make a selection from several choices displayed in a GUI **menu**. For example, a coffee shop might have four types of coffee to choose from. The statement

```
String[] coffeeChoices = {"Regular", "Decaf", "Expresso", "Latte"};
```

declares `coffeeChoices` as an array of four strings. Next, we pass this array as an argument to method `showOptionDialog()` (from class `JOptionPane` of `Swing`):

```
int coffeeKind = JOptionPane.showOptionDialog(null, "Select a coffee", "Menu",
        JOptionPane.YES_NO_CANCEL_OPTION, JOptionPane.QUESTION_MESSAGE, null,
        coffeeChoices , coffeeChoices[0]);
```

The call above has two null arguments and two constants (in uppercase) from class `JOptionPane`. The string `"Select a coffee"` is a prompt, and the string `"Menu"` is a label for the menu window. The elements of array `coffeeChoices` (the next-to-last argument) are button labels (see Fig. 5.26). Depending on which button is pressed, method `showOptionDialog()` returns a value from `0` (for `"Regular"`) through `3` (for `"Latte"`), which is saved in `coffeeKind`. The last argument defines `coffeeChoices[0]` as the default, so `0` will be returned if the user presses the Enter key. If you import class `KeyIn` of package `psJava`, you can use the simpler statement pair below:

```
String[] coffeeChoices = {"Regular", "Decaf", "Expresso", "Latte"};
int coffeeKind = KeyIn.getChoice("Select a coffee", coffeeChoices);
```

Often, programmers use a multiple-alternative decision to make a selection based on the value returned by a menu. For example, the `if` statement below could be used to set the coffee price (value of `price`) based on the value of `coffeeKind`. Assume the identifiers that start with `PRICE_` are type `double` constants.

Figure 5.26   Dialog window with a menu

```
if (coffeeKind == 0)
    price = PRICE_REGULAR;
else if (coffeeKind == 1)
    price = PRICE_DECAF;
else if (coffeeKind == 2)
    price = PRICE_EXPRESSO;
else if (coffeeKind == 3)
    price = PRICE_LATTE;
```

◆◆EXAMPLE 5.8 ───

The heading for method **main**

```
public static void main(String[] args)
```

declares its argument **args** as an array of **String** objects. This array provides a way for the user of the operating system to provide arguments to the entire program.

In the UNIX operating system, you can start an application called **MyApplication** by typing the command line

```
java MyApplication
```

Or you could provide command-line arguments by typing

```
java MyApplication this is way cool
```

The interface between the operating system and the Java Virtual Machine recognizes that you have typed four strings (separated by spaces). Notice that double quotes are not needed around these strings. They are stored in the array **args** (i.e., **args[0]** is "this", **args[1]** is "is", **args[2]** is "way", and **args[3]** is "cool").

Figure 5.27 provides a sample of what a program such as **MyApplication** could do with the strings. This program displays the input string in reverse order (in the console window), starting with **args[3]**. Because strings may be converted into any primitive type, you can pass virtually any kind of data to a program.

Figure 5.27 Application with command-line arguments

```
/* DisplayMainArgs.java          Authors: Koffman & Wolz
 * Application class for displaying command-line arguments
 */
public class DisplayMainArgs {

   public static void main(String[] args) {
      if (args.length > 0) {
         for (int i = args.length - 1; i >= 0; i--)
            System.out.println(args[i]);
      }
      else {
         System.out.println("No command line args - no fun!");
      }
   }
}
```

Array of Employee Objects

In Section 4.4, we wrote a payroll program that processed several employees. We stored each employee's payroll data in the same **Employee** object. Once we finished processing an employee, the employee's data was replaced with that of the next employee. Another approach to solving this problem is to create an array of **Employee** objects and to store each employee's data in a different **Employee** object.

The statement

```
Employee[] employees = new Employee[5];
```

declares an array **employees** that can reference five objects of type **Employee**. The array elements initially store the value **null**. The statements

```
employees[0] = new Employee(1111, 40.0, 15.5);
employees[1] = new Employee(1234, 50.0, 25.0);
```

create and store data in two new **Employee** objects referenced by **employees[0]** and **employees[1]** (see Fig. 5.28).

Figure 5.28   Array employees with two Employee objects

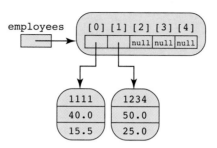

We can use the **for** statement below to calculate the total pay of the first two employees.

```
totalPay = 0.0;
for (int i = 0; i < 2; i++) {
   totalPay += (employees[i].getHours() *
               employees[i].getRate());
```

We apply these concepts next.

CASE STUDY COMPUTING PAYROLL USING AN ARRAY OF EMPLOYEES

PROBLEM   We have a company with several employees. We want to read and store all employee data and compute the total payroll for the company using an array of **Employee** objects.

ANALYSIS AND DESIGN   Our company has a collection of employees and also a payroll. Figure 5.29 shows a description of class **Company** with a data field, **employees**, that references an array of **Employee** objects and a data field **payroll** that stores the total payroll for the company. Class **Company** provides methods for processing the data stored in the array and for computing the company payroll.
     Method **setEmployee()** stores an **Employee** object at a specified position in the array; method **getEmployee()** returns the **Employee** object at the subscript specified by its argument. Method **readPayrollData()** reads the payroll data for the company. Method **computePayroll()** computes the total payroll for the company.

Figure 5.29   Class `Company`

Data Fields	Attributes
`Employee[] employees`	Array of employees
`double payroll`	Company payroll

Methods	Behavior
`Company(int)`	Creates a **company** object with an array **employees** whose size is specified by the argument
`void setEmployee(Employee, int)`	Stores the first argument in array **employees** at the position specified by the second argument
`void setPayroll(double)`	Stores its argument in **payroll**
`Employee getEmployee(int)`	Retrieves the employee at the position indicated by its argument
`double getPayroll()`	Returns the company payroll
`void readPayrollData()`	Reads the payroll data into array **employees**
`void computePayroll`	Computes the total payroll
`String toString()`	Represents the company's data as a string

Classes Used
`Employee`

IMPLEMENTATION   Figure 5.30 shows the class implementation. The constructor method allocates storage for an array whose size is set by the constructor argument. The private method **inRange()** tests whether its argument is a valid subscript for array **employees** and is called by both **setEmployee()** and **getEmployee()**.

Method **toString()** represents the contents of the array **employees** as a string, with line feed characters between individual employee objects. In the **for** statement, the line

```
empStr = empStr + employees[countEmp] + "\n";
```

appends the string representing the current employee to the string being formed. Notice that it is not necessary to explicitly call the current employee's **toString()** method; this is done automatically. The value of **payroll** is appended to the string after the array of employee information.

Method **readPayrollData()** reads the employee data and stores that data in array **employees**. During each iteration of the **for** statement, method **readOneEmp()**

(a `private static` method) reads a single employee's payroll data and stores this data in a new `Employee` object, which is returned as the method result. The statement

```
employees[countEmp] = readOneEmployee();
```

causes the current element of array `employees` to reference the new `Employee` object.

In method `computePayroll()`, the statement

```
payroll += (employees[index].getHours() *
            employees[index].getRate());
```

adds the current employee's pay to the sum being accumulated in data field `payroll`.

TESTING   Figure 5.31 shows an application class that tests class `Company`. Figure 5.32 shows the result of running this application.

PROGRAM STYLE: *Algorithm Simplification by Using Arrays*

The data structure used in a program can affect the complexity of the algorithm. Compare the payroll program in this section to the one in Section 4.4. Method `computePayTotals` (in Section 4.4) reads each employee's data and also processes it. Because we could only store one employee's data at a time, we had to process the current employee's data in its entirety before we could read the next employee's data. The array data structure enables us to save data for all the employees in memory, so we can separate the reading operation (done by methods `readPayrollData()` and `readOneEmployee()`) from the payroll processing operation (done by method `computePayroll()`). This results in a simplification of the algorithm for method `computePayroll()`.

CASE STUDY PHONE DIRECTORY

PROBLEM   You would like to be able to create a personal telephone directory that contains your friends' names and telephone numbers. You would like to be able to display this directory and also to retrieve a particular entry in the directory by specifying the person's name or a directory subscript.

Figure 5.30   Class Company

```
/* Company.java          Authors: Koffman & Wolz
 * Class for processing array of employees and computing
 * company payroll.
 * Uses Employee
 */
import psJava.KeyIn;

public class Company {

  // Data fields
  private Employee[] employees; // array of employees
  private double payroll;       // company payroll

  // Methods
  // postcondition: Allocates storage for an array of Employee objects
  //   of the specified size.
  public Company(int numEmp) {
     employees = new Employee[numEmp];
  }

  public void setPayroll(double totPay) {
    payroll = totPay;
  }

  // postcondition: Returns true if its argument
  //    is a valid subscript for array employees
  private boolean inRange(int index) {
    return index >= 0 && index < employees.length;
  }

  // postcondition: Stores the employee at the specified index if
  //     the index is a valid subscript.
  public void setEmployee(Employee emp, int index) {
    if (inRange(index))
       employees[index] = emp;
  }

  public double getPayroll() {
    return payroll;
  }

  // postcondition: If the index is valid, returns that employee
  //    otherwise, returns null.
```

Figure 5.30 Class Company, *continued*

```java
public Employee getEmployee(int index) {
   if (inRange(index))
     return employees[index];
   else
     return null;
}

// postcondition: Returns an Employee object after reading its data.
private static Employee readOneEmployee() {
   String id = KeyIn.readString("Employee id:");
   double hours = KeyIn.readDouble("Hours worked:");
   double rate = KeyIn.readDouble("Hourly rate $");
   return new Employee(id, hours, rate);
}

// postcondition: Stores all employee data in myCompany.
public void readPayrollData() {
   for (int countEmp = 0; countEmp < employees.length; countEmp++) {
      // Read data for a new employee and store
      //    the data in array employees
      employees[countEmp] = readOneEmployee();
   }
}

// postcondition: Compute the total payroll for the company.
public void computePayroll() {
   // Compute total gross pay.
   payroll = 0;
   for (int index = 0; index < employees.length; index++) {
      payroll += (employees[index].getHours() *
                employees[index].getRate());
   }
}

public String toString() {
   String empStr = "Employee information: \n";
   for (int countEmp = 0; countEmp < employees.length; countEmp++) {
      empStr = empStr + employees[countEmp] + "\n";
   }
   return empStr + "\nCompany payroll is $" + payroll;
}

}
```

Figure 5.31 Class `PayrollApp`

```
/* PayrollApp.java          Authors: Koffman & Wolz
 * Application class for testing class Company
 * Uses Payroll
 */
import psJava.KeyIn;      // used for input

public class PayrollApp {

    public static void main(String[] args) {
        // Create a new Company object.
        Company comp =
            new Company(KeyIn.readInt("How many employees?"));
        // Read the payroll data.
        comp.readPayrollData();
        // Compute the total payroll.
        comp.computePayroll();
        // Display the company information.
        System.out.println(comp.toString());
    }
}
```

Figure 5.32 Sample run of class `PayrollApp`

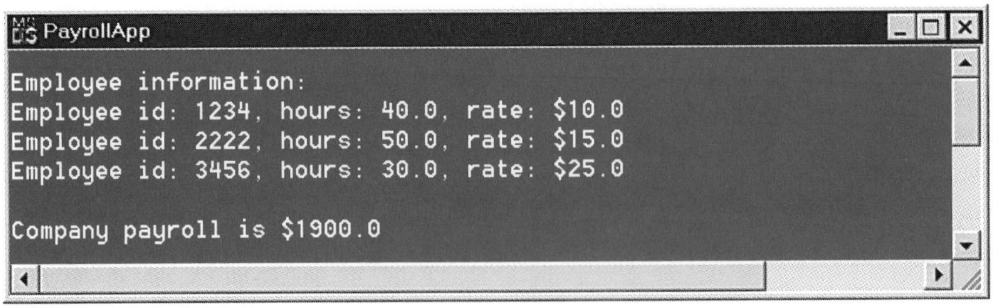

```
MS PayrollApp                                        _ □ ✕

Employee information:
Employee id: 1234, hours: 40.0, rate: $10.0
Employee id: 2222, hours: 50.0, rate: $15.0
Employee id: 3456, hours: 30.0, rate: $25.0

Company payroll is $1900.0
```

ANALYSIS   Because we don't know how big the directory is likely to get, we will make it expandable by adding a new page whenever the last page is filled. To make it easy to illustrate this expansion in the program output, we will make the page size relatively small (five entries per page). An actual directory would have a larger page size. We need a class **Friend** to represent each friend's information and a class **PhoneBook** to represent the telephone directory.

DESIGN

Class **Friend**

Fig. 5.33 shows a description of class **Friend**; a **Friend** object stores a person's name and phone number in two type **String** data fields. We have already discussed how to write classes that are similar to class **Friend**.

Class **PhoneBook**

Fig. 5.34 shows a description of class **PhoneBook**. Data field **directory** stores an array of **Friend** objects.

We have discussed how to write methods for searching an array and for retrieving selected array elements. We talk about the new methods next.

Method **addFriend()** first checks to see whether the current directory is filled. If so, it calls method **addPage()** to add a new page to the directory. In either case, the new friend is stored in the next available position (index **numFriends**) of the directory.

Figure 5.33   Class Friend

Data Fields	Attributes
String name	A name
String phone	A phone number
Methods	**Behavior**
Friend(String, String)	Creates a **Friend** object, storing its arguments in the new object's data fields
String getName()	Gets the friend's name
String getPhone()	Gets the friend's phone number
String toString()	Represents the friend's data as a string
Classes Used	
String	

Figure 5.34   Class `PhoneBook`

Data Fields	Attributes
`Friend[] directory`	The telephone directory
`int numPages`	The number of pages in the directory
`int numFriends`	The number of friends in the directory
Methods	**Behavior**
`PhoneBook()`	Creates a new `PhoneBook` object whose directory has one page and zero friends
`void addFriend(Friend)`	Adds a friend's data to the directory
`void setFriend(int, Friend)`	Stores the specified `Friend` object at the specified index
`Friend getFriend(int)`	Retrieves a friend from the directory given an index
`int findFriend(String)`	Finds the subscript of a friend in the directory given the friend's name
`String getNumber(String)`	Retrieves a friend's phone number given the friend's name
`void addPage()`	Adds a page to the directory
`int getNumPages()`	Gets the number of pages in the directory
`int getNumFriends()`	Gets the number of friends in the directory
`String toString()`	Represents the phone book data as a string
Classes Used	
`Friend`	

Algorithm for *addFriend()* (class *PhoneBook*)

1. `if` the directory is filled

   Add a new page.

2. Insert new friend at position `numFriends` of directory array.

3. Increment `numFriends`.

Method `addPage()` adds a page to the directory. It does this by creating a new directory array that has one more page than the current directory.

Algorithm for *addPage()* (class *PhoneBook*)

1. Increment the number of pages.

2. Create a new array of friends with one more page.

3. Copy all friends from the old array to the new array.

4. Reset directory to reference the new array.

IMPLEMENTATION   Figure 5.35 shows class `Friend`. Figure 5.36 shows class `PhoneBook`. The class constructor starts each new `PhoneBook` object with a directory of one page:

```
directory = new Friend[PAGE_SIZE];
numPages = 1;
```

In method `addFriend()`, the condition (`numFriends >= numPages * PAGE_SIZE`) is true if the current directory is full. If so, a new page is added.

Figure 5.35   Class `Friend`

```
/*
 * Friend.java        Authors: Koffman and Wolz
 * Represents a friend.
 */
public class Friend {
  // Data fields
  private String name;
  private String phone;

  // Methods
  public Friend() {
  }

  // postcondition: Stores its arguments in a new Friend object
  public Friend(String friendName, String friendPhone) {
    name = friendName;
    phone = friendPhone;
  }

  public String getName() {
    return name;
  }

  public String getPhone () {
    return phone;
  }

  public String toString() {
    return name + ", " + phone;
  }
}
```

Figure 5.36   Class PhoneBook

```java
/*
 * PhoneBook.java      Authors: Koffman and Wolz
 * Represents a telephone directory.
 */
public class PhoneBook {
  // Data fields
  private Friend[] directory;      // array of friends
  private static int PAGE_SIZE = 5; // friends on each page
  private int numPages;       // number of pages in directory
  private int numFriends;     // number of friends in directory

  // postcondition: Creates a new PhoneBook object with 1 page
  //    in its directory.
  public PhoneBook() {
    directory = new Friend[PAGE_SIZE];
    numPages = 1;
  }

  // postcondition: Adds its argument to the directory.
  //    Adds a new page if current page is filled.
  //    Increments numFriends.
  public void addFriend(Friend aFriend) {
    if (numFriends >= numPages * PAGE_SIZE)
      addPage();
    directory[numFriends] = aFriend;
    numFriends++;
  }

  // postcondition: Returns true if its argument is in range.
  public boolean inDirectory(int index) {
    return index >= 0 && index < numFriends;
  }

  // postcondition: Stores aFriend at position index.
  public void setFriend(int index, Friend, aFriend) {
    if (inDirectory(index))
      directory[index] = aFriend;
  }

  // postcondition: Returns the friend selected by its argument.
  //    Returns a null reference if the index is not in range.
  public Friend getFriend(int index) {
```

Figure 5.36 **Class** PhoneBook, *continued*

```
    if (inDirectory(index))
      return directory[index];
    else
      return null;
  }


  // postcondition: Returns the phone number (a string) of the
  //    friend whose name is referenced by its argument.
  //    Returns a null reference if the name is not found.
  public String getNumber(String friendName) {
    int index = findFriend(friendName);
    if (index >= 0)
      return directory[index].getPhone();
    else
      return null;
  }


  // postcondition: Returns the index of the friend whose
  //    name is referenced by its argument.
  //    Returns -1 if not found.
  public int findFriend(String friendName) {
    for (int index = 0; index < numFriends; index++) {
      if (directory[index].getName().equals(friendName))
        return index;
    }


    // friendName not found.
    return -1;
  }


  // postcondition: Increments numPages and adds a page to
  //    the directory array.
  public void addPage() {
    numPages++;

    // Create a new array of friends with one more page.
    Friend[] tempDirectory = new Friend[numPages * PAGE_SIZE];

    // Copy all friends from the old array to the new array.
    System.arraycopy(directory, 0, tempDirectory, 0, numFriends);
```

Figure 5.36   Class PhoneBook, *continued*

```
  // Reset directory to reference the new array.
  directory = tempDirectory;
}

public int getNumPages() {
  return numPages;
}

public int getNumFriends() {
  return numFriends;
}

// postcondition: Returns a String representing the telephone
//   directory. The page number is inserted at the beginning
//   of each new page.
public String toString() {
  String result = "";
  for (int index = 0; index < numFriends; index++) {
    if (index % PAGE_SIZE == 0)
      result = result + "\npage: " + (1 + index / PAGE_SIZE) +
               "\n";
    result = result + directory[index] + "\n";
  }
  return result;
}

}
```

In method **getFriend()**, the condition (inDirectory(index)) is **true** if index is within the valid subscript range. If so, the directory entry with that subscript is returned. If not, a null reference is returned.

In method **findFriend()**, the condition (directory[index].getName(). equals(friendName)) is **true** if the current friend's name matches the string referenced by argument **friendName**. If so, the subscript **index** is returned.

In method **addPage()**, the statement

```
System.arraycopy(directory, 0, tempDirectory, 0, numFriends);
```

copies the old directory into the new, larger directory.

Method `toString()` builds a string containing all of the friends' information, with a line separator character between friends. The condition **(index % PAGE_SIZE == 0)** is **true** when **index** accesses the first friend on a page. If so, the page number is calculated **(1+index / PAGE_SIZE)** and is inserted in the string before the first friend's information.

TESTING   Figure 5.37 shows class **PhoneBookApp**, which tests class **PhoneBook**. Figure 5.38 shows the result of running this application.

Figure 5.37   Class PhoneBookApp

```
/*
 * PhoneBookApp.java       Authors: Koffman and Wolz
 * Application to test class PhoneBook.
 */
public class PhoneBookApp {

  public static void main(String[] args) {
    PhoneBook myPB = new PhoneBook();

    myPB.addFriend(new Friend("Caryn", "215-555-1234"));
    myPB.addFriend(new Friend("Jane", "215-555-2222"));
    myPB.addFriend(new Friend("Robin", "215-555-2345"));
    myPB.addFriend(new Friend("Sam", "215-555-1867"));
    myPB.addFriend(new Friend("Elliot", "215-555-2222"));
    myPB.addFriend(new Friend("Deborah", "215-555-6543"));
    myPB.addFriend(new Friend("Sally", "215-555-8133"));

    System.out.println("pages: " + myPB.getNumPages() +
                   ", friends: " + myPB.getNumFriends());
    System.out.println(myPB.toString());
    System.out.println("Sam's number: " + myPB.getNumber("Sam"));
    System.out.println("last friend: " +
                   myPB.getFriend(myPB.getNumFriends() - 1));
  }
}
```

Figure 5.38   Sample run of PhoneBookApp

```
page: 1
Caryn, 215-555-1234
Jane, 215-555-2222
Robin, 215-555-2345
Sam, 215-555-1867
Elliot, 215-555-2222

page: 2
Deborah, 215-555-6543
Sally, 215-555-8133

pages: 2, friends: 7
Sam's number: 215-555-1867
last friend: Sally, 215-555-8133
```

EXERCISES FOR SECTION 5.5

SELF-CHECK

1. Draw a diagram showing object **myPB** (Fig. 5.37) after the first three friends have been inserted.

2. Trace the execution of method **readOneEmployee()** of class **Company** (Fig. 5.30).

3. Discuss how you would modify class **Company** (Fig. 5.30) to use your own methods **readDouble()** and **readInt()**.

PROGRAMMING

1. Write a method for class **Company** (Fig. 5.30) to find the mean gross salary.

2. Modify method **computeTotalGross()** of class **Company** to display each employee's data and gross salary as it is calculated.

3. Write a sorting method for class **Company** (Fig. 5.30) that rearranges the information in array **employees** so that the employee information is ordered by hours worked. The employee with the smallest number of hours should be first.

4. Write a method **readFriendsData()** for class **PhoneBook** (Fig. 5.37) that reads the data for a collection of friends and stores them in the phone book.

5.6 Multidimensional Arrays—Arrays of Arrays

The array data structure allows a programmer to organize information in arrangements that are more complex than the linear or one-dimensional arrays you've seen so far. We can declare and use arrays with several dimensions. Although **multidimensional arrays** give you more flexibility in arranging data than one-dimensional arrays, the rules for element types are the same: The array elements may be simple or structured, but they must all be the same type.

Two-dimensional arrays, the most common multidimensional arrays, store information that we normally represent in table form. An example is a seating plan for a classroom in which you list each student's name in the position (row and seat) where that student's desk is located in the classroom (see Fig. 5.39).

Figure 5.39   Classroom seating plan (11 rows and 9 seats per row)

	Seat 0	Seat 1	...	Seat 8
Row 0	Alice	Bill		Gerry
Row 1	Jane	Sue		Groucho
. .	.		.	
. .	.		.	
. .	.		.	
Row 10	Harpo	Sam		Jillian

Declaring Two-Dimensional Arrays

The next examples demonstrate how to declare and process two-dimensional arrays. To reference an element of a two-dimensional array, you must specify the array name and provide two index expressions. The first index is the row index, and the second index is the column index.

◆◆EXAMPLE 5.9

A familiar two-dimensional object is a tic-tac-toe board. The statement

```
char[][] ticTacToe = new char[3][3];
```

allocates storage for array `ticTacToe` (see Fig. 5.40). Array `ticTacToe` is a two-dimensional array with three rows and three columns. This array has nine elements, each of which must be referenced by specifying a row index (**0**, **1**, or **2**) and a column index (**0**, **1**, or **2**).

Figure 5.40   **A tic-tac-toe board stored as array `ticTacToe`**

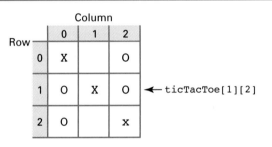

The indexed variable

```
ticTacToe[1][2]
```

selects the array element in row **1**, column **2** of the array in Fig. 5.40; it contains the character **O**.

◆◆EXAMPLE 5.10

Your instructor wants to store the seating plan (Fig. 5.39) for a classroom on a computer. The statements

```
String[][] seatPlan = new String[11][9];
```

allocate storage for a two-dimensional array of strings called **seatPlan**. Array **seatPlan** could be used to hold the first names of the students seated in a classroom with 11 rows and 9 seats in each row. The statement

```
seatPlan[5][4] = "Marilyn";
```

places a student named **Marilyn** in row **5**, seat **4**, the center of the classroom.

A two-dimensional array is really an array of arrays; therefore, variable **seatPlan** actually references a one-dimensional array. Each element of this array also references a one-dimensional array whose elements reference **String** objects (see Fig. 5.41).

Figure 5.41   Array **seatPlan**

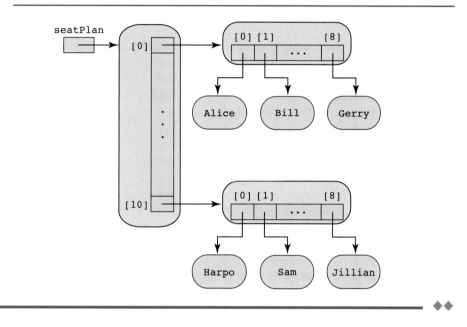

Initializing a Two-Dimensional Array

Just as for one-dimensional arrays, you can initialize the elements of a two-dimensional array when you declare it. You specify the element values for each row in braces and enclose all the row values in an outer pair of braces.

◆◆EXAMPLE 5.11 ─────────────────────────────────

The statements

```
double matrix[][] = {{5.0, 4.5, 3.0},
                     {-16.0, -5.9, 0.0}};
```

allocate storage for the array matrix with two rows and three columns. Each inner pair of braces contains the initial values for a row of the array matrix, starting with row 0, as shown next:

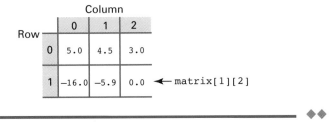

Processing Two-Dimensional Arrays Using Nested Loops

You must use nested loops to access the elements of a two-dimensional array in row or column order. If you want to access the array elements in row order (the normal situation), use the row index as the loop-control variable for the outer loop and the column index as the loop-control variable for the inner loop. The general form of such a loop is

> **for** each row **r** in the array
>   **for** each column **c** in the array
>   Process the element with indices **[r][c]**

For each value of **r** (normally from 0 to its maximum), the inner loop executes and cycles through all values of **c**. This means the nested loops process the elements of array **matrix** (see Example 5.11) in the sequence

```
matrix[0][0]  matrix[0][1]  matrix[0][2]  matrix[1][0]
matrix[1][1]  matrix[1][2]
```

This approach is called **row-major order**. If the outer **for** statement controls the column subscript and the inner for statement controls the row subscript, the array will be processed in **column-major order**.

◆◆EXAMPLE 5.12 ───

Method **toString()** in Fig. 5.42 creates a string (**result**) that represents the seating plan array from Fig. 5.39 in table format. Because the outer **for** loop initializes **row** to its largest value, the first row of the string contains the names of the students sitting in the last row of the classroom. The last row contains the names of the students sitting in the first row of the classroom (closest to the teacher). In the inner **for** loop, the statement

```
result = result + seatPlan[row][col] + "    ";
```

appends each name in a row to the string being formed. A new-line character is inserted at the end of each row.

Figure 5.42   Method `toString()` for seating plan array

```
// postcondition: returns a string representation of array seatPlan.
//    The last row in the array is placed first in the string.
//    New-line characters separate the rows.
public String toString() {
  String result = "";
  for (int row = seatPlan.length - 1; row >= 0; row--) {
    for (int col = 0; col < seatPlan[row].length; col++) {
      result = result + seatPlan[row][col] + "   ";
    }
    result += "\n";    // insert new-line character between rows
  }
  return result;
}
```

◆◆EXAMPLE 5.13

Method **sumMatrix** in Fig. 5.43 finds the sum of all elements of the two-dimensional array passed as the function argument (**twoDim**).

Figure 5.43   Method `sumMatrix()`

```
// postcondition: Returns the sum of all elements of
//    its matrix argument.
public static int sumMatrix (int[][] twoDim) {
  int sum = 0.0;

  for (int row = 0; row < twoDim.length; row++)
    for (int col = 0; col < twoDim[row].length; col++)
      sum = sum + twoDim[row][col];

  return sum;
}
```

Use of `length` Attribute with Two-Dimensional Arrays

In Figs. 5.42 and 5.43 we used the `length` attribute to make the methods general. In method `toString()`, the number of rows in the seating plan is represented by `seatPlan.length`. In method `sumMatrix()`, the number of rows in the matrix parameter is represented by `twoDim.length`. For each array, the subscript of the last row is 1 less than the number of rows. Because each row of a two-dimensional array is also an array, we can use the `length` attribute with the row name to get the number of elements in a row. For example, `twoDim[i].length` is the number of elements in row `i` of the matrix parameter `twoDim`. The subscript of the last column in the matrix is 1 less than this value.

Arrays with More Than Two Dimensions

There is no limit to the number of dimensions for Java arrays, but arrays with more than three dimensions occur infrequently. The three-dimensional array declared below can be used to store the monthly sales figures (12 per year) for the last five years for each of 10 salespeople.

```
int salesPeople = 10;
int years = 5;
double[][][] sales = new double[salesPeople][years][12];
```

The array `sales` has a total of 160 (10 × 5 × 12) elements. The array element `sales[0][4][11]` represents the amount of sales made by the first salesperson during the last month of the last year.

EXERCISES FOR SECTION 5.6

SELF-CHECK

1. For the two-dimensional array

   ```
   double[][] salesByQuarter = new double[5][4];
   ```

   a. How many elements are in array `salesByQuarter`?

   b. Write a statement to display the element in row **2**, column **3**.

   c. How would you reference the element in the last column of the last row?

PROGRAMMING

1. Write a `toString()` method that creates a string representation of a matrix. Each row should end with a `\n` character.

5.7   Vectors

Java provides a class called **Vector** that is like an array but with some additional features. Unlike an array, you don't need to declare the size of a vector, but you can let it grow and shrink as needed. Also, there are methods in the **Vector** class that let you add, retrieve, insert, or remove elements in the middle of a vector. The elements that you place in a vector must be objects, not primitive types. You must insert the statement

```
import java.util.Vector;
```

or

```
import java.util.*;
```

before the definition of a class that uses vectors.

◆◆EXAMPLE 5.14 ───

In this example, we show how to use the **Vector** class for storing a collection of employees. The data declaration

```
Vector employees = new Vector();
```

is all that is required to allocate storage for a vector named **employees**. We don't need to declare the type of object to be stored in the vector, or the size of the vector, because its size is automatically adjusted as new items are added and removed.
   The statements

```
employees.addElement(new Employee(1111, 40.0, 15.0));
employees.addElement(new Employee(1234, 50.0, 25.0));
```

append two new **Employee** objects at the end of vector **employees**. If vector **employees** is empty, the first employee would be at position 0 and the second employee would be at position 1. The method call **employees.size()** would return 2, the current size of vector **employees**. Figure 5.44 shows the vector **employees**.

Figure 5.44 Vector employees

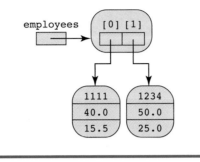

Even though vector elements have indexes, Java does not allow you to use an indexed variable to reference a vector element (that is, `employees[0]` is not allowed). Instead, use method `elementAt()` to access an element of a vector. The statement

```
Object tempEmp = employees.elementAt(1);
```

causes `tempEmp` (type `Object`) to reference the second object in vector `employees` (the object at index 1). You get an index out-of-bounds error if there is no vector element with that index. Notice that the data type of the reference is type `Object`, rather than type `Employee`. We discuss this further in the next section.

Three other useful methods for vectors are `setElementAt()`, `insertElementAt()`, and `removeElementAt()`. You use method `setElementAt()` to store an object in a specified element of a vector. The statement

```
employees.setElementAt(new Employee(2222, 40.0, 25.0), 1);
```

stores a reference to a new `Employee` object (the first argument) with ID **2222** at index **1** (the second argument). If there is no element with index **1**, you get an index out-of-bounds error.

You use method `insertElementAt()` to insert an element anywhere in a vector—the elements that follow it are shifted down one position to make room. The statement

```
employees.insertElementAt(new Employee(2345, 50.0, 25.0)), 0);
```

inserts a new `Employee` object at index 0, the employee formerly at index 0 moves to index 1, the employee formerly at index 1 moves to index 2. The vector size is **3** (see Fig. 5.45). You get an index out-of-bounds error if the index you insert at is larger than the vector size before the insertion. When the index equals the vector size, the new element is appended to the end of the vector.

Figure 5.45 Vector **employees** after insertion

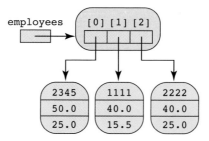

Similarly, you use **removeElementAt** to remove an element from the vector—the elements that follow it are shifted up one position to fill the vacated space. As you would expect, the vector size automatically decreases after a removal. The statement

```
Object tempEmp = employees.removeElement(1);
```

causes **tempEmp** to reference the second object in vector **employees** (the object at index **1**) and removes this element from the vector; the element at position **2** moves to position **1**. The vector size is now **2**.

The **Vector** class has a **toString()** method. If you apply this method to a **Vector** object, it returns a string enclosed in brackets consisting of the string representation of each of its elements separated by commas. In order for this string to make sense, each of the objects in the vector must have its own **toString()** method. Class **Employee** has a **toString()** method that forms a string containing the information for each employee (see Fig. 4.12). For the vector **employees** shown in Fig. 5.44, the method call

```
employees.toString()
```

returns the string containing the characters [**Employee id: 1111, hours: 40.0, rate: $15.0, Employee id: 1234, hours: 50.0, rate: $25.0**]. Table 5.3 summarizes the methods for the **Vector** class.

Casting Objects in a Vector

As we saw earlier, the expression

```
employees.elementAt(0)
```

returns a type **Object** reference to the first object in vector **employees**. (Recall that type **Object** is the superclass of all classes.) However, we know that vector **employees** stores references to type **Employee** objects. The expression

```
(Employee) employees.elementAt(0)
```

Table 5.3 Methods for `Vector` class

Method Header	Sample Call
`Vector()`	`Vector employees = new Vector();` Constructs an empty vector **employees**.
`void addElement(Object o)`	`employees.addElement(Emp1)` Appends object **Emp1** (type **Employee**) to vector **employees** and increments its size.
`Object elementAt(int i)`	`employees.elementAt(0)` Returns a type **Object** reference to the element at index **0** of vector **employees**. The argument must be less than the vector size.
`int indexOf(Object o)`	`employees.indexOf(Emp1)` Returns the location of the first occurrence of **Emp1** in vector **employees**.
`void insertElementAt(Object o, int i)`	`employees.insertElementAt(anEmp, 1)` Inserts object **anEmp** (type **Employee**) at index **1** of **employees**, moving the object formerly at index **1** to index **2**, and so on. Increments the size of **employees**. The argument must not be greater than the vector size.
`boolean removeElement(Object o)`	`employees.removeElement(anEmp)` Removes the first occurrence of **anEmp** from vector **employees**, shifting all elements following the one removed to fill the space. Returns **true** if **anEmp** was removed; otherwise, returns **false**.
`void removeElementAt(int i)`	`employees.removeElementAt(1)` Removes the element at index **1** from **employees**, moving the element at index **2** to index **1**, and so on. The argument must be less than the vector size. Decrements the size of **employees**.
`void setElementAt(Object o, int i)`	`employees.setElementAt(Emp2, 1)` Stores object **Emp2** at index **1** of vector **employees**. The argument must be less than the vector size.
`int size()`	`employees.size()` Returns the size of vector **employees**.
`String toString()`	`employees.toString()` Returns a string representation of vector **employees** enclosed in brackets. It forms this string by applying each object's **toString()** method starting with the object at index **0**. Places a comma between objects.

casts the type **Object** reference from type **Object** to type **Employee**, so we can use the statement below to store a reference to the first employee in variable **firstEmp**:

```
Employee firstEmp = (Employee) employees.elementAt(0);
```

The casting operation is required because without it, we would be attempting to store a reference to a type `Object` entity in a type `Employee` variable, and Java does not allow this. We discuss assignment and casting in an object hierarchy in Section 6.2.

The statement

```
int firstID = firstEmp.getID();
```

calls the `getID()` method of the object referenced by `firstEmp` and assigns the result to `firstID`. You can also accomplish this using a single statement:

```
int firstID = ((Employee) employees.elementAt(0)).getID();
```

In the expression above, the type `Employee` reference resulting from the type `cast` is **anonymous** or **unnamed** because it is not stored in a variable.

Storing Different Type Objects in a Vector

Unlike an array, a vector can store objects of different types. For example, the statement

```
employees.setElementAt("Harry", 2);
```

stores the string containing the characters `Harry` at element `2` of vector `employees`. This is generally not a good idea, because the programmer must remember what kind of object is stored in each vector element in order to process it correctly. For example, the expression

```
(Employee) employees.elementAt(2)
```

would cause an invalid cast error because an object of type `String` cannot be cast to an object of type `Employee`.

Class PhoneBook as a Vector

You can use vectors anywhere you use one-dimensional arrays. Often the use of vectors will simplify the code because vectors can grow as needed. In the phone book case study, we added a new page whenever the current directory was filled (see Fig. 5.36). If we implement the telephone directory class (`PhoneBook`) using a vector to store the telephone directory, we don't need to keep track of the number of friends in the phone directory or to add a new page when we fill the current page.

Fig. 5.46 shows class `PhoneBook`. The constructor method creates a new empty vector, `directory`. All methods call object `directory`'s `size()` method to determine the number of friends currently stored. Method `addFriend()` calls object `directory`'s `addElement()` method to add a new friend. Class `PhoneBookApp` (Fig. 5.37) and the output would be the same as before (see Fig. 5.38).

Figure 5.46   Class PhoneBook with a vector implementation

```java
/*
 * PhoneBook.java        Authors: Koffman and Wolz
 * Represents a telephone directory using a vector.
 */
import java.util.Vector;

public class PhoneBook {
  // Data fields
  private Vector directory;
  private static int PAGE_SIZE = 5;   // friends on each page

  // Methods
  // postcondition: directory references an empty vector
  public PhoneBook() {
    directory = new Vector();
  }

  // postcondition: Adds its argument to the directory.
  public void addFriend(Friend aFriend) {
    directory.addElement(aFriend);
  }

  // postcondition: Returns the friend selected by its argument.
  public Friend getFriend(int index) {
    if (inDirectory(index))
      return (Friend) directory.elementAt(index);
    else
      return null;
  }

  // postcondition: Returns the number of the friend whose
  //    name is referenced by its argument.
  public String getNumber(String friendName) {
    int index = findFriend(friendName);
    if (index >= 0)
      return ((Friend) directory.elementAt(index)).getPhone();
    else
      return null;
  }

  // postcondition: Returns the index of the friend whose
  //    name is referenced by its argument.
  //    Returns -1 if not found.
  public int findFriend(String friendName) {
```

Figure 5.46   Class `PhoneBook` with a vector implementation, *continued*

```
    for (int index = 0; index < directory.size(); index++) {
      if (((Friend) directory.elementAt(index)).getName().equals(friendName))
        return index;
    }

    // friendName not found.
    return -1;
  }

  // postcondition: Returns true if its argument is in range.
  public boolean inDirectory(int index) {
    return index >= 0 && index < directory.size();
  }

  // postcondition: Returns a String representing the telephone
  //    directory. The page number is inserted at the beginning
  //    of each new page.
  public String toString() {
    String result = "";
    for (int index = 0; index < directory.size(); index++) {
      if (index % PAGE_SIZE == 0)
        result = result + "\npage: " + (1 + index / PAGE_SIZE) + "\n";
      result = result + directory.elementAt(index).toString() + "\n";
    }
    return result;
  }

  // postcondition: Returns the number of friends in the directory.
  //    Added for compatibility with the array implementation.
  public int getNumFriends() {
    return directory.size();
  }

  // postcondition: Returns the number of pages in the directory.
  //    Added for compatibility with the array implementation.
  public int getNumPages() {
    return 1 + directory.size() / PAGE_SIZE;
  }

}
```

As we explained in the last section, we use the construct

```
(Friend) directory.elementAt(index)
```

several times in class **PhoneBook** to cast to type **Friend** the type **Object** reference returned by method **elementAt()**. Method **findFriend()**

```
public int findFriend(String friendName)
```

returns the directory index of the friend whose name is **friendName**. The condition

```
(((Friend) directory.elementAt(index)).getName().equals(friendName))
```

compares data field **name** (returned by **getName()**) of the friend at **index** to **friendName**.

In the statement

```
result = result + directory.elementAt(index).toString() + "\n";
```

it was not necessary to cast the vector element at **index** to type **Friend** because both the **Object** and **Friend** classes have **toString()** methods. Because the object that is referenced is type **Friend**, the Java run-time environment calls the correct **toString()** method (the one belonging to class **Friend**). If class **Object** did not have a **toString()** method, the compiler would not be able to translate this statement. If class **Friend** did not have a **toString()** method, the run-time environment would call the **toString()** method for class **Object**. We discuss this further in Section 6.2.

EXERCISES FOR SECTION 5.7

SELF-CHECK

1. Complete the **for** loop below that displays the information in vector **employees**, one object per line. Method **toString()** is defined in class **Employee**. Is the call to **toString()** necessary?

```
for (int i = 0; i < _____ ; i++)
    System.out.println(              .toString());
```

Write a single statement that accomplishes this without using a loop.

2. Explain each statement in the fragment below:

```
Vector n = new Vector();
n.addElement(new Friend("Jane", "555-1212"));
n.addElement(new Friend("Sally", "555-8484"));
n.setElementAt(new Friend("Jill", "555-3678"), 1);
n.insertElementAt(new Friend("Sarah", "555-0101"), 0);
Friend best = (Friend) n.elementAt(2);
n.removeElementAt(1);
System.out.println("Size is " + n.size());
System.out.println(n.toString());
```

3. Assume you have a vector of **Employee** objects. Write statements to replace the element at index 1 with **empC**. Insert **empB** at index 2. Then remove the element in the middle of the vector and move it to the end.

PROGRAMMING

1. Rewrite class **Company** (Fig. 5.29) using a vector to store the employee data.

5.8 Wrapper Classes for Primitive Type Data

You can store objects, but not primitive types, in vectors. Does this restriction mean that you can only store primitive types in arrays and not in vectors? Fortunately, Java provides a **wrapper class** for each primitive type that encapsulates a primitive type value in an object so it can be processed like other object types. Each wrapper class contains methods for converting back and forth between primitive types and objects. The wrapper classes for Java's primitive types are **Boolean**, **Character**, **Integer**, and **Double**. They are described in detail in Appendix C.

Table 5.4 describes some methods defined in class **Integer**. The other wrapper classes have counterparts to all of these methods, except for **parseInt()**. However, class **Double** has a comparable method **parseDouble()**. Use method **doubleValue()** to retrieve a type **double** value from a type **Double** object, method **charValue()** to retrieve a type **char** value from a type **Character** object, or method **booleanValue()** to retrieve a type **boolean** value from a type **Boolean** object. You can compare two wrapper objects of the same type using method **equals()** and build a string representation of any wrapper object using method **toString()**.

Table 5.4   Methods in wrapper class `Integer`

Header	Sample Call
`Integer(int n)`	`Integer i1 = new Integer(55)` Wraps the integer 55 in a type `Integer` object referenced by `i1`.
`Integer(String s)`	`Integer i2 = new Integer("55");` Wraps the integer 55 in a type `Integer` object referenced by `i2`. The argument must be a numeric string.
`String toString()`	`i1.toString()` Returns a string containing the characters 55.
`int intValue()`	`i1.intValue()` Gets the integer 55, which is wrapped in `Integer` object `i1`.
`boolean equals(Object obj2)`	`i1.equals(i2)` Value is `true` because both `Integer` objects wrap the integer 55.
`static int parseInt(String s)`	`Integer.parseInt("55")` Returns the integer 55. The argument must be a numeric string.

We previously used two methods defined in the wrapper classes for data entry: methods `Double.parseDouble()` and `Integer.parseInt()`. Both methods take a `String` argument and return a number if the string is numeric.

◆◆EXAMPLE 5.15 ─────────────────────────────────────

The statements

```
double x = 5.67;
double y = 7.92;
Double dX = new Double(x);
Double dY = new Double(y);
```

declare two type **double** variables (**x** and **y**) and wrap their values in type **Double** objects (**dX** and **dY**). Next, we store these objects in the first two elements of vector **numbers**:

```
Vector numbers = new Vector();
numbers.addElement(dX);
numbers.addElement(dY);
```

We can access the type **Double** objects stored in the vector using method **elementAt()** (for class **Vector**), and we can compare them using method **equals()** (for class **Double**):

```
if (numbers.elementAt(0).equals(numbers.elementAt(1)))
   System.out.println("First two numbers are the same");
else
   System.out.println("First two numbers are different");
```

We don't need to cast the two type `Object` references in the condition above to type `Double` because class `Double` and class `Object` both have `equals()` methods and Java knows which one to call. The `if` statement displays the message `First two numbers are different`.

Before we can process the numbers wrapped in these objects, we must extract them using method `doubleValue()`. The expression

```
((Double) numbers.elementAt(0)).doubleValue() +
((Double) numbers.elementAt(1)).doubleValue()
```

computes the sum (`13.59`) of the numbers stored in the first two elements of vector numbers. The parentheses in color ensure that method `doubleValue()` is applied to a type `Double` object. Without them, Java would attempt to apply the method before the casting operation and you would get a syntax error: `method DoubleValue() not found in class java.lang.Object`.

◆◆

EXERCISES FOR SECTION 5.8

SELF-CHECK

1. Write statements to wrap the integer **6**, the character **'z'**, and the real number **5.35** in object instances.

2. Write statements to read three data values and wrap them in three type `Integer` objects. Do this using method `parseInt()` and without using method `parseInt()`.

3. Trace the execution of this fragment:

```
Vector nums = new Vector();
nums.addElement(new Integer("30"));
nums.addElement(new Double(5.5));
double mystery = ((Integer) nums.elementAt(0)).intValue() +
                 ((Double) nums.elementAt(1)).doubleValue();
nums.removeElementAt(0);
nums.removeElementAt(1);
```

PROGRAMMING

1. Write a fragment that finds the sum of all the numbers stored in a vector of type `Integer` objects. Assume you don't know how many numbers are stored.

2. Display the contents of a vector in the console window assuming the vector elements reference type `Integer`, `Double`, or `String` objects. Display each object on a separate line.

3. Write your own method `equals()` for the `Integer` class (see Table 5.4).

4. Write a fragment that compares object `i1` (type `Integer`) to an array of `Integer` objects and displays the subscripts of all elements that wrap the same integer value as `i1` (use method `equals()` in Table 5.4).

5.9 The `Arrays` and `ArrayList` Collection Classes (Optional)

Java 2 provides a collection class framework that makes it easier to process collections of information because this framework implements a number of data structures that are often used by programmers. The availability of the collection class framework enables programmers to practice class reuse, incorporating off-the-shelf components in new programs instead of building their own. We will take a brief glimpse at two of the indexed collection classes in this section.

Arrays Class

The `Arrays` class provides a set of static methods that you can use to process arrays with elements of any data type. This class provides methods to fill an array with data (method `fill()`), to sort an array (method `sort()`), to search for a target item in a sorted array (method `binarySearch()`—see Programming Project 4 at the end of the chapter), and to compare two arrays (method `equals()`). Each method has at least one array argument. Method `fill()` has a second argument that indicates the value to be stored in all elements of the array. Method `binarySearch()` has a second argument that indicates the target item. Method `equals()` has two array arguments, which are the arrays to compare on an element-by-element basis.

Method `binarySearch()` can only be applied to an array that is sorted. You can use method `sort()` to do this. For an array of objects, the elements must implement the `Comparable` interface, which is described in Section 6.4.

Class `TestArrays` in Fig. 5.47 uses these methods to process arrays that store integers (array `ints`), real numbers (array `doubs`), and strings (array `months`). The class begins with the statement

```
import java.util.Arrays;
```

The statement

```
Arrays.fill(ints, (int) (10 * Math.random()));
```

fills array `ints` (type `int[]`) with a random integer less than 10. The statement

```
Arrays.sort(months);
```

sorts the array `months` (type `String[]`), which stores the names of the first six months. The statement

```
Arrays.sort(doubs);
```

sorts the array `doubs` (type `double[]`). The method call

```
Arrays.binarySearch(doubs, 7)
```

searches array `doubs` for the value `7`. The method call

```
Arrays.equals(ints, moreInts)
```

compares two arrays that happen to reference the same array object. Figure 5.48 shows a sample run of this application. Table 5.5 shows the methods discussed above.

Table 5.5 Methods of class `Arrays`

Sample Call	Behavior
`Arrays.binarySearch(nums, 10)`	Searches array `nums` for the target `10`. Array `nums` must be type `int[]` or `double[]`.
`Arrays.equals(nums, moreNums)`	Compares arrays `nums` and `moreNums` element by element. They must be the same type array.
`Arrays.fill(nums, 30)`	Stores `30` in all elements of array `nums` (type `int[]` or `double[]`).
`Array.sort(names)`	Sorts the elements in array `names`.

Class `ArrayList`

Next, we examine class `ArrayList`, which is an indexed collection that behaves like a vector. Class `ArrayList` has additional functionality that is beyond the scope of this discussion. Table 5.6 shows some `ArrayList` methods and their vector counterparts. You must import the `ArrayList` class from package `java.util` in order to use it. Figure 5.49 shows the `PhoneBook` class rewritten with `directory` as type `ArrayList` instead of type `Vector`.

Figure 5.47   Class `TestArrays`

```
/*
 * TestArrays.java       Authors: Koffman and Wolz
 * Application class to test collection class Arrays.
 */
import java.util.Arrays;

public class TestArrays {

  public static void main(String[] args) {

    int[] ints = new int[10];
    double doubs[] = {3.4, 55, 20, 65, 7};
    String months[] = {"January", "February", "March", "April", "May", "June"};

    // Fill array ints with a single random value.
    Arrays.fill(ints, (int) (10 * Math.random()));
    System.out.println("Contents of array ints:");
    for (int i = 0; i < ints.length; i++)
      System.out.print(ints[i] + "    ");
    System.out.println();

    // Sort three arrays.
    Arrays.sort(ints);
    Arrays.sort(months);
    Arrays.sort(doubs);

    // Display array months after sort.
    System.out.println("First six months in alphabetical order:");
    for (int i = 0; i < months.length; i++)
      System.out.print(months[i] + "    ");
    System.out.println();

    // Display result of searching for 7 in array doubs.
    System.out.println("Number 7 is at position " +
                     Arrays.binarySearch(doubs, 7));

    // Display result of comparing two equal arrays.
    int moreInts[] = ints;
    System.out.println("The value should be true - it is " +
                     Arrays.equals(ints, moreInts));
  }

}
```

Figure 5.48   Sample run of class `TestArrays`

```
TestArrays                                                    _ □ ✕
7    7    7    7    7    7    7    7    7    7
First six months in alphabetical order:
April    February    January    June    March    May
Number 7 is at position 1
The value should be true - it is true
```

Table 5.6   Methods of class `ArrayList`

ArrayList Method	Corresponding vector Method	Behavior
`ArrayList()`	`Vector()`	Creates an empty `ArrayList` object.
`void add(Object o)`	`void addElement(Object o)`	Adds its argument to the `ArrayList` object.
`Object get(int i)`	`Object elementAt(int i)`	Retrieves the object at position i in the `ArrayList` object.
`int indexOf(Object o)`	`int indexOf(Object o)`	Returns the position of the first occurrence of object o in the `ArrayList` object. Returns −1 if o is not found.
`boolean remove(Object o)`	`boolean removeElement (Object o)`	Removes the first occurrence of object o in the `ArrayList` object, shifting the elements that follow to fill the space, and returns `true`. Returns `false` if object o is not found.
`Object remove(int i)`	`void removeElementAt(i)`	Removes the element at position i of the `ArrayList` object, shifting the elements that follow to fill the space.
`void set(int i, Object o)`	`void setElementAt(Object o, int i)`	Stores object o at position i of the `ArrayList` object. The value of i must be between `0` and `size()` −1, inclusive.
`int size()`	`int size()`	Returns the size of the `ArrayList` object.
`String toString()`	`String toString()`	Represents the `ArrayList` object as a string enclosed in brackets. Commas are placed between elements.

Figure 5.49   Class PhoneBook using a directory of type ArrayList

```java
/*
 * PhoneBook.java       Authors: Koffman and Wolz
 * Represents a telephone directory using an ArrayList.
 */
import java.util.ArrayList;

public class PhoneBook {
  // Data fields
  private ArrayList directory;
  private static int PAGE_SIZE = 5;   // friends on each page

  // Methods
  // postcondition: directory references an empty vector
  public PhoneBook() {
    directory = new ArrayList();
  }

  // postcondition: Adds its argument to the directory.
  public void addFriend(Friend aFriend) {
    directory.add(aFriend);
  }

  // postcondition: Returns the friend selected by its argument.
  public Friend getFriend(int index) {
    if (inDirectory(index))
      return (Friend) directory.get(index);
    else
      return null;
  }

  // postcondition: Returns the number of the friend whose
  //    name is referenced by its argument.
  public String getNumber(String friendName) {
    int index = findFriend(friendName);
    if (index >= 0)
      return ((Friend) directory.get(index)).getPhone();
    else
      return null;
  }

  // postcondition: Returns the index of the friend whose
  //    name is referenced by its argument.
  //    Returns -1 if not found.
```

Figure 5.49   Class `PhoneBook` using a directory of type `ArrayList`, *continued*

```
public int findFriend(String friendName) {
  for (int index = 0; index < directory.size(); index++) {
    if (((Friend) directory.get(index)).getName().equals(friendName))
      return index;
  }

  // friendName not found.
  return -1;
}

// postcondition: Returns true if its argument is in range.
public boolean inDirectory(int index) {
  return index >= 0 && index < directory.size();
}

// postcondition: Returns a String representing the telephone
//    directory. The page number is inserted at the beginning
//    of each new page.
public String toString() {
  String result = "";
  for (int index = 0; index < directory.size(); index++) {
    if (index % PAGE_SIZE == 0)
      result = result + "\npage: " + (1 + index / PAGE_SIZE) + "\n";
    result = result + directory.get(index) + "\n";
  }
  return result;
}

// postcondition: Returns the number of friends in the directory.
//    Added for compatibility with the array implementation.
public int getNumFriends() {
  return directory.size();
}

// postcondition: Returns the number of pages in the directory.
//    Added for compatibility with the array implementation.
public int getNumPages() {
  return 1 + directory.size() / PAGE_SIZE;
}

}
```

EXERCISES FOR SECTION 5.9

SELF-CHECK

1. Complete the `for` loop below that displays the information in `ArrayList` `employees`, one object per line. Method `toString()` is defined in class `Employee`.

   ```
   for (int i = 0; i < _____ ; i++)
       System.out.println(               .toString());
   ```

   Write a single statement that accomplishes this without using a loop.

2. Explain the effect of each statement in the fragment below:

   ```
   ArrayList n = new ArrayList();
   n.add(new Friend("Jane", "555-1212"));
   n.add(new Friend("Sally", "555-8484"));
   n.set(1, new Friend("Jill", "555-3678"));
   n.add(new Friend("Sarah", "555-0101"));
   Friend best = (Friend) n.get(2);
   n.remove(1);
   System.out.println("Size is " + n.size());
   System.out.println(n.toString());
   ```

3. Assume you have an `ArrayList` of `Employee` objects. Write statements to replace the element at index 1 with `empC`. Insert `empB` at index 2. Then remove the object in the middle of the list and move it to the end.

PROGRAMMING

1. Write method `findMedian()` (Fig. 5.23) using the sort method of class `Arrays`.

2. Write method `search()` (Fig. 5.20) using the binary search method of class `Arrays`.

3. Rewrite class `Company` (Fig. 5.30) using an `ArrayList` object to store the employee data.

5.10 Common Programming Errors

When debugging programs (or methods) that process arrays (or vectors), it is best to test them on arrays (or vectors) with just a few elements. If constants are used in array size declarations, give these constants small values. After your program is error free, you can change the constants to their normal values.

The most common error in the use of arrays is an index expression whose value goes outside the allowable range during program execution. Index out-of-bounds errors most often are caused by an incorrect index expression. If the index is also the loop-control variable and it is incremented before each loop iteration, an index out-of-bounds error will occur if the loop does not terminate or if it executes an extra time.

Index out-of-bounds errors are most likely for index values at the loop boundaries. If these values are in bounds, it is likely that all other index values in the loop are in bounds as well. When debugging, you may want to place a variable or expression used as an array index in a watch window, particularly if the array reference is inside a loop. When processing an array (for example, array **x**) in a loop, a common error is using **x.length** for the last counter (or index) value instead of **x.length −
1**. If you use the counter as an array index, you will get an index out-of-bounds error after the last array element is processed.

As with all Java data types, make sure there are no type inconsistencies. The index type must be an integer expression. The element type must correspond to what is specified in the array declaration. Similarly, the element types of two arrays used in an array copy or assignment statement, or as a corresponding argument/parameter in a method call, must be the same.

Remember that you must both declare an array and create an instance of it. If you write

```
int[] a;
a[i] = 10;    // error
```

you will get a null pointer exception because you have declared the array but have not allocated storage space for it. It is perfectly reasonable to separate the array declaration and instantiation, but you must instantiate the array (using **new**) before you access its elements.

You can also get a null pointer exception if you forget to create an object to be stored in an array of objects. For example, the following will properly create an array of references to objects with array length equal to **aSize**. However, object **a[0]** does not exist, so you will get a null pointer exception when you try to call method **someOperation**.

```
class Demo {
    private SomeObject[] a; // array a will contain
                            //    SomeObjects

    public createArray(int aSize) {
        a = new SomeObject[aSize];
        a[0].someOperation();   // error
    }
```

Before you can access `a[0]`, you must create it using the statement

```
a[0] = new SomeObject();
```

If you use nested `for` loops to process the elements of a multidimensional array, make sure that loop-control variables used as array indices are in the correct order. The order of the loop-control variables determines the sequence in which the array elements are processed.

When using vectors, be careful not to remove more data than are actually stored in the vector. Don't forget to perform a type cast on each object that you retrieve from a vector. Also, don't attempt to store primitive types in a vector without placing their values in a wrapper object.

CHAPTER REVIEW

1. Arrays are data structures that store collections of data items of the same type.

2. You can reference the entire collection of data using the array name, and you can reference individual items using the array name followed by an index (an indexed variable). The subscript must be an integer constant or expression. The data field (attribute) `length` gives the size of the array and `length−1` is the subscript of the last element.

3. You can use a `for` statement to reference the individual elements of an array in sequence. Some common array operations written using `for` loops are initializing, reading, and printing arrays. You can also reference array elements in arbitrary or random order (called **random access**).

4. Methods can have array arguments and can return a reference to an array. You can modify the data stored in an array argument.

5. You can write methods that search an array for a specific target value. You can also sort an array so that its elements are ordered in an increasing or decreasing sequence.

6. You can store a collection of objects in an array that contains references to objects. When you allocate an array that will contain objects, initially all references are `null`. Make sure you create an object for an array element to reference (using `new`) before you attempt to store its data in the array.

7. You can store objects that have more than one dimension in an array. Two-dimensional arrays are commonly used to store tables of data. Each row of a two-dimensional array is itself an array. If `x` is a two-dimensional array, `x.length` is the number of rows in the array and `x[0].length` is the number of columns in the first row. We usually process two-dimensional arrays in

row-major order, starting with the first row and ending with the last row. We can accomplish this using nested **for** statements in which the outer counter variable is the row subscript and the inner counter variable is the column subscript.

8. You can store a collection of objects (not primitive types) in a vector. Make sure you insert the statement

```
import java.util.Vector;
```

before a class that uses a vector. The vector size adjusts automatically as new objects are stored and removed from the vector. If you insert an object in the middle of a vector, the ones that follow it are moved accordingly. You can use method **size()** to determine the size of a vector and **size()-1** is the index of the last element. The objects referenced by a vector's elements can have different data types.

New Java constructs

Construct	Effect
Array Declaration	
`int[] cube = new int[10];` `int[] count = new int[10];`	Allocates storage for arrays **cube** and **counts** with **10** type **int** elements each.
Array Initialization	
`int[] primes = {2, 3, 5, 7, 11};`	Stores the first five prime numbers in array **primes**.
Array Reference	

`for (int i = 0; i < 10; i++)`
`   cube[i]  = i * i * i;`
`if (cube[5] > 100)`
`   System.out.println(cube[5]);`
	Saves i cubed in the ith element of array **cube**. Displays **cube[5]** if it is greater than **100**.

Array Copy	
`System.arraycopy(cube, 0, count,` `0, 10);`	Copies contents of array **cube** to array **count**.
Array Assignment	
`count = cube;`	Variables **count** and **cube** reference the same array. They reference the array originally referenced by **cube**.

New Java constructs, *continued*

Construct	Effect

Array of Objects

`Employee[] people = new` `                Employee[10];`	Allocates storage for an array people that can reference 10 type `Employee` objects. Initializes each reference to `null`.
`people[0] = new Employee();`	Creates a new `Employee` object referenced by `people[0]`.

Vectors

`Vector names = new Vector();` `names.addElement("Robin");`	Creates a vector **names**. `names[0]` references "Robin." `names.size()` is 1.
`names.insertElementAt("Debbie", 0);`	Inserts `"Debbie"` at `names[0]` and shifts `"Robin"` to `names[1]`. `names.size()` is 2.
`names.setElementAt("Rich", 1);`	Stores `"Rich"` at `names[1]`, replacing `"Robin"`.
`String you =` `       (String) names.elementAt(0)`	String variable **you** references the string `"Debbie"`.
`names.removeElementAt(0);`	Removes the reference to string `"Debbie"` from `names[0]` and shifts `"Rich"` to `names[0]`. `names.size()` is 1.

Two-Dimensional Arrays

`int table[][] = new int[3][5];`	Allocates storage for an array **table** with three rows and five columns.
`table[0][0] = 5;` `table[2][4] = 5;`	Stores 5 in the first element and last element of array **table**.

`for (int i = 0; i < 3; i++)`
`   for (int j = 0; j < 5; j++)`
`      table[i][j] *= 2;`
	Doubles each element in array **table**.

✔ **QUICK-CHECK EXERCISES**

1. What is a data structure?

2. Can values of different types be stored in an array? In a vector?

3. If an array is declared to have 10 elements, must the program use all 10?

4. Show a way to declare an array of integers named **x** and define its size during run-time.

5. Explain the difference between assigning one array to another and copying the values of one array into another. Write statements that do both for arrays **x** and **y** (assign or copy **y** to **x**).

6. Fill in the initialization, repetition test, and update step for the following loop that accesses all elements of array **x** in sequential order:

```
for (int i = ___ ; _____ ; _____)
```

7. Write expressions that access the last character in string **x**, the last element of array **x**, and the last element of vector **x**.

8. Explain the purpose of the type cast `(Integer)` in

```
(Integer) x.elementAt(0)
```

What exactly is type `Integer` and why do we need it?

9. Why will you get a null pointer reference error if you do the following? How can you fix it?

```
Employee[] employees = new Employee[10];
employees[0].processEmpData();
```

10. Declare variables **names** and **ages** that can be used to store your friends' names and ages in separate arrays. Assume 50 names and ages need to be stored.

11. Write a **for** statement that reads data into these two arrays. Ask the user for a person's name and then that person's age. Use methods from class **KeyIn** to read each person's data.

ANSWERS TO QUICK-CHECK EXERCISES

1. A data structure is a grouping of related values in main memory.

2. No, Yes.

3. No, there can be some elements at the end whose values are undefined and not used.

4. `int[] x;`

```
x = new int[readInt("How many values in array?")];
```

or

```
String numStr = JOptionPane.showInputDialog("How many values in array?");
x = new int[Integer.parseInt(numStr)];
```

5. If you assign array **y** to array **x**(**x** = **y**;), the elements allocated to array **x** become inaccessible and arrays **x** and **y** will always reference the storage locations accessed by array **y**. If you copy array **y** to array **x** (`System.array-copy(y, 0, x, 0, y.length);`), the values in **y** are copied over to array **x**'s storage locations, which remain accessible.

6. `for (int i = 0; i < x.length; i++)`

7. `x.charAt(x.length()-1), x[x.length-1],`

   `x.elementAt(x.size()-1)`

8. (`Integer`) type casts the value returned by `elementAt` (type `Object`) to type `Integer`. Type `Integer` is a wrapper type for an integer value; we need it to represent an integer value as an object.

9. You will get a null pointer reference because there is no object allocated to `employees[0]`. You need to insert the statement

   ```
   employees[0] = new Employee();
   ```

   between the two listed.

10. ```
    String[] names = new String[50];

    int[] ages = new int[50];
    ```

11. ```
    for (int i = 0; i < ages.length; i++) {
        names[i] = KeyIn.readString("Enter name " + i);
        ages[i] = KeyIn.readInt("Enter age " + i);
    }
    ```

REVIEW QUESTIONS

1. Identify the error in the following code segment. When will the error be detected?

   ```
   int[] x = new int[9];
   for (int i = 0; i <= 9; i++)
       x[i] = i;
   ```

2. Indicate which of the statements in the following code segment are incorrect. For each incorrect statement, describe what the error is and when it will be detected:

```
int[] x = new int[10];
int[] y = new int[10];
i = 1;
x(i) = 7.5;
```

3. A method has one argument that is an array and it returns as its result an array of the same type (`int[]`). The method copies the elements in its argument array to the result array in reverse order. Write the method.

4. Write a method that reads in a collection of strings and stores them in a vector. Assume that the class that defines the method has a vector of strings as a data field.

5. Write a method that displays the collection of strings that were read in for Review Question 4 in the reverse order in which they were read. *Hint:* The last string read in is at index `size()-1` in the vector.

6. Write a method that writes the strings in the vector to the console window, starting with the first string in the vector. Write the number of strings as the first item.

7. Write a method that loads the vector from an array of strings. The first array element will be the first vector element, and so on.

8. How many exchanges are required to sort the following list of integers using selection sort? How many comparisons?

```
20 30 40 25 60 80
```

9. Create a two-dimensional array that you can use to store the names of friends that you called on the telephone during each day of the past week. Write a method that reads this data interactively into the array. The number of friends you call each day can vary.

10. Write a method that you can use to represent the contents of your array of friends from Review Question 9 as a string.

PROGRAMMING PROJECTS

1. Write a program to read data items into two arrays, **x** and **y**. Store the product of corresponding elements of **x** and **y** in a third array, **z**. Display a three-column table that shows corresponding elements of the arrays **x**, **y**, and **z**. Then compute and print the square root of the sum of the items in **z**.

2. Write a program for the following problem. You are given a collection of scores (type `int`) for the last exam in your computer course. You are to compute the average of these scores and assign grades to each student according to the following rules: If a student's score is within 10 points (above or below) of the median, assign a grade of `'C'`. If a student's score is more than 10 points higher than the median, assign a grade of `'A'`. If a student's score is more than 10 points below the median, assign a grade of `'F'`. The output from your program should consist of a labeled two-column list that shows each score and its corresponding grade. You will need methods to read the student data, to write the student data, to compute the median score, and to assign a letter grade based on the exam score and the median score.

3. Redo Programming Project 2, but this time assume that the data for each student contains a student's ID number (a string), the student name, and an exam score.

4. If an array is sorted, we can search for an item in the array much more quickly by dividing the array and searching decreasing halves. This technique is called a binary search. Given a beginning and an end in an array, the binary search determines a middle index and compares the middle value to the search value. If they are equal, the method can return the middle index. If the middle is less than the search value, we search to the right of the middle, repeating the same process. Write a binary search method for an array of integers and a test program that searches for each value in an ordered array of 1000 numbers (0 to 999). Have the program count the total number of comparisons required. Compare this number to the 5,005,000 comparisons required by the simple search method.

5. The results of a true-false exam given to a computer science class have been coded for input to a program. The information available for each student consists of a student identification number and the student's answers to 10 true-or-false questions. The available data are as follows:

Student Identification	Answer String
0080	FTTFTFTTFT
0340	FTFTFTTTFF
0341	FTTFTTTTTT
0401	TTFFTFFTTT
0462	TTFTTTFFTF
0463	TTTTTTTTTT
0464	FTFFTFFTFT
0512	TFTFTFTFTF
0618	TTTFFTTFTF
0619	FFFFFFFFFF
0687	TFTTFTTFTF
0700	FTFFTTFFFT
0712	FTFTFTFTFT
0837	TFTFTTFTFT

Write a program that first reads in the answer string representing the 10 correct answers (use **FTFFTFFTFT** as data). Next, read each student's data and compute and store the number of correct answers for each student in one array and store the student ID number in the corresponding element of another array. Determine the best score, **best**. Then print a three-column table that displays the ID number, the score, and the grade for each student. The grade should be determined as follows: if the score is equal to **best** or **best-1**, give an **A**; if it is **best-2** or **best-3**, give a **C**. Otherwise, give an **F**.

6. The results of a survey of the households in your township are available for public scrutiny. Each record contains data for one household, including a four-digit integer identification number, the annual income for the household, and the number of household members. Write a program to read the survey results into three arrays and perform the following analyses:

    a. Count the number of households included in the survey and print a three-column table displaying the data. (Assume that no more than 25 households were surveyed.)

    b. Calculate the average household income and list the identification number and income of each household that exceeds the average.

    c. Determine the percentage of households with incomes below the poverty level. Compute the poverty level income using the formula

$$p = \$6500.00 + \$750.00 \times (m - 2)$$

    where m is the number of members of each household. This formula shows that the poverty level depends on the number of family members, m, and that the poverty level income increases as m gets larger.

Test your program on the following data.

Identification Number	Annual Income	Household Members
1041	12,180	4
1062	13,240	3
1327	19,800	2
1483	22,458	8
1900	17,000	2
2112	18,125	7
2345	15,623	2
3210	3,200	6
3600	6,500	5
3601	11,970	2
4725	8,900	3
6217	10,000	2
9280	6,200	1

7. Assume that your computer has the very limited capability of being able to read and write only single-integer digits and to add together two integers consisting of one decimal digit each. Write a program that can read in two integers of up to 30 digits each, add these digits together, and display the result. Test your program using pairs of numbers of varying lengths. *Hints:* Store the two numbers in two integer arrays of length 30, one digit per array element. If the number is less than 30 digits in length, enter enough leading zeros (to the left of the number) to make the number 30 digits long. You will need a loop to add the digits in corresponding array elements starting with index 30. Don't forget to handle the carry digit if there is one. Use a **boolean** variable to indicate whether the sum of the last pair of digits is greater than 9.

8. A prime number is any number that is divisible only by 1 and itself. Write a program to compute all the prime numbers less than 2000. One way to generate prime numbers is to create an array of **boolean** values that are **true** for all prime numbers and **false** otherwise. Initially, set all the array entries to **true**. Then, for every number from 2 to 1000, set the array locations indexed by multiples of the number (but not the number itself) to **false**. When done, output all numbers whose array location is **true**. These numbers will be prime numbers.

9. Write a program that generates the Morse code for a sentence that ends in a period and contains no other characters except letters and blanks. After reading the Morse code into an array of strings, your program should read each word of the sentence and display its Morse equivalent on a separate line. The Morse code is as follows:

```
A .-  B -...  C -.-.  D -..  E .  F ..-.  G --.
H ....  I ..  J .---  K -.-  L .-..  M --  N -.
O ---  P .--.  Q --.-  R .-.  S ...  T -  U ..-
V ...-  W .--  X -..-  Y --.--  Z -..
```

10. Write a program that plays the game of Hangman. Read the letters of the word to be guessed into array **word**. The player must guess the letters belonging to **word**. The program should terminate when either all letters have been guessed correctly (player wins) or a specified number of incorrect guesses have been made (computer wins). *Hint:* Use array **solution** to keep track of the solution so far. Initialize **solution** to a string of symbols *****. Each time a letter in word is guessed, replace the corresponding ***** in **solution** with that letter.

11. An important data structure in computer science is a stack. A stack is like the dishes in a buffet line—you can only access the element at the top of a stack. You can implement a stack using a vector. In this case, the element at the top of the stack is the one with index **size()-1** in the vector. You insert an item by pushing it onto the stack (using method **push()**). Method **push()** should

be passed the item to be inserted as its argument and should call method `addElement()` to do the insertion. You remove an element by calling method `pop()`. Method `pop()` should return as its result the item removed from the top of the stack. You also need a method `empty()` that returns `true` if the stack is `empty()` and `false` if it is not. Write a class that can be used to process a stack of `String` objects. Then write an application that uses this class to read a collection of strings. Store them on a stack and then display them in the reverse order in which they were read. *Hint*: The element at the top of the stack is the last string read.

6

Class Hierarchies, Inheritance, and Interfaces

Throughout the book we followed object-oriented design techniques by using **abstraction**—modeling real-life entities by retaining only essential information. We also used **encapsulation**—clustering data and methods together into classes, providing safe and reliable boundaries. This chapter enhances our capability to use object-oriented design by introducing key features such as inheritance, polymorphism, and interfaces. These features will allow us to reuse existing code more effectively to create new applications. We also describe techniques for testing the individual methods and classes of a program system.

6.1   Class Hierarchies and Inheritance

We mentioned before that code reuse is a very important concept. If you build new applications using code that has already been written and tested, you are more likely to develop programs that are error free. In earlier programming languages, programmers could use libraries of functions (similar to class methods) that were provided by the language developers. Programmers could also create their own libraries of functions that could be reused in new applications.

We have demonstrated how object-oriented programming languages enable programmers to take further advantage of code reuse. Language developers provide packages (libraries of classes) and programmers create their own packages, all of which can be reused for writing new applications.

However, we have barely scratched the surface. If an application needs a new class that is similar to an existing class, the programmer can create it by **extending** the existing class, rather than rewriting the original class. The new class (called the **subclass**) can have additional data fields and methods for increased functionality. Its objects also **inherit** the data fields and methods of the original class (called the **superclass**).

Hierarchies and inheritance are rich concepts that appear often in science. In biology, hierarchical organizations capture essential information about relationships between living organisms. For example, living things can be divided into plants and animals. Animals in turn can be separated into vertebrates and invertebrates. Each level in the hierarchy is a refinement of the previous level (see Fig. 6.1).

Figure 6.1   **Hierarchical organizations in biology**

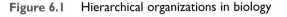

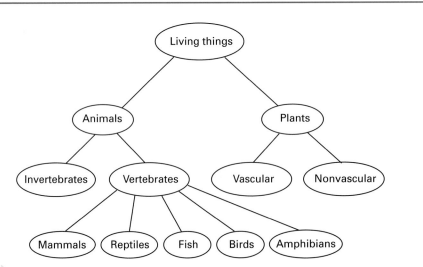

Inheritance, in combination with hierarchical organizations, allows you to capture the idea that one thing may be a refinement or extension of another. For example, an animal *is a* living thing. Such an "is a" relationship creates the right balance between too much and too little structure. The entities farther down the hierarchy are more complex and less general than those higher up. The entities farther down the hierarchy may inherit data fields (attributes) and methods from those farther up, but not vice versa.

is a versus *has a* **Relationships**

One misuse of inheritance is confusing the *has a* relationship with the *is a* relationship. The *is a* relationship between classes means that one class *is a* subclass of the other class. For example, "a car *is a* vehicle" means that the car class is a subclass of the vehicle class. The *is a* relationship is achieved by extending a class.

The *has a* relationship between classes means that one class *has* the second class as an attribute. For example, a mammal *has* fur, or a car *has* wheels. The *has a* relationship is achieved by declaring in one class a data field whose type is the other class.

We can combine *is a* and *has a* relationships. For example, a car *is a* vehicle and it *has a* wheel. A vehicle *has an* engine, so by extension a car *has an* engine. But a wheel is not an extension of a car; it is a part of a car. Consequently, it doesn't inherit the engine attribute from the vehicle. Note that not all vehicles have wheels; for example, snowmobiles do not.

Java allows you to capture both the inheritance (*is a*) relationship and the *has a* relationship. For example, a car class might be declared as follows:

```
public class Car extends Vehicle {
    Wheels[] w = new Wheels[4]; // cars have 4 wheels.
```

The keyword **extends** specifies that **Car** is a subclass of **Vehicle**.

CASE STUDY A HIERARCHY OF EMPLOYEE CLASSES

PROBLEM You have a class called **NewEmployee** that stores basic data about an employee: name, social security number, job title, address, phone number, age, starting year of employment, and total pay to date. Besides accessor and modifier methods, this class has a method to compute the employee's number of years with the company, one to compute the number of years to retirement, and one to update the total pay to date. It also has a **toString()** method.

Now suppose you decide to differentiate between two kinds of employees: salaried and hourly employees. Hourly employees are paid an hourly rate and their weekly pay varies depending on how many hours they work. Salaried employees, on the other hand, have a fixed annual salary and their weekly pay rate is the same regardless of how many hours they work.

ANALYSIS AND DESIGN

Class `NewEmployee`

Figure 6.2 shows a description of class `NewEmployee`. In addition to the methods described above, we added an `equals()` method that compares two `NewEmployee` objects.

Figure 6.2   Class `NewEmployee`

Data Fields	Attributes
`String name`	Name
`String socSecNum`	Social security number
`String jobTitle`	Job title
`String address`	Address
`String phoneNumber`	Phone number
`int age`	Age
`int startYear`	Starting year of employment
`double totalPay`	Total pay to date
Methods	**Behavior**
`int calcYearsService(int)`	Computes years with company. The current year is an argument.
`int calcYearsToRetire()`	Computes years until retirement.
`boolean equals(NewEmployee)`	Determines whether current employee has same social security number as the employee passed as argument.
`double updateTotalPay(double)`	Increases total pay by the amount specified (the argument).
`String toString()`	Represents a `NewEmployee` object as a string.
`String getName(),`	Accessors: Retrieve information in each data field.
`String getSocSecNum(),`	
`String getJobTitle(),`	
`String getAddress(),`	
`String getPhoneNumber(),`	
`int getAge(),`	
`int getStartYear(),`	
`double getTotalPay()`	
`setName(String),`	Modifiers: Update value in each data field.
`setSocSecNum(String),`	
`setJobTitle(String),`	
`setAddress(String),`	
`setPhoneNumber(String),`	
`setAge(int),`	
`setStartYear(int),`	
`setTotalPay(double)`	

Classes `SalaryEmployee` and `HourlyEmployee`

Let's create two new classes of employees: `SalaryEmployee` (Fig. 6.3) and `HourlyEmployee` (Fig. 6.4). Rather than duplicate the information and methods in your `NewEmployee` class in each of these new classes, you can extend the `NewEmployee` class and thereby inherit these data fields and methods. You can also declare additional data fields for each of these classes such as annual salary for `SalaryEmployee` and hours and rate for `HourlyEmployee`. Each of these classes would have its own `computeWeeklyPay()` and `toString()` methods, but the details of the method would be different for each kind of employee.

IMPLEMENTATION

Class `NewEmployee`

Figure 6.5 shows the `NewEmployee` class. The declaration statements for the type `String` data fields initialize them to the empty string (`""`). The numeric data fields are initialized to zero (the default value).

Notice there are three constructor methods with different argument lists. The first is the zero-parameter constructor. We also included a constructor that specifies just the name and social security number of a `NewEmployee` object. You can also create a new employee with all employee data fields defined using the third constructor.

Figure 6.3 Class `SalaryEmployee`

Data Fields	Attributes
`annualSalary`	Annual salary

Methods	Behavior
`void setSalary(double)`	Sets the salary data field
`double getSalary()`	Retrieves the salary
`double computeWeeklyPay()`	Computes weekly pay
`String toString()`	Represents a `SalaryEmployee` object as a string

Data Fields Inherited from `NewEmployee`

`name, socSecNum, jobTitle, address, phoneNumber, age, startYear, totalPay`

Methods Inherited from `NewEmployee`

`getName(), getSocSecNum(), getJobTitle(), getAddress(), getPhoneNumber(), getAge(), getStartYear(), getTotalPay(), setName(), setSocSecNum(), setJobTitle(), setAddress(), setPhoneNumber(), setAge(), setStartYear(), setTotalPay(), calcYearsService(), calcYearsToRetire(), equals(), updateTotalPay()`

Figure 6.4 Class `HourlyEmployee`

Data Fields	Responsibilities
hours	Hours worked
rate	Hourly rate

Methods	Behavior
double computeWeeklyPay()	Computes weekly pay
void setHours (double hours)	Sets hours worked
void setRate (double rate)	Sets hourly rate
double getHours()	Gets hours worked
double getRate()	Gets hourly rate
String toString()	Represents an `HourlyEmployee` object as a string

Data Fields Inherited from `NewEmployee`

name, socSecNum, jobTitle, address, phoneNumber, age, startYear, totalPay

Methods Inherited from `NewEmployee`

getName(), getSocSecNum(), getJobTitle(), getAddress(), getPhoneNumber(), getAge(), getStartYear(), getTotalPay(), setName(), setSocSecNum(), setJobTitle(), setAddress(), setPhoneNumber(), setAge(), setStartYear(), setTotalPay(), calcYearsService(), calcYearsToRetire(), equals(), updateTotalPay()

Figure 6.5 Class `NewEmployee`

```java
/* NewEmployee.java        Authors: Koffman & Wolz
 * Superclass of employee classes.
 * Uses String
 */
public class NewEmployee {

  // data fields
  private String name = "";
  private String socSecNum = "";
  private String jobTitle = "";
  private String address = "";
  private String phoneNumber = "";
  private int age;
  private int startYear;
  private double totalPay;

  // methods
  // constructors
```

Figure 6.5   Class NewEmployee, *continued*

```
public NewEmployee() {
}

public NewEmployee(String name, String social) {
   this.name = name;
   socSecNum = social;
}

public NewEmployee(String name, String social, String job,
                   String address, String phone,
                   int age, int year, double totPay) {
   this.name = name;
   socSecNum = social;
   jobTitle = job;
   this.address = address;
   phoneNumber = phone;
   this.age = age;
   startYear = year;
   totalPay = totPay;
}

// modifiers
public void setName(String name) {
   this.name = name;
}

public void setAge(int age) {
   this.age = age;
}

// Insert other modifiers here.
// . . .

// accessors
public String getName() {
   return name;
}

public String getSocial() {
   return socSecNum;
}

public int getAge() {
   return age;
}
```

Figure 6.5   Class `NewEmployee,` *continued*

```
// Insert other accessors here.
// . . .

// precondition: the argument is the current year
// postcondition: Returns the number of years worked
public int calcYearsService(int year) {
  return year - startYear;
}

// postcondition: Returns the number of years until employee
//    will reach the retirement age of 65. Returns 0 if
//    employee has reached retirement age.
public int calcYearsToRetire() {
  int RETIREMENT_AGE = 65;  // normal retirement age
  int yearsToRetire = RETIREMENT_AGE - age;
  if (yearsToRetire > 0)
    return yearsToRetire;
  else
    return 0;
}

public void updateTotalPay(double pay) {
  totalPay += pay;
}

// postcondition: Returns the object's state as a string
public String toString() {
  return "name: " + name + ", social security: " + socSecNum +
          ", job: " + jobTitle + "\naddress: " + address +
          ", phone: " + phoneNumber + ", age: " + age +
          ", year started: " + startYear +
          ", total pay $" + totalPay;
}

// postcondition: Returns true if this object has the same
//    social security number as the argument.
public boolean equals(NewEmployee emp) {
  return this.socSecNum.equals(emp.socSecNum);
}

}
```

Use of prefix *this* in *NewEmployee*

In both constructors and in method `setAge()`, the statement

```
this.age = age;
```

changes data field **age** of the current object. The prefix **this.** references the current object and is necessary in order to distinguish data field **age** from parameter **age**. Inside a method, parameters or local variables hide instance variables with the same name (the local declaration is assumed by Java), so the identifier **age** by itself refers to parameter **age**. We did not need to use the prefix **this.** in earlier classes because we were careful not to use the same name for both a parameter and a data field.

You can use the keyword **this** in three different ways inside a method. To reference a data field of the current object (say, **age**), you use **this.age**. You can also call a method by writing **this.***methodName(args)*; however, there is usually no reason to do so.

Finally, you can reference one constructor for a method from inside another using **this**(*args*). Figure 6.6 shows the multiple-parameter constructor written using the two-parameter constructor to initialize the data fields **name** and **socSecNum**. The method call

```
this(name, social);
```

calls the current object's two-parameter constructor to initialize data fields **name** and **socSecNum**. The arguments are passed on to the two-parameter constructor. The constructor call must be the first statement in the constructor being defined.

Figure 6.6 Calling one constructor from within another

```
public NewEmployee(String name, String social, String job,
                   String address, String phone,
                   int age, int year, double pay) {
    this(name, social);
    this.address = address;
    phoneNumber = phone;
    this.age = age;
    startYear = year;
    totalPay = pay;
}
```

The keyword `this`

> Form: `this.memberName`
>   `this(args)`
> Example: `this.age`
>   `this.name.equals(that.name)`
>   `this("Jim", "3456")`

Interpretation: The keyword `this` refers to the current object. The form `this.memberName` references a data field or calls a method of the current object. The form `this(args)` calls a constructor of the class.

Note: The call to the constructor must be the first statement in another constructor that is being defined for this class.

Method `equals()`

Method `equals()` compares two `NewEmployee` objects. It returns `true` if the current object's social security number matches the social security number of the `NewEmployee` object passed as an argument. This object is referenced by parameter `emp`. We ignore the other data fields because we assume that an employee's identity is based solely on social security number. The statement

```
return this.socSecNum.equals(emp.socSecNum);
```

uses the `String` class `equals()` method to compare the characters contained in the strings referenced by `this.socSecNum` (the current object's social security number) and `emp.socSecNum` (the social security number of the object referenced by `emp`). Method `equals()` for class `NewEmployee` returns as its result the value returned by `String` method `equals()`. The use of the prefix `this.` is not required; we included the prefix so that the two references to `socSecNum` would look symmetrical (that is, each has the form *object.socSecNum*).

Class `SalaryEmployee`

Figure 6.7 shows class `SalaryEmployee`. The class header

```
public class SalaryEmployee extends NewEmployee {
```

indicates that `SalaryEmployee` extends `NewEmployee` and is therefore a subclass of `NewEmployee` (its superclass). Class `SalaryEmployee` defines only data field `annualSalary`.

Class `SalaryEmployee` defines accessor and modifier methods for data field `annualSalary`. The accessors and modifiers for its inherited data fields are defined in class `NewEmployee` and inherited from that class. There is also a method `calcWeeklyPay()`, which computes weekly pay by dividing annual salary by 52. We discuss its constructor methods and the `toString()` method next.

Figure 6.7   Class `SalaryEmployee`

```
/* SalaryEmployee.java          Authors: Koffman & Wolz
 * Represents a salaried employee.
 * Extends NewEmployee
 */
public class SalaryEmployee extends NewEmployee {

  // data fields
  private double annualSalary;

  // methods
  // constructors
  public SalaryEmployee() {
  }

  public SalaryEmployee(String name, String social) {
    super(name, social);
  }

  public SalaryEmployee(String name, String social, String job,
                   String address, String phone, int age, int year,
                   double totPay, double salary) {
    super(name, social, job, address, phone, age, year, totPay);
    annualSalary = salary;
  }

  public void setSalary(double salary) {
    annualSalary = salary;
  }

  public double getSalary() {
    return annualSalary;
  }

  public double calcWeeklyPay() {
    if (annualSalary > 0)
      return annualSalary / 52;
    else
      return 0;
  }
```

Figure 6.7 Class `SalaryEmployee,` *continued*

```
public String toString() {
   return super.toString() +
           "\nannual salary $" + annualSalary;
}

}
```

Keyword **super**

The two-parameter constructor contains the statement

```
super(name, social);
```

The keyword **super** refers to the constructor for the superclass **NewEmployee**, so this statement calls the two-parameter constructor for **NewEmployee**. The superclass constructor sets the values of the inherited data fields **name** and **socSecNum** for the current object. Similary, the constructor with nine parameters begins with the statement

```
super(name, social, job, address, phone, age, year, totPay);
```

It calls the constructor for class **NewEmployee** with eight parameters. This constructor stores its argument values in the corresponding data fields of the current object. Notice that you would get a **method not found** syntax error if you tried to replace either statement above with a call to a constructor for class **NewEmployee**:

```
NewEmployee(. . .);      // invalid call to a constructor
```

The call to the superclass constructor must be the first statement in the method body. If it is omitted, the compiler inserts a call to the constructor for **NewEmployee** which has zero parameters. This is the case for the zero-parameter constructor shown for class **SalaryEmployee**.

You can use the prefix **super.** to call a method of the superclass. In **toString()**, the **return** statement begins with the method call **super.toString()**, which calls the **toString()** method defined in the superclass **NewEmployee**. This method places the information in the data fields inherited from **NewEmployee** (name, social security number, and so on) at the beginning of the string being formed to represent the current **SalaryEmployee** object.

You can also use the prefix **super** with a data field, but it is not necessary. For example, you should be able to use either **super.name** or **name** to reference the current object's **name** field. In Section 6.2, we discuss what the visibility of **name** should be (currently **private**) in order for this to happen.

The keyword `super`

Form: `super.memberName`
     `super(args)`

Example: `super.toString()`
     `super.name`
     `super("Sally", 1234)`

Interpretation: The keyword **super** refers to the superclass of the current object. The form **super.*methodName*(*argumentList*)** calls method ***methodName*()** defined in the superclass. The form **super(...)** calls a constructor of the superclass of the current object.

Note: The call to the superclass constructor must be the first statement in a constructor that is being defined. If it is omitted, Java inserts a call to the default constructor.

Class `HourlyEmployee`

Fig. 6.8 shows class **HourlyEmployee**, which also extends class **NewEmployee**. Objects of type **HourlyEmployee** have two additional data fields: **hours** and **rate**. Method **calcWeeklyPay()** returns the product of **hours** and **rate**.

TESTING

Figure 6.9 shows a class that tests all three employee classes. Method **main()** declares objects **clerk** (type **HourlyEmployee**), **manager** (type **SalaryEmployee**), and **spouseOfBoss** (type **NewEmployee**) and calls several of their methods. For convenience, we use four digits to represent a social security number. Figure 6.10 shows the console window after the class executes. We discuss some of the method calls in the next sections.

Figure 6.8   Class `HourlyEmployee`

```java
/* HourlyEmployee.java          Authors: Koffman & Wolz
 * Represents an hourly employee.
 * Extends NewEmployee
 */
public class HourlyEmployee extends NewEmployee {

  // data fields
  private double hours;
  private double rate;

  // methods
  // constructors
  public HourlyEmployee() {
  }

  public HourlyEmployee(String name, String social) {
    super(name, social);
  }

  public HourlyEmployee(String name, String social, String job,
                  String address, String phone, int age, int year,
                  double totPay, double hours, double rate) {
    super(name, social, job, address, phone, age, year, totPay);
    this.hours = hours;
    this.rate = rate;
  }

  public void setHours(double hours) {
    this.hours = hours;
  }

  public void setRate(double rate) {
    this.rate = rate;
  }

  public double getHours() {
    return hours;
  }

  public double getRate() {
    return rate;
  }
```

Figure 6.8   Class `HourlyEmployee,` *continued*

```java
public double calcWeeklyPay() {
  return hours * rate;
}

public String toString() {
  return super.toString() +
         "\nweekly hours: " + hours +
         ", hourly rate $" + rate;
}

}
```

Figure 6.9   Class `TestEmployeeClasses`

```java
/* TestEmployeeClasses.java        Authors: Koffman & Wolz
 * Application for testing hierarchy of employee classes.
 *  Uses NewEmployee, SalaryEmployee, HourlyEmployee
 */
public class TestEmployeeClasses {

  public static void main(String[] args) {

    HourlyEmployee clerk =
        new HourlyEmployee("Sam", "1234", "clerk", "", "",
                           30, 2000, 15000.00, 40.0, 15.0);
    SalaryEmployee supervisor =
        new SalaryEmployee("Jessica", "2222", "supervisor", "", "",
                           33, 1998, 40000.00, 52000.00);

    NewEmployee spouseOfBoss = new NewEmployee("George", "3456");

    double weekPay = clerk.calcWeeklyPay();
    clerk.updateTotalPay(weekPay);
    System.out.println(clerk.toString());
    System.out.println(clerk.getName() + "  " +
                       clerk.getSocial() +
                       ", weekly salary $" + weekPay + "\n");

    weekPay = supervisor.calcWeeklyPay();
    supervisor.updateTotalPay(weekPay);
```

Figure 6.9   Class `TestEmployeeClasses`, *continued*

```
        System.out.println(supervisor.toString());
        System.out.println(supervisor.getName() + "   " +
                        supervisor.getSocial() +
                        ", weekly salary $" + weekPay + "\n");


        spouseOfBoss.updateTotalPay(500.00);
        System.out.println(spouseOfBoss.toString() + "\n");


        if (clerk.equals(supervisor))
          System.out.println(clerk.getName() + " and " +
                        supervisor.getName() + " are same employee");
        else
          System.out.println(clerk.getName() + " and " +
                        supervisor.getName() + " are different employees");
    }
}
```

Figure 6.10   Sample run of class `TestEmployeeClasses`

```
TestEmployeeClasses                                           _ □ ×
name: Sam, social security: 1234, job: clerk
address: , phone: , age: 30, year started: 2000, total pay $15600.0
weekly hours: 40.0, hourly rate $15.0
Sam   1234, weekly salary $600.0

name: Jessica, social security: 2222, job: supervisor
address: , phone: , age: 33, year started: 1998, total pay $41000.0
annual salary $52000.0
Jessica  2222, weekly salary $1000.0

name: George, social security: 3456, job:
address: , phone: , age: 0, year started: 0, total pay $500.0

Sam and Jessica are different employees
```

EXERCISES FOR SECTION 6.1

SELF-CHECK

1. Explain why you cannot assign a variable of class **HourlyEmployee** to reference an object of type **SalaryEmployee** and vice versa.

2. Carefully trace the execution of the statements in method **main()** of Fig. 6.9.

3. Given the declarations in Fig. 6.9, describe the effect of inserting each valid statement below in method `main()`. Indicate what is wrong with each incorrect statement.

   a. `System.out.println(spouseOfBoss.name());`

   b. `String myName = spouseOfBoss.getName();`

   c. `clerk = supervisor;`

   d. `supervisor.setName(clerk.getName());`

   e. `double pay = supervisor.calcWeeklyPay();`

   f. `System.out.println("Weekly pay of " + clerk.getName() +`
                  `" is $" + clerk.calcWeeklyPay());`

   g. `supervisor.setSalary(1.2 * 2080 * clerk.getRate());`

   h. `System.out.println("Hourly rate is $" +`
               `supervisor.getRate());`

   i. `clerk.updateTotalPay(clerk.calcWeeklyPay());`

   j. `clerk.updateTotalPay(supervisor.calcWeeklyPay());`

   k. `clerk.updateTotalPay(spouseOfBoss.calcWeeklyPay());`

4. Show the new class hierarchy described in Programming Exercises 3 through 5 below.

5. Assume that the following statements appear in a method of class `SalaryEmployee`. Explain the effect of **this** and **super** in each statement below. Also, indicate any restrictions on the use of these statements and whether **this** or **super** could be omitted from the statement.

   a. `this.name = name;`

   b. `super("Sam", "3456");`

   c. `String res = super.toString() + this.toString();`

   d. `this("Sam", "3456");`

   e. `this.salary = super.totalPay;`

   f. `this.salary = super.getTotalPay();`

PROGRAMMING

1. Change method `equals()` of class `NewEmployee` to return **true** only if the objects being compared have the same social security number and the same name.

2. Provide a new method **equals()** for class **SalaryEmployee** that returns **true** only if the objects being compared are considered equal according to the method **equals()** in class **NewEmployee** and they also have the same salary.

*For Programming Exercises 3 through 5, provide each new class with constructors, accessors, modifiers, and a **toString()** method besides the specific methods described.*

3. Create a new subclass of **NewEmployee** called **Intern** with data fields that store the college attended, major, and years in college.

4. Create a subclass of **HourlyEmployee** called **TemporaryWorker** with data field **tempAgency** (type **String**).

5. Create a subclass of **SalaryEmployee** called **Management** with data fields **hasStockOptions** (type **boolean**), **stockShares** (type **double**), and **lifeInsurance** (type **double**). Write a method that calculates the life insurance amount for a **Management** employee (3 times the employee's salary) and a method that increases the value of **stockShares** by an additional 1000 shares per $10,000 of salary for a management employee who has stock options.

6.2 Operations in a Class Hierarchy

Fig. 6.11 shows the class hierarchy for the employee classes developed in the last section. Recall that all Java classes actually extend class **Object**, so **NewEmployee** is a subclass of **Object**, as are **HourlyEmployee** and **SalaryEmployee**, by extension. Figs. 6.12 through 6.14 show the data fields (instance variables) for each employee class in the hierarchy. For each class, the inherited data fields are shown in italics above the dotted line in the color block. The methods defined in each class are shown in the gray block, but the inherited methods are not shown.

Figure 6.11 Class hierarchy

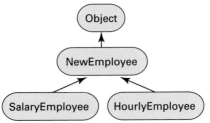

Figure 6.12 Data fields and methods for class `NewEmployee`

NewEmployee
(subclass of Object)

name, socSecNum jobTitle, address phoneNumber, age startYear, totalPay
setName(), setSocial(), setJobTitle(), setAddress(), setPhone(), setAge(), setStartYear(), setTotalPay(), getName(), getSocial(), getJobTitle(), getAddress(), getPhone(), getAge(), getStartYear(), getTotalPay(), calcYearsService(), calcYearsToRetire(), equals(), updateTotalPay(), toString()

Figure 6.13 Data fields and methods for class `SalaryEmployee`

SalaryEmployee
(subclass of NewEmployee)

name, socSecNum, *jobTitle, address,* *phoneNumber, age* *startYear, totalPay* - annualSalary
setSalary(), getSalary(), calcWeeklyPay(), toString()

Figure 6.14   Data fields and methods for class `HourlyEmployee`

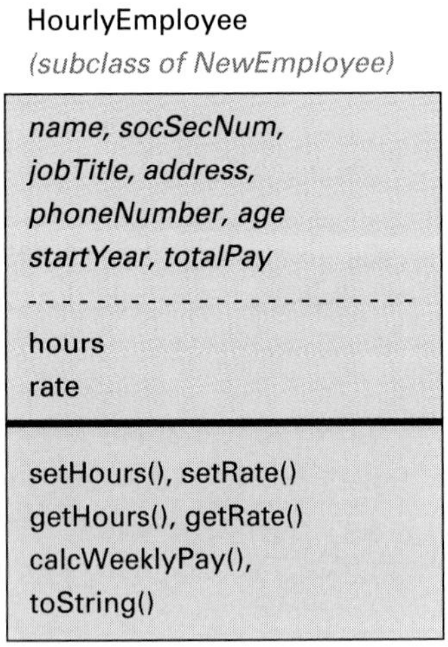

HourlyEmployee
(subclass of NewEmployee)

name, socSecNum,
jobTitle, address,
phoneNumber, age
startYear, totalPay

- -

hours
rate

setHours(), setRate()
getHours(), getRate()
calcWeeklyPay(),
toString()

Let's look more closely at the method calls in Fig. 6.4. There is no method **getName()** in class **HourlyEmployee**, so for the method call

```
clerk.getName()
```

the **getName()** method inherited from class **NewEmployee** executes.
    There are two **calcWeeklyPay()** methods. For the method call

```
clerk.calcWeeklyPay()
```

the method **calcWeeklyPay()** defined in class **HourlyEmployee** (the type of **clerk**) is the one that executes. For the method call

```
supervisor.calcWeeklyPay()
```

the **calcWeeklyPay()** method defined in class **SalaryEmployee** (the type of **supervisor**) is the one that executes.

Method Overloading

There are three constructor methods for each class. When a class has multiple methods with the same name, this is called **method overloading**. For the statement

```
HourlyEmployee clerk =
    new HourlyEmployee("Sam", "1234", "clerk", "", "",
                        30, 2000, 15000.0, 40.0, 15.0);
```

how does Java know which constructor to call? The answer is that it calls the constructor with the same **signature** as the method call. A method signature consists of the method name and its parameter list. The constructor in the above call has four **String** parameters followed by two **int** parameters and three **double** parameters, so its signature is

```
HourlyEmployee(java.lang.String, java.lang.String, Java.lang.String,
Java.lang.String, int, int, double, double, double)
```

If there is no method with the required signature, a **method not found** syntax error occurs.

Method Overriding

Each class defines a **toString()** method. For the method call

```
clerk.toString()
```

which **toString()** method executes? Because **clerk** is an instance of class **HourlyEmployee**, the **toString()** method for that class executes. The fact that a method defined in a subclass blocks the execution of a method with the same signature defined in its superclass is called **method overriding**. In a subclass, you can use the prefix **super.** to call a superclass method with the same signature as one in the subclass (for example, **super.toString()** in Figs. 6.7 and 6.8).

If method **toString()** were defined only in class **SalaryEmployee** and class **NewEmployee**, which one would execute for the method call **clerk.toString()**? The answer is the **toString()** method defined in the superclass (**NewEmployee**) because that is the one that would have been inherited by object **clerk**.

Protected Visibility

It is interesting to consider to what extent data fields defined in a superclass are visible in a subclass. Because all data fields in class **NewEmployee** have private visibility, they cannot be accessed directly in subclasses **HourlyEmployee** and **SalaryEmployee**. Therefore, you must use accessors and modifiers defined in class **NewEmployee** to manipulate these data fields. This restriction may seem strange given that Figs. 6.13 and 6.14 clearly show that storage is allocated in each subclass object for the data fields of class **NewEmployee**.

There is another category of visibility that removes this restriction: **protected visibility** as declared next for data field **name** in class **NewEmployee**.

```
protected String name;
```

Now, data field **name** can be accessed directly in any subclass of **NewEmployee** and, by extension, in any subclass of **HourlyEmployee** or **SalaryEmployee**.

Shadowing Data Fields

In the last section, we saw that if a data field happens to have the same name as a local variable or parameter in a method, the local variable **shadows** or **hides** the data field, preventing it from being accessed directly. However, you can still access the data field by using the prefix **this.**

If you happen to declare data fields in a subclass and in a superclass with the same name, the data field in the subclass will shadow the data field in the superclass and prevent it from being directly accessed in the subclass. However, you can still access the data field in the superclass by using the prefix **super.**

◆◆EXAMPLE 6.1 ─────────────────────────────────────

Assume a subclass and a superclass both declare a data field **name** of type **String**. Method **confuseNames()** below also declares **name** as a local variable. The effect of executing this method is to store a reference to the string **"Tom"** in local variable **name**, a reference to the string **"Dick"** in the current object's data field **name**, and a reference to the string **"Harry"** in the data field **name** inherited from the superclass. The method will write the line

```
Tom, Dick, and Harry
```

in the console window.

```
public void confuseNames() {
    String name = "Tom";     // local variable name
    this.name = "Dick";      // data field name
    super.name = "Harry";    // assume protected visibility
    System.out.println(name + ", " + this.name +
                    ", and " + super.name);
}
```

◆◆

Misnomer of Superclass and Subclass

Which class has more data fields or methods, the superclass or one of its subclasses? The answer, of course, is the subclass. This is somewhat confusing because it shows there is really nothing *super* about a superclass. When we draw a class hierarchy, the superclass appears above the subclass, which is why it is given the prefix *super*. Another reason for calling it the superclass is that it is normally defined first, and its subclasses are derived by extending it.

Assignment in a Class Hierarchy

It is interesting to consider assignment capability between a superclass and its subclasses. We illustrate this in the next examples.

◆◆EXAMPLE 6.2 ─────────────────────────────────────

Assume we have the following declarations:

```
Object obj;
NewEmployee anEmp = new NewEmployee("Sam", "1111");
HourlyEmployee hourEmp = new HourlyEmployee("Sally", "2222");
SalaryEmployee salEmp = new SalaryEmployee("Tony", "2345");
```

Can we make the following assignments?

```
obj = anEmp;
anEmp = hourEmp;
```

The answer is Yes. A variable can reference an object of its own type or of a subclass type. Fig. 6.15 shows the status of these variables before and after the assignments.
After the assignment

```
obj = anEmp;
```

variable **obj** references an object of type **NewEmployee**. However because **obj** is type **Object**, it is only possible to use data fields and methods defined in class **Object**. Therefore, **obj.getName()** would cause a **method not found** syntax error.

Because class **Object** has a **toString()** method, **obj.toString()** is a valid method call. However, the surprising result is that it calls the **toString()** method of class **NewEmployee** (the type of the object referenced by **obj**), not the **toString()** method of class **Object**. This happens because the object refer-

Figure 6.15 Assignments in a class hierarchy

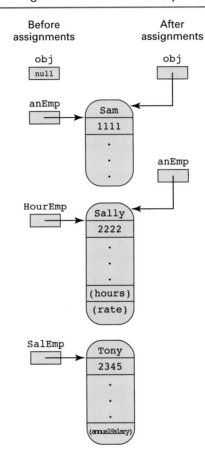

enced by **obj** is linked to the **toString()** method for class **NewEmployee**. (We explore this further in Section 6.3.) The statement

```
System.out.println(obj.toString());
```

would display

```
name: Sam, social security: 1111, job: ,
address: , phone: , age: 0, year started: 0, total pay $0.0
```

Similarly, after the assignment

```
anEmp = hourEmp;
```

variable **anEmp** references an object of type **HourlyEmployee**, complete with data fields **hours** and **rate** (see Fig. 6.10). Because **anEmp** is type **NewEmployee**, we can use **anEmp.getName()** to access the name field of this **HourlyEmployee** object. However, we cannot access the **hours** field of this object using **anEmp.getHours()** because method **getHours()** is not defined in class **NewEmployee**.

The method call **anEmp.toString()** applies the **toString()** method to the object referenced by **anEmp**. Because **anEmp** now references a type **HourlyEmployee** object, the **toString()** method defined in class **HourlyEmployee** executes, so the values of **hours** and **rate** would be part of the result. The statement

```
System.out.println(anEmp.toString());
```

would display

```
name: Sally, social security: 2222, job: ,
address: , phone: , age: 0, year started: 0, total pay $0.0,
weekly hours: 0.0, hourly rate $0.0
```

◆◆

Example 6.2 shows that we can assign *up* the class hierarchy; that is, a variable of a superclass type can reference an object of a subclass type. However, the converse is not true.

◆◆EXAMPLE 6.3 ───────────────────────────────────

Let's repeat the declarations in Example 6.2.

```
Object obj;
NewEmployee anEmp = new NewEmployee("Sam", "1111");
HourlyEmployee hourEmp = new HourlyEmployee("Sally", "2222");
SalaryEmployee salEmp = new SalaryEmployee("Tony", "2345");
```

We cannot make the assignment

```
salEmp = anEmp; // incompatible types
```

because after this assignment, variable **salEmp** (type **SalaryEmployee**) would reference an instance of its superclass (**NewEmployee**). This is not allowed because we should be able to access all data fields and methods of class **SalaryEmployee** through variable **salEmp**, including data field **annualSalary**. However, `salEmp.annualSalary` is not defined because a `NewEmployee` object does not have this data field. Similarly, we could not use the method call `salEmp.calcWeeklyPay()` if `salEmp` references a `NewEmployee` object. For this reason, assignment down a class hierarchy is not permitted and leads to an `incompatible types` syntax error.

◆◆

Can we assign across the class hierarchy? In other words, can we assign a variable of one subclass type to reference an object of another subclass type such as

```
salEmp = hourEmp; // incompatible types
```

The answer is No, and we ask you to explain why in Self-Check Exercise 1.

Casting in a Class Hierarchy

In working with class hierarchies, it is not unusual to make assignments similar to ones shown in Example 6.2. For example, we may want a variable **anEmp** of type `NewEmployee` to be able to reference either an `HourlyEmployee` object or a `SalaryEmployee` object. The statement

```
NewEmployee anEmp = new HourlyEmployee("Sam", "1234", "clerk", "",
                            "", 30, 2000, 15000.00, 40.0, 15.0);
```

declares a variable of type `NewEmployee` that references an `HourlyEmployee` object with the same data as the one shown in Fig. 6.9. In the last section we saw that it would not be possible to access data fields `hours` and `rate` in this object using the prefix `anEmp` because `anEmp` is type `NewEmployee`. However, we can use casting to solve this problem, as shown in the next example.

◆◆EXAMPLE 6.4 ─────────────────────────────

If variable **anEmp** declared above (type `NewEmployee`) references an object of type `HourlyEmployee`, the statement

```
((HourlyEmployee) anEmp).setHours(30.0);
```

stores the value **30.0** in data field **hours** for this object. The casting operation creates an **anonymous** (unnamed) **reference** of type `HourlyEmployee` to object **anEmp**. We can apply method **setHours()** to the reference created by the cast, but not to **anEmp**. Note the importance of the parentheses in color. Without them, method **setHours()** would be applied to **anEmp**, leading to a syntax error.

◆◆

◆◆EXAMPLE 6.5 ─────────────────────────────────

If variable **obj** (type **Object**) references a type **NewEmployee** object, the expression

```
((NewEmployee) obj).getName()
```

retrieves the **name** field of the object referenced by **obj**. If **obj** does not reference a type **NewEmployee** object (or an instance of a subclass of **NewEmployee**), we would get an **illegal cast exception** during program execution.

── ◆◆

Although we cannot assign down the class hierarchy as a general rule, casting allows us to assign down the class hierarchy in certain situations. In Example 6.3, we showed that the assignment

```
salEmp = anEmp;  // incompatible types
```

would not be permitted when **salEmp** is type **SalaryEmployee** (subclass) and **anEmp** is type **NewEmployee** (superclass). However, if **anEmp** actually references a type **SalaryEmployee** object, the assignment statement below is valid:

```
salEmp = (SalaryEmployee) anEmp;
```

We are assigning the type **SalaryEmployee** reference created by the cast to **salEmp**, a type **SalaryEmployee** variable, so all is fine. If **anEmp** does not reference a type **SalaryEmployee** object, we would get an **illegal cast exception** during program execution.

What about casting up the hierarchy? If **salEmp** references a type **SalaryEmployee** object, is the operation

```
(NewEmployee) salEmp
```

valid and, if so, what is its effect? The casting operation does create a valid type **NewEmployee** reference to the object referenced by **salEmp**. However, you can apply only the methods of class **NewEmployee** to this reference. Because Java allows you to assign an object of a subclass type to a superclass variable anyway, you should not have to cast up a class hierarchy.

Passing Objects as Arguments

We use similar reasoning to determine whether an argument of one class type can be passed to a parameter that is a different class type. You can pass an argument that is a subclass type to a parameter that is a superclass type, but the converse is not true. We will demonstrate this in the examples that follow.

First let's consider what happens when you pass an argument that is an object to a method. The address of the object referenced by the argument is actually stored in the parameter. This means that the parameter and the argument reference the same object during the execution of the method. If the method changes a data field value in the object, that change remains in effect after the method is exited.

This is different from the situation with parameters that are primitive types (`int`, `double`, `char`, and `boolean`). The value of a primitive variable (not its address) is passed to a method and stored in the corresponding parameter. If the method changes the value of the parameter, the argument value is unchanged.

◆◆EXAMPLE 6.6 ───

We defined method `equals()` (shown below) in class `NewEmployee`.

```
public boolean equals(NewEmployee emp) {
   return this.socSecNum.equals(emp.socSecNum);
}
```

In our test class (Fig. 6.4), we used the condition (`clerk.equals(supervi-sor)`) to compare the objects referenced by `clerk` (type `HourlyEmployee`) and the method argument, `supervisor` (type `SalaryEmployee`). The argument type, `SalaryEmployee`, is a subclass of the parameter type, `NewEmployee`. The condition above evaluates to `false`.

─── ◆◆

A surprising fact is that we can call method `equals()` with a type `Object` argument. For example, if `obj` is type `Object`, the method call `clerk.equals(obj)` is valid. We stated earlier that you cannot pass a parameter that is a superclass type to an argument that is a subclass type, so you might wonder why this method call is valid. Also, the method call `clerk.equals("Help!!!")` is valid, but it makes no sense to pass a `String` argument to a type `NewEmployee` parameter. What is happening? In both these situations, Java calls the `equals()` method with the signature `equals(Object)`, not the one with signature `equals(NewEmployee)`. The former method is defined in class `Object` and is inherited by all the employee classes.

The instanceof Operator

We can define our own `equals()` method with the signature `equals(Object)` and override the one defined in class `Object`. We show how to do this in the next example by using casting and the `instanceof` operator. The expression

```
object instanceof ClassName
```

tests whether *object* (an instance variable) is an instance of *className* (a class type). It evaluates to **true** if *object* is an instance of *className*.

◆◆EXAMPLE 6.7

Fig. 6.16 shows another method **equals()** for class **NewEmployee** that overrides the one defined in class **Object**. If the condition **(emp instanceof NewEmployee)** is **true**, the argument is cast to a type **NewEmployee** reference, which is stored in **tempEmp**. Next, the **String** class **equals()** method compares the current object's social security number to **tempEmp**'s social security number and the result (**true** or **false**) is returned. If the condition **(emp instanceof NewEmployee)** is **false**, the second **return** statement executes, so the result will be **false**.

Figure 6.16   Method **equals()** with type **Object** parameter

```
public boolean equals(Object emp) {
  if (emp instanceof NewEmployee) {
    NewEmployee tempEmp = (NewEmployee) emp;
    return this.socSecNum.equals(tempEmp.socSecNum);
  }
  else {
    return false;
  }
}
```

The **if** statement guards the casting operation so that it is performed only when it should be. The condition **(emp instanceof NewEmployee)** is **true** only when **emp** references an object that is an instance of **NewEmployee** (or one of its subclasses).

◆◆

instanceof operator

Form: *object* instanceof *ClassName*
Example: clerk instanceof HourlyEmployee
                 company[i] instanceof Payable

Interpretation: Evaluates to **true** if *object* is an instance of *ClassName*; otherwise, evaluates to **false**.

EXERCISES FOR SECTION 6.2

SELF-CHECK

1. Explain why you cannot assign a variable of class **HourlyEmployee** to reference an object of type **SalaryEmployee** and vice versa.

2. Explain what an anonymous reference to an object is and indicate one way of generating one.

3. Describe the effect of each valid statement below. Assume the valid statements execute in sequence.

    a. NewEmployee anEmp = new SalaryEmployee("Jane", "1234");

    b. SalaryEmployee salEmp = (SalaryEmployee) anEmp;

    c. System.out.println(anEmp instanceof NewEmployee);

    d. System.out.println(anEmp instanceof HourlyEmployee);

    e. System.out.println(anEmp instanceof SalaryEmployee);

    f. ((SalaryEmployee) anEmp).setSalary(25000.00);

    g. HourlyEmployee hourEmp = anEmp;

    h. hourEmp = (HourlyEmployee) anEmp;

    i. ((HourlyEmployee) anEmp).setHours(50.0);

4. Explain the terms *method overriding*, *method overloading*, and *shadowing*.

PROGRAMMING

1. Write a static method **findHours()** that returns the **hours** field of its argument (type **NewEmployee**) only if its argument references a type **HourlyEmployee** object. It should return **40.0** if its argument references a type **SalaryEmployee** object and zero otherwise. *Hint*: use the **instanceof** operator.

6.3 Polymorphism

We have studied a class hierarchy with three different types of employees. We also showed a test class (Fig. 6.4) that created and manipulated individual objects of these types. In this section, we show how we can store objects of different types in a single array and process them in a uniform way using a programming language feature called polymorphism.

━━━━━━━━━━━━━

CASE STUDY A COMPANY WITH AN ARRAY OF EMPLOYEES OF DIFFERENT TYPES

PROBLEM In Section 5.5, we showed how to process an array of employees in which each element was the same type (`Employee`). Now our company has several employees of different types (`NewEmployee`, `HourlyEmployee`, and `SalaryEmployee`). We want to store them in an array and compute the total company payroll.

ANALYSIS AND DESIGN In the last section, we determined that a variable of a superclass type can reference objects of its own type or of a subclass types, so we should be able to store employees of all types in an array with `NewEmployee` elements. Fig. 6.17 shows a description of a class `NewCompany` with a single data field `employees` that stores an array of `NewEmployee` objects. An individual array element, say `employees[i]`, can reference an object of type `NewEmployee`, `SalaryEmployee`, or `HourlyEmployee`.

The constructor allocates storage for an array whose size is specified by the constructor argument. Method `setEmployee()` stores an employee object in the array, and method `getEmployee()` retrieves an employee object from the array. There is also a method `computePayroll()` that calculates each employee's weekly pay, updates the total pay data field for all employees, and adds the weekly pay to the total payroll. It also displays each employee's ID number and weekly pay.

Figure 6.17 Class `NewCompany`

Data Fields	Attributes
`NewEmployee[] employees`	Array of employees
`double payroll`	Company payroll
Methods	**Behavior**
`NewCompany(int)`	Creates `NewCompany` object with array `employees` whose size is specified by the argument
`void setEmployee(Employee, int)`	Stores the first argument in array `employees` at the position specified by the second argument
`void setPayroll(double)`	Stores its argument in `payroll`
`Employee getEmployee(int)`	Retrieves the employee at the position indicated by its argument
`double getPayroll()`	Returns the company payroll
`void readPayrollData()`	Reads the payroll data into array `employees`
`void computePayroll()`	Computes the total payroll
`String toString()`	Represents the company's data as a string
Classes Used	
`NewEmployee, HourlyEmployee, SalaryEmployee`	

IMPLEMENTATION   Fig. 6.18 shows class **NewCompany**. In method **computePayroll()**, the first statement below stores a reference to the current employee in variable **emp**:

```
NewEmployee emp = employees[i];
if (emp instanceof HourlyEmployee)
    weekPay = ((HourlyEmployee) emp).calcWeeklyPay();
else if (emp instanceof SalaryEmployee)
    weekPay = ((SalaryEmployee) emp).calcWeeklyPay();
else
    weekPay = 0.0;
```

Figure 6.18   Class NewCompany

```
/* NewCompany.java          Authors: Koffman & Wolz
 * A class for processing an array of employees of
 * different types and for computing company payroll.
 * Uses NewEmployee, HourlyEmployee, SalaryEmployee.
 */
public class NewCompany {

  // Data fields
  private NewEmployee[] employees;  // array of employees
  private double payroll;           // company payroll

  // Methods
  // postcondition: Allocates storage for numEmp employees
  //    in a new NewCompany object.
  public NewCompany(int numEmp) {
    employees = new NewEmployee[numEmp];
  }

  // postcondition: Stores employee emp at position index
  //    of array employees if index is in range.
  public void setEmployee(NewEmployee emp, int index) {
    if (index >= 0 && index < employees.length)
      employees[index] = emp;
    else
      System.out.println("Index value " + index +
                         " is out of range");
  }

  // postcondition: Returns an employee at position index
  //    of employees. Returns null if index is not in range.
  public NewEmployee getEmployee(int index) {
```

Figure 6.18   Class `NewCompany`, *continued*

```
      if (index >= 0 && index < employees.length)
         return employees[index];
      else
         return null;
   }


   // postcondition: Computes weekly pay for each employee,
   //    adds it to payroll, and updates employee's total pay.
   //    Displays each employee's ID (social security number) and pay.
   public void computePayroll() {
      System.out.println("ID" + "\t" + "pay");
      for (int i = 0; i < employees.length; i++) {
         // Calculate weekly pay.
         double weekPay;
         NewEmployee emp = employees[i];
         if (emp instanceof HourlyEmployee)
            weekPay = ((HourlyEmployee) emp).calcWeeklyPay();
         else if (emp instanceof SalaryEmployee)
            weekPay = ((SalaryEmployee) emp).calcWeeklyPay();
         else
            weekPay = 0.0;

         // Add the weekly pay amount to employee's total pay.
         emp.updateTotalPay(weekPay);

         // Add the weekly pay amount to the payroll.
         payroll += weekPay;

         // Display ID and pay.
         System.out.println(emp.getSocial() +
                            "\t" + weekPay);
      }
   }

   public String toString() {
      String result = "Total payroll is $" + payroll +
                      "\n\nEmployee information:\n";
      for (int i = 0; i < employees.length; i++) {
         result = result + employees[i].toString() + "\n\n";
      }
      return result;
   }

}
```

The **if** statement calculates the weekly pay for each employee object that is type **HourlyEmployee** or type **SalaryEmployee** by calling the **calcWeeklyPay()** method for that object. For example, when **emp** references a type **HourlyEmployee** object, the casting operation creates a type **HourlyEmployee** reference, so the **calcWeeklyPay()** method for **HourlyEmployee** objects is called. After **weekPay** is calculated, the statement

```
emp.updateTotalPay(weekPay);
```

calls object **emp**'s **updateTotalPay()** method, passing it the value of **weekPay** just calculated (zero if the current employee is type **NewEmployee**).

TESTING   Fig. 6.19 shows an application class, and Fig. 6.20 shows the result of executing this class. The **main** method creates an object **myCompany** with storage for three employees. It calls object **myCompany**'s **setEmployee()** method to store three employee objects of different types in the array. The first argument in each call is the object to be stored; the second argument is the array subscript. Next method **computePayroll()** computes and displays the payroll information, and method **toString()** returns a string representation of object **myCompany**, which is then displayed.

Polymorphism and Late Binding of Method Calls

In Fig. 6.18, we define a **toString()** method that returns a string representing the information stored in a **NewCompany** object. The string begins with characters that represent the total payroll. In the **for** loop body, the statement

```
result = result + employees[i].toString() + "\n\n";
```

calls object **employees[i]**'s **toString()** method to represent the current employee as a string. The particular **toString()** method called depends on the type of object referenced by **employees[i]**. Java cannot determine at compile-time which **toString()** method to call because it does not know at compile-time what kind of employee object (type **NewEmpoyee**, **HourlyEmployee**, or **SalaryEmployee**) will be referenced by each array element. For example, in the application shown in Fig. 6.19, when **i** is 0, **employees[i]** references a type **HourlyEmployee** object, but it references a type **SalaryEmployee** object when **i** is 1.

Figure 6.19   Class `TestNewCompany`

```
/* TestNewCompany.java        Authors: Koffman & Wolz
 * An application class for class NewCompany.
 */
public class TestNewCompany {

  public static void main(String[] args) {
    // Create a Company object with 3 elements.
    NewCompany myCompany = new NewCompany(3);

    // Store 3 employees of different kinds in the array.
    myCompany.setEmployee(
            new HourlyEmployee("Sam", "1234", "clerk",
                "", "", 30, 2000, 15000.00, 40.0, 15.0), 0);
    myCompany.setEmployee(
            new SalaryEmployee("Jessica", "2222", "manager",
                "", "", 33, 1998, 40000.00, 52000.00), 1);
    myCompany.setEmployee(
            new NewEmployee("George", "3456",
            "spouse of boss",
                "", "", 55, 1990, 0.0), 2);

    // Update total pay for each employee.
    myCompany.computePayroll();

    // Display employee information.
    System.out.println(myCompany.toString());
  }

}
```

The feature that enables a particular method call to have different behavior at different times is called **polymorphism**, which means multiple forms. At run-time, Java determines which `toString()` method to call based on the data type of the object referenced by `employees[i]`. That object will be linked to the code for its `toString()` method and that is the one that executes. The feature that enables a programming language to select a code fragment to execute at run-time is called **dynamic binding**.

Figure 6.20   Execution of class `TestNewCompany`

```
TestNewCompany                                              _ □ ×
ID      pay
1234    600.0
2222    1000.0
3456    0.0
Total payroll is $1600.0

Employee information:
name: Sam, social security: 1234, job: clerk
address: , phone: , age: 30, year started: 2000, total pay $15600.0
weekly hours: 40.0, hourly rate $15.0

name: Jessica, social security: 2222, job: manager
address: , phone: , age: 33, year started: 1998, total pay $41000.0
annual salary $52000.0

name: George, social security: 3456, job: spouse of boss
address: , phone: , age: 55, year started: 1990, total pay $0.0
```

EXERCISES FOR SECTION 6.3

SELF-CHECK

1. Are the calls to `updateTotalPay()` and `calcWeeklyPay()` in method `computePayroll()` (Fig. 6.18) resolved at compile-time or run-time? Explain your answer.

2. In Fig. 6.18 is the call to method `toString()` (inside method `toString()`) required? Explain your answer.

3. Explain why you cannot use the `if` statement below in method `computePayroll()`.

```
if (emp instanceof HourlyEmployee ||
    emp instanceof SalaryEmployee)
  weekPay = emp.calcWeeklyPay();
else
  weekPay = 0.0;
```

PROGRAMMING

1. Write a static method for class **NewCompany** that reads an employee's data into a **NewEmployee** object (the method result). The method must ask the user what kind of employee is being processed before asking for the data. For all employees, read the name and social security number. In addition, for annual employees read the salary amount, and for hourly employees, read the hours worked and rate. The remaining data fields should be filled with their default values. Your method should create and return a new object of the specified type.

2. Write a method for class **NewCompany** that reads data into its array of employees. This method should use the one written for Programming Exercise 1.

6.4   Interfaces

In this section we introduce another kind of Java construct that is similar to a class; it is called an interface. An **interface** is used to specify a set of requirements that is imposed on a collection of classes. Classes that **implement an interface** are guaranteed to have certain functionality (behavior) and also inherit any constants that are defined in the interface. In the next example, we define an interface **Payable**. Classes that implement the **Payable** interface are guaranteed to know how to calculate weekly pay.

◆◆EXAMPLE 6.8 ──────────────────────────

We can declare an interface **Payable** that specifies the requirement that a class have a method to calculate weekly pay (method **calcWeeklyPay()**). Consequently, any class that implements the **Payable** interface must define a **calcWeeklyPay()** method. Figure 6.21 shows the declaration for interface **Payable**. It is similar to a class definition and would be saved in file **Payroll.java**.

Figure 6.21   Payable interface

```
/* Payable.java          Authors: Koffman & Wolz
 * The Payable interface.
 */
public interface Payable {
  public double calcWeeklyPay();
}
```

◆◆

The interface in Fig. 6.21 documents the fact that all classes that implement it have a method called `calcWeeklyPay()`. The interface body consists of only the heading for method `calcWeeklyPay()`. This is considered an **abstract method** because it is not defined in the interface. If an abstract method has parameters, the complete parameter list must be provided. If a class that implements the interface does not define method `calcWeeklyPay()`, the syntax error `class should be declared abstract` occurs when that class is compiled. Only abstract methods and constant definitions (indicated by the modifiers `static final`) are permitted in an interface; an interface cannot have data fields. Also, all methods must be public.

To indicate that classes `HourlyEmployee` and `SalaryEmployee` implement this interface, we change their headers to

```
public class HourlyEmployee extends NewEmployee implements Payable
public class SalaryEmployee extends NewEmployee implements Payable
```

A class can only extend one superclass, but it can implement multiple interfaces. Each interface name follows the word **implements** with commas as separators.

We can use interface `Payable` to simplify the `if` statement in method `computePayroll()` (Fig. 6.18). Before, we used separate conditions to test for objects of type `HourlyEmployee` and `SalaryEmployee`:

```
if (emp instanceof HourlyEmployee)
   weekPay = ((HourlyEmployee) emp).calcWeeklyPay();
else if (emp instanceof SalaryEmployee)
   weekPay = ((SalaryEmployee) emp).calcWeeklyPay();
else
   weekPay = 0.0;
```

Now, objects of type `HourlyEmployee` and `SalaryEmployee` are also considered to be type `Payable` because they implement the `Payable` interface, so we can use the simpler `if` statement:

```
if (emp instanceof Payable)
   weekPay = ((Payable) emp).calcWeeklyPay();
else
   weekPay = 0.0;
```

The condition is `true` if object `emp` implements the `Payable` interface. If so, the casting operation creates a type `Payable` reference to the object referenced by `emp`. Because the reference is type `Payable`, the call to method `calcWeeklyPay()` compiles. However, the particular method that is called is determined at run-time based on the actual type (`HourlyEmployee` or `SalaryEmployee`) of the object referenced by `emp`.

We summarize the steps to create and use the **Payable** interface next.

◆ Write the **Payable** interface (file **Payable.java**).

◆ Add **implements Payable** to all classes that implement it. Verify that these classes contain complete definitions for method **calcWeeklyPay()**.

◆ Use casting to ensure that all calls to method **calcWeeklyPay()** are applied only to type **Payable** references.

Interface definition

Form: ```
public interface InterfaceName {
    abstract method headings
    constant declarations
}
```

Example:   ```
public interface Payable {
    public void calcWeeklyPay();
    public static final double DEDUCT_PCT = 5.5;
}
```

Interpretation: Interface *InterfaceName* is defined. The interface body provides headings for abstract methods and constant declarations. Interfaces may extend other interfaces.

Declaring Constants in Interfaces

We can declare constants in an interface. These constants would be inherited by classes that implement the interface. For example, we could use the declaration

```
public static final double DEDUCT_PCT = 5.5;
```

in class **Payable** to declare **DEDUCT_PCT** as a constant with a value of **5.5**.

The Comparable Interface and Method compareTo()

Java provides a number of useful interfaces. One of these, the **Comparable** interface, ensures that the programmer will be able to compare objects in each class that implements it. Fig. 6.22 shows the **Comparable** interface.

Figure 6.22 Comparable interface

```
public interface Comparable {
  public int compareTo(Object obj);
}
```

All classes that implement the **Comparable** interface must have a **compareTo()** method that returns an integer value defined as follows:

◆ The result is negative if the object it is applied to is less than the argument.

◆ The result is zero if the object it is applied to is equal to the argument.

◆ The result is positive if the object it is applied to is greater than the argument.

The **String** class implements the **Comparable** interface and therefore has a **compareTo()** method. Table 6.1 shows the results of three calls of this method.

Table 6.1   Method compareTo() of class String

Method Call	Result	Reason
"this".compareTo("that")	Positive	"this" is greater than "that"
"that".compareTo("this")	Negative	"that" is less than "this"
"same".compareTo("same")	Zero	"same" is equal to "same"

Sorting Comparable Objects

We can use the fact that there is a **Comparable** interface to build generic sorting methods that can sort arrays whose elements reference type **Comparable** objects—objects whose classes implement the **Comparable** interface. In Fig. 5.22, we wrote methods **selectionSort()** and **findPosMin()**, which performed a selection sort on an array of integers. Fig. 6.23 shows a class **Sorts** that contains class methods **selectionSort()** and **findPosMin()**, modified to sort arrays whose elements are type **Comparable**. We only need to change a few statements in the original methods in Fig. 5.22. We change the headings for methods **selectionSort()**and **findPosMin()** to show that the arguments are type **Comparable[]** arrays.

```
public static void selectionSort(Comparable[] x)
private static int findPosMin(Comparable[] x, int fill)
```

In **selectionSort()**, we change the declaration of variable **temp** to

```
Comparable temp;   //temporary variable for exchange
```

Also, we replace the condition (x[i] < x[posMinSoFar]) in method **findPosMin()** with (x[i].compareTo(x[posMinSoFar]) < 0). This condition uses method **compareTo()** to test whether x[i] is less than x[posMinSoFar].

Figure 6.23   Class Sorts

```
/* Sorts.java          Authors: Koffman & Wolz
 * Contains method selectionSort() to sort Comparable[] arrays.
 * Part of package psJava.
 */
package psJava;

public class Sorts {

  // precondition: array x is defined
  // postcondition: elements in array x are in increasing order
  public static void selectionSort(Comparable[] x) {

    int posMin;        //index of next smallest element
    Comparable temp;   //temporary variable for exchange

    for (int fill = 0; fill < x.length-1; fill++) {
      /* invariant:
       *    The elements in x[0] through x[fill-1] are in
       *    their proper place and fill < x.length is true.
       */
      //Find index of smallest element in subarray
      //  starting at element x[fill].
      posMin = findPosMin(x, fill);

      //Exchange elements with indices fill and posMin.
      if (posMin != fill) {
        temp = x[fill];
        x[fill] = x[posMin];
        x[posMin] = temp;
      }
    }
  }


  private static int findPosMin(Comparable[] x, int fill) {
    int posMinSoFar = fill;
    for (int i = fill + 1; i < x.length; i++)
      if (x[i].compareTo(x[posMinSoFar]) < 0)
        posMinSoFar = i;

    return posMinSoFar;
  }
}
```

The first line

```
package psJava;
```

indicates that class **Sorts** is part of package **psJava**. We explain its significance in Section 6.7. Next, we use method **selectionSort()** to sort two arrays: an array of strings and an array of employees.

◆◆EXAMPLE 6.9 ───

Fig. 6.24 shows a class (**TestStringSorts**) that uses method **Sorts.selectionSort()** to sort an array of strings entered as data. The first **for** statement in the main method reads five strings and stores them in array **names**. The statement

```
Sorts.selectionSort(names);
```

sorts the array. Because class **String** implements the **Comparable** interface, we can call method **selectionSort()** with an array of **Strings** as its argument. Next, the second **for** statement displays the names in alphabetical order. Figure 6.25 shows the console window for a sample run.

◆◆

The next example shows how to use the **selectionSort()** method to sort an array of employees. This is possible only if we modify class **NewEmployee** so that it implements the **Comparable** interface.

◆◆EXAMPLE 6.10 ───

We can modify class **NewEmployee** (Fig. 6.5) to implement the **Comparable** interface by changing its header:

```
public class NewEmployee implements Comparable {
```

We must also provide a definition for the comparison method required by the interface, method **compareTo()**. Now class **NewEmployee** (and its subclasses by extension) implements the **Comparable** interface, so method **compareTo()** should compare two objects of type **NewEmployee** (or of its subclass types). The result will be based on the social security numbers of the objects being compared. The method heading required by the **Comparable** interface

```
public void compareTo(Object obj)
```

Figure 6.24   Class `TestStringSort`

```
/* TestStringSorts.java          Authors: Koffman & Wolz
 * Tests class Sorts.
 */
import psJava.Sorts;
import javax.swing.JOptionPane;

public class TestStringSort {

  public static void main(String[] args) {

    String[] names = new String[5];

    // Read in 5 names
    for (int i = 0; i < names.length; i++)
      names[i] = JOptionPane.showInputDialog("Enter name " + (i+1));

    // Sort the array names
    Sorts.selectionSort(names);

    // Display the names in alphabetical order
    System.out.println("Names in alphabetical order:");
    for (int i = 0; i < names.length; i++)
      System.out.println(names[i]);

  }
}
```

Figure 6.25   Sample run of class `TestStringSort`

shows that method **compareTo()** has a type **Object** parameter. In the new class **NewEmployee** (Fig. 6.26), method **compareTo()** casts the object referenced by its argument to type **NewEmployee**:

```
NewEmployee emp = (NewEmployee) obj;
```

Next, it calls method **compareTo()** (of class **String**) to compare the social security number of the current employee to the social security number of the object referenced by **emp**. Method **compareTo()** (of class **NewEmployee**) returns the result (an integer) of this string comparison.

Figure 6.26   Class **NewEmployee** with method **compareTo()**

```
/* NewEmployee.java          Authors: Koffman & Wolz
 * Superclass of employee classes.
 * Uses String
 */
public class NewEmployee implements Comparable {

  // Data fields
  private String name = "";
  private String socSecNum = "";
  . . .

  // Methods
  //    Insert methods here.
  //    . . .

  // postcondition: returns negative value, 0, or positive value
  //    depending on whether this employee's social security #
  //    is less than, equal to, or greater than its argument's
  //    social security #.
  public int compareTo(Object obj) {
     NewEmployee emp = (NewEmployee) obj;
     return this.socSecNum.compareTo(emp.socSecNum);
  }

}
```

We can insert a method to sort data field **employees** in class **NewCompany** (Fig. 6.18). Fig. 6.27 shows method **sortEmployees()**. If class **NewCompany** imports class **psJava.Sorts**, the statement

```
Sorts.selectionSort(employees);
```

sorts data field **employees**. After the sort, the elements of array **employees** will be in order by social security number. We could also use method **sort()** of class **java.util.Arrays**.

Figure 6.27   **Method** sortEmployees() **for class** NewCompany

```
// postcondition: sorts the employees by social security number
public void sortEmployees() {
  Sorts.selectionSort(employees);
}
```

EXERCISES FOR SECTION 6.4

SELF-CHECK

1. Show data field **employees** in class **NewCompany** (Fig. 6.18) after the sorting operation.

2. Assume **emp** is type **NewEmployee**. What would be the effect of executing the **if** statement below if the phrase **implements Payable** was deleted from class **SalaryEmployee**?

```
if (emp instanceof Payable)
   weekPay = ((Payable) emp).calcWeeklyPay();
else
   weekPay = 0.0;
```

3. Why can't we add **implements Payable** to the header for class **NewEmployee**?

PROGRAMMING

1. Modify method **compareTo()** to order a pair of **NewEmployee** objects by name instead of social security number.

2. Write method `computePayroll()` (Fig. 6.18) using the `Payable` interface. Make the modifications required to classes `HourlyEmployee` and `SalaryEmployee` and rerun class `TestNewCompany` to demonstrate that the `Payable` interface works correctly.

3. Make the modifications required to classes `NewEmployee`, `NewCompany`, and `TestNewCompany` to sort the array of employees and to demonstrate that the sorting operation works correctly.

6.5 Abstract Classes

One reason to use inheritance is that it allows you to reuse existing classes to build new classes. Another reason is that it allows you to cluster similar classes together. This clustering can help you design effective abstractions for large, complex systems.

For our hierarchy of employee classes, we had a superclass, `NewEmployee`, that was an actual class and could be instantiated. Sometimes we have to create a new class, called an **abstract class**, that should not be instantiated and whose sole purpose is to serve as the parent (superclass) of a group of classes. The parent class gives us a convenient place to declare all data fields and methods common to its subclasses.

An example of such an abstract class would be a class `Food` that has subclasses for the different food groups `Grains`, `Fruit`, `Vegetables`, `Meats`, `Fish`, `Poultry`, and `Dairy`. Each of these classes could be instantiated (for example, a pear would be a `Fruit` object, a chicken breast would be a `Poultry` object). All edible objects would be an instance of one of these food groups, so these classes should be instantiated, but not the `Food` class. We introduce another abstract class and show how to use it in the next case study.

Abstract class definition

Form: ```
public abstract class ClassName {
    data field declarations
    abstract method headings
    method definitions
}
```

Example:  ```
public abstract class Food {
    // Data field
    private double calories;

    // Abstract methods
    public abstract double percentProtein();
    public abstract double percentFat();
    public abstract double percentCarbohydrates();
```

```
// Methods
public double getCalories() {
   return calories;}
public void setCalories(double cal) {
    calories = cal;
}
}
```

Interpretation: Abstract class *ClassName* is defined. The class body may contain data field declarations, method definitions, and headings for abstract methods

CASE STUDY   AREAS OF GEOMETRIC FIGURES

PROBLEM   Consider the problem of finding the total area of a collection of geometric figures. This problem has many practical applications. For example, in calculating the paint needed for a house, a painter might visualize the interior walls as a series of rectangular and triangular shapes. In calculating the amount of fertilizer to buy, a landscaper might represent a garden as a collection of circle and triangular shapes.

ANALYSIS   One way to solve this problem would be to create an array of rectangular objects, an array of circular objects, and a separate array of triangular objects. Each object has an area, so we can calculate separately the sum of the areas of all objects in each array and then add the sums. However, what would happen if we needed to add a new geometric figure such as a circle? We would need to modify our code to define a new array of objects and to calculate the sum of the areas of the objects stored in this new array. Each new figure type would require us to define a new array type and to modify the area finding code.

There is a better way to add another geometric figure. If we could store objects of many different figure types in a single array, we would not need to modify our code when a new figure type was added. We can design a base class called `GeoFigure` and have all our figure types extend this class. `GeoFigure` should be an abstract class because we create a new geometric object by instantiating one of its subclasses, not by instantiating `GeoFigure`. Fig. 6.28 shows the class hierarchy.

DESIGN   An abstract class provides an "outline" of a class but leaves the complete definition to the subclasses that extend it. An abstract class contains method headings (similar to the headings in an interface) that must be defined by all of the classes that extend it. Fig. 6.29 shows a description for class `GeoFigure`. Figs. 6.30 through 6.32 show descriptions for its subclasses.

Figure 6.28   Class hierarchy for figures problem

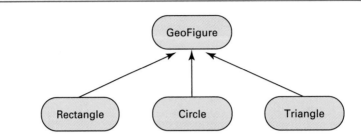

Figure 6.29   Abstract class GeoFigure

Methods	Behavior
abstract double computePerimeter()	Computes the perimeter; defined in subclasses
abstract double computeArea()	Computes the area; defined in subclasses

Figure 6.30   Class Rectangle

Data Fields	Attributes
int width	Width of rectangle
int height	Height of rectangle

Methods	Behavior
Rectangle()	Sets new object's data fields to their default values
Rectangle(int, int)	Sets new object's data fields to values of arguments
double computePerimeter()	Computes the perimeter
double computeArea()	Computes the area
void setWidth(int)	Sets data field width to its argument
void setHeight(int)	Sets data field height to its argument
int getWidth()	Retrieves the width
int getHeight()	Retrieves the height
String toString()	Returns a string representation of a rectangle

Figure 6.31   Class `Circle`

Data Fields	Attributes
`int radius`	Radius of circle
Methods	**Behavior**
`Circle()`	Sets new object's data field to its default value
`Circle(int)`	Sets new object's data field to value of its argument
`double computePerimeter()`	Computes the perimeter
`double computeArea()`	Computes the area
`void setRadius(int)`	Sets data field `radius` to its argument
`int getRadius()`	Retrieves the radius
`String toString()`	Returns a string representation of a circle

Figure 6.32   Class `Triangle`

Data Fields	Attributes
`int base`	Base of triangle
`int height`	Height of triangle
Methods	**Behavior**
`Triangle()`	Sets new object's data fields to their default values
`Triangle(int, int)`	Sets new object's data fields to values of arguments
`double computePerimeter()`	Computes the perimeter
`double computeArea()`	Computes the area
`void setBase(int)`	Sets data field `base` to its argument
`void setHeight(int)`	Sets data field `height` to its argument
`int getBase()`	Retrieves the base
`int getHeight()`	Retrieves the height
`String toString()`	Returns a string representation of a triangle

IMPLEMENTATION   Figure 6.33 shows the definition of the abstract class
`GeoFigure`. The first modifier **abstract** identifies `GeoFigure` as an abstract class.
The modifier **abstract** in a method heading identifies that method as abstract (to be
defined by the subclasses). Unlike an interface, the modifier **abstract** is required for
abstract method headings in an abstract class because you can provide real method
definitions as well as abstract method headings in an abstract class.

Figure 6.33 Abstract class `GeoFigure`

```
/* GeoFigure.java          Authors: Koffman & Wolz
 * Abstract superclass of geometric figures classes.
 */
public abstract class GeoFigure {
   public abstract double computePerimeter();
   public abstract double computeArea();
}
```

Figures 6.34 through 6.36 show definitions of three classes that extend abstract class **GeoFigure**: **Rectangle**, **Circle**, and **Triangle**. Each class has data fields that are appropriate for that class of objects (**width** and **height** for rectangles, **radius** for circles, **base** and **height** for right triangles). We gave the data fields protected visibility because we plan to extend these classes in Section 6.6. They all have default values of zero. Each class has **computePerimeter()** and **computeArea()** methods. Also, each contains a method **toString()**.

Figure 6.34 Class `Rectangle`

```
/* Rectangle.java          Authors: Koffman & Wolz
 * Represents a rectangle.
 * Extends GeoFigure
 */
public class Rectangle extends GeoFigure {

  // Data Fields
  protected int width;
  protected int height;

  // Methods
  // Constructors
  public Rectangle() {}

  public Rectangle(int wid, int hei) {
    width = wid;
    height = hei;
  }

  // Modifiers
  public void setWidth(int wid) {
    width = wid;
  }
```

Figure 6.34   **Class** `Rectangle`, *continued*

```
public void setHeight(int hei) {
  height = hei;
}

// Accessors
public int getWidth() {
  return width;
}

public int getHeight() {
  return height;
}

public double computeArea() {
  return height * width;
}

public double computePerimeter() {
  return 2 * (height + width);
}

public String toString() {
  return "Rectangle: width is
         " + width + ", height is " + height;
}

}
```

TESTING   Figure 6.37 implements an application that uses class `GeoFigure` and its subclasses. Method `main()` allocates storage for an array `gF` that contains four objects of different geometric types, each a subclass of abstract class `GeoFigure`. For example, array element `gF[0]` stores a right triangle with a base of `10` and a height of `20`. In the first `for` loop, method `main` uses the method call `gF[i].toString()` to display the category of each object in the array. In the second `for` loop, method `main` displays each object's area (returned by `geoFigure.computeArea()`) and adds it to the total area (`total`). In both cases, the particular `toString()` or `computeArea()` method that is called is determined at run-time. Figure 6.38 shows a sample run.

Figure 6.35 Class `Circle`

```
/* Circle.java          Authors: Koffman & Wolz
 * Represents a circle.
 * Extends GeoFigure
 */
public class Circle extends GeoFigure {

  // Data Fields
  protected int radius;

  // Methods
  // Constructors
  public Circle() {}

  public Circle(int rad) {
    radius = rad;
  }

  // Modifiers
  public void setRadius(int rad) {
    radius = rad;
  }

  // Accessors
  public int getRadius() {
    return radius;
  }

  // Operations
  public double computeArea() {
    return radius * radius * Math.PI;
  }

  public double computePerimeter() {
    return 2 * radius * Math.PI;
  }

  public String toString() {
    return "Circle: radius is " + radius;
  }

} // class Circle
```

Figure 6.36   Class `Triangle`

```java
/* Triangle.java          Authors: Koffman & Wolz
 * Represents a right triangle.
 * Extends GeoFigure
 */
public class Triangle extends GeoFigure {

  // Data Fields
  protected int base;
  protected int height;

  // Methods
  // Constructor
  public Triangle(int bas, int hei) {
    base = bas;
    height = hei;
  }

  public Triangle() {}

  // Modifiers
  public void setBase(int bas) {
    base = bas;
  }

  public void setHeight(int hei){
    height = hei;
  }

  // Accessors
  public int getBase() {
    return base;
  }

  public int getHeight() {
    return height;
  }

  // Operations
  public double computeArea()      {
    return height * base / 2.0;
  }
```

Figure 6.36   Class `Triangle`, *continued*

```java
public double computePerimeter() {
  return height + base +
         Math.sqrt(height*height + base*base);
}

public String toString() {
  return "Right Triangle: base is " + base +
         ", height is " + height;
}

}
```

Figure 6.37   Class `TestGeoFigure`

```java
/* TestGeoFigure.java          Authors: Koffman & Wolz
 * Tests a type GeoFigure[] array.
 * Uses GeoFigure, Triangle, Rectangle, and Circle.
 */

public class TestGeoFigure {

    public static void main(String[] args) {
        // Create an array of type GeoFigure
        GeoFigure gF[] = {new Triangle(10, 25),
                          new Circle(5),
                          new Rectangle(10, 20),
                          new Rectangle(30, 30)   };

        // Compute area of each figure and add it to total.
        // Display each figure and its area.
        double totalArea = 0;
        for (int i = 0; i < gF.length; i++) {
            double area = gF[i].computeArea();
            totalArea += area;
            System.out.println(gF[i].toString());
            System.out.println("Area is " + area + "\n");
        }

        System.out.println("\nTotal area is " + totalArea);
    }

}
```

Figure 6.38   Execution of `TestGeoFigure`

```
TestGeoFigure                                            _ □ ×
Right Triangle: base is 10, height is 25
Area is 125.0

Circle: radius is 5
Area is 78.53981633974483

Rectangle: width is 10, length is 20
Area is 200.0

Rectangle: width is 30, length is 30
Area is 900.0


Total area is 1303.539816339745
```

PROGRAM STYLE: *Balancing Flexibility and Protection*

The declaration of array `gF` with four different type elements perfectly balances flexibility and protection constraints. The ability to store objects of different types in a single array significantly simplifies the code. This kind of flexibility is not possible without inheritance. You would be forced to declare one array for each geometric class (type `Triangle[]`, type `Rectangle[]`, and so on).

The ability to declare an array of an abstract class type provides real protection for the programmer. Only instantiations of classes that extend the abstract class may be stored in the array. For example, if a class called `Ellipse` is defined that does not extend `GeoFigure`, the compiler will not allow it to be included in the array:

```
GeoFigure[] gF = {new Triangle(10, 20),
                  new Circle(10),
                  new Ellipse(10, 20), // syntax error
                  new Rectangle(10, 20)};
```

EXERCISES FOR SECTION 6.5

SELF-CHECK

1. Explain what makes a class abstract. Why are abstract classes useful? What may be declared in an abstract class?

2. Summarize the differences between an abstract class and an interface.

PROGRAMMING

1. Declare a class type **Square** that extends **Rectangle**. A square is a rectangle in which both dimensions are the same. You need to define a constructor that has the side dimension as its parameter. It should call its superclass constructor to set the dimensions of **width** and **height** to the side dimension.

6.6 Drawing Figures Using an Abstract Class and an Interface

Our next case study illustrates the use of an abstract class and an interface. After the case study, we discuss their similarities and differences.

CASE STUDY DRAWING GEOMETRIC FIGURES

PROBLEM We would like to draw geometric figures on the screen. Each figure object will be one of our standard shapes and can appear anywhere on the screen with any interior color or border color.

ANALYSIS A simple solution would be to extend classes **Circle**, **Rectangle**, and **Triangle** to get three new subclasses for drawable figures (**DrawableCircle**, **DrawableRectangle**, and **DrawableTriangle**). Figure 6.39 shows a new class hierarchy with a new base class **GeoFigure**. There is also an interface **Drawable** that must be implemented by each class that can draw its objects.

Figure 6.39   Class hierarchy for drawing figures

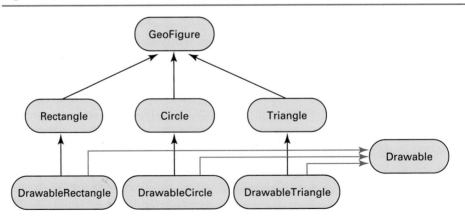

DESIGN   A drawable figure has three additional data fields: its position on the screen (x, y), its border color, and its interior color. It must also define accessor and modifier methods for each of these data fields. Rather than provide separate data fields and methods in each of the three new subclasses, we can declare them higher up in the hierarchy, by modifying abstract class `GeoFigure`. Figure 6.40 shows a description of our new class `GeoFigure`.

Notice that class `GeoFigure` now has three data fields and defines six actual methods. Recall that an abstract class can have data fields and actual methods as well as abstract methods.

Not all subclasses of `GeoFigure` have objects that can be drawn. To distinguish between those that can be drawn and those that can't, we provide a `Drawable` interface, and each class whose objects can be drawn must implement the `Drawable` interface. Figure 6.41 shows the `Drawable` interface. It has one abstract method `drawMe()`, which must be defined in each class that implements it. Method `drawMe()` is responsible for drawing a figure on the screen and has a parameter of type `Graphics` (a class defined in the Abstract Window Toolkit, or AWT).

Figure 6.42 shows a description of class `DrawableRectangle`. It extends class `Rectangle` and implements class `Drawable`, so it must provide a `drawMe()` method. It has no additional data fields beyond what it inherits from class `Rectangle` and class `GeoFigure`.

Figure 6.40   New class `GeoFigure`

Data Fields	Attributes
`Point pos`	(x, y) position on screen
`Color borderColor`	Border color
`Color interiorColor`	Interior color
Abstract Methods	**Behavior**
`double computePerimeter()`	Computes the perimeter
`double computeArea()`	Computes the area
Methods	**Behavior**
`void setPos(Point)`	Sets the (x, y) screen position to its argument
`void setBorderColor(Color)`	Sets the border color to its argument
`void setInteriorColor(Color)`	Sets the interior color to its argument
`Point getPos()`	Retrieves the (x, y) screen position
`Color getBorderColor()`	Retrieves the border color
`Color getInteriorColor()`	Retrieves the interior color

Figure 6.41 `Drawable` **interface**

```
/* Drawable.java        Authors: Koffman & Wolz
 * The Drawable interface.
 */
import java.awt.*;

public interface Drawable {
  public void drawMe(Graphics g);
}
```

Figure 6.42 Class `DrawableRectangle`

Methods	Behavior
`DrawableRectangle()`	No parameter constructor; sets a new object's data fields to default values
`DrawableRectangle(int, int, Point, Color, Color)`	Five parameter constructor; sets a new object's data fields (`width`, `length`, `pos`, `borderColor`, `interiorColor`) as specified by its arguments
`void drawMe(Graphics)`	Draws a rectangle object with top-left corner at `pos` and with colors specified by its data fields
`String toString()`	Represents attributes of a `DrawableRectangle` object as a string
Data Fields Inherited from `Rectangle` and `GeoFigure`	
`width, height, pos, borderColor, interiorColor`	
Methods Inherited from `Rectangle` and `GeoFigure`	
`computePerimeter(), computeArea(), setWidth(), setHeight(), setPos(), setBorderColor(), setInteriorColor(), getWidth(), getHeight(), getPos(), getInteriorColor(), getBorderColor()`	

The descriptions of classes `DrawableCircle` and `DrawableTriangle` are similar to class `DrawableRectangle`, so we will leave them as an exercise.

IMPLEMENTATION

Class `GeoFigure`

Figure 6.43 shows abstract class `GeoFigure`. Class `GeoFigure` imports the AWT because it uses two classes defined there: `Point` and `Color` (see Section 3.8). Data field **pos** (type **Point**) represents the screen position where a drawable object will appear.

The three data fields initially reference the objects `Point(0, 0)`, `Color.black`, and `Color.white`. `Point(0, 0)` represents the pixel at the top-left corner of the screen. An object of type `Point` has two public data fields, `x` and `y`. Initially `pos.x` and `pos.y` are zero.

Class `DrawableRectangle`

Fig. 6.44 shows class `DrawableRectangle`. The constructor with multiple arguments first calls the superclass constructor (`Rectangle()`) with two arguments to define the values of `width` and `height`. Then it defines the data fields inherited from abstract class `GeoFigure`.

Method `drawMe()` in Fig. 6.44 contains the code to draw a rectangle. It calls method `fillRect()` (of the `Graphics` class) to draw the filled rectangle first (color is `interiorColor`) and then calls method `drawRect()` to draw a border around it (color is `borderColor`).

Method `toString()` returns a string consisting of the characters `Drawable`, the string returned by the `toString()` method for the superclass `Rectangle`, characters that represent the *x* and *y* coordinate of the top-left corner of the rectangle (returned by the `toString()` method of class `Point`), and characters that represent the border color and interior color of the rectangle. The color characters are returned by the `toString()` method of class `Color` and consist of the RGB (red, green, blue) component values (0 through 255) for a color. The lines

```
DrawableRectangle dR = new DrawableRectangle(30, 40,
                          new Point(50,100), Color.magenta,
                          Color.blue)
System.out.println(dR.toString());
```

declare a `DrawableRectangle` object, `dR`, and call method `println()` to display its string representation. Figure 6.45 shows the lines displayed by method `println()`. The border color, `magenta`, has maximum values for its red and blue components.

Figure 6.46 shows the `DrawableTriangle` class. The `Graphics` class does not have a method for drawing triangles, but it does have methods for drawing polygons (`fillPolygon()` and `drawPolygon()`). We can use these methods because a triangle is a polygon with three vertices. First the `drawMe()` method creates a new `Polygon` object `tri`. It then calls `tri`'s `addPoly()` method three times to add the triangle vertices to `tri`. Finally, methods `fillPolygon()` and `drawPolygon()` draw triangle `tri`, which is passed as an argument. We leave class `DrawableCircle` as an exercise (Programming Exercise 1).

Figure 6.43   **Abstract class GeoFigure with data fields for drawable figures**

```
/* GeoFigure.java          Authors: Koffman & Wolz
 * Abstract superclass of geometric figures classes
 * and their drawable subclasses.
 * Uses AWT.
 */
import java.awt.*;

public abstract class GeoFigure {
  // Data Fields
  protected Point pos = new Point(0, 0);    // position on screen
  protected Color borderColor = Color.black;
  protected Color interiorColor = Color.white;

  // Abstract Methods
  public abstract double computePerimeter();
  public abstract double computeArea();

  // Actual Methods
  // Mutators
  public void setBorderColor(Color bor) {
    borderColor = bor;
  }

  public void setInteriorColor(Color inter) {
    interiorColor = inter;
  }

  public void setPos(Point p) {
    pos = p;
  }

  // Accessors
  public Point getPos() {
    return pos;
  }

  public Color getBorderColor() {
    return borderColor;
  }

  public Color getInteriorColor() {
    return interiorColor;
  }

}
```

Figure 6.44   Class DrawableRectangle

```
/* DrawableRectangle.java          Authors: Koffman & Wolz
 * Represents a drawable rectangle.
 * Extends Rectangle and implements Drawable.
 */
import java.awt.*;

public class DrawableRectangle extends Rectangle implements Drawable {

  // Data fields
  //   none

  // Methods
  // Constructors
  public DrawableRectangle() {}

  public DrawableRectangle(int wid, int hei,
                    Point p, Color bor, Color inter) {
    super(wid, hei);  // Define width and height fields
    pos = p;
    borderColor = bor;
    interiorColor = inter;
  }


  // Operations

  // postcondition: Draws a rectangular object with
  //   top-left corner at pos.x, pos.y
  public void drawMe(Graphics g) {
    g.setColor(interiorColor);
    g.fillRect(pos.x, pos.y, width, height);
    g.setColor(borderColor);
    g.drawRect(pos.x, pos.y, width, height);
  }

  public String toString() {
    return "Drawable " + super.toString() +
          "\nx coordinate is " + pos.x +
          ", y coordinate is " + pos.y +
          "\nborder color is " + borderColor +
          "\ninterior color is " + interiorColor;
  }

}
```

Figure 6.45   **Result of** `System.out.println(dR.toString())`

```
Drawable Rectangle: width is 30, height is 40
x coordinate is 50, y coordinate is 100
border color is java.AWT.Color[r=255,g=0,b=255]
interior color is java.AWT.Color[r=0,g=0,b=255]
```

Figure 6.46   **Class** `DrawableTriangle`

```java
/* DrawableTriangle.java         Authors: Koffman & Wolz
 * Represents a drawable triangle.
 * Extends Triangle and implements Drawable.
 */
import java.awt.*;

public class DrawableTriangle extends Triangle implements Drawable
{

  // Data fields
  //    none

  // Methods
  // Constructors
  public DrawableTriangle() {}

  public DrawableTriangle(int bas, int hei,
                    Point p, Color bor, Color inter) {
    super(bas, hei);  // Define width and height fields
    pos = p;
    borderColor = bor;
    interiorColor = inter;
  }

  // Operations

  // postconditon: Draws a triangle with right angle at
  //    pos.x and pos.y and with specified base and height.
  public void drawMe(Graphics g) {
    Polygon tri = new Polygon();
    tri.addPoint(pos.x, pos.y);
    tri.addPoint(pos.x, pos.y - height);
    tri.addPoint(pos.x + base, pos.y);
    g.setColor(interiorColor);
    g.fillPolygon(tri);
```

Figure 6.46   **Class DrawableTriangle,** *continued*

```
     g.setColor(borderColor);
     g.drawPolygon(tri);
   }

   public String toString() {
     return "Drawable " + super.toString() +
            "\nx coordinate is " + pos.x +
            ", y coordinate is " + pos.y +
            "\nborder color is " + borderColor +
            "\ninterior color is " + interiorColor;
   }

}
```

TESTING   Fig. 6.47 shows class **TestDrawFigures,** which tests our new class hierarchy. In the applet **paint()** method, array **gF** (type **GeoFigure[]**) stores a collection of figures, both drawable and not drawable. The **for** loop draws each drawable figure by first casting it to a type **Drawable** reference and then calling each **Drawable** object's **drawMe()** method. The **if** statement guards the casting operation.

Fig. 6.48 shows the execution of this class. Notice that only five of the six objects stored in array **gF** are drawn (Why?). You must provide an HTML file (see Section 3.7) in order to run the applet.

Just as we used both drawable and nondrawable figures in class **TestDrawFigures,** we can use both kinds of figures in class **TestGeoFigure** (Fig. 6.37). An object that is **Drawable** will have its area computed by the **computeArea()** method inherited from its nondrawable superclass.

Abstract Classes, Multiple Inheritance, and Interfaces

Abstract classes can help you organize collections of classes. Under some circumstances you may want to organize classes in more than one way. You may want to have classes extend more than one superclass. This type of extension is called **multiple inheritance** and is not supported in Java.

Figure 6.49 shows a classic example of multiple inheritance. A toy elephant has some attributes of an elephant and some of a toy. The question is how to resolve conflicts between data fields and methods that belong to both superclasses. (For example, should method **getColor()** be inherited from superclass **Elephant** or from superclass **Toy**?) Schemes for implementing multiple inheritance have been debated among designers of object-oriented languages for many years. There are no easy answers.

Figure 6.47 Class `TestDrawFigures`

```java
/* TestDrawFigures.java          Authors: Koffman & Wolz
 * Draws a collection of geometric objects stored in an array.
 * Uses GeoFigure, Triangle, Rectangle, Circle, Drawable,
 * DrawableRectangle, DrawableCircle,  DrawableTriangle,
 * and awt.
 */
import java.awt.*;
import java.applet.Applet;

public class TestDrawFigures extends Applet {

  public void paint(Graphics g) {
    // Create an array of type GeoFigure
    GeoFigure gf[] = {
        new DrawableRectangle(100, 100, new Point (0,0),
                              Color.blue, Color.green),
        new DrawableRectangle(100, 200, new Point (100,100),
                              Color.red, Color.yellow),
        new Triangle(10, 20),
        new DrawableRectangle(50, 100, new Point (200,300),
                              Color.black, Color.red),
        new DrawableCircle(30, new Point(300,200),
                           Color.orange, Color.gray),
        new DrawableTriangle(40, 60,
                             new Point(300,300),
                             Color.black, Color.magenta) };

    // Draw the drawable objects.
      for (int i = 0; i < gf.length; i++) {
        if (gf[i] instanceof Drawable)
          ((Drawable) gf[i]).drawMe(g);
      }
  }

}
```

Figure 6.48   Execution of class `TestDrawFigures`

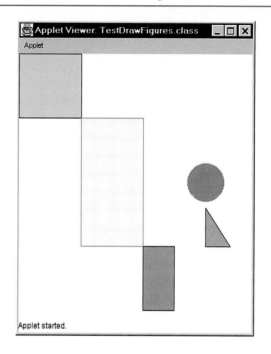

Figure 6.49   An example of multiple inheritance

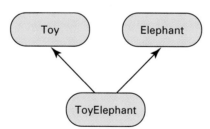

    As another example of multiple inheritance, a possible class hierarchy for the previous case study would have each class for a drawable figure (for example, `DrawableRectangle`) extend two superclasses. One would be the superclass without the capability to draw objects (for example, `DrawableRectangle` extends `Rectangle`) and the other would be an abstract class `Drawable` that contained the data fields and methods necessary for a figure to draw itself. The data fields `pos`, `interiorColor`, and `borderColor` would be defined in class `Drawable` (instead of class `GeoFigure`) and method `drawMe()` would be declared as an abstract method in class **Drawable**. This would be preferable to declaring these data fields in class **GeoFigure** because they are not relevant to the immediate subclasses of **GeoFigure** (**Rectangle**, **Circle**, **Triangle**) which cannot draw objects. To visualize the new hierarchy, replace interface **Drawable** in Fig. 6.39 with abstract class **Drawable**.

Although this new design makes sense, it is not possible in Java because multiple inheritance is not supported. However, interfaces provide some of the advantages of multiple inheritance without the problems. A class can extend only one superclass, but it can implement many interfaces. A class can inherit constants (defined as **static final**) from each interface. A class does not inherit instance variables (data fields) or methods from an interface. However, the interface imposes requirements for functionality through its abstract method definitions, and the compiler ensures that these requirements are met.

An object has the properties of its superclass type and of all the interface types that its class implements. An object can be referenced by a variable whose type is its class type, by a variable whose type is its superclass type, or by a variable whose type is an interface type that its class implements. Similary, an object of a particular class type can be passed as an argument to a parameter whose type is its own class type, its superclass type, or an interface type that its class implements.

EXERCISES FOR SECTION 6.6

SELF-CHECK

1. Provide descriptions for class **DrawableCircle** and class **DrawableTriangle**.

2. Replace the array referenced by **gF** in Fig. 6.37 with the array shown in Fig. 6.47. Show the result of the first three iterations of the **for** loop below:

```
for (int i = 0; i < gF.length; i++) {
    double area = gF[i].computeArea();
    totalArea += area;
    System.out.println(gF[i].toString());
    System.out.println("Area is " + area + "\n");
}
```

3. Why can a class implement multiple interfaces but extend only one class?

PROGRAMMING

1. Implement class **DrawableCircle**.

2. Discuss how you could implement the toy elephant example using an interface.

6.7 Packages and Visibility (Optional)

The package to which a class belongs is declared at the top of the file in which the class is defined using the keyword **package** followed by the package name. As an example, class **Sorts** in Fig. 6.23 begins with the line

```
package psJava;
```

Generally, all classes in the same package are stored in the same directory or folder. The directory should have the same name as the package. All the classes in the folder must declare themselves to be in the package.

Package declaration

> Form: **package** *packageName***;**
> Example: **package psJava;**

Interpretation: This declaration appears at the top of the file in which a class is defined. The class is now considered part of the package.

Classes that are not part of a package may access public members (data fields or methods) of classes in the package. For example, assume that **Rectangle** in Fig. 6.34 and **DrawableRectangle** in Fig. 6.44 are in package **figures**. Fig. 6.50 shows an application class that is not in the **figures** package. It compares the areas of **Rectangle r1** and **DrawableRectangle r2**. Because it is not in the package, the application class must reference the classes by their complete names. The complete name of a class is *packageName.ClassName*.

You may wonder why we don't have to use the complete name when comparing the areas. Shouldn't the code look like the following?

```
if (r1.figures.Rectangle.computeArea() ==
    r2.figures.DrawableRectangle.computeArea())
```

The compiler needs to know the complete name of the class to create the instance. But once the instance is bound to the variable name (such as **r1** or **r2**), the instance can be referred to by just the variable name. There is no longer any need to use the package name or the class name.

The **import** Statement

We have seen that the **import** statement allows class members to be referenced directly by their class name. If we insert the statement

```
import figures.*;
```

Figure 6.50   An application using package figures

```
/* PackageApp.java         Authors: Koffman & Wolz
 * Demonstrates use of a package.
 */
import java.awt.*;

public class AnApp {

   public static void main (String[] args) {
      Point p = new Point();

      figures.Rectangle r1 = new figures.Rectangle(5, 10);
      figures.DrawableRectangle r2 =
            new figures.DrawableRectangle(10, 20,
               new Point(0,3), Color.red, Color.blue);
      if (r1.computeArea() == r2.computeArea())
         System.out.println("same size");
      else
         System.out.println("different size");
   }
}
```

at the beginning of Fig. 6.50, we can write the declatation statements in a more compact way:

```
Rectangle r1 = new Rectangle(5, 10);
DrawableRectangle r2 = new DrawableRectangle(10, 20,
                          new Point(0,3), Color.red, Color.blue);
```

Default Visibility

We have used the modifiers **private**, **public**, and **protected** to specify the visibility of a class member (data field or method). There is a fourth kind of visibility, default visibility, which is indicated by the absence of a visibility modifier. **Default visibility** is also called **package visibility** and makes the class member visible in all classes of the same package, but not outside the package.

Visibility Supports Encapsulation

The rules for visibility control how encapsulation occurs in a Java program. Table 6.2 summarizes the rules in order of decreasing protection.

Notice that **private** visibility is for members of a class that should not be accessible to anyone but the class, not even classes that extend it. It doesn't make sense for a class to be **private**. It would mean that no other class can use it.

Also notice that package visibility (the default) allows the developer of a library to shield classes and class members from classes outside the package. Typically such classes have a supporting role that the **public** classes within the package exploit.

Use of **protected** visibility allows the package developer to give control to other programmers who want to extend classes in the package. Protected data fields are typically essential to an object. Similarly, **protected** methods are those that are essential to an extending class.

Table 6.2 shows that **public** classes and members are universally available. Within a package, the **public** classes are those that are essential to communicating with objects outside the package.

The No Package Declared Environment

In the previous chapters, packages were not specified, yet objects of one class could communicate with objects of another class. How did this work? Just as there is a default visibility, there is a default package. Files that do not specify a package are considered part of the default package. If all three classes, **Rectangle**, **DrawableRectangle**, and the application class did not contain a package declaration, all three would be in the same package and could refer to each other using short names.

Table 6.2   Summary of kinds of visibility

Visibility	Applied to Class	Applied to Class Members
private	Not applicable	Visible only within this class.
Default or package	Accessible to classes in this package	Accessible to classes in this package.
protected	Not applicable	Accessible to classes in this package and to classes outside the package that extend this class.
public	Accessible to all classes	Accessible to all classes. The class defining the member must also be **public**.

PROGRAM STYLE: *When to Package Classes*

The default package facility is intended for use during the early stages of implementing classes or for small prototype programs. If you are developing an application that has a few classes that will eventually be bundled into one package, you may use the default. However, as soon as you begin exploiting default visibility in your design, you should declare packages. The declaration will keep you from accidentally referring to classes by their short name in other classes that are outside the package.

6.8 Testing a Program System

Just as you can simplify the overall programming process by writing a large program system as a set of classes, you can simplify testing and debugging if you test in stages as the program system evolves. We show some techniques for testing in this section.

Top-Down Testing and Stubs

Whether a single programmer or a programming team is developing a program system, not all classes will be ready at the same time. Also, within a single class, not all methods will be finished at the same time. It is still possible to test and debug methods that are complete using a substitute, called a stub, for all methods that are not yet coded. A stub consists of a method heading followed by a minimal body, which should display a message identifying the method being executed. If the stub is a mutator method, it should assign simple values to any data fields it is supposed to modify. If the method calculates and returns a result, the stub should return a simple result. For example, we could use the stub below for method `computeArea()` in class `Triangle`.

```
public double computeArea() {
  System.out.println("Executing computeArea() in class Triangle");
  return 100.0;
}
```

The stub arbitrarily returns a value of 100.0, which is reasonable data to use in any remaining computations. Similarly, we could use the stub below for method `drawMe()` in class `DrawTriangle` if we didn't know how to draw a triangle but we wanted to test the other `drawMe()` methods. This method displays a string at the position of the triangle.

```
public void drawMe(Graphics g) {
  g.drawString(interiorColor + " triangle goes here ", pos.x, pos.y);
}
```

The process of using stubs in this way is called **top-down testing**. Top-down testing enables us to test the overall flow of control in an application and to verify that the completed methods are working correctly.

Bottom-Up Testing and Drivers

When a method is completed, it can be substituted for its stub. However, we often perform a preliminary test of a new method because it is easier to locate and correct errors when dealing with a single method than with a complete program system. We can perform such a **unit test** by writing a short driver to call it.

Don't spend a lot of time creating an elegant driver because you will discard it as soon as the new method is tested. A driver should be a small **main** method that contains only the declarations and executable statements necessary to test a single method. A driver should create a test object, apply the method(s) being tested to the object, and display the results. Next, we show a driver for method **computeArea()** that could be inserted in class **Triangle**:

```
public static void main(String[] args) {
   Triangle tr = new Triangle(10, 20);

   System.out.println("Triangle area is " + tr.computeArea());
}
```

It may seem strange that the **main** method above can be part of class **Triangle** and also instantiate class **Triangle**. This presents no problems to Java. Each class that you write can have a **main** method, not just the application class.

The process of separately testing individual methods before inserting them in a class is called **bottom-up testing**. You can carry the process of unit testing one step further by testing each class as a unit, adding a **main** method to the class that tests all its other methods. This will enable you to use the class with confidence in a larger program system. When you are finished testing, you can bracket the **main** method with comment delimiters (**/***, ***/**), so that it is available for later use if you need it.

Once the individual classes have been tested, you can incorporate them in the program system and test the system as a whole. Tests of the entire system are called **system integration tests**.

By following a combination of top-down and bottom-up testing, a programming team can be fairly confident that the complete program system will be relatively free of errors when it is finally put together. Consequently, the final debugging sessions should proceed quickly and smoothly. A list of suggestions for debugging a program system follows:

1. Carefully document each method parameter and local variable using comments as you write the code. Also describe the method's purpose using comments.

2. Create a trace of execution by displaying the method name as you enter it.

3. Trace or display the values of all arguments upon entry to a method. Check that these values make sense.

4. Trace or display the values of all method results after returning from a method. Verify that these values are correct by hand computation.

You should plan for debugging as you write each method rather than adding debugging statements later. Include statements to display console output that will help you determine that the method is working. When you are satisfied that the method works as desired, you can remove these debugging statements or make them comments.

Identifier Scope and Watch Window Variables

You can use a debugger to trace values passed into a method's parameters and the value returned by a function. The values displayed in the `Watch` window are determined by the normal scope rules for identifiers. Consequently, a method's local variables and formal parameters will be considered undefined until that function begins execution. Upon exit from the method, its local variables and formal parameters will again become undefined.

Black-Box versus White-Box Testing

There are two basic ways to test a completed method or an entire program system: black-box and white-box testing. In **black-box** (or **specification-based**) **testing** we assume that the program tester has no information about the code inside the method or system. The tester's job is to verify that the method or system meets its specifications. For each method, the tester must ensure that its postconditions are satisfied whenever its preconditions are met. Because the tester cannot look inside the method, the tester must prepare sufficient sets of test data to verify that the system output is correct for all valid input values. The tester should also determine that the method or system does not crash for invalid data. The tester should especially check the boundaries of the system, or particular values where the system performance changes. For example, a boundary for a salaried employee would be the value of hours worked that triggers overtime pay. Black-box testing is most often done by a special testing team or by program users.

In **white-box** (or **glass-box**) **testing**, the tester has full knowledge of the code for the method or system and must ensure that each section of code has been thoroughly tested. For a selection statement (`if` or `switch`), this means checking all possible paths through the selection statement. The tester must determine that the correct path is chosen for all possible values of the selection variable, taking special care at the boundary values where the path changes.

For a loop, the tester must make sure that the loop always performs the correct number of iterations and that the number of iterations is not off by 1. Also, the tester should verify that the computations inside the loop are correct at the boundaries, that is, for the initial and final values of the loop-control variable. Finally, the tester should make sure that the method or system still meets its specification when a loop executes zero times and that under no circumstances can the loop execute forever.

EXERCISES FOR SECTION 6.8

SELF-CHECK

1. Explain the difference between black-box and white-box testing.

2. What is a unit test and what is system integration testing?

3. Explain the difference between a stub and a driver.

PROGRAMMING

1. Write a driver function to test method `computePerimeter()` of class `Triangle`.

2. Write a stub for method `computePerimeter()` of class `Triangle`.

6.9 Common Programming Errors

Be conservative with the visibility of data fields. Think carefully about whether they should be something other than **private**. If you define them with either **public** or **protected** visibility, they become unprotected and a client can tamper with them. These kinds of errors are very hard to track down.

Make sure you use the prefix **this.** to reference a data field that has the same name as a method parameter or a local variable. Be careful not to declare a data field as a local variable by mistake. For example, assume **payroll** is a data field and we use the statement

```
double payroll = 0;
```

in method **computeTotalPay()** to initialize **payroll** to zero. The effect is to create a local variable **payroll** that will hide data field **payroll** so that **computeTotalPay()** will modify the local variable, not the data field.

You can use **this(. . .)** or **super(. . .)** to call a constructor from within another constructor. The constructor call must be the first statement. In a subclass constructor, the default is to call the superclass constructor with no parameters, so make sure you declare one if it is needed.

In a class hierarchy, you often need to cast down the hierarchy to apply an instance method. For example, if **obj** is type **Object** and **getName()** is an instance method of class **NewEmployee**, the statement

```
((NewEmployee) obj).getName()
```

retrieves the name field of the object referenced by **obj**. If object **obj** does not reference an object of type **NewEmployee** (or one of its subclass), we would get an **illegal cast exception**.

You can use an **if** statement with a condition involving the **instanceof** operator to eliminate casting errors. For example, the statement

```
if (obj instanceof NewEmployee)
   myName = ((NewEmployee) obj).getName()
else
   myName = "";
```

is a safe way to retrieve an employee's name.

If you fail to implement all abstract methods in a subclass, the compiler will display an error message saying that your subclass should be declared abstract. It will tell you which method has not been implemented. If you think you properly defined the method, check to make sure the method signature (the return type and the parameter list) matches the abstract method declaration.

CHAPTER REVIEW

1. An abstraction provides a way of clustering data and methods. Traditionally, computer science views an **abstract data type** as one that collects the essential components of an entity in one place. Classes provide a mechanism for creating abstract data types in Java. Encapsulation builds a wall around an object's private data, allowing users of an object to access its data only through the public methods of the object's class.

2. Inheritance, in combination with hierarchical organizations, allows you to capture the idea that one thing may be a refinement or extension of another. For example, an animal *is a* living thing. Such *is a* relationships create the right balance between too much and too little structure. Think of inheritance as a means of creating a refinement of an abstraction. The entities farther down the hierarchy are more complex and less general than those higher up. The entities farther down the hierarchy may inherit data members (attributes) and methods from those farther up, but not vice versa.

3. Encapsulation and inheritance impose structure on object abstractions. Polymorphism means "many forms." It captures the idea that methods may take on a variety of forms to suit different purposes. Polymorphism provides a degree of flexibility in defining methods. It loosens the structure a bit to make methods more accessible and useful.

4. Three types of polymorphism are possible. Polymorphism across classes occurs when two classes define the same method. Method overriding occurs when a

subclass redefines a method of a superclass. Method overloading occurs when a method name within a class has more than one signature.

5. The keyword **abstract** defines an abstract class or method. The reserved word **interface** defines an interface. A class that uses an interface *implements* the interface. Interfaces provide an alternative to multiple inheritance in Java. You can declare data fields and actual methods in an abstract method. However, you can only declare abstract methods and constants in an interface.

6. Visibility is influenced by the package in which a class is declared. You assign classes to a package by including the reserved word **package** at the top of the file. You can refer to classes within a package by their direct names when the package is imported through an **import** statement.

New Java constructs

Construct	Effect
Interface	

``
public interface Payable {
   public void calcWeeklyPay();
   public static final double
           DEDUCT_PCT = 5.5;
 	
}
``
	Defines an interface **Payable** with one abstract method (**calcWeeklyPay()**) and one constant. Method **calcWeeklyPay()** must be defined by all classes that implement **Payable**. The constant can be referenced in all sub-classes.

Abstract Class	

``
public abstract class Food {
   // Data field
   private double calories;
 	
   // Abstract methods
   public abstract double
           percentProtein();
   public abstract double
           percentFat();
   public abstract double
           percentCarbs();
 	
   // Methods
   public void setCalories(double cal) {
     calories = cal;
   }
   public double getCalories()
}
``
	Defines an abstract class that may be the ancestor for a class hierarchy but cannot be instantiated. Class **Food** contains data field **calories** and an accessor and mutator method for this field. Classes that extend **Food** must define the three abstract methods.

✔ **QUICK-CHECK EXERCISES**

1. What does polymorphism mean? Describe the three kinds of polymorphism.

2. What is a method signature? Describe how it is used in method overloading.

3. Describe the use of the keywords **super** and **this**.

4. When would you use an abstract class and what should it contain?

5. When would you use an interface? Can a class implement more than one interface? What does an interface contain?

6. Describe the difference between *is a* and *has a* relationships.

7. Which can have more data fields and methods, the superclass or the subclass?

8. You can reference an object of a(n) _____ type through a variable of a(n) _____ type.

9. You cast an object referenced by a(n) _____ type to an object of a(n) _____ type in order to apply methods of that type to the object.

10. You use a(n) _____ in place of a method that has not yet been completed when testing a class. The method you use to perform _____ tests of individual methods is called a(n) _____ .

ANSWERS TO QUICK-CHECK EXERCISES

1. Polymorphism means many forms. There are three kinds of polymorphism: polymorphism across classes, method overriding, method overloading. Polymorphism across classes means that the same method appears in different, unrelated classes. Method overriding means that the same method appears in a subclass and a superclass. Method overloading means that the same method appears with different signatures in the same class.

2. A signature is the form of a method determined by its return type, name, and arguments. For example, **void doIt(int, double)** is the signature for method **doIt()**, which has one type **int** argument and one type **double** argument and returns no result. If several methods in a class have the same name (method overloading), Java applies the one whose signature matches the signature implied by the method call.

3. The keyword **this** means use the member (data field or method) of the current object. The keyword **super** means use the method (or data field) with this name that is defined in the superclass of the object, not the one belonging to the object. Using **super** as a method call in a constructor tells Java to call a constructor for the superclass of the object being created.

4. An abstract class is used as a parent class for a collection of related subclasses. An abstract class cannot be instantiated. The abstract methods (identified by modifier **abstract**) defined in the abstract class act as placeholders for the actual methods. Also, you should define data fields that are common to all the subclasses in the abstract class. An abstract class can have actual methods as well as abstract methods.

5. An interface is used to specify that a collection of classes has some common functionality. It allows the definition of abstract methods and constants (identified by modifiers **static final**) for the subclasses of a hierarchy of classes. It provides all the advantages of using an abstract class without putting the classes that implement it in a subclass relationship. Therefore, a class can implement multiple interfaces and it is Java's alternative to multiple inheritance.

6. An *is a* relationship between classes means that one class is a subclass of a parent class. A *has a* relationship means that a class has data members for representing the attribute being described.

7. subclass

8. subclass, superclass

9. superclass, subclass

10. stub, unit, driver

REVIEW QUESTIONS

1. Define encapsulation and information hiding.

2. List the three kinds of visibility and explain the difference between them.

3. What is default or package visibility?

4. Explain how the compiler determines which method to use when a method definition is overridden in several classes that are part of an inheritance hierarchy.

5. Like a rectangle, a parallelogram has opposite sides that are parallel, but it has a corner angle, theta, that is less than 90 degrees. Discuss how you would add parallelograms to the class hierarchy for geometric figures (see Fig. 6.33). Write a definition for class **Parallelogram** and make whatever modifications are required to the classes **GeoFigure** and **TestGeoFigure** (Fig. 6.37) to include parallelograms.

6. Explain what multiple inheritance means. How does Java support behavior that is similar to multiple inheritance?

7. Explain how assignments can be made within a class hierarchy and the role of casting in a class hierarchy.

PROGRAMMING PROJECTS

1. A veterinary office wants to produce information sheets on the pets it treats. Data includes diet, whether it is nocturnal or not, whether its bite is poisonous (e.g., snakes), whether it flies, and so on. Use a superclass **Pet** with abstract methods and create appropriate subclasses to support about 10 animals of your choice.

2. A student is a person and so is an employee. Create a class **Person** that has the data attributes common to both students and employees (name, social security number, age, gender, address, and telephone number) and appropriate method definitions. A student has a grade-point average (GPA), major, and year of graduation. An employee has a department, job title, and year of hire. In addition, there are hourly employees (hourly rate, hours worked, and union dues) and nonsalaried employees (annual salary). Define a class hierarchy and write an application class that you can use to first store the data for an array of people and then display that information in a meaningful way.

3. Create a pricing system for a computer company that sells personal computers over the Internet. There are two kinds of computers, laptops and desktop computers. Each computer has a processor (0.8, 1, 1.2, or 1.5 gigahertz), memory (128, 256, 394, or 512K), hard drive (20, 40, or 60 gigabytes), CD drive (CD-ROM, CD-RW, or DVD). Laptops have 14- or 15-inch screens. Desktops have 15-, 17-, or 19-inch monitors. Options are a modem, a network card, and a zip drive. You should have an abstract class **Computer** and subclasses **DeskTop** and **LapTop**. Each subclass should have methods for calculating the price of a computer given the base price plus the cost of the different options. You should have methods for calculating memory price, hard drive price, and so on. There should be a method to calculate shipping cost.

4. Write a banking program that simulates the operation of your local bank. You should declare the following collection of classes:

   Class **Account**
   Data fields: **customer** (type **Customer**), **balance**, **accountNumber**,
              transactions array (type **Transaction[ ]**)

   Methods: **getBalance( )**, **getCustomer( )**, **toString( )**,
           setCustomer( ), **setBalance( )**, **toString( )**

   Class **SavingsAccount** extends **Account**
   Methods: **deposit( )**, **withdraw( )**, **addInterest( )**

   Class **CheckingAccount** extends **Account**
   Methods: **withdraw( )**, **deposit( )**, **addInterest( )**

Class `Customer`
Data fields: `name`, `address`, `age`, `telephoneNumber`, `customerNumber`
Methods: accessors and mutators for data fields

Classes `Senior`, `Adult`, `Student`, all these classes extend `Customer`
Each has constant data fields—`SAVINGS_INTEREST`, `CHECK_INTEREST`,
`CHECK_CHARGE`, and `OVERDRAFT_PENALTY` —that define these values for
customers of that type.

Class `Bank`
Data field: `accounts` array (type `Account[ ]`)
Methods: `addAccount()`, `makeDeposit()`, `makeWithdrawal()`,
       `getAccount()`

Class `Transaction`
Data fields: `customerNumber`, `transactionType`, `amount`, `fees` (a
       string describing unusual fees)
Methods: `processTran()`

You need to write all these classes and an application class that interacts with
the user. In the application, you should first open several accounts and then
enter and process several transactions.

Graphical User Interfaces (GUIs)

In our programs so far, the user interacts with a running program by entering data in response to prompts displayed by the program. This model promotes a "stop-and-wait" mindset. The program, and by extension, the CPU, stop and wait for input before proceeding with the steps that follow. This simple model is rapidly becoming obsolete.

The microcomputer industry dramatically changed the way software developers viewed the input and output of a program. Instead of just typing in data in response to prompts from the program (as in the old "stop-and-wait" model), the user controls what the program does by mouse clicks and other actions. Therefore, the effectiveness of the user interface becomes as important to the success of a program solution as the efficiency of its code.

This chapter describes how to use Java features to develop graphical user interfaces (GUIs). In the new world of programming, a good program solution must have mechanisms for communicating with users and with other processes. Therefore, the program must be able to handle actions, or **events**, initiated by the user. We discuss the GUI components provided in the AWT and `Swing` packages. We also describe Java's **event model** and **event handling**.

7.1 AWT, `Swing`, and Browser-Applet Interaction

The study of GUI design serves as a vehicle to reinforce some important ideas about object-oriented programming. This is because GUI design involves the use of a number of predefined components (buttons, check boxes, text fields, etc.) that are part of a class hierarchy. Therefore, each of these components is able to access data fields and methods that are defined elsewhere in the hierarchy. A GUI is a collection of instances (objects) of these components.

Earlier versions of Java used the Abstract Window Toolkit (AWT) and its components to build GUIs. However, Java 1.2 introduced the more flexible `Swing` API with `Swing` components as an improved alternative to the AWT components. Because Java developers recommend that new programs use `Swing` components, we will focus on them in this textbook. However `Swing` and AWT are quite intertwined because `Swing` relies on features of the AWT. Keep in mind that the principles of using AWT components are similar to those for using `Swing` components.

The major difference between AWT and `Swing` components is that AWT components match exactly the form of corresponding components in the operating system for the platform (computer) you are using, so their appearance is **platform dependent**. Components drawn using the `Swing` API may look the same regardless of the platform being used (**platform independent**), and they may have a different appearance from the components used by the operating system for that platform. (It is also possible for `Swing` components to look the same as their counterparts in the platform's operating system.) The reason AWT components are platform dependent is that each AWT component relies on a corresponding component in the platform's operating system (called a **peer component**) to draw it. Components in the `Swing` API inherit the `paint()` method defined in class `JComponent`, which is written entirely in Java, and this `paint()` method is used to draw the component. A component that uses a pure Java method to draw itself is called a **lightweight component**.

Categories of Classes in Swing and AWT

In the rest of this chapter, we will study four kinds of classes used for building GUIs:

1. **Swing** GUI component classes: Includes basic window objects like buttons, text fields, menu items. Also included are panels and applets that act as containers (groupings) for the basic window objects.

2. AWT layout manager classes: Used to determine the placement of objects in a container.

3. AWT event classes: Define the events that are generated when users do things such as click buttons, select menu items, and move the mouse.

4. AWT listener classes: Contain methods that are activated by the operating system when events occur.

GUI Component Classes

Class **DistanceConverter** (see Fig. 7.1) contains methods to convert a distance measurement in miles to kilometers (method **toKilometers()**) and a distance measurement in kilometers to miles (method **toMiles()**). The GUI in Fig.7.2 could be used with this class. The GUI enables the user to enter a distance value and then press a button to start a conversion operation. The GUI contains, from top to bottom, a label (the prompt **input distance >>**), a text field for data entry with the number 100 typed in, two buttons that are used to select a conversion operation, and a text area for output. The output shown in the text area appears after the user presses the button containing text **Convert to kms**.

Each GUI component in Fig. 7.2 is an instance (object) of a class in API **Swing**. Table 7.1 describes each component in Fig. 7.2.

Table 7.1 GUI components in Fig. 7.2

GUI Component	Component Type	Purpose
Label Input distance >>	JLabel	Provides information to the user
Text field with number 100	JTextField	Place where user enters data (100)
Button with text Convert to kms	JButton	Starts conversion to kilometers
Button with text Convert to miles	JButton	Starts conversion to miles
Two-line text area at bottom of GUI	JTextArea	Place where user views results

Figure 7.1   Class `DistanceConverter`

```
/* DistanceConverter.java          Authors: Koffman & Wolz
 * Class that converts miles to kilometers and vice versa.
 */

public class DistanceConverter {
  // Data field
  private static final double CONVERT_FACTOR = 1.609;

  // Methods
  // precondition: A distance in kilometers is passed as an
  //    argument.
  // postcondition: Returns the equivalent value in miles
  public double toMiles(double kms) {
    return kms / CONVERT_FACTOR;
  }

  // precondition: A distance in miles is passed as an argument.
  // postcondtion: Returns the equivalent value in kilometers.
  public double toKilometers(double miles) {
    return miles * CONVERT_FACTOR;
  }

}
```

Figure 7.2   A GUI for converting distances

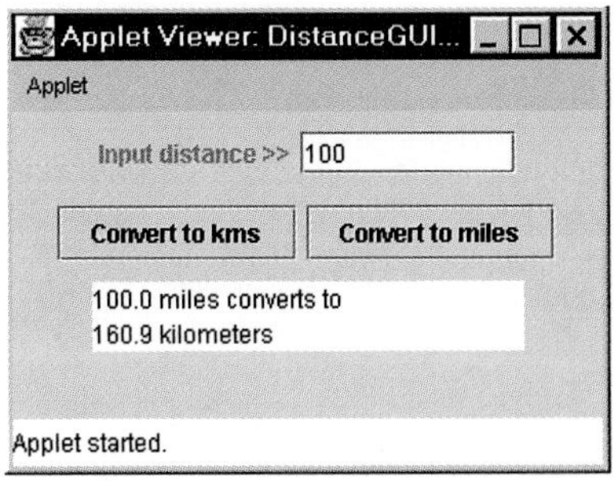

Applet Viewer: DistanceGUI...
Applet

Input distance >> 100

Convert to kms   Convert to miles

100.0 miles converts to
160.9 kilometers

Applet started.

Overview of AWT and Swing Hierarchy

Figure 7.3 shows part of the AWT and **Swing** class hierarchy. Several **Swing** classes at the bottom of the diagram (**JLabel**, **JOptionPane**, and so on) extend **Swing** class **JComponent**, which in turn extends AWT class **Container**. Also, class **JApplet** (from **Swing**) extends class **Applet** (from AWT), so you can see that the AWT and

Swing APIs are intertwined. The AWT classes are in gray, and the **Swing** classes are in color.

There are four abstract classes in Fig. 7.3: *Container*, *Component*, *JComponent*, and *AbstractButton*. Recall that abstract classes serve as the parent class for a group of classes that share common properties and functionality. For example, abstract class **AbstractButton** is the parent of classes **JButton**, **JToggleButton**, and **JMenuItem** (not shown). As such, **AbstractButton** defines the common behaviors for its derived classes: **JButton**, **JToggleButton**, **JMenuItem**, **JCheckbox**, and **JRadioButton**.

In **Swing**, the objects that are part of a GUI are all derived from class **JComponent**. Each instance of an actual class that extends **JComponent** is an **atomic component**.

Figure 7.3   Part of AWT and Swing hierarchy

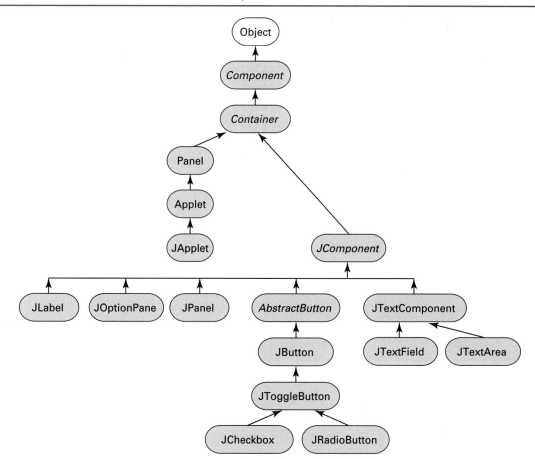

Applets and Panels Are Containers

The `JComponent` class extends `Container`, which extends `Component`. Containers are components that can hold other components. There are two types of containers: panels and windows. Windows are the top-level element displayed by an operating system. Panels are containers that cluster related components within a larger object such as an applet or an application window.

An applet (instance of `Applet` class in AWT or `JApplet` class in `Swing`) is a special kind of panel. An applet inherits all of its interactive functionality from class `Panel` and, by extension, from classes `Container` and `Component`. Because an applet is a panel, it is contained within another window object, such as a browser. An applet is also a container, so it may include any number of other components such as buttons. It may also contain other panels that are used to group its components. Although not shown, there are two panels (objects of class `JPanel`) in Fig. 7.3. One contains the label and text field used for data entry, and the other contains the two buttons.

Browser and Applet Interaction

An applet context is a program such as a browser or applet viewer (see Section 3.7). You tell the applet context to run an Applet by providing it with an HTML file or page. The browser interprets the HTML file and displays the information in the file in a readable form. An HTML file consists of text and HTML formatting tags. A tag is a delimiter (for example, `<TITLE>`, `</TITLE>`) that defines how a string of text should be interpreted. Delimiters occur in pairs, and the closing delimiter begins with a slash. In the HTML file shown in Fig. 7.4, we show the tags in color and a comment follows each line describing its purpose.

You use the applet tag (`<applet code = ... >`) to insert an applet in an HTML file. In order for the applet to execute properly, the applet tag must contain the following attributes:

> `code`—identifies the bytecode file defining the applet to instantiate and execute (`FileName.class`)
>
> `width`—the width of the rectangle in the applet context in which the applet will appear
>
> `height`—the height of the rectangle in the applet context in which the applet will appear

Figure 7.4 An `HTML` file with an applet tag

```
<HTML>
<TITLE>Distance Conversion Applet </TITLE>      title of html file
<applet code = DistanceGUI.class width = 300 height = 200> applet
</applet>                                    end of applet specification
</HTML>                                          end of html file
```

When the tag contains only these three attributes, the HTML file and the `.class` file for the applet must reside in the same directory. Appendix A shows other attributes.

The applet context (browser of applet viewer) controls the execution of the applet by calling the applet's methods. For example, when the user loads an HTML file with an applet tag, the browser displays the entire file and instantiates and displays the applet in the specified rectangle. It then starts up the applet and lets it run.

When the HTML page in Fig. 7.4 executes, the browser creates a `DistanceGUI` object and then executes the `init()` method for that object if one is provided. It is as if the browser executes the statements

```
DistanceGUI dGUI = new DistanceGUI();
dGUI.init();
```

The second line above calls applet `dGUI`'s `init()` method.

When the user leaves the HTML page, for example, by loading a different page or by overlaying the browser with a different application such as a word processor, the browser stops or suspends the applet. When the user returns to the page, the browser restarts the applet. Finally, when the user exits the browser, the browser must destroy the applet.

The methods in class `JApplet` that the browser calls to perform these actions are described in Table 7.2. Fig. 7.5 shows how a browser calls these methods as a user visits and leaves a page. When you define an applet, you do not need to concern yourself with the order in which the applet's methods are called by the browser. Your job is to properly override the `JApplet init()` method so that your applet behaves properly. The statements in your `init()` method create the initial applet and determine what text and components will appear inside the applet.

Table 7.2   `JApplet` methods called by the browser

Method	Action
`init()`	Initializes the applet. You usually override this method when defining an applet.
`start()`	Makes the applet "active"; that is, it starts the applet running. You usually do not override this method.
`stop()`	Makes the applet "inactive"; that is, it stops the applet. You usually do not override this method.
`destroy()`	Destroys the applet so that its resources can be recycled. The applet context calls this method when the user exits the applet context. You usually do not override this method.

Figure 7.5 A browser calls the `Applet` methods

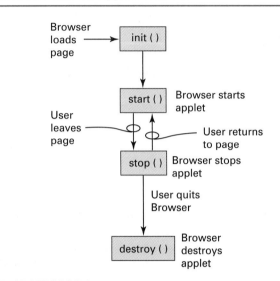

EXERCISES FOR SECTION 7.1

SELF-CHECK

1. List the four methods of **Applet** called by the applet context and explain what they do.

2. What is a container and what is an atomic component? Name three container classes shown in Figure 7.3.

3. Explain the difference between a peer component and a lightweight component. Which kind is used by the AWT and which kind is used by **Swing**?

PROGRAMMING

1. Write an HTML file to load an applet called **MyApplet** in a window of height 200 and width 300.

7.2 Designing a First GUI

In the GUIs we write, our goal is to design an interface that enables the program user to effectively interact with the program (the applet). An interface, whether it is for a program, a home appliance, an automated teller machine (ATM), or vending machine, generally provides

- Instructions or information for the user

- A way for the user to provide input to the device

◆ An area for the device to display outputs

◆ A way for the user to control the interaction with the device

In a GUI, we can use labels to provide single lines of information or prompts. We can use text areas to display more complicated instructions; text fields, text areas, or check boxes to provide input; text fields and text areas to display outputs; and buttons to control the interaction.

The Containment Hierarchy for a First GUI

Earlier we showed a sample GUI that contains a label, a text field, two buttons, and a text area. We show the GUI again in Fig. 7.6. We include two panels (class **JPanel**) that cluster the objects. The panel titled **Data panel** contains the label and text field objects, and the panel titled **Control panel** contains the two buttons that control the interaction. We show how to put borders and titles around components at the end of this section.

The applet is a **top-level container**. It exists mainly to provide a place for other Swing components to draw themselves. Other top-level containers are frames (main windows) and dialogs.

The two panels are **intermediate-level containers**. Their purpose is to simplify the positioning of the label, text field, and buttons.

Fig. 7.7 shows the containment hierarchy for the GUI in Fig. 7.2. This diagram shows each container used by the GUI, along with the components it contains. There are two panels (the **JPanel** components). Notice also that the applet has an intermediate container called its **content pane**. We usually don't distinguish between the applet and its content pane. However, when we add components to an applet, we must add them to the applet's content pane, not to the applet itself.

Figure 7.6   A first GUI and its panels

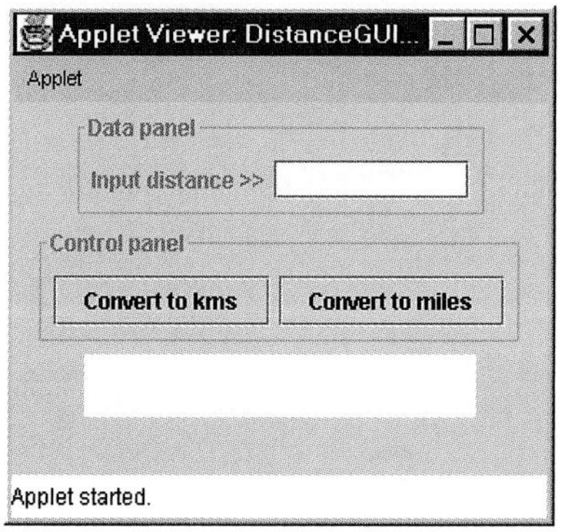

Figure 7.7   Containment hierarchy for GUI in Fig. 7.2

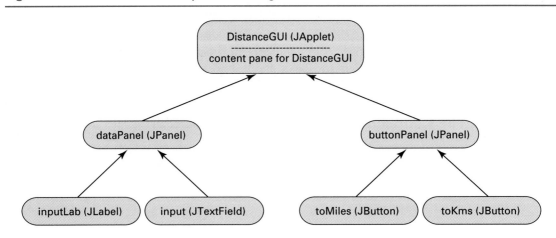

Declaring the GUI Components

To build the applet, we must first declare each GUI component and provide statements that add these components to the applet. Fig. 7.8 shows the declaration for class `DistanceGUI`, including method `init()`. We declare as data fields the four components that need to be referenced throughout the class: the input text field (`input`), the output area (`output`), and the control buttons (`toKms` and `toMiles`). The input label (`inputLabel`) and the two panels (`dataPanel` and `buttonPanel`) are declared as local variables in method `init()`.

Figure 7.8   Class `DistanceGUI` with method `init()`

```
/* DistanceGUI.java          Authors: Koffman & Wolz
 * Applet for distance conversion.
 * Uses DistanceConverter, Swing, and AWT.
 */
import javax.swing.*;
import java.awt.*;
import java.awt.event.*;

public class DistanceGUI extends JApplet
                    implements ActionListener {
    // Data fields
    private JTextField input = new JTextField(10);
    private JTextArea output = new JTextArea(2, 20);
    private JButton toKms = new JButton("Convert to kms");
    private JButton toMiles = new JButton("Convert to miles");
```

Figure 7.8   Class `DistanceGUI` with method `init()`, *continued*

```
// Methods
// postcondition: Overrides JApplet init() method.
public void init() {
  // Declare local variables
  JLabel inputLab = new JLabel("Input distance > ");
  JPanel dataPanel = new JPanel();
  JPanel buttonPanel = new JPanel();

  // Define the layout manager for the applet
  getContentPane().setLayout(new FlowLayout());

  // Fill dataPanel and add it to applet
  dataPanel.add(inputLab);
  dataPanel.add(input);
  getContentPane().add(dataPanel);

  // Give the focus (cursor) to the input text field
  input.requestFocus();

  // Fill buttonPanel and add it to applet
  buttonPanel.add(toKms);
  buttonPanel.add(toMiles);
  getContentPane().add(buttonPanel);

  // Add output text area to applet
  getContentPane().add(output);

  // Register applet as listener for button presses
  toMiles.addActionListener(this);
  toKms.addActionListener(this);
} // end init

// Insert method actionPerformed() (Fig. 7.12).
```

The lines

```
import javax.swing.*;
import java.awt.*;
```

import the **Swing** and AWT packages. The line

```
import java.awt.event.*;
```

imports the classes that support the Java event model that enables the applet to respond to user-generated events.

The first four lines of the class definition and the first three lines of method **init()** create atomic objects defined in the **Swing** package. Table 7.3 summarizes the constructor calls used in Fig. 7.8 and describes the constructor arguments that are optional. If they are omitted, the defaults are used.

Table 7.3   Constructors for GUI components in Fig. 7.8

Constructor	Behavior
`JTextField(String str, int col)` Example: `JTextField(10)`	Creates an editable text field with **col** columns and string **str** as its initial contents. Either or both arguments may be omitted. The defaults are null and 0. If the dimension argument is omitted, the width will be determined by the string argument.
`JTextArea(String str, int row, int col)` Example: `JTextArea(2, 20)`	Creates an editable text area with **row** rows and **col** columns and string **str** as its initial contents. Either the string or both dimension arguments may be omitted. The defaults are null and 0. If the dimension arguments are omitted, the text area will fit the string argument.

`JButton(String str, Icon pic)`
Examples:
`JButton("Convert to miles")`
`JButton("Convert to kms")`
	Creates a "push" button showing the text in **str** and the image in file **pic**. Either or both arguments may be omitted. The defaults are null.

`JLabel(String str, Icon pic)` Example: `JLabel("Input distance >")`	Creates a display area for the text in string **str** or the image in file **pic**. Either or both arguments may be omitted. The defaults are null.
`JPanel(LayoutManager lM)` Example: `JPanel(new BorderLayout())`	Creates a new container for components using the layout manager specified by its argument. The argument may be omitted. The default for a panel is `FlowLayout`.

Placing the Components in the Applet

After the local variable declarations, method `init()` specifies the placement of components within the applet. A container has an associated object called a layout manager that determines where to place the individual components in a container. The statement

```
getContentPane().setLayout(new FlowLayout());
```

sets the layout manager for the applet's content pane (accessed by method `getContentPane()`) to `FlowLayout`, which positions components in a left-to-right, top-to-bottom order. There is a lot going on in this statement. Method `getContentPane()` is applied to this applet. Method `setLayout()` (defined in AWT class `Container`) sets the layout manager for a container (the applet's content pane). In this call, its argument is a new, unnamed object of type `FlowLayout` (`new FlowLayout()`). Each call to method `setLayout()` has the form

```
container.setLayout(LayoutManager lM)
```

`LayoutManager` is an interface that is implemented by each of the layout managers, including `FlowLayout`. The `FlowLayout` manager positions components in left-to-right order, starting at the top of the applet and moving down to the bottom of it.

To add a component to container, you use the **add()** method, which is defined in AWT class `Container`. Each call to method **add()** has the form

```
container.add(Component component)
```

where the argument (a *component*) is added to the object (a *container*) whose `add()` method executes. Because each of `Swing`'s atomic components is a subclass of `Component`, we can use an atomic component as an argument. We begin by adding the label (`inputLab`) and text field (`input`) to panel `dataPanel` using the statements

```
dataPanel.add(inputLab);
dataPanel.add(input);
```

The `FlowLayout` layout manager is used by default in `dataPanel` (type `JPanel`). Because `dataPanel` is a GUI component (as well as a container), we add it to the applet's content pane using the statement

```
getContentPane().add(dataPanel);
```

The next statement

```
input.requestFocus();
```

calls method **requestFocus()** to "give the focus" to text field **input**. This means that the input cursor will be placed in text field **input** when the applet is started.

Next, we add the two buttons (**toKms** and **toMeters**) to the button panel (**buttonPanel**), add the button panel to the applet's content pane, and the text area (**output**) to the applet's content pane. Table 7.4 summarizes the methods introduced in this section.

The order we followed in adding components was not arbitrary. You must add each component to a panel before adding that panel to the applet's content pane. We added the two panels to the applet in the order (top to bottom) in which we wanted them to appear in the GUI. We added the output text area last because we wanted it to appear at the bottom of the GUI.

Recall that the applet context (such as a browser) creates or instantiates the applet. This example does not allow the user to do anything yet. It merely assembles the GUI components of the applet. The construction must occur within the **init()** method so that when the applet's **start()** method is invoked, the components will be visible. We discuss the last two statements of method **init()** in Section 7.3 where we discuss how the applet responds to user actions or **events**.

Adding Color and Borders to Components

Class **JComponent** defines methods for setting a component's background color (**setBackground()**) and text color (**setForeground()**) as well as for adding a border around a component (**setBorder()**). These methods are inherited by all **Swing** components and are described in Table 7.5.

Table 7.4   Methods in method **init()** in Fig. 7.8

Method Calls in **init()**	Behavior

container.setLayout(LayoutManager *lM*);
 Examples:
 getContentPane().setLayout(new FlowLayout());
	Sets the layout manager for the container to the layout manager object *lM*. Each of Java's layout manager classes implements the interface **LayoutManager**.

container.add(Component *c*);
 Examples:
 dataPanel.add(input);
 getContentPane().add(dataPanel);
	Adds component **c** to the container whose **add()** method is called. Each of **Swing**'s atomic components is a subclass of **Component**.

component.requestFocus(); Example: **input.requestFocus()**	Gives the focus (the input cursor) to the object whose **requestFocus()** method is called.

Table 7.5   Methods for adding borders and colors

Method	Behavior
`component.setBorder(Border bor);`	Draws a border around the component. The argument must be type **Border** and can be created using methods in class **BorderFactory**.
`component.setBackground(Color col);`	Changes the background color of the component to its argument.
`component.setForeground(Color col);`	Changes the color of text in the component to its argument.

◆◆EXAMPLE 7.1

Figure 7.9 shows the effect of the following two calls to method **setBorder()**:

```
dataPanel.setBorder(
    BorderFactory.createTitledBorder("Data panel"));
buttonPanel.setBorder(
    BorderFactory.createTitledBorder("Control panel"));
```

The **setBorder()** method takes a type **Border** argument. We use method **createTitledBorder()** of the **BorderFactory** class to create a border and give it a title.

Figure 7.9   Adding a titled border

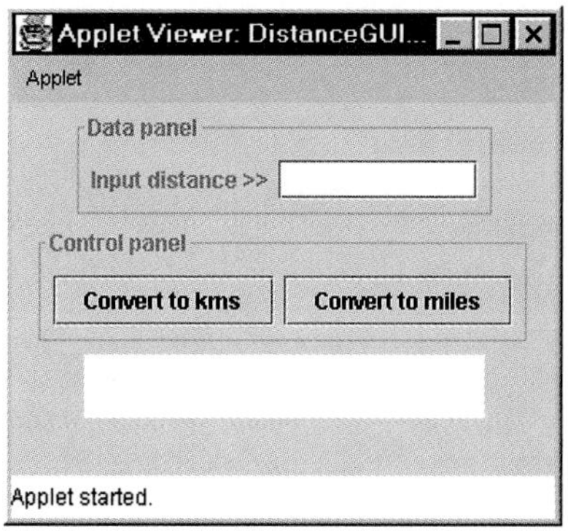

◆◆

◆◆EXAMPLE 7.2 ──────────────────────────

Figure 7.10 shows the effect of the following calls to methods `setBackground()`
and `setForeground()`:

```
dataPanel.setBackground(Color.black);
toKms.setForeground(Color.green);
toMiles.setBackground(Color.green);
```

They change the background color of panel `dataPanel` and button `toMiles` and
the text color of button `toKms`.

Figure 7.10   Changing background and foreground color

── ◆◆

EXERCISES FOR SECTION 7.2

SELF-CHECK

1. What is a containment hierarchy?

2. List the steps in creating a containment hierarchy.

3. What is the purpose of calling method `getContentPane()`? When do you
   need to call it?

PROGRAMMING

1. Design a GUI interface that contains three buttons and a text field. The text
   field appears below a panel that contains the three buttons. The buttons have
   colors red, yellow, and green.

2. Add a `quit` button to the button panel for class `DistanceGUI`.

7.3 The Java Event Model

The previous section showed how to build up a container (applet) of components. This section shows you how to make the applet respond to user-generated events such as button presses, mouse movement or clicks, and keystrokes. Each of these events is represented in Java by a class that extends the **AWTEvent** class.

Recall that the statement

```
import java.awt.event.*;
```

imports the classes that support the Java event model. The way events are handled in a programming language constitutes the **event model** for that language. Java uses the model of event generators and event listeners. An **event generator** is an object that initiates an event (an object of some **Event** type). Many GUI components are event generators. For example, a button has a visual representation on the screen. When a mouse click occurs within the area of the button, some action should take place in a program. The button therefore generates an "action event." An **event listener** is an object that listens for and then responds to events of a particular type. For example, the applet (an object created by the browser) will typically respond to action events generated by its buttons. Figure 7.11 illustrates this process for button **toMiles** and object **dGUI** (an instance of **DistanceGUI**).

Registering as an Event Listener

The event generator and event listener must know about each other in order to establish their relationship. For example, an applet (the event listener) creates a button (the event generator). The applet can refer to the button through a variable. The applet then calls the button's **addActionListener()** method to register itself as a listener for that button's events. The last two statements in method **init()**

```
toMiles.addActionListener(this);
toKms.addActionListener(this);
```

Figure 7.11   Java event model

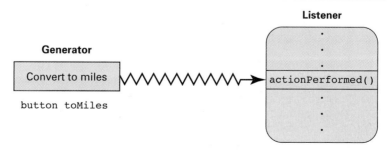

call a button's `addActionListener()` method (defined in class `AbstractButton`) to register the method argument (`this` applet) as a listener for action events generated by that button. These statements have the form below; the `listener object` must be type `ActionListener`.

```
generatorObject.addActionListener(listenerObject);
```

The `ActionListener` Interface

In order for an object to be a listener for a particular event, that object must follow certain protocols. The Java compiler can guarantee that those protocols are followed if the listener has the proper attributes. For example, a listener of action events must be type `ActionListener`. However, our applet (type `DistanceGUI`) already extends class `JApplet`. Because most classes (such as applets) already extend some other class, the `ActionListener` type is an interface rather than a class, and the heading for class `DistanceGUI` correctly indicates that it implements class `ActionListener`:

```
public class DistanceGUI extends JApplet implements ActionListener {
```

For now, we will use the applet as the listener object. However, it is possible to create other objects whose sole purpose is to listen for and respond to events.

Method `actionPerformed()`

We have solved half of the problem. We have registered the applet as a listener for action events generated by the two buttons. Now we have to finish the job by defining how the listener responds to these events.

We mentioned that an action listener implements the `ActionListener` interface. Typically, an interface contains abstract methods, and an implementer must define those methods. The definition for interface `ActionListener` below shows that each implementer must define an `actionPerformed()` method with a single argument of type `ActionEvent` that represents an action event object. (The class heading shows that interface `ActionListener` also extends `EventListener`, another interface class.)

```
public interface ActionListener extends EventListener {

    public void actionPerformed(ActionEvent e);
}
```

Whenever a button generates an action event, the `actionPerformed()` method of the listener for that button's action events automatically executes. This method specifies the response to the event. The programmer does not explicitly call the `actionPerformed()` method; rather, it is automatically called whenever an action event occurs for which there is a registered listener. (If an action event is generated by an object with no registered action listener, there will be no response to that event.)

The statements below describe what we want method `actionPerformed()`to do when a button is pressed:

Get the input distance from text field `input`
Create a `DistanceConverter` object
`if` the `toMiles` button is pressed
   Convert input distance to miles using `DistanceConverter` method `toMiles()`
   Show the values in kilometers and miles in the output text area
`else` if the `toKms` button is pressed
   Convert the input distance to kilometers using `DistanceConverter` method `toKilometers()`
   Show the values in kilometers and miles in the output text area

Recall that class `DistanceConverter` (Fig. 7.1) contains the distance conversion methods. The implementation of this algorithm is complicated by the fact that the input data is a string, so we need to change that string to a type `double` value before we can do the distance conversion. Next, we need to determine which button was pressed. Class `ActionEvent` has a `getSource()` method, which returns a reference to the object that generated the event.

Figure 7.12 shows the `actionPerformed()` method, which implements the above algorithm. The method body declares three Java objects: `dc` (type `DistanceConverter`), `inputStr` (type `String`), and `buttonPressed` (type `Object`). The method has a parameter `aE`, which represents the action event object that is being processed.

The statement

```
String inputStr = input.getText();
```

calls method `getText()` (defined in class `JTextField`) to get the data typed in the text field `input` and store it in `inputStr`. Next, the statement

```
double inputDist = Double.parseDouble(inputStr);
```

calls the `parseDouble()` method (a static method defined in class `Double`) to extract the type `double` value that is represented by the string. For example, if `inputStr` contains the characters `100.34`, `inputDist` will get the real number 100.34. Now that we have a numeric representation of the input distance, the `if` statement can call one of object `dc`'s conversion methods to calculate the desired output distance.

The statement

```
Object buttonPressed = aE.getSource();
```

calls method `getSource()` to return a reference to the generator of the event object being processed. The reference returned is stored in `buttonPressed`. The condition (`buttonPressed == toMiles`) is `true` when the event generator is the button object `toMiles`. If the condition is `true`, object `dC` converts the input distance to miles; if the condition (`buttonPressed == toKilometers`) is `true`, object `dC` converts the input distance to kilometers. The two statements that have the form

```
output.setText(". . .");
```

call the `setText()` method to store the string argument in text area `output`.
   The last line

```
input.requestFocus();    // Gives the focus to input
```

calls method `requestFocus()` to give the focus back to text field `input` so that the user can enter another distance.

Figure 7.12   Method `actionPerformed()` of class `DistanceGUI`

```
// precondition: Text field input contains numeric
//    information and a button is pressed.
// postcondition: Performs the conversion requested by
//    user, placing the result in text area output.
public void actionPerformed(ActionEvent aE) {
    String inputStr = input.getText();
    double inputDist = Double.parseDouble(inputStr);
    double outputDist;
    DistanceConverter dC = new DistanceConverter();
    Object buttonPressed = aE.getSource();
    if (buttonPressed == toMiles) {
        outputDist = dC.toMiles(inputDist);
        output.setText(inputDist + " kilometers converts to\n" +
                    outputDist + " miles");
    }
    else if (buttonPressed == toKms) {
        outputDist = dC.toKilometers(inputDist);
        output.setText(inputDist + " miles converts to\n" +
                    outputDist +  " kilometers");
    }

    input.requestFocus();    // Gives the focus to input
}
```

Table 7.6 summarizes the methods that are used in Fig. 7.12. As you can see, building and using GUIs requires you to be familiar with several of the classes in the AWT and `Swing` packages, their methods, and how these classes interact.

Handling Other Events

Notice that other kinds of events can occur when this applet is running. For example, you can pull down the File menu on the browser and select an operation. That event would be handled by the browser, not by the applet.

Also, pressing the Carriage Return in text field **input** (type **JTextField**) causes the text field to generate an action event. However, there is no object registered as a listener for action events generated by text field **input**, so carriage returns in the text field are ignored. If you have written an **actionPerformed()** method that does not seem to respond properly to a user action, the problem may not be with the **actionPerformed()** method. Check carefully to verify that a listener is registered for the event generated by that user action.

Running the Applet

The complete source file for class **DistanceGUI** contains methods **init()** (Fig 7.8) and **actionPerformed()** (Fig. 7.12). You should put file **DistanceConverter. java** (Fig. 7.1) in the same folder. You can compile the two source files, creating

Table 7.6   Methods and classes in Fig. 7.12

Methods	Behavior

component.getText();
Example:
input.getText();
	Returns the text in a component. Examples of components with getText() methods include buttons, labels, text fields, and text areas.

component.setText(String str);
Example:
output.setText("I like Java");
	Sets the text displayed in a component to the characters contained in string **str**. Examples of components with setText() methods include buttons, labels, text fields, and text areas.

anEvent.getSource(); Example: aE.getSource()	Returns a reference to the atomic component that is the generator of the event that caused the current method to execute. Method getSource() may be called in method **actionPerformed()** or **itemStateChanged()** and is applied to that method's parameter (an event type such as **ActionEvent**)

`.class` files for each. If you use a browser to load and run the applet, the HTML file (see Fig. 7.4) and the `.class` files must be in the same folder.

Fig. 7.2 showed a sample run of the applet. We entered a data value of 100 and pressed the `Convert to kms` button. If you press a convert button when the text field is empty or when it contains nonnumeric data, you will get a run-time error. We discuss how to prevent this kind of error in Section 8.1.

Comparison of Event-Driven Programming and "Stop-and-Wait" Programming

One advantage of event-driven programming is that we can execute an applet as many times as we want to without providing a loop. After each run, the applet is still active and the user can perform any of the following operations:

◆ Enter new input data

◆ Press button `toMiles`

◆ Press button `toKilometers`

◆ Close the applet

◆ Select one of the options under the Applet menu

The first user action changes the input data. The next two user actions generate another action event, causing the `actionPerformed()` method to execute again. Finally, the user can close the applet (by pressing the close button) or can select one of the options under the Applet menu. The browser, not the applet, responds to the event generated by selecting an option under the Applet menu.

It takes some time to get used to the idea that you can repeatedly execute an event-driven program without writing a loop, but you have been doing that all along when you interact with a Windows-based operating system or commercial software. These programs are also event-driven and will repeat an operation (such as searching for a text string in a document) as many times as you specify.

EXERCISES FOR SECTION 7.3

SELF-CHECK

1. Explain the difference between an event generator and an event listener. Give an example of each one.

2. How is an event listener created?

3. If `aText` is an instance of the class `JTextField`, what does the following statement do within a method in an applet:

   `aText.addActionListener(this);`

4. In an `actionPerformed()` method, with argument `ActionEvent aE`, what does `aE.getSource()` return?

5. If your applet does not respond when you press a button, what is one possible reason for this?

6. Explain the purpose of the `ActionListener` interface.

PROGRAMMING

1. Write an `actionPerformed()` method for Programming Exercise 1 of Section 7.2. If you press the red button, the text "stop - wait until red light changes to green" should appear. If you press the yellow button, the text "proceed with care - yellow light changes to red" should appear. If you press the green button, the text "go - green changes to yellow" should appear.

2. Write an `actionPerformed()` method for Programming Exercise 2 of Section 7.2. This method should execute the method call `System.exit(0)` when the quit button is pressed.

7.4 Using a GUI in an Application

You may be wondering whether you can include GUIs in application programs. The answer is Yes. If we make two minor changes and one major change to the applet code shown earlier, we can use our GUI in an application. First, we need to change the class heading to

```
public class DistanceGUIFrame extends JFrame
                             implements ActionListener
```

The new heading indicates that we are using the **Swing** component `JFrame` as the container for the GUI objects rather than `JApplet`. A `JFrame` container (a frame) is required for a GUI application. A frame resembles a typical window that appears when you run an application program such as Microsoft Word. It has a border, a title, and small buttons on the top right (see Fig. 7.13) for iconifying the window (button ■), expanding the window to full screen (button ▢), or closing it (button ✖). Iconifying a window temporarily removes it from your desktop and causes a small icon to appear on the desktop toolbar. You can redisplay the window by deiconifying it—clicking on the icon.

The second minor change is to replace the applet's method `init()` with a constructor (see Fig. 7.14) for class `DistanceGUIFrame`, which has the same body as method `init()`. The reason for this is that the application must create a `DistanceGUIFrame` object and execute statements to add the required components to the GUI container and to register the event listeners. In an application, this code belongs in a constructor.

Figure 7.13 Frame for `DistanceGUIFrame` application

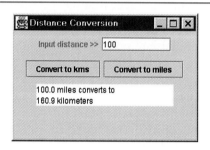

Figure 7.14 Class `DistanceGUIFrame`

```java
/* DistanceGUIFrame.java          Authors: Koffman & Wolz
 * Application for distance conversion.
 * Uses DistanceConverter, Swing, and AWT.
 */
import javax.swing.*;
import java.awt.*;
import java.awt.event.*;

public class DistanceGUIFrame extends JFrame
                              implements ActionListener {

   // Data fields
   private JTextField input = new JTextField(10);
   private JTextArea output = new JTextArea(2, 20);
   private JButton toKms = new JButton("Convert to kms");
   private JButton toMiles = new JButton("Convert to miles");

   // Methods
   // Constructor
   // postcondition: Places the GUI in a window.
   public DistanceGUIFrame() {
      // Declare local variables
      JLabel inputLab = new JLabel("Input distance > ");
      JPanel dataPanel = new JPanel();
      JPanel buttonPanel = new JPanel();

      // Define the layout manager for the frame
      getContentPane().setLayout(new FlowLayout());
```

Figure 7.14   Class `DistanceGUIFrame`, *continued*

```
        // Fill dataPanel and add it to frame
        dataPanel.add(inputLab);
        dataPanel.add(input);
        getContentPane().add(dataPanel);

        // Give the focus (cursor) to the input text field
        input.requestFocus();

        // Fill buttonPanel and add it to the frame
        buttonPanel.add(toKms);
        buttonPanel.add(toMiles);
        getContentPane().add(buttonPanel);

        // Add output text area to the frame
        getContentPane().add(output);

        // Register frame as listener for button presses
        toMiles.addActionListener(this);
        toKms.addActionListener(this);


    }

    // Insert method actionPerformed (Fig. 7.12)
    // Insert method main (Fig. 7.15).
```

Method `actionPerformed()` (Fig. 7.12) should be inserted in the class without modification. The major change is to write a main method for the application class (Fig. 7.15). The application class creates the `DistanceGUIFrame()` object and takes care of closing it when the user presses the "close window" icon. You can execute the application directly; there is no need to provide an HTML file.

The first statement in Fig. 7.15 creates a `DistanceGUIFrame` object `dGUI` as a new frame. Next we set the size of the frame to 300 pixels (horizontal) by 200 pixels (vertical) and set the title for the frame to `Distance Conversion`. The statement

```
dGUI.setVisible(true);
```

makes the frame appear on the screen so we can see it. Figure 7.13 shows the frame after we type in some data and press the `Convert to kms` button.

The call to method `addWindowListener()` in Fig. 7.15 is rather complicated and we will not explain it in too much detail. Its purpose is to close the application when the user presses the close button on the frame. It adds a window listener that listens for a `WindowEvent`. It also defines the `windowClosing()` method, which

Figure 7.15 Method `main()` for class `DistanceGUIFrame`

```
// Creates the frame and closes the frame.
public static void main(String[] args) {
    DistanceGUIFrame dGUI = new DistanceGUIFrame();
    dGUI.setSize(300, 200);
    dGUI.setVisible(true);
    dGUI.setTitle("Distance Conversion");
    dGUI.addWindowListener(
        new WindowAdapter() {
            public void windowClosing(WindowEvent e) {
                System.exit(0);
            }
        }
    );
}
```

executes when the "close window" button is pressed. In this case, the window disappears and system exit occurs. Table 7.7 lists the steps followed in this section to incorporate a GUI of **Swing** components in an application.

Table 7.7 Steps to incorporate a GUI frame in an application

1. Define an application class that extends **JFrame** and implements **ActionListener**.
2. Write a constructor that performs the same steps as method **init()** for a GUI in an applet.
3. Write a **main** method that creates a new GUI object as shown in Fig. 7.15. Place the **main** method in the application class.

EXERCISES FOR SECTION 7.4

SELF-CHECK

1. What do classes **JApplet** and **JFrame** have in common? When do you extend each one?

2. When do you use an **init()** method to place and initialize GUI components and when do you use a constructor?

PROGRAMMING

1. Write the assignment for the three colored buttons (Programming Exercises 1 for Sections 7.2 and 7.3) as an application.

2. Write the assignment for adding a quit button (Programming Exercises 2 for Sections 7.2 and 7.3) as an application.

7.5 Components for Making Choices

In this section, we introduce some GUI components for making choices. We study check boxes (class **JCheckBox**) and radio buttons (class **JRadioButton**), which are subclasses of **JToggleButton**. A toggle button is like a switch that has two states. Each time the button is pressed, it changes its state. Normally we say the two states are "off" and "on." You press a toggle button by clicking on the text that follows the button icon. We also discuss combo boxes, which implement pull-down lists.

Check Boxes

Check boxes provide **boolean** data to a program. If the check box is checked, its state is on, corresponding to **true**; if the check box is not checked, its state is off, corresponding to **false**. You can use check boxes when you have a list of one or more items that you want to include or not include. Each item will be represented by a check box. Only the items corresponding to check boxes that are checked will be included.

◆◆EXAMPLE 7.3 ──

Figure 7.16 shows a group of check boxes that can be used to indicate current weather conditions. The state of check boxes **cold**, **wet**, and **mix** is **true**; the state of all other check boxes is **false**. The check boxes indicate that the weather is cold and wet, with a mix of snow and rain.

Figure 7.17 shows the source code for applet **CheckBoxDemo**. There are nine check boxes and each row of check boxes is placed in a separate panel.

Figure 7.16   Applet with check boxes

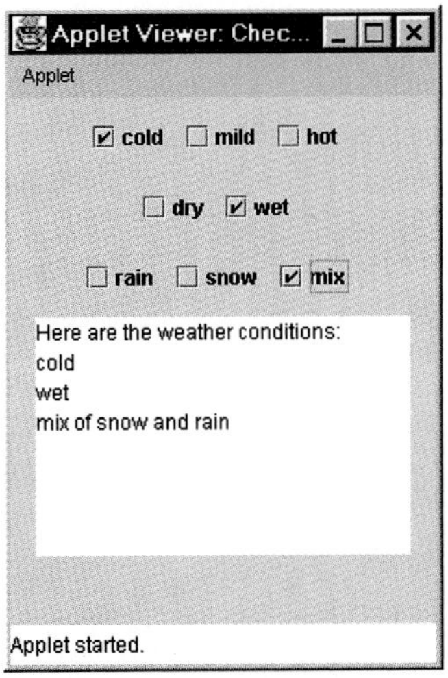

Figure 7.17 **Class** CheckBoxDemo

```java
/* CheckBoxDemo.java        Authors: Koffman & Wolz
 * Applet for demonstrating check boxes.
 * Uses Swing and AWT.
 */
import javax.swing.*;
import java.awt.event.*;
import java.awt.*;

public class CheckBoxDemo extends JApplet
                         implements ItemListener {
  // Data fields
  private JCheckBox temp1 = new JCheckBox("cold");
  private JCheckBox temp2 = new JCheckBox("mild");
  private JCheckBox temp3 = new JCheckBox("hot");
  private JCheckBox precip1 = new JCheckBox("dry");
  private JCheckBox precip2 = new JCheckBox("wet");
  private JCheckBox precipKind1 = new JCheckBox("rain");
  private JCheckBox precipKind2 = new JCheckBox("snow");
  private JCheckBox precipKind3 = new JCheckBox("mix");
  private JTextArea weather = new JTextArea(8, 20);


  // Methods
  // postcondition: Builds a GUI with check boxes in 3 panels.
  public void init() {
    // Define the layout manager for the applet
    getContentPane().setLayout(new FlowLayout());

    // Define panel for temperature check boxes
    JPanel tempPanel = new JPanel();
    tempPanel.add(temp1);
    tempPanel.add(temp2);
    tempPanel.add(temp3);
    getContentPane().add(tempPanel);

    // Define panel for precipitation check boxes
    JPanel precipPanel = new JPanel();
    precipPanel.add(precip1);
    precipPanel.add(precip2);
    getContentPane().add(precipPanel);

    // Define panel for kind of precipitation check boxes
    JPanel precipKindPanel = new JPanel();
```

Figure 7.17   **Class** `CheckBoxDemo`, *continued*

```
      precipKindPanel.add(precipKind1);
      precipKindPanel.add(precipKind2);
      precipKindPanel.add(precipKind3);
      getContentPane().add(precipKindPanel);

      // Add the output text area to the applet
      getContentPane().add(weather);

      // Register the applet as an item listener for all check boxes
      temp1.addItemListener(this);
      temp2.addItemListener(this);
      temp3.addItemListener(this);
      precip1.addItemListener(this);
      precip2.addItemListener(this);
      precipKind1.addItemListener(this);
      precipKind2.addItemListener(this);
      precipKind3.addItemListener(this);
   }


   // postcondition: Displays information about weather conditions
   //    selected by check boxes in output text area.
   public void itemStateChanged(ItemEvent e) {
      String weatherStr = "Here are the weather conditions:\n";
      if (temp1.isSelected())
         weatherStr += "cold\n";
      if (temp2.isSelected())
         weatherStr += "mild\n";
      if (temp3.isSelected())
         weatherStr += "hot\n";
      if (precip1.isSelected())
         weatherStr += "dry\n";
      if (precip2.isSelected())
         weatherStr += "wet\n";
      if (precipKind1.isSelected())
         weatherStr += "rain\n";
      if (precipKind2.isSelected())
         weatherStr += "snow\n";
      if (precipKind3.isSelected())
         weatherStr += "mix of snow and rain\n";
      weather.setText(weatherStr);
   }
}
```

The applet implements the **ItemListener** interface because check boxes generate item events (objects of class **ItemEvent**), not action events. The method call

```
temp1.addItemListener(this);
```

registers the applet as a listener for item events generated by check box **temp1**. A class that implements **ItemListener** must define the abstract method **itemStateChanged()**.

Method **itemStateChanged()** in Fig. 7.17 executes whenever the state of a check box changes. The method builds an output string (**weatherStr**) and copies it to the text area, **weather**. Each **if** statement has a condition of the form

```
(checkbox.isSelected())
```

The condition is **true** if the state of the indicated checkbox is on. If the condition is **true**, the assignment statement (its consequent) appends a string representing that weather situation to the output string.

◆◆

Radio Buttons

◆◆EXAMPLE 7.4

Radio buttons are used in a manner similar to check boxes. Figure 7.18 shows radio buttons that correspond to the check boxes in Fig. 7.16.

Figure 7.18 Applet with radio buttons

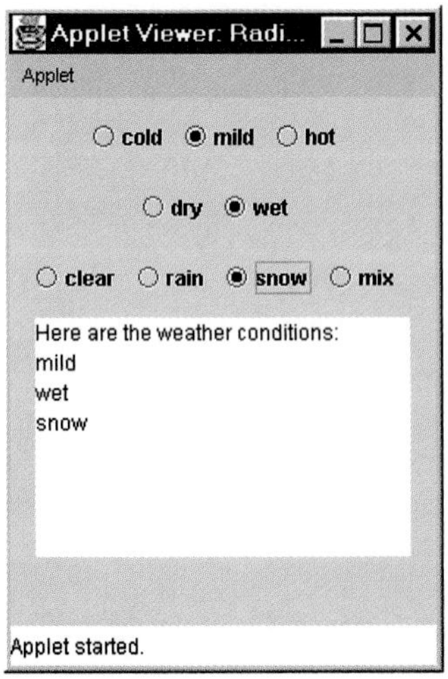

Radio buttons have one additional feature that check boxes do not have. They can be part of a button group (**Swing** class **ButtonGroup**). For radio buttons that are part of a button group, only one of the buttons in a group can be on. If a button that is currently off is pressed, its state changes to on, and the other buttons in the group are set to off. The **ButtonGroup** object takes care of resetting the state of the other buttons. In Fig. 7.18, it would make sense to have three button groups, one for each row of buttons. The last row has an extra button with the text "clear." Figure 7.19 shows the applet code. Radio buttons generate both action events and item events; however, the convention is to listen for action events.

Although we could have written class **RadioButtonDemo** to look very similar to class **CheckBoxDemo** in Fig. 7.17, we decided to use three arrays of radio buttons to streamline the code. The statement

```
private JRadioButton[] temp = {new JRadioButton("cold"),
                               new JRadioButton("mild"),
                               new JRadioButton("hot")};
```

creates an array of three radio buttons referenced by **temp**.

The statements

```
JPanel tempPanel = new JPanel();
ButtonGroup tempGr = new ButtonGroup();
for (int butNum = 0; butNum < temp.length; butNum++) {
   tempPanel.add(temp[butNum]);
   tempGr.add(temp[butNum]);
   temp[butNum].addActionListener(this);
}
```

create a new panel (**tempPanel**) and a new button group (**tempGr**). The **for** statement performs all the initialization operations required for the radio buttons referenced by array **temp**. It adds each radio button to panel **tempPanel** and to button group **tempGr** and registers the applet as a listener for that button. Similar statements are provided for the other two arrays of radio buttons.

Each time the user selects a radio button, method **actionPerformed()** executes. In **actionPerformed()**, the **for** statement

```
for (int butNum = 0; butNum < temp.length; butNum++) {
   if (temp[butNum].isSelected())
      weatherStr += (temp[butNum].getText() + "\n");
}
```

determines which button referenced by array **temp** is selected and appends its text to the weather string. We provide similar **for** statements for arrays **precip** and **precipKind**.

Figure 7.19   Class `RadioButtonDemo`

```
/* RadioButtonDemo.java          Authors: Koffman & Wolz
 * Applet for demonstrating radio buttons.
 * Uses Swing and AWT.
 */
import javax.swing.*;
import java.awt.event.*;
import java.awt.*;

public class RadioButtonDemo extends JApplet implements ActionListener {
  // Data fields
  private JRadioButton[] temp = {new JRadioButton("cold"),
                                 new JRadioButton("mild"),
                                 new JRadioButton("hot")};

  private JRadioButton[] precip = {new JRadioButton("dry"),
                                   new JRadioButton("wet")};

  private JRadioButton[] precipKind = {new JRadioButton("clear"),
                                       new JRadioButton("rain"),
                                       new JRadioButton("snow"),
                                       new JRadioButton("mix")};
  private JTextArea weather = new JTextArea(8, 20);

  // Methods
  public void init() {
    // Define the layout manager for the applet
    getContentPane().setLayout(new FlowLayout());

    // Define panel and button group for temperature radio buttons.
    //    add each button to panel and to button group and
    //    register applet as a listener for each button,
    JPanel tempPanel = new JPanel();
    ButtonGroup tempGr = new ButtonGroup();
    for (int butNum = 0; butNum < temp.length; butNum++) {
      tempPanel.add(temp[butNum]);
      tempGr.add(temp[butNum]);
      temp[butNum].addActionListener(this);
    }
    getContentPane().add(tempPanel);

    // Define panel and button group for precipitation radio buttons,
    //    add each button to panel and to button group and
    //    register applet as a listener for each button.
    JPanel precipPanel = new JPanel();
    ButtonGroup precipGr = new ButtonGroup();
    for (int butNum = 0; butNum < precip.length; butNum++) {
```

Figure 7.19 Class `RadioButtonDemo`, *continued*

```
        precipPanel.add(precip[butNum]);
        precipGr.add(precip[butNum]);
        precip[butNum].addActionListener(this);
      }
      getContentPane().add(precipPanel);

      // Define panel and button group for precipitation
      //    kind radio buttons,
      //    add each button to panel and to button group and
      //    register applet as a listener for each button,
      JPanel precipKindPanel = new JPanel();
      ButtonGroup precipKindGr = new ButtonGroup();
      for (int butNum = 0; butNum < precipKind.length; butNum++) {
        precipKindPanel.add(precipKind[butNum]);
        precipKindGr.add(precipKind[butNum]);
        precipKind[butNum].addActionListener(this);
      }
      getContentPane().add(precipKindPanel);

      // Add the output text area to the applet
      getContentPane().add(weather);
    }


    public void actionPerformed(ActionEvent e) {

      String weatherStr = "Here are the weather conditions:\n";
      for (int butNum = 0; butNum < temp.length; butNum++) {
        if (temp[butNum].isSelected())
          weatherStr += (temp[butNum].getText() + "\n");
      }

      for (int butNum = 0; butNum < precip.length; butNum++) {
        if (precip[butNum].isSelected())
          weatherStr += (precip[butNum].getText() + "\n");
      }

      for (int butNum = 0; butNum < precipKind.length; butNum++) {
        if (precipKind[butNum].isSelected())
          weatherStr += (precipKind[butNum].getText() + "\n");
      }
      weather.setText(weatherStr);
    }
  }
```

◆◆

Combo Boxes

A **combo box** (type `JComboBox`) allows the user to select one of several options and is used to represent a drop-down menu. When the user clicks on the option bar, a list of options drops down and the user can make a selection. For example, a combo box can be used to allow a user to select one title from among several (Mr., Ms., Mrs., Dr.) or to select your state of residence from among the 50 possible choices. Making a selection generates an item event. Applying method `getSelectedIndex()` to the combo box returns the index of the selection, starting with 0 for the first option in the drop-down menu; applying method `getSelectedItem()` returns the selected item (type `Object`).

You can initialize a combo box's options using an array of strings. You can also use method `addItem()` to add individual options (strings). When the combo box is initially displayed, the first option will be shown.

◆◆EXAMPLE 7.5 ────────────────────────────────

Figure 7.20 shows an application class `ComboBoxDemo` that illustrates the use of a combo box. The combo box `titleList` is a private data field. In the constructor, the statements

```
String[] titles = {"Mr.", "Ms.", "Mrs.", "Dr."};
titleList = new JComboBox(titles);
titleList.addItem("Professor");
```

create a new combo box whose initial selections are specified by array `titles`. The first selection, `Mr.`, is displayed on the option bar. We add a fifth selection using method `addItem()`. Figure 7.21 shows the drop-down list.

Figure 7.20   **Class** `ComboBoxDemo`
──

```
/* ComboBoxDemo.java          Authors: Koffman & Wolz
 * Application demonstrating use of a combo box.
 * Uses Swing, AWT.
 */
import javax.swing.*;
import java.awt.event.*;
import java.awt.*;

public class ComboBoxDemo extends JFrame
                          implements ItemListener {
```

Figure 7.20   Class `ComboBoxDemo,` *continued*

```java
private JComboBox titleList;
private JTextField greeting = new JTextField(20);

// Creates a GUI with a combo box for selecting a title
//   and a text field for output.
public ComboBoxDemo() {
  getContentPane().setLayout(new FlowLayout());
  String titles[] = {"Mr.", "Ms.", "Mrs.", "Dr."};
  titleList = new JComboBox(titles);
  titleList.addItem("Professor");
  getContentPane().add(titleList);
  getContentPane().add(greeting);
  titleList.addItemListener(this);
}

// postcondition: Displays a greeting that includes the title
//   selected from the combo box.
public void itemStateChanged(ItemEvent itEv) {
  if (itEv.getSource() == titleList) {
    String titleStr = (String) titleList.getSelectedItem();
    greeting.setText("Dear " + titleStr + " Jones;");
  }
}

// Creates the frame and closes the frame.
public static void main(String[] args) {
  ComboBoxDemo cBD = new ComboBoxDemo();
  cBD.setSize(400, 200);
  cBD.setVisible(true);
  cBD.setTitle("Combo box demo");
  cBD.addWindowListener(
      new WindowAdapter() {
        public void windowClosing(WindowEvent e) {
          System.exit(0);
        }
      }
  );
}
}
```

Figure 7.21 Drop-down list in GUI for class ComboBoxDemo

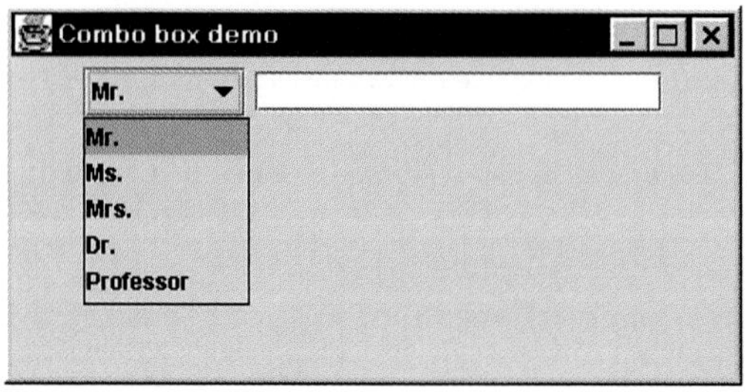

In method **itemStateChanged( )**, the statement

```
String titleStr = (String) titleList.getSelectedItem();
```

retrieves the item that is selected (type **Object**), casts it to type **String**, and stores a reference to the type **String** object in **titleStr**. Fig. 7.22 shows the result of selecting **Professor** from the drop-down list. Table 7.8 lists some methods for the components introduced in this section.

Figure 7.22 Selecting **Professor** from drop-down list

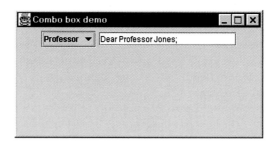

Table 7.8 Methods for making choices

Methods	Behavior
JCheckBox Methods	
JCheckBox(String)	Creates a new check box with the specified text
checkbox.isSelected()	Returns **true** if the check box to which it is applied has been checked
checkbox.addItemListener(this)	Registers the applet as a listener for item events generated by *checkbox*
checkbox.getText()	Gets the text for *checkbox*
JRadioButton Methods	
JRadioButton(String)	Creates a new radio button with the specified text
radbutton.isSelected()	Returns **true** if *radbutton* is on
radbutton.addActionListener(this)	Registers the applet as a listener for action events generated by *radbutton*
radbutton.getText()	Gets the text for *radbutton*
ComboBox Methods	
JComboBox();	Creates a new combo box with no selections
JComboBox(Object[])	Creates a new combo box that contains the elements in the specified array
JComboBox(Vector)	Creates a new combo box that contains the elements in the specified vector
combobox.addItem(Object)	Adds the argument to the selections for *combobox*
combobox.addItemListener(this)	Registers the applet as a listener for item events generated by *combobox*
combobox.getSelectedItem()	Returns a type **Object** reference to the item selected by *combobox*
combobox.getSelectedIndex()	Returns the index (type **int**) of the item selected by *combobox*
combobox.setSelectedIndex(int)	Selects the item whose index is specified
ButtonGroup Methods	
ButtonGroup()	Creates a new **ButtonGroup** object; only one of the buttons in a group can be on
buttgroup.add(AbstractButton)	Adds the specified button to *buttgroup*
ItemListener Methods	
itemStateChanged(ItemEvent)	Required by **ItemListener** interface; automatically executes when an item event with a registered listener is generated

EXERCISES FOR SECTION 7.5

SELF-CHECK

1. What characteristic do button groups and combo boxes share?

2. Which of the components used in this section are subclasses of `JToggleButton`?

3. Which of the components used in this section had registered listeners for item events and which had registered listeners for action events?

PROGRAMMING

1. Rewrite `CheckBoxDemo` as an application. Use three arrays of check boxes.

2. Rewrite `RadioButtonDemo` as an application.

3. Rewrite `ComboBoxDemo` as an applet.

7.6   Designing a GUI for an Existing Class

In this section, we revisit the `PhoneBook` class that we wrote in Section 5.5. We will design a GUI for interacting with this class.

CASE STUDY A GUI FOR THE PHONEBOOK CLASS

PROBLEM   We would like a GUI that interacts with a user of the `PhoneBook` class (Fig. 5.36). The user should be able to add new entries (type `Friend`, see Fig. 5.35) to the phone directory, retrieve a person's phone number, or change a phone number for a person who is in the phone directory.

ANALYSIS   The problem inputs are the person's name and, possibly, number (for a new entry). The output is a message indicating the result of an operation. The user also needs to be able to select one of three operations: add an entry, get a number, or change a number. We already have classes `PhoneBook` and `Friend`, so we only need to design the interface.

Data Requirements

Problem Inputs

Friend's name
Friend's number
Operation selected

Problem Outputs

Friend's number
Instructions and results

DESIGN   We can use radio buttons in a button group to enable the user to select an operation. We need two text fields to enter the person's name and number. As an alternative to typing in the name of a person already in the directory, we can provide a combo box whose selection list is an array containing the names of all persons in the directory. We also need a text area for displaying instructions to the user and results of operations. Figure 7.23 shows the initial GUI; Fig. 7.24 provides a description for class **PhoneBookGUI**.

To interact with the GUI, the user should press a radio button and then follow the instructions for that operation. After typing in the data (or selecting a name), the user must press the submit button to process the new entry. Method **init()** creates the GUI shown in Fig. 7.23. The algorithm follows.

*Algorithm for **init()***

1. Set the layout manager to flow layout.

2. Place the radio buttons in a panel and in a button group and add the panel.

3. Add the data area for displaying instructions.

4. Place the name and number text fields in a panel and add the panel.

5. Place the combo box and submit button in a panel and add the panel.

6. Register the applet as an action listener for all buttons and as an item listener for the combo box.

Figure 7.23   GUI for phone book class

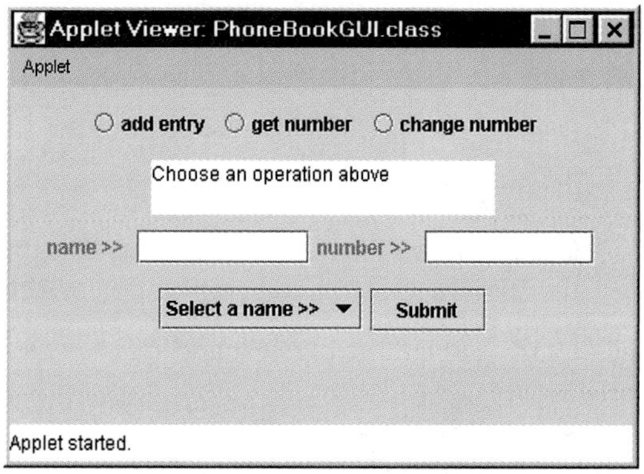

Figure 7.24   Class `PhoneBookGUI`

Data Fields	Attributes
`JTextField nameText`	A name
`JTextField numberText`	A phone number
`JRadioButton addRB`	Radio button for adding a friend
`JRadioButton getRB`	Radio button for getting a number
`JRadioButton changeRB`	Radio button for changing a number
`JTextArea instruct`	Text area for displaying instructions and results
`JComboBox nameList`	Combo box for selecting a name
`JButton submit`	A button to initiate processing an operation
`PhoneBook myPhoneBook`	A phone book object

Methods	Behavior
`void init()`	Creates a GUI object
`void actionPerformed()`	Responds to action events generated by pressing a radio button or the submit button
`void itemStateChanged()`	Responds to item events generated by making a selection from the combo box

Classes Used
`PhoneBook, Friend, String, JTextField, JRadioButton, JTextArea, JComboBox, ButtonGroup, JApplet, ItemListener, ActionListener`

Method `actionPerformed()` responds to button presses. If a radio button is pressed, instructions for performing that operation should be displayed in the text area. If the submit button is pressed, the selected operation must be performed using the name and number data. The algorithm for `actionPerformed()` follows.

Algorithm for `actionPerformed()`

1. **if** a radio button is pressed

    Display instructions for performing the selected operation.

    else if `submit` is pressed and **add entry** is selected

    Get the friend's name and number, add the friend to the directory, and add the friend's name to the combo box selection list.

    else if `submit` is pressed and **get number** is selected

    Get the friend's name and retrieve the friend's number from the directory.

    else if `submit` is pressed and **change number** is selected

    Get the friend's name and new number.

if the friend is in the directory

>Replace the entry at that location with one containing the friend's name and new number.

else

>Display an error message.

Method `itemStateChanged()` executes when the user selects a name from the combo box list. The name selected should be placed in text field `nameText`.

Algorithm for `itemStateChanged()`

1. **if** a name is selected from the combo box list

>Store the name selected in data field `nameText`.

IMPLEMENTATION   Figure 7.25 shows the data field declarations and method `init()` for class `PhoneBookGUI`.

Figure 7.26 shows method `actionPerformed()`, which is implemented as a nested **if** statement. If a radio button is pressed, one of the first three conditions will be **true** and the appropriate instructions will appear in text area `instruct`.

If the **submit** button is pressed, one of the last three conditions will be **true**. For example, the condition

```
(but == submit && addRB.isSelected())
```

is **true** if the **add entry** radio button is selected when **submit** is pressed. If either the name or number text field is empty, an error message is displayed. Otherwise the statements

```
aFriend = new Friend(name, number);
myPhoneBook.addFriend(aFriend);
nameList.addItem(name);  // add name to combo box list
```

execute, adding **aFriend** to the directory and the friend's name to the combo box list. If the condition

```
(but == submit && getRB.isSelected())
```

is **true** and **name** is not empty, the statement

```
number = myPhoneBook.getNumber(name);
```

Figure 7.25   Data fields and method `init()` for PhoneBookGUI

```java
/* PhoneBookGUI.java           Authors: Koffman & Wolz
 * GUI for Using the PhoneBook class.
 * Uses Swing, AWT, and PhoneBook.
 */
import javax.swing.*;
import java.awt.event.*;
import java.awt.*;

public class PhoneBookGUI extends JApplet
                          implements ActionListener, ItemListener {
  // Data fields
  private JTextField nameText = new JTextField(10);
  private JTextField numberText = new JTextField(10);
  private JRadioButton addRB = new JRadioButton("add entry");
  private JRadioButton getRB = new JRadioButton("get number");
  private JRadioButton changeRB = new JRadioButton("change number");
  private JTextArea instruct = new JTextArea(2, 20);
  private JComboBox nameList = new JComboBox();
  private JButton submit = new JButton("Submit");
  private PhoneBook myPhoneBook = new PhoneBook();

  // Methods
  public void init() {
    // Define the layout manager for the applet.
    getContentPane().setLayout(new FlowLayout());

    // Define operations panel and button group for radio buttons.
    JPanel radButPanel = new JPanel();
    radButPanel.add(addRB);
    radButPanel.add(getRB);
    radButPanel.add(changeRB);
    getContentPane().add(radButPanel);
    ButtonGroup operations = new ButtonGroup();
    operations.add(addRB);
    operations.add(getRB);
    operations.add(changeRB);

    // Add instructions text area to applet.
    instruct.setText("Choose an operation above");
    getContentPane().add(instruct);
```

Figure 7.25   Data fields and method `init()` for `PhoneBookGUI`, *continued*

```
// Define panel for entering name and number.
JPanel dataPanel = new JPanel();
JLabel nameLabel = new JLabel("name >> ");
dataPanel.add(nameLabel);
dataPanel.add(nameText);
JLabel numberLabel = new JLabel("number >> ");
dataPanel.add(numberLabel);
dataPanel.add(numberText);
getContentPane().add(dataPanel);

// Define panel for combo box and submit button.
JPanel controlPanel = new JPanel();
nameList.addItem("Select a name >"); // first selection
controlPanel.add(nameList);
controlPanel.add(submit);
getContentPane().add(controlPanel);

// Register event listeners.
addRB.addActionListener(this);
getRB.addActionListener(this);
changeRB.addActionListener(this);
submit.addActionListener(this);
nameList.addItemListener(this);
} // end init
```

retrieves the person's number, which is then displayed. If the condition

```
(but == submit && changeRB.isSelected())
```

is **true** and **name** and **number** are not empty, the statement

```
int index = myPhoneBook.findFriend(name);
```

gets the index of the directory entry with the specified name. If the index is not negative, the statement

```
myPhoneBook.setFriend(index, aFriend);
```

stores the modified entry (**aFriend**) at that location.

Figure 7.26 Method `actionPerformed()` for `PhoneBookGUI`

```
// postcondition: Displays instructions for performing
//    an operation when a radio button is pressed.
//    Performs the selected operation when the submit button
//    is pressed.
public void actionPerformed(ActionEvent e) {
  String name;
  String number;
  Friend aFriend;
  Object but = e.getSource();
  if (but == addRB)
    instruct.setText("Enter name and number and " +
                     "\nPress submit");
  else if (but == getRB)
    instruct.setText("Select name or enter name." +
                     "\nPress submit");
  else if (but == changeRB)
    instruct.setText("Select name or enter name." +
                     "\nEnter new number and press submit");
  else if (but == submit && addRB.isSelected()) {
    // add new friend
    name = nameText.getText();
    number = numberText.getText();
    if (name.equals("") || number.equals("")) {
      instruct.setText("Missing name or number - " +
                       "\nTry again");
      return;
    }
    aFriend = new Friend(name, number);
    myPhoneBook.addFriend(aFriend);
    nameList.addItem(name);  // add name to combo box list
    instruct.setText("Added: " + aFriend +
                     "\nChoose another operation above" );
    nameText.setText("");
    numberText.setText("");
  }
  else if (but == submit && getRB.isSelected()) {
    // Retrieve a number
    name = nameText.getText();
    if (name.equals("")) {
      instruct.setText("Missing name - " +
                       "\nTry again");
      return;
```

Figure 7.26   Method `actionPerformed()` for `PhoneBookGUI`, *continued*

```
      }
      number = myPhoneBook.getNumber(name);
      instruct.setText("Number is " + number +
                       "\nChoose another operation above");
      nameText.setText("");
    }
    else if (but == submit && changeRB.isSelected()) {
      // change an entry
      name = nameText.getText();
      number = numberText.getText();
      if (name.equals("") || number.equals("")) {
        instruct.setText("Missing name or number - " +
                         "\nTry again");
        return;
      }
      aFriend = new Friend(name, number);
      int index = myPhoneBook.findFriend(name);
      if (index > -1) {
        myPhoneBook.setFriend(index, aFriend);
        instruct.setText("Entry changed to: " + aFriend +
                         "\nChoose another operation above" );
      }
      else {
        instruct.setText(name + " not found - " +
                         "\nTry again");
      }
      nameText.setText("");
      numberText.setText("");
    }

    nameText.requestFocus();
    nameList.setSelectedIndex(0); // Reset combo box message
  } // end actionPerformed()
```

Method `itemStateChanged()` (Fig. 7.27) executes when a selection is made from the combo box list. The condition

```
(e.getSource() == nameList &&
 nameList.getSelectedIndex() != 0)
```

is **true** if the element at position 0 (**Select a name >>**) is not selected. The statements

```
String name = (String) nameList.getSelectedItem();
nameText.setText(name);
```

retrieve the name selected and store it in data field **nameText**.

TESTING   To test this applet, choose **add entry** several times to add a collection of names to the directory. Once you have added several names, try the **get name** and **change number** options. Test these options by typing in a name and by selecting one from the combo box list. Figure 7.28 shows the GUI just before a name is selected (operation is **get number**). Figure 7.29 shows the GUI after the name is selected and **submit** is pressed.

Figure 7.27   Method itemStateChanged() for PhoneBookGUI

```
// postcondition: Stores the name selected from the combo box list
//    in nameText.
public void itemStateChanged(ItemEvent e) {
  if (e.getSource() == nameList &&
      nameList.getSelectedIndex() != 0) {
    String name = (String) nameList.getSelectedItem();
    nameText.setText(name);
  }
}
```

Figure 7.28   Phone book GUI just before selecting a name

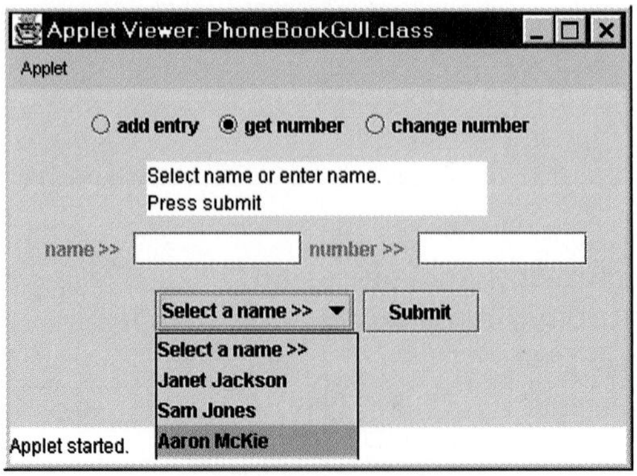

Figure 7.29   Phone book GUI after selecting a name and pressing `submit`

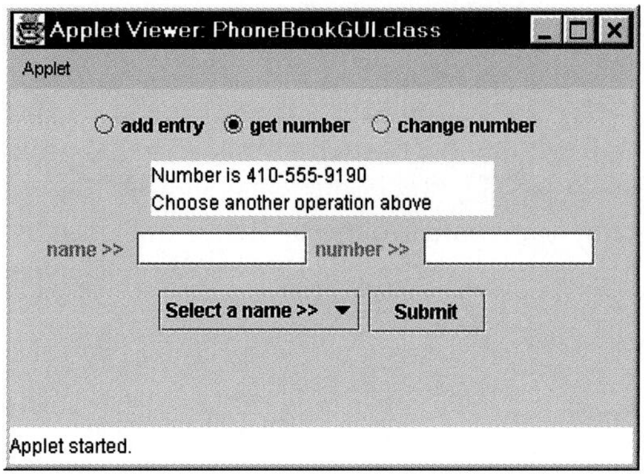

EXERCISES FOR SECTION 7.6

SELF-CHECK

1. What is displayed in text area `instruct` after the phone number for a friend named Aaron McKie is successfully changed to 215-555-3256? Trace through each statement that executes in method `actionPerformed()` when the `submit` button is pressed (`chargenumber` is selected) and indicate its effect.

2. Answer Self-Check Exercise 1 when the `submit` button is pressed and the operation is to get the phone number for a friend named Aaron McKie who is in the directory.

3. What is displayed in text area `instruct` after the radio button `change number` is selected?

4. Indicate how you would change the GUI to be able to delete a friend from the directory. What changes would be required in method `actionPerformed()`? What changes would be required in class `PhoneBook`?

PROGRAMMING

1. Assume that there is a method `removeEntry(int)` in class `PhoneBook` that removes the entry at a specified position. Implement your answer to Self-Check Exercise 4. Provide the code for the changes needed in methods `init()` and `actionPerformed()`.

7.7 Listener Classes as Inner Classes

The `actionPerformed()` method in Fig. 7.26 is quite lengthy and complicated because it processes all of the possible action events that might occur. Another approach is to use separate listener classes to respond to individual action events or to respond to a group of action events. For this problem, it makes sense to use separate listener classes for the events generated by the radio buttons and for the events generated by the control button. The listener classes should be **inner classes** that are wholly contained within the GUI class. This enables the inner classes to reference private data fields of the GUI.

Figure 7.30 shows inner class `submitButtonListener`, and Fig. 7.31 shows inner class `radioButtonListener`. The classes have private visibility because they are referenced only within the GUI class. Each class implements the **ActionListener** interface and defines an `actionPerformed()` method only. Notice that we don't bother to test the event source in method `actionPerformed()` for class `SubmitButtonListener` because this class only responds to **submit** button events. The conditions determine which radio button was selected before **submit** was pressed.

Figure 7.30   Inner class `SubmitButtonListener`

```
/* inner class SubmitButtonListener for class PhoneBookGUI
 * Listens for a submit button event.
 */
private class SubmitButtonListener implements ActionListener {

  // precondition: Button submit was pressed.
  // postcondition: Performs the selected operation.
  public void actionPerformed(ActionEvent e) {
    String name;
    String number;
    Friend aFriend;
    if (addRB.isSelected()) {
      // add new friend
      name = nameText.getText();
      number = numberText.getText();
      if (name.equals("") || number.equals("")) {
        instruct.setText("Missing name or number - " +
                          "\nTry again");
        return;
      }
      aFriend = new Friend(name, number);
      myPhoneBook.addFriend(aFriend);
      nameList.addItem(name);  // add name to combo box list
      instruct.setText("Added: " + aFriend +
                        "\nChoose another operation above" );
```

Figure 7.30   Inner class `SubmitButtonListener`, *continued*

```
         nameText.setText("");
         numberText.setText("");
      }
      else if (getRB.isSelected()) {
         // get a number
         name = nameText.getText();
         if (name.equals("")) {
            instruct.setText("Missing name - " +
                              "\nTry again");
            return;
         }
         number = myPhoneBook.getNumber(name);
         instruct.setText("Number is " + number +
                          "\nChoose another operation above");
         nameText.setText("");
      }
      else if (changeRB.isSelected()) {
         // change an entry
         name = nameText.getText();
         number = numberText.getText();
         if (name.equals("") || number.equals("")) {
            instruct.setText("Missing name or number - " +
                              "\nTry again");
            return;
         }
         aFriend = new Friend(name, number);
         int index = myPhoneBook.findFriend(name);
         if (index > -1) {
            myPhoneBook.setFriend(index, aFriend);
            instruct.setText("Entry changed to: " + aFriend +
                              "\nChoose another operation above" );
         }
         else {
            instruct.setText(name + " not found - " +
                              "\nTry again");
         }
         nameText.setText("");
         numberText.setText("");
      }

      nameText.requestFocus();
      nameList.setSelectedIndex(0); // Reset combo box message
   }

} // end SubmitButtonListener
```

Figure 7.31 Inner class `RadioButtonListener`

```
/* inner class RadioButtonListener for class PhoneBookGUI
 * Listens for a radio button event.
 */
private class RadioButtonListener implements ActionListener {

  public void actionPerformed(ActionEvent e) {
    Object but = e.getSource();
    if (but == addRB)
       instruct.setText("Enter name and number and " +
                          "\nPress submit");
    else if (but == getRB)
       instruct.setText("Select name or enter name." +
                          "\nPress submit");
    else if (but == changeRB)
       instruct.setText("Select name or enter name." +
                          "\nEnter new number and press submit");
    nameText.requestFocus();
  }

}  // end RadioButtonListener
```

Because the applet no longer listens for action events, it should not implement the **ActionListener** interface, and its **actionPerformed()** method should be deleted. Its new heading would be

```
public class PhoneBookGUI extends JApplet
                            implements ItemListener {
```

The statements in method **init()** that register the applet as an action listener should be replaced by the statements below. These statements create two listener objects, **sBL** and **rBL**. They register **SubmitButtonListener sBL** as a listener for action events generated by the **submit** button and **RadioButtonListener rBL** as a listener for action events generated by the three radio buttons.

```
SubmitButtonListener sBL = new SubmitButtonListener();
submit.addActionListener(sBL);

RadioButtonListener rBL = new RadioButtonListener();
addRB.addActionListener(rBL);
getRB.addActionListener(rBL);
changeRB.addActionListener(rBL);
```

PROGRAM STYLE: *Placement of Inner Classes*

The inner class definitions must be nested somewhere within class `PhoneBookGUI`. The exact placement does not matter, but an inner class should not be defined inside a method. Two convenient locations for the inner classes would be at the very beginning of class `PhoneBookGUI` (after the heading) or after the last method in class `PhoneBookGUI`.

EXERCISES FOR SECTION 7.7

SELF-CHECK

1. If there was a separate listener for combo box `NameList` events, what would be the new heading for applet `PhoneBookGUI`? Write the statements in method `init()` that create and register the listener for the combo box.

2. Explain the advantage of using inner listener classes.

PROGRAMMING

1. Create a separate listener object for combo box `nameList` in class `PhoneBookGUI`. Write the inner class.

2. Rewrite class `RadioButtonDemo` (Fig. 7.19) using a separate listener class for each button group. Each time an event occurs, you should display only the text in the button that was selected.

7.8 Layout Managers

A **layout manager** is an object that determines the size and placement of objects in a container. Every container has a default layout manager. For example, the default layout for class `Applet` (from AWT) is flow layout, the default layout for class `JApplet` (from `Swing`) is border layout, and the default layout for class `Panel` or `JPanel` is flow layout (see Table 7.9). We can change the layout manager for a container by applying its `setLayout()` method. Make sure you apply this method to the content pane of a `JApplet` or `JFrame` object.

◆◆EXAMPLE 7.6 ────────────────────────────────

The statements below change the layout manager for applet `LayoutDemo` to flow layout and the layout manager for panel `pan` to border layout:

```
public class LayoutDemo extends JApplet {
   public void init() {
      getContentPane().setLayout(new FlowLayout());
      JPanel pan = new JPanel();
      pan.setLayout(new BorderLayout());
```

In each case, the argument for method **setLayout()** is a new layout manager object of the desired type.

◆◆

Flow Layout

Flow layout is the simplest form of layout and is the default for the **JPanel** and **Applet** classes. Flow layout puts as many components on a row as will fit. When a row is filled, the next row of components is assembled.

Within each row, the components are either centered, left-justified, or right-justified. The default is centered, but you can specify a different alignment when you create the flow layout object. Use the predefined constant **FlowLayout.LEFT** to specify left-justified alignment; use the predefined constant **FlowLayout.RIGHT** to specify right-justified alignment:

```
setLayout(new FlowLayout(FlowLayout.RIGHT))
```

Border Layout

Border layout sets up five areas in which components can be placed and is the default for class **JApplet**. Figure 7.32 shows the position of the five areas. You can only put one component in each area, so if you want to put two or more components in an area,

Table 7.9 Layout managers

Layout Manager	Description
`java.awt.BorderLayout`	Arranges objects in five areas of the container: North, West, Center, East, and South
`javax.swing.BoxLayout`	Arranges objects in a single row or column
`java.awt.FlowLayout`	Arranges objects in left-to-right order across the container, flowing down to the next row when a row is filled
`java.awt.GridLayout`	Arranges objects in a two-dimensional grid

you need to first place them in a panel and then place the panel in that area. If an area contains no components, the Center area will expand to fill that space. To specify border layout for a container, use the method call

```
setLayout(new BorderLayout())
```

Figure 7.33 shows the applet for the phone directory with the radio button panel (`radButPanel`) in the North, the text area `instruct` in the West, the data panel in the Center, and the control panel (containing the combo box and `submit` button) in the South. The Center area expands to fill the empty East area. The applet should begin with the statement

```
getContentPane().setLayout(new BorderLayout());
```

The statements that control the placement in the applet follow:

```
getContentPane().add(radButPanel, BorderLayout.NORTH);
getContentPane().add(instruct, BorderLayout.WEST);
getContentPane().add(dataPanel, BorderLayout.CENTER);
getContentPane().add(controlPanel, BorderLayout.SOUTH);
```

Figure 7.32   Five areas for border layout

North		
West	Center	East
South		

Figure 7.33   Phone book GUI with border layout

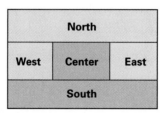

Box Layout

Box layout is a new layout manager introduced in **Swing**. It enables placement of components in either a single row or a single column. For example, the statements below use box layout to align the radio buttons in a single column in panel `radButPanel` (see Fig. 7.34):

```
JPanel radButPanel = new JPanel();
radButPanel.setLayout(new BoxLayout(radButPanel,
                    BoxLayout.Y_AXIS));
radButPanel.add(addRB);
radButPanel.add(getRB);
radButPanel.add(changeRB);
getContentPane().add(radButPanel, BorderLayout.NORTH);
```

Notice that the container name is passed as the first argument in the call to the `BoxLayout` constructor. If the second argument is `BoxLayout.Y_AXIS`, the components are placed in a column; if the second argument is `BoxLayout.X_AXIS`, the components are placed in a row.

Figure 7.34   Phone book GUI with border layout and box layout for panel
`radButPanel`

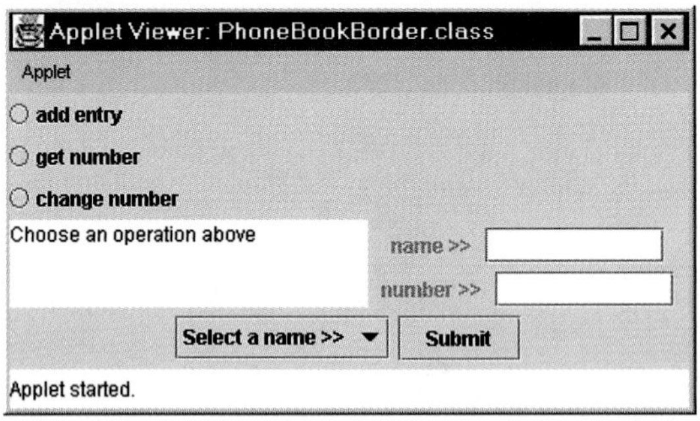

◆◆EXAMPLE 7.7 ──────────────────────────────

This example shows a menu planner in which breakfast food selections are presented as vertically aligned check boxes in a frame with box layout. Each time a box is selected or deselected, total calories are calculated and displayed. Figure 7.35 shows the `FoodItem` class. Figure 7.36 shows the `CalorieCounter` class. Figure 7.37 shows a sample display. This example illustrates a number of important ideas:

1. A class `FoodItem` is defined that associates a food description with a check box.

2. An array of `FoodItem` objects is created "in-line" in the applet.

3. In method `init()`, the array of `FoodItem` objects is traversed to set up the GUI display and to register the applet as an `ItemListener` for each menu item's check box.

4. We use method `getBox()` to return a reference to a menu item's check box.

Figure 7.35 The `FoodItem` class

```java
/* FoodItem.java        Authors: Koffman & Wolz
 * Class for storing a food description, calorie amount, and check box.
 * Uses Swing.
 */
import javax.swing.*;

public class FoodItem {
  // Data fields
  private String description;
  private int calorieAmount;
  private JCheckBox box;

  // Methods
  // Creates a new FoodItem item whose check box has text desc
  FoodItem(String desc, int cal) {
    description = desc;
    calorieAmount = cal;
    box = new JCheckBox(desc);
  }

  public JCheckBox getBox() {
    return box;
  }

  public int getCalories() {
    return calorieAmount;
  }

  public String getDescription() {
    return description;
  }

  public String toString() {
    return description + ", calories " + calorieAmount +
           ", selected: " + box.isSelected();
  }
}
```

Figure 7.36   The `CalorieCounter` GUI

```java
/* CalorieCounter.java          Authors: Koffman & Wolz
 * GUI for counting calories.
 * Uses Swing, AWT, and FoodItem.
 */
import javax.swing.*;
import java.awt.event.*;

public class CalorieCounter extends JFrame
                            implements ItemListener {

  // Data fields
  private JLabel calories = new JLabel("Calories: 0          ");
  // Array of FoodItem items.
  private FoodItem[] foods = {
      new FoodItem("8 oz. orange juice", 80),
      new FoodItem("1 cup black coffee", 0),
      new FoodItem("1 serving cornflakes with 1/2 cup skim milk", 120),
      new FoodItem("1 delicious sugar coated donut", 600),
      new FoodItem("8 oz. of skim milk", 70),
      new FoodItem("2 slices white toast, lightly buttered", 200)
      };

  // Methods
  // postcondition: Creates the calorie counter GUI.
  public CalorieCounter() {

    // Define layout manager as box layout with vertical align.
    getContentPane().setLayout(
      new BoxLayout(getContentPane(), BoxLayout.Y_AXIS));

    // Add each check box to frame and register it.
    for(int i = 0; i < foods.length; i++) {
      getContentPane().add(foods[i].getBox());
      foods[i].getBox().addItemListener(this);
    }

    // Add label calories to frame.
    getContentPane().add(calories);
  }
```

Figure 7.36 The `CalorieCounter` GUI, *continued*

```java
// postcondition: Calculates and displays total calories
//    when a check box changes state.
public void itemStateChanged(ItemEvent itEv) {
    // Add total calories for all boxes that are checked.
    int total = 0;
    for (int i = 0; i < foods.length; i++) {
        JCheckBox box = foods[i].getBox();
        if (box.isSelected())
            total += foods[i].getCalories();
    }
    calories.setText("Calories: " + total);
}

// Creates the frame and closes the frame.
public static void main(String[] args) {
    CalorieCounter cal = new CalorieCounter();
    cal.setSize(300, 200);
    cal.setVisible(true);
    cal.setTitle("Calorie Counter");
    cal.addWindowListener(
        new WindowAdapter() {
            public void windowClosing(WindowEvent e) {
                System.exit(0);
            }
        }
    );
}
}
```

Figure 7.37 A sample display for the calorie counter

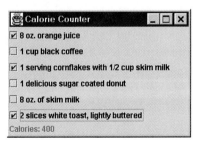

The constructor in the `FoodItem` class stores the food description and the calorie amount and creates a check box for that food item. In method `init()`, the statement

```
getContentPane().setLayout(
    new BoxLayout(getContentPane(), BoxLayout.Y_AXIS));
```

sets up a box layout for the frame with one column, creating a display that is easy to read. The **for** loop goes through the array of `FoodItem` objects. The statements

```
getContentPane().add(foods[i].getBox());
foods[i].getBox().addItemListener(this);
```

add the check box for each `FoodItem` object to the frame and register the applet as its listener. Finally, within `init()`, a label for total calories is added to the applet.

The `itemStateChanged()` method recalculates total calories every time a check box changes state. The **for** loop goes through the array, retrieving the `JCheckBox` object associated with each `FoodItem` object:

```
JCheckBox box = foods[i].getBox();
```

If the box is checked, the calories for this food are added to the total

```
if (box.isSelected())
    total += foods[i].getCalories();
```

After loop exit, the label **calories** is updated to show the new total.

◆◆

Grid Layout

Grid layout is used to position components in a two-dimensional grid. Most often it is used to place buttons in a grid pattern. For example, we might want to create a grid pattern of four rows and three columns for a calculator applet. Buttons for the digit characters 1 through 9 would be placed in the first three rows and the fourth row would contain buttons with text C (for clear), the digit 0, and the decimal point (period) character (see Fig. 7.38).

In class `CalculatorButtons` (see Fig. 7.39), method `init()` builds the applet shown in Fig. 7.38. The statement

```
buttonGrid.setLayout(new GridLayout(4, 3));
```

creates a grid layout manager for this panel that places objects in a grid with four rows and three columns.

Figure 7.38   Using grid layout for a calculator's buttons

Array `digitButtons` is an array of `JButton` objects. The `for` statement below creates all the buttons for array `digitButtons` and adds them to panel `buttonGrid`.

```
for (int nextBut = 0; nextBut < digitButtons.length; nextBut++) {
   digitButtons[nextBut] = new JButton(buttonLabels[nextBut]);
   buttonGrid.add(digitButtons[nextBut]);
   digitButtons[nextBut].addActionListener(this);
}
```

The first statement in the loop creates the next button (subscript `nextBut`); the button's text is the next string in array `buttonLabels`. The second statement adds the new button to panel `buttonGrid`. The last statement registers the applet as a listener for action events generated by this button. The first three buttons added to the panel will be placed in row 1, the next three buttons will be placed in row 2, and so on.

In method `actionPerformed()`, the `if` statement condition below is `true` when `nextBut` is the subscript of the button that was pressed:

```
if (whichButton == digitButtons[nextBut])
   result.setText("You pressed " +
                  digitButtons[nextBut].getText());
```

The button text (a string) is retrieved (by `getText()`) and placed in text field result.

Figure 7.39   Class `CalculatorButtons`

```java
/* CalculatorButtons.java          Authors: Koffman & Wolz
 * Applet for demonstrating grid layout.
 * Uses Swing and AWT.
 */
import javax.swing.*;
import java.awt.event.*;
import java.awt.*;

public class CalculatorButtons extends JApplet
                               implements ActionListener {

  // Data fields
  private JButton[] digitButtons;
  private JTextField result = new JTextField(10);

  // Methods
  // postcondition: Displays a 4 X 3 grid of buttons in the applet.
  //    The buttons in the first row have labels 1, 2, 3.
  public void init() {
    String[] buttonLabels =  {"1", "2", "3", "4", "5", "6",
                              "7", "8", "9", "C", "0", "."};

    // Create an array of buttons.
    digitButtons = new JButton[buttonLabels.length];

    // Create a 4 x 3 grid for placement of buttons.
    JPanel buttonGrid = new JPanel();
    buttonGrid.setLayout(new GridLayout(4, 3));

    // Create a button with each button label, add it to buttonGrid,
    //    and register the applet as a listener.
    for (int nextBut = 0; nextBut < digitButtons.length; nextBut++) {
      digitButtons[nextBut] = new JButton(buttonLabels[nextBut]);
      digitButtons[nextBut].addActionListener(this);
      buttonGrid.add(digitButtons[nextBut]);
    }

    JLabel instruct = new JLabel("Press a button");
    getContentPane().add(instruct, BorderLayout.NORTH);
```

Figure 7.39 Class `CalculatorButtons,` *continued*

```
   getContentPane().add(buttonGrid, BorderLayout.CENTER);
   getContentPane().add(result, BorderLayout.SOUTH);
 }

 // postcondition: Displays the label of the button pressed.
 public void actionPerformed(ActionEvent aE) {
   Object whichButton = aE.getSource();
   for (int nextBut = 0; nextBut < digitButtons.length; nextBut++) {
     if (whichButton == digitButtons[nextBut])
       result.setText("You pressed " +  digitButtons[nextBut].getText());
   }
 }
}
```

In the next case study, we use different layout managers. We also write a GUI for an application involving a class we have seen before.

CASE STUDY A GUI FOR A PAYROLL APPLICATION

PROBLEM   In Section 4.4, we wrote a payroll application with a loop that processed the pay data for a collection of employees (type `Employee`). We want to write a GUI that interacts with the program user to get the data and display results (see Fig. 7.40). We will write the GUI as an application.

ANALYSIS   The GUI will be a client of class `Employee`, the class that knows how to calculate gross pay and net pay. If we write this application as a GUI, we do not need a loop. The problem inputs and outputs are listed below.

Problem Inputs

Employee ID number
Hours worked
Hourly rate
Employee is a union member (true/false)
Overtime rate

Problem Outputs

Gross pay for each employee
Net pay

The program input consists of each employee's ID, hours, and rate, an indication of whether the employee is a union member, and the employee's overtime rate. The program output consists of each employee's gross pay and net pay as well as the total gross payroll amount.

DESIGN Class **Employee** has already been designed and implemented. However, it must be modified slightly because the original version assumed that all employees were union members and that the overtime rate was a constant. We leave this as an exercise (see Programming Exercise 3).

The GUI class contains the following components:

◆ A label and text field for the ID number

◆ A label and text field for the hours worked

◆ A label and text field for the hourly rate

◆ A check box for indicating employee's union status

◆ Three radio buttons for selecting the employee's overtime rate (1.0, 1.5, or 2.0)

◆ Three buttons for controlling the operations (view data, compute pay, clear total payroll)

◆ A text area to show the outputs

Figure 7.40 **GUI for payroll program**

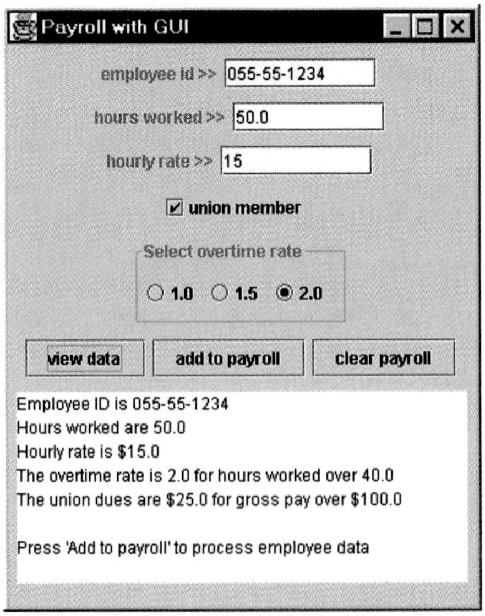

The GUI consists of four methods:

1. The constructor builds the GUI.

2. Method `actionPerformed()` responds to events that are generated by pressing a control button or selecting a radio button.

3. Method `itemStateChanged()` responds to events that are generated by changing the check box state.

4. Method `main()` creates an instance of the GUI and closes it when the user is done.

Method `actionPeformed()` executes when a control button or radio button is pressed. In the following algorithm, the first three conditions test whether a control button is pressed; the last condition is true when a radio button is pressed.

> *Algorithm for `actionPerformed()`*
>
> `if` the view data button is pressed
>   Store the data in an `Employee` object
>   and display the state of the `Employee` object.
> `else if` the add to payroll button is pressed
>   Store the data in an `Employee` object.
>   Calculate gross pay and net pay.
>   Add gross pay to total gross pay.
>   Show the state of the `Employee` object and display total pay so far.
> `else if` the clear payroll button is pressed
>   Display final value of total payroll.
>   Reset total payroll to 0.
> `else if` a radio button is pressed
>   Reset the overtime rate as specified.

IMPLEMENTATION   Figure 7.41 shows the data field declarations and constructor for class `PayrollGUI`. The constuctor uses box layout for the data panel and flow layout for the frame's content pane and the other panels.

Figure 7.42 shows method `actionPerformed()`. In method `actionPerformed()`, variable `buttonPressed` references the button object that generates the action event. The condition

```
(buttonPressed == r1 && r1.isSelected())
```

is **true** if radio button `r1` was selected and if its state is on. If so, the statements

```
overtimeRate = Double.parseDouble(r1.getText());
programmer.setOvertimeRate(overtimeRate);
```

set the employee's overtime pay rate to the value indicated by the text for radio button `r1`.

Figure 7.41   Class `PayrollGUI` data fields and constructor

```java
import javax.swing.*;
/* PayrollGUI.java          Authors: Koffman & Wolz
 * Payroll application with a GUI.
 * Uses Employee.
 */
import javax.swing.*;
import java.awt.event.*;
import java.awt.*;

public class PayrollGUI extends JFrame
                        implements ActionListener, ItemListener {
  // Data fields
  private JTextField empIDText = new JTextField(10);
  private JTextField hoursText = new JTextField(10);
  private JTextField rateText = new JTextField(10);
  private JCheckBox c1 = new JCheckBox("union member");
  private JRadioButton r1 = new JRadioButton("1.0");
  private JRadioButton r2 = new JRadioButton("1.5");
  private JRadioButton r3 = new JRadioButton("2.0");
  private JTextArea output = new JTextArea(8, 30);
  private JButton viewData = new JButton("view data");
  private JButton addPayroll = new JButton("add to payroll");
  private JButton clearPayroll = new JButton("clear payroll");
  private double payroll;   // accumulating payroll amount
  Employee programmer = new Employee();


  // Creates the initial payroll GUI
  public PayrollGUI() {
    // Define the layout manager for the frame.
    getContentPane().setLayout(new FlowLayout());

    // Fill idPanel and add it to frame.
    JPanel dataPanel = new JPanel();
    dataPanel.setLayout(new BoxLayout(dataPanel, BoxLayout.Y_AXIS));
    JPanel idPanel = new JPanel();
    JLabel askEmpID = new JLabel("employee id >> ");
    idPanel.add(askEmpID);
    idPanel.add(empIDText);
    dataPanel.add(idPanel);
```

Figure 7.41   Class `PayrollGUI` data fields and constructor, *continued*

```
// Fill hoursPanel and add it to frame.
JPanel hoursPanel = new JPanel();
JLabel askHours = new JLabel("hours worked >> ");
hoursPanel.add(askHours);
hoursPanel.add(hoursText);
dataPanel.add(hoursPanel);

// Fill ratePanel and add it to frame.
JPanel ratePanel = new JPanel();
JLabel askRate = new JLabel("hourly rate >> ");
ratePanel.add(askRate);
ratePanel.add(rateText);
dataPanel.add(ratePanel);

// Fill unionPanel and add it to dataPanel.
JPanel unionPanel = new JPanel();
unionPanel.add(c1);
dataPanel.add(unionPanel);
getContentPane().add(dataPanel);

// Fill overtimePanel and add it to frame.
JPanel overtimePanel = new JPanel();
overtimePanel.add(r1);
overtimePanel.add(r2);
overtimePanel.add(r3);
overtimePanel.setBorder(
   BorderFactory.createTitledBorder("Select overtime rate"));
getContentPane().add(overtimePanel);

// Add each radio button to buttonGroup rates.
ButtonGroup rates = new ButtonGroup();
rates.add(r1);
rates.add(r2);
rates.add(r3);

// Fill buttonPanel and add it to frame.
JPanel buttonPanel = new JPanel();
buttonPanel.add(viewData);
buttonPanel.add(addPayroll);
buttonPanel.add(clearPayroll);
getContentPane().add(buttonPanel);
```

Figure 7.41   Class `PayrollGUI` data fields and constructor, *continued*

```
    // Add output text area to Frame().
    getContentPane().add(output);

    // Register applet as listener for action events
    //   on all buttons.
    viewData.addActionListener(this);
    addPayroll.addActionListener(this);
    clearPayroll.addActionListener(this);
    r1.addActionListener(this);
    r2.addActionListener(this);
    r3.addActionListener(this);

    // Register applet as listener for item events
    //   on checkbox
    c1.addItemListener(this);
}
```

Figure 7.42   Method `actionPerformed()`

```
// postcondition: Performs the operation requested if a
//   control button is pressed. If a radio button is pressed,
//   sets the overtime rate to the value in the button.
public void actionPerformed(ActionEvent aE) {
    String empID;
    String hoursStr;
    String rateStr;
    double hours;
    double rate;
    double overtimeRate;

    Object buttonPressed = aE.getSource();
    if (buttonPressed == viewData) {
        // Get data.
        empID = empIDText.getText();
        hoursStr = hoursText.getText();
        hours = Double.parseDouble(hoursStr);
        rateStr = rateText.getText();
        rate = Double.parseDouble(rateStr);
```

Figure 7.42   Method `actionPerformed()`, *continued*

```
   // Store data in programmer.
   programmer.setPayData(empID, hours, rate);
   output.setText(programmer.toString() + "\n" +
      "Press 'Add to payroll' to process employee data\n");
}
else if (buttonPressed == addPayroll) {
   // Get data, calculate gross and net, and add
   //   gross to total.
   empID = empIDText.getText();
   hoursStr = hoursText.getText().trim();
   hours = Double.parseDouble(hoursStr);
   rateStr = rateText.getText().trim();
   rate = Double.parseDouble(rateStr);

   // Store data and compute gross pay.
   programmer.setPayData(empID, hours, rate);
   double gross = programmer.computeGross();

   // Compute net pay, given gross pay.
   double net = programmer.computeNet(gross);

   // Add gross pay to payroll
   payroll = payroll + gross;

   // Display pay amounts and payroll so far.
   output.setText(programmer.toString() +
                  "Gross pay is $" + gross +
                  "\nNet pay is $" + net +
                  "\n\nTotal gross payroll is $" + payroll);
   empIDText.setText("");
   rateText.setText("");
   hoursText.setText("");
}
else if (buttonPressed == clearPayroll) {
   // Clear payroll
   output.setText("Final gross payroll is $" + payroll +
                  "\nGross payroll reset to 0");
   payroll = 0;
   empIDText.setText("");
   rateText.setText("");
   hoursText.setText("");
}
```

Figure 7.42   Method `actionPerformed()`, *continued*

```
   else if (r1.isSelected()) {
      overtimeRate = Double.parseDouble(r1.getText());
      programmer.setOvertimeRate(overtimeRate);
   }
   else if (r2.isSelected()) {
      overtimeRate = Double.parseDouble(r2.getText());
      programmer.setOvertimeRate(overtimeRate);
   }
   else if (r3.isSelected()) {
      overtimeRate = Double.parseDouble(r3.getText());
      programmer.setOvertimeRate(overtimeRate);
   }

}  // end actionPerformed()
```

Fig. 7.43 shows methods `itemStateChanged()` and `main()`. Method `itemStateChanged()` executes when an item event occurs. If the item event was caused by the user selecting the check box **(choice == c1** is **true)**, method `setInUnion()` is called to set the employee's union status to the check box state (**true** or **false**).

TESTING   Fig. 7.44 shows the GUI after the data for an employee are typed in and the **view data** button is pressed. The employee is a union member whose overtime rate is 1.5 times the normal hourly rate. If the data are incorrect, the user can edit the data by editing the text fields or by changing the state of the check box or radio buttons and can then view it again. Or the user can press the **add to payroll** button to process the data (see Fig. 7.40). The user can process as many employees as needed before pressing the **clear payroll** button, causing the total payroll amount to be displayed and then reset to zero.

Figure 7.43 Methods `itemStateChanged()` and `main()`

```
// postcondition: The employee's union status is set
//   to match the check box state.
public void itemStateChanged(ItemEvent iE) {
  Object choice = iE.getItemSelectable();
  if (choice == c1)
    programmer.setInUnion(c1.isSelected());
}


// Creates the frame and closes the frame.
public static void main(String[] args) {
  PayrollGUI pay = new PayrollGUI();
  pay.setSize(350, 430);
  pay.setVisible(true);
  pay.setTitle("Payroll with GUI");
  pay.addWindowListener(
      new WindowAdapter() {
          public void windowClosing(WindowEvent e) {
              System.exit(0);
          }
      }
  );
}
}
```

Figure 7.44   GUI after pressing `add to payroll` button

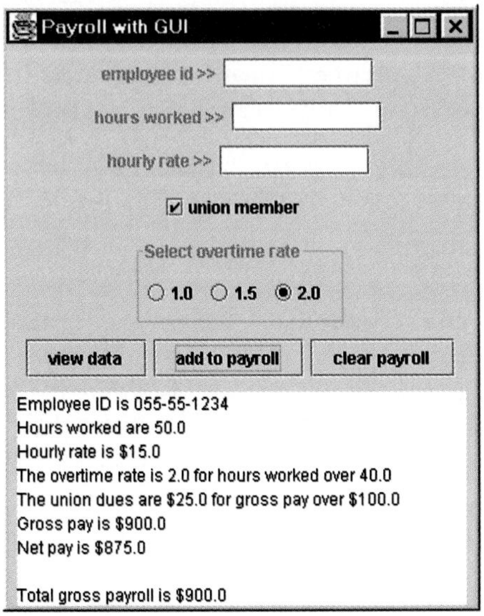

EXERCISES FOR SECTION 7.8

SELF-CHECK

1. Describe the characteristics of the following layout managers:

   `BorderLayout`

   `BoxLayout`

   `FlowLayout`

   `GridLayout`

2. What is the default layout for class `JApplet`? For class `Applet`? For class `JPanel`?

3. Why are layout managers useful?

4. How will the following buttons be displayed?

```
pan.setLayout(new GridLayout(3, 2));
pan.add(new Button("1"));
pan.add(new Button("2"));
pan.add(new Button("3"));
pan.add(new Button("4"));
pan.add(new Button("5"));
pan.add(new Button("6"));
```

PROGRAMMING

1. Create an applet that has a grid of buttons that looks like this:

		red		
	orange		purple	
yellow		white		blue
		green		

2. Use box layout for the panels in class **PhoneBookGUI**. Place the radio buttons in vertical alignment in panel **radButPanel**. Create a new name panel with a name label and name text field in horizontal alignment. Create a new number panel with a number label and number text field in horizontal alignment. Place both these panels in a data panel in vertical alignment. Place the **submit** button and combo box in vertical alignment in a control panel. Place all these panels in vertical alignment in the applet.

3. Modify class **Employee** (Fig. 4.12). Change the constant **OVERTIME_RATE** to a variable. Also, add a **boolean** variable **inUnion** that represents an employee's union status. Add the additional mutator (setter) methods: **setPayData()**, **setOvertimeRate**, and **setUnionStatus()**. Finally, modify method **computeNet()** to take into account the fact that not all employees are in the union.

7.9 Common Programming Errors

Don't forget to create a listener for an event generator (for example, a button) by registering the applet, or a listener object, using methods **addActionListener()** or **addItemListener()**. If your GUI does not seem to respond to an event, the first thing to do is to check that you did indeed register a listener for the event generator. For buttons, use action listeners and for check boxes and combo boxes, use item listeners. If the action performed is not the correct one, look further into method `actionPerformed()` (or `itemStateChanged()`).

Make sure you indicate that your applet (or listener class) implements the required interface (`ActionListener` for action events, `ItemListener` for item events). You must also define the abstract method that is specified by that interface (`actionPerformed()` or `itemStateChanged()`). If you do not, you will get a syntax error stating that your class must be declared abstract.

If you get a `class not found` error when attempting to load and execute an applet, make sure the `.html` file and all `.class` files for the applet are in the same folder. Also make sure that you have spelled the applet file name correctly in the `.html` file. Remember, case matters.

If you attempt to process numeric data in a text field before the text field has been filled or when the text field contains nonnumeric characters, you will get a run-time error. Often this will be an `ArithmeticException` error. We will discuss how to prevent these kinds of errors at the beginning of the next chapter.

When adding GUI components to a top-level container (applet or frame), make sure you add the component to the content pane for that container. You can access the content pane using method `getContentPane()`.

If an applet or frame is not displayed properly, you can adjust the dimensions by changing the `.html` file (for an applet) or the arguments of method `setSize()` (for a frame). This is a trial-and-error process. You can also improve the appearance of the applet by using a different layout manager.

CHAPTER REVIEW

1. The AWT and `Swing` provide a number of classes for building GUIs. Java developers recommend the use of `Swing` classes and components, but `Swing` is still intertwined with the AWT. AWT components are drawn using native code for a particular platform (called peer components), whereas `Swing` components are drawn using code that is written in Java (called lightweight components). This means that AWT components are platform dependent, whereas `Swing` components have a uniform look and feel.

2. The GUI components we studied were containers and atomic components. Containers are used to group or contain other components. They included applets (class `JApplet`), frames (class `JFrame`), and panels (class `JPanel`). We use the `add()` method to add a component to a container and a method call has the form *container*`.add(`*component*`)`. For an applet or frame, a method call has the form `getContentPane().add(`*component*`)` because we always add components to the content pane associated with an applet or frame.

3. The atomic components we studied were components for displaying or entering text: labels (class **JLabel**), text fields (class **JTextField**), and text areas (class **JTextArea**). We also studied components for selecting operations or making choices: buttons (class **JButton**), check boxes (class **JCheckBox**), radio buttons (class **JRadioButton**), button groups (class **ButtonGroup**), and combo boxes (class **JComboBox**).

4. The AWT event model is based on event listeners and event generators. An event is a button press, a mouse click or mouse movement, or an item selection. We studied two kinds of events: action events (pressing a button) and item events (selecting an item). Components in a GUI are event generators. To respond to an event generated by a component, the applet must be registered as a listener for events generated by that component. The applet must also implement the interface associated with that kind of event (**ActionListener** for action events, **ItemListener** for item events). Implementing the interface requires that the applet have an **actionPerformed()** method (for **ActionListener**), an **itemStateChanged()** method (for **ItemListener**), or both. When an action event occurs for which the applet is a registered listener, the **actionPerformed()** method executes; when an item event occurs for which the applet is a registered listener, the **itemStateChanged()** method executes. These methods must contain code to identify the event source and to take appropriate action.

5. To simplify the code, you can declare inner listener classes and create instances of these class that serve as event listeners. Each inner class can implement a listener interface and contain an **actionPerformed()** or **itemStateChanged()** method. An object whose type is an inner class can be registered as a listener for events generated by a subset of the GUI components. The **actionPerformed()** or **itemStateChanged()** method for this class will respond only to events generated by this subset of components. In this way, the task of responding to events can be parceled out to several classes instead of just the applet.

6. You can use layout managers to position components and containers within an applet or frame. The default layout for applets and frames is border layout, but the easiest layout to use is flow layout (the default for panels). We also studied box layout, which positions components in a row or column, and grid layout, which positions components in a two-dimensional grid.

✔ **QUICK-CHECK EXERCISES**

1. Contrast the "stop-and-wait" model of user interaction with the event model.

2. Explain the difference between a component and a container.

3. What is a layout manager?

4. How do event generators and listeners interact?

5. What does the method `actionPerformed()` do in an action event listener and which class declares it as an abstract method?

6. What does the method `itemStateChanged()` do in an item event listener and which class declares it as an abstract method?

7. We use method _____ to retrieve information from a text field, text area, or check box. We use method _____ to store information in a text field, text area, or check box.

8. If you have three radio buttons that represent choices, can more than one be selected? If your answer is Yes, explain how you can ensure that only one will be selected.

9. Can you change the number of choices available using an array of check boxes? Can you change the number of choices available using a combo box?

10. Describe the manner of layout provided by the border layout manager, the box layout manager, and the grid layout manager.

ANSWERS TO QUICK-CHECK EXERCISES

1. In the "stop-and-wait" model, the program and perhaps even the CPU literally stop and wait for the user to respond to a prompt. In the event model, the operating system informs processes that events have occurred.

2. A component is any GUI object that can be displayed. A container is a kind of GUI component that can contain other components. For example, a panel is a container.

3. A layout manager is an object associated with a container that determines how the components in the container will be arranged.

4. An event generator creates an event object when the user interacts with it. A specific method of an event listener is called to inform the listener that the event has occurred. The event listener must register with the generator in order to be informed of events.

5. The `actionPerformed()` method is automatically called when an action event occurs. The listener's `actionPerformed()` method contains the statements that are to be executed as a result of the event. It is an abstract method in interface `ActionListener`.

6. The `itemStateChanged()` method is automatically called when an item event occurs. The listener's `itemStateChanged()` method contains the statements that are to be executed as a result of the event. It is an abstract method in interface `ItemListener`.

7. `getText()`, `setText()`

8. Yes, you need to put them in a button group (type `ButtonGroup`) using method `add()` to ensure that only one can be selected.

9. No, an array has a fixed size. Yes, you can use method `addItem()` to add a choice to the list of choices displayed by a combo box.

10. Using the border layout manager, you can put components in one of five areas in a container (North, West, Center, East, South). Using box layout, you can put components in a row or in a column. Using grid layout, you can put components in a two-dimensional grid.

REVIEW QUESTIONS

1. Is HTML a programming language?

2. Describe the use of the `add()` method of the `Container` class.

3. If `b1` and `b2` are buttons declared as data fields within an applet, write statements to register the applet as a listener for events generated by pressing these buttons.

4. Write an `actionPerformed()` method that increments `b1Count` when `b1` is pressed and `b2Count` when `b2` is pressed. Also display a message in a data field indicating which button was pressed.

5. Assume you have declared an array `choices` of type `JCheckBox[]`. Write a loop that adds each check box to a panel and registers the applet as a listener for each check box.

6. Write code that adds the check boxes to the panel in a single column.

7. List the steps needed to "convert" an applet to a frame. Do you still need an HTML file for the frame?

8. Write code that places an array of 10 buttons in a 2×5 grid pattern. Set the text for the first row to the letters *a* through *e* and the text for the second row to the digits 1 through 5.

9. Create a combo box that contains the vowels as choices and contains `select a vowel` as its initial choice. Write an `itemStateChanged()` method that increments `countA`, `countE`, and so on, depending on which vowel is selected. After each selection, reset the combo box so that `select a vowel` is the selection.

10. Pressing the Enter key when the cursor is in a text field generates an action event. Write an `actionPerformed()` method that appends the text typed into text field `input` to the text shown in text area `output` whenever the Enter key is pressed in text field `input`.

PROGRAMMING PROJECTS

1. Using `TextFields`, write an applet that requests a name, street address, city name, and zip code from a user. A **submit** button collects all the data from the text fields, stores it in a vector, and asks for data for another person. A **quit** button ends the session and displays all of the information within a text area of the applet.

2. Modify the payroll GUI and methods in Section 7.8 to interact with class **NewCompany** as described in Section 6.3. You should have control buttons with the text **view data**, **store data**, and **calculate payroll**. Pressing **view data** should show what data have been entered; pressing **store data** should store the data entered in the next array element; pressing **calculate payroll** should cause the total payroll amount to be computed and displayed.

3. Design a GUI for a simple calculator with a panel similar to the one in Fig. 7.38 for entering a number. As each character is typed in, append it to the numeric string so far and display the numeric string so far in a text field. When you finish typing in a number, press the control button **store first number** (or **store second number**). After typing in both numbers, select a radio button (+, -, *, /, ^), perform the selected operation (^ means raise to a power), and display the result in the text field. If both numbers have not been entered, display an appropriate error message in the text field. You should declare a **Calculator** class as well as a GUI class.

4. Write a GUI that can be used with a collection of CDs. Enter the CD data (name, artist, year, price) using the GUI, display the CD, and store it in an array of CDs. Besides **view** and **store**, you should have control buttons that allow you to retrieve all the data for a particular CD given its title, calculate the total value of your collection, view all the CDs by a particular artist, and delete a CD from your collection.

5. Assume you have a collection of CDs, cassette tapes, and vinyl records. Create an abstract class, **MusicMedia**, for this collection that stores the title, artist's name, year, cost, category of music, and number of songs. For a CD, also store the number of tracks. For a record, also store the size of the record (78, 45, 33). For a cassette, also store the length of the tape in minutes. Store your collection in an array of **MusicMedia** elements. You should be able to display all the entries, display all the entries by a particular artist, display all the entries for a particular title, display all the entries for a particular kind of media, and so on. Provide a GUI for this project.

8

Exceptions, Streams, and Files

All our example programs have received input data from the keyboard or through options selected by a mouse. All program output was displayed on the screen. This is fine for small programs, but they limit the effectiveness of programs that process large amounts of data. If we need to run a program many times (for example, during debugging), we have to type in the program data each time. Also, the program results disappear when the program finishes execution.

We can use files to solve both of these problems. We can save the data for a program in a semipermanent form in a file and have the program read its data from this **input file**. If we want to change the data for a new program run, we can edit the input file using a text editor before we run the program. Also, we can write the program results to an **output file** instead of just displaying them in a window.

In this chapter we discuss the use of data files (Java streams) for storing program input and output. Java can process two kinds of data files:

text and binary. We will learn the differences between these two types of files and how to use both types.

We begin by discussing exceptions. **Exceptions** are run-time errors that can occur in Java programs. Exceptions are common when using files, and these programs must include steps to handle exceptions.

8.1   Exceptions

Using `if` Statements to Prevent Errors

We have practiced **defensive programming**. By this we mean being careful to prevent the occurrence of run-time errors that terminate execution of a program. The `if` statement below **guards** the first assignment statement and prevents it from executing when `count` is 0. If `count` is 0, we display an error message and set the average to 0.

```
if (count != 0) {
    average = sum / count;
}
else {
    average = 0;
    System.out.println("Error - count is zero");
}
```

Without guarding the first assignment statement, we would get a run-time error when `count` is 0. The Java Virtual Machine (JVM) would terminate the program and display the error message

```
Arithmetic exception: / by zero
```

Exception Classes

An attempt to divide by zero causes a `/ by zero` exception, which is an instance of the class `ArithmeticException`. The process of creating an exception instance is called **throwing** an exception. Table 8.1 lists some common run-time exceptions (subclasses of `RuntimeException`) that you may have seen in your programming.

`try-catch` Statement

As we demonstrated earlier, we can use `if` statements to prevent the occurrence of errors or exceptions that we can anticipate. However, sometimes we may know that an error might occur, but we have no way to guard against its occurrence using an `if` statement. Java provides a mechanism called the **`try-catch`** statement, which

Table 8.1   Class `RuntimeException` and some subclasses

Exception Class	Kind of Error
`RuntimeException`	Superclass of run-time exceptions
`ArithmeticException`	Division by zero or some other arithmetic error
`ArrayIndexOutOfBoundsException`	An array index is outside the allowable range
`ClassCastException`	An attempt to perform an invalid casting operation
`IllegalArgumentException`	Calling a method with an improper argument
`NegativeArraySizeException`	Declaring an array with a negative size
`NullPointerException`	Attempt to access an object that does not exist (reference is `null`)
`NumberFormatException`	Signals an illegal number format.

enables us to "catch" exceptions and to handle them, thereby preventing an exception from terminating the program.

Exceptions often occur during program input. The first statement in Figure 8.1 prompts for an integer value, storing it in the string referenced by **numStr**. The **try** block contains a statement that attempts to convert the string to a type **int** value. If **numStr** does not contain a numeric string (for example, 1oo instead of 10), a **NumberFormatException** is thrown. The **catch** block executes when a number format exception occurs and **catches** (or handles) the exception that was thrown.

The first line of the catch block

```
catch (NumberFormatException ex) {
```

resembles a method header. The formal parameter type is **NumberFormat-Exception** and its name is **ex**. The body of the **catch** block displays an error message window (see Fig. 8.2) and sets **children** to its default value of 1, and program execution continues with the first statement after the **catch** block.

Figure 8.1   A fragment with a `try-catch` statement

```
String numStr = JOptionPane.showInputDialog("Number of children:");
int children = 1;        // problem input, default is 1
try {
   children = Integer.parseInt(numStr);
}
catch (NumberFormatException ex) {   // handle number format exception
   JOptionPane.showMessageDialog(null,
            "Invalid integer " + numStr + " - default is 1",
            "Error", JOptionPane.ERROR_MESSAGE);
}
```

Figure 8.2   Error message window for `try-catch` statement in Fig. 8.1

In the call to `showMessageDialog()`, the second argument forms the error message, which is displayed. The third argument sets the window title to **Error**. The fourth argument indicates that this is an error message window and causes the stop sign to be displayed.

`try-catch` statement syntax

```
try {
        // Statements that may throw an exception
        . . .
}
catch (exceptionType1 parameterName) {
        // statements to execute for exceptionType1
        . . .
}
catch (exceptionType2 parameterName) {
        // statements to execute for exceptionType2
        . . .
}
. . .



catch (exceptionTypek parameterName) {
        // statements to execute for exceptionTypek
        . . .
}
finally {
        // Statements to execute after try block and catch block
}
```

Example:

```
try {
   z = x / y;
}
catch (ArithmeticException ex) {
   System.out.println("Illegal arithmetic operation");
}
```

Interpretation: The **try** block executes. If there are no exceptions, all **catch** blocks that follow the **try** block are skipped. However, if an exception is thrown, we exit the **try** block and execute the statements in the first **catch** block whose exception type (**catch** parameter) matches the one thrown or whose exception type is a superclass of the one thrown. If there is no **catch** block for that exception type, Java displays an error message in the console window, indicating the type of exception that was thrown and halts program execution.

The **finally** block is optional and is used to do any "clean-up" that might be necessary. If no exceptions are thrown, the **finally** block executes after the **try** block executes. If an exception is thrown, the **finally** block executes after the appropriate **catch** block executes.

Note: At least one **catch** block or a **finally** block must follow the **try** block.

◆◆EXAMPLE 8.1 ─────────────────────────────────

Figure 8.3 shows the use of a **try–catch** statement to **catch** an attempt to convert a string stored in **inputStr** that is not numeric to a number. In the **try** block, the statement

```
inputDist = Double.parseDouble(inputStr);
```

raises a **NumberFormatException** if **inputStr** is not numeric. The **catch** block causes the error message **Bad numeric string – try again** to be displayed in the output text area (see Fig. 8.4). Method **actionPerformed()** is exited immediately, and the user can edit the input data and press a control button to execute **actionPerformed()** again. This method is based on Fig. 7.12; the part that follows the **try–catch** statement is unchanged.

Figure 8.3   Method `actionPerformed()` with `try-catch`

```
// precondition: Text field input contains numeric
//    information.
// postcondition: Performs the conversion requested by
//    user, placing the result in text area output.
public void actionPerformed(ActionEvent aE) {

   double inputDist;  // input, number to convert
   String inputStr = input.getText();
   // Convert a valid numeric string to a number.
   try {
      inputDist = Double.parseDouble(inputStr);
   }
   catch (NumberFormatException ex) {
      output.setText("Bad numeric string - try again");
      return;
   }


   // Create DistanceConverter object and do conversion.
   double outputDist; // output, result of conversion
   DistanceConverter dC = new DistanceConverter();
   Object buttonPressed = aE.getSource();
   if (buttonPressed == toMiles) {
      outputDist = dC.toMiles(inputDist);
      output.setText(inputDist + " kilometers converts to\n" +
                     outputDist + " miles");
   }
   else if (buttonPressed == toKms) {
      outputDist = dC.toKilometers(inputDist);
      output.setText(inputDist + " miles converts to\n" +
                     outputDist +  " kilometers");
   }

   input.requestFocus();   // Gives the focus to input
}
```

Figure 8.4   Effect of `try-catch` statement in Fig. 8.3

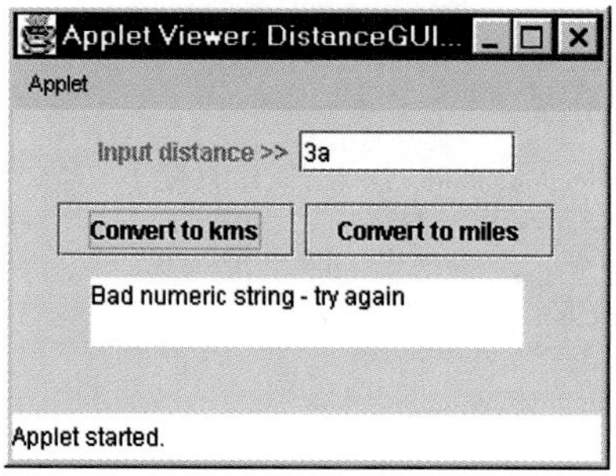

Order of catch Blocks

If different kinds of exceptions can occur when executing the statements in a **try** block, you should provide a **catch** block for each kind of exception. A **catch** block will handle any exceptions that match its exception type (parameter). It will also handle exception types that are subclasses of its exception type (parameter). The order of the **catch** blocks is important. Only the first **catch** block that will handle a particular exception type executes, so the most specific exception type should come first. You may get a **catch is unreachable** syntax error if your catch blocks do not follow this order. We illustrate this in the next example.

◆◆EXAMPLE 8.2 ━━━━━━━━━━━━━━━━━━━━━━━━━━━━━━━━━━━━

The **main()** method in class **MyException** (Fig. 8.5) contains a **try-catch** statement with two catch blocks. The first **catch** block handles a number format exception as we described earlier. Class **Exception** is the superclass of all exception classes, so the second **catch** block executes for all other exception types. We include it as a precaution because we don't know what other exception types may occur.

The first statement in the **try** block

```
double oneShare = 100.0 / children;
```

calculates each child's share of an estate as a percentage. It throws a "division by zero" exception if the user enters 0 as the value of **children**. The **catch** block with parameter type **Exception** executes because we did not provide an **if** statement to guard against "division by zero" errors or a **catch** block with parameter type **ArithmeticException** (see Programming Exercise 2). Figure 8.6 shows the console window when **children** is zero.

Figure 8.5 Class `MyException` with two `catch` blocks

```java
/* MyException.java         Authors: Koffman & Wolz
 * Demonstrates try/catch.
 * Uses Swing.
 */
import javax.swing.JOptionPane;

public class MyException {

  public static void main(String[] args) {
    String numStr =
        JOptionPane.showInputDialog("Number of children:");

    int children = 1;    // problem input, default is 1
    try {
      children = Integer.parseInt(numStr);
      double oneShare = 100.0 / children;
      System.out.println("Each child's share is " +
                         oneShare + " percent");
    }
    catch (NumberFormatException ex) {
      // Handle number format exception.
      JOptionPane.showMessageDialog(null,
              "Invalid integer " + numStr + " - default is 1",
              "Error", JOptionPane.ERROR_MESSAGE);
    }
    catch (Exception ex) {
      // Handle all other exception types.
      System.out.println(ex.getMessage());
      ex.printStackTrace();
    }
    finally {
      System.out.println("Number of children is " + children);
    }
  }
}
```

◆◆

Methods `getMessage()` and `printStackTrace()`

In the second `catch` block of Fig. 8.5, the statements

```
System.out.println(ex.getMessage());
ex.printStackTrace();
```

call two methods of the object referenced by parameter `ex`. Method `getMessage()` retrieves a message indicating the type of the exception (`/ by zero`), which is displayed in the console window.

Method `printStackTrace()` displays the exception type (`java.lang.ArithmeticException: / by zero`) and indicates which step threw the exception (execution of line 16 of method `main()` in class `MyException.java`). If more than one method was involved, it would show the sequence of method calls leading to an exception in reverse order, ending with method `main()`. This sequence of method calls is derived from the internal **call stack** (maintained by the Java Virtual Machine), which stores this information and is referred to as a **call stack trace**.

The `finally` block displays the value of `children`. It executes after the `try` block finishes execution or after a `catch` block executes.

◆◆EXAMPLE 8.3 ──────────────────────────────

The call stack trace

```
java.lang.NumberFormatException
    at Inner.funny(Inner.java:15)
    at Outer.useFunny(Outer.java:7)
    at OuterApp.main(OuterApp.java:9)
```

shows that a number format exception was raised at line 15 of method `funny()` (defined in class `Inner`), which was called at line 7 of method `useFunny()` (defined in class `Outer`), which was called at line 9 of method `main()` (defined in

Figure 8.6   Console window when `children` is 0

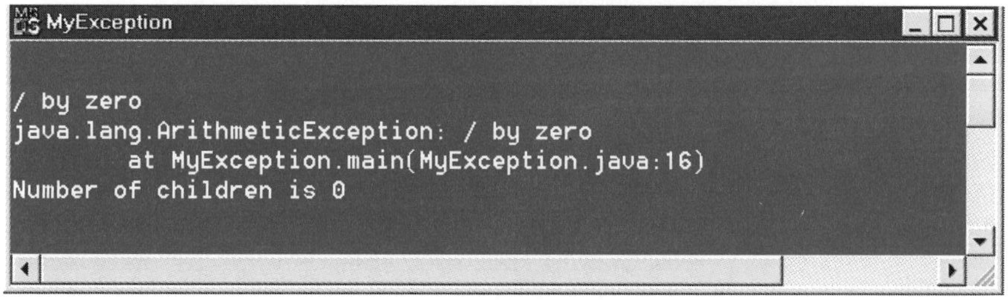

class **OuterApp**). This type of trace is displayed automatically by the JVM when it catches an exception.

◆◆

Exception Propagation and **throws** Clause

Sometimes we prefer not to handle an exception inside a method but to let the caller of the method handle the exception instead. As an example, Fig. 8.7 contains a static method **getDepend()** that may throw a number format exception when converting a string to an integer, but it does not catch this exception. The call to **getDepend()** occurs in the **try** block of method **main()**, so method **main()** handles the exception in its **catch** block, displaying an error message window similar to the one in Fig. 8.2. If method **main()** did not have a **catch** block for number format exceptions, the exception would be handled by its caller (in this case, the JVM), which would terminate execution and display an error message and a trace of the call stack.

In general, if the enclosing block of code does not have an appropriate **catch** block, Java checks the next higher enclosing block of code in the method, and so on. If the method does not handle the exception, the JVM stops running the current method, and returns to the caller of this method, and looks for an appropriate **catch** block in the same way. This process continues until an exception handler is found or the JVM handles the exception itself.

The **throws** clause in the header of method **getDepend()** tells the compiler that the method may throw a number format exception. This clause may be required for certain kinds of exceptions, as discussed in the next section.

throws clause syntax

throws *exceptionType*₁, *exceptionType*₂, · · ·

Example:

throws NumberFormatException, ArithmeticException

Interpretation: The **throws** clause comes at the end of a method header, and it declares to the Java compiler that the method may throw an exception of the type(s) listed.

Checked Exceptions

There is a special category of exceptions called **checked exceptions**. For checked exceptions, the compiler checks to see whether an exception is either caught or declared (using **throws**) in the current method or in a caller of that method. If this is not the case, the compiler will display an error message such as **unreported exception,** *exceptionType* **must be caught or declared to be thrown**. The

Figure 8.7   Class `PropagateException`

```
/* PropagateException.java        Authors: Koffman & Wolz
 * Demonstrates exception propagation.
 * Uses Swing.
 */
import javax.swing.JOptionPane;

public class PropagateException {

  // postcondition: Returns int value of a numeric data string.
  //    Throws an exception if string is not numeric.
  public static int getDepend() throws NumberFormatException {
    String numStr =
            JOptionPane.showInputDialog("Number of dependents:");
    return Integer.parseInt(numStr);
  }


  // postcondition: Calls getDepend() and handles its exceptions.
  public static void main(String[] args) {

    int children = 1;     // problem input, default is 1
    try {
      children = getDepend();
    }
    catch (NumberFormatException ex) {
      // Handle number format exception.
      JOptionPane.showMessageDialog(null,
              "Invalid integer - default is 1",
              "Error", JOptionPane.ERROR_MESSAGE);
      ex.printStackTrace();
    }
  }
}
```

subclasses of **ArithemeticException** are not checked, but the subclasses of **IOException** (exceptions caused by input/output errors) are checked. This is because the compiler cannot determine whether an arithmetic operation can generate an exception, but any input/output operation can cause an exception.

Throwing an Exception Using a `throw` Statement

If you know an exception is going to occur, you can throw it yourself using a throw statement rather than waiting for the JVM to throw it. Figure 8.8 shows a **try-catch** statement that attempts to cast an object reference (**tempEmp**) to type **Employee** using the statement

```
Employee emp = (Employee) tempEmp;
```

The assumption is that **tempEmp** (type **Object**) references some object that may or may not be type **Employee**.

We guard this casting operation using an **if** statement with the condition

```
!(tempEmp instanceof Employee)
```

This condition is **true** if object **tempEmp** is not an instance of **Employee**. We know that attempting to cast such a reference to type **Employee** would throw a cast exception error. Rather than let this happen, the **throw** statement creates a new object of type **ClassCastException** and specifies the error message (the constructor argument) associated with this exception. The **try** block is exited immediately.. If the condition above is **false**, the **throw** statement does not execute and the casting operation takes place as desired. The class cast exception should be caught by a method in the call sequence.

Figure 8.8   **try-catch** statement with **throw** statement

```
// assertion: tempEmp is type Object and references some object
   if (!(tempEmp instanceof Employee)) {
      throw new
         ClassCastException("Can't cast " +
                               tempEmp + " to type Employee");
   }
   Employee emp = (Employee) tempEmp;
```

throw statement syntax

```
throw new exceptionType(errorMessage);
```

Example:

```
throw new ArithmeticException("Divisor is 0 or negative");
throw new NumberFormatException();
```

Interpretation: The **throw** statement creates a new exception object of the type specified. The message associated with this exception may be specified as the constructor argument (optional).

PROGRAM STYLE

You may be wondering why we bother to throw an exception given that the JVM will throw an exception if the cast operation fails. One advantage is that we can specify a descriptive error message for this particular cast exception, rather than accepting the default provided by Java. Also, the **throw** statement reminds us that an exception is likely and should be caught by a method in the call sequence if we want the program to continue running.

EXERCISES FOR SECTION 8.1

SELF-CHECK

1. Can you reverse the order of the **catch** blocks in Fig. 8.5? Explain your answer.

2. Compare the calls to **showMessageDialog()** in Fig. 8.5 and 8.7. Explain why **numStr** cannot appear as an argument in the call to **showMessageDialog()** in Fig. 8.7.

3. Assume that method **getDepend()**, which is called at line 23 of the **main()** method, throws an exception at line 14. What would be displayed by the method call **ex.printStackTrace()**?

4. What is the difference between a checked exception and a regular exception?

5. Explain the difference between the **throw** statement and the **throws** declaration. Which one requires the creation of a new object?

PROGRAMMING

1. Rewrite method **actionPerformed()** in Fig. 7.42 to include **try-catch** statements that handle invalid numeric strings in **hoursStr** and **rateStr** by displaying the error message **Not a numeric string - try again** in the output text area.

2. Insert an **if** statement in the **try** block of method **main()** (Fig. 8.5) to prevent division by zero errors. Also, add a **catch** block to catch arithmetic exceptions. Be careful where you place this block.

8.2 Streams and Text Files

A **stream** is a sequence of characters or bytes used for program input or output. Java provides many different input and output stream classes in the **java.io** API. We will examine a few of them in this chapter.

The Standard Output Stream: System.out

So far, we have used the **standard output stream System.out**, which is declared in class **System** and is associated with the console window. Writing characters to **System.out** using method **print()** or **println()** displays these characters on your screen.

Any character, whether printable or not, may be read from or written to a stream. Thus, nonprintable control characters such as **'\t'** and **'\n'** may also be read from or written to streams. As their name suggests, these characters are not displayed. Rather, they cause special actions to occur, such as inserting blanks to reach the next tab position (**'\t'**) or advancing to the next line (**'\n'**).

◆◆EXAMPLE 8.4 ───

The **new-line character** **'\n'** partitions a stream into a sequence of lines. We call this a **logical partition** because it reflects the way we often think and talk about a stream. Don't forget, however, that a stream is physically just a sequence of characters with the new-line character interspersed. For example, the following represents a stream of two lines of data consisting of letters, blank characters, . (a period), and ! (an exclamation point).

```
This is a stream!\nIt would be displayed as two lines.\n
```

The character \n separates one line of data in the stream from the next. The letter I following the first \n is the first character of the second line. If we display this stream, each \n character terminates a line, so everything that follows it appears at the beginning of a new line. The displayed stream would appear as follows:

```
This is a stream!
It would be displayed as two lines.
```

─── ◆◆

A stream has no fixed size. As we write (insert) information to a stream, we are simply adding characters to the end of the stream (increasing its size). The stream output methods keep track of the size of the stream. As we read information from a stream, the stream input methods keep track of the last character read using an **input stream pointer**. Each new attempt to get information from an input stream begins at the current position of this pointer.

When writing a value stored in memory to **System.out**, method **print()** or **println()** must first convert its internal representation to a sequence of characters and then write this character sequence to the output stream.

◆◆EXAMPLE 8.5 ──

For the statement

```
System.out.println("Age is " + age + "\nName is " + name);
```

the **String** expression in parentheses is evaluated and the characters it contains are appended to the standard output stream. During the evaluation process, the binary number stored in **age** (type **int**) is converted to a sequence of decimal digit characters that are inserted in the string being formed. Method **println()** (but not method **print()**) inserts a new-line character after the last character in the string referenced by **name**. Figure 8.9 shows the characters that are added to the standard output stream when age contains the binary number shown. If you know the binary number system, you can verify that **011001** (binary or base 2) is **25** (decimal or base 10).

Figure 8.9   **Effect of call to `println()` in Example 8.5**

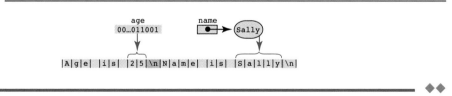

A stream has no fixed size.

Writing to an Output Text File

Writing to an Output Text File

It is relatively easy to use the standard output stream because the statements that declare **System.out** and associate it with the console are part of **java.io**. In this section, we see how to declare our own stream of characters (an output text file) and write information to it.

Regardless of what kind of file we process, we must carry out the following steps:

1. Create a stream object and associate it with a disk file
2. Give the stream object the desired functionality
3. Read information from an input file or write information to an output file
4. Close the file

We show how to do this in the next example.

◆◆EXAMPLE 8.6 ──

Fig. 8.10 shows a **main()** method that uses a **try–catch** statement to write four lines of information to an output file. The **try** block begins with the statement pair

```
FileWriter outStream = new FileWriter("myOut.txt");
PrintWriter outs = new PrintWriter(outStream);
```

which performs steps 1 and 2 above. The first statement declares **outStream** as a new object of type **FileWriter** (a stream for writing text files) and associates it with the disk file named **myOut.txt** in the current directory. A **FileWriter** object can only write strings, characters, and integer values to an output stream using method **write()**. The second statement wraps **outStream** in a new PrintWriter object **outs**, which has methods **print()** and **println()** for writing representations of **String** objects and all primitive data types (**int**, **double**, and so on). (We explain the purpose of wrapping stream objects after the example.) You use these methods with object **outs** in exactly the same way that you use them with object **System.out**. Just as all information written to object **System.out** appears in the console window, all information written to object **outs** is written to disk file **myOut.txt**, which is saved in the current directory. Any information previously stored in this file will be lost.

   Each value of **age** is a random integer between 0 and 99. The information is organized logically into four lines (Fig. 8.11). After writing the information to the output stream, the **try** block also calls method **println()** of object **System.out** to display the message **File written** in the console window.

   The last statement in the **try** block

```
outs.close();
```

closes output stream **outs**, ensuring that the information written to it is saved in file **myOut.txt**. If you don't close an output stream, all the information written may not be copied to the associated disk file. We discuss the **catch** block in the next section.

Figure 8.10   Class `TextFileOutput`

```java
/* TextFileOutput.java          Authors: Koffman & Wolz
 * Demonstrates writing to an output stream.
 * Uses PrintWriter and FileWriter.
 */
import java.io.*;

public class TextFileOutput {

    // postcondition: Writes two lines to file myOut.txt.
    public static void main(String[] args) {
        try {
            FileWriter outStream = new FileWriter("myOut.txt");
            PrintWriter outs = new PrintWriter(outStream);

            // Write 2 lines to the output file.
            outs.println("Age is " + (int) (Math.random() * 100));
            outs.println("Name is " + "Sally");
            outs.println("Age is " + (int) (Math.random() * 100));
            outs.println("Name is " + "Sam");

            // Write a console message and close the output file.
            System.out.println("File written");
            outs.close();
        }
        catch (IOException ex) {
            System.out.println("i/o error: " + ex.getMessage());
        }
    }
}
```

After this program runs, you can view file **myOut.txt** using a text editor. Figure 8.11 shows a sample file created by running class **TextFileOutput**. The values for **age** are randomly generated and should change each time you run the program.

Figure 8.11   File `myOut.txt`

```
Age is 60
Name is Sally
Age is 34
Name is Sam
```

PROGRAM STYLE: *Wrapping Stream Objects in Other Stream Objects*

The `try` block in Fig. 8.10 declares two stream objects, `outStream` (type `FileWriter`) and `outs` (type `PrintWriter`). Wrapping object `outStream` in object `outs` enables us to take advantage of the easier to use methods defined in class `PrintWriter` for writing sequences of characters to the output stream. We cannot declare a type `PrintWriter` object without first declaring a type `FileWriter` object. However, sometimes programmers combine these two statements as:

```
PrintWriter outs = new PrintWriter(new FileWriter("myOut.txt"));
```

The line above wraps an anonymous (unnamed) `FileWriter` object in a type `PrintWriter` object. We will see more examples of wrapping one stream type in another to gain additional functionality. This process is analogous to wrapping a type `int` value in a type `Integer` object. Doing this allows us to use the methods of class `Integer` (the wrapper class) to process the type `int` value.

Input/Output Exceptions

Class `IOException` is the most general input/output exception and may be thrown by any statement that reads from or writes to a file. It is a checked exception, so it must be caught or declared in every method that processes a file. Table 8.2 describes class `IOException` and some of its subclasses.

Reading Data from the Console

The console is defined as `System.in`, the standard input stream. Instead of using `System.in` for data entry, we have used dialog windows and methods from class `JOptionPane` to enter program data. However, it is useful to learn how to process console data as an input stream.

Table 8.2 Class `IOException` and some subclasses

Exception Class	Kind of Exception
`IOException`	Any kind of input/output exception
`EOFException`	An end-of-file exception caused by attempting to read beyond the last record in the file
`FileNotFoundException`	An error caused because a file cannot be found

◆◆EXAMPLE 8.7 ────────────────────────────

In Fig. 8.12 the first statements in the **try** block

```
InputStreamReader inStream = new InputStreamReader(System.in);
BufferedReader ins = new BufferedReader(inStream);
```

associate the console (**System.in**) with object **inStream** (type **InputStreamReader**). Class **InputStreamReader** can only read individual characters from a stream, so we wrap object **inStream** in object **ins** (type **BufferedReader**). Class **BufferedReader** has methods that enable more efficient reading of characters and data lines.

Next, we prompt the user for the output filename and read the filename from the console using the statement

```
String outFileName = ins.readLine();
```

The characters entered by the user are stored in the string referenced by **outFileName**. The user should not type in any quotes and must press the Enter key when done.

We create object **outs** (type **PrintWriter**) in the same way as in Example 8.6. It is connected to the disk file whose name is stored in the string referenced by **outFileName**.

In the statement

```
int numLines = Integer.parseInt(ins.readLine());
```

ins.readLine() reads the number of data lines to be entered as a numeric string. This string is converted to type **int** and stored in **numLines**. The **for** statement repeats **numLines** times. During each iteration, the first statement below

```
String dataLine = ins.readLine();
outs.println(dataLine);
```

calls method **readLine()** of object **ins** to read the next line of data from the console into the string **dataLine**. Then that string is written as a new line to object **outs** (the output stream). After loop exit, we display a message on the console and close the output stream.

Figure 8.13 shows the console window for a sample run. File **outFile2.txt** contains the three lines of data typed in after the prompt **Type 3 lines.**

Figure 8.12   Class `ConsoleInput`

```java
/* ConsoleInput.java          Authors: Koffman & Wolz
 * Demonstrates reading data from the console.
 * Uses InputStreamReader, BufferedReader,
 * FileWriter, and PrintWriter.
 */
import java.io.*;

public class ConsoleInput {

    public static void main(String[] args) {

        try {
            // Create object ins and connect it to the console.
            InputStreamReader inStream = new InputStreamReader(System.in);
            BufferedReader ins = new BufferedReader(inStream);

            // Read name of output file.
            System.out.print("Enter output file name: ");
            String outFileName = ins.readLine();

            // Create object outs — the output file.
            FileWriter outStream = new FileWriter(outFileName);
            PrintWriter outs = new PrintWriter(outStream);

            // Get the number of data lines.
            System.out.println("How many data lines?");
            int numLines = Integer.parseInt(ins.readLine());

            // Read the data lines from the console
            //    and write them to the output file.
            System.out.println("Type " + numLines + " lines:");
            for (int lineCount = 0; lineCount < numLines; lineCount++)  {
                String dataLine = ins.readLine();
                outs.println(dataLine);
            }

            // Write message to console and close files.
            System.out.println(numLines + " data lines written to file " +
                                outFileName);
            ins.close();
            outs.close();
        }
```

Figure 8.12   Class `ConsoleInput,` *continued*

```
      catch (IOException ex) {
        System.out.println("i/o error: " + ex.getMessage());
        ex.printStackTrace();
      }
      catch (NumberFormatException ex) {
        System.out.println(ex.getMessage());
        ex.printStackTrace();
      }
    }
  }
}
```

Figure 8.13   Console window for sample run of `ConsoleInput`

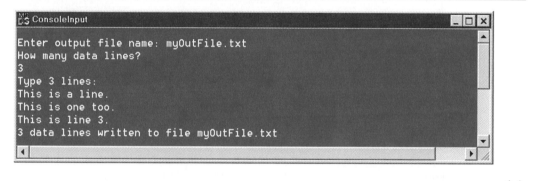

PROGRAM STYLE: *Stream Processing Inside* **try** *Block*

The **main()** method of Fig. 8.12 consists of a **try-catch** statement. All operations involving stream **ins** and stream **outs** can cause exceptions of type **IOException**, which is a checked exception. If these statements are not within the **try** block, you get the syntax error: **unreported exception: IOException must be caught or thrown**. Because **inStream** is associated with the predefined stream **System.in**, the declaration for objects **instream** and **ins** could come before the **try** block.

EXERCISES FOR SECTION 8.2

SELF-CHECK

1. Explain why we wrap one stream object inside another.

2. With what kind of object do you associate `System.out`? Answer the question also for `System.in`.

3. What is the purpose of the `close()` operation? What can happen if you omit it after writing information to an output file?

PROGRAMMING

1. Rewrite the `main()` method in Fig. 8.12 to use a sentinel string to indicate the end of the data. Write all data lines except for the sentinel to the output file.

8.3   Using Text Files

Next we consider reading data for a Java program from a text file that we have prepared beforehand by entering and saving its lines using an editor. We can associate a text file with a `BufferedReader` object and read data from a text file in the same way that we read data from the console. If we change the first two lines in the `try` block of Fig. 8.12 to

```
FileReader inStream = new FileReader("myData.txt");
BufferedReader ins = new BufferedReader(inStream);
```

Object `ins` is now associated with text file `myData.txt` instead of `System.in`, so method call `ins.readLine()` reads the next data line from file `myData.txt` instead of the console. Notice that we associate a text file used for input with a `FileReader` object instead of an `InputStreamReader` object.

◆◆EXAMPLE 8.8 ───────────────────────────

Fig. 8.14 shows class `ReadTextFile`, which reads data lines from an input text file and writes them to an output text file. The names of the input and output files are read using dialog windows. Because we are reading from a file, there are no console prompts.

Figure 8.14   Class `ReadTextFile`

```
/* ReadTextFile.java          Authors: Koffman & Wolz
 * Demonstrates reading data from a text file.
 * Uses FileReader, BufferedReader,
 * FileWriter, and PrintWriter.
 */
import java.io.*;
import javax.swing.JOptionPane;
```

Figure 8.14   Class `ReadTextFile,` *continued*

```java
public class ReadTextFile {

    public static void main(String[] args) {

        try {
            // Create object ins — the input file.
            String inFileName =
                    JOptionPane.showInputDialog("Input file name?");
            FileReader inStream = new FileReader(inFileName);
            BufferedReader ins = new BufferedReader(inStream);

            // Create object outs — the output file.
            String outFileName =
                    JOptionPane.showInputDialog("Output file name?");
            FileWriter outStream = new FileWriter(outFileName);
            PrintWriter outs = new PrintWriter(outStream);

            // Read the number of data lines.
            int numLines = Integer.parseInt(ins.readLine());

            // Read the data lines from the input file.
            //    and write them to the output file
            for (int lineCount = 0; lineCount < numLines; lineCount++)  {
                String dataLine = ins.readLine();
                outs.println(dataLine);
            }

            // Write message to console and close files.
            System.out.println(numLines + " data lines written to file " +
                               outFileName);
            ins.close();
            outs.close();
        }
        catch (IOException ex) {
            System.out.println("i/o error: " + ex.getMessage());
            ex.printStackTrace();
        }
        catch (NumberFormatException ex) {
            System.out.println(ex.getMessage());
            ex.printStackTrace();
        }
    }
}
```

Assume file **myData.txt** stores the following data:

```
3
This is a line.
This is one too.
This is line 3.
```

If we enter **myData.txt** as the input filename and **myOutput.txt** as the output filename, the number **3** would be stored in **numLines** and the three data lines that follow would be written to file **myOutput.txt**. The console output would consist of the line

```
3 data lines written to file myOutput.txt
```

◆◆

CASE STUDY USING TEXT FILES WITH A DVD COLLECTION

PROBLEM You want to be able to keep track of your ever-expanding collection of DVDs. You have prepared an initial text file that contains the data for the first three DVDs in your collection (see Fig. 8.15). You would like to be able to perform some basic operations on this file. These operations include searching for a particular title, listing the titles in a category, listing the titles for a year, adding a new DVD to the collection, modifying the data stored for a particular DVD, deleting a DVD, and so on. In this case study, we will write a method that reads the data from this file into memory so that it can be processed and a method that writes the data back out again. We will also write a method that searches for a particular title and a method that displays the titles in a specified category. Programming Project 1 at the end of this chapter asks you to write methods to perform the other processing steps.

Figure 8.15 File myDVDFile.txt

```
Gone with the Wind
Drama
1939
3.67
Toy Story
Animation
1995
1.33
Shrek
Animation
2001
1.5
```

ANALYSIS   The problem input is the text file containing the DVD collection, the operations selected by the user, and any new DVD data typed in by the user. The problem output is the text file containing the DVD collection after it has been modified.

Data Requirements

Problem Inputs

Text file for DVD collection
Data for a single DVD
User selection of operations

Problem Outputs

Text file for DVD collection
Data for a single DVD
List of DVDs by category
List of DVDs by title

We need a class **DVD** that represents and stores the information for a DVD (title, category, year, time) in its data fields. This class should contain constructor methods with and without arguments. It should also have accessor methods for each data field and a **toString()** method.

We also need a class **DVDCollection** that stores all the DVD information. Finally, we need a user interface class. We will discuss this class after we code and test classes **DVD** and **DVDCollection**.

DESIGN

Class **DVD**

Class **DVD** (Fig. 8.16) is straightforward and will contain the usual constructor and accessor methods.

Class **DVDCollection**

For class **DVDCollection** (Fig. 8.17), we will store the DVD collection in a vector because the size of the collection keeps changing. This class contains methods to read the data for the DVD collection from a text file into the vector and to write the DVD data from the vector to a text file. It also contains methods to perform other operations that may be selected by the user.

We provide the algorithms for the first five methods next. We leave the others to the exercises.

Algorithm for **readDVDFile()**

1. Read the title of the first DVD

2. **while** there are more DVDs

   3. Read the rest of the DVD data

4. Store the DVD data in the vector

5. Read the title of the next DVD

6. Close the input file

Figure 8.16   Specification of DVD class

Data Fields	Attributes
`String title`	Title of DVD
`String category`	Category of DVD
`int year`	Year of release
`double time`	Running time in hours
Methods	**Behavior**
`DVD()`	Default constructor
`DVD(String, String, int, double)`	Constructor that initializes all data fields
`String getTitle()`	Retrieves title
`String getCategory()`	Retrieves category
`int getYear()`	Retrieves year of release
`double getTime()`	Retrieves running time
`String toString()`	Represents the DVD data as a string

Figure 8.17   Specification of DVDCollection class

Data Fields	Attributes
`Vector DVDs`	Vector storing the collection of DVDs
Methods	**Behavior**
`void readDVDFile(BufferedReader)`	Reads data from the specified input file into the vector
`void writeDVDFile(PrintWriter)`	Writes DVD information to the specified output file
`DVD searchDVD(String)`	Searches for a specified title
`void addDVD(DVD)`	Adds the specified DVD to the collection
`String listInCategory(String)`	Returns a string listing all DVDs in a category
`String toString()`	Represents the collection as a string
`void deleteDVD(String)`	Deletes a DVD with the specified title
`void modifyDVD(DVD)`	Replaces a DVD's information with the specified data
`String listInYear(int)`	Returns a string listing all DVDs in a year

Algorithm for **writeDVDFile()**

1. **for** each DVD in the collection

    2. Write the DVD data to object outs

3. Close the output file

Algorithm for **searchDVD()**

1. **for** each DVD in the collection

    2. **if** this DVD has the target title

        Return a reference to this DVD

3. Return null

Algorithm for **addDVD()**

1. Append the DVD data to vector **DVDs**

Algorithm for **listInCategory()**

1. Set the result string to the empty string

2. **for** each DVD in the collection

    3. **if** this DVD has the target category

        Append this DVD's title to the result string

4. Return the result string

IMPLEMENTATION   Figure 8.18 shows class **DVD**. All methods should be familiar to you. Figure 8.19 shows class **DVDCollection**. Data field **DVDs** (a vector) is used to store the information about your DVD collection. Method **readDVDs()** reads all DVD data from a text file and saves this information in vector **DVDs**. Each data item is on a separate line of the text file (Fig. 8.15).

The **try** block in **readDVDs()** has a **while** loop that continues to execute as long as there are data lines remaining in the text file passed as the argument. If the file is empty, the first statement

```
title = ins.readLine();
```

returns a value of null to the string title, causing the loop repetition condition (**title != null**) to become **false** and loop exit to occur immediately. Otherwise, the **while** loop reads four lines of information for each DVD, starting with its title. The statement

```
DVDs.addElement(new DVD(title, category, year, time));
```

Figure 8.18   Class DVD

```
/* DVD.java          Authors: Koffman & Wolz
 * Class that stores DVD information.
 */
import java.io.*;

public class DVD {
  // Data fields
  private String title;
  private String category;
  private int year;
  private double time;

  // Methods
  // Constructors
  public DVD() {}
  public DVD(String titleStr, String cat, int aYear, double aTime) {
    title = titleStr;
    category = cat;
    year = aYear;
    time = aTime;
  }

  public String getTitle() {return title;}

  public String getCategory() {return category;}

  public int getYear() {return year;}

  public double getTime() {return time;}

  public String toString() {
    return title + ", " + category + ", " + year +
          ", " + time + " hours\n";
  }
}
```

stores the information just read in a new DVD object and appends the object to vector **DVDs**. The loop continues to read and store DVDs until the last data item for the last DVD is read. After the last line of the data file is read, the next execution of

```
title = ins.readLine();
```

at the bottom of the loop returns a value of `null` to string `title`, causing loop exit to occur. After loop exit, the input file is closed.

Method `writeDVDs()` in Fig. 8.19 writes the DVD information stored in vector `DVDs` to the output text file passed as an argument. The `for` statement body writes each DVD to the output file. The statement

```
DVD nextDVD = (DVD) DVDs.elementAt(next);
```

retrieves the object at element `next` from vector `DVDs`, and assigns `nextDVD` to reference it. We call the `println()` method for object `outs` (type `PrintWriter`) four times to write the data for each DVD to the output file. The output file will be similar to the original file shown in Fig. 8.15.

Methods `searchDVD()` and `listInCategory()` contain a loop that stores each DVD's information in the object referenced by `nextDVD`. In `searchDVD()`, the `if` statement

```
if (nextDVD.getTitle().equals(aTitle))
    return nextDVD;
```

returns a reference to `nextDVD` if its title is the one we are seeking (string parameter `aTitle`); the return occurs as soon as the desired title is found. If the title is not found, the loop is exited in the normal way and the method returns a `null` reference.

In method `listInCategory()`, the `if` statement

```
if (nextDVD.getCategory().equals(targetCat))
    result += nextDVD.getTitle() + "\n";
```

appends the title of each DVD whose category field matches `targetCat` (a `String` parameter) to the string being formed (`result`).

TESTING   Class `DVDCollection` (Fig. 8.19) contains a `main()` method that executes when this class is compiled and run. Method `main()` serves as a driver program to test the methods of class `DVDCollection`. Its creates an object of type `DVDCollection`. Then it reads the input filename, associates object `ins` with the input file, and calls `readDVDs()` to read the data in the input file. Next, it calls `toString()` to verify that the information has been stored correctly and also calls `listInCategory()`. After displaying the information returned by these methods in the console window (Fig. 8.20), `main()` associates object `outs` with an output file and calls method `writeDVDs()` to write the DVD information to the output file. You can open the output file with a text editor to verify that it contains the same information as the input file.

Method `main()` also catches an `IOException`. It displays an error message and a trace of the call stack when an exception occurs.

Figure 8.19 Class DVDCollection

```java
/* DVDCollection.java          Authors: Koffman & Wolz
 * Class that stores a collection of DVDs.
 * Uses FileReader, BufferedReader,
 * FileWriter, and PrintWriter.
 */
import javax.swing.*;
import java.io.*;
import java.util.*;

public class DVDCollection {
    // Data field
    Vector DVDs = new Vector();

    // Methods

    // postcondition: Reads all data from specified input file into
    //    vector DVDs.
    public void readDVDs(BufferedReader ins) {
        try {
            // Read and store data for DVD collection
            String title = ins.readLine();
            while (title != null) {
                String category = ins.readLine();
                int year = Integer.parseInt(ins.readLine());
                double cost = Double.parseDouble(ins.readLine());
                DVDs.addElement(new DVD(title, category, year, cost));
                title = ins.readLine();
            }
            ins.close();
        } // catch exceptions
        catch (NumberFormatException ex) {
            System.out.println("bad numeric string");
            ex.printStackTrace();
        }
        catch (IOException ex) {
            System.out.println("i/o error " + ex.getMessage());
            ex.printStackTrace();
        }
    }
```

Figure 8.19   **Class** DVDCollection, *continued*

```
// precondition: Vector DVDs stores a DVD collection
// postconditon: Writes the collection to the specified file.
public void writeDVDs(PrintWriter outs) {
    // Write the DVD collection to the output file
    for (int next = 0; next < DVDs.size(); next++) {
        DVD nextDVD = (DVD) DVDs.elementAt(next);
        outs.println(nextDVD.getTitle());
        outs.println(nextDVD.getCategory());
        outs.println(nextDVD.getYear());
        outs.println(nextDVD.getTime());
    }

    outs.close();
    System.out.println("Output file written");
}

// postcondition: Adds the specified DVD to the collection.
public void addDVD(DVD aDVD) {
    DVDs.addElement(aDVD);
}

// postcondition; Returns a string of all DVD titles
//    in a specified category.
public String listInCategory(String targetCat) {
    String result = "";
    for (int next = 0; next < DVDs.size(); next ++) {
        DVD nextDVD = (DVD) DVDs.elementAt(next);
        if (nextDVD.getCategory().equals(targetCat))
            result += nextDVD.getTitle() + "\n";
    }
    return result;
}

// postcondition: Returns the DVD with a specified title.
//    Returns a null reference if not found.
public DVD searchDVD(String aTitle) {
    for (int next = 0; next < DVDs.size(); next ++) {
        DVD nextDVD = (DVD) DVDs.elementAt(next);
        if (nextDVD.getTitle().equals(aTitle))
            return nextDVD;
    }
```

Figure 8.19   Class DVDCollection, *continued*

```
        // Assertion: DVD with aTitle not found.
        return null;
    }


    // postcondition: Represents the collection as a string.
    public String toString() {
        return DVDs.toString();
    }


    // Driver program to test the DVDCollection class.
    public static void main(String[] args) {
      try {
          // Create DVD collection and read and store DVDs.
          DVDCollection myDVDs = new DVDCollection();

          // Create object ins and connect it to the input file
          String inFileName =
              JOptionPane.showInputDialog("Input file:");
          FileReader inStream = new FileReader(inFileName);
          BufferedReader ins = new BufferedReader(inStream);

          // Read DVD data from the input file, store it, and
          //   display the data stored.
          myDVDs.readDVDs(ins);
          System.out.println(myDVDs.toString());

          // Display DVDs in a specified category.
          String targetCat =
              JOptionPane.showInputDialog("Enter target category:");
          System.out.println("\nDVDs in category " + targetCat + "\n" +
                                myDVDs.listInCategory(targetCat));

          // Create object outs and connect it to the output file
          String outFileName =
              JOptionPane.showInputDialog("Output file name:");
          FileWriter outStream = new FileWriter(outFileName);
          PrintWriter outs = new PrintWriter(outStream);
```

Figure 8.19   Class `DVDCollection`, *continued*

```
    // Write DVDs to the output file.
    myDVDs.writeDVDs(outs);
  } // catch exceptions
  catch (IOException ex) {
    System.out.println(ex.getMessage());
    ex.printStackTrace();
  }
}

}
```

Figure 8.20   Console window for sample run of class `DVDCollection`

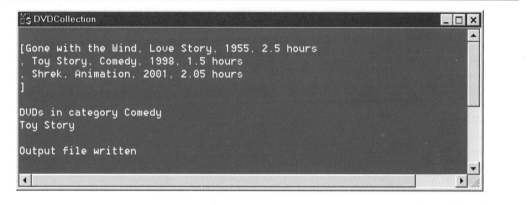

PROGRAM STYLE

Rather than write a separate application class that has a **main()** method, we inserted method **main()** in class **DVDCollection** (Fig. 8.19) to enable us to test its methods. This is a perfectly legitimate way to test the methods of a class. Some Java programmers write **main()** methods in every class so that they can test the class and its methods in isolation (not as part of a larger system). For example, you could insert the **main()** method below in class **DVD** to test its constructor and **toString()** method. This **main()** method would execute when you run class **DVD.java**. The **main()** method in Fig. 8.19 would execute when you run class **DVDCollection.java**.

```
// driver method to test class DVD
public static void main(String[] args) {
    DVD aDVD = new DVD("hi", "me", 5, 50);
    System.out.println(aDVD.toString());
}
```

You can temporarily remove a **main()** method by placing comment delimiters around it.

EXERCISES FOR SECTION 8.3

SELF-CHECK

1. In **readDVDFile()**, why is the title for the first DVD read before the **while** loop is reached?

2. What would happen if the input DVD file was empty?

3. Explain what happens if the user types in an invalid filename.

4. Do you think you can use the same name for both the input file and the output file? Explain your answer.

PROGRAMMING

1. Modify method **main()** in Fig. 8.14 to prompt the user for the input and output file names using dialog windows and to copy all lines of the input file to the output file. Assume that the number of lines is not known beforehand.

8.4 A GUI for Processing the DVD Collection

The user interface must get the data for a new DVD from the user (through text fields) and must enable the user to select operations (using control buttons and combo boxes). It also needs to display results to the user (through a text area). We could also enter the input and output filenames through text fields, but **Swing** provides a file chooser dialog to facilitate the selection of a file.

Fig. 8.21 shows the user interface after the data file has been read and the user has selected the **List all titles** operation. There are text fields for data entry (**titleText**, **yearText**, and **timeText**) and a combo box for the category selection (**catChooser**). There are control buttons for opening (**open file**) and saving a file (**save file**). There is a text area with a vertical scroll bar for showing results (**output**). There is also a combo box for the user to select an operation (**opChooser**).

Fig. 8.22 shows a description of class DVDGUI and Fig. 8.23 shows the data field declarations and method **init()**. The applet uses a box layout manager to place its panels in a single column of the GUI. The applet is registered as an item listener for the **opChooser** combo box and as an action listener for the two control buttons.

Figure 8.21 User interface for managing a DVD collection

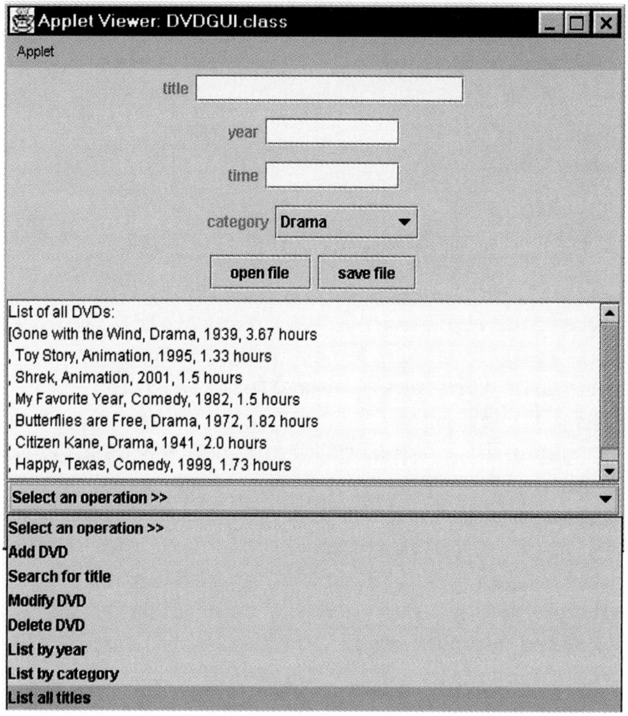

Figure 8.22 Class DVDGUI

Data Fields	Attributes
JTextField titleText	Text area for entering movie title
JTextField yearText	Text area for entering year of release
JTextField timeText	Text area for entering running time
JComboBox catChooser	Combo box for selecting movie category
JComboBox opChooser	Combo box for selecting operation
JButton open	Control button for open file dialog
JButton save	Control button for save file dialog
JTextArea output	Text area for results
DVDCollection DVDdata	The DVD collection

Methods	Behavior
init()	Builds the GUI
actionPerformed()	Responds to open and save button events
itemStateChanged()	Responds to combo box **opChooser** selections

Figure 8.23   Method `init()` of class DVDGUI

```java
/* DVDGUI.java          Authors: Koffman & Wolz
 * GUI for class DVDCollection.
 * Uses DVDCollection, swing, io.
 */
import javax.swing.*;
import java.awt.event.*;
import java.io.*;

public class DVDGUI extends JApplet
                    implements ActionListener, ItemListener {
  private JTextField titleText = new JTextField(20);
  private JTextField yearText = new JTextField(10);
  private JTextField timeText = new JTextField(10);
  private String[] categories = {"Drama", "Comedy", "Love Story",
           "Suspense", "Action", "Science Fiction", "Horror",
           "Animation"};
  private JComboBox catChooser = new JComboBox(categories);
  private JComboBox opChooser = new JComboBox(operations);
  private JButton open = new JButton("open file");
  private JButton save = new JButton("save file");
  private JTextArea output = new JTextArea(8, 30);
  private String[] operations = {"Select an operation >> ", "Add DVD",
           "Search for title", "Modify DVD", "Delete DVD",
           "List by year", "List by category", "List all titles"};
    private DVDCollection DVDdata = new DVDCollection();

  // Builds the GUI.
  public void init () {
    // Define the layout manager for the applet
    getContentPane().setLayout(
      new BoxLayout(getContentPane(), BoxLayout.Y_AXIS));

    // Fill the panels and add them to the applet.
    JPanel titlePanel = new JPanel();
    JLabel titleLab = new JLabel("title");
    titlePanel.add(titleLab);
    titlePanel.add(titleText);
    getContentPane().add(titlePanel);

    JPanel yearPanel = new JPanel();
    JLabel yearLab = new JLabel("year");
    yearPanel.add(yearLab);
```

Figure 8.23 Method `init()` of class DVDGUI, *continued*

```
yearPanel.add(yearText);
getContentPane().add(yearPanel);

JPanel timePanel = new JPanel();
JLabel timeLab = new JLabel("time");
timePanel.add(timeLab);
timePanel.add(timeText);
getContentPane().add(timePanel);

JPanel catPanel = new JPanel();
JLabel catLab = new JLabel("category");
catPanel.add(catLab);
catPanel.add(catChooser);
getContentPane().add(catPanel);

JPanel filePanel = new JPanel();
filePanel.add(open);
filePanel.add(save);
getContentPane().add(filePanel);

// Add output with scroll bars and operation chooser
JScrollPane outputScroll = new JScrollPane(output,
        ScrollPaneConstants.VERTICAL_SCROLLBAR_AS_NEEDED,
        ScrollPaneConstants.HORIZONTAL_SCROLLBAR_AS_NEEDED);
getContentPane().add(outputScroll);
getContentPane().add(opChooser);

// Register applet as listener for action events
//    on all buttons
open.addActionListener(this);
save.addActionListener(this);


// Register applet as listener for item events
//    on combo box opChooser
opChooser.addItemListener(this);
}
```

The statements

```
JScrollPane outputScroll = new JScrollPane(output,
        ScrollPaneConstants.VERTICAL_SCROLLBAR_AS_NEEDED,
        ScrollPaneConstants.HORIZONTAL_SCROLLBAR_AS_NEEDED);
getContentPane().add(outputScroll);
```

create a new **JScrollPane** object **outputScroll** that consists of text area **output** with vertical and horizontal scroll bars as needed. The **JScrollPane** object is added to the applet's content pane, causing text area **output** to be displayed with scroll bars when they are needed and without them when they are not.

Method **itemStateChanged()** (Fig. 8.24) responds to item events generated by combo box **opChooser**. The **switch** statement uses the selector expression **opChooser.getSelectedIndex()** to select a case, so each case label corresponds to the element of array **operations** with that index. Case 1 implements **Add DVD**. The DVD data is taken from the three GUI text fields and combo box **catChooser**. The conversion of numeric strings for year and time are performed in a **try-catch** block; the **catch** block catches a number format exception. The statement

```
DVDdata.addDVD(aDVD);
```

calls object **DVDdata**'s **addDVD()** method to add the DVD to the vector of DVDs.

Case 2 implements **Search for title**. It uses the statement

```
aDVD = DVDdata.searchDVD(title);
```

to search for the DVD whose title matches the one in **titleText**. If successful, the corresponding data fields of **aDVD** are copied to text fields **yearText** and **timeText** and the statement

```
catChooser.setSelectedItem(aDVD.getCategory());
```

sets **catChooser** to show **aDVD**'s category data field.

Cases 3, 4, and 5 (modify DVD, delete DVD, list by year) are part of Programming Project 1. To delete a DVD, just enter its title before selecting **Delete DVD**. To modify a DVD, you should first enter the title of the DVD you want to modify and then select **Search for title** to get the current information for that DVD. Edit the data displayed in the GUI input fields to contain the updated information before selecting **Modify DVD**.

Case 6 gets the category selected by `catChooser` and passes it to `DVDdata`'s `listInCategory()` method. Any data items in the input fields are ignored. All the DVDs in the selected category are show in the output text area.

Method `actionPerformed()` (Fig. 8.25) executes when the user presses the `open file` or `save file` button. The method begins with the line

```
JFileChooser fileChooser =
    new JFileChooser("H:\\Java2ndEd\\Chapter8\\DVDCollection");
```

which creates a new `JFileChooser` object `fileChooser`. Class `JFileChooser` provides methods for opening and saving a file using file dialog windows. The constructor argument specifies the directory path for the file chooser object. Notice that the backslash character (for the Microsoft Windows operating system) is represented by \\ in the argument string. If there is no argument, the directory path is the user's home directory.

Because the file operations can raise checked exceptions, the rest of the method is in a **try** block. The statement

```
int result = fileChooser.showOpenDialog(this);
```

displays a file open dialog (Fig. 8.26) and the statement

```
int result = fileChooser.showSaveDialog(this);
```

displays a file save dialog (Fig. 8.27). You can select a file by highlighting it or by typing in its name. Pressing button `Open` (or `Save`) or `Cancel` in the dialog returns an integer value, which is stored in `result`. If `Open` or `Save` was pressed, `result` gets the constant `JFileChooser.APPROVE_OPTION`. The condition `(result == JFileChooser.APPROVE_OPTION)` is `true` and the statements

```
File aFile = fileChooser.getSelectedFile();
String inFileName = aFile.getName();
```

execute. `File` variable `aFile` references the file selected and the characters in the file name are stored in string `inFileName` (for `Open`) or `outFileName` (for `Save`). Next we call method `readDVDs()` (for `Open`) or method `writeDVDs()` (for `Save`) to process the file.

Figure 8.24   Method `itemStateChanged()` of class `DVDGUI`

```
// postcondition: Responds to selection from opChooser.
public void itemStateChanged(ItemEvent op) {
   if (op.getSource() == opChooser) {
      switch (opChooser.getSelectedIndex()) {
         case 0: // Select an operation >>
            break;
         case 1: // Add DVD
            DVD aDVD;
            String title = titleText.getText();
            String cat = (String) catChooser.getSelectedItem();
            try {
              int year = Integer.parseInt(yearText.getText());
              double time = Double.parseDouble(timeText.getText());
              if (!title.equals("")) {
                aDVD = new DVD(title, cat, year, time);
                DVDdata.addDVD(aDVD);
                output.setText("Added: " + aDVD.toString());
              }
              else {
                output.setText("Title is missing");
              }
            }
            catch (NumberFormatException nfe) {
              output.setText(
                  "year or time is an invalid numeric string");
            }
            break;
          case 2: // Search for title
            title = titleText.getText();
            aDVD = DVDdata.searchDVD(title);
            if (aDVD == null) {
              output.setText(title + " not in collection");
            }
            else {    //Display DVD information
              catChooser.setSelectedItem(aDVD.getCategory());
              yearText.setText("" + aDVD.getYear());
              timeText.setText("" + aDVD.getTime());
              output.setText(title + " found");
            }
            break;
```

Figure 8.24 Method `itemStateChanged()` of class `DVDGUI`, *continued*

```
          case 3: case 4: case 5:
              output.setText("not implemented yet");
              break;
          case 6: // List DVDs in selected category
              cat = (String) catChooser.getSelectedItem();
              output.setText("DVDs in category " + cat + ":\n" +
                          DVDdata.listInCategory(cat));
              break;
          case 7: // List all DVDs
              output.setText("List of all DVDs:\n" +
                          DVDdata.toString());
              break;
          default:
              output.setText("Invalid operation");
      }  // end switch
      if (opChooser.getSelectedIndex() != 0)
          opChooser.setSelectedIndex(0);    // Reset chooser bar
  }  // end if
}
```

Figure 8.25 Method `actionPerformed()` of class `DVDGUI`

```
// postcondition: If open was pressed, opens data file and
//    reads it. If save was pressed, writes DVD information to
//    output file and saves the output file.
public void actionPerformed(ActionEvent aE) {
   JFileChooser fileChooser =
       new JFileChooser("H:\\Java2ndEd\\Chapter8\\DVDCollection");
   Object command = aE.getSource();
   try {
     if (command == open) {
        int result = fileChooser.showOpenDialog(this);
        if (result == JFileChooser.APPROVE_OPTION) {
           File aFile = fileChooser.getSelectedFile();
           String inFileName = aFile.getName();
           FileReader inStream = new FileReader(inFileName);
           BufferedReader ins = new BufferedReader(inStream);
           DVDdata.readDVDs(ins);
           output.setText("Reading data from file " +
                        inFileName);
```

Figure 8.25 Method `actionPerformed( )` of class `DVDGUI`, *continued*

```
      }
      else {
         output.setText("File open cancelled");
      }
   } // end open
   else if (command == save) {
      int result = fileChooser.showSaveDialog(this);
      if (result == JFileChooser.APPROVE_OPTION) {
         File aFile = fileChooser.getSelectedFile();
         String outFileName = aFile.getName();
         FileWriter outStream = new FileWriter(outFileName);
         PrintWriter outs = new PrintWriter(outStream);
         DVDdata.writeDVDs(outs);
         output.setText("Writing data to file " +
                        outFileName);
      }
      else {
         output.setText("File save cancelled");
      }
   }  // end save
}
// end try
catch (IOException ex) {
  System.out.println(ex.getMessage());
  ex.printStackTrace();
}

}
```

Figure 8.26 `JFileChooser` file open dialog

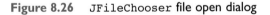

Figure 8.27   `JFileChooser` file save dialog

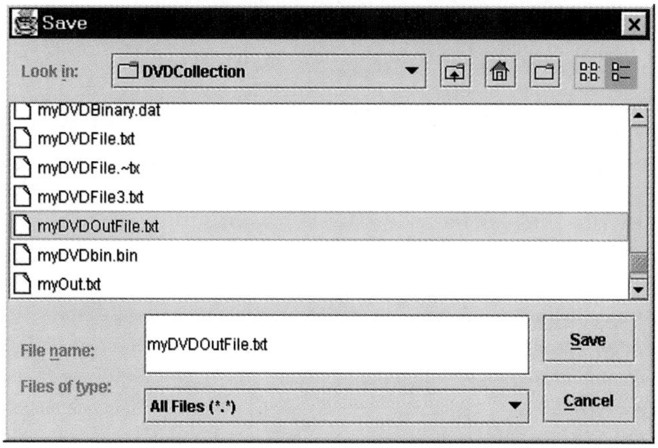

EXERCISES FOR SECTION 8.4

SELF-CHECK

1. What happens if the user presses **Cancel** in the open file or save file dialog window?

2. Discuss the changes that would be required to add a **Submit** button that the user could press to start an operation after all selections were made and all data items were entered. Would you need to change **itemStateChanged()**, **actionPerformed()**, or both if you had this button?

3. There is no listener registered for **catChooser** events. Is this an oversight or is it not necessary to have a listener for these events? Explain your answer. How is a selection from this combo box currently processed by method **itemStateChanged()**?

PROGRAMMING

1. Modify the search operation so that the results of a search are shown in text area **output** as well as in the text fields.

8.5 Binary Files

Java also supports binary files. **Binary files (or byte streams)** store binary images of information that are identical to the binary images stored in main memory. When you write the value of a type **int** variable to a binary file, the actual binary representation is stored in the file. Recall that when you write a type `int` variable to a text file, the binary representation is converted to a sequence of decimal digit characters and the digit characters are stored in the file. For example, the binary number 11001 (decimal value is 25) would be written as 00...011001 in a binary file, but it would be written as a Unicode character 2 followed by a Unicode character 5 in a text file. Similarly, when you read the binary image of an integer value from a binary file, the binary image is stored directly in memory, whereas you must first read an integer as a numeric string from a text file and then convert that string to a type `int` value. Also, you can write (or read) all the data fields for an object or all the information in an array as a single entity (called a **record**) in a binary file. In a text file, each data field would be written as a separate line. Therefore, binary files are more efficient in terms of processing time and space utilization than are text files.

The disadvantages of binary files are that you cannot create binary files using a text editor (or display them on a screen) because the binary images cannot be read by humans. For this reason binary files are more useful when you need to store information between successive runs of a program. For example, if you have a collection of data (or **database**) that is modified or updated by a program that you run on a regular basis (for example, a DVD collection, an address book, or a stock portfolio), you can store the database as a binary file.

You must be especially careful using binary files. In a text file, each "record" is a string of characters, and you can write each record on a separate line using methods `print()` or `println()`. Also, you can read each record (line) using method `readLine()`. However, in a binary file, each binary image depends on the kind of information it represents. If you write the binary image of an integer value to a binary file using method `writeInt()` (a method for writing a type `int` value), you can only read that image as a type `int` value (using method `readInt()`). Attempting to do otherwise will throw an `IOException`.

Table 8.3 shows the eight methods we will use for reading and writing information to a binary file. They are defined in classes `DataInputStream` and `DataOutputStream`. Methods `writeUTF()` and `readUTF()` use a special format for strings that is compatible with ASCII. Method `writeChar()` has a type `int` parameter. This means that a character written using `writeChar()` is represented in binary format rather than as an ASCII or Unicode character.

Creating a Binary File

You cannot create a binary file using a text editor. However, you can read data from a text file (created using an editor) into memory and then write the corresponding binary images to a binary output file.

Table 8.3   `DataInputStream` and `DataOutputStream` methods for input/output

I/O Method	Description
`readUTF()`	Reads a string of Unicode characters
`readInt()`	Reads an `int` value
`readDouble()`	Reads a `double` value
`readChar()`	Reads a character
`readBoolean()`	Reads a `boolean` value
`writeUTF(String s)`	Writes a string of Unicode characters
`writeInt(int i)`	Writes an `int` value
`writeDouble(double d)`	Writes a `double` value
`writeChar(int c)`	Writes a character
`writeBoolean(boolean b)`	Writes a `boolean` value

◆◆EXAMPLE 8.9 ─────────────────────────────────────

Figure 8.28 shows an instance method `writeDVDBinaryFile()` for class `DVDCollection` to write the DVD data to a binary file. Before the method is called, we must associate an output stream object with a binary file using statements such as

```
FileOutputStream outStream = new FileOutputStream(outFileName);
DataOutputStream outs = new DataOutputStream(outStream);
```

These statements wrap object `outStream` (type `FileOutputStream`) in a `DataOutputStream` object that is referenced by `outs`. The constructor for `FileOutputStream` takes a `String` argument.

Assume that the DVD collection has been read and stored in object `myDVDs` (type `DVDCollection`). We can use the method call

```
myDVDs.writeDVDBinaryFile(outs);
```

to write a binary file that stores the information in vector `DVDs` of object `myDVDs`.

Method `writeDVDBinaryFile()` consists of a `try-catch` statement. The `try` block contains a `for` loop that repeats the statements below:

```
DVD nextDVD = (DVD) DVDs.elementAt(next);
nextDVD.writeDVD(outs);
```

The first statement stores a reference to the next DVD in variable `nextDVD`. The second statement calls object `nextDVD`'s `writeDVD()` method (see Fig. 8.29) to write the data in `nextDVD` to the binary output file (the method argument). After the last DVD has been written, the `for` loop is exited and the output file is closed.

Figure 8.28 Method `writeDVDBinaryFile` (for class `DVDCollection`)

```
// postcondition: Writes the DVD information stored in vector DVDs
//   to binary file outs.
public void writeDVDBinaryFile(DataOutputStream outs) {
   try {
      // Write each DVD to binary file outs.
      for (int next = 0; next < DVDs.size(); next++) {
         DVD nextDVD = (DVD) DVDs.elementAt(next);
         nextDVD.writeDVD(outs);
      }

      outs.close();
   }
   catch (IOException ex) {
      System.out.println("i/o error: " + ex.getMessage());
      ex.printStackTrace();
   }
}
```

Fig. 8.29 shows methods `writeDVD()` and `readDVD()`, which we include in class **DVD** because their purpose is to write and read the data for a **DVD** object. Both methods declare that they can throw an `IOException` (a checked exception). Any `IOException` is handled in the corresponding **catch** block of the caller (`writeDVDBinaryFile()` or `readDVDBinaryFile()`). The input or output stream being processed is passed as an argument to each method. Note the symmetry between the two method bodies.

◆◆

Now we describe method `readDVDBinaryFile()` (Fig. 8.30), which reads the binary file created by method `writeDVDBinaryFile()`. Parameter **ins** references a type `DataInputStream` object, which must be declared before the method is called using statements such as

```
FileInputStream inStream = new FileInputStream(inFileName);
DataInputStream ins = new DataInputStream(inStream);
```

These statements wrap object **inStream** (type `FileInputStream`) in a `DataInputStream` object, which is referenced by **ins**. The constructor for `FileInputStream` takes a `String` argument. We can use the method call

```
myDVDs.readDVDBinaryFile(ins);
```

Figure 8.29   Class DVD with methods writeDVD( ) and readDVD( )

```
/* DVD.java          Authors: Koffman & Wolz
 * Class that stores DVD information.
 */
public class DVD implements Serializable {
  // Data fields
  private String title;
  private String category;
  private int year;
  private double time;

  // Methods
  // Insert methods from Fig. 8.18 here.

  // Additional methods for reading and writing binary objects.

  // postcondition: writes the binary images for this object
  //    to binary stream outs.
  public void writeDVD(DataOutputStream outs) throws IOException {
    outs.writeUTF(title);
    outs.writeUTF(category);
    outs.writeInt(year);
    outs.writeDouble(time);
  }

  // postcondition: Reads binary images from binary stream ins
  //    into this object.
  public void readDVD(DataInputStream ins) throws IOException {
    title = ins.readUTF();
    category = ins.readUTF();
    year = ins.readInt();
    time = ins.readDouble();
  }
}
```

to read a binary file and store its information in vector **DVDs** of object **myDVDs**.

In **readDVDBinaryFile( )**, an inner **try-catch** statement is used to read all the DVDs. Its **try** block contains a **while** statement that executes "forever" because the **while** condition is **true**. Each iteration of the **while** loop body creates a new **DVD** object referenced by **aDVD**. The statement

```
aDVD.readDVD(ins);
```

calls object **aDVD**'s **readDVD( )** method to read the information for each DVD. This information is stored in vector **DVDs**.

How do we exit the **while** loop? After the last record has been read, the next call to method **readDVD( )** throws an end of file exception (type **EOFException**). This exception is caught by the inner **catch** block, which closes the input file. Next, we exit the inner **catch** block, the outer **try** block, and the method itself.

Writing and Reading Objects in a Binary File

In this section we show how to write (and read) all of an object's data fields as a single entity (record) in a binary file. Streams **ObjectInputStream** and **ObjectOutputStream** provide methods **writeObject( )** and **readObject( )** for this purpose. To be able to write or read the next DVD object, class **DVD** (see Fig. 8.29) must implement the predefined **Serializable** interface. This interface provides methods for reading and writing individual objects from a file that consists of a sequence of DVD objects, a process called **object serialization**.

Figure 8.30   Method **readDVDBinaryFile( )** (for class **DVDCollection**)

```
// postcondition: Reads a collection of DVDs from binary file ins
//    and stores the information in vector DVDs.
public void readDVDBinaryFile(DataInputStream ins) {
   try {
      // Read data for DVD collection and store it in DVDs.
      try {
         while (true) {
            DVD aDVD = new DVD();
            aDVD.readDVD(ins);
            DVDs.addElement(aDVD);
         }
      }
      catch (EOFException eof) {
         System.out.println("end of input file reached");
         ins.close();
      }
   }
   catch (IOException ex) {
      System.out.println("i/o error: " + ex.getMessage());
      ex.printStackTrace();
   }
}
```

◆◆EXAMPLE 8.10 ─────────────────────────────────────

To write each DVD's information as a single record to a file of objects, we need to wrap the `FileOutputStream` object referenced by `outStream` in an `ObjectOutputStream` object instead of a `DataOutputStream` object:

```
FileOutputStream outStream = new FileOutputStream(outFileName);
ObjectOutputStream outs = new ObjectOutputStream(outStream);
```

Similarly, to read each record in this binary file, we need to wrap the `FileInputStream` object (referenced by `inStream`) in an `ObjectInputStream` object instead of a `DataInputStream` object:

```
FileInputStream inStream = new FileInputStream(inFileName);
ObjectInputStream ins = new ObjectInputStream(inStream);
```

Figure 8.31 shows method `writeDVDBinaryObjectFile()`, and Fig. 8.32 shows method `readDVDBinaryObjectFile()`.

Figure 8.31   Method `writeDVDBinaryObjectFile()` (for class `DVDCollection`)

```java
// postcondition: Writes the DVD information stored in vector DVDs
//    to binary object file outs.
public void writeDVDBinaryObjectFile(ObjectOutputStream outs) {
   try {
      // Write each DVD to binary object file outs.
      for (int next = 0; next < DVDs.size(); next++) {
         DVD nextDVD = (DVD) DVDs.elementAt(next);
         nextDVD.writeDVD(outs);
      }

      outs.close();
   }
   catch (IOException e) {
      System.out.println("i/o error: " + e.getMessage());
      e.printStackTrace();
   }
}
```

Figure 8.32 Method `readDVDBinaryObjectFile()` (for class `DVDCollection`)

```
// postcondition: Reads a collection of DVDs from binary object
//    file ins and stores the information in vector DVDs.
public void readDVDBinaryObjectFile(ObjectInputStream ins) {
   try {
      // Read data for DVD collection and store it in DVDs.
      try {
         while (true) {
            DVD aDVD = new DVD();
            aDVD.readDVD(ins);
            DVDs.addElement(aDVD);
         }
      }
      catch (EOFException eof) {
         System.out.println("end of input file reached");
         ins.close();
      }
   }  // Catch errors
   catch (IOException ex) {
      System.out.println("i/o error: " + ex.getMessage());
      ex.printStackTrace();
   }
   catch (ClassNotFoundException ex) {
      System.out.println(ex.getMessage());
      ex.printStackTrace();
   }
}
```

Method **writeDVDBinaryObjectFile()** uses the statement

```
nextDVD.writeDVD(outs);
```

to write each object and method **readDVDBinaryObjectFile()** uses the statement

```
aDVD.readDVD(ins);
```

to read each object. Fig. 8.33 provides versions of these methods that write and read entire objects as records. These methods overload the ones shown in Fig. 8.29 because they have the same names but different parameter types. In **writeDVD()**, the statement

```
outs.writeObject(this);
```

writes the current object (**this**) to stream **outs**.
      In **readDVD()**, the statement

```
DVD aDVD = (DVD) ins.readObject();
```

reads the next record (type **Object**) from stream **ins** and casts it to type **DVD** before storing it in object **aDVD**. The remaining statements in **readDVD()** copy each data field of **aDVD** into the corresponding data field of the current **DVD** object (referenced by **this**). Notice that **readDVD()** declares that it can throw a **ClassNotFoundException** (a checked exception). A **catch** block for this exception type must be provided in method **readDVDBinaryObjectFile()** (Fig. 8.32).

Figure 8.33   Methods **writeDVD()** and **readDVD()** for **DVD** objects (insert in class **DVD**)

```
// postcondition: writes this DVD as a binary object
//    to binary stream outs.
public void writeDVD(ObjectOutputStream outs) throws IOException {
    outs.writeObject(this);
}


// postcondition: Reads the next object from binary stream ins
//    into this object.
public void readDVD(ObjectInputStream ins)
        throws IOException, ClassNotFoundException {
    DVD aDVD = (DVD) ins.readObject();
    this.title = aDVD.title;
    this.category = aDVD.category;
    this.year = aDVD.year;
    this.time = aDVD.time;
}
```

Writing and Reading Arrays to a Binary File (Optional)

You can also write an entire array as a single record to an **ObjectOutputStream** object and read this record into an **ObjectInputStream** object. Assume there is a class **DVDArray** (Fig. 8.34) that stores a DVD collection in an array instead of a vector. Data field **DVDs** (type **DVD[]**) is the data field for class **DVDArray**. Method **readDVDs()** reads the DVD data from a text file into array **DVDs**. This method is

Figure 8.34 Class `DVDArray` with methods `writeDVDArray()` and `readDVDArray()`

```java
/* DVDArray.java          Authors: Koffman & Wolz
 * Class that stores DVD information in an array of DVDs.
 */
import java.io.*;

public class DVDArray {

   // Data field
   private DVD[] DVDs;    // array of DVDs

   // Methods
   // Constructors
   public DVDArray() {}

   // Allocates an array with mySize elements.
   public DVDArray(int mySize) {
      DVDs = new DVD[mySize];
   }

   // postcondition: Reads a DVD collection from text file ins
   //    into array DVDs.
   public void readDVDs(BufferedReader ins) {
      try {
         // Read and store the data for DVD collection in array DVDs.
         String title = ins.readLine();
         int count = 0;
         while (title != null && count < DVDs.length) {
            String category = ins.readLine();
            int year = Integer.parseInt(ins.readLine());
            double time = Double.parseDouble(ins.readLine());
            DVDs[count] = new DVD(title, category, year, time);
            count++;
            title = ins.readLine();
         }

         ins.close();
      } // catch exceptions
      catch (NumberFormatException ex) {
         System.out.println("bad numeric string");
         ex.printStackTrace();
      } catch (IOException ex) {
         System.out.println("i/o error: " + ex.getMessage());
         ex.printStackTrace();
      }
   }
```

Figure 8.34   Class `DVDArray` with methods `writeDVDArray()` and `readDVDArray()`, *continued*

```
// postcondition: Writes the array DVDs as
//   a single object to binary file outs.
public void writeDVDArray (ObjectOutputStream outs) {
    try {
        // Write array DVDs as a record to binary output file
        outs.writeObject(DVDs);

        outs.close();
    }
    catch (IOException ex) {
        System.out.println("i/o error: " + ex.getMessage());
        ex.printStackTrace();
    }
}


// postcondition: Reads a single object (type DVD[]) from
//   binary stream ins into array DVDS.
public void readDVDArray(ObjectInputStream ins) {
    try {
        // Read DVD array as a record from binary stream ins.
        try {
            DVDs = new DVD[DVDs.length];
            DVDs = (DVD[]) ins.readObject();
        }
        catch (EOFException eof) {
            System.out.println("end of input file reached");
            ins.close();
        }
    } // catch errors
    catch (IOException ex) {
        System.out.println("i/o error: " + ex.getMessage());
        ex.printStackTrace();
    }
    catch (ClassNotFoundException ex) {
        System.out.println("object in binary file is not DVD[]");
        ex.printStackTrace();
    }

}
}
```

similar to method **ReadDVDs( )** for class **DVDCollection** (Fig. 8.19), which reads the DVD data into vector DVDs.

Method **writeDVDArray( )** writes array **DVDs** to its binary file argument. The statement

```
outs.writeObject(DVDs);
```

writes array **DVDs** as a single record to stream **outs**.

In method **readDVDArray( )** (Fig. 8.34), the first statement below

```
DVDs = new DVD[DVDs.length];
DVDs = (DVD[]) ins.readObject();
```

creates a new array of **DVD** objects (referenced by **DVDs**) with the same number of elements as the original. Next, we read a single record from the binary file, casting it to type **DVD[ ]** (an array of **DVD** objects) before storing it in array **DVDs**.

EXERCISES FOR SECTION 8.5

SELF-CHECK

1. What is the difference between a text file and a binary file? What are the advantages of each?

2. What stream type and methods would you use to write a file storing binary images for each data field in an object. Assume the object has one data field of type **String**, **int**, **char**, and **double**. What stream type and methods would you use to read the data in this file?

3. Answer Self-Check Exercise 2 assuming you are writing each object as a single record to the binary file.

PROGRAMMING

1. Write a **main( )** method that creates a **DVDCollection** object and uses method **writeBinaryFile( )** to read a DVD collection from a text file and create a binary file with the DVD data. Next, it calls method **readBinaryFile( )** to read the file that was just created back into the DVD collection. Finally it displays the contents of object **DVDCollection**. *Hint:* In your **main( )** method, you will need to create stream objects of the appropriate types before calling the methods. Assume **writeBinaryFile( )** and **readBinaryFile( )** are instance methods of class **DVDCollection**.

2. Do Programming Exercise 1 using methods `writeBinaryObjectFile()` and `readBinaryObjectFile()`.

3. Do Programming Exercise 1 for a `DVDArray` object using methods `writeDVDArray()` and `readDVDArray()`. Assume these methods are instance methods of class `DVDArray`.

8.6 Common Programming Errors

You should try to prevent an error from occurring by using an `if` statement. However, if you can't write an `if` condition that will guard a potentially erroneous statement, the next best thing is to try to catch or trap the error using a `try-catch` statement.

You will get a `catch is unreachable` syntax error if a `catch` block exception type is a subclass of the exception type for an earlier block. The earlier `catch` block prevents the later one from executing; hence, the error. Reorder the `catch` blocks so that the most specific exception type (the subclass type) comes first.

You must either handle a checked exception inside a method where it might occur or declare it as thrown using a `throws` clause in the method header. If not, you will get a syntax error such as `unreported exception, ExceptionType must be caught or declared to be thrown`.

When you throw an exception, make sure that the caller of the method throwing the exception catches it or declares it to be thrown. If not, you will get an `unreported exception, ExceptionType must be caught or declared to be thrown` error.

Stream and file processing are potential sources of error, and the exceptions that they raise are checked exceptions. Therefore, you must place your file processing statement in a `try-catch` statement with a `catch` block that handles exceptions of type `IOExceptionType`. This is the superclass of all input/output exceptions, so it should follow the catch blocks for more specific input/output errors.

We discussed several stream types in this chapter. Be careful how you use them. For example, you should associate an input text file with a `FileReader` object and wrap it in a `BufferedReader` object. The chapter review will summarize the combinations discussed in this chapter and the methods that can be used with each stream type.

If you create a file as a particular output stream type, you should read it using only its corresponding input stream type. For example, a file that is written as a type `BufferedWriter` stream should be read using methods for a `BufferedReader` stream. You cannot read a text file using stream types and methods for binary files or read a binary file using stream types and methods for text files. Also, after you write an image to a binary file, you can only read that image with a method that is compatible with the one used to write it. For example, if an image is written using `writeUTF()`, it can only be read using `readUTF()`.

CHAPTER REVIEW

1. Exceptions are raised when a statement that causes a run-time error is executed. Use the **try-catch** statement to handle or trap errors that may occur in your programming. By handling these errors in your program, you enable it to continue running and take corrective measures. If your program doesn't handle an exception, it will be handled by the JVM and will cause program execution to terminate.

2. A **try-catch** statement can have many **catch** blocks. Each **catch** block begins with the phrase **catch(*ExceptionType* ex)**. If an exception occurs, the JVM executes the first **catch** block whose *ExceptionType* is the same as the exception type or is a superclass of the exception type. For this reason, you should order the **catch** blocks so that a superclass exception type follows all its subclass exception types. A **finally** block that executes after the **try** block or a **catch** block can follow all the **catch** blocks.

3. You don't have to handle an exception in the method that raises it. If an exception is not handled in the method where it occurs, it will propogate to the caller of this method. If a **catch** block that handles this exception type is present in the caller, that block will execute. If not, the exception will propogate to the caller of this method, and so on. This process continues until either a **catch** block that handles the exception is found or the **main()** method is reached. If there is no **catch** block for the exception in any of the methods in the call stack, the JVM handles the method and terminates program execution.

4. Checked exceptions must be handled in the method where they occur or must be explicitly declared as being thrown using **throws *ExceptionType*** in the method heading. Examples of checked exceptions are exceptions caused by input/output operations. You can use the **throw** statement (**throw new *ExceptionType* (*Stringmess*)**) to actually throw an exception. The **String** argument becomes the error message associated with the exception that is thrown. One of the methods in the call sequence must catch a checked exception.

5. Streams are used for data input and output in Java. **System.out** is a predefined stream type that represents console output. **System.in** (type **InputStreamReader**) is a predefined stream that represents console input. It is appropriate to study exceptions and streams in the same chapter because stream processing often causes input/output exceptions. These are checked exceptions.

6. We saw that in stream processing, it is useful to wrap one primitive stream type in a second stream type that provides more user-friendly methods. We show a summary of these stream types and methods at the end of the review.

7. You can create a text file using an editor or by running a program. Text files are sequences of ASCII characters. Text files can be read by humans. We write a `String` expression as a line of information to a text file (a `PrintWriter` object) using method `println()`; we read a line of information from a text file (a `BufferedReader` object) into a `String` variable using method `readLine()`. We use `Integer.parseInt()` and `Double.parseDouble()` to convert a numeric string to a type `int` or `double` value, respectively. If the string is not numeric, the attempt to convert it raises a `NumberFormatException`.

8. Binary files consist of binary images of storage space allocated to individual data items or objects. They cannot be read by humans; however, they are more efficient in terms of processing time and space utilization. We can create a binary file that stores binary images of strings and primitive values. We use method `writeUTF()` (for strings), `writeInt()`, `writeDouble()`, `writeChar()`, or `writeBoolean()` to write a binary image to a binary file (a `DataOutputStream` object). We use a corresponding method that begins with `read` to read a binary image from a binary file (a `DataInputStream` object). We use `writeObject()` to write a binary image of an object or an array to a binary file (an `ObjectOutputStream` object). We use `readObject()` to read a binary image of an object or an array from a binary file (an `ObjectInputStream` object).

New Java constructs

Construct	Effect
`try-catch` Block	

``
try {
    int num = Integer.parseInt(str);
}
catch (NumberFormatException ex) {
    System.out.println(ex.getMessage());
    ex.printStackTrace();
}
``
	Attempts to convert string `str` to type `int` and store the result in `num`. If `str` does not reference a valid numeric string, the `catch` block displays an error message in the console window and displays a trace of the call stack.

Console Input	

``
InputStreamReader inStream = new
    InputStreamReader(System.in);
BufferedReader ins = new
    BufferedReader(inStream);
``
	Use method `readLine()` to read data lines from the console. To test for end of data, use the condition (`str != null`) where `str` references the data line just read.

Text File Input	

``
FileReader inStream = new
    FileReader("data.txt");
BufferedReader ins = new
    BufferedReader(inStream);
``
	Use method `readLine()` to read data lines from text file `data.txt`. To test for end of data, use the condition (`str != null`) where `str` references the data line just read.

New Java constructs, *continued*

Text File Output

```
FileWriter outStream = new
    FileWriter("out.txt");
PrintWriter outs = new
    PrintWriter(outStream);
```

Use method `print(String)` or method `println(String)` to write to text file **out.txt**.

Binary File Input

```
FileInputStream inStream = new
    FileInputStream("data.bin");
DataInputStream ins = new
    DataInputStream(inStream);
```

Use method `readUTF()`, `readChar()`, `readInt()`, `readDouble()`, `readBoolean()` to read a binary image from file **data.bin**. An `EOFException` is raised if you attempt to read an item after the end of the file has been reached.

Binary File Output

```
FileOutputStream outStream = new
    FileOutputStream("out.bin");
DataOutputStream outs = new
    DataOutputStream(outStream);
```

Use method `writeUTF(String)`, `writeChar(int)`, `writeInt(int)`, `writeDouble()`, `writeBoolean(boolean b)` to write a binary image from memory to file **out.bin**.

Object File Input

```
FileInputStream inStream = new
    FileInputStream("data.bin");
ObjectInputStream ins = new
    ObjectInputStream(inStream);
```

Use method `readObject()` to read the next object from a binary file. Cast the result to the type of object that was read. An `EOFException` occurs if you attempt to read an object after the end of the file has been reached. The object being read must implement the **Serializable** interface.

Object File Output

```
FileOutputStream outStream = new
    FileOutputStream("out.bin");
ObjectOutputStream outs = new
    ObjectOutputStream(outStream);
```

Use method `writeObject()` to write an object to a binary file. The object being written must implement the **Serializable** interface.

✔ QUICK-CHECK EXERCISES

1. If you can do both, is it better to use an `if` statement to prevent an error or to use a `try-catch` to handle an error when it occurs?

2. What can happen if you don't close an output file?

3. Why do we wrap one stream object inside of another?

4. If a **try-catch** statement contains **catch** blocks with exception types **IOException**, **FileNotFoundException**, and **EOFException**, in what order must these blocks appear?

5. Objects of which stream class have the same methods as **System.out**?

6. Complete the declarations for object **ins**, which represents the console.

    _____ inStream = new _____ (_____);
    _____ ins = new _____ (inStream);

7. Complete the declarations for object **outs**, which represents an output text file.

    _____ outStream = new _____ (outFileName);
    _____ outs = new _____ (outStream);

8. Complete the declarations for object **ins**, which represents an input text file.

    _____ inStream = new _____ (inFileName);
    _____ ins = new _____ (inStream);

9. Complete the declarations for object **ins**, which represents a binary input file with separate images for each primitive type data item.

    _____ inStream = new _____ (inFileName);
    _____ ins = new _____ (inStream);

10. Complete the declarations for object **outs**, which represents a binary output file with a single record for each object.

    _____ outStream = new _____ (outFileName);
    _____ outs = new _____ (outStream);

ANSWERS TO QUICK-CHECK EXERCISES

1. Preventing an error is better than handling it.

2. You may not store all the information written to that file on disk.

3. This allows us to use more user-friendly methods to read and write information.

4. **IOException** (the superclass for input/output exceptions) must be last.

5. `PrintWriter`

6. `InputStreamReader`
   ```
   inStream = new InputStreamReader(System.in);
   BufferedReader ins = new BufferedReader(inStream);
   ```

7. ```
   FileWriter outStream = new FileWriter(outFileName);
   PrintWriter outs = new PrintWriter(outStream);
   ```

8. ```
   FileReader inStream = new FileReader(inFileName);
   BufferedReader ins = new BufferedReader(inStream);
   ```

9. `FileInputStream`
   ```
   inStream = new FileInputStream(inFileName);
   DataInputStream ins = new DataInputStream(inStream);
   ```

10. `FileOutputStream`
    ```
    outStream = new FileOutputStream(outFileName);
    ObjectOutputStream
    outs = new ObjectOutputStream(outStream);
    ```

REVIEW QUESTIONS

Use class `Date` for the following questions:

```
public class Date implements Serializable {
   private String month;
   private int day;
   private int year;
```

1. Write an instance method to write a `Date` object to a text file (a parameter).

2. Write an instance method to read a `Date` object from a text file (a parameter). Make sure you check for number format exceptions.

3. Write an instance method to write a `Date` object to a binary file (a parameter). Write each data field separately.

4. Write an instance method to read a `Date` object from a binary file (a parameter). Read each data field separately.

5. Write an instance method to write a `Date` object to a binary file (a parameter). Write the object as a file record.

6. Write an instance method to read a `Date` object from a binary file (a parameter). Read the object as a file record.

7. Class **Calendar** stores an array of **Date** objects in data field **myDates**. Write an instance method for this class to read a collection of **Date** objects into array **myDates** from a text file.

8. For class **Calendar**, write an instance method for this class to read a collection of **Date** objects into array **myDates** from a binary file with separate binary images for each field.

9. For class **Calendar**, write an instance method for this class to read a collection of **Date** objects into array **myDates** from a binary file assuming each object is stored as a single record.

10. For class **Calendar**, write an instance method for this class to read a collection of **Date** objects into array **myDates** from a binary file that stores the array as a single object.

PROGRAMMING PROJECTS

1. Complete the methods for **DVDCollection** shown in Figure 8.17. Test your final class using class **DVDGUI**. If the file selected to be opened or saved has an extension **.txt**, use text file methods. If the file selected to be opened or saved has an extension **.bin**, use binary file methods.

2. Modify class **PhoneBook** and **PhoneBookGUI** (Section 7.6) to enable the phone book data to be read from a text file and stored in a text file after you are done.

3. Add methods to class **Company** (Fig. 5.30) that enable information about a company's employees to be read from text files, from binary files, from binary files of objects, and as a single record from a binary file. Provide corresponding file write methods. Write a driver program that tests all these file processing methods.

4. Each year the state legislature rates the productivity of the faculty of each of the state-supported colleges and universities. The rating is based on reports submitted by the faculty members that indicate the average number of hours worked per week during the school year. Each faculty member is rated, and the university receives an overall rating. The faculty productivity ratings are computed as follows:

   a. Highly productive means over 55 hours per week reported.

   b. Satisfactory means reported hours per week are between 35 and 55.

   c. Overpaid means reported hours per week are less than 35.

   d. Read the following data from a text file:

Names	Hours
Herm	63
Flo	37
Jake	20
Maureen	55
Saul	72
Tony	40
Al	12

Write each faculty member's name, hours, and productivity rating to an output text file.

5. Whatsamata U. offers a service to its faculty in computing grades at the end of each semester. A program will process three weighted test scores and will calculate a student's average and letter grade (A is 90 to 100, a B is 80 to 89, etc.). Write a program system that will read the student data from a text file and write each student's ID, test score, average, and grade to a binary output file. The data will consist of the three test weights followed by three test scores and a student ID number (four digits) for each student. Calculate the weighted average for each student and the corresponding grade. This information should be written out along with the three test scores. The weighted average for each student is equal to

    weight1 × score1 + weight2 × score2 + weight3 × score3

    For summary statistics, display the "highest weighted average," "lowest weighted average," "average of the weighted averages," and "total number of students processed." Sample data:

    ```
    0.35   0.25   0.40         (test weights)
    100    76    88   1014     (test scores and ID)
    ```

6. Because text files can grow very large, some computer systems supply a handy utility program that displays the head and tail of a file, where the head is the first four lines, and the tail is the last four lines. Write a program that asks the user to type in a filename and then displays the head of the file, a line of dots (three or four dots will do), and the tail of the file. If the file is eight lines long or less, just display the entire file.

7. Write a program to manage a dictionary. Your dictionary should be stored in a text file named **diction.txt** and consist of an alphabetized list of words, one per line. When a user enters a word, scan the dictionary looking for the word. If the word is in the dictionary, say so. If not, display the dictionary word immediately preceding and the word immediately following so the user can see

words that are close in spelling. Then ask if the user wants to add this new word to the dictionary. If the answer is Yes, do so and go back to request the next word.

To insert a word into a file in alphabetical order, simply copy the file to a new, temporary file named `diction.txt` and move words one at a time from this temporary file back to the original file, inserting the new word when you reach its correct position alphabetically.

9

Recursion

A recursive method is one that calls itself. Each time it is called, the recursive method can operate on different arguments. You can use recursion as an alternative to iteration (looping). Generally, a recursive solution is slightly less efficient, in terms of computer time, than an iterative one because of the overhead for the extra method calls. In many instances, however, recursion enables us to specify a natural, simple solution to a problem that otherwise would be difficult to solve. For this reason, recursion is an important and powerful tool in problem solving and programming. Recursion is used widely in solving problems that are not numeric, such as proving mathematical theorems, writing compilers, and in searching and sorting algorithms.

9.1   Recursive Methods

In this section we demonstrate recursion using a simple method and we develop rules for writing **recursive methods**, or methods that call themselves. Consider the computer solution to the problem "Raise 6 to the power 3." A computer can multiply, but it cannot perform the operation "Raise to the power." However, we know that 6^3 is 6 times 6^2 and 6^2 is 6 times 6. Therefore, the problem "Raise 6 to the power 3" can be split into the problems:

Subproblems Generated from "Raise 6 to the power 3":

Problem 1   Raise 6 to the power 2

Problem 2   Multiply the result of problem 1 by 6

Because a computer can multiply, we can solve problem 2 but not problem 1. However, problem 1 is an easier version of the original problem. We can split it into two problems, 1.1 and 1.2, leaving three problems to solve (1.1, 1.2, and 2), two of which are multiplications:

Subproblems Generated from "Raise 6 to the power 2":

Problem 1.1   Raise 6 to the power 1

Problem 1.2   Multiply the result of problem 1.1 by 6

You can program a computer to recognize that the result of raising any number to the power 1 is that number. Therefore, we can solve problem 1.1 (the answer is 6) and then solve problem 1.2 (the answer is 36), which gives us the solution to problem 1. Multiplying this result by 6 (problem 2) gives us 216, which is the solution to the original problem.

Figure 9.1 implements this approach to raising a number to a power as the recursive Java method **power()**, which returns the result of raising its first argument, **m**, to the power indicated by its second argument, **n**. If **n** is greater than **1**, the statement

```
return m * power(m, n-1);      // Recursive step
```

executes, splitting the original problem into the two simpler problems as desired:

Problem 1   Raise **m** to the power **n-1** (**power(m, n-1)**)

Problem 2   Multiply the result by **m**

If the new second argument is greater than **1**, there will be additional calls to method **power()**. We call this case the **recursive step** because it contains a call to method **power()**.

The first case in Fig. 9.1 causes an immediate return from the method when the condition **n <= 1** becomes **true**. We call this a **stopping case** because it ends the recursion. A condition that is true for a stopping case is called a **terminating condition**.

Figure 9.1 Recursive method power

```
//   precondition : m and n are defined and n > 0.
//   postcondition: Returns m raised to the power n.
public static int power(int m, int n) {
    if (n <= 1)
        return m;                       // Stopping case
    else
        return m * power(m, n-1); // Recursive step
}
```

Tracing a Recursive Method

Hand-tracing an algorithm's execution demonstrates how that algorithm works. We can trace the execution of the method call **power(6, 3)** by drawing an activation frame that corresponds to each call of the method. An **activation frame** is a logical device that shows the argument values for each call and summarizes its execution.

Fig. 9.2 shows the three activation frames generated to solve the problem of raising 6 to the power 3. The part of each activation frame that executes before the next recursive call is in color; the part that executes after the return from the next call is in gray.

The value returned from each call appears alongside each black arrow. The return arrow from each method call points to the operator * because the multiplication is performed just after the return.

Figure 9.2 Trace of method power()

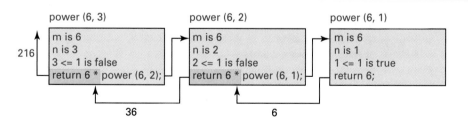

Figure 9.2 shows that there are three calls to method **power()**. Argument **m** has the value **6** for all calls; argument **n** has the values **3** , **2**, and finally **1**. Because n is **1** in the third call, the value of **m** (**6**) is returned as the result of that call. After the return to the second activation frame, the value of **m** is mulitiplied by this result, and the product (**36**) is returned as the result of the second call. After the return to the first activation frame, the value of **m** is multiplied by this result, and the product (**216**) is returned as the result of the original call to method **power()**.

Properties of Recursive Problems and Solutions

Problems that can be solved by recursion have the following characteristics:

- One or more stopping cases have a simple, nonrecursive solution.

- The other cases of the problem can be reduced (using recursion) to problems that are closer to stopping cases.

- Eventually the problem can be reduced to only stopping cases, which are relatively easy to solve.

    Follow these steps to solve a recursive problem:

1. Try to express the problem as a simpler version of itself.

2. Determine the stopping cases.

3. Determine the recursive steps.

The recursive algorithms that we write generally consist of an **if** statement with the form

if the stopping case is reached

　　　Solve it.

else

　　　Split the problem into simpler cases using recursion.

Fig. 9.3 illustrates these steps. Assume that for a particular problem of size n, we can split the problem into a problem of size 1, which we can solve (a stopping case), and a problem of size $n - 1$. We can split the problem of size $n - 1$ into another problem of size 1 and a problem of size $n - 2$, which we can split further. If we split the problem n times, we end up with n problems of size 1, all of which we can solve.

In some situations, we represent a recursive algorithm as an **if** statement whose consequent is the recursive step. The condition tests whether the stopping case has been reached. If not, the recursive step executes; otherwise, an immediate return occurs.

if the stopping case is not reached

　　　Split the problem into simpler cases using recursion.

Figure 9.3   Splitting a problem into smaller problems

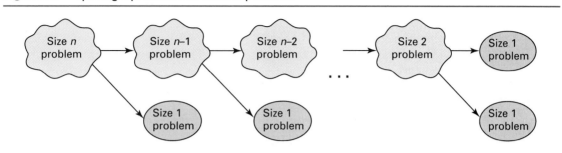

EXERCISES FOR SECTION 9.1

SELF-CHECK

1. Show how the problem generated by the method call **power(5, 4)** can be split into smaller problems as in Fig. 9.3.

2. Trace the execution of **power(5, 4)**.

3. Given the following method and the call **whatDo(4)**, what would be the output?

```
public static void whatDo(int i) {
    if (i > 1) {
        displayResult(i);
        whatDo(i - 1);
        displayResult(i)
    }
}
```

PROGRAMMING

1. Write a recursive method **multiply(int a, int b)** to compute the same result as **a * b** without using the operator *****.

2. Write a recursive method **divide(int a, int b)** to compute the same result as **a / b** without using the operator **/** or **%**.

9.2 Recursive Mathematical Methods

Many mathematical methods are defined recursively. An example is the factorial of a number *n* (represented as *n*!).

◆ 0! is 1.

◆ n! is $n \times (n - 1)!$ for $n > 0$.

This is the definition of n! Thus, $4! = 4 \times 3! = 4 \times 3 \times 2!$, and so on. In Section 6.7 (see Fig. 6.23) you saw how to implement this recursive mathematics definition as a recursive method.

◆◆EXAMPLE 9.1 ━━━━━━━━━━━━━━━━━━━━━━━━━━━━━━━━━━━━

The **greatest common divisor (gcd)** of two integers is the largest integer that divides them both. A recursive definition of Euclid's algorithm for finding the greatest common divisor of two positive integers, m and n, follows.

◆ `gcd(m, n)` is `gcd(n, m)` if `m < n`.

◆ `gcd(m, n)` is n if n `<=` m and n divides m.

◆ Otherwise, `gcd(m, n)` is `gcd(n,` remainder of m divided by n).

This algorithm states the following: If m is the smaller number, the **gcd** determination should be performed with the arguments transposed. If n is less than or equal to m and n divides m, the result is n. If n does not divide m, the answer is obtained by finding the **gcd** of n and the remainder of m divided by n. Fig. 9.4 shows method **gcd()**.

Figure 9.4   Method gcd()

```
//      precondition : m and n are defined and both are > 0.
//      postcondition: Returns greatest common divisor of m & n.
public static int gcd(int m, int n) {
     if (m < n)
          return gcd(n, m);
     else if (m % n == 0)
          return n;
     else
          return gcd(n, m % n);
}
```

◆◆

◆◆EXAMPLE 9.2 ───

The Fibonacci numbers are a sequence of numbers that have varied uses. They were originally intended to model the growth of a rabbit colony. We will not describe the model here, but you can see that the Fibonacci sequence 1, 1, 2, 3, 5, 8, 13, 21, 34, . . . increases rapidly. The 15th number in the sequence is 610 (that's a lot of rabbits!). The Fibonacci sequence is defined as follows:

◆ Fib_1 is 1.

◆ Fib_2 is 1.

◆ Fib_n is $Fib_{n-2} + Fib_{n-1}$, for $n > 2$.

Verify for yourself that the sequence of numbers in the preceding paragraph is correct. Fig. 9.5 shows a recursive method that computes the nth Fibonacci number.

Figure 9.5   Recursive method `fibonacci()`

```
//     precondition : n is defined and n > 0.
//     postcondition: Returns the nth Fibonacci number.
public static int fibonacci(int n) {
    if (n <= 2)
        return 1;
    else
        return fibonacci(n-2) + fibonacci(n-1);
}
```

─── ◆◆

Although easy to write, the **fibonacci()** method is very inefficient because each recursive step generates two calls to method **fibonacci()**. Also, we must evaluate the two recursive calls independently. This means that for a particular value of **n**, we cannot use the result of the earlier call to **fibonacci(n-2)** to reduce the effort needed to calculate the value of **fibonacci(n-1)**. We have to recalculate **fibonacci(n-2)** all over again.

EXERCISES FOR SECTION 9.2

SELF-CHECK

1. What does method `puzzle()` compute? What is its result when **n** is 2?

```
public static int puzzle(int n) {
    if (n == 1)
        return 0;
    else
        return 1 + puzzle(n / 2);
}
```

2. If a program had the statement `f = fibonacci(5)`, how many calls to `fibonacci` would be performed?

3. Complete the following recursive method, which calculates the result of raising an integer (**base**) to an exponent (**exp**). The value of **exp** can be positive, negative, or zero. You should provide two stopping cases.

```
public static double powerRaiser(int base, int exp) {
        if (base == 0)
            return _____;
        else if (exp == 0)
            return _____;
        else if (exp < 0)
            return 1.0 / _____;
        else
            return _____;
}
```

4. What would happen if the terminating condition for method `fibonacci()` is `n <= 1`?

PROGRAMMING

1. Write a recursive method, `findSum()`, that calculates the sum of successive integers starting at 1 and ending at n (e.g., `findSum(n) = 1 + 2 + . . . + (n - 1) + n`).

2. Write an iterative version of the `fibonacci()` method. *Hint:* First determine the least number of calculations you need to remember.

3. Write an iterative method that calculates the greatest common divisor.

9.3   Use of the Stack in Recursion

Displaying Characters in Reverse Order

Method **reverse()** in Fig. 9.6 is an unusual recursive method because it has no argument, and it does not return a value. It reads in a sequence of individual characters and displays the sequence in reverse order. If the user enters the data characters a, b, c, d, e, * (the sentinel), they will be displayed as **edcba**.

The body of method **reverse()** first stores a data character in **next**. Then it executes the **if** statement. The stopping case is reached when **next** contains the character *. Otherwise, the recursive step executes:

```
reverse();
System.out.print(next);
```

The character just read is not displayed until later. This is because the call to **print()** follows the recursive method call; consequently, **print()** is not called until after the recursive call to **reverse()** is completed. For example, the first character that is read is not displayed until after the method execution for the second character is done. Hence, the first character is displayed after the second character, which is displayed after the third character.

To see why this is so, let's trace the execution of method **reverse()** assuming the characters c, a, t, * are entered as data. The trace (Fig. 9.7) shows three activation frames for method **reverse()**. Each activation frame shows the value of **next** for that frame. Note that the sentinel character * is not displayed.

The statements that execute for each frame are shown next. The statements in color are recursive method calls and result in a new activation frame, as indicated by the colored arrows. A method return is indicated by a black arrow that points to the statement in the calling frame to which the method returns. Tracing the colored arrows and then the black arrows in Fig. 9.7 gives us the sequence of events listed in

Figure 9.6   Method reverse()

```
//  postcondition: displays characters in reverse
//     of the order in which they are entered.
public static void reverse()  {
    String nextStr =
        JOptionPane.showInputDialog("Next character or *");
    char next = nextStr.charAt(0);
    if (next != '*')  {
        reverse();
        System.out.print(next);
    }
}
```

Figure 9.7   Trace of method `reverse`

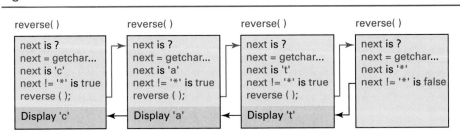

Fig. 9.8. To help you understand this list, all the statements for a particular activation frame are indented to the same column.

As shown, there are four calls to method **reverse()**. The method returns always occur in the reverse order of the method calls; that is, we return from the last call first, then we return from the next to last call, and so on. After we return from a particular execution of the method, we display the character that was read into **next** just prior to that method call. The process of returning from a succession of recursive calls is called **unwinding the recursion**.

Figure 9.8   Sequence of events for trace of `reverse()`

Call **reverse()**.

    Read the first character (**c**) into **next**.

    next is not *—Call **reverse()**.

        Read the second character (**a**) into **next**.

        next is not *—Call **reverse()**.

        Read the third character (**t**) into **next**.

        next is not *—Call **reverse()**.

            Read the fourth character (*) into **next**.

            next is *—Return from fourth call.

        Display the third character (**t**).

        Return from third call.

    Display the second character (**a**).

    Return from second call.

Display the first character (**c**).

Return from original call.

Stack for Method Calls

Java uses a special data structure called a **stack** to keep track of critical data for a recursive method as it changes from call to call. A stack is analogous to a stack of dishes or trays. In a stack of dishes in a buffet line, clean dishes are always placed on top of the stack. When you need a dish, you always remove the last one placed on the stack. This causes the next-to-last dish placed on the stack to move to the top of the stack.

Whenever a method call occurs (recursive or otherwise), a number of items are placed onto the stack. They include the argument values for that call, a storage location for each local variable during that call, and the instruction to return to after that call is finished. Whenever **next** is referenced in method **reverse( )**, Java accesses the top storage location for **next** allocated on the stack. When a method return occurs, the storage locations for that call at the top of the stack are removed, and the storage locations for the previous call "move" to the top.

Let's look at the stack right after the first call to **reverse( )**. To simplify our discussion, we consider only the storage locations for local variable **next** that are allocated on the stack. There is one storage location on the stack and the letter **c** is read into it:

Stack after first call to reverse():

Right after the second call to **reverse( )**, another storage location for **next** is allocated on the stack and the letter **a** is read into it:

Stack after second call to reverse():

a
c

Right after the third call to **reverse( )**, another storage location for **next** is allocated on the stack and the letter **t** is read into it:

Stack after third call to reverse():

t
a
c

Right after the fourth call to **reverse( )**, another storage location for **next** is allocated on the stack and the character ***** is read into it:

Stack after fourth call to reverse():

Because next is * (the stopping case), an immediate return occurs. The method return causes the value at the top of the stack to be removed, as shown next.

Stack after first return from reverse():

Control returns to the statement that calls method **print()**, so the value of **next** (**t**) at the top of the stack is displayed. Another return from method **reverse()** occurs, causing the value currently at the top of the stack to be removed.

Stack after second return from reverse():

Again, control returns to the statement that calls method **print()**, and the value of **next**   (**a**) at the top of the stack is displayed. Another return from method **reverse()** occurs, causing the value currently at the top of the stack to be removed.

Stack after third return from reverse():

Again, control returns to the statement that calls method **print()**,   and the value of **next** (**c**) at the top of the stack is displayed. Another return from method **reverse()** occurs, causing the value currently at the top of the stack to be removed. Now, the stack is empty and control returns to the statement in the application that follows the original call to method **reverse()**.

Chapter 10 shows you how to declare and manipulate stacks yourself. Because these steps are all done automatically by Java, we can write recursive methods without worrying about the stack.

EXERCISES FOR SECTION 9.3

SELF-CHECK

1. Assume the characters **q, w, e, r,*** are entered when method **reverse()** is called. Show the contents of the stack immediately after each recursive call and return.

2. For the method call **power(5, 4)**, show the stack after each recursive call. Place a new pair of values on the stack for each call. Remove the top pair after returning from each call.

3. Modify method **reverse()** so that it also displays the sentinel character.

PROGRAMMING

1. Write an application that calls method `reverse()`.

9.4 Recursive Methods with Arrays, Vectors, and Strings

So far our recursive examples have used arguments that are integers. Recursive methods also can process arguments that are data structures or objects.

CASE STUDY SUMMING THE VALUES IN AN ARRAY

PROBLEM   Write a recursive method that finds the sum of the values in an array `x` of size `n` (elements `x[0]` through `x[n-1]`).

ANALYSIS   The stopping case occurs when `n` is `1`, that is, the sum is `x[0]` for an array with one element. If `n` is not `1`, we must add `x[n-1]` to the sum we get when we add the values in the subarray with indices `0` through `n-2` (a simpler version of the problem).

Data Requirements

Problem Inputs

`int[] x`—array of integer values
`int n`—number of elements to be added

Problem Output

The sum of the array values

DESIGN

Algorithm for *findSum()*

`if` (n is 1)
    The sum is `x[0]`.
`else`
    Add `x[n-1]` to the sum of values in the subarray with indices `0` through `n-2`.

IMPLEMENTATION   Method `findSum()` in Fig. 9.9 implements this algorithm.

Figure 9.9   Using recursive method `findSum()`

```
//    precondition : Array x is defined and n >= 1.
//    postcondition: Returns sum of first n elements of x.
public static int findSum(int[] x, int n) {
  if (n <= 1)
    return x[0];
  else
    return x[n-1] + findSum(x, n-1);
}
```

TESTING   Fig. 9.10 traces the method call **findSum(x, 3)** for the array **x** shown next:

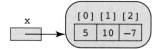

As before, the colored part of each activation frame executes before the next recursive method call, and each colored arrow points to a new activation frame. The gray part of each activation frame executes after the return from a recursive call, and each black arrow indicates the return point (the operator **+**) after a method execution. The value returned is indicated alongside the black arrow. The value returned for the original call, **findSum(x, 3)**, is **8**.

Figure 9.10   Trace of `findSum(x, 3)`

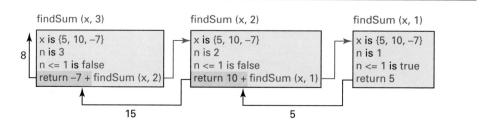

◆◆EXAMPLE 9.3

Method **search()** in Fig. 9.11 returns the location (array index) where the argument **target** occurs in the array with elements **x[0]** through **x[n-1]**. If **target** is not found, method **search()** returns the value **-1**. The target cannot be present if the array is empty, so the empty array (**n == 0**) is a stopping case. For nonempty arrays, the result is **true** if the last element, **x[n-1]**, equals **target** (another stop-

Figure 9.11   Recursive method `search()`

```
// precondition : target, n, and array x are defined & n >= 0.
// postcondition: Returns position of the
//    last occurrence of target in elements x[0] through x[n-1]
//    if target is found; otherwise, returns -1.
public static int search(int[] x, int target, int n) {
   if (n == 0)
      return -1;          // target not in empty array.
   else if (x[n-1] == target)
      return n-1;         // Found! - return location.
   else  // Search rest of array.
      return search(x, target, n-1);
}
```

ping case). Otherwise, the result depends on whether **target** occurs in the sub-array **x[0]** through **x[n-2]**, as indicated by the recursive step.

Fig. 9.12 traces the method call **search(x, 10, x.length)** for the array **x** shown next:

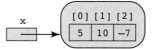

The value returned is **true**, because the expression **x[n-1] == target** is **true** when **n** is **1** (the second activation frame).

Figure 9.12   Trace of method `search()`

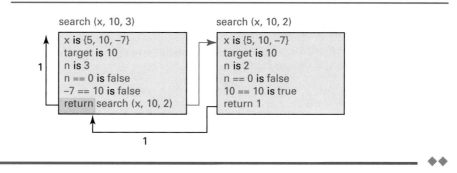

Comparison of Iterative and Recursive Methods

In method `searchIt()` (Fig. 9.13), the iterative version of `search()`, a loop is needed to examine each array element, starting with the last. If `target` is found at element `x[i]`, the array search terminates and the method returns the index `i`. If all array elements are examined without success, the method returns **-1**.

The iterative method would execute a bit faster than the recursive version. However, many programmers would argue that the recursive version is aesthetically more pleasing. It is certainly more compact (a single `if` statement). Once you are accustomed to thinking recursively, the recursive form is somewhat easier to read and understand than the iterative form.

Some programmers like to use recursion as a conceptual tool. Once they have written the recursive form of a method, they can always translate it into an iterative version if run-time efficiency is important. In Section 9.5, we describe a much more efficient searching algorithm.

Figure 9.13   Iterative method `searchIt()`

```
// precondition: target, n, and array x are defined & n >= 0.
// postcondition: Returns position of the last occurrence of target
//    in array elements x[0] through x[n-1] if target is found in array
//    x; otherwise, returns -1.
public static int searchIt(int[] x, int target, int n) {
  for (int i = n-1; i >= 0; i--)
     if (x[i] == target)
        return i;     // Found! - return location.

  // Assert: All elements examined & target not found.
  return -1;
}
```

A Recursive `boolean` Method

Methods that return `boolean` values (`true` or `false`) also can be written using recursion. These methods do not perform a computation; however, the method result is still determined by evaluating an expression (type `boolean`) containing a recursive call.

◆◆EXAMPLE 9.4 ───

The `boolean` method `isEqual()` (Fig. 9.14) returns `true` if two arrays, say, `x` and `y`, of `n` elements are the same (e.g., `x[0] == y[0]`, `x[1] == y[1]`, `x[n-1] == y[n-1]`). There are three stopping cases: If the array lengths are not equal, the result is `false`. For single-element arrays, the result depends on whether `x[0]` and `y[0]` have the same value. For larger arrays, the result is **false** if the last elements of each array have different values. If they are equal, we still have to compare the first **n-1** elements of both arrays (a simpler version of the problem).

Figure 9.14   Recursive method `isEqual()`

```
// precondition: Arrays x & y are defined and n > 0.
// postcondition: Returns true if arrays
//    x & y are equal;
//    otherwise, returns false.
public static boolean isEqual(int[] x, int[] y, int n) {
    if (x.length != y.length)
        return false;              // Array sizes unequal.
    else if (n == 1)
        return (x[0] == y[0]); // Compare 1-element arrays.
    else if (x[n-1] != y[n-1])
        return false;              // Found an unequal pair.
    else  // Compare rest of arrays.
        return isEqual(x, y, n-1);
}
```

A Recursive Vector Search

Figure 9.15 shows a recursive method, **searchVec()**, that searches a vector. If **names** is a vector of strings, you can use the method call

```
searchVec(names, "Sally", names.size());
```

to search for the string **"Sally"** in vector **names**.

The stopping cases for **searchVec()** are similar to recursive method **search()** (Fig. 9.11). The first condition tests for an empty vector (**n == 0**). The second condition tests whether the last element matches **target**. The recursive step calls **searchVec()** to search a smaller-sized vector. Note that method **equals()** must be defined for the objects being compared.

Recursion with Strings

Figure 9.16 shows a recursive method, **searchStr()**, that searches for a character in a string. It is very similar to the other search methods. Notice that we don't need to pass the string length as an argument. The statement

```
int posLast = s.length() - 1; // index of last character.
```

defines the position of the last character in the string when **searchStr()** is entered. If the string is not empty (first stopping case) and the last character in string **s** does not match the target (second stopping case), the recursive step

```
return searchStr(s.substring(0, posLast), target);
```

searches for **target** in the substring of **s** that excludes the last character.

Figure 9.15   Method searchVec()

```
// precondition: target, n, & vector v are defined & n >= 0.
// postcondition: Returns position of its last occurrence
//    if target is found in
//    vector v; otherwise, returns -1.
public static int searchVec(Vector v, Object target, int n) {
   if (n == 0)
      return -1;
   else if (v.elementAt(n-1).equals(target))
      return n-1;          // Found! - return location.
   else  // Search rest of vector.
      return searchVec(v, target, n-1);
}
```

Figure 9.16   Method searchStr()

```
// precondition: target & string s are defined.
// postcondition: Returns position of its last occurrence
//    if target is located in string s; otherwise, returns -1.
public static int searchStr(String s, char target) {
   int posLast = s.length() - 1; // index of last character.

   if (posLast == -1)
      return -1;                      // empty string.
   else if (s.charAt(posLast) == target)
      return posLast;                 // Found - return location.
   else  // Search rest of string.
      return searchStr(s.substring(0, posLast), target);
}
```

◆◆EXAMPLE 9.5 ────────────────────────

Method **reverse()** in Fig. 9.4 displayed a sequence of data characters in the reverse of the order in which they were entered. In this example, we show how to reverse a string that is already stored in a **String** object. The recursive algorithm follows.

Algorithm for *reverseStr()*

if the string is empty
> Return the empty string.

else
> Return the string formed by concatenating (joining) the last character with the reverse of the rest of the string (all but the last character).

Fig. 9.17 shows the implementation. For the method call

```
reverseStr("Happy Birthday Dustin")
```

the result is the string formed by concatenating the string **"n"** with the reverse of the string **"Happy Birthday Dusti"**. After reversing all substrings and performing all concatenations, the result is **"nitsuD yadhtriB yppaH"**.

Figure 9.17   Method reverseStr()

```
// precondition: string s is defined.
// postcondition: Returns the reverse of string s.
public static int reverseStr(String s) {
    int posLast = s.length() - 1; // index of last character.

    if (posLast == -1)
        return "";                          // Return the empty string.
    else
        return s.charAt(posLast) +
                reverseStr(s.substring(0, posLast));
}
```

──────────────────────────────────── ◆◆

EXERCISES FOR SECTION 9.4

SELF-CHECK

1. Trace the execution of recursive method `isEqual()` for the three-element arrays **x** (element values **1, 15, 10**) and **y** (element values **1, 5, 7**).

2. Trace the execution of the recursive method `search()` on array **x** in Self-Check Exercise 1 when searching for **15** and for **3**.

3. What does the following recursive method do? Trace its execution on array **x** in Self-Check Exercise 1. *Hint:* Method `Math.min()` returns the smaller of its two arguments.

```
public static int mystery (int[] x, int n) {
   if (n == 1)
      return x[0];
   else
      return Math.min(x[n-1], mystery(x, n-1));
}
```

4. Trace the execution of the method call `searchStr("happy", 'p')`.

5. Trace the execution of the method call `reverseStr("tick")`.

PROGRAMMING

1. Write a recursive method that returns the largest value in an array.

2. Write a recursive method that returns the *index of* the largest value in an array.

3. Answer Programming Exercise 1 for a vector of **Integer** objects.

4. Answer Programming Exercise 2 for a vector of **Integer** objects.

9.5 Binary Search

This section describes another recursive search algorithm called binary search. Binary search is an example of an $O(\log_2 n)$ algorithm—a significant improvement over the sequential search algorithm, which is $O(n)$ (see Section 7.5).

CASE STUDY RECURSIVE BINARY SEARCH

Methods `search()` and `searchIt()` implement a *linear* or *sequential search* for a target key in an array, examining the elements in sequence from last to first. Because the method requires an average of $n/2$ comparisons to find a target in an array of n elements, and n comparisons to determine that a target is not in the array, sequential search is not very efficient for large arrays ($n > 100$). If the elements of the array being searched have been sorted and are in sequence by key value, we can make use of a more efficient search algorithm known as binary search.

PROBLEM   Write an improved search algorithm that takes advantage of the fact that the array is sorted.

ANALYSIS   The *binary search algorithm* uses the ordering of array elements to eliminate half the array elements with each probe into the array. Consequently, if the array has 1000 elements, it either locates the target value or eliminates 500 elements with its first probe, 250 elements with its second probe, 125 elements with its third probe, and so on. The maximum number of probes requierd to search an array with n elements is approximately $\log_2 n$. This means that you could use the binary search algorithm to find a name in a large metropolitan telephone directory using 30 or fewer probes (2^{30} is approximately equal to 1,000,000,000).

Because the array is sorted, we only need to compare the target value with the middle element of the subarray we are searching. If their values are the same, we are done. If the middle element value is larger than the target value, we should search the lower half of the subarray next; otherwise, we should search the upper half of the subarray.

The subarray being searched has indices `first` through `last`. The variable `middle` is the index of the middle element in this range. Fig. 9.18 shows an example in which the target is `35`, `first` is `0`, `last` is `8`, and `middle` is `4`. The upper half of the array (indices `middle` through `last`) is eliminated by the first probe.

The argument `last` needs to be reset to `middle - 1` to define the new subarray to be searched, and `middle` should be redefined as shown in Fig. 9.19. The target value, `35`, would be found on this probe.

Data Requirements

Problem Inputs

Array to search
Target value
Index of first element in subarray
Index of last element in subarray

Problem Output

Location of target value in array if found, or −1

Figure 9.18   First probe of binary search

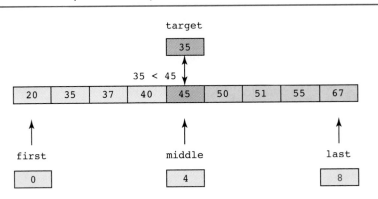

Figure 9.19   Second probe of binary search

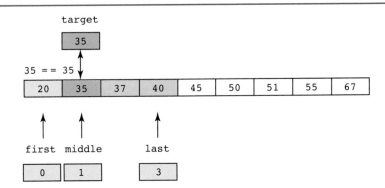

DESIGN   We can write the binary search algorithm without too much effort using recursion. The stopping cases are

◆ The array bounds are improper (**first > last**).

◆ The middle value is the target value.

   In the first case, the method returns **−1** to indicate that the target is not present in the array. In the second case, **middle** is returned as the index of the target value. The recursive step is to search the appropriate subarray (a simpler problem).

Binary Search Algorithm

1. Compute the index of the middle element of the array.

2. **if** the array bounds are improper

3.   Target not present, return −1.

else if target is the middle value

4.   Return `middle`.

else if target is less than the middle value

5.   Search subarray with indices `first` through `middle-1`.

else

6.   Search subarray with indices `middle+1` through `last`.

For each of the recursive steps (steps 5 and 6), the bounds of the new subarray must be listed as actual arguments in the recursive call. The actual arguments define the search limits for the next probe into the array.

IMPLEMENTATION   In the initial call to the recursive method, `first` and `last` should be defined as the first and last elements of the entire array, respectively. For example, you could use the method call

```
binSearch(x, 35, 0, 8)
```

to search an array **x** with nine elements for the target value **35**. The position of the target element in array **x** will be returned as the method result if **35** is found. Method `binSearch()` is shown in Fig. 9.20.

The statement

```
int middle = (first + last) / 2;
```

computes the index of the middle element by finding the average of `first` and `last`. The value has no meaning when `first` is greater than `last`, but it does no harm to compute it.

TESTING   Check for targets in the first and last elements of the array. Check for targets that are not present. Check the algorithm for even- and odd-length arrays. Also check arrays with multiple target values. See what happens when the array size gets very large, say, 1000.

Figure 9.20   Recursive binary search method

```
// precondition: The elements of table are sorted &
//    first and last are defined.
// postcondition: If target is in the array, return its
//    position; otherwise, returns -1.
public static int binSearch(int[] table,
                            int target,
                            int first,
                            int last) {
   int middle = (first + last) / 2; // middle of array

   if (first > last)
       return -1;                    // unsuccessful search
   else if (target == table[middle])
       return middle;                // successful search
   else if (target < table[middle])
       return binSearch(table, target, first, middle-1);
   else  // search upper half of array
       return binSearch(table, target, middle+1, last);
}
```

EXERCISES FOR SECTION 9.5

SELF-CHECK

1. Trace the execution of `binSearch()` for the array shown in Fig. 9.18 and a `target` value of 40.

2. What would happen if `binSearch()` were called with the precondition of elements in increasing order violated? Would `binSearch()` still find the item?

PROGRAMMING

1. Sorting algorithms need to know where in a sorted array a new item should be inserted. Write a recursive method `insertLocation()` that returns a location where `target` could be inserted into an array and still maintain correct ordering.

9.6 Solving Towers of Hanoi with Recursion

In this section, we develop an elegant recursive solution to a problem that would be very difficult to solve without recursion. Our analysis will show that the solution to the original problem can be expressed readily in terms of simpler versions of itself, so a recursive solution is called for.

CASE STUDY TOWERS OF HANOI PROBLEM

PROBLEM   Solve the Towers of Hanoi problem for *n* disks, where *n* is an argument.

ANALYSIS   To solve the Towers of Hanoi problem you must move a specified number of disks of different sizes from one tower (or peg) to another. Legend has it that the world will come to an end when the problem is solved for 64 disks. You may be familiar with a children's game that is a three-disk version of this puzzle.

In the version of the problem shown in Fig. 9.21, there are five disks (numbered 1 through 5) and three towers or pegs (lettered A, B, and C). The goal is to move the five disks from peg A to peg C subject to the following rules:

- ◆ Only one disk may be moved at a time, and this disk must be the top disk on a peg.

- ◆ A larger disk can never be placed on top of a smaller disk.

A stopping case of the problem is the movement of only one disk (e.g., "move disk 2 from peg A to peg C"). Simpler problems than the original would be to move four disks subject to the rules above, to move three disks, and so on. Therefore, we want to split the original five-disk problem into one or more problems involving fewer disks. Let's consider splitting the original problem into three problems:

1. Move four disks from peg A to peg B.

2. Move disk 5 from peg A to peg C.

3. Move four disks from peg B to peg C.

Step 1 moves all disks but the largest to tower B, an auxiliary tower. Step 2 moves the largest disk to the goal tower, tower C. Step 3 then moves the remaining disks from B to the goal tower, where they will be placed on top of the largest disk. Let's assume that we can perform steps 1 and 2 (a stopping case); Figure 9.22 shows the status of the three towers after completion of these steps. At this point it should be clear that we can solve the original five-disk problem if we can complete step 3 (Move four disks from peg B to peg C). In step 3, peg C is the goal tower and peg A becomes the auxiliary tower.

Unfortunately, we still don't know how to perform step 1 or step 3. Both steps, however, involve four disks instead of five, so they are easier than the original problem. We should be able to split them into even simpler problems. In step 3 we must

Figure 9.21 Towers of Hanoi

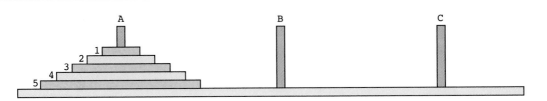

Figure 9.22 Towers of Hanoi after steps 1 and 2

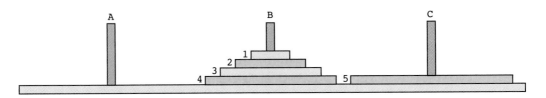

move four disks from peg B to peg C, so we can split it into two three-disk problems and a single one-disk problem:

3.1 Move three disks from peg B to peg A.

3.2 Move disk 4 from peg B to peg C.

3.3 Move three disks from peg A to peg C.

Fig. 9.23 shows the towers after completion of steps 3.1 and 3.2. The two largest disks are now on peg C. Once we complete step 3.3, all five disks will be on peg C. Although we still do not know how to solve steps 3.1 and 3.3, they are at least simpler problems than the four-disk problem from which they are derived.

By splitting each n-disk problem into two problems involving $n - 1$ disks and a one-disk problem, we eventually reach the point where all the cases manipulate only one disk, cases that we know how to solve. Next, we use this process to write a Java method that solves the Towers of Hanoi problem.

Figure 9.23 Towers of Hanoi after steps 1, 2, 3.1, and 3.2

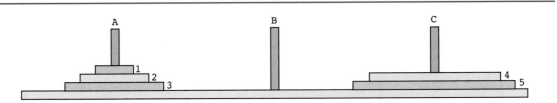

The solution to the Towers of Hanoi problem consists of a printed list of individual disk moves. *We need a method to read the problem data.* We also need a recursive method that moves any number of disks from one peg to another, using the third peg as an auxiliary. The role of each peg (source, destination, auxiliary) changes with each call.

Data Requirements

Problem Inputs

The source peg, destination peg, and spare peg
The number of disks

Problem Output

A list of individual disk moves

DESIGN

Class `TowersOfHanoi`

Data Fields	Attributes
`int numDisks`	The count of disks
`char sourcePeg`	The peg that has the disks
`char destinationPeg`	The peg where the disks will end up
`char sparePeg`	The peg that has no disks at the beginning or at the end

Methods	Behavior
`void readTowerdata()`	Reads the count of disks and the letter for each peg.
`void tower(char, char, char, int)`	Determines and displays the sequence of disk moves.

Algorithm for `tower()`

1. `if n is 1`

    2. Move disk **1** from the *from* peg to the *to* peg.

    `else`

    3. Move **n-1** disks from the *from* peg to the *auxiliary* peg using the *to* peg as an intermediary.

    4. Move disk **n** from the from peg to the to peg.

    5. Move **n-1** disks from the *auxiliary* peg to the *to* peg using the *from* peg as an intermediary.

If **n** is **1**, a stopping case is reached. If **n** is greater than **1**, the recursive step splits the original problem into three smaller subproblems (steps 3, 4, and 5), one of which is a stopping case (step 4). Each stopping case displays a move instruction. Verify that the recursive step generates the three subproblems shown earlier and repeated below when **n** is **5**, the *from* peg is A, and the *to* peg is C.

3. Move four disks from peg A to peg B.

4. Move disk 5 from peg A to peg C.

5. Move four disks from peg B to peg C.

IMPLEMENTATION   The implementation of this algorithm is shown as recursive method **tower()** in Fig. 9.24. Method **tower()** has four parameters. The method call statement

```
tower('A', 'C', 'B', 5)
```

solves the problem posed earlier of moving five disks from peg A to peg C using B as an auxiliary peg.

The stopping case in method **tower()** ("Move disk 1 from peg...") is written as a call to **println()**. Each recursive step consists of two recursive calls to **tower()**, with a call to **println()** sandwiched between them. The first recursive call solves the problem of moving **n-1** disks to the *auxiliary* peg. The call to **println()** displays a message to move disk **n** to the *to* peg. The second recursive call solves the problem of moving the **n-1** disks back from the *auxiliary* peg to the *to* peg.

There is a second **tower()** method that has no parameters. This is called a **starter method**; its sole purpose is to make the initial call of the recursive method **tower()** with four parameters. An application would call the public starter method, which would then call the private recursive method.

Method **readTowerData()** should be called before method **tower()**. It uses class **KeyIn** methods to read the number of disks and the source and destination pegs. The **while** loop with repetition condition (**sourcePeg   == destinationPeg**) continues to read a destination peg until the source and destination pegs are different. The **for** loop sets the auxiliary peg to the peg that is neither the source nor the destination. The string **pegsUsed** is the concatenation of the source and destination pegs. The condition (**pegsUsed.indexOf(nextCh) < 0**) is **true** when **nextCh** is the peg that is not yet used.

TESTING   Fig. 9.25 traces the solution to a simpler problem: move three disks from peg A to peg C. Fig. 9.26 shows the output generated by method **tower**. Verify for yourself that this list of steps solves the problem.

Figure 9.24   Class `TowersOfHanoi`

```
/* TowersOfHanoi.java          Authors: Koffman & Wolz
 * Class that solves the Towers of Hanoi problem.
 * Uses KeyIn and JOptionPane.
 */
import psJava.KeyIn;
import javax.swing.JOptionPane;

public class TowersOfHanoi {
  // Data fields
  private int numDisks;
  private char sourcePeg;
  private char destinationPeg;
  private char sparePeg;

  // Methods
  // precondition: fromPeg, toPeg, auxPeg, and
  //   n are defined.
  // postcondition: Displays a list of instructions to
  //   move n disks from fromPeg to toPeg
  //   using auxPeg as an intermediary.
  private void tower(char fromPeg, char toPeg,
                     char auxPeg, int n) {
    if (n == 1)
      System.out.println("Move disk 1 from peg " +
                         fromPeg + " to peg " + toPeg);
    else {  // recursive step
      tower(frompeg, auxPeg, toPeg, n-1);
      System.out.println("Move disk " + n +
            " from peg " + fromPeg + " to peg " toPeg);
      tower(auxPeg, toPeg, fromPeg, n-1);
    }
  }

  // postcondition: Starts the recursive method.
  public void tower() {
    tower(sourcePeg, destinationPeg, sparePeg, numDisks);
  }
```

Figure 9.24 Class `TowersOfHanoi,` *continued*

```
// postcondition: Reads the number of disks and sourcePeg
//    and destinationPeg. Sets sparePeg to the unused peg.
public void readTowerData() {
  numDisks = KeyIn.readInt("How many disks", 1, 8);

  // Get source and destination pegs.
  sourcePeg = KeyIn.readChar("Enter the source peg (A,B,C)");
  destinationPeg =
      KeyIn.readChar("Enter the destination peg (A,B,C)");
  while (sourcePeg == destinationPeg) {
    JOptionPane.showerMessageDialog(null,
        "source and destination can't be the same!",
        "Error", JOptionPane.ERROR_MESSAGE);
    destinationPeg =
        KeyIn.readChar("Enter destination (A,B,C)");
  }

  // Set sparePeg to the unused peg.
  String pegsUsed = "" + sourcePeg + destinationPeg;
  // Find peg that is not used.
  for (char nextCh = 'A'; nextCh <= 'C'; nextCh++) {
    if (pegsUsed.indexOf(nextCh) < 0) {
      sparePeg = nextCh;
      return;
    }
  }
}
```

Figure 9.25   Trace of `tower('A', 'C', 'B', 3);`

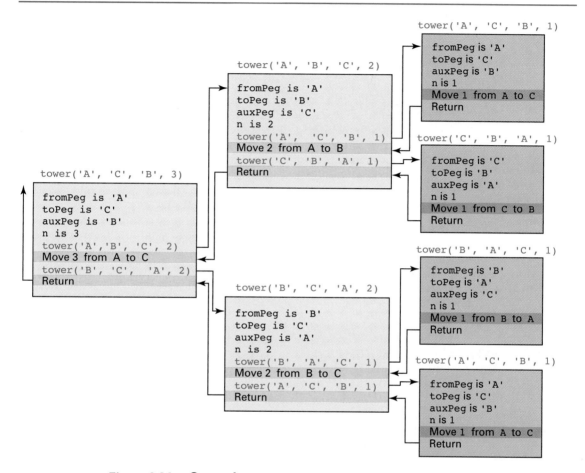

Figure 9.26   Output for `tower('A', 'C', 'B', 3);`

```
MS TowersApp                                              _ □ ✕
Move disk 1 from peg A to peg C
Move disk 2 from peg A to peg B
Move disk 1 from peg C to peg B
Move disk 3 from peg A to peg C
Move disk 1 from peg B to peg A
Move disk 2 from peg B to peg C
Move disk 1 from peg A to peg C
```

Comparison of Iterative and Recursive Methods

It is interesting to consider that method **tower()** in Fig. 9.24 will solve the Towers of Hanoi problem for any number of disks. The three-disk problem results in a total of seven calls to method **tower()** and is solved by seven disk moves. The five-disk problem would result in a total of 31 calls to method **tower()** and is solved in 31 moves. In general, the number of moves required to solve the n-disk problem is $2^n - 1$. Because each method call requires the allocation and initialization of a local data area in memory, the computer time increases exponentially with the problem size. For this reason, be careful about running the program with a value of **n** larger than 10 (2^{10} is 1024).

The dramatic increase in processing time for larger numbers of disks results because of the problem, not because of recursion. In general, however, if there are recursive and iterative solutions to the same problem, the recursive solution requires a bit more time and space because of the extra method calls.

Although recursion was not really needed to solve many of the simpler problems in this chapter, it was extremely useful in formulating an algorithm for the Towers of Hanoi. For certain problems, recursion leads naturally to solutions that are much easier to read and understand than their iterative counterparts. In those cases, the benefits gained from increased clarity far outweigh the extra cost in time and memory of running a recursive program.

EXERCISES FOR SECTION 9.6

SELF-CHECK

1. What problems are generated when you attempt to solve the problem "Move three disks from peg B to peg A"? Answer the same question for the problem "Move three disks from peg A to peg C."

2. How many moves are needed to solve the six-disk problem?

PROGRAMMING

1. Write an application for the Towers of Hanoi problem.

2. There is no error checking in method **readTowerData()**; consequently, a user may attempt to use a peg for more than one purpose. Discuss how you might incorporate error checking into **readTowerData()** to eliminate this possibility.

9.7 A Recursive Program with a GUI

In this section, we develop a recursive solution to an image processing problem. We incorporate a GUI in the solution.

CASE STUDY COUNTING CELLS IN A BLOB

PROBLEM We have a two-dimensional array of cells, each of which may be empty or filled. The filled cells that are connected form a blob. There may be several blobs on the array. We would like a method (**findBlob()**) that accepts as input the row and column of a particular cell and returns the size of the blob containing the cell. The filled cells might represent islands of land surrounded by water or malignant cells in a tissue sample.

There are three blobs in the sample array shown in Fig. 9.27. If the method arguments represent the row and column of a cell, the result of **findBlob(0, 0)** is **5**; the result of **findBlob(5, 1)** is **2**; the result of **findBlob(5, 2)** is **0**; the result of **findBlob(3, 4)** is **5**.

Figure 9.27   **Applet with three blobs**

ANALYSIS Method **findBlob()** must test the cell specified by its arguments to see whether it is filled. There are two stopping cases: The cell is not in the array or the cell is empty; in either case, the value returned by **findBlob()** is **0**. If the cell is in the array and filled, the value returned is **1** plus the size of the blobs containing each of its eight neighbors. The recursive algorithm for **findBlob()** follows.

Algorithm for **findBlob()**

if the cell is not in the array
    Return a count of **0**.
else if the cell is empty then
    Return a count of **0**.
else
    Mark the cell as empty.
    Return **1** plus the size of the blob containing any of its 8 neighbors.

The recursive step (following **else**) marks the cell as empty before visiting its neighbors. If this were not done first, a filled cell would be counted more than once because it is a neighbor of all its neighbors. A worse problem is that the recursion would not terminate. When each neighbor of the current cell is visited, **findBlob()** is called again with the row and column of the current cell as arguments (the current cell is a neighbor of its neighbors). If the current cell had not been marked as empty, the recursive step would be executed erroneously. Eventually all memory allocated to the stack would be used up (a stack overflow error).

DESIGN   Let's see how we can take advantage of Java's graphics capabilities to design a solution that incorporates a GUI. We will represent the array of cells as a two-dimensional grid of smart buttons. We will use the color gray (for land) to represent a filled cell and the color green (for vegetation) to represent an empty cell. These colors are stored as the background color of the button (defined in the **Component** class). A smart button also knows its row and column position in the grid and its current color. The current color of an empty cell is always the same as its background color; the current color of a filled cell should change temporarily to green when it is marked empty.

Class **SmartButton** (Extends **JButton**)

Data Fields	Attributes
int row	Row position of button
int column	Column position of button
Color curColor	Its current color
Methods	**Behavior**
int getRow()	Gets row
int getColumn()	Gets column
Color getStoredColor()	Gets current color
void setStoredColor(Color)	Sets current color
String toString()	Returns its stored information as a string

We also need an applet. The applet defines a two-dimensional grid of smart buttons (**buttons**) and a **Label** field (**result**). The applet has an **init()** method that creates a panel. Method **init()** allocates storage for the array of buttons and adds a grid to the panel with the same dimensions as this array. Method **init()** must create each button, define its characteristics, and add it to the panel. It also registers the applet as a listener for actions from each button. Finally, `init()` adds the panel and label to the applet.

The applet also needs an `actionPerformed()` method. It determines the button that was pressed, finds the size of the blob containing that button (using method `findBlob()`), resets any button colors that were changed (using method `recolorMap()`), and defines the `JLabel` field `result`.

Class `BlobApplet` (Extends `Applet`)

Data Fields	Attributes
`smartButton[][] buttons`	The grid of smart buttons
`JLabel result`	A label that shows the position and color of the button selected and the blob size

Methods	Behavior
`void init()`	Sets up the applet and defines the array of buttons
`void actionPerformed(ActionEvent)`	Responds to the user selection, calls `findBlob()` and `recolorMap()`, and defines the result field
`int findBlob(int int)`	Finds the blob size, resetting the color of each button in the blob to green
`void recolorMap()`	Resets the current color of each button to its background color

We showed the algorithm for `findBlob()` earlier. The algorithms for `init()` and `actionPerformed()` follow.

Algorithm for `init()`

1. Construct the panel.

    1.1. Create a two-dimensional array of smart buttons. Call the `GridLayout` constructor to build a grid with the same dimensions.

    1.2. Set the characteristics of each button. Add it to the panel and register the applet as an action listener for actions from the button.

2. Add the panel to the applet.

3. Add the label to the applet.

Algorithm for `actionPerformed()`

1. Determine which button was selected.

2. Find the size of the blob that contains it.

3. Recolor the array of buttons.

4. Define the `JLabel result`.

5. Declare that `result` is invalid.

6. Have the applet redo the layout.

IMPLEMENTATION   Fig. 9.28 shows class `SmartButton`, and Fig. 9.29 shows the applet.

Method `init()` allocates storage for panel `Map` and defines a two-dimensional array (`bitMap`) of 0s and 1s. The `for` loops traverse the array of buttons, setting each button's background color to green or gray based on the value of the corresponding element of array `bitMap` (gray for `1`, green for `0`).

In method `findBlob()`, if the cell being visited is off the grid or is empty (current color is green), a value of zero is returned immediately. Otherwise, the recursive step executes causing method `findBlob()` to call itself eight times. Each time a different neighbor of the current cell is visited. The method result is defined as the sum of all values returned from these recursive calls plus `1` (for the current cell). These problems are simpler than the original because the current cell has been marked as empty.

The sequence of operations performed in `findBlob()` is very important. The `if` statement tests whether the current cell is on the grid before testing whether it is empty. If the order were reversed, an index-out-of-bounds error would occur whenever the current cell was off the grid.

TESTING   Earlier (Fig. 9.27) we showed a result of running the applet. Each time you click on a new button, the result changes. You should try clicking on buttons that are filled and empty and buttons that are near the borders of the grid. Also, make sure you click on two buttons that are in the same blob.

Figure 9.28 Class `SmartButton`

```
/*    SmartButton.java.      Authors: Koffman & Wolz.
 *    Class that represents a button with a position (row, column) and color.
 *    Extends JButton.
 */
import java.awt.*;
import javax.swing.*;
public class SmartButton extends JButton {
    // Data fields
    private Color curColor;
    private int row;
    private int column;

    // Methods
    // Constructor
    public SmartButton(String s, Color col, int r, int c) {
        super(s);            // Call JButton constructor -
                             //    define text field
        curColor = col;
        row = r;
        column = c;
        setBackground(col);  // Define background color.
    }

    // Accessors
    public int getRow() {return row;}
    public int getColumn() {return column;}
    public Color getStoredColor() {return curColor;}

    // Modifier
    public void setStoredColor(Color col) {curColor = col;}

    // toString
    public String toString() {
        String col;
        if (curColor == Color.gray)
           col = "gray";
        else
           col = "green";
        return row + "," + column + " (" + col + ")";
    }
} // class SmartButton
```

Figure 9.29   Class `BlobApplet`

```
/*   BlobApplet.java.      Authors: Koffman & Wolz.
 *   Applet for counting cells in a blob.
 *   Extends JApplet.
 */
import java.awt.*;
import javax.swing.*;
import java.awt.event.*;

public class BlobApplet extends JApplet
                   implements ActionListener {

    private SmartButton[][] buttons;    // array of buttons
    private JLabel result = new JLabel(); // label for result

    public void init() {
       //Define applet layout manager
         getContentPane.setLayout(new FlowLayout());

         JPanel map  = new JPanel();

         // Define bitMap array
         int[][] bitMap = {  {1,1,0,0,0},
                             {0,1,1,0,0},
                             {0,0,1,0,1},
                             {0,0,0,0,1},
                             {1,0,0,0,1},
                             {0,1,0,1,1}
                          };

         // Create an array of the proper size.
         buttons = new
             SmartButton[bitMap.length][bitMap[0].length];

         // Create the grid.
         map.setLayout(new
             GridLayout(buttons.length, buttons[0].length));

         // Traverse the array of buttons. Create each
         //   button, add it to the panel, and register it.
         for (int r = 0; r < buttons.length; r++)
             for (int c = 0; c < buttons[r].length; c++) {
                 Color col;
```

Figure 9.29   Class `BlobApplet`, *continued*

```
                    if (bitMap[r][c] == 1)
                        col = Color.gray;
                    else
                        col = Color.green;
                    // Make a new smart button
                    buttons[r][c] = new SmartButton(r + "," + c,
                                              col, r, c);
                    // Add it to the panel and register the
                    //    applet as the listener.
                    map.add(buttons[r][c]);
                    buttons[r][c].addActionListener(this);
            }

        getContentPane().add(map);      // Add the grid to the applet.
        getContentPane().add(result);   // Add the label to the applet.
    }


    public void actionPerformed(ActionEvent aE) {
        SmartButton b = (SmartButton) aE.getSource();

        // Find the size of the blob.
        int count = findBlob(b.getRow(), b.getColumn());

        // Reset the colors.
        recolorMap();

        // display the result.
        result.setText("Button " + b +
                    ", cells in blob: " + count);
    }

    // For each button reset the current color field to
    //    the background color.
    private void recolorMap() {
        for(int r = 0; r < buttons.length; r++)
            for(int c = 0; c < buttons[r].length; c++)
                buttons[r][c].setStoredColor(
                    buttons[r][c].getBackground());
    }
```

Figure 9.29   Class `BlobApplet`, *continued*

```
// Find the size of the blob.
private int findBlob(int r, int c) {
    if (r < 0 || c < 0 || r >= buttons.length ||
        c >= buttons[0].length)
        return 0;                       // Cell is not in array.
    else if (buttons[r][c].getStoredColor() == Color.green)
        return 0;                       // Cell is empty.
    else {
        // Mark cell empty.
        buttons[r][c].setStoredColor(Color.green);
        // Count it and its filled neighbors.
        return 1 + findBlob(r-1,c-1) +
                findBlob(r,c-1) + findBlob(r+1,c-1) +
                findBlob(r-1,c) + findBlob(r+1,c) +
                findBlob(r-1,c+1) + findBlob(r,c+1) +
                findBlob(r+1,c+1);
    }
}

} // class BlobApplet
```

EXERCISE FOR SECTION 9.7

SELF-CHECK

1. Trace the execution of method `findBlob()` for the buttons at positions [1, 1] and [2, 1] in the sample grid in Fig. 9.27.

2. Is the order of the two tests performed in method `findBlob()` critical? What happens if we reverse them or combine them into a single condition?

PROGRAMMING

1. Instead of using the array `bitMap` to set the color of each button, consider how you would write a method that enabled the user to indicate a filled button by clicking on it. The initial color for each button would show that it was empty.

9.8   Common Programming Errors

The most common problem that occurs with a recursive method is that it may not terminate properly. For example, if the terminating condition is not correct or is incomplete, the method may call itself indefinitely or until all available memory is used up. Normally, a **stack overflow** run-time error indicates that a recursive method is not terminating. Make sure you identify all stopping cases and provide a terminating condition for each one. Also be sure that each recursive step leads to a situation that is closer to a stopping case and that repeated recursive calls eventually lead to stopping cases only.

When debugging, you may find it helpful to display the value of the argument that is supposed to be getting smaller during each call as the first statement in a recursive method. This will help you determine whether the method is being called correctly and whether it will eventually terminate.

CHAPTER REVIEW

1. A recursive method is one that calls itself. You can use recursion to solve problems by splitting them into smaller versions of themselves.

2. Each recursive method has one or more stopping cases and recursive steps. The stopping cases can be solved directly; the recursive steps lead to recursive calls of the method.

3. Recursive methods can be used with arguments that are simple types or structured types. Recursive methods can implement mathematical operations that are defined by recursive definitions.

4. Binary search is a recursive search method that can search a large array very efficiently.

✔ **QUICK-CHECK EXERCISES**

1. How are stacks used in recursion?

2. Can the stopping case also have a recursive call in it?

3. In Java, which control statement is always in a recursive method?

4. What is the relation between a terminating condition and a stopping case?

5. Returning from a series of recursive calls is called _____ the recursion.

6. What causes a **stack overflow** error?

7. What can you say about a recursive algorithm that has the following form?

   `if` (*condition*)
   Perform recursive step.

ANSWERS TO QUICK-CHECK EXERCISES

1. The stack is used to hold all argument and local variable values and the return point for each execution of a recursive method.

2. No. If it did, recursion would continue.

3. `if` statement

4. A recursive method reaches a stopping case when a terminating condition is true.

5. unwinding

6. A stack overflow error occurs when there are too many recursive calls. Usually recursion doesn't terminate.

7. The method is exited immediately when the stopping case is reached.

REVIEW QUESTIONS

1. Differentiate between a recursive step and a stopping case in a recursive algorithm.

2. Discuss the time and space efficiency of recursive methods versus iterative methods.

3. What basic characteristics must a problem have for a recursive solution to be applicable?

4. Write a recursive method that prints the accumulating sum of ordinal values corresponding to each character in a string. For example, if the string is "a boy", the first value printed would be the ordinal number of a, then the sum of ordinals for a and the space character, then the sum of ordinals for a, space, b, and so on.

5. Write a recursive method that calculates an approximate value for *e*, the base of the natural logarithms, by summing the series

$$1 + \frac{1}{1!} + \frac{1}{2!} + ... + \frac{1}{n!}$$

   until additional terms do not affect the approximation.

PROGRAMMING PROJECTS

1. The expression for computing $c(n,r)$, the number of combinations of n items taken r at a time, is

$$c(n,r) = \frac{n!}{r!(n-r)!}$$

Write and test a method for computing $c(n,r)$, given that $n!$ is the factorial of n.

2. A palindrome is a word that is spelled exactly the same when the letters are reversed (for example, level, deed, and mom). Write a recursive method that returns the **boolean** value **true** if a word, passed as an argument, is a palindrome.

3. Write a recursive method that lists all subsets of pairs of letters for a given set of letters, for example,

```
['A','C','E','G'] => ['A','C'], ['A','E'],
                     ['A','G'], ['C','E'],
                     ['C','G'], ['E','G']
```

4. Write a method that accepts an 8×8 array of characters that represents a maze. Each position can contain either an **X** or a blank. Starting at position **[0,0]**, list any path through the maze to get to location **[7,7]**. Only horizontal and vertical moves are allowed (no diagonal moves). Make sure your algorithm avoids retracing previously tried paths. If no path exists, write a message indicating this.

   Moves can be made only to locations that contain a blank. If an **X** is encountered, that path is blocked and another must be chosen. Use recursion.

5. The bisection method finds an approximate root for the equation $f(x) = 0$ on the interval **xLeft** to **xRight**, inclusive (assuming that function $f(x)$ is continuous on this interval). The interval endpoints (**xLeft** and **xRight**) and the tolerance for the approximation (**epsilon**) are input by the user.

   One stopping criterion for the bisection method is the identification of an interval **[xLeft, xRight]** that is less than **epsilon** in length over which $f(x)$ changes sign (from positive to negative or vice versa). The midpoint **[xMid = (xLeft + xRight)/2.0)]** of the interval will be an approximation to the root of the equation when **f(xMid)** is very close to zero. Of course, if you find a value of **xMid** such that **f(xMid)** = 0, you have found a very good approximation of the root, and the algorithm should also stop.

To perform the recursive step, replace either **xLeft** or **xRight** with **xMid**, depending on which one has the same sign as **xMid**. Write a program that uses the bisection method to determine an approximation to the equation

$$5x^3 - 2x^2 + 3 = 0$$

over the interval **[-1,1]** using **epsilon = 0.0001**.

6. Write a program that, given a list of up to 10 integer numbers and a sum, will find a subset of the numbers whose total is that sum if one exists or otherwise will indicate that none exists. For example, for the list: **5, 13, 23, 9, 3, 3** and sum = **28**, your program should find: **13, 9, 3, 3**.

7. A **mergeSort** is a sorting technique with the following recursive algorithm (*mergeSort*):

if the array to sort has more than one element
    mergeSort the left half of the array.
    mergeSort the right half of the array.
    Merge the two sorted subarrays to form the sorted array.

For example, **mergeSort** the array **10, 20, 15, 6, 5, 40** by following these steps:

mergeSort the subarray **10, 20, 15**, giving **10, 15, 20**.
mergeSort the subarray **6, 5, 40**, giving **5, 6, 40**.
Merge the two sorted subarrays, giving **5, 6, 10, 15, 20, 40**.

Of course, each call to **mergeSort** above will generate two more recursive calls (one for a one-element array and one for a two-element array). **mergeSort** for a one-element array is a stopping case.

8. Do Programming Project 4 using an array of smart buttons. Green buttons correspond to empty cells, and red buttons correspond to cells that contain **X**. As the program traces out a path through the maze, it should select only buttons that are green and reset the color of the buttons on the path to white.

10

Linked Data Structures

In this chapter we focus on linked data structures that are also dynamic data structures. Unlike static structures, in which the size of the data structure is determined when the storage is initially allocated and remains unchanged throughout program execution (like an array), dynamic data structures expand and contract as a program executes.

The first dynamic data structure we will study is called a *linked list*. A linked list is a collection of elements (called *nodes*) that are objects. Each node has a reference field, called a *link*, that connects it to the next node in the list.

Linked lists are extremely flexible. It is easy to add new information by creating a new node and inserting it between two existing nodes. It is also relatively easy to delete a node.

In this chapter we study three special kinds of linked lists: stacks, queues, and trees. All three data structures have many applications in computer science. We will show how to implement them and how to use them.

10.1   Linked Lists

We can arrange groups of dynamically allocated nodes into a flexible data structure called a **linked list**. Linked lists are like chains of children's "pop beads." Each bead has a hole at one end and a plug at the other (see Fig. 10.1). We can connect the beads in the obvious way to form a chain. After a chain has been created, we can easily modify it. We can remove a bead by disconnecting the two beads at both its ends and re-attaching this pair of beads. We can add a new bead by connecting it to the bead at either end of the chain. Or we can break the chain somewhere in the middle (between beads A and B) and insert a new bead by connecting one end to bead A and the other end to bead B. We show how to perform these operations to rearrange the nodes in a linked list next.

Building a Linked List

Although a link to a node is a new term, it is not really a new concept. For example, the statement

```
Employee emp = new Employee();
```

actually allocates a new **Employee** object and stores a reference to it in the memory cell named **emp**. We say that **emp** references this object or is a **link** to this object.

We can define a list node as a class with data fields that represent the data stored in the node and its link to the next node. Figure 10.2 shows a class **ListNode** that stores any kind of object in its **info** field. We will use **ListNode** as an inner class, so its data fields can be accessed directly by methods of an outer class.

Figure 10.1   Children's pop beads in a chain

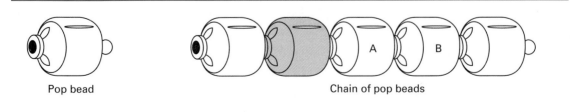

Pop bead   Chain of pop beads

Figure 10.2　Class `ListNode`

```java
/* ListNode.java              Authors: Koffman & Wolz
 * Represents a node with information and link fields.
 */
private class ListNode {

   // Data field
   private Object info;        // data stored in the node
   private ListNode link;      // link to next node

   // Methods
   // Constructors
   // postcondition: Creates a new empty node.
   public ListNode() {
     info = null;
     link = null;
   }

   // postcondition: Creates a new node storing obj.
   public ListNode(Object obj) {
     info = obj;
     link = null;
   }

   // postcondition: Creates a new node storing obj
   //    and linked to node referenced by next.
   public ListNode(Object obj, ListNode next) {
     info = obj;
     link = next;
   }
}
```

Because data field `link` has type `ListNode`, it can store a reference to another node of type `ListNode`. The default constructor initializes `info` and `link` to `null`. The second constructor stores its single argument (type `Object`) in the `info` field of a new node (the `link` field is `null`). The third constructor stores its argument values in both fields of a new node, thereby linking the new node to another node.

Connecting Nodes

The statements

```
ListNode p = new ListNode("the");
ListNode q = new ListNode("hat");
```

allocate storage for two objects of type **ListNode** referenced by **p** and **q**. The node referenced by **p** stores the string **"the"**, and the node referenced by **q** stores the string **"hat"** (see Fig. 10.3). The link fields of both nodes are **null**.

The statement

```
p.link = q;
```

stores the address of node **q** in the link field of node **p**, thereby connecting node **p** to node **q** (see Fig. 10.4). The link field of node **p** is now a link to node **q**. Because **p.link** references node **q**, we can use either **q.info** or **p.link.info** to access the data in node **q**.

Programmers often represent the value null by drawing a diagonal line in a **link** field (Fig. 10.5). The linked list referenced by **p** contains the strings **"the"**, **"hat"**.

Figure 10.3   Nodes referenced by p **and** q

Figure 10.4   Connecting nodes p **and** q

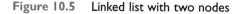
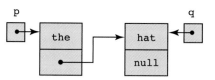

Figure 10.5   Linked list with two nodes

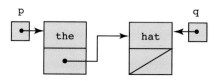

Inserting a Node in a List

To insert a new node between nodes **p** and **q**, we can use the statement

```
// Insert a new node between nodes p and q.
p.link = new ListNode("top", q);
```

This statement allocates a new node that is referenced by **p.link**. The new node stores the string **"top"** and its **link** field references node **q**. Fig. 10.6 shows the effect of this statement. The color arrows show the new values of the **link** fields; the gray arrow shows an old value. The new linked list referenced by **p** contains the strings **"the"**, **"top"**, **"hat"**.

Figure 10.6   Inserting a new node in a list

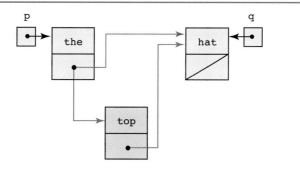

We can access the data in each node directly or by following a trail of links. Table 10.1 shows some expressions that reference the list data in Fig. 10.6.

Table 10.1   References to list data in Fig. 10.6

Expression	Data Referenced
p.info	info field of first node ("the")
p.link.info	info field of second node ("top")
q.info, p.link.link.info	info field of third node ("hat")

Insertion at the head of a list

We usually insert new data items at the end of an array or vector. However, it is normally easier to insert a new item at the front or **head of a list**. If we assume that head has been declared as type **ListNode**, the statement

```
// Insert a new node at head of list.
head = new ListNode("in", p);
```

links **head** to a new node with **info** field **"in"** and **link** field **p**, so the new node is connected to the list in Fig. 10.6. Node **head** becomes the first element of the expanded list containing the strings **"in"**, **"the"**, **"top"**, **"hat"** (see Fig. 10.7).

Insertion at the end of a list

The reason it is less efficient to insert an item at the end of a list is that we usually do not have a link to the last list element. Consequently, we often need to follow the trail of links from the list head to the last list node and then perform the insertion. However, in this example, **q** is a link to the last list node, so the statement

```
// Attach a new node to the end of the list.
q.link = new ListNode("box");
```

links the node referenced by **q** to a new node that stores the string **"box"** (see Fig. 10.8). The new list contains the strings **"in"**, **"the"**, **"top"**, **"hat"**, **"box"**. We have no direct reference to the node that contains **"box"**, but we can access its data using the expression **q.link.info**.

Removing a Node

To remove or delete a node from a linked list, we simply change the **link** field of the node that references it (its **predecessor**). We want to link the predecessor to the node

Figure 10.7   New list of four nodes

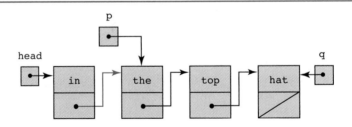

Figure 10.8   Insertion at the end of a list

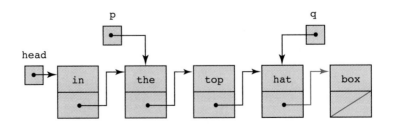

that follows the one being removed (its **successor**). For example, to remove the node referenced by **p** from the five-element list in Fig. 10.8, we change the **link** field of the first node so that it references the same node as the **link** field of node **p**:

```
head.link = p.link;      // Bypass node p.
```

Next, we use the statement

```
p.link = null;     // Disconnect p from the list.
```

to disconnect node **p** from the list. The new list (Fig. 10.9) contains the strings `"in"`, `"top"`, `"hat"`, `"box"`.

Traversing a List

In many list-processing operations, we must process each node in the list in sequence; this is called **traversing a list**. To traverse a list, we must start at the list head and follow the trail of links until we reach the last list node, the one whose **link** field is **null**. We can do this using a loop with the form

```
ListNode next = head;
while (next != null) {
   // Perform some operation on the node referenced by next
   //   . . .
   next = next.link;  // Advance to the next node.
}
```

In the loop above, the control variable **next** (type **ListNode**) references the next list node. It starts at the list head. The update step at the end of the loop advances **next** down the list. The loop repetition condition **(next != null)** is true after the last list node has been processed in the loop. Sometimes we want to stop when we reach the last node, rather than after we have passed it. We can use the repetition condition **(next.link != null)** to do this.

Figure 10.9   Removing a list node

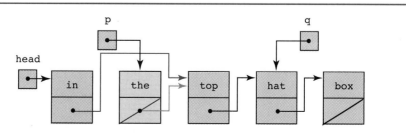

A Linked List Class

We will create a linked list class (class `LinkedList`) with a number of useful methods. The specification for this class follows.

Class `LinkedList`

Data Field	Attribute
head	References the first list node

Methods	Behavior
void addFirst(Object)	Adds its argument to the front of the list
void addLast(Object)	Adds its argument to the end of the list
void getFirst()	Retrieves the object stored in the first list node
void getLast()	Retrieves the object stored in the last list node
int size()	Returns the length of the list
String toString()	Returns a string representation of the information stored in the list

Using these methods, we can insert an object at the front or at the end of a list. We can retrieve the information stored in the first and last nodes. We can also count the number of nodes and get a string representing the contents of the list.

Implementing Class `LinkedList`

Fig. 10.10 shows class `LinkedList` with class `ListNode` (Fig. 10.2) declared as a private inner class.

Constructor, `addFirst()`, and `addLast()`

The constructor creates a new linked list object with data field **head** storing a value of **null**. In method **addFirst()**, the statement

```
ListNode newHead = new ListNode(obj, head);
```

creates a new list node (referenced by **newHead**) that stores **obj** is linked to the current head of the list. The statement

```
head = newHead;
```

changes **head** to reference the new node.

Figure 10.10   Class LinkedList

```
/*  LinkedList.java         Authors: Koffman & Wolz
 *  Represents a linked list whose first node is referenced
 *  by head.
 */

public class LinkedList {

  // Insert inner class ListNode (Fig. 10.2) here.

  // Data field for LinkedList
  private ListNode head;    // first list node

  // Methods
  // constructor
  public LinkedList() {
     head = null;
  }

  // postcondition: Adds a node storing obj at front of this list.
  public void addFirst(Object obj) {
    ListNode newHead = new ListNode(obj, head);
    head = newHead;
  }

  // postcondition: Adds a node storing obj at end of this list.
  public void addLast(Object obj) {
    if (head == null)
       addFirst(obj);   // insert in empty list
    else {
       // Advance next to end of list
       ListNode next = head;
       while (next.link != null)
          next = next.link;

       // At last element - insert obj
       next.link = new ListNode(obj);
    }
  }

  // postcondition: Returns object stored at head of this list.
  public Object getFirst() {
    if (head == null)
       return null;
```

Figure 10.10   Class `LinkedList`, *continued*

```
    else
       return head.info;
  }

  // postcondition: Returns object stored at end of this list.
  public Object getLast() {
    if (head == null)
       return null;
    else {
       // Advance next to end of list
       ListNode next = head;
       while (next.link != null)
          next = next.link;

       // At last element - retrieve its info.
       return next.info;
    }
  }

  // postcondition: Returns the length of this list.
  public int size() {
    ListNode next = head;
    int count = 0;
    while (next != null) {
       count++;
       next = next.link;
    }
    return count;
  }

  // precondition: The last list node has a null link.
  // postcondition: Returns a string formed by concatenating the
  //    data fields of all list nodes.
  public String toString() {
    String result = "";
    ListNode next = head;
    while (next != null) {
       result = result + next.info + "\n";
       next = next.link;
    }
    return result;
  }

} // class LinkedList
```

Method `addLast()` checks to see if the list is empty. If so, it calls `addFirst()` to insert `obj` at the front of the list. Otherwise, the `while` loop traverses the list, advancing `next` to the last list node. The loop repetition condition is `(next.link != null)`. The statement

```
next.link = new ListNode(obj);
```

connects the last node to a new node that stores `obj`.

Methods `getFirst()`, `getLast()`, `size()`, and `toString()`

Method `getFirst()` retrieves the object in the `info` field of the node referenced by `head`. In method `getLast()`, the `while` loop traverses the list, advancing `next` to the last list node. It then returns the object stored in that node's `info` field.

Method `size()` traverses the list, adding 1 to count until it reaches the end of the list. Method `toString()` traverses the list, appending the `info` field of the node selected by `next` to the string being formed. The loop repetition condition for both these methods is `(next != null)`.

Using the `LinkedList` Class

Method `main()` in Fig. 10.11 creates the linked list shown in Fig. 10.8. Data field `head` of object `lL` would reference the first list node. Executing this method would display the words `in the top hat box` on separate lines followed by the lines

```
List has 5 elements
First element is in, last element is box
```

Figure 10.11   Method `main()` for testing `LinkedList` class

```
public static void main(String[] args) {
    LinkedList lL = new LinkedList();
    lL.addFirst("top");
    lL.addLast("hat");
    lL.addLast("box");
    lL.addFirst("the");
    lL.addFirst("in");
    System.out.println(lL.toString());
    System.out.println("List has " + lL.size() + " elements");
    System.out.println("First element is " + lL.getFirst() +
                       ", last element is " + lL.getLast());
}
```

Circular Lists and Two-Way Lists (Optional)

You can move in only one direction in a list, and you can't move past the last element. To get around these restrictions, programmers sometimes use circular lists or two-way lists.

Circular lists

A **circular list** is a list in which the last list node references the list head. In the circular list below, you can start anywhere in the list and still access all list elements.

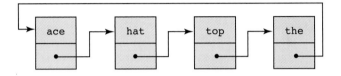

Two-way lists

In a **two-way** or **doubly linked list**, each node has two links: one to the node's successor and one to the node's predecessor. The node **next** below has two link fields, named **left** and **right**.

The statement

```
next = next.right;
```

resets link **next** to the successor node, and the statement

```
next = next.left;
```

resets link **next** to the predecessor node.

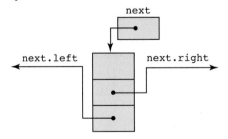

EXERCISES FOR SECTION 10.1

SELF-CHECK

1. For the four-element list in Fig. 10.7, explain the effect of each fragment. Assume the list is restored to its initial state before each fragment executes.

a. `p.link = q;`

b. `head.link = q;`

c. `head = p.link;`

d. `p.info = p.link.info;`

e. `p.info = p.link.link.info;`

f. `q.link = new ListNode("zzz");`

g. `p.link = q.link;`

h. `p.info = q.info;`

i. `p.link.link = null;`

j.
```
ListNode next = head;
int count = 0;
while (next != null) {
    count++;
    next = next.link;
}
```

2. How would you delete the node at the head of a list?

3. Sketch the linked list formed by the following **main()** method. What is displayed when this method executes?

```
public static void main(String[] args) {
    LinkedList lL = new LinkedList();
    lL.addLast("them");
    lL.addLast("me");
    lL.addLast("you");
    lL.addFirst("us");
    System.out.println(lL.toString());
    System.out.println(lL.size());
    System.out.println(lL.getFirst() + ", " + lL.getLast());
}
```

PROGRAMMING

1. Write a **main** method that reads in some strings and stores them in a linked list in the order in which they were read. The first list node should contain the first data string, the second list node the second data string, and so on.

10.2 Stacks

A **stack** is a data structure in which only the top element can be accessed. The plates stored in the spring-loaded device in a buffet line perform like a stack. A customer always takes the top plate; when a plate is removed, the plate beneath it moves to the top.

The diagram below shows a stack of three characters. The letter **c** is the character at the top of the stack and is the only character that we can access. We must remove the letter **c** from the stack in order to access the symbol **+**. Removing a value from a stack is called **popping the stack**. Storing a data item in a stack is called **pushing** it onto the stack.

Implementing Stacks as Linked Lists

We can think of a stack as a linked list in which all insertions and deletions are performed at the list head. A list representation of the stack containing **c**, **+**, and **2** follows:

Variable **top** is a reference to the list head (the top of the stack). We can access only the character referenced by **top**, the letter **c**. Next we draw the stack after we push the symbol ***** onto it. Now the only character we can access is the symbol *****:

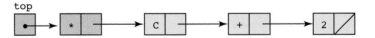

If we pop this stack, we retrieve the symbol ***** and restore the stack to its earlier state. A stack is called a **last-in, first-out (LIFO)** structure because the last element stored in a stack is always the first one removed.

Specification for Class `StackList`

Next we provide a specification for class `StackList`. Besides operators `push` and `pop`, we include operators `peek` and `isEmpty`. Operator `peek` accesses the top element on a stack without removing it. Operator `isEmpty` determines whether or not a stack has any elements.

Class `StackList`

Data Field	Attribute
`ListNode top`	A reference to the top of the stack
Methods	**Behavior**
`void push(Object)`	Place the argument at the top of the stack
`Object pop()`	Returns the object at the top of the stack and removes it
`Object peek()`	Returns the object at the top of the stack without removing it
`boolean isEmpty()`	Returns `true` if the stack is empty; otherwise, returns `false`

Implementing StackList

Figure 10.12 shows class `StackList` with class `ListNode` declared as a private inner class.

In method `push()`, the statement

```
top = new ListNode(item, top);
```

creates a new node at the top of the stack, copies `item` into its `info` field, and links the new node to the old top of the stack.

Method `peek()` returns the information at the top of a stack without changing the stack. Method `peek()` uses the condition `(isEmpty())` to test whether the stack is empty before returning the data in its top element (accessed by `top.info`). Method `isEmpty()` returns `true` when the boolean expression `top == null` is `true`. Method `peek()` throws a `NullPointerException` if the stack is empty.

Method `pop()` uses the statement

```
Object item = peek();        // Retrieve item at top.
```

to retrieve the item at the top of the stack. Next, it removes the current top of the stack by executing the statement

```
top = top.link;       // Link top to second element.
```

Figure 10.12   Class StackList

```
/*  StackList.java.          Authors: Koffman & Wolz.
 *  A stack class implemented as a linked list.
 *  Data field top references the top of the stack.
 */

public class StackList {
   // Insert class ListNode (Fig. 10.2) here.

   // Data fields
   private ListNode top;            // top of stack

   // Methods
   // constructor
   public StackList() {top = null;

   // precondition: item is defined.
   // postcondition: pushes item onto the top of this stack.
   public void push(Object item) {
      // Allocate a new node, store item in it, and
      //  link it to old top of stack.
      top = new ListNode(item, top);
   }


   // precondition: This stack is defined.
   // postcondition: Returns item at top of stack and removes it from the
   //    stack. Old second stack element is at top of stack.
   public Object pop() {
       Object item = peek();   // Retrieve item at top.

       //Remove old top of stack
       top = top.link;        // Link top to second element.

       return item;           // Return data at old top.
   }


   // precondition: This stack is defined.
   // postcondition: Returns item at top of this stack without removing it.
   //    Throws an exception if this stack is empty.
```

Figure 10.12   Class `StackList,` *continued*

```
   public Object peek() {
      if (isEmpty())
         throw new NullPointerException();
      return top.info;        // Return top item.
   }



   // postcondition: Returns true if this stack is empty;
   //   otherwise, return false.
   public boolean isEmpty() {
      return (top == null);
   }
} // class StackList
```

Displaying a Collection of Strings in Reverse Order

Next we write a class `StringsInReverse` (Fig. 10.13) with methods `main()`, `readStringStack()`, and `showStringStack()`. Method `main()` creates a new stack `StackOfStrings` (type `StackList`) and then calls `readStringStack()` and `showStringStack`, passing `StackOfStrings` as an argument. Method `readStringStack()` reads each string through the sentinel (`"***"`) and pushes it onto its stack argument, excluding the sentinel. Method `showStringStack()` pops each string off its stack argument and displays it. Because the last string stored on the stack is the first one removed, the strings are displayed in reverse order. Figure 10.14 shows a sample run.

Implementing a Stack Using a Vector

You may be wondering why we called our class `StackList` instead of just `Stack`. We chose `StackList` because Java provides a `Stack` class (in package `java.util`). Instead of using a linked list, Java implements class `Stack` as an extension of a vector. This is quite natural because the size of a vector automatically increases as elements are appended. In a vector representation of a stack, the element with subscript `size() - 1` is considered the element at the top of the stack.

Fig. 10.15 sketches stack `StackOfStrings` using a vector representation. Stack `StackOfStrings` contains the three data strings `"first"`, `"is"`, `"last"`, and the top of the stack (element with index 2) contains the string `"last"`. Fig. 10.16 shows class `StackVector`. Notice that class `StackVector` does not have a data field or a constructor. When a new `StackVector` object is created, it is represented as an empty vector.

Figure 10.13   Class `StringsInReverse`

```
/* StringsInReverse.java          Authors: Koffman & Wolz
 * Reads and stores a collection of strings on a stack
 * and displays them in reverse order.
 * Uses StackList and JOptionPane.
 */
import javax.swing.*;
import java.util.*;

public class StringsInReverse  {

  // Methods
  // postcondition: Reads a group of strings & pushes
  //    them onto its stack argument
  public static void readStringStack(StackList s) {
     String next =
         JOptionPane.showInputDialog("Enter a string or ***:");
     while (!next.equals("***")) {
        s.push(next);
        next = JOptionPane.showInputDialog("Enter a string or ***:");
     }
  }

  // postcondition: Pops strings off its stack
  //    argument and displays them.
  public static void showStringStack(StackList s) {
     // Pop each string and display it.
     while (!s.isEmpty()) {
        Object next = s.pop();
        System.out.println(next);
     }
  }

  // postcondition: Fills a stack and then empties it,
  //    displaying its contents.
  public static void main(String[] args) {

    // Create a new stack.
    StackList stackOfStrings = new StackList();
```

Figure 10.13   **Class StringsInReverse,** *continued*

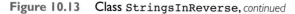

```
  // Fill the stack.
  readStringStack(stackOfStrings);

  // Empty it, displaying its contents.
  showStringStack(stackOfStrings);
 }
}
```

Figure 10.14   **Sample run of StringsInReverse**

Figure 10.15   **Stack StackOfStrings as a vector**

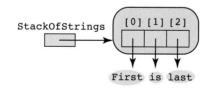

Our class **StackVector** differs from class **Stack** in folder **java.util** in two ways. Class **Stack** has a method **empty()** instead of **isEmpty()**. Also, method **push()** in class **Stack** returns as its result the item pushed onto the stack. Hence, method **push()** in class **Stack** is type **Object** (instead of type **void**).

Figure 10.16   Class StackVector

```
/* StackVector.java.          Authors: Koffman & Wolz.
 * A stack class implemented as a vector.
 */
import java.util.*;

public class StackVector extends Vector {
  // Methods
  // precondition: item is defined.
  // postcondition: Pushes item onto the top of the stack.
  public void push(Object item) {
    addElement(item);
  }


  // precondition: This stack is defined and is not empty.
  // postcondition: Returns item at top of this stack and removes it from the
  //    stack. Old second stack element is at top of stack.
  public Object pop() {
    Object item;

    item = peek();                    // Retrieve item at top.
    removeElementAt(size() - 1);  // Remove top element.
    return item;
  }


  // precondition: This stack is defined and is not empty.
  // postcondition: Returns item at top of stack without removing it.
  public Object peek() {
    if (isEmpty())
        throw new NullPointerException();
    return elementAt(size() - 1);
  }


   // postcondition: Returns true if this stack is empty; otherwise, returns
   //    false.
  public boolean isEmpty() {
    return (size() == 0);
  }
} // class StackVector
```

EXERCISES FOR SECTION 10.2

SELF-CHECK

1. Explain the difference between methods `pop()` and `peek()`.

2. Assume stack **s** is a stack of characters. Perform the following sequence of operations. Indicate the result of each operation and the new stack if it is changed. Rather than draw the stack each time, use the notation |2+C/ to represent a stack of four characters, where the last symbol on the right (/) is at the top of the stack.

   ```
   StackList s = new StackList();
   s.push("$");
   s.push("-");
   nextCh = (String) s.pop();
   nextCh = (String) s.peek();
   boolean success = s.isEmpty();
   ```

3. It is helpful to include a field `numItems` in type `StackList`, which contains a count of the number of elements on the stack. What changes would be required to the data fields and methods if field `numItems` is included?

4. How could a stack be implemented using an array instead of a linked list or vector? What are two disadvantages to this approach?

PROGRAMMING

1. Write a method `toString()` for class `StackList`. Append the `info` field of the node referenced by `top` first.

10.3 Queues

A **queue** (pronounced "Q") is a list-like structure in which items are inserted at one end and removed from the other. In contrast, stack elements are inserted and removed from the same end (the top of the stack).

A queue consists of a collection of elements that are all the same data type. The elements of a queue are ordered according to time of arrival. The element that was inserted first is the only one that may be removed or examined. Elements are removed from the front of the queue and inserted at the rear of the queue.

Because the element that was stored first is removed first, a queue is called a **first-in, first-out (FIFO)** structure. A queue can be used to model a line of customers waiting at a checkout counter or a stream of jobs waiting to be printed by a printer.

Figure 10.17   Queue of customers (a), after insertion (b), and removal (c)

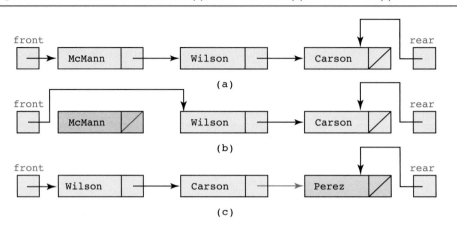

Fig. 10.17a shows a queue of three customers waiting for service at a bank. The name of the customer who has been waiting the longest is **McMann** (referenced by **front**); the name of the most recent arrival is **Carson** (referenced to by **rear**). Customer **McMann** in the node referenced to by **front** will be the first one removed from the queue when a teller becomes available, and link **front** will be reset to reference **Wilson** (Fig. 10.17b). Any new customers will be inserted after **Carson** in the queue, and link **rear** will be adjusted accordingly (Fig. 10.17c).

Specification for Class Queue

Next we provide the specification for class **Queue**. A queue is a class with two reference fields, **front** and **rear**. Variable **front** references the node at the front of the queue, and variable **rear** references the node at the rear of the queue. Because we might also want to know how many elements are in a queue, we will add a third data field, **size**. Each queue node (object of class **ListNode**) has an information field and a link to the next queue node. The only methods are constructors.

Class **Queue**

Data Fields	Attributes
ListNode front	A reference to the front of the queue
ListNode rear	A reference to the rear of the queue
int size	The size of the queue

Methods	Behavior
`void insert(object)`	Inserts its argument at the rear of the queue
`Object peek()`	Returns the element at the front of the queue without removing it
`Object remove()`	Returns the element at the front of the queue and removes it
`boolean isEmpty()`	Returns `true` if the queue is empty; otherwise, returns `false`
`int getSize()`	Returns the size of the queue
`String toString()`	Represents the queue as a string.

Implementing Queue

Figure 10.18 shows class `Queue` with class `ListNode` declared as a private inner class. For each new object of class `Queue`, data fields `front`, `rear`, and `size` are set to their defaults (`null`, `null`, and `0`).

Method `insert()` treats insertion of a node in an empty queue as a special case. For an empty queue, it uses the statements

```
rear = new ListNode(item);
front = rear;
```

to create a new node (with `item` in its `info` field) and to link both `front` and `rear` to this node. If the queue is not empty, the statements

```
rear.link = new ListNode(item);
rear = rear.link;   // Move rear to new node.
```

link `rear` to a new node (with `item` in its `info` field) and reset `rear` to reference the new node (Fig. 10.17c). Next, the statement

```
size++;                      // Increment queue size.
```

increments the queue size.

If a queue is empty, method `peek()` throws a `NullPointerException`. Otherwise, it returns the data at the front of the queue (`front.info`).

Method `remove()` uses method `peek()` to retrieve the queue data. Next, the statements

```
front = front.link;   // Delete first node.
size--;               // Decrement queue size.
```

reset `front` to reference the second node in the queue (Fig. 10.17b).

Figure 10.18   **Class** Queue

```
/*  Queue.java.            Authors: Koffman & Wolz.
 *  A class that represents a queue implemented as a linked list.
 */
public class Queue {
    // Insert inner class ListNode (Fig. 10.12) here.
    // Data Fields
    private ListNode front;   // Reference to front of queue
    private ListNode rear;    // Reference to rear of queue
    private int size;          // Size of queue

    // Methods
    //  postcondition: Inserts item in a new node and resets
    //      rear to reference the new node. If this queue has
    //      1 element, front references the new node also.
    public void insert(Object item) {
        if (isEmpty()) { // Empty queue
            // Link rear and front to only node.
            rear = new ListNode(item);
            front = rear;
        }
        else { // extend a nonempty queue
            rear.link = new ListNode(item);
            rear = rear.link;  // Move rear to new node.
        }

        size++;                    // Increment queue size.
    }

    // postcondition: If this queue is not empty, returns its
    // first element & front references new first element.
    public Object remove() {
        Object item = peek();      // Retrieve first item.

        // Remove first element.
        front = front.link;        // Delete first node.
        size--;                    // Decrement queue size.

        return item;
    }
```

Figure 10.18 Class Queue, *continued*

```
        // precondition: The queue has been created.
        // postcondition: If this queue is not empty, returns its
        //    first element; otherwise, throws an exception.
     public Object peek() {
            if (isEmpty())
                throw new NullPointerException();
            return front.info;
     }

       //  postcondition: Returns true if this queue is empty; otherwise,
       //           returns false.
     public boolean isEmpty() {
          return (size == 0);
     }

     // postcondition: Returns to the size of this queue.
     public int getSize() {
            return size;
     }
   public String toString() {
     String result = "";
     ListNode next = front;     start at front
     while (next != null) {
        result = result + next.info + "\n";
        next = next.link;
     }
     return result;
   }
} // class Queue
```

Testing the queue Class

Figure 10.19 shows an application program that tests the **queue** class. It begins by storing four names in the queue and then removes and displays the first name stored (**Chris**), stores a new name (**Dustin**), and removes and displays the second name stored (**Robin**). Finally, it displays the queue size (**3**) after a total of five insertions and two removals. Figure 10.20 shows a sample run.

Figure 10.19   Class QueueTest

```
/*  QueueTest.java.          Authors: Koffman & Wolz.
 *  Tests class Queue.
 */

public class QueueTest {

    public static void main (String[] args) {
        Queue q = new Queue();
        String name;

        // Insert 4 names
        q.insert("Chris");
        q.insert("Robin");
        q.insert("Debbie");
        q.insert("Richard");
        System.out.println(q.toString());

        name = (String) q.remove();
        System.out.println("Removed" + name);    // Displays Chris.
        q.insert("Dustin");
        System.out.println ("Inserted Dustin");

        name = (String) q.remove();
        System.out.println("Removed" + name);    // Displays Robin.

        System.out.println("size of q is " + q.getSize());
        System.out.println(q.toSize());
    }
} // class QueueTest
```

Figure 10.20   Sample run of class QueueTest

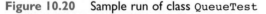

EXERCISES FOR SECTION 10.3

SELF-CHECK

1. Redraw the queue in Fig. 10.17 after the insertion of customer **Harris** and the removal of one customer from the queue. Which customer is removed? How many customers are left? Show links **first** and **rear** after each operation.

2. Trace the operation of methods **insert()** and **remove()** as the operations in Self-Check Exercise 1 are performed. Show before and after values for all links.

3. What changes would be made to method **insert()** to create a new **rudeInsert()** method that inserts at the front of the queue rather than the end?

4. A circular queue is a queue in which the node at the rear of the queue references the node at the front of the queue. (See circular lists in Section 10.1.) Draw the queue in Fig. 10.17 as a circular queue with just one link field named **rear**. Explain how you would access the queue element at the front of a circular queue.

PROGRAMMING

1. Is it possible to simulate the operation of a queue using two stacks? Write a class **QueueStacks** assuming two stacks are used for storing the queue. What performance penalty do we pay for this implementation?

10.4 Binary Trees

A binary tree has the following recursive definition: A **binary tree** is either empty or it consists of a node called the **root node** and two disjoint binary trees called its **left subtree** and **right subtree**.

Figure 10.21 shows two binary trees. For the tree (a), each node stores a three-letter string. The nodes on the bottom of the tree have zero successors and are called **leaf nodes**. All other nodes have two successors. For tree (b), each node stores an integer. The nodes containing **40** and **45** have a single successor; all other nodes have zero or two successors.

In the definition for binary tree, the phrase *disjoint subtrees* means that a node cannot be in both a left and right subtree of the same root node. For the trees shown in Fig. 10.21, the values **"FOX"** and **35** are stored in the root nodes of each tree. The node with **info** field **"DOG"** is the root of the left subtree of the tree whose root has the **info** field **"FOX"**; the node with info field **"CAT"** is the root of the left subtree of the tree whose root has the **info** field **"DOG"**; the node with **info** field **"CAT"** is a leaf node because both its subtrees are empty trees.

Figure 10.21   Binary trees

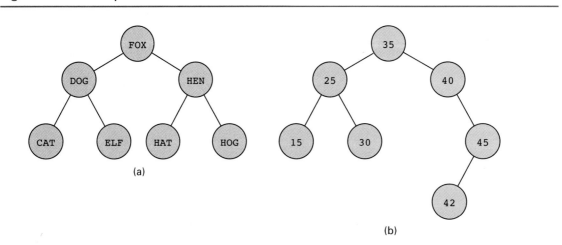

(a)

(b)

A binary tree resembles a family tree, and the relationships among the members of a binary tree are described with similar terminology. In Fig. 10.21 the node with `info` field `"HEN"` is the **parent** of the nodes with `info` fields `"HAT"` and `"HOG"`. Similarly, the nodes with `info` fields `"HAT"` and `"HOG"` are **siblings**, because they are both **children** of the same parent node. The root of a tree is an **ancestor** of all other nodes in the tree, and they in turn are **descendants** of the root node.

For simplicity, we did not show the link fields in Fig. 10.21. Be aware that each node has two link fields and that the nodes in (b) with `info` fields `45` and `42` are stored as follows:

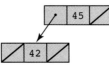

Binary Search Tree

In the rest of this chapter, we focus our attention on a particular kind of binary tree called a binary search tree. A **binary search tree** is a tree structure that stores data in such a way that it can be retrieved very efficiently. Every item stored in a binary search tree has a unique key.

The trees in Fig. 10.21 are examples of binary search trees; each node has a single data field that is its key. For tree (a), the string stored in every node is alphabetically larger than all strings in its left subtree and alphabetically smaller than all strings in its right subtree. For tree (b), the number stored in every node is larger than all numbers in its left subtree and smaller than all numbers in its right subtree. Notice that this must be true for every node in a binary search tree, not just the root node. For example, the number `40` must be smaller than both numbers stored in its right subtree (`45`, `42`).

Searching a Binary Search Tree

Next we explain how to search for an item in a binary search tree. To find a particular item, say `target`, we compare `target`'s key to the root item's key. If `target`'s key is smaller, we know that `target` can only be in the left subtree, so we search it. If `target`'s key is larger, we search the root item's right subtree. We write this recursive algorithm in pseudocode below; the first two cases are stopping cases.

Algorithm for searching a binary search tree

`if` the tree is empty
> The target key is not in the tree.

`else` `if` the target key is in the root item
> The target key is found in the root item.

`else` `if` the target key is smaller than the root's key
> Search the left subtree.

`else`
> Search the right subtree.

Figure 10.22 traces the search for **42** in a binary search tree containing integer keys. The argument **root** indicates the root node whose key is being compared to **42** at each step. The color arrows show the search path. The search proceeds from the top (node **35**) down to the node containing **42**.

Building a Binary Search Tree

Before we can retrieve an item from a binary search tree, we must, of course, build the tree. To do this, we must process a collection of data items that is in no particular order and insert each one individually, making sure that the expanded tree is a binary search tree. We build a binary search tree from the root node down, so we must store the first data item in the root node. To store each subsequent data item, we must find its parent node in the tree, attach a new node to the parent, and then store that data item in the new node.

When inserting an item, we must search the existing tree to find that item's key or to locate its parent node. If the item's key is already in the tree, we will not insert the item (duplicate keys are not allowed). If the item's key is not in the tree, the search will terminate at a **null** reference in the parent node of the item. If the item's key is smaller than its parent's key, we attach a new node as the parent's left subtree and insert the item in this node. If the item's key is larger than its parent's key, we attach a new node as the parent's right subtree and insert the item in this node. The following recursive algorithm maintains the binary search tree property; the first two cases are stopping cases.

Figure 10.22   Searching for key 42

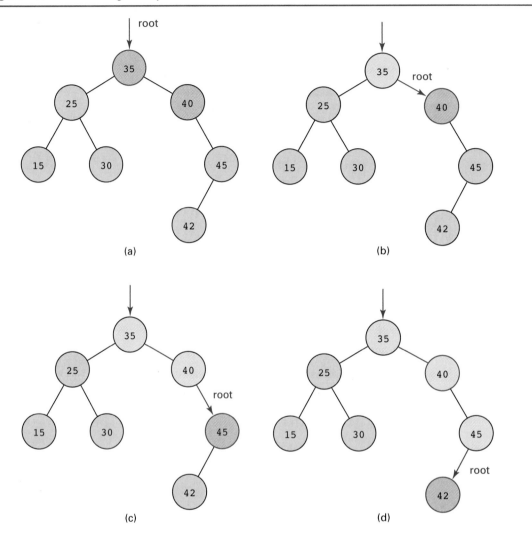

Algorithm for insertion in a binary search tree

if the tree is empty
    Insert the new item in the tree's root node.
else if the current node's key matches the new item's key
    Skip insertion—duplicate key.
else if the new item's key is smaller than the current node's key
    Insert the new item in the left subtree of the current node.
else
    Insert the new item in the right subtree of the current node.

Figure 10.23 builds a tree from the list of keys: **40**, **20**, **10**, **50**, **65**, **45**, **30**. The search path followed when inserting each key is shown in color.

The last node inserted (bottom-right diagram) contains the key **30** and is inserted in the right subtree of node **20**. Let's trace how this happens. Target key **30** is smaller than **40**, so we insert **30** in the left subtree of node **40**; this tree has **20** in its root. Target key **30** is greater than **20**, so we insert **30** in the right subtree of node **20**, an empty tree. Because node **20** has no right subtree, we allocate a new node and insert target **30** in it; the new node becomes the root of **20**'s right subtree.

Be aware that we would get a very different tree if we changed the order in which we inserted the keys. For example, if we inserted the keys in increasing order (**10**, **20**, **30**, ...), each new key would be inserted in the right subtree of the previous key and all left links would be **null**. The resulting tree would resemble a linked list. We will see later (Section 10.5) that the insertion order also affects search efficiency.

Traversing a Binary Search Tree

To display the contents of a binary search tree so that its items are listed in order by key value, use the recursive algorithm below.

Algorithm for traversing a binary search tree

1. **if** the tree is not empty
    2. Traverse left subtree.
    3. Display root item.
    4. Traverse right subtree.

Figure 10.23   Building a binary search tree

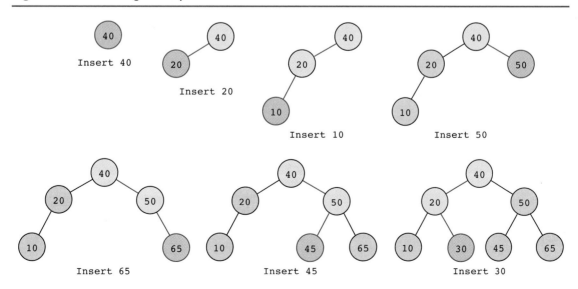

For each node, the items in its left subtree are displayed before the item in its root; the items in its right subtree are displayed after the item in its root. Because the root key value lies between the key values in its left and right subtrees, the algorithm displays the items in order by key value as desired. Because the nodes' data components are displayed in order, this algorithm is also called an **in-order traversal**.

Table 10.2 traces the sequence of calls generated by applying the traversal algorithm to the last tree in Fig. 10.23. The trace so far displays the item keys in the sequence 10, 20, 30, 40. Completing the sequence of calls for the last step shown in Table 10.2—"Traverse right subtree of node 40."—is left as an exercise.

Table 10.2 Trace of tree display algorithm

Traverse left subtree of node 40.
    Traverse left subtree of node 20.
        Traverse left subtree of node 10.
            Tree is empty—return from traversing left subtree of node 10.

        Display item with key 10.
        Traverse right subtree of node 10.
            Tree is empty—return from traversing right subtree of node 10.
        Return from traversing left subtree of node 20.
    Display item with key 20.
    Traverse right subtree of node 20.
        Traverse left subtree of node 30.
            Tree is empty—return from traversing left subtree of node 30.
        Display item with key 30.
        Traverse right subtree of node 30.
            Tree is empty—return from traversing right subtree of node 30.
        Return from traversing right subtree of node 20.
    Return from traversing left subtree of node 40.
    Display item with key 40.
    Traverse right subtree of node 40.

EXERCISES FOR SECTION 10.4

SELF-CHECK

1. Are the trees below binary search trees? Show the list of keys as they would be displayed by an in-order traversal of each tree. If the trees below were binary search trees, what key values would you expect to find in the left subtree of the node containing key 50?

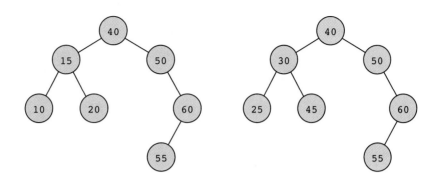

2. Complete the trace started in Table 10.2.

3. Show the binary search trees that would be created from the lists of keys below. Which tree do you think would be the most efficient to search? What can you say about the binary search tree formed in parts (b) and (c)? What can you say about the binary search tree formed in part (d)? How do you think searching it would compare to searching a linked list with the same keys?

    a. 25, 45, 15, 10, 60, 55, 12

    b. 25, 12, 55, 10, 15, 45, 60

    c. 25, 12, 10, 15, 55, 60, 45

    d. 10, 12, 15, 25, 45, 55, 60

4. What would be displayed by an in-order traversal of each tree in Self-Check Exercise 3?

10.5   A Binary Search Tree Class

A binary search tree is a collection of elements (nodes) such that each element has a unique key value. Each node of a binary tree has zero, one, or two subtrees connected to it. The key value in each node of a binary search tree is larger than all key values in its left subtree and smaller than all key values in its right subtree.

Next, we write the specification for a binary search tree class. Each binary search tree node (object of class **TreeNode**) has an information field (**info**) and two link fields (**left** and **right**).

Data field **info** is type **Comparable**. This means that any object stored in the search tree must implement the **Comparable** interface (see Section 6.4):

```
public interface Comparable {
    int compareTo(Object obj);
}
```

Recall that classes that implement the **Comparable** interface must have a **compareTo()** method that returns an integer value defined as follows:

◆ The result is negative if the object it is applied to is less than the argument.

◆ The result is zero if the object it is applied to is equal to the argument.

◆ The result is positive if the object it is applied to is greater than the argument.

Because **info** is type **Comparable**, we know that we can apply the **compareTo()** method to any object in a binary search tree.

Class **TreeNode**

Data Fields	Attributes
info	The node's key
TreeNode left	A reference to the left subtree of this node
TreeNode right	A reference to the right subtree of this node

Class **SearchTree**

Data Field	Attribute
TreeNode root	A reference to the root of the tree.
Methods	**Behavior**
boolean search(object)	Searches a tree to find a node with the same key as its argument. If found, returns **true**; otherwise, returns **false**.
boolean insert(object)	Inserts its argument into the binary search tree and returns **true**. If there is already an element with the same key, returns **false** and no insertion is performed.
Object peek(object)	Returns the tree element with the same key as its argument. If there is no tree element with that same key, returns **null**.
boolean isEmpty()	Returns **true** if the tree is empty; otherwise, returns **false**.

Implementing Class **TreeNode**

Figure 10.24 shows inner class **TreeNode** with two constructors and method **insertNode()**. The zero paramater constructor (the default) leaves the three data fields set at their default values (**null**). The one-parameter constructor casts its argument to type (**comparable**) before storing a reference to it in **info**. The link fields **left** and **right** are **null**.

Method `insertNode()` is called by method `insert` of `SearchTree` to perform steps 2 through 4 of the recursive tree insertion algorithm illustrated in Fig. 10.23. We explain why `insertNode()` is needed shortly.

Figure 10.24   Class `TreeNode`

```
private class TreeNode {
    // Data Fields
    private Comparable info;
    private TreeNode left;   //link to left subtree
    private TreeNode right;  //link to left subtree

    // Methods
    // Constructors
    public TreeNode() {};

    public TreeNode(Object obj) {
        info = (Comparable) obj;       // cast obj
        left = null;
        right = null;
    }

    // postcondition: Returns true if item is inserted.
    public boolean insertNode(Object item) {
        if (info.compareTo(item) == 0)
            return false;
        else if (info.compareTo(item) > 0)
            // item key < root key - check left subtree
            if (left == null) {
                left = new TreeNode(item); // Insert item.
                return true;
            } else  // Insert item in left subtree.
                return left.insertNode(item);
        // item key > root key - check right subtree
        else if (right == null) {
            right = new TreeNode(item);    // Insert item.
            return true;
        } else  // Insert item in right subtree.
            return right.insertNode(item);
    }
}
```

Implementing Class `SearchTree`

Figure 10.25 shows class `SearchTree` with methods `insert()` and `isEmpty()`
(returns `true` if root is `null`).

Methods `insert()` and `insertNode()`

Method `insert()` (Fig. 10.25) tests for an empty tree (a stopping case). If so, it uses
the statement

```
root = new TreeNode(item); // Insert item in root.
```

to create a root node and insert `item` in it. If the tree is not empty, method `insert()`
calls `insertNode` (Fig. 10.24) to find the insertion point for `item` and to insert `item`
in the tree.

Figure 10.25   Class `SearchTree()` with methods `insert()` and `isEmpty()`

```java
/* SearchTree.java.          Authors: Koffman & Wolz.
 * Class for binary search tree that stores Comparable objects.
 */

public class SearchTree {

    // Insert inner class TreeNode (Fig. 10.24) here.

    // Data fields
    private TreeNode root;

    // Methods
    // postcondition: Returns true if the insertion is performed. Returns
    //    false if there is a node with the same key as item.
    public boolean insert(Object item) {
        if (isEmpty()) { // Empty search tree
            root = new TreeNode(item); // Insert item in root.
            return true;
        }
        else  // Find insertion point and insert item.
            return root.insertNode(item);
    }

    // postcondition: Returns true if this tree is empty.
    public boolean isEmpty() {
        return (root == null);
    }

    // Insert methods search and display (Fig. 10.27) here.
```

The first condition of `insertNode()`

```
(info.compareTo(item) == 0)
```

tests whether the current node contains the same key as `item`, a stopping case. If so, `insertNode()` returns `false` (no insertion) because we don't allow duplicate items in the tree.

If a stopping case is not reached, method `insertNode()` must determine whether to insert `item` in the left subtree or the right subtree of the current node. The condition

```
(info.compareTo(item) > 0)
```

is `true` if `item`'s key is less than the key in the current node. In this case, we must insert in its left subtree. Before doing this, we test whether the left subtree is empty using the condition `left == null`. If the left subtree is empty, the statement

```
left = new TreeNode(item); // Insert item.
```

links a new node to the left subtree and inserts `item` in it. If the left subtree is not empty, the statement

```
return left.insertNode(item);
```

causes the insertion path to follow the left subtree of the current node. There are similar statements for inserting in the right subtree that execute when `item`'s key is greater than the current node's key.

Figure 10.26 illustrates the insertion of `"same"` in a binary search tree. The left subtree of the node containing `"smoke"` is empty before the insertion takes place.

Figure 10.26   Inserting a node in a tree

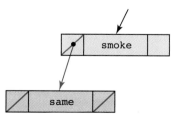

Method search()

Method **search()** (Fig. 10.29) implements the recursive search algorithm illustrated in Fig. 10.22. Notice that there are two methods named **search()**. The first method would be called in an application class to initiate the search. The public **search()** method calls the private **search()** method, passing it the tree root and target as arguments, and returns the result of the private **search()** method to the application.

The private **search()** method actually performs the recursive search. The first two conditions test for stopping cases. If the tree is empty, **search()** returns **false**. If the root node contains the target key, the condition

```
(root.info.compareTo(target) == 0)
```

is **true**, and method **search()** returns **true**.

If either stopping case above is not reached, method **search()** must determine whether to search the left subtree or the right subtree. The condition

```
(root.info.compareTo(target) > 0)
```

is **true** if the target key is less than the key in the root node. In this case, we must search the left subtree. Before doing so, we test whether the left subtree is empty using the condition **root.left == null** and return **false** if it is. Otherwise, the statement

```
return search(root.left, target);
```

applies method **search()** to the left subtree and returns the result of this search.

If the condition shown earlier is **false**, the target key is greater than the key in the current root node, so we must search the right subtree. If it is empty, we return **false**; otherwise, we search it.

Method toString()

We also provide two **toString()** methods. The public one is called by the application object and it, in turn, calls the private **toString** method, which builds a string that represents the result of the recursive in-order traversal discussed earlier.

The public **toString()** method (Fig. 10.28) just returns the string that is built by calling the recursive one, passing it the search tree root as its argument. The stopping case for the recursive method is reached when **root** is **null** (an empty tree); the method returns the empty string (**""**). Otherwise, it forms a string with three components. The first component is the string representation of its argument's left subtree, the middle component is the root node's information followed by the new line character, and the last component is the string representation of its argument's right subtree. When each node's information is inserted in the string being formed, there is an implicit call to the **toString()** method for data field **root.info**.

Figure 10.27   Method `search()`

```
// postcondition: Returns true if target's key is found;
//    otherwise, returns false.
public boolean search(Object target) {
    return search(root, target);
}


private boolean search(TreeNode root, Object target) {
    if (isEmpty())
        return false;              // Tree is empty.
    else if (root.info.compareTo(target) == 0)
        return true;               // Target is found.
    else if (root.info.compareTo(target) > 0)
        // target key < root key - check left subtree
        if (root.left == null)
            return false;          // Left subtree empty.
        else  // Search left.
            return search(root.left, target);
    // target key > root key - check right subtree
    else if (root.right == null)
        return false;              // Right subtree empty.
    else  // Search right.
        return search(root.right, target);
}
```

Figure 10.28   Method `toString()`

```
public String toString() {
   return toString(root);
}


// postcondition: Returns string showing in order traversal.
private String toString(TreeNode root) {
   if (root == null)
      return "";
   else {
      // Concatenate string formed from left subtree
      //    with root node's info field and with string
      //    formed from right subtree.
      return toString(root.left) +
             root.info + "\n" +
             toString(root.right);
   }
}
```

You may be wondering why we didn't provide a recursive insertion method in class `SearchTree` instead of writing method `insertNode()` (in class `TreeNode`). A recursive insertion method in `SearchTree` would require the root of the current tree as its argument. The root would change as we moved down the tree and would eventually become `null` when we reached the insertion point (the parent node). Next, we need to link the parent node to a new node containing `item`. However, Java does not allow us to change a method's argument, so the parent node's actual link would remain `null`.

Method `peek()` (see Programming Exercise 1) returns the tree element with the same key as `target`. Its implementation would be similar to `search()`. When `peek()` locates the `target`'s key, use the statement

```
return root.info;      // Return tree data with same key.
```

to return the tree data instead of returning `true`.

Testing the `SearchTree` Class

Figure 10.29 shows an application class that tests class `SearchTree`. Method `main()` stores 12 strings in the tree and then displays the tree. Figure 10.30 shows that the names are displayed in lexicographical order even though they were not entered that way.

Efficiency of a Binary Search Tree

Searching a binary search tree can be a very efficient process. If the left and right subtrees of every node are exactly the same size, each move to the left or the right during a search eliminates the elements of the other subtree from the search process. Because they need not be searched, the number of nodes we do have to search is cut in half in each step. This is a *best-case analysis* because, in reality, it is unlikely that a binary search tree will have exactly the same number of nodes in the left and right subtrees of each node. But this best-case analysis is useful for showing the power of the binary search tree.

As an example, if n is 1023 it will require searching 10 trees ($n = 1023, 511, 255, 127, 63, 31, 15, 7, 3, 1$) to determine that a target is missing. It should require fewer than 10 probes to find a target that is in the tree. The number 1024 is a power of 2 (1024 is 2 raised to the power 10). Keep in mind that not all binary search trees will have left and right subtrees of equal size.

Figure 10.29 Application class `TreeTest`

```
/*  TreeTest.java.              Authors: Koffman & Wolz.
 */ Tests class SearchTree.

public class TreeTest {

    public static void main (String[] args) {
        SearchTree t = new SearchTree();

        // Insert 12 names and nicknames in the tree.
        t.insert("Richard");
        t.insert("Debbie");
        t.insert("Robin");
        t.insert("Chris");
        t.insert("Jacquie");
        t.insert("Jeff");
        t.insert("Dustin");
        t.insert("Richie");
        t.insert("Deborah");
        t.insert("Jeffrey");
        t.insert("Jacqueline");
        t.insert("Christopher");

        // Display the tree contents.
        System.out.println(t.toString());
    }
} // class TreeTest
```

Figure 10.30 Output from running `TreeTest`

EXERCISES FOR SECTION 10.5

SELF-CHECK

1. Explain the effect of each statement in the following fragment if **myTree** is type **SearchTree**. Draw the tree built by the sequence of insertions. What values would be displayed?

    ```
    myTree.insert("hit");
    myTree.insert("apple");
    myTree.insert("toy");
    myTree.insert("this");
    myTree.insert("cat");
    myTree.insert("dog");
    myTree.insert("goat");
    myTree.insert("can");
    myTree.insert("tin");
    myTree.insert("cat");
    System.out.println(myTree.toString());
    ```

2. Draw the tree created by the sequence of insertions in Fig. 10.29.

3. Deletion of an entry in a binary tree is more difficult than insertion. Given any node in a tree that is to be deleted, what are the three cases for deletion and what must be done in each case? Be sure your approach preserves the binary search tree order.

4. Given the binary tree below, how many comparisons are needed to find each of the following keys or to determine that the key is not present? List the keys compared to the target for each search.

    a. 50   d. 65

    b. 55   e. 52

    c. 10   f. 48

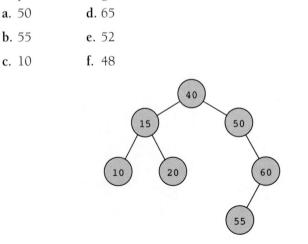

5. Why is it unlikely that a given binary tree will have exactly the same number of elements in the left and right subtrees of every node? For what numbers of nodes is this possible?

6. If the elements of a binary tree are inserted in order, what will the resulting tree look like?

7. The binary search introduced in Section 9.5 also performed efficient searches. Name two advantages of a binary tree over the binary search. Name one disadvanatge.

PROGRAMMING

1. Write method `peek()` that returns a reference to the search tree item whose key matches its argument's key. Return `null` if the search is unsuccessful.

2. Write an application class that stores a sequence of integers in a binary tree. You will need to wrap each integer value in an `Integer` object.

3. Define a `Student` class that implements the `Comparable` interface. Assume that a student has a `name` field (a string), an `id` (an integer), and `gPA` (grade-point average). Let the relative order of two student objects be determined by their names. If their names are the same, use their `id`'s as a tie-breaker.

10.6 `LinkedList` Collection Class and List Iterators (Optional)

As an alternative to developing your own linked list class, you can use the `LinkedList` collection class (see Section 5.9) provided in package `java.util`. This class has the methods described in Section 10.1 and many additional methods. It provides methods to get, remove, and insert an element at the beginning and end of a linked list. Therefore, a linked list object can be used as a stack or a queue. It also provides methods to get, set, and remove the element at a specified position (index) in the list. Finally, you can convert a linked list object to an array. Table 10.3 describes some of the `LinkedList` collection class methods.

List Iterators

In Section 10.1, we showed how to traverse the elements of a linked list using a reference variable `next` (type `ListNode`) and a loop of the form

```
while (next != null) {
  // Process the next node
  // . . .
  next = next.link;
}
```

Table 10.3 Methods of class `LinkedList`

Method	Behavior
`void add(int index, Object obj)`	Inserts the specified element at the specified position in the list.
`void add(Object obj)`	Appends the specified element to the end of the list.
`void addFirst(Object obj)`	Inserts the specified element at the beginning of the list.
`void addLast(Object obj)`	Inserts the specified element at the end of the list.
`boolean contains(Object o)`	Returns **true** if this list contains the specified element.
`Object get(int index)`	Returns the element in this list at the specified position.
`Object getFirst()`	Returns the first element in this list.
`Object getLast()`	Returns the last element in this list.
`int indexOf(Object o)`	Returns the position of the first occurrence of the specified element in this list (**-1** if not found).
`int lastIndexOf(Object o)`	Returns the position of the last occurrence of the specified element in this list (**-1** if not found).
`LinkedList()`	Creates an empty list.
`ListIterator listIterator(int index)`	Returns a list iterator for this list. The iterator selects the element specified or the first element if there is no argument.
`Object remove(int index)`	Removes and returns the specified element from this list.
`boolean remove(Object obj)`	Removes the first occurrence of the specified element from this list, returning **true** if found and **false** if not found.
`void removeFirst()`	Removes and returns the first element of this list.
`void removeLast()`	Removes and returns the last element of this list.
`Object set(int index, Object obj)`	Replaces the element at the specified position with the specified element. Returns the element previously at this position.
`int size()`	Returns the size of this list.
`Object[] toArray()`	Returns an array containing all the elements in this list in the correct order.
`String toString()`	Returns a string representation of this list. The list is enclosed in brackets and the elements are separated by commas.

Java provides a better way. In package `java.util`, there is an interface `ListIterator` (an extension of interface `Iterator`) that enables a programmer to easily traverse a list in either direction (forward or backward).

The statements

```
LinkedList myList = new LinkedList();
. . .
ListIterator iter = myList.listIterator();
```

declare a linked list `myList` with a list iterator `iter`. You can think of `iter` as an internal cursor that selects a particular element of list `myList`. You can move the cursor one position forward using method `next()`, and you can move the cursor one position back using method `previous()`. Both `next()` and `previous()` return the element at the cursor position. You can test whether the cursor has passed the last element in the list using method `hasNext()`, and you can test whether it has passed the first element in the list using method `hasPrevious()`. You can use method `add()` to insert an element at the cursor position, `remove()` to delete the element at the cursor position, and `set()` to replace the element at the cursor position with a new one. Finally, you can use method `nextIndex()` to return the index of the element that would be accessed by the next call to `next()`. Method `previousIndex()` returns the index of the element that would be accessed by the next call to `previous()`. Table 10.4 shows the methods of interface `ListIterator`.

Table 10.4 Methods of `ListIterator` interface

Method	Behavior
`void add(Object o)`	Inserts the specified element into the list (optional operation).
`boolean hasNext()`	Returns `true` if this list iterator has more elements when traversing the list in the forward direction.
`boolean hasPrevious()`	Returns `true` if this list iterator has more elements when traversing the list in the backward direction.
`Object next()`	Returns the next element in the list.
`int nextIndex()`	Returns the index of the element that would be returned by a subsequent call to `next()`.
`Object previous()`	Returns the previous element in the list.
`int previousIndex()`	Returns the index of the element that would be returned by a subsequent call to `previous()`.
`void remove()`	Removes from the list the last element that was returned by `next()` or `previous()` (optional operation).
`void set(Object obj)`	Replaces the last element returned by `next()` or `previous()` with the specified element (optional operation).

◆◆EXAMPLE 10.1

The program in Fig. 10.31 uses class `LinkedList` and interface `ListIterator`. It displays the lines

```
[first, she, ciao, hello, middle, them, me, you, last]
[first, she, good-bye, hello, middle, them, we, you, last]
```

After the initial list is built and displayed (see first output line above), we declare **iter** as a list iterator for list **myList**:

```
ListIterator iter = myList.listIterator();
```

Linked list **myList**'s **listIterator()** method returns an iterator to the linked list. Subsequent references to the linked list are through this iterator. The **while** loops traverse the list, replacing each word **me** with **we** and each word **ciao** with **good-bye** (see second output line above). Initially, the cursor is set just before the first element, so the first loop traverses the list in the forward direction. Loop exit occurs just after the cursor advances past the last list element. Because of this, the second loop must traverse the list in the backward direction (using method **previous()**).

After the list iterator has been created, you cannot modify the structure of the loop except through the iterator's own **add()** or **remove()** methods. If you attempt to, you will get a **ConcurrentModificationException**.

Figure 10.31   Class TestListIterator

```
/* TestListIterator.java          Authors: Koffman & Wolz
 * Tests the ListIterator interface.
 * Uses LinkedList, ListIterator.
 */
import java.util.*;

public class TestListIterator {

  public static void main(String[] args) {

    LinkedList myList = new LinkedList();
    myList.addFirst("hello");
    myList.addFirst("ciao");
    myList.addLast("them");
    myList.addLast("me");
    myList.addLast("you");
    myList.addFirst("she");
    myList.add(myList.size(), "last");
    myList.add(0, "first");
    myList.add(myList.size() / 2, "middle");
    System.out.println(myList);

    ListIterator iter = myList.listIterator();
    while (iter.hasNext())
      if (iter.next().equals("me"))
```

Figure 10.31   Class `TestListIterator`, *continued*

```
            iter.set("we");

        while (iter.hasPrevious()) {
          if (iter.previous().equals("ciao")) {
              iter.remove();
              iter.add("good-bye");
          }
        }

        System.out.println(myList);
      }
    }
```

EXERCISES FOR SECTION 10.6

SELF-CHECK

1. Explain the effect of each statement in the **main** method below. What is displayed?

```
public static void main(String[] args) {
    LinkedList lL = new LinkedList();
    lL.addLast("hello");
    lL.add(1, "good");
    lL.remove("good");
    lL.add(lL.size(), "more");
    lL.set(1, "greetings");

    ListIterator it = lL.listIterator();
    int count = 0;
    while (it.hasNext()) {
        count++;
        String temp = (String) it.next();
        it.set(temp + temp);
    }

    System.out.println(lL.toString() + ", " + lL.size() + ", count);
}
```

PROGRAMMING

1. Write a main method that creates and populates a linked list. Use a list iterator to display the list contents in reverse order.

2. Write a main method that creates a linked list of **Integer** objects. Use a list iterator to double the number stored in each list element.

10.7 Common Programming Errors

Several run-time errors can occur when traversing linked data structures. For example, if link **next** is supposed to reference each node in the linked list, make sure **next** is initialized to reference the list head.

Watch out for infinite loops caused by failure to advance a link down a list. The **while** statement

```
while (next != null)
  System.out.println(next.info);
  next = next.link;
```

executes forever. That happens because the link assignment statement is not included in the loop body, so **next** is not advanced down the list.

A **NullPointerException** can occur when the link **next** is advanced too far down the list and **next** takes on the value **null**, indicating the end of the list. If link **next** has the value **null**, the while condition

```
while ((next.info != "9999") && (next != null))
```

causes a run-time error because **next.info** is undefined when **next** is **null**. The **while** condition should be rewritten as

```
while ((next != null) && (next.info != "9999"))
```

Problems with heap management can also cause run-time errors. If your program gets stuck in an infinite loop while you are creating a linked data structure, your program could consume all the memory cells on the storage stack. This situation leads to a **stack overflow** error.

Similar problems can occur with recursive methods. If a recursive method does not terminate, you can get a **stack overflow** error.

Make sure your program does not attempt to reference a list node after the node is disconnected from the list. All links to a node being disconnected should be set to **null** so that the node can never be accessed unless it is reallocated.

Debugging Tips

When writing driver programs to test and debug linked data structures, you can create small linked structures by allocating several objects and linking them together using assignment statements (see Section 10.1). You also can use assignment statements to store information in the nodes.

CHAPTER REVIEW

1. If object **p** contains a link field, you can connect it to another object of the same type, thereby building a linked data structure. We considered linked lists, stacks, queues, and binary search trees.

2. Linked lists are flexible data structures that shrink and expand as a program executes. It is relatively easy to insert and delete nodes of a linked list.

3. A stack is a LIFO (last-in-first-out) structure in which all insertions (push operations) and deletions (pop operations) are done at the list head. Stacks have many varied uses in computer science, including saving argument lists for recursive methods and for translation of arithmetic expressions.

4. A queue is a FIFO (first-in-first-out) structure in which insertions are done at one end and deletions (removals) at the other end. Queues are used to save lists of items waiting for the same resource (e.g., a printer).

5. A binary tree is a linked data structure in which each node has two link fields leading to the node's left and right subtrees. Each node in the tree belongs to either the left or right subtree of an ancestor node, but it cannot be in both subtrees of an ancestor node.

6. A binary search tree is a binary tree in which each node's key is greater than all keys in its left subtree and smaller than all keys in its right subtree. Searching for a key in a binary search tree is an $O(\log_2 n)$ process.

QUICK-CHECK EXERCISES

1. If a linked list contains the three strings **"him"**, **"her"**, and **"its"** and h is a reference to the list head, what is the effect of the following statements? Assume the data field is **info**, the link field is **link**, and n and p are links.

```
n = h.link;
n.info = "she";
```

2. Answer Quick-Check Exercise 1 for the following fragment:

```
p = h.link;
n = p.link;
p.link = n.link;
```

3. Answer Quick-Check Exercise 1 for the following fragment:

```
n = h;
h = new ListNode("his");
h.link = n;
```

4. When is it advantageous to use a linked list data structure? When would an array be a better choice?

5. If A, B, and C are inserted into a stack and a queue, what would be the order of removal for the stack? For the queue?

6. Often computers allow you to type characters ahead of the program's use of them. Should a stack or a queue be used to store these characters?

7. Write a fragment that removes the element just below the top of a stack **s**. Use the stack operators.

8. Assume each left link of the tree below is **null**. Is it a binary search tree? What would be displayed by its in-order traversal? Write a sequence for inserting these keys that would create a binary search tree whose **null** links were all at the lowest level. Is there more than one such sequence?

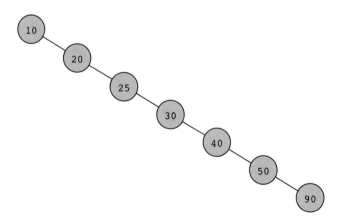

9. If a binary search tree has an in-order traversal of **1**, **2**, **3**, **4**, **5**, **6**, and the root node contains **3** and has **5** as the root of its right subtree, what do we know about the order that numbers were inserted in this tree?

10. Each node in a binary search tree has two children. True or false?

11. What is the relationship between the left child and the right child in a binary search tree? Between the left child and the parent? Between the right child and the parent? Between a parent and all descendants in its left subtree?

ANSWERS TO QUICK-CHECK EXERCISES

1. **"her"** is replaced by **"she"**.

2. The third list element is deleted.

3. A new list node with value **"his"** is inserted at the front of the list.

4. It is advantageous to use a linked list data structure when the number of elements is variable and there are frequent insertions and deletions. An array is a better choice when elements must be accessed in random order.

5. For stack: C, B, A; for queue: A, B, C.

6. A queue should be used.

7. ```
String x = (String)s.pop();

s.pop();

s.push(x);
```

8. Yes; **10**, **20**, **25**, **30**, **40**, **50**, **90**; **30**, **20**, **10**, **25**, **50**, **40**, **90**; yes.

9. **3** was inserted first and **5** was inserted before **4** and **6**.

10. False. One or more of its links can be null.

11. left child < parent < right child; parent > all descendants in left subtree.

## REVIEW QUESTIONS

1. Why are recursive methods often used for processing linked data structures?

2. Why is it more efficient to insert at the front of a list than at the end? How can insertion at the end of a list be made more efficient?

3. If a linked list of data elements is in sorted order, would we be able to search it more effciently? Why or why not?
```

4. Show the effects of each of the following operations on stack **s**:

```
s.push("hit");
s.push("hat");
system.out.println(s.peek().toString());
system.out.println(s.pop().toString());
s.push("top");
while (!s.isEmpty())
      system.out.println(s.pop().toString());
```

5. Write a stack operator that reverses the order of the top two stack elements if the stack has more than one element. Use **push()** and **pop()**.

6. Answer Review Question 4 for a queue **q** of characters. Replace **push()** with **insert()** and **pop()** with **remove()**.

7. Write a queue method **moveToRear()** that moves the element currently at the front of the queue to the rear of the queue. The element that was second in line will be at the front of the queue. Do this using methods **insert()** and **remove()**.

8. Write a queue method **moveToFront()** that moves the element at the rear of the queue to the front of the queue. Do this using insert and remove.

9. Discuss the differences between a simple linked list and a binary tree. Consider the number of link fields per node, search technique, and insertion algorithm.

10. How can you determine if a binary tree node is a leaf?

11. Trace an in-order traversal of the following tree. In what sequence would the nodes be diplayed?

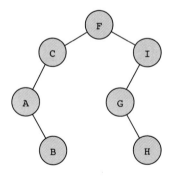

12. What happens when all the elements in a binary search tree are inserted in order. In reverse order? How does this affect the future performance of search and insertion methods?

PROGRAMMING PROJECTS

1. Write an application program that uses a queue to simulate a typical session for a bank teller. Store the customer's name, the transaction type, and the amount in a customer record. After every five customers are processed, display the size of the queue and the names of the customers who are waiting.

2. Carry out Programming Project 1 using a stack instead of a queue.

3. Write a program to monitor the flow of an item into and out of a warehouse. The warehouse will have numerous deliveries and shipments for this item (a widget) during the time period covered. A shipment out is billed at 50 percent over the cost of a widget. Unfortunately, each shipment received may have a different cost associated with it. The accountants for the firm have instituted a last-in, first-out system for filling orders. This means that the newest widgets are the first ones sent out to fill an order. This method of inventory can be represented using a stack. The **push** method will insert a shipment received. The **pop** method will delete a shipment going out. Each data record will consist of the following items:

   shipIn: shipment received (**true**) or order to be sent (**false**)

   quantity: quantity received or shipped out

   cost: cost per widget (for a shipment received only)

   vendor: string that names company sent to or received from

   Write the necessary methods to store shipments received and to process orders. The output for an order will consist of the quantity and the total cost for all widgets in the order. *Hint:* Each widget price is 50 percent higher than its cost. The widgets used to fill an order may come from multiple shipments with different costs.

4. Redo Programming Project 3 assuming widgets are shipped using a first-in, first-out strategy. Use a queue to store the widget orders.

5. A *dequeue* might be described as a double-ended queue, that is, a structure in which elements can be inserted or removed from either end. Write and test class **Dequeue**.

6. The radix sorting algorithm uses an array of 10 queues (numbered 0 through 9) to simulate the operation of the old card-sorting machines. The algorithm requires one pass to be made for every digit of the numbers being sorted. For example, a list of three-digit numbers would require three passes through the list. During the first pass, the least significant digit (the ones digit) of each number is examined and the number is inserted at the rear of the queue whose subscript matches the digit. After all numbers have been processed, the elements of each queue, beginning with the first queue, are copied one at a time

to the end of an eleventh queue prior to beginning the next pass. The process is repeated for the next most significant digit (the tens digit) using the order of the numbers in the eleventh queue. Repeat the process for the third most significant digit (the hundreds digit). After the final pass, the eleventh queue will contain the numbers in sorted order. Write a program that implements radix sort using class `Queue`.

7. Use a binary search tree to maintain an airline passenger list. Each passenger record should contain the passenger name and number of seats. The main program should be menu driven and allow the user to display the data for a particular passenger, display the entire list, create a list, insert a node, delete a node, and replace the data for a particular passenger. When deleting a node, simply change the number of assigned seats to zero and leave the passenger's node in the tree.

8. Save each word appearing in a block of text in a binary search tree. Also save the number of occurrences of each word and the line number for each occurrence. Use a stack for the line numbers. After all words have been processed, display each word in alphabetical order. Along with each word, display the number of occurrences and the line number for each occurrence.

9. The fastest binary tree is one that is as close to balanced as possible. However, there is no guarantee that elements will be inserted in the right order. It is possible to build a balanced binary tree if the elements to be inserted are in order in an array. Write a method and test program that, given a sorted array of elements, builds a balanced binary tree. Augment the binary search tree to keep a count of the number of nodes that are searched to find an element and display the number of nodes that are searched to find each item in the tree. *Hint:* The root of the tree should be the middle (median) of the array. This project is easier to do if you use recursion.

10. Write a method that performs an in-order traversal of a binary tree without using recursion. It will be necessary to use a stack. Write a suitable test program for your method.

11. Write a method that uses the selection sort strategy to create a sorted copy of a linked list.

12. A polynomial can be represented as a linked list, where each node contains the coefficient and the exponent of a term of the polynomial. The polynomial $4x^3 + 3x^2 - 5$ would be represented as the following linked list:

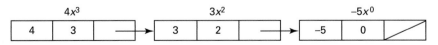

Write a class **Polynomial** that has operators for creating a polynomial, reading a polynomial, and adding and subtracting a pair of polynomials. *Hint:* To add or subtract two polynomials, traverse both lists. If a particular exponent value is present in either one, it also should be present in the result polynomial unless its coefficient is zero.

13. There are many programs that create multiple, overlapping windows on the screen. With overlapping windows comes the concept of a window being on top and a front-to-back ordering of windows. If windows are drawn from back to front, their appearance matches the expected results. Write a program that maintains a linked list of colored rectangles representing windows in back-to-front order. Your program should have a menu that allows the user to enter a letter for a rectangle, the color of the rectangle, and its screen location. Other menu options should allow the screen to be redrawn and any window to be moved to the top.

Java Resources, Package **psJava**, **JBuilder**, and HTML Resources

Java Resources
Package **psJava**
Using **JBuilder**
HTML Resources

Java Resources

Java is a proprietary product of Sun Microsystems, Incorporated. To find out more about Java, visit the company's website: http://java.sun.com/. If you select Products and APIs, you can obtain much of the documentation about the APIs in Java, which is similar to what is provided in Appendixes C, D, and E.

Addison-Wesley has developed a Web site called Java Place specifically for students who are learning Java. The preface provides instructions about accessing Java Place, and you can access materials for this textbook from it. The URL is www.javaplace.net.

There are many textbooks available for advanced features of Java. Addison-Wesley has developed a series of books on Java written by members of the JavaSoft team at Sun Microsystems, Inc. The URL for this series is www.aw.com/cseng/javaseries.

Package **psJava**

The package **psJava** provides classes from this textbook. Principally, it contains a class called **KeyIn**, which you can use to facilitate reading data typed in at the keyboard. This class and its methods are described in Section 3.6. There is also a class in the package called **UserOut**, which contains methods for displaying information in message windows and in table output form. The documentation for using this class is

provided at the beginning of the class. You can download this package from
www.aw.com/cssupport..

Using `JBuilder`

The CD that accompanies this textbook contains `JBuilder`, an Integrated
Development Environment for writing, running, and debugging Java programs. When
you install it, select typical installation. Make sure the path to the folder where you
install it does not contain a folder with a space in its name.

Projects

You need a project for each Java program. You should place each program and its files
in a separate folder in directory `myprojects`. To create a new project, select **File,
New Project** (Fig. A-1).

Figure A-1

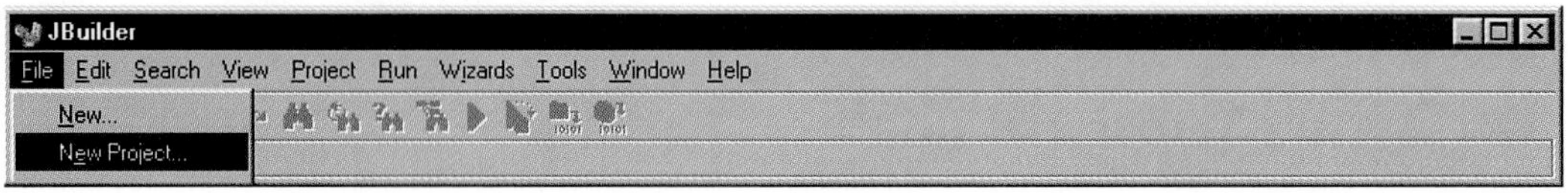

You can browse to select the folder in which the project will be placed. You can
use the same name for the folder and the project. Don't use spaces in any folder or
project names. Also, case matters. The project file has a `.jpr` extension. After typing
in the project name (but not the extension), select **Finish** from the project wizard (Fig.
A-2).

Figure A-2

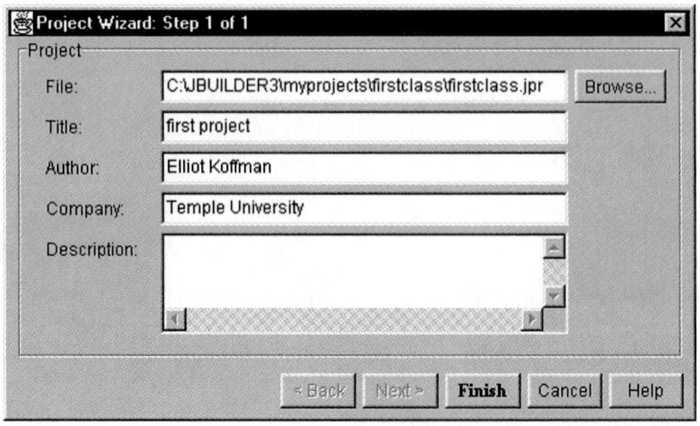

When a new project is created, an `.html` file that has the same name as the project is automatically placed in the project. It shows up in the edit window (Fig. A-3), but you should ignore it except when writing applets (more on this later).

Figure A-3

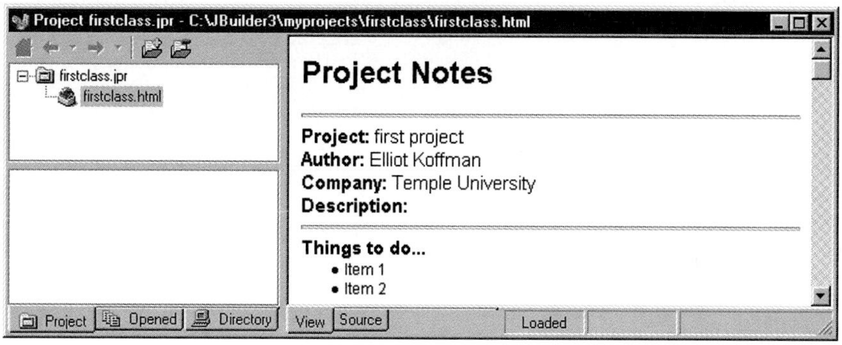

Classes

To create Java classes for your project, select **File, New,** and click on the **Class icon** (Fig. A-4).

Figure A-4

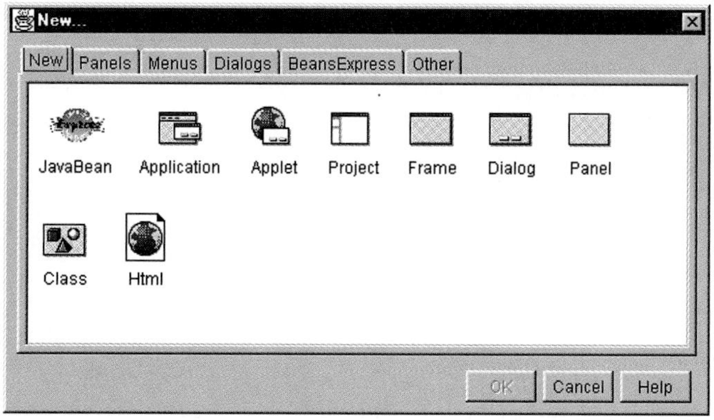

You will have a file window in which you can type in the class name in the field with label **Class Name** (Fig. A-5). Java will give the file the same name as the class name and adds a `.java` extension (see **File Name** field). After you select **OK**, an edit window will pop up with the skeleton for a `.java` file (Fig. A-6). You can delete the package line at the top. The default constructor is provided for you as shown in the edit window in the figure.

Figure A-5

```
┌─ New Java File ────────────────────────────────────┬─ X ─┐
│  ┌─Class──────────────────────────────────────────────┐  │
│  │  Package:      │firstclass                       │  │  │
│  │                                                    │  │
│  │  Class Name:   │FirstClass│                       │  │  │
│  │                                                    │  │
│  │  File Name:    │C:\JBuilder3\myprojects\firstclass\FirstClass.java│  │
│  │                                                    │  │
│  │  Extends:      │java.lang.Object                 │  │  │
│  └────────────────────────────────────────────────────┘  │
│                                                          │
│  ┌─Style──────────────────────────────────────────────┐  │
│  │  ☐  Generate header comments                       │  │
│  │                                                    │  │
│  │  ☑  Public                                         │  │
│  │                                                    │  │
│  │  ☑  Generate parameterless constructor             │  │
│  │                                                    │  │
│  │  ☐  Generate main function                         │  │
│  └────────────────────────────────────────────────────┘  │
│                                                          │
│                     ┌────────┐ ┌────────┐ ┌────────┐     │
│                     │   OK   │ │ Cancel │ │  Help  │     │
│                     └────────┘ └────────┘ └────────┘     │
└──────────────────────────────────────────────────────────┘
```

Figure A-6

```
┌─ Project firstclass.jpr - C:\JBuilder3\myprojects\firstclass\FirstClass.java ──┬─□ X ─┐
│ ▓ ← · → · │ ░ ░          │ package firstclass;                                 ▲│
│ ┌──────────────────────┐ │                                                     ││
│ ⊟─▣ firstclass.jpr      │ │ public class FirstClass {                          ││
│    ├─▓ firstclass.html  │ │                                                    ││
│    └─▓ FirstClass.java  │ │   public FirstClass() {                            ││
│                         │ │   }                                                ││
│                         │ │ }                                                  ││
│ ⊟─▨ FirstClass          │ │                                                    ││
│    ├─▨ Object           │ │                                                    ││
│    └─▨ FirstClass()     │ │                                                    ││
│ ⊟─▨ Imports             │ │                                                    ││
│    └─▨ firstclass       │ │                                                    ▼│
│                         │ │ ◄ ░                                              ► │
│ ▣ Project │▒ Opened│▣ Directory│ Source │ Doc │        8: 1 │ Modified │ Insert │
└────────────────────────────────────────────────────────────────────────────────┘
```

Type in one class in each file. If you need more files for a project, use **File, New** and click on the **Class icon** again. Each file will automatically be added to the project. To add other Java files to the project that are already on your disk (or in other folders), click on the green + icon or select **Project, Add to project**. This will allow you to browse through your directory to find the file. Open it to add it to the project. It should show up in the Project window described below.

Project and Opened Tabs

To the left of the edit window, there is a window with two tabs. The default tab is **Project**, which shows all the files for the current project. If you select the tab **Opened**, you will see all the files that are currently opened.

Compiling and Running

When you are all done, select the edit window for the file that has the main method (the starting point) and click on the **run** button (a green arrow pointing to the right) or select **Run, Run** (Fig. A-7). Your classes will be compiled and run if there are no errors. Error messages will show up under the edit window. Click on an error message to go to the line that is causing it. When your program runs, the message **Running:** or **Running: Compiled with warnings** will appear in the **JBuilder** menu, and the console window will pop up with some program output in it (Fig. A-8). Close the console window when you are done if it is not closed automatically. You will get a warning message window that you may lose unsaved information, but it is OK to do this (select **Yes—I want to close down**).

Figure A-7

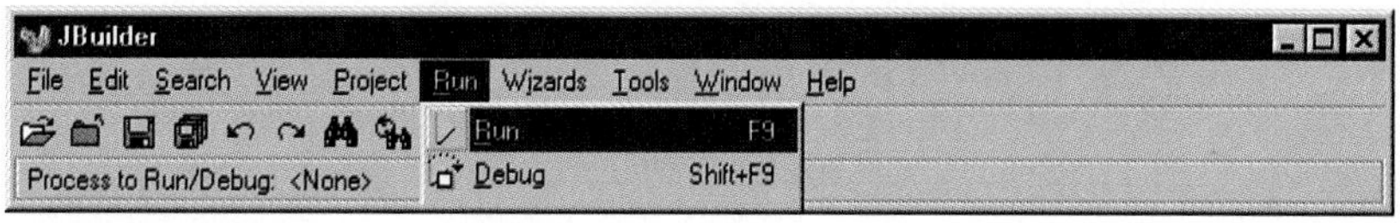

Project Properties Menu

You can select **Project, Properties** to change the properties for this project or **Project, Default Properties**, to change the defaults (Fig. A-9). You can select properties for a specific project that are different from the ones you set as the default, but all new projects will be given the default properties when the project is created.

The **Paths** tab usually shows up first; it shows the **Source** directory (where Java looks for your classes) and the **Output** directory (where it puts the .class or compiled bytecode files). If all your Java class files are stored in folder **myprojects**, make that the default source directory (Fig. A-10). You can type it in or select the button to the right of the field to browse for a Source directory. You can have more than one Source directory, but only one Output directory. The default is to place the compiled files (.class or bytecode files) in a folder called **myclasses**, but you may want to put them in the project folder (particularly for applets). You can accomplish this by making the project folder the Output directory (Fig. A-10).

Figure A-8

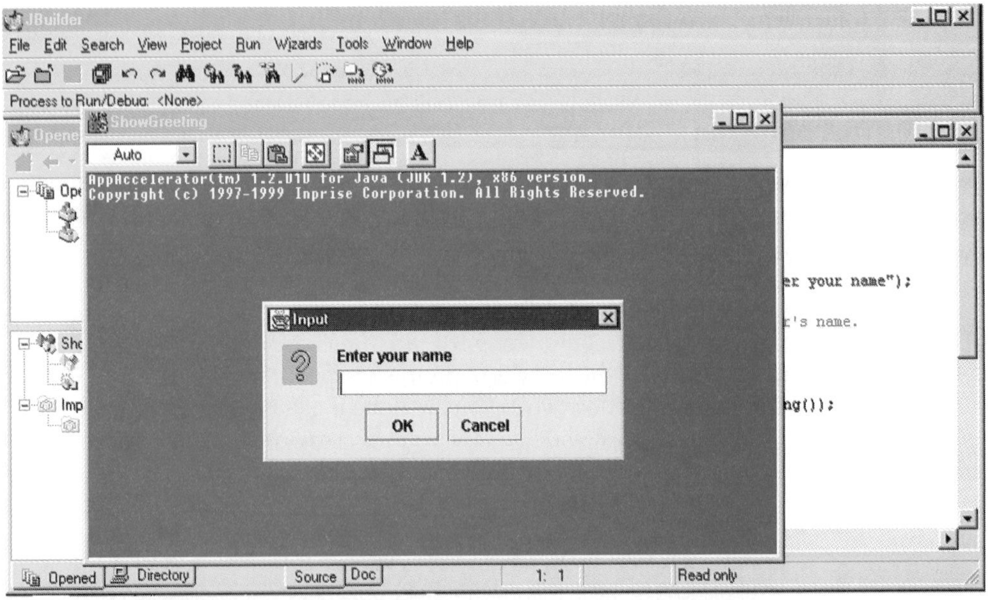

Figure A-9

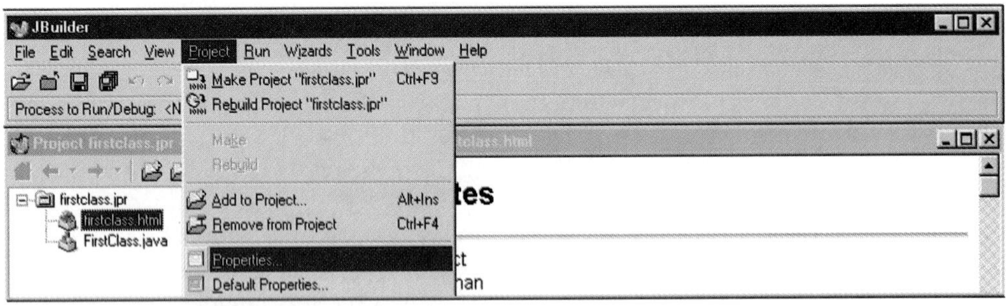

Under the **Compiler** tab, you may want to deselect the check box for **Show warn-ings** if there are lots of warning messages that are displayed each time you compile a project (Fig. A-11). You may also want to select the check box **Autosave all files before compiling**. This will ensure that you don't lose everything if there is a crash during compilation or execution.

Figure A-10

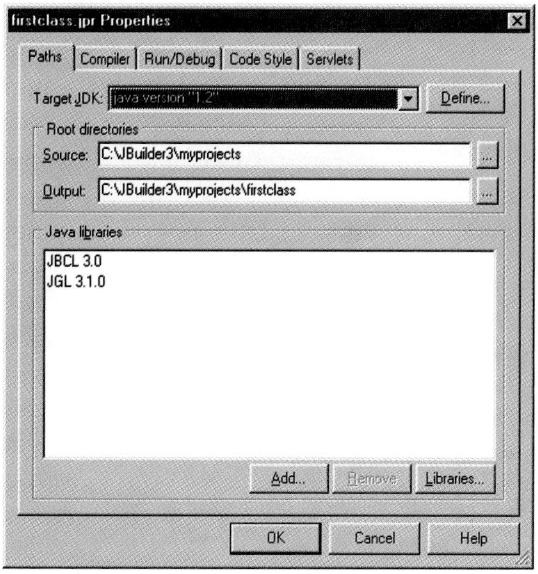

Figure A-11

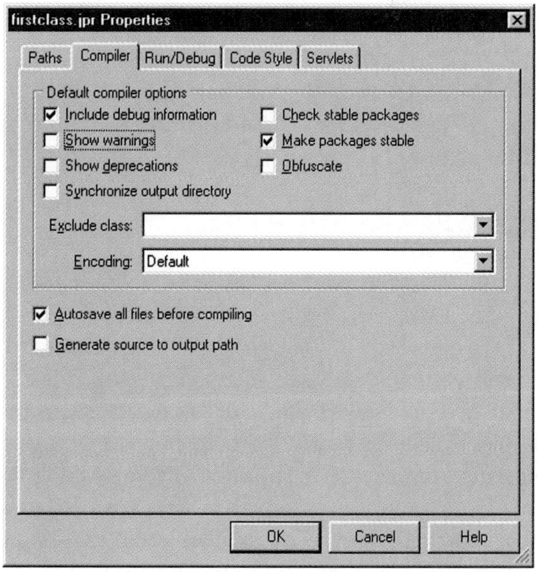

Under **Run/Debug**, you may want to deselect the check box **Close Console window on exit** (Fig. A-12). This will keep your console window open until you shut down the application. Otherwise, your console window may close down immediately, before you can read see your console output.

Figure A-12

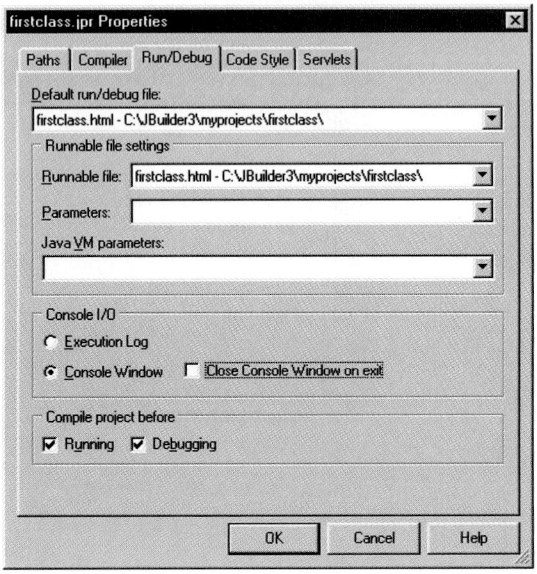

Under **Code style**, you can choose whether you want open braces on the same line as the header (select **End of line**) or on the line following the header (select **Next line**) (Fig. A-13).

Applets

To run an applet, you need an `.html` file for your project. You can edit the one that was provided when the project was first created (Fig. A-3). Select the **Source tab** to see the HTML code for this file (Fig. A-14). Delete most of this code and type in what you need to run your applet. Make sure you save this file each time you modify it by pressing the **disk save** icon. Select the edit window for this file and then select **Run** to execute the applet. The applet viewer should pop up. If you get a **class not found error**, you have specified the wrong `.class` file or it is saved in a different directory. For applets, make sure your project output path is set so the `.class` files (the compiled bytecode) are in the same folder as the `.html` file; otherwise, Java may not find the `.class` file. This is particularly true if you try to run the applet using a browser program.

Figure A-13

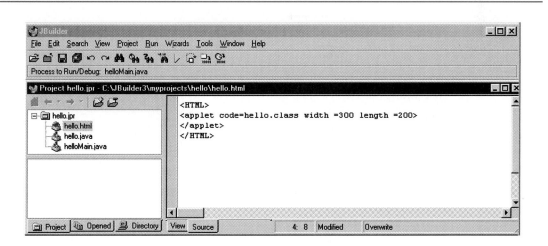

Figure A-14

Using the Debugger

Using the debugger enables you to execute your program incrementally instead of all at once. To use the debugger, select **Run** and then **Trace Into** or **Step Over** from the **Run** menu. This will cause the debugger to pause before executing the first line of your main method (Fig. A-15).

Figure A-15

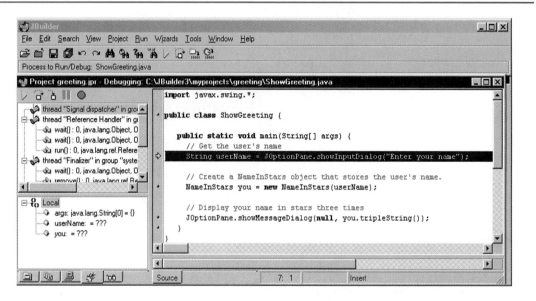

At this point you can select any of the choices from the **Run** menu, or you can click on the **Step Over** icon, which executes a method body in a single step, or click on the **Trace Into** icon, which allows you to execute individual lines of a method. Unless you are sure you are tracing into your own method, you are better off not selecting **Trace Into** because you may end up tracing a system library method. You can place the cursor at a particular program line and then select **Run to Cursor** to execute to that line (Fig. A-16). Or you can click on several different lines to set breakpoints in your program and then select **Run** to execute to the next breakpoint. To remove a breakpoint, click on it a second time.

The whole purpose of using the debugger is to be able to see the effect of each program statement on your program variables. As you step through your program, the debugger updates the values of the program variables shown in the **Debug** window (bottom left of Fig. A-16). Click on the + icons to view more information about a variable.

Figure A-16

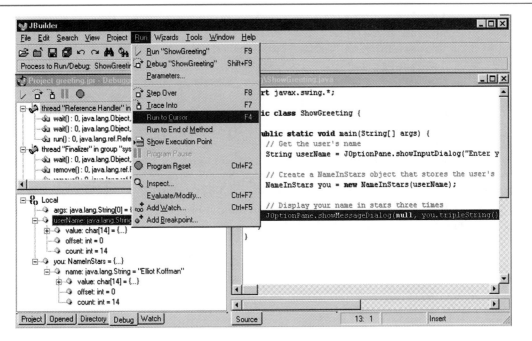

HTML Resources

You can learn about HTML from many sources. There are a multitude of "how to" books. Many browsers such as Internet Explorer and Netscape Communicator allow you to construct HTML pages through icons and menus. The JBuilder environment contains some resource material as well as support for building HTML files.

Tags related to applets are summarized here.

`<applet> </applet>`	Defines the boundaries of the applet tag.

`<param name =`
`unquotedString value =`
`"quotedString"/>`
	Appears within applet boundaries; specifies parameters for the applet.

`code`	The class name of the applet.
`height`	The initial height of the applet in pixels.
`object`	The filename containing a serialized version of the applet; see resource materials for details.
`width`	Specifies the initial width of the applet in pixels.
`align`	The alignment of the applet within the browser, value may be: `left`, `right`, `top`, `texttop`, `middle`, `absmiddle`, `baseline`, `bottom`, and `absbottom`.
`alt`	Text to display if the browser understands the applet tag but cannot run Java applets.
`archive`	A list of comma-separated archive files in JAR format; see resource materials for details.
`codebase`	The applet's code base (where the applet class file is stored).
`hspace`	Horizontal space to the left and right of the applet.
`name`	The applet's name.
`vspace`	Vertical space on the top and bottom of the applet.

Java Language Summary

Basic Syntax and Structure of the Java Language
Reserved Words
Operator Precedence
The Unicode Character Set
Primitive Types

Basic Syntax and Structure of the Java Language

Although the Java Class Libraries make Java a huge language, the basic forms and syntax of Java are simple. They are summarized here within the context of (1) class definitions, (2) variable and method declarations and object instantiations, (3) statements and control structures, (4) array declarations and element reference, and (5) package declarations.

Class Definitions

A class definition consists of a class declaration and a body. The body contains data field and method declarations.

    The declaration consists of keywords and identifiers. Reserved words appear in color. Examples of identifiers appear in plain text.

```
/* The simplest form of a class definition */

class SimplestClass {

    // Data field and method declarations go here.

} // class SimplestClass

/* A simple class that extends anotherClass */

public class SimpleClass extends anotherClass {

    // Data field and method declarations go here.

} // class SimplestClass

/* A complicated object with all the options */

public abstract class MyClass extends anotherClass
    implements interfaceOne, interfaceTwo {

    // Data field and method declarations go here.

} // class MyClass
```

Variable and Method Declarations, and Object Instantiations

In Java, variables may be declared (1) as data fields of a class, (2) as arguments to a method, or (3) as local variables within a block.

Data field and method variable declarations

You declare a variable by giving its type and its identifier. The type may be one of the primitive types or it may be a class. Data field and local variable declarations may include assignment of an initial value. Arguments get their initial value when the method is called.

```
// Examples of data field or method variable declaration

int x;                     // Identifier x is of type int
char myInitial = 'C';      // myInitial is of type char
                           //   with initial value 'C'
String answer = "Hello";   // Answer is of type String
                           //   with initial value "Hello"
boolean flag = true;
```

Creating an instance of a class

To create an initial value for a variable whose type is an object, you must create an instance of the class. The reserved word **new**, followed by a constructor for the class, allocates space for the object and initializes the data fields of the object.

```
SomeClass x = new SomeClass(); // x is an instance of a
                               //  SomeClass object.
```

Visibility of data fields and methods

Data fields are accessible from any method within the class. Depending on the declared visibility, other objects may also access the data fields. Data fields that are not given an explicit initial value are set to the appropriate default (see the data type summary below).

```
/* Examples of data field declarations */
public class Example1 {
    // Data fields
    public int y = 10;    // Will be accessible to any
                          //  other class

    AnotherObject x;  // Default visibility, accessible
                      //  within package
                      // Set to the default value null.

    protected int x;  // Accessible within the package
                      //  and by subclasses
                      // Set to the default value 0.

    private SomeObject y = new SomeObject();
                  // Only accessible within the class.
                  // Creates an instance of a
                  //  SomeObject.
} // class Example1
```

Summary of default data field values

Type	Value
Number (integer or real)	0
boolean	false
char	The null character
String	null
Object	null

Method declarations

Simple method declarations, also called method signatures, consist of a return type, an identifier, and an argument list. The return type may be a valid type (including a class) or the type **void** if nothing will be returned. The argument list consists of type declarations (without initial values) separated by commas. The argument list may be empty. Methods may also be given an explicit visilibity.

```java
public class Example2 {
    // No data fields declared

/* The simplest method declaration: returns nothing, is
    not passed any arguments */
    private void calculateX() {
        // Method body
    }

/* A method with a single argument of type double that returns an
integer */
    public int calculateY(double x) {
        // Method body
    }

/* A method that returns an object of type MyObj, given
    an integer and string as input */
    protected MyObj translateIT(int x, String y) {
        // Method body
    }
} // class Example2
```

Method calls

When these methods are called, arguments of the proper type must be provided. The returned value must be handled properly:

```java
// Within a method:
{ calculateX();      // A simple statement (returns
                     // void), no arguments required.

  int w = calculateY(15.7); //Returns an int, requires a
                            //   double as an argument.

  MyObj x = translateIT(5, "Hello"); // Returns a MyObj.
                                     // Requires an int and a
                                     //  string.

  ...
}
```

Constructor declarations

The declaration of a constructor differs in one important way from an ordinary method. It does not include a return type. If no constructors are declared for a class, a default constructor is automatically created. If any constructors are declared, the default constructor is not automatically generated. For example,

```
public class SimpleClass {
    int x;
    void incrementX() { x = x + 1;}
}
```

This class may be instantiated and used as follows:

```
{ SimpleClass anObj = new SimpleClass();
    // An object is created, x is initially set to 0.
    anObj.incrementX();
    // The value of anObj.x will be 1.
}
```

```
public class ConstructorClass {
    int x;

    public ConstructorClass(int s) { x = s;}

    void incrementX() { x = x + 1;}
}
```

This class may be instantiated and used as follows:

```
{ ConstructorClass anObj = ConstructorClass(10);
  // This is not allowed:
  //   ConstructorClass anObj = ConstructorClass();
  //   because the default constructor
  //   has not been built.

  anObj.incrementX();
  // The value of anObj.x will be 11.
}
```

The reserved words this and super

When used within a constructor, the reserved words **this** and **super** refer to this class and the superclass, respectively. The reserved word **this** may also be used to refer to the current object, for example to pass this object as an argument.

Instance vs. class members, final members

Data fields or methods may be instance or class members. Instance members are unique to each instance; class members are shared by all instances of the class. Both data fields and methods may be declared `final`. `Final` data fields may not have their initial value changed. `Final` methods may not be overridden by a subclass.

```java
// All members have default visibility.
public class Example3 {
    int x = 3;             // Instance data field,
                           //  may be modified.

    final int y = 10;      // Instance data field,
                           //  may not be modified.

    static int z = 4;      // Class data field,
                           //   shared by all instances,
                           //  may be modified.

    static final int w = 7; // Final class data field,
                           //   shared by all instances,
                           //  may not be modified.

} // class Example3
```

A `static` method may be referenced by the class name as well as by an instance of the class.

Abstract class and interface declarations

An abstract class is one in which at least one method is declared abstract.

```java
public class anAbstractClass {

    int x; // An abstract class may have data fields.
    // The method fillInLater will be defined by
    //  a subclass of this class.
    public abstract void fillInLater();

}
```

An interface only contains abstract method definitions and **final** class data fields.

```
public interface anInterface {
    public static final x = 3; // Only final class data
                               //  fields allowed.

    public void fillInLater(); // Doesn't need to be
                               //  declared abstract.
}
```

Method declarations that throw exceptions

A method may either handle an exception or "throw it" to the method that called it. See the discussion of **try-catch** below for exception handling. A method throws an exception by adding the reserved word **throws** and the exception to throw to the end of the method declaration. For example,

```
public void myFileMethod(int x) throws IOException {
    // method body
}
```

Statements and Control Structures

A method body consists of one or more program statements. Statements contain identifiers, reserved words, and expressions. Variable declarations are the simplest kind of statement.

Assignment statements

An assignment statement assigns the value of the expression on the right-hand side to the variable on the left-hand side. For example,

```
x = (5 + y) * 21;  // The sum of 5 and y is multiplied
                   //  by 21 and assigned to variable x.
```

Return statements

Return statements provide an exit from a method with a non-**void** return value. Return statements may not appear in a method with return type **void**. Return statements may appear anywhere in a control structure; they cause an immediate return from the method. The value of the expression following the return must match the return type of the method. All possible paths (for example, in a selection statement) through the method must contain a valid return value. For example,

```
public int calculateSum(int x, int y) {
        return x + y;
}
```

Compound statements

Compound statements are enclosed in **{ }** and cause sequential execution of the statements within the block. For example,

```
{ int x = 5;      // Assigns the value 5 to x.
  int y = 10;     // Assigns the value 10 to y.
  int z = x + y; // Assigns the value 15 (10 + 5) to z.
}
```

The `if` and `if-else` statements

Selection statements provide control over alternative paths based on the **boolean** value of an expression. In general,

- **if** Statement (One Consequent)

```
if (condition) // Only do statement if
               //   condition is true.
    statement_T;
```

For example,

```
if (x > 0.0)
      posProd = posProd * x;
```

- **if** Statement (Two Alternatives)

```
if (condition)      // If condition is true,
                    //   then do statement_T'
      statement_T;

else                //   otherwise do statement_F.
      statement_F;
```

Example:

```
if (x >= 0.0)
      System.out.println("Positive");

else
      System.out.println("Negative");
```

The `switch` *statement*

In a **switch** statement the *selector* expression is evaluated and compared to each `case label`. Each `case label` is a single, constant value, and each `case label` must be different from the others. If the value of the *selector* expression matches a *case label*, execution begins with the first statement following that `case label`. To prevent executing the statements associated with another `case label`, you must place a **break** statement before each new set of `case labels`. Control passes out of the **switch** statement when a **break** statement executes. If the value of the *selector* does not match any `case label`, no *statement* is executed unless a **default** `case label` is provided. If present, the **default** statements (*statement*$_d$) are executed. Each `case label` must be a unique value. The type of each `case label` must correspond to the type of the *selector* expression. Type **int** or **char** are permitted as the *selector* type. If a **break** statement is missing, execution "falls through" to the statements associated with the next set of `case labels`.

```
switch (selector) {
    case label₁:
        statements₁;
        break;
    case label₂:
        statements₂;
        break;
            ...
    case labelₙ:
        statementₙ;
        break;
    default:
        statementₔ;
} // End switch
```

For example,

```
switch (n) {
    case 1:
    case 2:
        message = "1, 2, Buckle my shoe";
        break;
    case 3:
    case 4:
        message = "3, 4, Shut the door";
        break;
    case 5:
    case 6:
        message = "5, 6, Pick up sticks";
        break;
    default:
        message = n + " is out of range";
} // End switch
```

The try-catch block sequence

The **if** and **switch** statements handle normal program flow. Occasionally, exceptions to normal flow occur. These may be handled with try-catch blocks as follows:

1. Create a **try** block containing *statements* that may cause an exception. A **try** block has the form

   ```
   try {
       // Statements that may cause an exception
       statements;
   }
   ```

2. Follow the **try** block by one or more **catch** blocks. Each **catch** block contains *statements* that handle a particular exception. A **catch** block has the form

   ```
   catch (exceptionType exceptionIdentifier) {
       // Statements that handle an exception
       statements;
   }
   ```

For example,

```java
public void delete() {
        String out = getString("Enter string to delete:");
        int posOut = text.indexOf(out);

        try {
                text = text.substring(0, posOut) +
                        text.substring(posOut +
                                        out.length());
        } catch (StringIndexOutOfBoundsException e) {
                System.out.println("String not found " +
                                " - no deletion performed");

        }
}
```

where the part in parentheses is like an argument list. The first item is the type of the exception being handled. The second item is a name that can be used to refer to the exception by the statements that handle it. Appendix C lists the standard exception types.

The *while* statement

The **while** statement is used to create repetition in the program flow. The *repetitionCondition* is tested; if it is **true**, the loop body is executed and the *repetitionCondition* is retested. When the *repetitionCondition* becomes **false**, the loop is exited, and the next program statement after the **while** statement is executed. If *repetitionCondition* evaluates to false the first time it is tested, the loop body is not executed. The **while** statement has the following form:

```java
while (repetitionCondition)
        loop body
```

For example,

```java
countStar = 0;
while (countStar < n) {
        displayResult("*");
        countStar = countStar + 1;
}
```

The do-while statement

The **do-while** statement is used for repetition when the loop body should be executed at least once. After each execution of the loop body, the *repetitionCondition* is evaluated. If the *repetitionCondition* is **true**, the loop body is repeated. If the *repetitionCondition* is **false**, loop exit occurs and the next program statement is executed. The **do-while** statement has the following form:

```
do {
      loop body
} while (repetitionCondition);
```

For example,

```
do {
      ch = getChar("Enter a digit");
} while (ch < '0' || ch > '9');
```

The for statement

The **for** loop header summarizes the loop-control operations. The *initialization statement* executes when the **for** statement begins execution. Prior to each loop repetition, including the first, the *repetitionCondition* is tested. If it is true, the loop body executes. If it is false, loop exit occurs. The *update statement* executes right after each repetition of the loop body. The **for** statement has the following form:

```
for (initialization statement; repetitionCondition; update statement)
      loop body
```

For example,

```
sum = 0;
for (int n = 0; n < 5; n++) {
      nextNum = getInt("Enter an integer:");
      sum += nextNum;
}
```

Scope of variables

The scope of a data field is determined by its visibility.

The scope of a method argument is the method.

The scope of a local variable is the block in which it is declared. A block is delimited by {}.

For example,

```
public int myMethod(int arg) { // arg may be accessed
                               // anywhere in the method.
    int x = 10;     // x can be accessed anywhere in
                    //  the method.
    if (x > 3) {
        int y = 3; // y can only be accessed within
                   //  this clause.
    }
    else {
        x = 15;     // y cannot be accessed here.
    }
    for (int w = 0; w < 10; w++)  { // The scope of w
                                    //  is the for loop.
        if (w > 5)
            x = x + 1;
    }
}
```

Array Declarations and Element Reference

Arrays provide a data structure in which elements of the same type may be stored.

Array element reference

The index of an array must be an integer expression. If the expression value is not in the allowable range of values, an **Out of bounds error** occurs during runtime. The form is

```
array[index]
```

For example,

```
x[3 * i - 2]
```

Multidimensional arrays are referenced with the following form:

```
array[index₁][index₂].....
```

For example,

```
matrix[5][3] // This refers to position 5, 3 in the matrix.
```

Array declaration

An array declaration may take one of three forms:

elementType [ ] *arrayName* ;

elementType [ ] *arrayName* = **new** *elementType* [*size*] ;

elementType [ ] *arrayName* = {*list-of-values*} ;

The identifier *arrayName* represents a collection of array elements; each element can store an item of type *elementType*. In the first example, the identifier is declared, but no space is allocated for the array. In the second example, enough space for an array of *size* elements is allocated, but the elements themselves are not specified. In the third form, the array size is not explicitly specified, but is implied by the size of the *list-of-values* enclosed in braces. These values are stored sequentially (one after the other) in the array elements and their data type must be *elementType*. The *elementType* can be any primitive type or class. If the element type is a class, the array elements contain references to objects, each of which must be separately instantiated. For example,

```
public class ArrayExample {
    int totals[]; // Totals will be an array,
                  //  with no size specified.

   // salary will contain 50 double values,
   //  the array contents is undefined.
    double[] salary = new double[50];

   // coinValues contains 5 integers,
   //  the values shown are stored in order.
    int[] coinValues = {1, 5, 10, 25, 50};

    Person[] employees; // employees will be an array
                        //  of class Person.

   // managers will contain two people, "Fred" and "Ethel"
    Person[] managers = { new Person("Fred"),
                          new Person("Ethel")
                        }
```

```
public void loadPeople(int number) {
    // Allocate enough space for the number
    //   of people specified.
    Person[] people = new Person[number];
    // Load each array element with an
    //   unnamed Person object.
    for (int i = 0; i < people.length; i++) {
        people[i] = new Person();
    }
}
}
```

Multidimensional arrays are declared by adding [ ] for each dimension. Note that Java supports arrays of arrays rather than true multidimensional arrays.

Package Declarations

A package is a collection of classes that reside in the same folder. The source file for each class must contain the following statement at the top of the file:

```
package packageName;
```

Other classes may import the classes in the package by including the following statement at the top of the source file. The * indicates that all classes may be referenced.

```
import packageName.*;
```

Any classes defined in source files that do not include the **package** reserved word are considered part of the default package. All such default classes that reside in the same folder (directory) are considered to be part of the same package and may access each other's protected and default visibility data fields and methods.

Reserved Words

The following reserved words may not be used as identifiers. Words in italics have no meaning in current versions of Java but are reserved for future use.

abstract	else	int	static
boolean	extends	interface	super
break	false	long	switch
byte	final	native	synchronized
byvalue	finally	new	this
case	float	null	throw
cast	for	*operator*	throws
catch	*future*	*outer*	transient
char	*generic*	package	true
class	*goto*	private	try
const	if	protected	*var*
continue	implements	public	void
default	import	*rest*	volatile
do	*inner*	return	while
double	instanceof	short	

Operator Precedence

The following table summarizes operators used in this text in order of precedence.

Operator	Description
method call	
type cast	
!, + (unary), − (unary)	Logical not, unary plus, unary minus
*, /, %	Multiplication, division, modulus
+, −, +	Addition, subtraction, string concatenation
<, <=, >=, >	Relational inequality
==, !=	Equal, not equal
&&	Logical and
||	Logical or
+, +=, −=, etc.	Assignment, addition then assignment, subtraction then assignment, and so on.

The Unicode Character Set

Java uses the Unicode character set for representing characters and strings. Unicode supports characters in many languages. A Unicode character is encoded as a 16-bit unsigned numeric value. This means there are 2^{16} possible characters, or approximately 65,000 of them. A subset of Unicode is ASCII, the American Standard Code for Information Interchange. ASCII is based on an 8-bit representation. Table B-1 lists the first 128 Unicode characters with their corresponding numeric values. These are also ASCII characters. Only printable characters are listed (some standard nonprintable ones such as carriage return are also included). These nonprintable characters appear in italics.

Primitive Types

The eight primitive types are listed here with their corresponding sizes.

	Type	Bits Used	Minimum Value	Maximum Value
Integers	byte	8	−128	127
	short	16	−32,768	32,767
	int	32	−2,147,483,648	2,147,483,647
	long	64	−9,223,372,036,854,755,808	−9,223,372,036,854,755,807
Real numbers	float	32	Approximately -3.4^{38} with 7 significant digits	Approximately 3.4^{38} with 7 significant digits
	double	64	Approximately -1.7^{308} with 15 significant digits	Approximately 1.7^{308} with 15 significant digits
Text characters	char	16		65,534 unique characters
Boolean	boolean			true or false

Table B-1   ASCII code

0	*null*	32		64	@	96	`
1		33	!	65	A	97	a
2	l	34	"	66	B	98	b
3		35	#	67	C	99	c
4		36	$	68	D	100	d
5		37	%	69	E	101	e
6		38	&	70	F	102	f
7	*bell*	39	'	71	G	103	g
8	*backspace*	40	(	72	H	104	h
9	*tab*	41	)	73	I	105	i
10	*line feed*	42	*	74	J	106	j
11		43	+	75	K	107	k
12	*form feed*	44		76	L	108	l
13	*carriage returrn*	45	−	77	M	109	m
14		46	.	78	N	110	n
15		47	/	79	O	111	o
16		48	0	80	P	112	p
17		49	1	81	Q	113	q
18		50	2	82	R	114	r
19		51	3	83	S	115	s
20		52	4	84	T	116	t
21		53	5	85	U	117	u
22		54	6	86	V	118	v
23		55	7	87	W	119	w
24		56	8	88	X	120	x
25		57	9	89	Y	121	y
26		58	:	90	Z	122	z
27	*escape*	59	;	91	[	123	{
28		60	<	92	\	124		
29		61	=	93	]	125	}
30		62	>	94	^	126	~
31		63	?	95	_	127	*delete*

Packages `java.lang` and `java.util`

Class Wrappers for the Primitive Types
- `Boolean` Class
- `Double` Class
- `Integer` Class
- `Math` Class
- `Object` Class
- `Runnable` Interface
- `String` Class
- `System` Class
- `Vector` Class (from `java.util`)

Class Wrappers for the Primitive Types

The following classes correspond to the primitive types. These classes are useful when a data type must be an object, for example, to be stored in a vector. Methods associated with these classes can be used to convert between primitive types.

Not all data fields and methods associated with each class are listed here. For complete definitions, see your online documentation or one of the resources listed in Appendix A. We describe only the wrapper classes for the objects and primitive numeric types discussed in this book (`int` and `double`).

◆◆Boolean Class

```
public final class Boolean extends Object implements Serializable
```

The **Boolean** class wraps a value of the primitive type **boolean** in an object.

Data fields

```
public static final Boolean TRUE
```

Corresponds to the primitive value **true**.

```
public static final Boolean FALSE
```

Corresponds to the primitive value **false**.

Constructors

```
public Boolean(boolean value)
public Boolean(String s)
```

Creates a **Boolean** object representing the value **true** if the string argument is not **null** and is equal (ignoring case) to the string **"true"**; otherwise, a **false** value is represented.

Methods

```
public boolean booleanValue()
```

Returns the value of this Boolean object as a **boolean**.

```
public boolean equals(Object obj)
```

Returns **true** if and only if the argument is not null and is a **Boolean** object that contains the same boolean value as this object.

```
public String toString()
```

Returns either the string **"true"** or **"false"** depending on the **Boolean** value of this object.

```
public static Boolean valueOf(String s)
```

Returns the **boolean** value represented by the specified string using the same rules as the constructor with a string argument.

◆◆Double Class

```
public final class Double extends Number
```

The **double** class wraps a value of the primitive type **double** in an object.

Data fields
```
public static final double POSITIVE_INFINITY
```

Positive infinity of type **double**.

```
public static final double NEGATIVE_INFINITY
```

Negative infinity of type **double**.

```
public static final double NaN
```

Represents "not a number."

```
public static final double MAX_VALUE
```

Largest positive value of type **double**.

```
public static final double MIN_VALUE
```

Smallest positive value of type **double**.

Constructors
```
public Double(double value)
```

Constructs a newly allocated **Double** object from a primitive double.

```
public Double(String s) throws NumberFormatException
```

Constructs a newly **Double** object represented by the string.

Methods
```
public byte byteValue()
```

Returns the value of this **Double** as a byte (by casting to a **byte**).

`public double doubleValue()`

Returns the **double** value of this **Double**.

`public boolean equals(Object` *obj*`)`

Compares this object against the specified object.

`public float floatValue()`

Returns the **float** value of this **Double**.

`public int intValue()`

Returns the value of this **Double** as an **int** (by casting to an **int**).

`public boolean isInfinite()`

Returns **true** if this **Double** is infinitely large.

`public static boolean isInfinite(double` *v*`)`

Returns **true** if the number is one of the infinite values.

`public boolean isNaN()`

Returns **true** if this **Double** is the **NaN** value.

`public static boolean isNaN(double` *v*`)`

Returns **true** if the specified number is **NaN**.

`public long longValue()`

Returns the long value of this **Double** (by casting to a **long**).

`public short shortValue()`

Returns the value of this **Double** as a **short** (by casting to a **short**).

`public String toString()`

Returns a string representation of this **Double** object.

```
public static String toString(double d)
```

Creates a string representation of the double argument.

```
public static Double valueOf(String s) throws
NumberFormatException
```

Returns a new **Double** value based on the string.

◆◆Integer Class

```
public final class Integer extends Number
```

The **Integer** class wraps a value of primitive type **int** in an object.

Data fields

```
public static final int MIN_VALUE
```

Smallest value of type **int**.

```
public static final int MAX_VALUE
```

Largest value of type **int**.

Constructors

```
public Integer(int value)
```

Constructs an **Integer** object that represents the primitive **int** argument.

```
public Integer(String s) throws NumberFormatException
```

Constructs an **Integer** object for the value represented by the string.

Methods

```
public byte byteValue()
```

Returns the value of this **Integer** as a **byte**.

```
public double doubleValue()
```

Returns the value of this `Integer` as a **double**.

`public boolean equals(Object obj)`

Compares this object to the specified object.

`public float floatValue()`

Returns the value of this `Integer` as a `float`.

`public int intValue()`

Returns the value of this `Integer` as an `int`.

`public long longValue()`

Returns the value of this `Integer` as a `long`.

`public static int parseInt(String s)`
`throws NumberFormatException`

Parses the string argument as a signed decimal integer.

`public static int parseInt(String s, int radix)`
`throws NumberFormatException`

Parses the string argument as a signed integer in the radix (base) specified by the second argument.

`public short shortValue()`

Returns the value of this `Integer` as a `short`.

`public static String toBinaryString(int i)`

Creates a string representation of the integer as an unsigned integer in base 2.

`public static String toHexString(int i)`

Creates a string representation of the integer as an unsigned integer in base 16.

`public static String toOctalString(int i)`

Creates a string representation of the integer as an unsigned integer in base 8.

```
public String toString()
```

Returns a string object representing this **Integer**'s value.

```
public static String toString(int i)
```

Creates a string representation of the integer.

```
public static String toString(int i, int radix)
```

Creates a string representation of the first argument in the radix (base) specified by the second argument.

```
public static Integer valueOf(String s)
                  throws NumberFormatException
```

Returns an **Integer** object initialized to the value of the string; assumes base 10.

◆◆Math Class

```
public final class Math extends Object
```

The **Math** class provides **static** methods and constraints used in numerical computations and cannot be instantiated.

Datafields
```
public static final double E
```

The base of all natural algorithms; it is represented as 2.7182818284590452354.

```
public static final double PI
```

The ratio of the circumference of a circle to its diameter; it is represented as 3.14159265358979323846.

Constructors
None. The class **Math** may not be instantiated.

Methods
```
public static double abs(double d)
public static float abs(float f)
```

```
public static int abs(int i)
public static long abs(long l)
```

Returns the absolute value of the argument.

```
public static native double acos(double d)
```

Returns the arc cosine of an angle, in the range of 0.0 through pi.

```
public static native double asin(double d)
```

Returns the arc sine of an angle, in the range of –pi/2 through pi/2.

```
public static native double atan(double d)
```

Returns the arc tangent of an angle, in the range of –pi/2 through pi/2.

```
public static native double atan2(double y, double x)
```

Converts rectangular coordinates (y, x) to polar (r, θ), returning θ, r. Can be calculated from the square root of the sum of the squares of x and y.

```
public static native double ceil(double d)
```

Returns the smallest whole number greater than or equal to d.

```
public static native double cos(double d)
```

Returns the trigonometric cosine of d.

```
public static native double exp(double d)
```

Returns e^d.

```
public static native double floor(double d)
```

Returns the largest whole number less than or equal to x.

```
public static native double IEEEremainder(double x, double y)
```

Computes the remainder of dividing x by y as defined by the IEEE 754 standard.

```
public static native double log(double x)
```

Returns $\log_e x$.

```
public static double max(double x, double y)
public static float  max(float x, float y )
public static int    max(int x, int y)
public static long   max(long x, long y)
```

Returns the greater of the two values.

```
public static double min(double x, double y)
public static float  min(float x, float y )
public static int    min(int x, int y)
public static long   min(long x, long y)
```

Returns the lesser of the two values.

```
public static native double pow(double x, double y)
```

Returns x^y. If $x = 0$, y must be greater than 0. If $x <= 0$, y must be a whole number.

```
public static syncronized random()
```

Returns a random number between 0.0 and 1.0.

```
public static native double rint(double d)
```

Returns a **double** that is the closest integer to d.

```
public static long round(double d)
```

Returns a **long** that is the closest **long** to d.

```
public static int round(float d)
```

Returns an **int** that is the closest **int** to d.

```
public static native double sin(double d)
```

Returns the trigonometric sine of angle d measured in radians.

```
public static native double sqrt(double d)
```

Returns the square root of d.

```
public static native tan(double d)
```

Returns the trigonometric tangent of angle *d* measured in radians.

◆◆Object Class

```
public class Object
```

Class **Object** is the root of the class hierarchy. Every class has **Object** as a super-class. All objects, including arrays, implement the methods of this class.

Constructors

```
public Object()
```

Methods

```
public final native Class getClass()
```

Returns the run-time class of an object.

```
public boolean equals(Object obj)
```

Compares two **Objects** for equality.

```
public String toString()
```

Returns a **String** representation of the object.

◆◆Runnable Interface

```
public interface Runnable
```

This interface is used to implement a thread when a class already extends an-other class. See Chapter 8.

◆◆String Class

`public final class String extends Object implements Serializable`

The `String` class represents character strings. All string literals in Java programs, such as `"abc"`, are implemented as instances of this class.

Constructors

`public String()`

Allocates a new `String` containing no characters.

`public String(String s)`

Allocates a new `String` that contains the same sequence of characters as `s`.

`public String(char a[])`

Allocates a new `String` that represents the sequence of characters in the array `a`.

`public String(char a[], int offset, int count)`

Allocates a new `String` that contains `count` characters from `a`, beginning at position `offset`.

`public String(StringBuffer buffer)`

Converts a `StringBuffer` to a `String`.

Methods

`public char charAt(int index)`

Returns the character at the specified index.

```
public int compareTo(String anotherString)
```

Compares two strings lexicographically.

```
public String concat(String str)
```

Concatenates **String str** to the end of this string.

```
public static String copyValueOf(char data[])
public static String copyValueOf
                    (char data[], int offset,int count)
```

Returns a **String** that is equivalent to **data**, beginning at **offset** for **count** characters. If **offset** and **count** are not specified, the entire array is used.

```
public void getChars(int sourceOffset, int sourceEnd,
                     char destination[], int dstOffset)
```

Copies characters from **sourceOffset** to **sourceEnd** into the character array **destination**, beginning at position **dstOffset**.

```
public boolean endsWith(String suffix)
```

Tests to see if this **String** ends with the suffix.

```
public boolean equals(Object anObject)
```

Compares this **String** to the specified object.

```
public boolean equalsIgnoreCase(String anotherString)
```

Compares this **String** to another, ignoring case.

```
public int indexOf(int ch)
public int indexOf(int ch, int offset)
public int indexOf(String str)
public int indexOf(String str, int offset)
```

Returns the index of the first occurrence of the character or string within this **String**. If **offset** is not specified, search begins at position 0 and returns −1 if not found.

```
public int lastIndexOf(int ch)
public int lastIndexOf(int ch, int offset)
public int lastIndexOf(String str, int offset)
public int lastIndexOf(String str)
```

Returns the index of the last occurrence of the character or string within this **String**. If **offset** is specified, search begins from there proceeding to the front of the string and returns −1 if not found.

```
public int length()
```

Returns the length of this string.

```
public boolean regionMatches(int offset1, String str2,
                             int offset2, int length)
public boolean regionMatches(boolean ignoreCase,
                             int offset1, String str2,
                             int offset2, int length)
```

Compares two string regions of length, beginning with **offset1** of this string and **offset2** of **str2**. If **ignoreCase == false**, case matters.

```
public String replace(char oldChar, char newChar)
```

Returns a new **String** in which all occurrences of **oldChar** are replaced by **newChar**.

```
public String trim()
```

Removes white space from both ends of this String.

```
public String toLowerCase()
```

Converts this **String** to lowercase.

```
public String toUpperCase()
```

Converts this **String** to uppercase.

```
public char[] toCharArray()
```

Converts this **String** to a new character array.

```
public String toString()
```

Returns this object.

```
public boolean startsWith(String prefix)
public boolean startsWith(String prefix, int offset)
```

Tests to see if this **String** starts with the specified prefix. If **offset** is not specified, start at position 0.

```
public String substring(int offset)
public String substring(int offset, int endIndex)
```

Returns a new **String** that is a substring of this string, beginning at **offset** and ending at the length of the string if **endIndex** is not specified.

```
public static String valueOf(boolean b)
public static String valueOf(char c)
public static String valueOf(int i)
public static String valueOf(long l)
public static String valueOf(float f)
public static String valueOf(double d)
```

Returns the **String** representation of the argument.

```
public static String valueOf(Object obj)
```

Returns the **String** representation of the object (returns the **toString()** value).

```
public static String valueOf(char data[])
```

Returns the **String** representation of the **char** array.

```
public static String valueOf(char data[],int offset,
                             int count)
```

Returns the **String** representation of the subarray **data**, beginning at **offset** for a length of **count**.

◆◆System Class

```
public final class System extends Object
```

The **System** class contains some general methods and datafields.

Datafields

```
public static final InputStream in
```

The "standard" input stream.

```
public static final PrintStream out
```

The "standard" output stream.

```
public static final PrintStream err
```

The "standard" error output stream.

Constructors

None. The class **System** may not be instantiated.

Methods

```
public static native void arraycopy (Object source,
                            int sourceStart,
                            Object dest, int destStart,
                            int length)
```

Copies array **source** beginning at position **sourceStart** to array **dest** beginning at position **destStart**, copying **length** array elements.

```
public static native long currentTimeMillis()
```

Returns the current time in milliseconds.

```
public static void exit(int status)
```

Terminates the currently running Java Virtual Machine; a zero argument indicates normal termination.

```
public static void gc()
```

Runs the garbage collector.

```
public static void setErr(PrintStream err)
```

Resets the "standard" error output stream.

```
public static void setIn(InputStream in)
```

Resets the "standard" input stream.

```
public static void setOut(PrintStream out)
```

Resets the "standard" output stream.

◆◆Vector Class (from `java.util`) ─────────────

```
public class Vector extends Object implements Cloneable,
Serializable
```

The size of a vector is the number of elements it currently holds. The capacity of a vector is the number of elements it may hold before the capacity must be increased.

Constructors

```
public Vector()
public Vector(int initialCapacity)
public Vector(int initialCapacity,
              int capacityIncrement)
```

Constructs an empty vector; default capacity is 10. If `initialCapacity` is not specified, the capacity is doubled whenever the capacity is reached; otherwise, the capacity is incremented by `capacityIncrement`.

Methods

```
public final synchronized void addElement(Object obj)
```

Adds `obj` to the end of this vector.

```
public final int capacity()
```

Returns the current capacity of this vector.

```
public final synchronized void copyInto(Object anArray[])
```

Copies the elements of this vector into the specified array.

```
public final boolean contains(Object elem)
```

Tests if the specified object is an element in this vector.

```
public final synchronized Object elementAt(int index)
```

Returns the element at the specified index.

```
public final synchronized void ensureCapacity(int minCapacity)
```

Increases the capacity of this vector, if necessary, to ensure that it can hold at least the number of elements specified by `minCapacity`.

```
public final synchronized Object firstElement()
```

Returns the first element in this vector.

```
public final int indexOf(Object elem)
public final synchronized int indexOf(Object elem, int offset)
```

Returns the index of the first occurrence of `elem` in the vector, and returns −1 if it is not found. Begins at the offset (if specified).

```
public final synchronized void insertElementAt (Object obj,
                                                int index)
```

Inserts `obj` at position `index` in this vector, shifting to the right all elements whose index is greater than or equal to `index`.

```
public final boolean isEmpty()
```

Tests to see if this vector has no elements.

```
public final synchronized Object lastElement()
```

Returns the last element in this vector.

```
public final int lastIndexOf(Object elem)
public final synchronized int lastIndexOf(Object elem,
                                          int offset)
```

Returns the index of the last occurrence of **elem** in the vector and returns −1 if it is not found. Begins at the **offset** (if specified), searching forward in the vector.

```
public final synchronized void removeAllElements()
```

Removes all elements from this vector and sets its size to zero.

```
public final synchronized boolean removeElement (Object obj)
```

Removes the first occurrence of **obj**, shifting to the left all elements to the left of **obj**.

```
public final synchronized void removeElementAt (int index)
```

Deletes the element at the specified index, shifting left all elements to the right of the removed element.

```
public final synchronized void setElementAt(Object obj,
                                            int index)
```

Places the object at position **index** in this vector, discarding the element previously in that position.

```
public final synchronized void setSize(int newSize)
```

Sets the size of this vector, adding null items or discarding elements in positions beyond **newSize** as necessary.

```
public final int size()
```

Returns the number of elements in this vector.

```
public final synchronized String toString()
```

Returns a string representation of this vector.

```
public final synchronized void trimToSize()
```

Trims the capacity of this vector to be the vector's current size.

D

Package `java.io`

Overview of the `java.io` Package

Data transfer in Java is handled through **streams**. Input streams bring data into a process, and output streams send data out. The data may be bytes or characters. The classes `InputStream`, `OutputStream`, and their subclasses provide rich functionality for handling bytes of data. See the resources in Appendix A for more detail. The **Reader** class provides basic methods for reading characters. The **Writer** class provides basic methods for writing characters. Selected subclasses of **Reader** and **Writer** are presented here. Note that only the classes and methods that might be relevant to a first-semester course are included. Others may be found in the resource materials listed in Appendix A.

The Reader Class and Selected Subclasses

◆◆Reader Class

```
public abstract class Reader extends Object
```

This **Abstract** class is used for reading character streams. Subclasses must implement **read(char[ ]**, **int**, **int)**, and **close( )**.

Methods
```
public abstract void close() throws IOException
```

Closes the stream.

```
public void mark(int readAheadLimit) throws IOException
```

Marks the present position in the stream. Later calls to **reset( )** will attempt to reposition the stream at this point.

```
public boolean markSupported()
```

Tells whether this stream supports the **mark( )** operation.

```
public int read() throws IOException
```

Reads a single character.

```
public int read(char cbuf[]) throws IOException
public abstract int read(char cbuf[], int offset,
                         int length) throws IOException
```

Reads characters into an array, starting at **offset** and reading **length** characters, if specified.

```
public boolean ready() throws IOException
```

Tells whether this stream is ready to be read.

```
public void reset() throws IOException
```

Resets the stream to either the mark or the starting point. Position is dependent upon the type of character input stream.

```
public long skip(long n) throws IOException
```

Skips **n** characters.

◆◆BufferedReader Class ——————————————————

```
public class BufferedReader extends Reader
```

Reads text from a character-input stream, buffering characters for the efficient reading of characters, arrays, and lines.

Constructors

```
public BufferedReader(Reader in)
public BufferedReader(Reader in, int size)
```

Creates a buffered reader for in. If size is not specified, then size is 8K characters.

Methods (that do not override Reader methods)

```
public String readLine() throws IOException
```

Reads a line of text (a line terminates by line feed (`'\n'`), a carriage return (`'\r'`), or a carriage return followed immediately by a linefeed).

◆◆CharArrayReader Class ——————————————————

```
public class CharArrayReader extends Reader
```

Creates a character buffer so that you can read from an array of characters as if it were a buffered input stream.

Constructors

```
public CharArrayReader(char buf[])
public CharArrayReader(char buf[], int offset, int length)
```

Creates a **CharArrayReader** from the specified array of chars, starting at **off-set** and continuing for **length**, if specified.

Methods

All methods override **Reader** methods.

◆◆FileReader Class ───────────────────────

```
public class FileReader extends InputStreamReader
```

Used for reading character files.

Constructors

```
public FileReader(String fileName) throws FileNotFoundException
public FileReader(File file) throws FileNotFoundException
public FileReader(FileDescriptor fd)
```

Opens the file specified by the (1) system-dependent filename, (2) the file object, or (3) the file descriptor. See resources in Appendix A for a discussion of file objects and descriptors.

Methods

No methods are defined.

◆◆InputStreamReader Class ───────────────────

```
public class InputStreamReader extends Reader
```

Allows conversion from a byte stream to a character stream. The character encoding scheme may be specified.

```
public InputStreamReader(InputStream in)
public InputStreamReader(InputStream in, String enc)
                    throws UnsupportedEncodingException
```

Creates an **InputStreamReader** that uses the character encoding scheme specified. If none is specified, it uses the default.

Methods:

```
public String getEncoding()
```

Returns the name of the encoding being used by this stream.

◆◆LineNumberReader Class

```
public class LineNumberReader extends BufferedReader
```

A buffered character-input stream keeps track of line numbers (terminated by a line feed (`'\n'`), a carriage return (`'\r'`), or a carriage return followed immediately by a linefeed).

Constructors

```
public LineNumberReader(Reader in)
public LineNumberReader(Reader in,int size)
```

Creates a new line-numbering reader, using the default input-buffer size, or size specified.

Methods (that do not override BufferedReader or Reader)

```
public void setLineNumber(int lineNumber)
```

Sets the current line number.

```
public int getLineNumber()
```

Returns the current line number.

◆◆StringReader Class

```
public class StringReader extends Reader
```

Converts a string to a character input stream.

Constructors

`public StringReader(String s)`

Creates a new string reader.

Methods

There are none that do not override **Reader** methods.

The `Writer` Class and Selected Subclasses

◆◆Writer Class ————————————————————————

`public abstract class Writer extends Object`

An abstract class for writing to character streams. Subclasses must implement `write(char[], int, int)`, `flush()`, and `close()`.

Methods

`public void write(int c) throws IOException`

Writes a single character based on the 16 low-order bits of the integer **c**.

```
public void write(char cbuf[]) throws IOException
public abstract void write(char cbuf[], int offset,
                           int length) throws IOException
```

Writes an array of characters, starting at **offset** for **length** specified; writes the entire array otherwise.

```
public void write(String str) throws IOException
public void write(String str, int off,int len) throws IOException
```

Writes a string, from **offset** for **length**, if specified; writes the entire string otherwise.

`public abstract void flush() throws IOException`

Flushs the stream, that is, empties it of characters.

```
public abstract void close() throws IOException
```

Closes the stream, flushing it first.

◆◆BufferedWriter Class

```
public class BufferedWriter extends Writer
```

Writes text to a character-output stream, buffering characters.

Constructors

```
public BufferedWriter(Writer out)
public BufferedWriter(Writer out, int size)
```

Creates a new buffered character-output stream. If **size** is not specified, buffer is 8K characters.

Methods (that do not override Writer methods)

```
public void newLine() throws IOException
```

Writes a line separator defined by the system property **line.separator**.

◆◆CharArrayWriter Class

```
public class CharArrayWriter extends Writer
```

Implements a character buffer that can be used as a **Writer**. The data can be retrieved using **toCharArray()** and **toString()**.

Constructors

```
public CharArrayWriter()
public CharArrayWriter(int initialSize)
```

Creates a new **CharArrayWriter**. If size is not specified, default buffer is 32 characters.

Methods (that do not override `Writer` methods)

```
public void writeTo(Writer out) throws IOException
```

Writes the contents of the buffer to another character stream.

```
public void reset()
```

Resets the buffer so that it can be used again.

```
public char[] toCharArray()
```

Returns a copy of the input data.

```
public int size()
```

Returns the current size of the buffer.

```
public String toString()
```

Converts data in array buffer to a string.

◆◆**FileWriter Class**

```
public class FileWriter extends OutputStreamWriter
```

Used for writing characters to a file.

Constructors

```
public FileWriter(String fileName) throws IOException
public FileWriter(String fileName, boolean append)
                                    throws IOException
public FileWriter(File file) throws IOException
public FileWriter(FileDescriptor fd)
```

Opens the file specified by the (1) system-dependent filename, (2) the file object, or (3) the file descriptor. See the resources in Appendix A for a discussion of file objects and descriptors. If **append** is true, append to rather than overwrite the file.

Methods

No methods defined.

◆◆PrintWriter Class ────────────────────

```
public class PrintWriter extends Writer
```

Prints formatted representations of objects to a text-output stream.

Constructors
```
public PrintWriter(Writer out)
public PrintWriter(Writer out, boolean autoFlush)
public PrintWriter(OutputStream out)
public PrintWriter(OutputStream out, boolean autoFlush)
```

Creates an output stream. Automatic flushing occurs after **println** if autoFlush is **true**.

Methods (that do not override Writer)

```
public boolean checkError()
```

Flushes the stream and checks its error state.

```
protected void setError()
```

Indicates that an error has occurred.

```
public void print(boolean b)
public void print(char c)
public void print(int i)
public void print(long l)
public void print(float f)
public void print(double d)
public void print(char s[])
public void print(String s)
public void print(Object obj)
```

Prints the specified object using its **toString** method.

```
public void println()
public void println(boolean x)
public void println(char x)
public void println(int x)
public void println(long x)
public void println(float x)
public void println(double x)
public void println(char x[])
public void println(String x)
public void println(Object x)
```

Prints the specified object, and then finishes the line.

E

Package `java.awt`

Applet Class
AppletContext Interface
Component Class
Container Class
Panel Class
Graphics Classes
    Color Class
    Dimension Class
    Graphics Class
    Point Class
    Polygon Class
Layout Manager Classes
    BorderLayout Class
    BoxLayout (see Appendix F)
    FlowLayout Class
    GridLayout Class
Events and Listeners
    ActionEvent Class
    ActionListener Interface
    ItemEvent Class
    ItemListener Interface
    WindowEvent Class
    WindowListener Interface

This appendix contains brief summaries of classes from the Java Class Libraries that support graphical user interface programming including applets. Only methods and data fields relevant to novice programming are included. See the online and text support materials listed in Appendix A for more complete coverage.

◆◆Applet Class

```
public class Applet extends Panel
```

An applet is a small program that is embedded in an applet context (another application such as a Web browser or applet viewer).

Constructors

```
public Applet()
```

Creates an instance of an applet.

Methods

```
public void destroy()
```

Called by the applet context to inform this applet that it is being reclaimed and that it should destroy any resources (such as threads) that it has allocated.

```
public AppletContext getAppletContext()
```

Gets the applet context for this applet (the browser or applet viewer in which it is embedded).

```
public String getAppletInfo()
```

Returns information about this applet. It should be overridden by subclasses to include information about the author, version, and copyright of the applet.

```
public AudioClip getAudioClip(URL url)
public AudioClip getAudioClip(URL url,String name)
```

Returns the **AudioClip** object specified by the URL argument. This method returns immediately even if the URL is not completely loaded. See resources in Appendix A for more information on how to use audio clips.

```
public URL getCodeBase()
```

Gets the base URL of the applet itself.

```
public URL getDocumentBase()
```

Gets the document URL in which the applet is embedded.

```
public Image getImage(URL url)
public Image getImage(URL url, String name)
```

Returns an **Image** object that can then be painted on the screen. This method returns immediately even if the URL is not completely loaded. See resources in Appendix A for more information on how to use images.

```
public String getParameter(String name)
```

Returns the value of the named parameter in the HTML tag.

```
public String[][] getParameterInfo()
```

Returns an array of strings corresponding to information about the applet's parameters. It should be overridden by subclasses that are understood by this applet. The form is { { *"parameterName1"* ,*"description1"*}, { *"parameterName2"*, *"description2"*} ...}.

```
public void init()
```

Called by the browser or applet viewer to inform this applet that it has been loaded into the system. It should be overridden by **Applet** subclasses to perform initializations.

```
public boolean isActive()
```

Determines if this applet is active; an applet is active just before **start()** is called and is inactive immediately after **stop()** is called.

```
public void play(URL url)
public void play(URL url, String name)
```

Plays the audio clip at the specified absolute URL.

```
public void resize(Dimension d)
public void resize(int width, int height)
```

Requests that the applet context resize this applet.

```
public void showStatus(String msg)
```

msg should be displayed in the "status window" of the applet context.

```
public void start()
```

Called by applet context to inform this applet that it should start its execution. It is called after the **init** method and each time the applet is revisited in a Web page.

```
public void stop()
```

Called by the applet context to inform this applet that it should stop its execution.

◆◆AppletContext Interface ──────────────

```
public interface AppletContext
```

Corresponds to the document (the HTML) that contains the applet.

Methods

```
public abstract Applet getApplet(String name)
```

Finds and returns the named applet if it exists in the applet context document. Note that an HTML page may contain more than one applet.

```
public abstract AudioClip getAudioClip(URL url)
```

Creates an audio clip.

```
public abstract Image getImage(URL url)
```

Returns an **Image** object that can then be painted on the screen.

```
public abstract void showDocument(URL url)
```

Replaces the Web page currently being viewed with the given URL.

```
public abstract void showStatus(String status)
```

Requests that the status string be displayed in the "status window."

◆◆Component Class

```
public abstract class Component extends Object
        implements ImageObserver, MenuContainer, Serializable
```

A component is an object that has a graphical representation and can interact with a user. The **Component** class is the abstract superclass of the non-menu-related Abstract Window Toolkit components.

Data fields

```
public static final float TOP_ALIGNMENT
public static final float CENTER_ALIGNMENT
public static final float BOTTOM_ALIGNMENT
public static final float LEFT_ALIGNMENT
public static final float RIGHT_ALIGNMENT
```

Specifies an alignment of the component.

Methods

```
public synchronized void add(PopupMenu popup)
```

Adds the specified popup menu to the component.

```
public synchronized void
            addComponentListener(ComponentListener l)
```

Adds the specified component listener to receive component events from this component.

```
public synchronized void addFocusListener(FocusListener l)
```

Adds the specified focus listener to receive focus events from this component.

```
public synchronized void addKeyListener(KeyListener l)
```

Adds the specified key listener to receive key events from this component.

```
public synchronized void addMouseListener(MouseListener l)
```

Adds the specified mouse listener to receive mouse events from this component.

```
public synchronized void
            addMouseMotionListener(MouseMotionListener l)
```

Adds the specified mouse motion listener to receive mouse motion events from this component.

```
public boolean contains(int x, int y)
public boolean contains(Point p)
```

Checks whether this component "contains" the specified point, where *x* and *y* are defined to be relative to the coordinate system of this component.

```
public void doLayout()
```

Prompts the layout manager to lay out this component. Usually called when the component (more specifically, container) is validated.

```
public Color getBackground()
```

Gets the background color of this component.

```
public Rectangle getBounds()
```

Gets the bounds of this component. A **Rectangle** object has fields width, height, *x*, and *y*.

```
public Component getComponentAt(Point p)
public Component getComponentAt(int x, int y)
```

Determines if this component or one of its immediate subcomponents contains the (*x*, *y*) location, and if so, returns the containing component.

```
public Font getFont()
```

Gets the font of this component.

```
public FontMetrics getFontMetrics(Font font)
```

Gets the font metrics for the specified font.

```
public Color getForeground()
```

Gets the foreground color of this component.

```
public Graphics getGraphics()
```

Creates a graphics context for this component.

```
public Point getLocation()
```

Gets the location (top-left corner) of this component relative to the parent's coordinate space.

`public Point getLocationOnScreen()`

Gets the location (top-left corner) of this component relative to the screen's coordinate space.

`public Dimension getMaximumSize()`

Gets the maximum size of this component. A **Dimension** object *x* has public width and height fields (e.g., **x.width, x.height**).

`public Dimension getMinimumSize()`

Gets the minimum size of this component. A **Dimension** object *x* has public width and height fields (e.g., **x.width, x.height**).

`public String getName()`

Gets the name of the component.

`public Container getParent()`

Gets the parent of this component, the container in which this component resides.

`public Dimension getPreferredSize()`

Gets the preferred size of this component. A **Dimension** object *x* has public width and height fields (e.g., **x.width, x.height**).

`public Dimension getSize()`

Returns the size of this component. A **Dimension** object *x* has public width and height fields (e.g., **x.width, x.height**).

`public void invalidate()`

Invalidates this component so that its parent will lay it out again.

`public boolean isEnabled()`

Determines whether this component is enabled. Can respond to user input and generate events.

```
public boolean isShowing()
```

Determines whether this component is showing on screen.

```
public boolean isValid()
```

Determines whether this component is valid. Components are invalidated when they are first shown on the screen.

```
public boolean isVisible()
```

Determines whether this component is visible.

```
public void paint(Graphics g)
```

Paints this component and defines the "picture" that you see.

```
public void paintAll(Graphics g)
```

Paints this component and all of its subcomponents.

```
protected String paramString()
```

Returns the parameter string representing the state of this component. Useful for debugging.

```
public synchronized void remove(MenuComponent popup)
```

Removes the specified popup menu from the component.

```
public synchronized void
        removeComponentListener(ComponentListener l)
```

Removes the specified component listener so that it no longer receives component events from this component.

```
public synchronized void removeFocusListener(FocusListener l)
```

Removes the specified focus listener so that it no longer receives focus events from this component.

`public synchronized void removeKeyListener(KeyListener l)`

Removes the specified key listener so that it no longer receives key events from this component.

`public synchronized void removeMouseListener(MouseListener l)`

Removes the specified mouse listener so that it no longer receives mouse events from this component.

`public synchronized void`
`        removeMouseMotionListener(MouseMotionListener l)`

Removes the specified mouse motion listener so that it no longer receives mouse motion events from this component.

`public void repaint()`

Repaints this component. Called by update.

`public void repaint(int x, int y, int width, int height)`

Repaints the specified rectangle of this component.

`public void requestFocus()`

Requests that this component get the input focus.

`public void setBackground(Color c)`

Sets the background color of this component.

`public void setBounds(Rectangle r)`
`public void setBounds(int x, int y, int width, int height)`

Moves and resizes this component.

`public void setEnabled(boolean b)`

Enables or disables this component.

```
public synchronized void setFont(Font f)
```

Sets the font of this component.

```
public void setForeground(Color c)
```

Sets the foreground color of this component.

```
public void setLocation(int x, int y)
public void setLocation(Point p)
```

Moves this component to a new location (top-left corner).

```
public void setName(String name)
```

Sets the name of the component to the specified string.

```
public void setSize(Dimension d)
public void setSize(int width, int height)
```

Resizes this component.

```
public void setVisible(boolean b)
```

Shows or hides this component.

```
public String toString()
```

Returns a **String** representation of this component and its values.

```
public void validate()
```

Ensures that this component has a valid layout.

```
public void update(Graphics g)
```

Updates this component: clears this component by filling it with the background color, sets the color of the graphics context to be the foreground color of this component, calls this component's paint method to completely redraw this component.

◆◆Container Class ───────────────

```
public abstract class Container extends Component
```

A generic Abstract Window Toolkit (AWT) that can contain other AWT components.

Methods

```
public Component add(Component comp)
```

Adds the specified component to the end of this container.

```
public Component add(Component comp, int index)
```

Adds the specified component to this container at the given position.

```
public synchronized void
          addContainerListener(ContainerListener l)
```

Adds the specified container listener to receive container events from this container.

```
public Component getComponent(int n)
```

Gets the nth component in this container.

```
public int getComponentCount()
```

Gets the number of components in this panel.

```
public Component[] getComponents()
```

Gets all the components in this container.

```
public Insets getInsets()
```

Determines the insets of this container, which indicate the size of the container's border.

`public LayoutManager getLayout()`

Gets the layout manager for this container.

`public boolean isAncestorOf(Component c)`

Checks to see if the component is contained in the component hierarchy of this container.

`public void paintComponents(Graphics g)`

Paints each of the components in this container.

`public void remove(int index)`

Removes the component, specified by index, from this container.

`public void remove(Component comp)`

Removes the specified component from this container.

`public void removeAll()`

Removes all the components from this container.

`public void removeContainerListener(ContainerListener l)`

Removes the specified container listener so that it no longer receives container events from this container.

`public void setLayout(LayoutManager mgr)`

Sets the layout manager for this container.

`protected void validateTree()`

Recursively descends the container tree and recomputes the layout for any sub-trees marked as needing it (those marked as invalid).

◆◆Panel Class ————————————————————————

```
public class Panel extends Container
```

Panel is the simplest container class. A panel provides space in which an application can attach any other component, including other panels.

Constructors

```
public Panel()
public Panel(LayoutManager layout)
```

Creates a new panel. The default layout manager is **FlowLayout**.

Graphics Classes

This section contains classes that are used for creating graphics.

◆◆Color Class ————————————————————————

```
public class Color extends Object implements Serializable
```

This class represents colors using the RGB (red, green, blue) format in which each color is represented by a range 0–255 (absence of color to complete saturation of that color). Note that HSB (hue, saturation, brightness) conversion methods are also available. See the resources in Appendix A for more detail.

Data fields

Numbers in parentheses are the red, green, blue values for each color.

```
public static final Color black        (0,0,0)
public static final Color blue         (0,0,255)
public static final Color cyan         (0,255,255)
public static final Color darkGray     (64,64,64)
public static final Color gray         (128,128,128)
public static final Color green        (0,255,0)
public static final Color lightGray    (192,192,192)
public static final Color magenta      (255,0,255)
public static final Color orange       (255,200,0)
public static final Color pink         (255,175,175)
public static final Color red          (255,0,0)
public static final Color white        (255,255,255)
public static final Color yellow       (255,255,0)
```

Constructors

```
public Color(int r, int g, int b)
```

Creates a color with the specified red, green, and blue components. The integers must be in the range 0–255.

```
public Color(int rgb)
```

Creates a color with the specified RGB value, where the red component is in bits 16–23 of the argument, the green component is in bits 8–15 of the argument, and the blue component is in bits 0–7.

```
public Color(float r, float g, float b)
```

Creates a color with the specified red, green, and blue values, where each of the values is in the range 0.0–1.0. This is *not* an HSB constructor.

Methods

```
public Color brighter()
```

Creates a brighter version of this color.

```
public Color darker()
```

Creates a darker version of this color.

```
public boolean equals(Object obj)
```

Determines whether another object is equal to this color.

```
public int getBlue()
```

Gets the blue component of this color.

```
public int getGreen()
```

Gets the green component of this color.

```
public int getRed()
```

Gets the red component of this color.

```
public int getRGB()
```

Gets the RGB value representing the color. Bits 16–23 are for the red value, bits 8–15 are for the green value, and bits 0–7 are for the blue value.

```
public String toString()
```

Creates a **String** representation of this color.

◆◆Dimension Class

```
public class Dimension extends Object implements Serializable
```

The Dimension class encapsulates the width and height of a component.

Data fields
```
public int width
```

The width dimension.

```
public int height
```

The height dimension.

Constructors

```
public Dimension()
```

Creates a **Dimension** with a width of zero and a height of zero.

```
public Dimension(Dimension d)
```

Creates a **Dimension** whose width and height are the same as for the specified dimension.

```
public Dimension(int width, int height)
```

Creates a **Dimension** and initializes it to the specified width and height.

Methods

```
public Dimension getSize()
```

Gets the size of this **Dimension** object.

```
public boolean equals(Object obj)
```

Checks whether two **Dimension** objects have equal values.

```
public void setSize(Dimension d)
public void setSize(int width, int height)
```

Sets the size of this **Dimension** object.

```
public String toString()
```

Returns a string that represents this **Dimension** object's values.

◆◆Graphics Class

```
public abstract class Graphics extends Object
```

A **Graphics** object encapsulates state information needed for the basic rendering operations that Java supports. This class contains many sophisticated methods for graphics. See the resources in Appendix A for more detail.

Constructors

Because **Graphics** is an abstract class, applications cannot call this constructor directly. Graphics contexts are obtained from other graphics contexts or are created by calling **getGraphics** on a component.

Methods

```
public abstract void copyArea(int x, int y, int width,
                              int height, int dx, int dy)
```

Copies an area of the component by a distance specified by *dx* and *dy*.

```
public abstract Graphics create()
```

Creates a graphics object that is a copy of this object.

```
public abstract void dispose()
```

Disposes of this graphics context and releases any system resources that it is using.

```
public void draw3DRect(int x, int y, int width,
                       int height,
                       boolean raised)
```

Draws a 3D highlighted outline of the specified rectangle. The edges of the rectangle are highlighted so that they appear to be beveled and lit from the upper-left corner. The **boolean raised** determines whether the rectangle appears to be raised above the surface or sunk into the surface.

```
public abstract void drawArc(int x, int y,int width,
               int height, int startAngle, int arcAngle)
```

Draws the outline of a circular or elliptical arc covering the specified rectangle.

```
public abstract void drawLine(int x1, int y1,
                              int x2, int y2)
```

Draws a line, using the current color, between the points $(x1, y1)$ and $(x2, y2)$

```
public abstract void drawOval(int x, int y, int width, int height)
```

Draws the outline of an oval.

```
public void drawRect(int x, int y, int width, int height)
```

Draws the outline of the specified rectangle.

```
public abstract void drawRoundRect(int x, int y, int width,
              int height, int arcWidth, int arcHeight)
```

Draws an outlined round-cornered rectangle.

```
public abstract void drawPolyline(int xPoints[],
                                  int yPoints[],
                                  int nPoints)
```

Draws a sequence of **npoints** connected lines defined by arrays of *x* and *y* coordinates, where each pair of (*x*, *y*) coordinates defines a point.

```
public abstract void drawPolygon(int xPoints[], int yPoints[],
                                 int nPoints)
```

Draws a closed polygon defined by arrays of *x* and *y* coordinates using **nPoints** − 1 pairs and closing the first and last points.

```
public abstract void drawString(String str, int x, int y)
```

Draws the text given by the specified string starting at position (*x*, *y*).

```
public void drawPolygon(Polygon p)
```

Draws the outline of a polygon defined by the specified **Polygon** object.

```
public void fill3DRect(int x, int y, int width,
    int height, boolean raised)
```

Paints a 3D highlighted rectangle filled with the current color. The edges of the rectangle will be highlighted so that it appears as if the edges were beveled and lit from the upper-left corner. The argument **raised** determines whether the rectangle appears to be raised above the surface or etched into the surface.

```
public abstract void fillArc(int x, int y,int width,
              int height, int startAngle,int arcAngle)
```

Fills a circular or elliptical arc covering the specified rectangle.

```
public abstract void fillOval(int x, int y, int width,
                                          int height)
```

Fills an oval bounded by the specified rectangle with the current color.

```
public void fillPolygon(Polygon p)
```

Fills a closed polygon based on *p*.

```
public abstract void fillPolygon(int xPoints[], int yPoints[],
                                 int nPoints)
```

Fills a closed polygon defined by arrays of *x* and *y* coordinates. See
drawPolygon.

```
public abstract void fillRect(int x, int y, int width, int height)
```

Fills the specified rectangle.

```
public abstract void fillRoundRect(int x, int y,
   int width, int height, int arcWidth, int arcHeight)
```

Fills the specified rounded-corner rectangle with the current color.

```
public abstract Color getColor()
```

Gets this graphics context's current color.

```
public abstract Font getFont()
```

Gets the current font.

```
public FontMetrics getFontMetrics()
```

Gets the font metrics of the current font.

```
public abstract FontMetrics getFontMetrics(Font f)
```

Gets the font metrics for the specified font.

```
public abstract void setColor(Color c)
```

Sets this graphics context's current color to the specified color.

```
public abstract void setFont(Font font)
```

Sets this graphics context's font to the specified font.

`public abstract void setPaintMode()`

Sets the paint mode of this graphics context to overwrite the destination with this graphics context's current color. Sets the logical pixel operation function to the paint or overwrite mode.

`public abstract void setXORMode(Color c1)`

Sets the paint mode of this graphics context to alternate between this graphics context's current color and the new specified color. The logical pixel operations are performed in the XOR mode, which alternates pixels between the current color and `c1`.

`public String toString()`

Returns a **String** object representing this **Graphics** object's value.

`public abstract void translate(int x, int y)`

Translates the origin of the graphics context to the point (x, y) in the current coordinate system.

◆◆Point Class ────────────────────────

`public class Point extends Object implements Serializable`

The **Point** class represents a location in a two-dimensional (x, y) coordinate space.

Data fields

`public int x`

The x coordinate.

`public int y`

The y coordinate.

Constructors

```
public Point()
```

Constructs and initializes a point at the origin (0, 0) of the coordinate space.

```
public Point(Point p)
```

Constructs and initializes a point with the same location as *p*.

```
public Point(int x, int y)
```

Constructs and initializes a point at the specified (x, y) location.

Methods

```
public boolean equals(Object obj)
```

Determines whether two points are equal.

```
public Point getLocation()
```

Returns the location of this point

```
public void move(int x, int y)
```

The same as **setLocation(int, int)**.

```
public void setLocation(Point p)
public void setLocation(int x, int y)
```

Changes the point to have the specified location.

```
public String toString()
```

Returns a representation of this point and its location.

```
public void translate(int dx, int dy)
```

Translates this point, at location (x, y), by dx along the x axis and by dy along the y axis so that it now represents the point $(x + dx, y + dy)$.

◆◆Polygon Class

```
public class Polygon extends Object implements Shape, Serializable
```

The `Polygon` class describes a closed, two-dimensional region within a coordinate space, bounded by an arbitrary number of line segments, each of which is one side of the polygon.

Data fields

```
public int npoints
```

The total number of points.

```
public int xpoints[]
```

The array of *x* coordinates.

```
public int ypoints[]
```

The array of *y* coordinates.

Constructors

```
public Polygon()
```

Creates an empty polygon.

```
public Polygon(int xpoints[], int ypoints[], int npoints)
```

Constructs and initializes a polygon from the specified parameters where each *x,y* pair represents a point.

Methods

```
public void addPoint(int x, int y)
```

Appends a point to this polygon.

```
public boolean contains(Point p)
public boolean contains(int x, int y)
```

Determines whether the specified point is inside the `Polygon`.

```
public void translate(int deltaX, int deltaY)
```

Translates the vertices by **deltaX** along the *x* axis and by **deltaY** along the *y* axis.

Layout Manager Classes

◆◆BorderLayout Class

```
public class BorderLayout extends Object
                          implements LayoutManager2, Serializable
```

A border layout lays out a container, arranging and resizing its components to fit in five regions: North, South, East, West, and Center [Variables].

Data fields

```
public static final String NORTH
public static final String SOUTH
public static final String EAST
public static final String WEST
public static final String CENTER
```

Constructors

```
public BorderLayout()
```

Constructs a new border layout with no gaps between components.

```
public BorderLayout(int hgap, int vgap)
```

Constructs a border layout with the specified gaps between components.

Methods

```
public int getHgap()
```

Returns the horizontal gap between components.

```
public int getVgap()
```

Returns the vertical gap between components.

```
public void setHgap(int hgap)
```

Sets the horizontal gap between components.

```
public void setVgap(int vgap)
```

Sets the vertical gap between components.

◆◆FlowLayout Class

```
public class FlowLayout extends Object
                        implements LayoutManager, Serializable
```

A flow layout arranges components in a left-to-right flow, text in a paragraph.

Data fields

```
public static final int LEFT
```

Each row of components should be left-justified.

```
public static final int CENTER
```

Each row of components should be centered.

```
public static final int RIGHT
```

Each row of components should be right-justified.

Constructors

```
public FlowLayout()
```

Constructs a new **Flow Layout** with a centered alignment and a default five-unit horizontal and vertical gap.

```
public FlowLayout(int align)
```

Constructs a new **Flow Layout** with the specified alignment and a default five-unit horizontal and vertical gap.

```
public FlowLayout(int align, int hgap, int vgap)
```

Creates a new flow layout manager with the given alignment and horizontal and vertical gaps.

Methods

`public int getAlignment()`

Gets the alignment for this layout.

`public int getHgap()`

Gets the horizontal gap between components.

`public int getVgap()`

Gets the vertical gap between components.

`public void setAlignment(int align)`

Sets the alignment for this layout.

`public void setHgap(int hgap)`

Sets the horizontal gap between components.

`public void setVgap(int vgap)`

Sets the vertical gap between components.

◆◆GridLayout Class

```
public class GridLayout extends Object
                        implements LayoutManager, Serializable
```

The `GridLayout` class lays out a container's components in a rectangular grid.

Constructors

`public GridLayout()`

Creates a grid layout in a single row with a default of one column per component.

`public GridLayout(int rows, int cols)`

Creates a grid layout with the specified number of rows and columns.

```
public GridLayout(int rows, int cols,
                  int hgap, int vgap)
```

Creates a grid layout with the specified number of rows and columns and horizontal and vertical gaps.

Methods

```
public int getColumns()
```

Gets the number of columns in this layout.

```
public int getHgap()
```

Gets the horizontal gap between components.

```
public int getRows()
```

Gets the number of rows in this layout.

```
public int getVgap()
```

Gets the vertical gap between components.

```
public void setColumns(int cols)
```

Sets the number of columns in this layout to the specified value.

```
public void setHgap(int hgap)
```

Sets the horizontal gap between components to the specified value.

```
public void setRows(int rows)
```

Sets the number of rows in this layout to the specified value.

```
public void setVgap(int vgap)
```

Sets the vertical gap between components to the specified value.

Events and Listeners

Events and Listeners go hand in hand. Therefore, the events and listeners are paired in this section.

◆◆ActionEvent Class————————————————————

```
public class ActionEvent extends AWTEvent
```

The action semantic event.

Data fields
```
public static final int SHIFT_MASK
```

The shift modifier constant.

```
public static final int CTRL_MASK
```

The control modifier constant.

```
public static final int META_MASK
```

The meta modifier constant.

```
public static final int ALT_MASK
```

The alt modifier constant.

Constructors
```
public ActionEvent(Object source, int id,String command)
public ActionEvent(Object source, int id,
                   String command, int modifiers)
```

Constructs an **ActionEvent** object with the object where the event originated, the type of event, the command string for this action event, and if present, the modifiers held down during this action.

Methods

`public String getActionCommand()`

Returns the command name associated with this action.

`public int getModifiers()`

Returns the modifiers held down during this action event.

◆◆ActionListener Interface

`public interface ActionListener extends EventListener`

The listener interface for receiving action events.

Methods

`public abstract void actionPerformed(ActionEvent e)`

The method is invoked when an action occurs.

◆◆ItemEvent Class

`public class ItemEvent extends AWTEvent`

The item event emitted by **ItemSelectable** objects. This event is generated when an item is selected or deselected.

Data fields

`public static final int ITEM_FIRST`

Marks the first integer ID for the range of item event IDs.

`public static final int ITEM_LAST`

Marks the last integer ID for the range of item event IDs.

`public static final int ITEM_STATE_CHANGED`

The item state changed event type.

```
public static final int SELECTED
```

The item selected state change type.

```
public static final int DESELECTED
```

The item deselected state change type.

Constructors

```
public ItemEvent(ItemSelectable source, int id,
                 Object item, int stateChange)
```

Constructs an **ItemEvent** object with the specified **ItemSelectable** source, type, item, and item select state.

Methods

```
public Object getItem()
```

Returns the item where the event occurred.

```
public ItemSelectable getItemSelectable()
```

Returns the **ItemSelectable** object where this event originated.

```
public int getStateChange()
```

Returns the state change type that generated the event.

◆◆ItemListener Interface ────────────

```
public interface ItemListener extends EventListener
```

The listener interface for receiving item events.

Methods

```
public abstract void itemStateChanged(ItemEvent e)
```

Is invoked when an item's state has been changed.

◆◆WindowEvent Class ————————————————

```
public class WindowEvent extends ComponentEvent
```

The window-level event.

Data fields

```
public static final int WINDOW_ACTIVATED
```

The window activated event type.

```
public static final int WINDOW_DEACTIVATED
```

The window deactivated event type.

```
public static final int WINDOW_CLOSED
```

The window closed event type.

```
public static final int WINDOW_CLOSING
```

The window closing event type.

```
public static final int WINDOW_DEICONIFIED
```

The window deiconified event type.

```
public static final int WINDOW_FIRST
```

Marks the first integer ID for the range of window event IDs.

```
public static final int WINDOW_ICONIFIED
```

The window iconified event type.

```
public static final int WINDOW_LAST
```

Marks the last integer ID for the range of window event IDs.

```
public static final int WINDOW_OPENED
```

The window opened event type.

Constructors

```
public WindowEvent(Window source,int id)
```

Constructs a WindowEvent object with the specified source window and type.

Methods

```
public Window getWindow()
```

Returns the window where this event originated.

◆◆WindowListener Interface ────────────

```
public interface WindowListener extends EventListener
```

The listener interface for receiving window events.

Methods

```
public abstract void windowActivated(WindowEvent e)
```

Is invoked when a window is activated.

```
public abstract void windowClosed(WindowEvent e)
```

Is invoked when a window has been closed.

```
public abstract void windowClosing(WindowEvent e)
```

Is invoked when a window is in the process of being closed.

```
public abstract void windowDeactivated(WindowEvent e)
```

Is invoked when a window is deactivated.

```
public abstract void windowDeiconified(WindowEvent e)
```

Is invoked when a window is deiconified.

```
public abstract void windowIconified(WindowEvent e)
```

Is invoked when a window is iconified.

```
public abstract void windowOpened(WindowEvent e)
```

Is invoked when a window has been opened.

Package `javax.swing`

JApplet Class
BorderFactory Class
BoxLayout Class
JComponent and Subclasses
JComponent Class
AbstractButton Class
JButton Class
JCheckBox Class
JComboBox Class
JFileChooser Class
JLabel Class
JOptionPane Class

◆◆JApplet Class

```
public class JApplet extends Applet implements Accessible,
RootPaneContainer
```

A layout manager that allows multiple components to be laid out either vertically or horizontally. The components will not wrap, so a vertical arrangement of components, for example, will stay vertically arranged when the frame is resized.

Constructors

```
public JApplet()
```

Creates a **Swing** applet instance.

Methods

```
protected void addImpl(Component comp, Object constraints, int
index)
```

By default, children may not be added directly to a this component; they must be added to its **contentPane** instead.

```
protected JRootPane createRootPane()
```

Called by the constructor methods to create the default **rootPane**.

```
public AccessibleContext getAccessibleContext()
```

Gets the **AccessibleContext** associated with this **JApplet**.

```
public Container getContentPane()
```

Returns the **contentPane** object for this applet.

```
public Component getGlassPane()
```

Returns the **glassPane** object for this applet.

```
public JMenuBar getJMenuBar()
```

Returns the **menuBar** set on this applet.

```
public JLayeredPane getLayeredPane()
```

Returns the **layeredPane** object for this applet.

```
public JRootPane getRootPane()
```

Returns the **rootPane** object for this applet.

```
protected  boolean isRootPaneCheckingEnabled()
```

Returns **true** if **add** and **setLayout** should be checked.

`protected String paramString()`

Returns a string representation of this **JApplet**.

`protected  void processKeyEvent(KeyEvent e)`

Overrides **processKeyEvent** in class **Component**.

`public void setContentPane(Container contentPane)`

Sets the **contentPane** property.

`public void setGlassPane(Component glassPane)`

Sets the **glassPane** property.

`public void setJMenuBar(JMenuBar menuBar)`

Sets the **menubar** for this applet.

`public void setLayeredPane(JLayeredPane layeredPane)`

Sets the **layeredPane** property.

`public void setLayout(LayoutManager manager)`

By default, the layout of this component may not be set; the layout of its **contentPane** should be set instead.

`protected  void setRootPane(JRootPane root)`

Sets the **rootPane** property.

`protected void setRootPaneCheckingEnabled(boolean enabled)`

If **true**, calls to **add()** and **setLayout()** will cause an exception to be thrown.

`public void update(Graphics g)`

Calls **paint(g)**.

◆◆BorderFactory Class ───────────────────────

```
public class BorderFactory extends Object
```

Methods

```
public static TitledBorder createTitledBorder(Border border)
```

Creates a new title border with an empty title specifying the border object, using the default text position (sitting on the top line) and default justification (left) and using the default font, text color, and edge determined by the current look and feel.

```
public static TitledBorder createTitledBorder(Border border,
String title)
```

Adds a title to an existing border, specifying the text of the title, using the default positioning (sitting on the top line) and default justification (left) and using the default font and text color determined by the current look and feel.

```
public static TitledBorder createTitledBorder(Border border,
String title, int titleJustification, int titlePosition)
```

Adds a title to an existing border, specifying the text of the title along with its positioning, using the default font and text color determined by the current look and feel.

```
public static TitledBorder createTitledBorder(Border border,
String title, int titleJustification, int titlePosition, Font
titleFont)
```

Adds a title to an existing border, specifying the text of the title along with its positioning and font, using the default text color determined by the current look and feel.

```
public static TitledBorder createTitledBorder(Border border,
String title, int titleJustification, int titlePosition, Font
titleFont, Color titleColor)
```

Adds a title to an existing border, specifying the text of the title along with its positioning, font, and color.

```
public static TitledBorder createTitledBorder(String title)
```

Creates a new title border specifying the text of the title, using the default border (etched), the default text position (sitting on the top line) and default justification (left), and the default font and text color determined by the current look and feel.

◆◆BoxLayout Class

```
public class BoxLayout extends Object implements LayoutManager2,
Serializable
```

Constructors

```
public BoxLayout(Container target, int axis)
```

Creates a layout manager that will lay out components either left to right or top to bottom, as specified in the axis parameter.

Methods

```
public float getLayoutAlignmentX(Container target)
```

Returns the alignment along the *x* axis for the container.

```
public float getLayoutAlignmentY(Container target)
```

Returns the alignment along the *y* axis for the container.

```
public void invalidateLayout(Container target)
```

Indicates that a child has changed its layout-related information, and thus any cached calculations should be flushed.

```
public void layoutContainer(Container target)
```

Called by the AWT when the specified container needs to be laid out.

```
public Dimension maximumLayoutSize(Container target)
```

Returns the maximum dimensions the target container can use to lay out the components it contains.

```
public Dimension minimumLayoutSize(Container target)
```

Returns the minimum dimensions needed to lay out the components contained in the specified target container.

```
public Dimension preferredLayoutSize(Container target)
```

Returns the preferred dimensions for this layout, given the components in the specified target container.

JComponent and Subclasses

◆◆JComponent Class ─────────────────────────────

```
public abstract class JComponent extends Container implements
Serializable
```

The base class for the **Swing** components.

Variables and constants

```
protected AccessibleContext accessibleContext
protected EventListenerList listenerList
public static String TOOL_TIP_TEXT_KEY
protected ComponentUI ui
public static int UNDEFINED_CONDITION
public static int WHEN_ANCESTOR_OF_FOCUSED_COMPONENT
public static int WHEN_FOCUSED
public static int WHEN_IN_FOCUSED_WINDOW
```

Constructors

```
public JComponent()
```

Default **JComponent** constructor.

Methods:

```
public void addAncestorListener(AncestorListener listener)
```

Registers listener so that it will receive **AncestorEvents** when it or any of its ancestors move or are made visible or invisible.

```
public void addNotify()
```

Notification to this component that it now has a parent component.

```
public void addPropertyChangeListener(PropertyChangeListener
listener)
```

Adds a **PropertyChangeListener** to the listener list.

```
public void addVetoableChangeListener(VetoableChangeListener
listener)
```

Adds a **VetoableChangeListener** to the listener list.

```
public void computeVisibleRect(Rectangle visibleRect)
```

Returns the component's "visible rect rectangle"—the intersection of the visible rectangles for this component and all of its ancestors.

```
public boolean contains(int x, int y)
```

Gives the UI delegate an opportunity to define the precise shape of this component for the sake of mouse processing.

```
public JToolTip createToolTip()
```

Returns the instance of **JToolTip** that should be used to display the tool tip.

```
public void firePropertyChange(String propertyName, boolean
oldValue, boolean newValue)
```

Reports a bound property change.

```
public void firePropertyChange(String propertyName, byte oldValue,
byte newValue)
```

Reports a bound property change.

```
public void firePropertyChange(String propertyName, char oldValue,
char newValue)
```

Reports a bound property change.

```
public void firePropertyChange(String propertyName, double
oldValue, double newValue)
```

Reports a bound property change.

```
public void firePropertyChange(String propertyName, float
oldValue, float newValue)
```

Reports a bound property change.

```
public void firePropertyChange(String propertyName, int oldValue,
int newValue)
```

Reports a bound property change.

```
public void firePropertyChange(String propertyName, long oldValue,
long newValue)
```

Reports a bound property change.

```
protected  void firePropertyChange(String propertyName, Object
oldValue, Object newValue)
```

Support for reporting bound property changes.

```
public void firePropertyChange(String propertyName, short
oldValue, short newValue)
```

Reports a bound property change.

```
protected void fireVetoableChange(String propertyName, Object
oldValue, Object newValue)
```

Support for reporting constrained property changes.

```
public AccessibleContext getAccessibleContext()
```

Gets the **AccessibleContext** associated with this **JComponent**.

```
public ActionListener getActionForKeyStroke(KeyStroke aKeyStroke)
```

Returns the object that will perform the action registered for a given keystroke.

```
public float getAlignmentX()
```

Overrides **Container.getAlignmentX** to return the vertical alignment.

```
public float getAlignmentY()
```

Overrides **Container.getAlignmentY** to return the horizontal alignment.

```
public boolean getAutoscrolls()
```

Returns **true** if this component automatically scrolls its contents when dragged, (when contained in a component that supports scrolling, like **JViewport**).

```
public Border getBorder()
```

Returns the border of this component or null if no border is currently set.

public Rectangle `getBounds(`**Rectangle rv)**

Stores the bounds of this component into "return value" rv and return rv.

public `Object` `getClientProperty(Object key)`

Returns the value of the property with the specified key.

protected Graphics `getComponentGraphics(`**Graphics g)**

Returns the graphics object used to paint this component.

`int getConditionForKeyStroke(`**KeyStroke aKeyStroke)**

Returns the condition that determines whether a registered action occurs in response to the specified keystroke.

public int `getDebugGraphicsOptions()`

Returns the state of graphics debugging.

public Graphics `getGraphics()`

Returns this component's graphics context, which lets you draw on a component.

public int `getHeight()`

Returns the current height of this component.

public Insets `getInsets()`

If a border has been set on this component, returns the border's insets; else it calls **super.getInsets**.

public Insets `getInsets(`**Insets insets)**

Returns an **Insets** object containing this component's inset values.

public Point `getLocation(`**Point rv)**

Stores the *x, y* origin of this component into "return value" rv and returns rv.

```
public Dimension getMaximumSize()
```

If the **maximumSize** has been set to a non-null value, just return it.

```
public Dimension getMinimumSize()
```

If the **minimumSize** has been set to a non-null value, just return it.

```
public Component getNextFocusableComponent()
```

Returns the next focusable component or null if the focus manager should choose the next focusable component automatically.

```
public Dimension getPreferredSize()
```

If the **preferredSize** has been set to a non-null value, just return it.

```
public KeyStroke[] getRegisteredKeyStrokes()
```

Returns the **KeyStrokes** that will initiate registered actions.

```
public JRootPane getRootPane()
```

Returns the **JRootPane** ancestor for a component.

```
public Dimension getSize(Dimension rv)
```

Stores the width/height of this component into "return value" rv and returns rv.

```
public Point getToolTipLocation(MouseEvent event)
```

Returns the tool tip location in the receiving component coordinate system. If **null** is returned, **Swing** will choose a location.

```
public String getToolTipText()
```

Returns the tool tip string that has been set with **setToolTipText()**.

```
public String getToolTipText(MouseEvent event)
```

Returns the string to be used as the tool tip for event.

```
public Container getTopLevelAncestor()
```

Returns the top-level ancestor of this component (either the containing window or applet) or null if this component has not been added to any container.

```
public String getUIClassID()
```

Returns the **UIDefaults** key used to look up the name of the **swing.plaf.ComponentUI** class that defines the look and feel for this component.

```
public Rectangle getVisibleRect()
```

Returns the component's "visible rectangle"—the intersection of this components visible rectangle: **new Rectangle(0, 0, getWidth(), getHeight());**, and all of its ancestor's visible **Rectangle**s.

```
public int getWidth()
```

Returns the current width of this component.

```
public int getX()
```

Returns the current *x* coordinate of the component's origin.

```
public int getY()
```

Returns the current *y* coordinate of the component's origin.

```
public void grabFocus()
```

Sets the focus on the receiving component.

```
public boolean hasFocus()
```

Returns **true** if this component has the keyboard focus.

```
public boolean isDoubleBuffered()
```

Returns whether the receiving component should use a buffer to paint.

```
public boolean isFocusCycleRoot()
```

Overrides this method and returns **true** if your component is the root of a component tree with its own focus cycle.

`public boolean isFocusTraversable()`

Identifies whether or not this component can receive the focus.

`public static boolean isLightweightComponent(Component c)`

Returns **true** if this component is a lightweight component.

`public boolean isManagingFocus()`

Overrides this method and returns **true** if your **JComponent** manages focus.

`public boolean isOpaque()`

Returns **true** if this component is completely opaque.

`public boolean isOptimizedDrawingEnabled()`

Returns **true** if this component tiles its children.

`public boolean isPaintingTile()`

Returns **true** if the receiving component is currently painting a tile.

`public boolean isRequestFocusEnabled()`

Returns whether the receiving component can obtain the focus by calling **requestFocus**.

`public boolean isValidateRoot()`

If this method returns **true**, **revalidate()** calls by descendants of this component will cause the entire tree beginning with this root to be validated.

`public void paint(Graphics g)`

This method is invoked by **Swing** to draw components.

`protected  void paintBorder(Graphics g)`

Paints the component's border.

```
protected  void paintChildren(Graphics g)
```

Paints this component's children.

```
protected  void paintComponent(Graphics g)
```

If the UI delegate is non-null, calls its paint method.

```
public void paintImmediately(int x, int y, int w, int h)
```

Paints the specified region in this component and all of its descendants that over-lap the region, immediately.

```
public void paintImmediately(Rectangle r)
```

Paints the specified region now.

```
protected  String paramString()
```

Returns a string representation of this **JComponent**.

```
protected  void processComponentKeyEvent(KeyEvent e)
```

Processes any key events that the component itself recognizes.

```
public void putClientProperty(Object key, Object value)
```

Adds an arbitrary key/value "client property" to this component.

```
public void registerKeyboardAction(ActionListener anAction,
KeyStroke aKeyStroke, int aCondition)
```

Calls **registerKeyboardAction(ActionListener, String, KeyStroke, condition)** with a null command.

```
public void registerKeyboardAction(ActionListener anAction, String
aCommand, KeyStroke aKeyStroke, int aCondition)
```

Registers a new keyboard action.

```
public void removeAncestorListener(AncestorListener listener)
```

Unregisters listener so that it will no longer receive **AncestorEvents** This method will migrate to **java.awt.Component** in the next major JDK release.

```
public void removeNotify()
```

Notification to this component that it no longer has a parent component.

```
public void removePropertyChangeListener(PropertyChangeListener
listener)
```

Removes a **PropertyChangeListener** from the listener list.

```
public void removeVetoableChangeListener(VetoableChangeListener
listener)
```

Removes a **VetoableChangeListener** from the listener list.

```
public void repaint(long tm, int x, int y, int width, int height)
```

Adds the specified region to the dirty region list if the component is showing.

```
public void repaint(Rectangle r)
```

Adds the specified region to the dirty region list if the component is showing.

```
public boolean requestDefaultFocus()
```

Requests the focus for the component that should have the focus by default.

```
public void requestFocus()
```

Sets focus on the receiving component if **isRequestFocusEnabled** returns **true**.

```
public void resetKeyboardActions()
```

Unregisters all keyboard actions.

```
public void reshape(int x, int y, int w, int h)
```

Moves and resizes this component.

```
public void revalidate()
```

Support for deferred automatic layout.

```
public void scrollRectToVisible(Rectangle aRect)
```

Forwards the **scrollRectToVisible()** message to the **JComponent**'s parent.

```
public void setAlignmentX(float alignmentX)
```

Sets the the vertical alignment.

```
public void setAlignmentY(float alignmentY)
```

Sets the the horizontal alignment.

```
public void setAutoscrolls(boolean autoscrolls)
```

If **true**, this component will automatically scroll its contents when dragged if contained in a component that supports scrolling, such as **JViewport**.

```
public void setBackground(Color bg)
```

Sets the background color of this component.

```
public void setBorder(Border border)
```

Sets the border of this component.

```
public void setDebugGraphicsOptions(int debugOptions)
```

Enables or disables diagnostic information about every graphics operation performed within the component or one of its children.

```
public void setDoubleBuffered(boolean aFlag)
```

Sets whether the receiving component should use a buffer to paint.

```
public void setEnabled(boolean enabled)
```

Sets whether or not this component is enabled.

```
public void setFont(Font font)
```

Sets the font for this component.

```
public void setForeground(Color fg)
```

Sets the foreground color of this component.

```
public void setMaximumSize(Dimension maximumSize)
```

Sets the **maximumSize** of this component to a constant value.

```
public void setMinimumSize(Dimension minimumSize)
```

Sets the **minimumSize** of this component to a constant value.

```
public void setNextFocusableComponent(Component aComponent)
```

Specifies the next component to get the focus after this one, for example, when the Tab key is pressed.

```
public void setOpaque(boolean isOpaque)
```

If **true**, the components background will be filled with the background color.

```
public void setPreferredSize(Dimension preferredSize)
```

Sets the preferred size of the receiving component.

```
public void setRequestFocusEnabled(boolean aFlag)
```

Sets whether the receiving component can obtain the focus by calling **requestFocus**.

```
public void setToolTipText(String text)
```

Registers the text to display in a tool tip.

```
public protected void setUI(ComponentUI newUI)
```

Sets the look and feel delegate for this component.

```
public void setVisible(boolean aFlag)
```

Makes the component visible or invisible.

`public void unregisterKeyboardAction(KeyStroke aKeyStroke)`

Unregisters a keyboard action.

`public void update(Graphics g)`

Calls `paint(g)`.

`public void updateUI()`

Resets the `UI` property to a value from the current look and feel.

◆◆AbstractButton Class ──────────────

`public abstract class AbstractButton extends JComponent implements ItemSelectable, SwingConstants`

Defines the common behaviors for the `JButton`, `JToggleButton`, `JCheckbox`, and the `JRadioButton` classes.

Methods

`public void addActionListener(ActionListener l)`

Adds an `ActionListener` to the button.

`public void addChangeListener(ChangeListener l)`

Adds a `ChangeListener` to the button.

`public void addItemListener(ItemListener l)`

Adds an `ItemListener` to the checkbox.

`protected int checkHorizontalKey(int key, String exception)`

Verifies that `key` is a legal value for the `horizontalAlignment` properties.

`protected int checkVerticalKey(int key, String exception)`

Ensures that the key is a valid.

`protected ItemListener createItemListener()`

```
protected  void fireActionPerformed(ActionEvent event)
protected  void fireItemStateChanged(ItemEvent event)
protected  void fireStateChanged()
public String getActionCommand()
```

Returns the action command for this button.

```
public Icon getDisabledIcon()
```

Returns the icon used by the button when it's disabled.

```
public Icon getDisabledSelectedIcon()
```

Returns the icon used by the button when it's disabled and selected.

```
public int getHorizontalAlignment()
```

Returns the horizontal alignment of the icon and text.

```
public int getHorizontalTextPosition()
```

Sets the horizontal position of the text relative to the icon.

```
public Icon getIcon()
```

Returns the default icon.

```
public String getLabel()
```

Deprecated; replaced by **getText()**.

```
public Insets getMargin()
```

Returns the margin between the button's border and the label.

```
public int getMnemonic()
```

Gets the keyboard mnemonic from the the current model.

```
public ButtonModel getModel()
```

Gets the model that this button represents.

```
public Icon getPressedIcon()
```

Returns the pressed icon for the button.

```
public Icon getRolloverIcon()
```

Returns the rollover icon for the button.

```
public Icon getRolloverSelectedIcon()
```

Returns the rollover selection icon for the button.

```
public Icon getSelectedIcon()
```

Returns the selected icon for the button.

```
public Object[] getSelectedObjects()
```

Returns an array (length 1) containing the label or null if the button is not selected.

```
public String getText()
```

Returns the button's text.

```
public ButtonUI getUI()
```

Returns the button's current **UI**.

```
public int getVerticalAlignment()
```

Returns the vertical alignment of the text and icon.

```
public int getVerticalTextPosition()
```

Returns the vertical position of the text relative to the icon. Valid keys: CENTER (the default), TOP, BOTTOM.

```
protected  void init(String text, Icon icon)
public boolean isBorderPainted()
```

Returns whether the border should be painted.

`public boolean isContentAreaFilled()`

Checks to see whether the "content area" of the button should be filled.

`public boolean isFocusPainted()`

Returns whether focus should be painted.

`public boolean isRolloverEnabled()`

Checks whether rollover effects are enabled.

`public boolean isSelected()`

Returns the state of the button.

`protected void paintBorder(Graphics g)`

Paints the button's border if **BorderPainted** property is **true**.

`protected String paramString()`

Returns a string representation of this **AbstractButton**.

`public void removeActionListener(ActionListener l)`

Removes an **ActionListener** from the button.

`public void removeChangeListener(ChangeListener l)`

Removes a **ChangeListener** from the button.

`public void removeItemListener(ItemListener l)`

Removes an **ItemListener** from the button.

`public void setActionCommand(String actionCommand)`

Sets the action command for this button.

`public void setBorderPainted(boolean b)`

Sets whether the border should be painted.

`public void setContentAreaFilled(boolean b)`

Sets whether the button should paint the content area or leave it transparent.

`public void setDisabledIcon(Icon disabledIcon)`

Sets the disabled icon for the button.

`public void setDisabledSelectedIcon(Icon disabledSelectedIcon)`

Sets the disabled selection icon for the button.

`public void setEnabled(boolean b)`

Enables (or disables) the button.

`public void setFocusPainted(boolean b)`

Sets whether focus should be painted.

`public void setHorizontalAlignment(int alignment)`

Sets the horizontal alignment of the icon and text.

`public void setHorizontalTextPosition(int textPosition)`

Sets the horizontal position of the text relative to the icon.

`public void setIcon(Icon defaultIcon)`

Sets the button's default icon.

`public void setLabel(String label)`

Deprecated; replaced by `setText(text)`.

`public void setMargin(Insets m)`

Sets space for margin between the button's border and the label.

`public void setMnemonic(char mnemonic)`

Specifies the mnemonic value.

`public void setMnemonic(int mnemonic)`

Sets the keyboard mnemonic on the current model.

`public void setModel(ButtonModel newModel)`

Sets the model that this button represents.

`public void setPressedIcon(Icon pressedIcon)`

Sets the pressed icon for the button.

`public void setRolloverEnabled(boolean b)`

Sets whether rollover effects should be enabled.

`public void setRolloverIcon(Icon rolloverIcon)`

Sets the rollover icon for the button.

`public void setRolloverSelectedIcon(Icon rolloverSelectedIcon)`

Sets the rollover selected icon for the button.

`public void setSelected(boolean b)`

Sets the state of the button.

`public void setSelectedIcon(Icon selectedIcon)`

Sets the selected icon for the button.

`public void setText(String text)`

Sets the button's text.

`public void setUI(ButtonUI ui)`

Sets the button's `UI`.

`public void setVerticalAlignment(int alignment)`

Sets the vertical alignment of the icon and text.

```
public void setVerticalTextPosition(int textPosition)
```

Sets the vertical position of the text relative to the icon.

```
public void updateUI()
```

Gets a new **UI** object from the default **UIFactory**.

◆◆JButton Class

```
public class JButton extends AbstractButton implements Accessible
```

An implementation of a "push" button.

Constructors

```
public JButton()
```

Creates a button with no set text or icon.

```
public JButton(Icon icon)
```

Creates a button with an icon.

```
public JButton(String text)
```

Creates a button with text.

```
public JButton(String text, Icon icon)
```

Creates a button with initial text and an icon.

Methods

```
public AccessibleContext getAccessibleContext()
```

Get the **AccessibleContext** associated with this **JComponent**.

```
public String getUIClassID()
```

Returns a string that specifies the name of the look and feel class that renders this component.

```
public boolean isDefaultButton()
```

Returns whether or not this button is the default button on the **RootPane**.

```
public boolean isDefaultCapable()
```

Returns whether or not this button is capable of being the default button on the **RootPane**.

```
protected String paramString()
```

Returns a string representation of this **JButton**.

```
public void setDefaultCapable(boolean defaultCapable)
```

Sets whether or not this button is capable of being the default button on the **RootPane**.

```
public void updateUI()
```

Notification from the **UIFactory** that the look and feel has changed.

◆◆JCheckBox Class

```
public class JCheckBox extends JToggleButton implements Accessible
```

Constructors
```
public JCheckBox()
```

Creates an initially unselected check box button with no text, no icon.

```
public JCheckBox(Icon icon)
```

Creates an initially unselected check box with an icon.

```
public JCheckBox(Icon icon, boolean selected)
```

Creates a check box with an icon and specifies whether or not it is initially selected.

```
public JCheckBox(String text)
```

Creates an initially unselected check box with **text**.

```
public JCheckBox(String text, boolean selected)
```

Creates a check box with **text** and specifies whether or not it is initially selected.

```
public JCheckBox(String text, Icon icon)
```

Creates an initially unselected check box with the specified **text** and **icon**.

```
public JCheckBox(String text, Icon icon, boolean selected)
```

Creates a check box with **text** and **icon**, and specifies whether or not it is initially selected.

Methods

```
public AccessibleContext getAccessibleContext()
```

Gets the **AccessibleContext** associated with this **JComponent**.

```
public String getUIClassID()
```

Returns a string that specifies the name of the L&F class that renders this component.

```
protected String paramString()
```

Returns a string representation of this **JCheckBox**.

```
public void updateUI()
```

Notification from the **UIFactory** that the L&F has changed.

◆◆**JComboBox Class** ━━━━━━━━━━━━━━━━━━━━━━

```
public class JComboBox extends JComponent implements
ItemSelectable, ListDataListener, ActionListener, Accessible
```

Swing's implementation of a ComboBox—a combination of a text field and drop-down list that lets the user either type in a value or select it from a list that is displayed when the user asks for it.

Constructors

```
public JComboBox()
```

Creates a **JComboBox** with a default data model.

```
public JComboBox(ComboBoxModel aModel)
```

Creates a **JComboBox** that takes its items from an existing **ComboBoxModel**.

```
public JComboBox(Object[] items)
```

Creates a **JComboBox** that contains the elements in the specified array.

```
public JComboBox(Vector items)
```

Creates a **JComboBox** that contains the elements in the specified **Vector**.

Methods

```
public void actionPerformed(ActionEvent e)
```

This method is **public** as an implementation side effect.

```
public void addActionListener(ActionListener l)
```

Adds an **ActionListener**.

```
public void addItem(Object anObject)
```

Adds an item to the item list.

```
public void addItemListener(ItemListener aListener)
```

Adds an **ItemListener**.

`protected  void fireActionEvent()`

Notifies all listeners that have registered interest for notification on this event type.

`protected void fireItemStateChanged(ItemEvent e)`

Notifies all listeners that have registered interest for notification on this event type.

`public Object getItemAt(int index)`

Returns the list item at the specified index.

`public int getItemCount()`

Returns the number of items in the list.

`public int getSelectedIndex()`

Returns the index of the currently selected item in the list.

`public Object getSelectedItem()`

Returns the currently selected item.

`public Object[] getSelectedObjects()`

Returns an array containing the selected item.

`public void insertItemAt(Object anObject, int index)`

Inserts an item into the item list at a given index.

`public boolean isEditable()`

Returns **true** if the **JComboBox** is editable.

`public boolean isPopupVisible()`

Determines the visibility of the pop-up.

`protected String paramString()`

Returns a string representation of this **JComboBox**.

```
public void removeActionListener(ActionListener l)
```

Removes an **ActionListener**.

```
public void removeAllItems()
```

Removes all items from the item list.

```
public void removeItem(Object anObject)
```

Removes an item from the item list.

```
public void removeItemAt(int anIndex)
```

Removes the item at **anIndex**. This method works only if the **JComboBox** uses the default data model.

```
public void removeItemListener(ItemListener aListener)
```

Removes an **ItemListener**.

```
protected void selectedItemChanged()
```

This method is called when the selected item changes.

```
public void setEditable(boolean aFlag)
```

Determines whether the **JComboBox** field is editable.

```
public void setEnabled(boolean b)
```

Enables the combo box so that items can be selected.

```
public void setSelectedIndex(int anIndex)
```

Selects the item at index **anIndex**.

```
public void setSelectedItem(Object anObject)
```

Sets the selected item in the **JComboBox** by specifying the object in the list.

◆◆JFileChooser Class

```
public class JFileChooser extends JComponent implements Accessible
```

JFileChooser provides a simple mechanism for the user to choose a file.

Constructors

```
public JFileChooser()
```

Creates a **JFileChooser** pointing to the user's home directory.

```
public JFileChooser(File currentDirectory)
```

Creates a **JFileChooser** using the given file as the path.

```
public JFileChooser(String currentDirectoryPath)
```

Creates a **JFileChooser** using the given path.

Methods

```
public boolean accept(File f)
```

Returns **true** if the file should be displayed.

```
public void addActionListener(ActionListener l)
```

Adds an **ActionListener** to the button.

```
public void addChoosableFileFilter(FileFilter filter)
```

Adds a filter to the list of user choosable file filters.

```
public void approveSelection()
```

Called by the **UI** when the user hits the approve (Open or Save) button.

```
public void cancelSelection()
```

Called by the **UI** when the user hits the cancel button.

```
public void changeToParentDirectory()
```

Changes the directory to be set to the parent of the current directory.

`protected  void fireActionPerformed(String command)`

Notifies all listeners that have registered interest for notification on this event type.

`public String getApproveButtonText()`

Returns the text used in the **ApproveButton** in the **FileChooserUI**.

`public File getCurrentDirectory()`

Returns the current directory.

`public String getDescription(File f)`

Returns the file description.

`public String getDialogTitle()`

Gets the string that goes in the **FileChooser**'s titlebar.

`public int getDialogType()`

Returns the type of this dialog.

`public String getName(File f)`

Returns the filename.

`public File getSelectedFile()`

Returns the selected file.

`public File[] getSelectedFiles()`

Returns a list of selected files if the filechooser is set to allow multi-selection.

`public String getTypeDescription(File f)`

Returns the file type.

`protected  String paramString()`

Returns a string representation of this **JFileChooser**.

```
public void removeActionListener(ActionListener l)
```

Removes an **ActionListener** from the button

```
public void setApproveButtonText(String approveButtonText)
```

Sets the text used in the **ApproveButton** in the **FileChooserUI**.

```
public void setCurrentDirectory(File dir)
```

Sets the current directory.

```
public void setDialogTitle(String dialogTitle)
```

Sets the string that goes in the **FileChooser** window's title bar.

```
public void setDialogType(int dialogType)
```

Sets the type of this dialog.

```
public void setSelectedFile(File selectedFile)
```

Sets the selected file.

```
public int showDialog(Component parent, String approveButtonText)
```

Pops up a custom file chooser dialog with a custom **ApproveButton**.

```
public int showOpenDialog(Component parent)
```

Pops up an "Open File" file chooser dialog.

```
public int showSaveDialog(Component parent)
```

Pops up a "Save File" file chooser dialog.

◆◆JLabel Class ───────────────────────────────

```
public class JLabel extends JComponent implements SwingConstants,
Accessible
```

A display area for a short text string, an image, or both.

Constructors

`public JLabel()`

Creates a **JLabel** instance with no image and with an empty string for the title.

`public JLabel(Icon image)`

Creates a **JLabel** instance with the specified image.

`public JLabel(String text)`

Creates a **JLabel** instance with the specified text.

`public JLabel(String text, Icon icon, int horizontalAlignment)`

Creates a **JLabel** instance with the specified text, image, and horizontal alignment.

Methods

`public Icon getIcon()`

Returns the graphic image (glyph, icon) that the label displays.

`public String getText()`

Returns the text string that the label displays.

`protected  String paramString()`

Returns a string representation of this **JLabel**.

`public void setIcon(Icon icon)`

Defines the icon this component will display.

`public void setLabelFor(Component c)`

Set the component this is labeling.

`public void setText(String text)`

Defines the single line of text this component will display.

◆◆ JOptionPane Class ─────────────────────────────────

```
public class JOptionPane extends JComponent implements Accessible
```

JOptionPane makes it easy to pop up a standard dialog box that prompts users for a value or informs them of something.

Constructors

```
public JOptionPane()
```

Creates a **JOptionPane** with a test message.

```
public JOptionPane(Object message)
```

Creates a instance of **JOptionPane** to display a message using the plain-message message type and the default options delivered by the **UI**.

```
public JOptionPane(Object message, int messageType, int
optionType, Icon icon, Object[] options)
```

Creates an instance of **JOptionPane** to display a message with the specified message type, icon, and options.

```
public JOptionPane(Object message, int messageType, int
optionType, Icon icon, Object[] options, Object initialValue)
```

Creates an instance of **JOptionPane** to display a message with the specified message type, icon, and options, with the inititially selected option specified.

Method summary

```
public static int showConfirmDialog(Component parentComponent,
Object message)
```

Brings up a modal dialog with the options Yes, No, and Cancel; with the title ″Select an Option″.

```
public static int showConfirmDialog(Component parentComponent,
Object message, String title, int optionType)
```

Brings up a modal dialog where the number of choices is determined by the **optionType** parameter.

```
static int showConfirmDialog(Component parentComponent, Object
message, String title, int optionType, int messageType)
```

Brings up a modal dialog where the number of choices is determined by the `optionType` parameter, where the `messageType` parameter determines the icon to display.

```
public static int showConfirmDialog(Component parentComponent,
Object message, String title, int optionType, int messageType,
Icon icon)
```

Brings up a modal dialog with a specified `icon`, where the number of choices is determined by the `optionType` parameter.

```
public static String showInputDialog(Component parentComponent,
Object message)
```

Shows a question-message dialog requesting input from the user parented to `parentComponent`.

```
public static String showInputDialog(Component parentComponent,
Object message, String title, int messageType)
```

Shows a dialog requesting input from the user parented to `parentComponent` with the dialog having the title `title` and message type `messageType`.

```
public static Object showInputDialog(Component parentComponent,
Object message, String title, int messageType, Icon icon, Object[]
selectionValues, Object initialSelectionValue)
```

Prompts the user for input in a blocking dialog where the initial selection, possible selections, and all other options can be specified.

```
public static String showInputDialog(Object message)
```

Shows a question-message dialog requesting input from the user.

```
public static void showMessageDialog(Component parentComponent,
Object message)
```

Brings up a confirmation dialog—a modal information-message dialog titled `"Confirm"`.

```
public static void showMessageDialog(Component parentComponent,
Object message, String title, int messageType)
```

Brings up a dialog that displays a message using a default icon determined by the `messageType` parameter.

```
public static void showMessageDialog(Component parentComponent,
Object message, String title, int messageType, Icon icon)
```

Brings up a dialog displaying a message, specifying all parameters.

```
public static int showOptionDialog(Component parentComponent,
Object message, String title, int optionType, int messageType,
Icon icon, Object[] options, Object initialValue)
```

Brings up a modal dialog with a specified icon, where the initial choice is determined by the `initialValue` parameter and the number of choices is determined by the `optionType` parameter.

Answers to Odd Self-Check Exercises

Chapter 1

Section 1.1

1. Microcomputer, minicomputer, mainframe, supercomputer.

Section 1.2

1. | Address | Contents |
    |---------|----------|
    | 0 | 75.625 (changed from –27.2) |
    | 2 | 0.005 |
    | 999 | 75.62 |

3. Bit, byte, floppy disk (approximately 1 megabyte), RAM (>= 64 megabytes), hard disk (>= 10 gigabytes).

5. Memory cells 6 to 8 contain instructions to add two numbers (retrieve the contents of cell 001, add the contents of cell 003, and store the result in 001).

7. | | |
    |----------|---------------|
    | ROM | permanent |
    | RAM | temporary |
    | Floppy disk | semipermanent |
    | Zip disk | semipermanent |
    | CD-ROM | permanent |
    | Hard disk | semipermanent |

9. File servers, print servers, gateways, and workstations.

11. Java is the first programming language to exploit the networked programming environment. Java programs are platform independent, which makes Java desirable for programming on the World Wide Web. You can transfer a compiled Java program (a bytecode file) from a server computer on the Web to a user's computer and execute it on the user's computer. The server and user computers can be different kinds of computers. Java also enables you to embed applets (small programs) inside a Web document (an HTML file).

Section 1.3

1. The values in memory cells a, b, and c are added and stored in the memory cell represented by x.

    The value in memory cell y is divided by the value in memory cell z, and the result is stored in the memory cell represented by x.

    The value in memory cell b is subtracted from the value in memory cell c, the value in a is added, and the result is stored in memory cell d.

    The value in the memory cell represented by z has 1 added to it and is stored in the same location.

    The value in the memory cell represented by **celsius** has 273.15 added to it, and the result is stored in the memory cell represented by **kelvin**.

3. Methods and data.

5. A class is an entity that defines the attributes of an objects; these attributes include data fields and methods. A class is the prototype for a number of objects with the same attributes.

    Objects are instances of a class. An object is an actual entity that has all the attributes described by the class definition.

    A class definition, or class, describes the properties of an abstract or hypothetical object.

    Objects are instances of the class.

Section 1.4

1. A C program is compiled specifically for the underlying machine (IBM PC, Apple Macintosh, UNIX, etc.). A compiled C program is a file consisting of machine language instructions for that machine and is ready to run. A Java program is compiled to byte code, which is platform independent. The Java

Virtual Machine (JVM) for a particular computer interprets and executes each byte code instruction.

3. A virtual machine allows cross-platform transparency by allowing many different models of computers to emulate a standard Java computer.

Section 1.5

1. Specify the problem requirements.

   Analyze the problem.

   Design the classes to solve the problem by:
   - Locating relevant classes in existing libraries.
   - Modifying existing classes where necessary.
   - Designing new classes where necessary.

   Implement the new and modified classes.

   Test and verify the completed program.

   Maintain and update the program.

3. Algorithms are developed in the Design phase. Problem inputs and outputs are identified in the Analysis phase.

5. Data fields (attributes)

   Methods (behavior)

   Algorithms for methods

Chapter 2

Section 2.1

1. Integers (type `int`), real numbers (type `double`), boolean (value `true` or `false`) (type `boolean`), characters (type `char`).

3. Valid: `15` (`int`), `'*'` (`char`), `25.123` (`double`), `15.` (`double`), `-999` (`int`), `.123` (`double`), `'x'` (`char`), `"X"` (`String`), `'9'` (`char`), `true` (`boolean`).

   Invalid: `'XYZ'`, `$`, `'-5'`, `'True'`.

5. The integer type (`int`) represents numbers, whereas the character type (`char`) represents characters.

a. `r = 3.5 + 5.0;`

   Valid; `r = 8.5`

b. `i = 2 * 5;`

   Valid; `i = 10`

c. `c = 'my name';`

   Invalid.

d. `c = "y";`

   Invalid; will result in an incompatible type error.

e. `b = boolean;`

   Invalid.

f. `r = c;`

   Invalid.

g. `c = 's';`

   Valid; char `'s'` is assigned to `c`.

h. `r = i;`

   Valid; `r = 10.0`

i. `i = r;`

   Invalid; results in compile-time error possible loss of precision.

j. `r = 10 + i;`

   Valid; `r = 20.0`

Section 2.2

1.   a. `22/7 = 3`   `7/22 = 0`   `22%7 = 1`   `7%22 = 7`

   b. `15/16 = 0` `16/15 = 1`   `15%16 = 15`   `16%15 = 1`

   c. `3/23 = 0`   `23/3 = 7`   `3%23 = 3`   `23%3 = 2`

   d. `-4/16 = 0`   `16/-4 = -4`   `-4%16 = 12`   `16%-4 = 0`

3. a. i = a % b; // 3

    b. i = (990 - maxI) / a; //-3

    c. i = a % y; // invalid

                    // y double

    d. x = pi * y; // -3.14159

    e. i = a / b;   // 0

    f. x = a / b;   // 0.0

    g. x = a % (a / b); //invalid

                        // division by 0

    h. i = b / 0;   // div by 0

    i. i = a % (990 - maxI);   // 3

    j. i = (maxI - 990) / a;   // 3

    k. x = a / y;   // -3.0

    l. i = pi * a;   // invalid - assign

                    // double to int

    m. x = pi / y;   // -3.14159

    n. x = - y * a / b;   // 0.75

    o. i = (maxI - 990) % a; // 1

    p. i = a % 0;   // invalid

                    // division by 0

    q. i = a % (maxI - 990);   // 3

5. a. x = 4.0 * a * c;

    b. a = a * c;

    c. i = 2 * -j;

    This will compile as written, but it would be clearer to write it as
    i = 2 * (-j);.

    d. k = 3 * (i + j);

    e. x = (5 * a) / (b * c);

    f. i = 5 * j * 3;

Section 2.3

1. $f(x) = x^2 + x + 1$

   $f(5) = 5^2 + 5 + 1 = 25 + 5 + 1 = 31$

   $f(7) = 7^2 + 7 + 1 = 49 + 7 + 1 = 57$

3. Class methods belong to the class rather than to individual class instances (objects) and therefore are not applied to an object. We also use dot notation to call class methods, but we prefix the method name with the class name instead of an object name:

   `ClassName.methodName(arguments)`

   Instance methods belong to an object instance and are applied to an object. The following is the form used to call instance methods:

   `objectName.methodName(arguments)`

Section 2.4

1. a. `"value of x is 35"`

   b. `"value of x is 57"`

   c. `"value of x is 12"`

   d. `T`

3. a. `word2 = word1.substring(0, 5);`

   b. `word2 =  "A" + word1.substring(2, 5) + "Z";`

   c. `word2 = word1.substring(4);`

   d. `word2 = word1.substring(word1.length() / 2);`

Section 2.5

1.

a.
```
String str2 = JOptionPane.showInputDialog("Enter your age");
double n = Double.parseDouble(str2);
```
b.
```
String str3 = JOptionPane.showInputDialog("Enter your choice");
char choice = str3.charAt(0);
```
c.
```
String str = JOptionPane.showInputDialog("Enter your name");
```
d.
```
String str2 = JOptionPane.showInputDialog("What is your salary?");
double x = Double.parseDouble(str2);
```

3.
```
String message = "Hi, I am " + name + " and" +
                 "\n my address is " + address +
                 "\n My age is  " + age +
                 "  but I feel much older today ";
JOptionPane.showMessageDialog(null, message);
```

Section 2.6

1.

```
word =     "Love";
pigLatin = "oveLay";
message =  "Love is oveLay in pig Latin\n";
```

```
word =     "Java";
pigLatin = "avaJay";
message =  "Love is oveLay in pig Latin\n Java is avaJay in pig Latin";
```

Section 2.7

1. Reserved words are words that have some special meaning to the Java compiler and that you are not allowed to use as identifier names.

3. a. `new, private, extends, static`

b. `Bill, program, Rate, Start, XYZ_123, ThisIsALongOne`

c. `Sue's, 123_XYZ,  Y=Z, Prog#2, 'MaxScores'`

5. It is not necessary to comment each and every line of the program because some part of the program could be easily understood without a comment. Overuse of comments could lead to a cluttered program that is hard to read.

Section 2.8

1. a. `u + v * Math.pow(w , 2)` or `u + v * w * w`

   b. `Math.log(Math.pow(x, y))`

   c. `Math.pow((x-y) , 3)`

   d. `Math.abs( x * y -  w / z)`

Section 2.9

1. a. Syntax—need quotes around `amy`.
   b. Logical—need parentheses around `x + y`.

   c. Run-time—division by 0.

   d. Syntax—`message` declared twice.

   e. Syntax—`println()` not defined in `JOptionPane`.

   f. Syntax—`showInputDialog()` returns string that can't be assigned to `int`.

   g. Syntax—missing first argument `null`.

   h. Syntax—comma should be `+`.

   i. Syntax—missing quote.

   j. Syntax—`x + y` is not a variable.

   k. Run-time—`"2.5"` cannot be converted to type `int`.

Chapter 3

Section 3.1

1. a. Result is `"Snickers, size: 6.5, price $ 0.55"`
   b. Result is `0.55`.

   c. Result is `0.084615`.

   d. The price for Snickers will change from 0.55 to 0.5.

Section 3.2

1. showInputDialog()—Reads "This is a sentence with 7 words." into sent.

   WordExtractor()—Creates wordExtractor object wE1 and stores the input sentence in data field sentence.

   getFirst()—Gets the first word (This).

   println()—Displays first word: This.

   getRest()—Returns a reference to a string containing is a sentence with 7 words.

   WordExtractor()—Creates wordExtractor object wE2 and stores is a sentence with 7 words. in data field sentence.

   getFirst()—Gets the second word is.

   println()—Displays second word: is.

   getRest()—Returns a reference to a string containing a sentence with 7 words.

   WordExtractor()—Creates wordExtractor object wE2 and stores a sentence with 7 words. in data field sentence.

   getFirst()—Gets the third word a.

   println()—Displays third word: a.

Section 3.3

1. CoinChanger()—Creates a new CoinChanger object cC.

   ShowInputDialog()—reads in the string "200".

   parseInt()—converts "200" to 200.

   setPennies()—sets pennies in cC to 200.

   ShowInputDialog()—reads in the string "30".

   parseInt()—converts "30" to 30.

   setNickels()—sets nickels in cC to 30.

   . . .

   setDimes()—sets dimes in cC to 5.

   . . .

setQuarters()—sets **quarters** in **cC** to 8.

toString()—places 200 pennies, 30 nickels, 5 dimes, 8 quarters in **message**.

findDollars()—places 6 in **message**.

findChange()—places 0 in **message**.

showMessageDialog()—displays 200 pennies, 30 nickels, 5 dimes, 8 quarters.

Coin collection value is $6.0.

Section 3.4

1. An accessor is a method that returns the value of an object's data field.

3.

Data Fields	Attributes
int height	Height of the box
int width	Width of the box
int length	Length of the box

Methods	Behavior
Box()	Creates a box with zero lengths for all sides
Box(int)	Creates a cube with side length specified by its argument
Box(int, int)	Creates a box with width and length specified by its first argument and height specified by its third argument
Box(int, int, int)	Creates a box—height is first argument, width is second argument, length is third argument.
void setWidth()	Sets the width
void setLength()	Sets the length
void setHeight()	Sets the height
int getWidth()	Gets the width
int getLength()	Gets the length
int getHeight()	Gets the height
int computeSurfArea()	Calculates the surface area
int computeVolume()	Calculates the volume
String toString()	Represents the box as a string

7. If data fields are declared public, it is true that accessors and mutators are not needed. But these data fields then become subject to accidental modification by other classes. If you are writing long, complicated programs or working with other programmers, this is a risk you won't want to take.

9. You may want to force classes to establish initial values for data fields when they establish a new instance of your class. By not providing a default constructor, you force other classes to use one of your constructors with arguments.

Section 3.5

1. They are used to read and return a type **double** data value (**readDouble()**) and a type **int** data value (**readInt()**). The modifier **static** is needed because these methods are class methods. They do not require an instance of class **WasherApp** to be called. One could call them by prefixing the class name as in

    ```
    WasherApp.readDouble(promptString)
    ```

Section 3.6

1. a. Displays a dialog window with prompt **Enter your age:**. The type **int** data entered must lie between **21** and **100** inclusive, and is stored in **n**.

    b. The character entered must be between letter **a** to letter **e**, and is stored in **ch**.

    c. Displays a prompt to enter your name and stores it in string **s**.

    d. Displays a dialog window to enter your salary and stores the **double** data item entered by the user in the variable **x**.

Section 3.7

1. Because on most computer screens the height (*y* value) is smaller than the width (*x* value).

3. It represents an instance of the **Graphics** class (the graphics context or drawing surface passed by the browser or applet viewer) so that we may call the methods of the **Graphics** class.

5. `g.drawRect(150, 250, 50, 50);`

   `g.drawRect(400, 250, 50, 50);`

7. Method `setColor()` sets the drawing color. It is in effect until changed by another call to that method.

Chapter 4

Section 4.2

1. a. `true`
    b. `false`
    c. `true`
    d. `true`

3. a. `true`.
    b. `false || true` is `true`.
    c. `true || true` is `true`.
    d. `false and false` is `false`.
    e. `!(false or false)` is `true`.

5. a. `true`
    b. `true`
    c. `false`
    d. `false`
    e. `true`
    f. a positive number
    g. a negative number
    h. `false`
    i. `true`

Section 4.3

1. **a.** `Not less`

   b. `>`

3. **a.** `Hi Kiddo`

     `How was your day?`

   b. `Hi Kiddo`

5. The `if` clause will consist of only one statement (`x = x + 10.0;`). The `if` statement is completed, and the word `else` will cause a syntax error: `statement cannot begin with else`.

7. It stores the product of three numbers in `product` if `add` is `false` (`!add` is `true`) and stores the sum of three numbers in `sum` if `add` is `true`.

```
if (add) {
    sum = num1 + num2 + num3;
    System.out.println("sum is " + sum);
}
else {
    product = num1 * num2 * num3;
    System.out.println("product is " + product);
}
```

Section 4.4

1. net pay = gross pay

   If union dues are required

      subtract union dues from net pay

3. If `gross` were declared as a data field of the `Employee` class, there would be no guarantee that it would be assigned a value by `computeGross()` before another class method referenced it. For example, if `computeNet()` were called before `computeGross()`, the value of `gross` used by `computeNet()` wouldn't have been properly assigned. The way the program example has been written guarantees that `gross` will have been assigned the proper value before other methods can access it.

Section 4.5

1. Condition (**salary** <= **15000.00**) is the first **true** condition:

   tax = (13500.00 − 8000.00) * 0.25 + 1425.00

   = 2800

Section 4.6

1. The loop is repeated three times. It displays

   ```
   9
   81
   6561
   6561  after loop exit
   ```

3. If you omitted the last statement in loop header, it will loop forever because **count** is no longer increased and remains at 0.

5. If we enter **x** = 5 and **y** = 3, the fragment displays **result** = **125**.

   It calculates **x** raised to the power **y**.

Section 4.7

1. Assuming the sentinel score of −1 is entered after 80:

   After reading and adding first score: **score** is 50, **sum** is 50, **count** is 1.

   After reading and adding second score: **score** is 70, **sum** is 120, **count** is 1.

   After reading and adding second score: **score** is 80, **sum** is 200, **count** is 2.

Section 4.10

1.
   ```
   for (int count = 0; count <= n; count++) {
       System.out.println("**** " + count);
       sum  += count;
       System.out.println("**** " + sum);
   }
   ```

Chapter 5

Section 5.1

1.  ```
    double y;
    double x3;
    double[] x = new double[4];   // or > 4
    ```

3.

a. ```
    double[] roomSize = new double[numRooms];
    ```

b. ```
    int[] numStudent = new int[5];
    ```

c.  ```
    char[] color = new char[30];
    ```

d. ```
    Color[] javaColors = new Color[30];
    ```

e.  ```
    String[] daysOfWeek = {"Sunday", "Monday", "Tuesday",
              "Wednesday", "Thursday", "Friday", "Saturday"};
    ```

f. ```
    String[] family = {"Mom", "Dad", "Micky", "Vandana"};
    ```

## Section 5.2

1.

```
x [i] = x [i] + 10.0; // adds 10.0 to x[3],
                      // new value is 36.0
x[i - 1] = x[2 * i - 1]; // change the value of x[2] to 12.0
x[i + 1] = x[2 * i] + x[2 * i + 1]; // change x[4] to -40.5
for (i = 5; i < 7; i++)
    x[i] = x[i + 1]; // copies x[6] ... x[7] into x[5] ... x[6]
for ( i = 3; i >= 1; i --)
    x[i + 1] = x[i]; // copies x[3] ... x[1] into x[4] ... x[2]
```

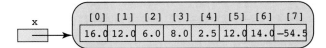
```

Section 5.3

1. First statement declares array **x** with values shown. Second statement declares array **y**, which initially stores 10 zeros. Third statement declares array **z**, which initially stores 10 zeros. Fourth statement copies first 5 elements of **x** into last 5 of **y**. Fifth statement copies last 5 elements of x into the first 5 of **y**. Last statement stores element-by-element sum of arrays **x** and **y** in array **z**. **x** is unchanged.

```
int[] y = {6, 7, 8, 9, 10, 1, 2, 3, 4, 5};
int[] z = {7, 9, 11, 13, 15, 7, 9, 11, 13, 15};
```

Section 5.4

1.   **a.** It will return the index of the last score, which is the first one to match the target.

   b. It will return the index of the first score that matches the target.

3. Finding the median should not change the original array. We sorted the copy, not the original.

5. The subscript(s) of the elements in array **copyX** are 2 and 3.

   If the array has five elements, the subscript will be 2, and if it has seven elements, it will be 3.

Section 5.5

1.

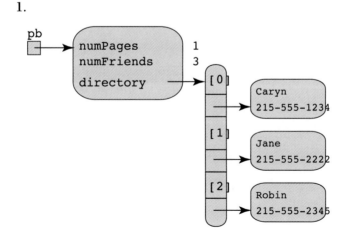

Section 5.6

1.   a. 20

b. `salesByQuarter[2][3]`

c. `salesByQuarter[4][3]`

Section 5.7

1. The method call **toString()** is not required in the call to **println()**. It is automatically called when the argument of **println()** is an object.

```
for (int i = 0; i <  employees.size(); i++)
   System.out.println( ((Employee) employees.elementAt(i)).toString());
```

Without using a loop, using the **Vector** class **toString()** method:

```
employees.toString();
```

3. Vector **v** stores **Employee** objects.

```
v.setElementAt(empC, 1);
v.insertElementAt(empB, 2);
Employee anEmp = (Employee) v.elementAt(v.size() / 2 );
                                            //Get middle emp.
v.removeElement(vsize() / 2);
v.addElement(anEmp); // Insert it at end.
```

Section 5.8

1.  ```
Integer i = new Integer(6);
Character c = new Character('z');
Double d = new Double(5.35);
```
```

3.

```
Vector nums = new Vector(); // nums is an empty vector
nums.addElement(new Integer("30")); // Integer object with value 30
                                    //   is added to nums (index 0)
nums.addElement(new Double(5.5)); // double object is added to nums
                                  //     (index 1)
double mystery = ((Integer) nums.elementAt(0)).intValue() +
                 ((Double) nums.elementAt(1)).doubleValue();
// the values stored in the integer object and double object are
//   added and the sum (35.5) is stored in variable mystery.
nums.removeElementAt(0); // the Integer object is removed from nums
                         //   and the Double object is moved up.
nums.removeElementAt(1); // index-out-of bounds exception - only 1
                         //   element in vector
```

Section 5.9

1.

```
for (int i = 0; i < employees.size(); i++)
   System.out.println(((Employee) employees.get(i)).toString());
```

A single statement that accomplishes this without using a loop:

```
System.out.println(employees.toString());
```

3.

```
employees.set(1, empc);
employees.add(2,  empB);
Employee oEmployee = (Employee) employees.remove(employees.size()/2) ;
employees.add(oEmployee);
```

Chapter 6

Section 6.1

1. This assignment would cause a compile-time error because these are incompatible data types. After the assignment, the variable of class **HourlyEmployee** would reference an instance of the class **SalaryEmployee**. This is not allowed because we should be able to access all the data fields and methods of class **HourlyEmployee** through its variable, including **hours** and **rate**. However, these data fields are not defined in class **SalaryEmployee**.

And methods like `setHours()`, `getHours()` cannot be used because after the assignment, the variable of class `HourlyEmployee` references an object of class `SalaryEmployee`. This is why such assignment is not permitted and leads to an incompatible types syntax error.

3. a. `System.out.println(spouseOfBoss.name());`

    Invalid; `name()` is not a method of class `NewEmployee`.

    b. `String myName = spouseOfBoss.getName();`

    Stores the string returned by the method `getName()` in the variable `myName`.

    c. `clerk = supervisor;`

    Invalid; incompatible types.

    d. `supervisor.setName(clerk.getName());`

    Sets the data field `name` for object `supervisor` with the string returned by object `clerk`'s method `getName()`.

    e. `double pay = supervisor.calcWeeklyPay();`

    `calcWeeklyPay()` is called and the `double` value returned is stored in variable `pay`.

    f. `System.out.println("Weekly pay of " + clerk.getName()`
       `+ " is $" + clerk.calcWeeklyPay());`

    Displays the string returned by the method call `clerk.getName()` and the `double` value returned by the method call `clerk.calcWeeklyPay()`.

    g. `supervisor.setAnnualSalary(1.2 * 2080 *`
       `clerk.getRate());`

    Calls the `clerk`'s method `getRate()`, and the value returned is multiplied with other values and passed to the `supervisor`'s method `setAnnualSalary()`.

    h. `System.out.println("Hourly rate is $" +`
       `supervisor.getRate());`

    Invalid; method `getRate()` is not defined in class `SalaryEmployee`.

    i. `clerk.updateTotalPay(clerk.calcWeeklyPay());`

    Updates the `totalPay` of `clerk`.

j. `clerk.updateTotalPay(supervisor.calcWeeklyPay());`

The value returned by the method `calcWeeklyPay()` of the `SalaryEmployee` class is passed to method `updateTotalPay()` of the `HourlyEmployee` class.

k. `clerk.updateTotalPay(spouseOfBoss.calcWeeklyPay());`

Invalid; `calcWeeklyPay()` is not a method of class `NewEmployee`.

5. **a.** `this.name = name;`

`this` is required. Sets the data field `name` to the string referenced by `name` (a local variable or parameter).

b. `super("Sam", "3456");`

Calls constructor for `NewEmployee` with two parameters. Must be the first statement in a constructor. `super` is required.

c. `String res = super.toString() + this.toString();`

Calls the `toString()` method for `NewEmployee` and then the `toString()` method for `SalaryEmployee`. Only `super` is required.

d. `this("Sam", "3456");`

Calls the constructor for `SalaryEmployee` with two parameters. Must be the first statement in a constructor. `this` is required.

e. `this.annualSalary = super.totalPay;`

Assigns the value of `totalPay` to `annualSalary`. `this` and `super` are not required. `totalPay` should have protected visibility.

f. `this.annualSalary = super.getTotalPay();`

Assigns the value returned by the method `getTotalPay()` to `annualSalary`. `this` and `super` are not required.

Section 6.2

1. If this assignment took place, the variable of type `HourlyEmployee` would reference an instance of its superclass (`NewEmployee`). This is not allowed because we should be able to access all data fields and methods of class `HourlyEmployee`, which are not found in class `NewEmployee`. This would lead to an incompatible type error.

Yes. However, after the assignment, we will not be able to access the variables and methods of class `HourlyEmployee` through the `NewEmployee` object.

3.   a. `NewEmployee anEmp = new SalaryEmployee("Jane", "1234");`

   Valid; the object of type `SalaryEmployee` is assigned to variable `anEmp`.

   b. `SalaryEmployee salEmp = (SalaryEmployee) anEmp;`

   Valid; `salEmp` references the object of type `SalaryEmployee` referenced by `anEmp`.

   c. `System.out.println(anEmp instanceof NewEmployee);`

   Displays `true` because `anEmp` is of type `NewEmployee`.

   d. `System.out.println(anEmp instanceof HourlyEmployee);`

   Displays `false` because `anEmp` is not an instance of `HourlyEmployee`.

   e. `System.out.println(anEmp instanceof SalaryEmployee);`

   Displays `true` because the object referenced by `anEmp` is an instance of type `SalaryEmployee`.

   f. `((SalaryEmployee) anEmp).setAnnualSalary(25000.00);`

   Valid; `anEmp` is type cast to `SalaryEmployee` and the method `setAnnualSalary()` for class `SalaryEmployee` is called.

   g. `HourlyEmployee hourEmp = anEmp;`

   Invalid; incompatible types; compile-time error.

   h. `hourEmp = (HourlyEmployee) anEmp;`

   Invalid; `ClassCastException` occurs at run-time. Variable `anEmp` cannot be cast to type `HourlyEmployee`.

   i. `((HourlyEmployee) anEmp).setHours(50.0);`

   Invalid; `ClassCastException` occurs at run-time.

Section 6.3

1.   Compile-time. The compiler knows what kind of object `calcWeeklyPay()` is being applied to because the cast operation occurs before the call. There is only one `updateTotalPay()` method (defined in class `NewEmployee`).

3.   `emp.calcWeeklyPay()` will not compile because `emp` is type `NewEmployee` and there is no `calcWeeklyPay()` method in this class.

Section 6.4

1. `employees[0]`
   name: Sam, social security: 1234, job: clerk
   address: null, phone: null, age: 30, year started: 2000, total pay 15600.0
   weekly hours: 40.0, hourly rate 15.0

   `employees[1]`
   name: Jessica, social security: 2222, job: manager
   address: , phone: , age: 33, year started: 1998, total pay 41000.0
   annual salary 52000.0

   `employees[2]`
   name: George, social security: 3456, job: spouse of boss
   address: , phone: , age: 55, year started: 1990, total pay 0.0

Section 6.5

1. An abstract class is abstract because it cannot be instantiated. Its sole purpose is to serve as the parent of a group of classes, and it gives us a convenient place to declare all data fields and methods common to its subclasses. You can declare data fields, methods, and abstract methods in an abstract class.

Section 6.6

1.

`DrawableCircle`

Methods	Behavior
`DrawableCircle()`	No-parameter constructor—sets a new object's data fields to default values
`DrawableCircle(int, Point, Color, Color)`	Four-parameter constructor—sets a new object's data fields (`radius`, `pos`, `borderColor`, `interiorColor`) as specified by its arguments
`void drawMe(Graphics)`	Draws a circle object inside a square with top-left corner at `pos` and with colors specified by its data fields
`String toString()`	Represents attributes of a `DrawableCircle` object as a string

`DrawableTriangle`

Methods	Behavior
`DrawableTriangle()`	No-parameter constructor—sets a new object's data fields to default values
`DrawableTriangle(int, int, Point, Color, Color)`	Five-parameter constructor—sets a new object's data fields (`base`, `height`, `pos`, `borderColor`, `interiorColor`) as specified by its arguments
`void drawMe(Graphics)`	Draws a right-triangle object with right-angle at `pos` and with colors specified by its data fields
`String toString()`	Represents attributes of a `DrawableTriangle` object as a string

Section 6.8

1. Black-box testing
   - No information about the code.
   - Tester has to verify the method or system.
   - Tester must prepare sufficient sets of test data.
   - Black-box testing is often done by special testing team or by program users.

   White-box testing
   - Full knowledge of the code.
   - Each section of code must be thoroughly tested.
   - Tester much check all the possible paths through selection statements.
   - Tester should take special care at boundary values.
   - Tester should make sure that loops perform the correct number of iterations.

3. Stub—a substitute for a method that is not yet written consisting of a heading followed by a minimal body, which should display a message identifying the method being executed and return a simple value. The overall flow of control and other methods that are complete can be tested and debugged if stubs are used for incomplete methods.

   Driver—a small main method that contains only the declarations and executable statements necessary to test a single method. A driver should create a test object, apply the methods being tested to the object, and display the results.

Chapter 7

Section 7.1

1. `init()`: Initializes the applet. One usually overrides this method when defining an applet.

   `start()`: Makes the applet "active," that is, it starts the applet running.

   `stop()`: Makes the applet "inactive," that is, it stops the applet.

   `destroy()`: Destroys the applet so that is resources can be recycled.

3. A component that relies on a corresponding component in the platform's operating system to draw itself is called a peer component.

   A component that uses a pure Java method to draw itself is called a lightweight component.

   Peer components are used by the AWT, and `Swing` uses lightweight components.

Section 7.2

1. A containment hierarchy is a hierarchical structure that shows the main container used, along with the components it contains.

3. You cannot add components directly to an applet. You use an intermediate container called the applet's content pane, which is accessed by calling method `getContentPane()`. You need to call it before adding a component to the applet (add to the content pane) or before creating a layout manager object (create a layout manager for the content pane).

Section 7.3

1. An event generator is an object that initiates an event. An event listener is an object that listens for and then responds to events.

   A button is an event generator.

   An applet is an event listener.

3. The applet (specified by `this`) is registered as a listener for action events generated by `aText`. An action event is generated if the user presses the Enter key when the cursor is in the text field.

5. If there is no action listener registered for that button, there will be no response to that event.

Section 7.4

1. **JApplet** and **JFrame** are both top-level containers for swing components. You extend **JApplet** when writing an applet. You extend **JFrame** when writing an application.

Section 7.5

1. Only one button in a button group can be on. Only one of the listed items can be selected using a combo box.

3. The check boxes and combo box had registered listeners for item events.

    The Radio button registered had registered listeners for action events.

Section 7.6

1. After the phone number for Aaron McKie is successfully changed, the following is displayed in text area **instruct**:

    ```
    Entry changed to: Aaron McKie, 215-555-3256

    Choose another operation above
    ```

    To change a number, select **changeRB** and press the Submit button. Control is passed to the **actionPerformed( )** method. The statement

    ```
    Object but = e.getSource( );
    ```

    sets **but** to reference the event generator (button **changeRB**). All the **if** conditions fail except the last one (**but   ==   submit   &&   changeRB.isSelected( )**).

    The name and number are retrieved from the **JTextField** objects and stored in the variables **name** and **number**.

    ```
    name = nameText.getText( );
    number = numberText.getText( );
    ```

A new object of type `friend` is created with the values from `name` and `number`:

```
aFriend = new Friend(name, number);
```

The index of the name is obtained by searching the phone book:

```
int index = myPhoneBook.findFriend(name);
```

Because the index is not −1, store the new object created in that index and display the message shown at the beginning:

```
if (index > -1) {
    myPhoneBook.setFriend(index, aFriend);
    instruct.setText("Entry changed to: " + aFriend +
                     "\nChoose another operation above" );
}
```

Set the information in text fields `nameText` and `numberText` to `""`:

```
nameText.setText("");
numberText.setText("");
```

Give the focus to `nameText`, and reset the combo box selection to the one at index 0:

```
nameText.requestFocus();
nameList.setSelectedIndex(0);
```

3. When the radio button `change  number` is selected, the following is displayed in text area `instruct`:

```
Select name or enter name.
Enter new number and press submit
```

Section 7.7

1. ```
   public class PhoneBookGUI extends JApplet
                               implements ActionListener {
   ```
   ```

The statement in method `init()` that registers the listener for the combo box:

```
ComboListener cBL = new ComboListener();
nameList.addItemListener(cBL);
```

Section 7.8

1. **BorderLayout**: Arranges objects in five areas of the container: North, West, Center, East, and South.

   BoxLayout: Arranges objects in a single row or column.

   FlowLayout: Arranges objects in left-to-right order across the container, flowing down to the next row when a row is filled.

   GridLayout: Arranges objects in a two-dimensional grid.

3. The advantage of layout managers is that they free the programmer from having to manage the low-level details of placing components in a user interface; these decisions and operations are carried out by the layout manager's methods.

Chapter 8

Section 8.1

1. No, we cannot reverse the order of the **catch** blocks in Fig. 8.5 because only the first **catch** block that will handle a particular exception type executes, so the most specific exception type should come first. In Fig. 8.5, **NumberFormatException** is the most specific exception type.

3. Assuming the characters **test** are entered instead of a number, the statement that performs the division is at line 14 (in method **getDepend()**) and the statement that calls method **getDepend()** is at line 23 (in method **main()**).

```
java.lang.NumberFormatException: test
        at java.lang.Integer.parseInt(Compiled code)
        at java.lang.Integer.parseInt(Integer.java:458)
        at
PropagateException.PropagateException.getDepend(PropagateException.java:14)
        at
PropagateException.PropagateException.main(PropagateException.java:23)
```

5. The **throws** declaration comes at the end of a method header, and it tells the Java compiler that the method may throw an exception of the type(s) listed. The **throw** statement is used to raise an exception by creating a new exception object of the type specified. The programmer does this instead of executing a particular statement that would cause an exception to occur. One advantage of a **throw** statement is that we can specify a descriptive error message for this particular exception, rather than using the default that would be provided by Java.

Section 8.2

1. We wrap one stream object inside another so that we can apply the more user-friendly methods defined in the wrapper class rather than the more primitive methods defined in the original stream class.

3. The **close()** operation closes the connection between the output stream and your program. It ensures that all information written to the output file is actually saved in the output file. If you don't close an output stream, all the information written may not be copied to the associated disk file.

Section 8.3

1. This will ensure that data is present for the first title to be read in **readDVDFile()**. Again at the end of the **while** loop we read the title of the next DVD, and we repeat the loop if the title is available.

3. A **FileNotFoundException** would be raised.

Section 8.4

1. When the user presses **Cancel** in the open file or save file dialog window, the dialog window is closed and method **actionPerformed()** displays a **File open cancelled** or **File save cancelled** method.

3. We don't need a listener for **catChooser** events because there is no program action that should occur as a result of making a category selection. Method **itemStateChanged()** is called when the user selects an operation. Method call **catChooser.getSelected()** and method call **catChooser.setSelected()** are used to get and set the category as needed in **itemStateChanged()**.

Section 8.5

1. Each data field is written as a sequence of characters to a text file. In a binary file, binary images are read and written to disk. Therefore, binary files are more efficient in terms of processing time and space utilization than are text files. Text files can be created using a text editor and can be read by humans because they are sequences of characters.

   A binary file cannot be created using a text editor. Also binary files cannot be read by humans. Therefore binary files are more useful for storing information between successive runs of a program.

3. To read and write all of an object's data fields as a single entity in a binary file, we can use `writeObject()` and `readObject()`, which are methods provided in classes `ObjectInputStream` and `ObjectOutputStream`.

Chapter 9

Section 9.1

1. Calculate 5^4 ⟶ Calculate 5^3 ⟶ Calculate 5^2 ⟶ Calculate 5^1

   Multiply 5^3 by 5 ⟶ Multiply 5^2 by 5 ⟶ Multiply 5^1 by 5

3. 4

   3

   2

   2

   3

   4

Section 9.2

1. Method `puzzle()` computes the log (base 2) of n or the number of times n can be divided by 2. When n is 2, the result is 1.

3.
```
public static double powerRaiser(int base,
                                 int power) {
    if (base == 0)
        return 0;
    else if (power == 0)
        return 1;
    else if (power < 0)
        return 1.0 /
            (double) powerRaiser(base, -power);
    else
        return power *
                powerRaiser(base, power - 1);
}
```

Section 9.3

1. Stack after first recursive call: |q.

   Stack after second recursive call: |qw.

   Stack after third recursive call: |qwe.

   Stack after fourth recursive call: |qwer.

   Stack after fifth recursive call: |qwer*.

   Stack after first return: |qwer, so r is popped and displayed.

   Stack after second return: |qwe, so e is popped and displayed.

   Stack after third return: |qw, so w is popped and displayed.

   Stack after fourth return: |q, so q is popped and displayed.

3. Change the if statement as follows:

```
if (next == '*')
    System.out.print(next);
else {
    reverse();
    System.out.print(next);
}
```

Section 9.4

1. `int[] x = {1, 15, 10}; int[] y = {1, 5, 7};`

   `isEqual(x, y, 3)`—returns `false` from the initial call, `x[2] != y[2]` is `true`.

3. It returns the smallest value in elements 0 through $n - 1$ of its array argument.

5. `reverseStr("tick")`—generates the following sequence of recursive calls: `'k' + (reverseStr("tic"))` →
   `'k' + ('c' + reverseStr("ti"))` →
   `'k' + ('c' + ('i' + reverseStr("t")))` →
   `'k' + ('c' + ('i' + 't')))`. The resulting string is: `"kcit"`.

Section 9.5

1. `binSearch(table, 40, 0, 8)`, middle value is `45` →
   `binsearch(table, 40, 0, 3)`, middle value is `35` →
   `binsearch(table, 40, 2, 3)`, middle value is `37` →
   `binsearch(table, 40, 3, 3)`, middle value is `40`, so method call returns `3`, which is passed all the way up.

Section 9.6

1. Problems generated from "Move three disks from peg B to peg A":

   1. Move two disks from peg B to peg C.

      1.1   Move 1 disk from B to A.

      1.2   Move disk 2 from B to C.

      1.3   Move 1 disk from A to C.

   2. Move disk 3 from B to A.

3. Move two disks from peg C to peg A.

    3.1 Move 1 disk from C to B.

    3.2 Move disk 2 from C to A.

    3.3 Move 1 disk from B to A.

Problems generated from "Move three disks from peg A to peg C":

1. Move two disks from peg A to peg B.

    1.1 Move 1 disk from A to C.

    1.2 Move disk 2 from A to B.

    1.3 Move 1 disk from C to B.

2. Move disk 3 from A to C.

3. Move two disks from peg B to peg C.

    3.1 Move 1 disk from B to A.

    3.2 Move disk 2 from B to C.

    3.3 Move 1 disk from A to C.

Section 9.7

1. The button at grid point [1, 1] is filled, so we generate calls to `findBlob()` for each of its eight neighbors. Four of them are filled: [0, 0], [0, 1], [1, 2], and [2, 2]. In visiting each filled cell, we come across no other cells that are filled, so the final answer will be 5.

    The button at grid point [2, 1] is empty, so we return 0.

Chapter 10

Section 10.1

1. a. Deletes node containing `"top"`.

    b. Deletes two middle nodes. List contains `"in"`, `"hat"`.

    c. Head references node containing `"top"`.

    d. Node referenced by `p` contains `"top"`, not `"the"`.

    e. Node referenced by `p` contains `"hat"`, not `"the"`.

    f. Appends a new node with `"zzz"` to the end of the list.

g. Stores **null** in the link field of the node referenced by **p**. List now has just two nodes.

h. Stores **"hat"** in the node referenced by **p**.

i. Deletes the last list element.

j. Counts the number of nodes (4) in the list.

3. In object **1L,** data field **head** references the node whose **info** field is **"us"** (the first list node). This node references one whose **info** field is **"them"** (the second list node), which references one whose **info** field is **"you"** (the third list node), which references one whose **info** field is **"you"** (the last list node). This method displays the line

```
us, you
```

Section 10.2

1. Method **pop( )** retrieves the value at the top of the stack and removes it from the stack, whereas method **peek( )** just retrieves the value at the top of the stack without removing it.

3. Add a data field:

```
private int numItems;
```

Method **push( )** should increment **numItems** by 1, and method **pop( )** should decrement **numItems** by 1. There should be an accessor for field **numItems**.

Section 10.3

1. After insertion, queue contents is **McMann, Wilson, Carson, Harris**; **first** references **McMann** and **rear** references **Harris**. After removal (of **McMann**), queue contents is **Wilson, Carson, Harris**; **first** references **Wilson** and **rear** references **Harris**. There are three customers in the queue.

3.
```
public void insert(Object item) {
    if (isEmpty()) { //empty queue
        // Link rear and front to only node.
        front = new QueueNode(item);
        rear = front;
    } else // insert at front of a non-empty queue
```

```
                    front = new QueueNode(item, front);

            size++;                         //Increment queue size.
        }
```

Section 10.4

1. The tree on the left is a binary search tree, the tree on the right is not. In-order traversal of left tree: 10, 15, 20, 40, 50, 55, 60. In-order traversal of right tree: 25, 30, 45, 40, 50, 55, 60.

   You would expect to find key values less than 50 in the left subtree of the node containing key 50.

3.

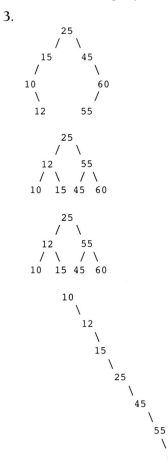

```
        25
       /  \
     15    45
    /        \
  10          60
    \         /
     12     55
```

```
         25
        /  \
      12    55
     / \   / \
   10  15 45  60
```

```
         25
        /  \
      12    55
     / \   / \
   10  15 45  60
```

```
      10
        \
         12
           \
            15
              \
               25
                 \
                  45
                    \
                     55
                       \
                        60
```

Trees (b) and (c) would be most efficient to search because they are full binary trees (no holes). Searching these trees is an O(log*n*) process. Each node in the tree in (d) has an empty left subtree. Searching it would be an O(*n*) process, the same as for a linked list.

Section 10.5

1. Each method call would insert its string argument in the tree, except for the second attempt to insert string `"cat"`.

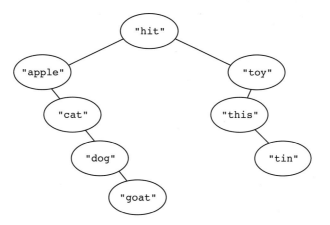

    Displays the strings: `"apple"`, `"cat"`, `"dog"`, `"goat"`, `"hit"`, `"this"`, `"tin"`, `"toy"`, on separate lines.

3. The first case is deleting a node with no subtrees—just delete the node. The second case is deleting a node with only one subtree—the link from the parent node to the node being deleted should be changed to connect the parent node to the subtree of the node being deleted. The third case is deleting a node with two subtrees—overwrite the key in the node to be deleted with the value in the leftmost node of the right subtree and delete that node instead.

Section 10.6

1. First statement creates a new, empty list.

   Second statement inserts `"hello"`.

   Second statement inserts `"good"` after `"hello"`.

   Third statement removes `"good"`.

   Fourth statement inserts `"more"` after `"hello"`.

   Fifth statement changes node with `"more"` to store `"greetings"`.

   The loop changes each node to store its contents joined to its contents.

   The list contains `"hellohello"` in the first node and `"greetingsgreetings"` in the second node. Variable **count** is incremented each time we process a node and finishes with a value of 2.

   We display the line:

   ```
   [hellohello, greetingsgreetings], 2
   ```

Index

A

`abs()`, 87
abstract classes, 404, 414, 421
abstract method, 396
Abstract Window Toolkit, 157, 440
`AbstractButton`, 443
abstraction, 22, 359
accessors, 109, 135
accumulate a sum, 231
accumulator, 231
`ActionEvent`, 457
`ActionListener`, 456
`actionPerformed()`, 456, 469, 479, 486, 519, 555
activation frame, 581
`add()`, 451, 666, 667, 668
`addActionListener()`, 455, 475
`addElement()`, 332
`addFirst()`, 666
`addItem()`, 472
`addLast()`, 666
`addPoly()`, 417
address, 5
`addWindowListener()`, 463, 464
algebra, 45
algorithm simplification, 311
algorithm, 23
allocate storage, 273
Altair, 3

alternatives, 197
analog signals, 10
analyze a problem, 21
ancestor, 650
anonymous, 384
apostrophes, 93
Apple, 3
applet viewer, 157, 444
`Applet`, 157, 442, 443, 444, 489
applet, 11, 20, 21, 158, 444
application class, 22, 74
application software, 14
application, 14, 20, 461
`APPROVE_OPTION`, 553
`args`, 78, 307
argument correspondence, 293
argument list, 114
argument, 53, 114, 117, 385
argument/parameter correspondence, 114
arithmetic drill and practice, 243
arithmetic overflow, 95
`ArithmeticDrill`, 89
`ArithmeticException`, 510, 516, 517
array, 271-328
array arguments, 293
array assignment, 292
array declarations, 272, 273
array elements, 272, 279
array file, 565

S

scientific notation, 38
scope, 430
scope of a variable, 213
screen, 9
scroll bars, 551
SDK, 19
search tree, 650
search(), 592, 656
searching a string, 204
searching a tree, 662
searching and sorting, 297
searchStr(), 596
SearchTree, 658
searchVec(), 596
secondary memory, 4–5, 7–8
secondary storage, 7
selection control, 182
selection sort, 299, 399
selectionSort(), 301, 400
selector, 222
semicolon, 36
sentinel value, 239
sentinel-controlled loops, 239
separation of concerns, 23, 149
sequence of if's, 216
Serializable, 562
server, 10
set(), 666, 667
setBackground(), 452
setBorder(), 452, 453
setColor(), 160
setElementAt(), 332
setForeground(), 452
setLayout(), 451, 489, 491, 496
setSize(), 464
setText(), 458
setVisible(), 463, 464
shadowing data fields, 380
short-circuit evaluation, 189

showConfirmDialog(), 185
showInputDialog(), 26, 66
showMessageDialog(), 26, 69
ShowNameInStars, 25
showOpenDialog(), 553
showSaveDialog(), 553
siblings, 650
signature, 379
simplifying a solution, 141
size(), 332
SmartButton, 612, 615
software, 2, 3, 8, 12, 14, 15, 16, 18, 19,
    21, 27, 28
software development method, 24
software piracy, 29
software **reuse**, 65
software tools, 20
sort(), 340
sorting, 298, 398
source code, 19
source file, 74
source program, 18
SOUTH, 491
spaces, 81
specification, 21
specification-based, 430
sqrt(), 87
stack, 587, 589, 636, 639
stack as linked list, 636
stack overflow, 619, 670
stack using a vector, 639
StackVector, 642
standard deviation, 283
standard input stream, 532
standard output stream, 528
start(), 445, 452
starter method, 606
state of object, 16, 52, 106, 117
state-controlled loop, 238
static, 78, 209, 396